# Introduction
# to Corrections

# Introduction to Corrections

*Fourth Edition*

## Vernon B. Fox

*Professor Emeritus*
*Florida State University*
*Tallahassee, FL*

## Jeanne B. Stinchcomb

*Associate Professor of Criminal Justice*
*Barry University*
*Miami, FL*

Prentice Hall Career & Technology
Englewood Cliffs, NJ 07632

**Library of Congress Cataloging-in-Publication Data**

Fox, Vernon Brittain
    Introduction to corrections / by Vernon B. Fox, Jeanne B.
Stinchcomb. -- 4th ed.
      p.    cm.
    Includes bibliographical references and index.
    ISBN 0-13-056458-3
    1. Corrections.  I. Stinchcomb, Jeanne B.  II. Title.
HV8665.F725  1994                           93-46214
364.6'0973--dc20                              CIP

Editorial/production supervision, interior design,
   and electronic composition: *Julie Boddorf*
Cover design: *Laura Ierardi*
Cover photo: *C. J. Pickerell*
Director of production and manufacturing: *David Riccardi*
Production coordinator: *Ed O'Dougherty*
Acquisitions editor: *Robin Baliszewski*
Editorial assistant: *Rose Mary Florio*

Prentice Hall Career & Technology
© 1994, 1985, 1977, 1972 by Prentice-Hall, Inc.
A Paramount Communications Company
Englewood Cliffs, NJ 07632

Printed in the United States of America

10  9  8  7  6  5  4  3  2  1

ISBN   0-13-056458-3

PRENTICE-HALL INTERNATIONAL (UK) LIMITED, *London*
PRENTICE-HALL OF AUSTRALIA PTY. LIMITED, *Sydney*
PRENTICE-HALL CANADA INC., *Toronto*
PRENTICE-HALL HISPANOAMERICANA, S.A., *Mexico*
PRENTICE-HALL OF INDIA PRIVATE LIMITED, *New Delhi*
PRENTICE-HALL OF JAPAN, INC., *Tokyo*
SIMON & SCHUSTER ASIA PTE. LTD., *Singapore*
EDITORA PRENTICE-HALL DO BRASIL, LTDA., *Rio de Janeiro*

*DEDICATION*

*To everyone who has made a difference in someone's life;*
*and especially those who have made such a difference in ours,*
*most notably,*

*Laura Fox*
*and Jim Stinchcomb*

# Contents

PREFACE     xxi

❖ **Part I: The Nature, Scope, and Function of Corrections**     1

**1**   THE CORRECTIONAL FRAMEWORK     4

Chapter Overview     4

The Correctional Conglomerate     5
    *Custodial Institutions, 7*
    *Noncustodial Alternatives, 8*
    *Juvenile Programs and Facilities, 10*
    *Corrections Defined, 11*

The Criminal Justice System and Corrections     13
    *Beginning the Process: Arrest, 14*
    *Next Stop: The Jail, 15*
    *The Process Continues: Initial Appearance,*
      *Preliminary Hearing, and Arraignment, 17*
    *The Process Adjudicates: Trial, 19*
    *The Process Concludes: Sentencing, 20*
    *Corrections: First and Last Stop, 23*

Government, Society, and Corrections    24
  *Jurisdictional Separation and Functional
    Fragmentation, 25*
  *Interactions within Criminal Justice, 26*
  *Criminal Justice Impact Assessment, 27*

Conflicting Correctional Goals    30
  *The Public's Role in Policymaking, 31*
  *Changing Public Policies, 31*
  *Implications for Corrections, 34*

Summary    36

2   CRIME AND THE CORRECTIONAL PROCESS    38

Chapter Overview    38

Deviance and the Law    39
  *Differing Perspectives on Crime, 40*
  *Determining Criminality, 42*

Definition of Crime    44
  *Necessary Conditions, 44*
  *Relativity of Crime, 46*

Extent of Crime    46
  *The* Uniform Crime Reports, *47*
  *Factors Affecting the Crime Rate, 49*
  *The* National Crime Survey, *51*
  *Implications for Corrections, 51*

Society's Response to Crime    54
  *Retribution, 54*
  *Deterrence, 57*
  *Incapacitation, 59*
  *Rehabilitation, 61*
  *Reintegration, 67*

Summary    69

3   THE CORRECTIONAL CLIENT    70

Chapter Overview    70

Nature of Correctional Clientele    71
    *Identifying the Correctional Client, 72*
    *Responding to the Correctional Client, 73*

Early Criminological Thought    74
    *The Classical School, 74*
    *The Positive School, 75*

Physiological Approaches    76
    *Physical Abnormalities, 77*
    *Body Types, 77*
    *Chromosome Abnormalities, 78*
    *Biochemical Theories, 79*
    *Biology and the Environment, 80*

Psychological Approaches    81
    *Psychoanalytic Theory, 81*
    *Clinical Psychology, 84*
    *Behavioralism, 85*
    *Intelligence and Education, 86*

Sociological Approaches    88
    *The Chicago School: Ecological Theory, 88*
    *Differential Association, 90*
    *Alienation, Adaptation, and Opportunity Theory, 90*
    *Containment Theory, 92*
    *Labeling Theory, 93*

Summary    95


**4**   THE DEVELOPMENT OF CORRECTIONS      96

Chapter Overview    96

Primitive Law    97
    *Blood Feuds, 97*
    *Written Codes, 98*
    Lex Talionis, *98*
    *The Roman Empire, 99*
    *The Rise of Religions and Confinement, 99*

Medieval Practices    100

*Church Influence, 100*
*Anglo-Saxon England, 100*
*Medieval Punishments, 101*
*Confinement Practices, 103*
*Early English Jails, 103*
*Breakdown of the Feudal System, 104*
*Banishment and Exile, 106*

Early American Corrections        107
*Colonial Punishments, 107*
*Colonial Correctional Institutions, 108*

From Vengeance to Justice        109
*John Howard's Prison Reforms, 110*
*Bentham, Beccaria, and Blackstone, 111*
*The U.S. Constitution, 111*

The Penitentiary Emerges        113
*The Walnut Street Jail, 113*
*The Auburn System, 116*

U.S. Prison Developments        119
*Regional Developments, 119*
*The Reform Era, 121*
*The Industrial Era, 124*

Corrections Today        127
*The Rehabilitative Era, 129*
*Impact of the 1960s, 130*
*The Past as Prologue, 134*

Summary        135


❖ Part II: Correctional Services, Practices, and Institutions        137

5   COMMUNITY-BASED ALTERNATIVES        140

Chapter Overview        140

Pretrial Intervention        142
*The Diversion Process, 143*
*Formal and Informal Diversion, 144*
*Advantages and Disadvantages of Diversion, 145*

Home Confinement and Electronic Monitoring    150

*Electronically Monitored Clients, 152*

*Advantages, 152*

*Disadvantages, 154*

Probation Services    156

*History of Probation, 157*

*Probation Today, 158*

*Conditions of Probation, 160*

*Probation Eligibility, 161*

*Presentence Investigations, 164*

*The Role of Probation Officers, 167*

*Probation Caseloads, 175*

Summary    182

**6   JAILS: PRETRIAL DETENTION AND SHORT-TERM CONFINEMENT    184**

Chapter Overview    184

Number and Types of Jails    186

*Eliminating Old Jails, 186*

*Accounting for the Jail Population, 187*

*Consolidating Small Jails, 189*

Functions of the Jail    191

*Pretrial Detention and Convicted Offenders, 191*

*Other Jail Inmates, 193*

*Offenses of Jail Inmates, 194*

*Length of Time Served, 197*

Direct-Supervision (New-Generation) Jails    198

*Philosophy, 198*

*Architecture and Inmate Supervision, 199*

*Physical Features, 201*

*Costs and Effectiveness, 203*

*Training and Management, 205*

Jail Administration and Operations    206

*Two Models of Jail Administration, 208*

*The Administrator's Role: Setting the Tone for Staff, 209*

*Staff Roles: Setting the Tone for Inmates, 211*

*Intake Procedures, 212*

*Operational Considerations, 213*
*Treatment and Industrial Programs, 213*
*Medical Services, 214*
*Suicide Vulnerability, 215*
*The Mentally Ill, 218*
*Classification, 219*
*Crowding, 220*

Summary     226


**7**   PRISONS AND OTHER CORRECTIONAL FACILITIES      228

Chapter Overview     228

Number and Types of Institutions     229
*Federal, State, and Military Facilities, 230*
*The Costs of Imprisonment, 230*
*Offender Fees, 232*
*Time Served, 233*

Security Classifications     234
*Maximum Security, 235*
*Medium Security, 236*
*Minimum Security, 236*
*Security Distribution, 238*
*Classification Procedures, 239*

The Prison Population     241
*Number of Inmates, 241*
*Prison Crowding, 242*
*Characteristics of Inmates, 245*
*Offenses of Inmates, 246*

The Purpose of Prisons     248
*Social Compromise, 248*
*Public Opinion, 250*

Prison Organization     251
*Political Influence, 251*
*Institutional Organization, 252*

Prison Administration     255
*Administrative Styles, 256*

*Operational Impact*, 257
*Inmate Control*, 260
*Informal Social Control*, 263
*Participatory Management*, 263
*Inmate Self-Governance*, 264
*Self-Governance Critique*, 265

Summary          268


❖ Part III: Correctional Institutions:
   Custody, Treatment, Confinement, and Release                          271

**8**   INSTITUTIONAL PROCEDURES: CUSTODY                                    274

Chapter Overview          274

Functions of Custody          275
   *Purposes of Custody*, 276
   *Custody/Treatment Relationships*, 276
   *Security Techniques*, 277

Architectural Design          278
   *External Security*, 278
   *Internal Security*, 280

Control Procedures          281
   *Segregation*, 283
   *Controlled Movement*, 284
   *Conducting Counts*, 288
   *Escapes*, 289

Contraband, Searches, and Equipment Control          291
   *Contraband*, 292
   *Cell Searches (Shakedowns)*, 293
   *Personal Searches*, 294
   *Tool Control*, 296
   *Key Control*, 296
   *Inmate Supervision*, 297

Contacts with the Outside          299
   *Telephone*, 300
   *Mail*, 301
   *Visiting*, 301

*Conjugal Visits, 303*
*Furloughs, 304*

Institutional Rules and Discipline    305
*Rules and Regulations, 306*
*Disciplinary Procedures, 306*

Inmate Management    309
*Rules and Relationships, 310*
*Overenforcement, 311*
*Underenforcement, 312*
*Corrupt Alliance, 313*
*Changing Supervisory Styles, 315*
*Balanced Enforcement, 315*
*Consistency, 316*
*Informal Controls, 317*
*Social Distance, 317*
*Interpersonal Communications, 318*

Summary    320

**9** INSTITUTIONAL PROCEDURES: TREATMENT    323

Chapter Overview    323

Inmate Classification    325
*Historical Developments, 326*
*Reception and Diagnosis, 328*
*Classification Decisions, 328*
*Relationship to the Medical Model, 329*
*Institutional Implications, 330*
*Classification Developments, 331*

Religious Services    336
*Inmate Acceptance, 337*
*Staff Acceptance, 338*
*Personnel Recruitment, 338*
*Treatment Impact, 339*

Education, Training, and Other Services    340
*Institutional Programs    341*
*Basic Education, 341*
*Computer-Assisted Instruction, 344*

*College Education, 345*

*Library Services, 346*

*Vocational Training, 347*

*Private-Sector Involvement, 350*

*Recreation, 351*

Counseling, Casework, and Clinical Services     353

*Treatment Availability, 353*

*Counseling, 356*

*Group Methods, 357*

*Self-Help Groups, 360*

*Sensitivity Training, 362*

*Psychodrama Role-Playing, 364*

*Family Therapy, 364*

*Behavior Modification, 365*

*Cosmetic Surgery, 366*

*Contingency Contracts, 367*

*Reality Therapy, 369*

*Psychiatric and Psychoanalytic Treatment, 369*

*Social Casework, 370*

*Nontraditional and Multiple Techniques, 370*

Summary     373

**10**    THE EFFECTS OF INSTITUTIONAL LIFE         376

Chapter Overview     376

The Process of Prisonization     378

*Importation or Deprivation?, 379*

*The Institutionalized Personality, 383*

Adaptations to Confinement     387

*Individual Adjustments, 387*

*Inmate Attitudes and Values, 389*

The Inmate Subculture     391

*Prison Language (Argot), 392*

*The Inmate Code, 392*

*Inmate Gangs, 396*

Prison Violence     400

*Riots and Disturbances, 401*

*Predisposing Conditions, 403*
*Precipitating Event, 405*
*Stages of a Riot, 405*
*Riot Control: Planning and Negotiating, 410*
*Riot Prevention, 411*

Summary     416

**11**   TRANSITION FROM CONFINEMENT TO COMMUNITY     419

Chapter Overview     419

Historical Background     421
*Parole Developments, 421*
*Parole Defined, 423*

Parole Authority     423
*Objectives of Parole, 424*
*Eligibility for Parole, 426*
*Parole Boards, 427*
*Administrative Models, 429*

Selection Procedures     430
*Due Process Considerations, 431*
*Selection Criteria, 432*
*Decision-making Criticisms, 433*
*Impact of the Justice Model, 435*

Parole Supervision     446
*Prerelease Planning, 447*
*Conditions of Parole, 452*
*Functions of Parole Officers, 455*
*Parole Revocation, 459*
*Recidivism, 461*

Summary     463

❖ Part IV: Special Topics, Current Issues, and the Future     466

**12**   SPECIAL POPULATIONS IN CORRECTIONS     469

Chapter Overview     469

Female Offenders     471

     *Female Inmates, 472*
     *Concerns for Children, 475*
     *Adaptation to Confinement, 477*
     *Comparisons to Past Practices, 479*
     *Current Conditions of Confinement, 480*
     *Co-correctional (Coed) Prisons, 482*

AIDS (Acquired Immune Deficiency Syndrome)     485

     *AIDS in Corrections, 486*
     *Correctional Responses, 487*

Other Special Offender Populations     494

     *Drug Abusers, 494*
     *Alcohol Abusers, 499*
     *Mentally Disordered Offenders, 501*
     *Sex Offenders, 507*
     *Physically Impaired Offenders, 511*
     *The Elderly in Prison, 514*

Summary     516

**13**    JUVENILE CORRECTIONS     519

Chapter Overview     519

Historical Background     521

     *Houses of Refuge and Reform Schools, 522*
     *The Child-Saving Movement, 523*
     *Origin of the Juvenile Court, 524*
     *Prevention and Treatment, 527*

Juvenile Justice Transformation     528

     *Due Process Considerations, 529*
     *Status Offenders and Delinquents, 532*
     *Juveniles in Adult Court, 533*
     *Juvenile Court Jurisdiction, 535*

The Juvenile Justice Process     537

     *Initial Contact and Referral, 537*
     *Intake Procedures, 538*
     *Juvenile Detention, 541*
     *Juveniles in Adult Jails, 542*

*Adjudication, 546*

*Dispositions, 549*

*Children in Custody, 552*

*Juvenile Institutions, 554*

*Effects of Confinement, 558*

*Shock Incarceration Programs, 560*

*Aftercare Programs, 562*

Alternative Approaches    564

*Diversion, 564*

*Decriminalization, 568*

*Deinstitutionalization, 570*

Summary    574

**14**    STAFF: THE KEY INGREDIENT    577

Chapter Overview    577

Correctional Personnel    579

*Numbers and Characteristics, 579*

*Implications of a Changing Workforce, 581*

*Staff Turnover and Retention, 582*

Administrative Practices    584

*Recruitment, 584*

*Selection, 586*

*Training, 589*

Line and Staff Supervision    597

*Motivation, 597*

*Discipline, 598*

*Direction, 600*

Correctional Management    603

*Planning and Decision Making, 603*

*Budgeting and Resource Allocation, 606*

*Organization and Administration, 607*

Personnel Issues    608

*Legal Liability, 609*

*Sexual Integration, 613*

*Officer Stress, 618*

*Labor Unions, 622*

Summary    624

**15**  CURRENT TRENDS AND FUTURE ISSUES                          626

Chapter Overview    626

Legal Issues    627
*Freedom of Religion, 630*
*Mail Privileges and Freedom from Censorship, 634*
*Freedom from Unreasonable Search and Seizure, 635*
*Freedom from Cruel and Unusual Punishment, 638*

Current Trends    649
*Accreditation, 650*
*Privatization, 652*

Future Issues    659
*Urbanization, Economics, and the Quality of Life, 660*
*Drugs and Related Crime, 661*
*Implications for the Justice Model, 661*
*Learning from Past Mistakes, 662*
*International Implications, 663*
*Projecting Correctional Trends, 664*

Summary    670

INDEX                                                            673

# Preface

It was the home stretch. Almost time to relax after more than a year of painstaking work. The fourth revision of this book was coming to a close. The last chapters were about to be typed on a home computer in a suburb of Miami. But it was also the summer of 1992. The greatest natural disaster in U.S. history was about to hit South Florida.

We were among the most fortunate. Hurricane Andrew spared us (and the computer). Nothing but damage from uprooted trees. The book was safe. Many people were not. Overnight, much of South Florida was simply gone. A mere day earlier, it had been a scenic tourist attraction. Now it was a scene of total destruction.

A population the size of Dayton, Ohio, was left homeless, jobless, and hungry. They wandered through rubble, searching for rain-soaked reminders of a former life. They waited patiently in long lines, scavanging for food and ice. They lived without roofs or windows, sleeping inside the few standing walls of what had once been home.

Some had lived comfortable lives in beachfront homes and upper-class suburbs. Some had struggled for survival as farmers and migrant workers. Some were newborn infants. Some were elderly invalids. Some had virtually nothing to begin with. Now they did not have even that. Hurricane Andrew did not discriminate. But those who had the least to lose, lost the most. Already on the brink of poverty and despair, Andrew's winds blew them over the edge.

The summer of 1992 seems like a long time ago. But many of those victims are still trying to rebuild their lives. Just as are many others in communities everywhere—people who are victimized routinely by life's hardships. These smaller scale misfortunes and personal tragedies do not get national news coverage. They do not rate presidential visits. They do not qualify for military assistance. Until one of them becomes an arrest statistic or a correctional client, they rarely capture public attention.

An outpouring of help came to South Florida in the wake of our disaster. People pulled together. Neighbors helped neighbors. Strangers helped strangers. We owe no less generosity to those whose lives are equally tragic every day. It is for them that this book is written—and for those who devote their own lives to helping others. For in the final analysis, it is largely fate or the power of a higher being that separates "us" from "them." In the summer of 1992, we learned how fragile and meaningless that separation truly is.

# part I

# The Nature, Scope, and Function of Corrections

*Justice in a democracy demands fair treatment of all citizens, neither ignoring victims nor degrading prisoners.*[1]

*American Correctional Association*

Courtesy of the Dade County Department of Corrections and Rehabilitation, Miami, Florida.

[1]*The American Prison: From the Beginning . . . A Pictorial History* (Laurel, MD: American Correctional Association, 1983), p. 253.

C orrections is both fascinating and frustrating. Changing the direction of an offender's life can be an exciting challenge. Helping a juvenile get back on the right track, guiding an ex-offender toward a law-abiding lifestyle, offering treatment to an alcoholic, or simply making time in a correctional facility more tolerable for an inmate can all be very personally rewarding experiences. Corrections offers unlimited opportunities for such meaningful social contributions—for work that has a purpose and makes a difference.

At the same time, when corrections does not function effectively, it can be a frustrating experience. When the same offenders keep reappearing in the correctional system, when needed resources are unavailable, when there is controversy over what corrections should be accomplishing, when the public is unconcerned and unsupportive, when even other agencies in the criminal justice system do not work cooperatively together, much of the fascination is diminished. Facing such obstacles can create confusion and conflict. It can also provide the potential for change—if obstacles are seen as opportunities.

Certainly, there is considerable opportunity for change in corrections. But before exploring where corrections might be tomorrow, it is essential to determine where this field is today and how it got there. Only with an understanding of the past and the present can we can begin to shape the future. Thus, Part I of this book focuses on an overview of the nature, scope, and function of corrections. The framework is set in Chapter 1 with a description of what is included in this vast collection of facilities, programs, and services called "corrections." With a better understanding of the correctional conglomerate, we follow a case through the criminal justice process, developing a more detailed appreciation for just how interdependent all phases of the justice system are. By looking at several different outcomes for the offenders involved, we see where corrections fits in the process and how its caseload is generated. Turning from criminal justice to government in general, we describe the fragmented functions and separate jurisdictions that have emerged from our democratic system of local government control. The public's role in shaping correctional practices is illustrated further by considering the impact of two conflicting models of correctional policymaking. Should corrections be treating and attempting to rehabilitate criminals, as the medical model would advocate? Or is corrections simply expected to constrain criminal behavior through incapacitation or to achieve retribution by implementing punishment, as the justice model would support? Pursuing these issues, we realize how criminal sanctions have changed over time as social opinion has fluctuated, along with the implications of such change in terms of correctional practices.

With that foundation, in Chapter 2 we explore in more detail the very reason for the existence of corrections—that is, crime. Without criminal behavior there would be no need for corrections. But just what is "crime," and how does it differ from "deviant behavior"? Since there is no universal agreement on what should be considered criminal, the chapter begins with the difference between "conflict" and "consensus" views of the development of criminal law—illustrating that there is no clear-cut distinction between what is merely socially unacceptable and what is actually criminal. Turning to the official definition of crime, we explore what must be involved for behavior to be considered criminal from a legal perspective, and thus, generate action by the criminal justice system. If defining crime is difficult, we next discover that accurately counting its frequency is nearly impossible. The nature and extent of crime as reflected in the *Uniform Crime Reports* is presented, together with factors that affect the reporting of crime. More recent efforts to uncover the volume of unreported crime through the victimization studies of the *National Crime Survey* are also addressed. Since it is society's response to crime that is of greatest concern to corrections, Chapter 2 concludes with a review of the various perspectives that have guided public opinion—from retribution, deterrence, and incapacitation to rehabilitation and reintegration.

In Chapter 3, attention shifts to a closer look at correctional clients and what it is that causes offenders to commit crime. While an all-encompassing theory explaining criminal behavior has yet to be developed, the search for causes has been directed largely toward the three general areas discussed in this chapter:

- *Physiological.* Is it something within the body itself that creates criminal tendencies: the genes we inherit? the food we eat?
- *Psychological.* Is it some condition of the mind that generates criminal behavior: personality disorders? emotional immaturity?
- *Sociological.* Is it the environment in which we live that is the culprit: dysfunctional families? poverty? inadequate opportunities?

All of these theories have influenced both society and its criminal justice decisionmakers at some point in time, which means that they have also influenced social policy concerning how we deal with criminals—which, in turn, means that theories have had a direct impact on correctional practices.

With this background on where corrections is today, how it is influenced by public policy, and what clients it serves, we take a step back in time to see how corrections has evolved through the years. Although it may be difficult to imagine living in a society without jails or prisons, as Chapter 4 points out, these have been relatively recent "inventions." The harshness of punishment practices in ancient, medieval, and colonial times is described in vivid detail—in contrast to the more humanitarian forces that eventually resulted in the evolution of correctional institutions, the reform movement, the industrial prison, and the rehabilitative era. Historical developments are reviewed in the context of changing public opinion, to explore further the relationship between corrections and social policy. Appropriately, the section concludes with a consideration of how the past has shaped the present, along with a challenge for the future—accommodating demands for punishment without abandoning directions toward positive change. In corrections, as in any endeavor, it is easy to resign oneself to the frustrations. The challenge is to rekindle the fascinations!

# chapter 1

# The Correctional Framework

*Corrections remains a world almost unknown to law-abiding citizens, and even those within it often know only their own particular corner.*[1]

President's Commission on Law Enforcement
and Administration of Justice

## ❖ CHAPTER OVERVIEW

Much of the confusion surrounding corrections and what it should be accomplishing is related to the wide variety of institutions, programs, and services provided within what is broadly viewed as "corrections." We therefore begin this chapter with a consideration of just what *is* included within this vast correctional conglomerate—what exactly *is* corrections? But even understanding the nature of corrections reveals only part of its complexity, for corrections does not operate in isolation. As a component of the criminal justice system, corrections interacts with—and is affected by—both law enforcement and the courts. The criminal justice system, in turn, is part of a broader network of government. As an agency of government, corrections is related to the executive, legislative, and judicial functions of government in general, along with the criminal justice system in particular.

Government is, in turn, influenced by the values, opinions, and interests of society. As a public service ultimately responsive to the community, corrections is also subject to various political and social pressures. At times, these have created conflicting expectations of corrections. When society demands public policies that emphasize goals ranging from retribution and punishment to treatment and rehabilitation, it is sometimes difficult to determine exactly what corrections is supposed to be accomplishing. The question therefore becomes not just what corrections *is*, but more important, what it is expected to *do*. As a member of

[1]President's Commission on Law Enforcement and Administration of Justice, *Task Force Report: Corrections* (Washington, DC: U.S. Government Printing Office, 1967), p. 1.

**4**

society, you have not only a personal stake in the answers, but also a role in shaping them.

---

*LEARNING GOALS*

*Do you know:*
- *How diverse correctional services are?*
- *The three levels of government at which corrections functions?*
- *The difference between prisons and jails?*
- *The percentage of inmates under correctional supervision who are confined in custodial institutions, as compared with those under community supervision?*
- *The difference between probation and parole?*
- *The definition of "corrections"?*

---

## ❖ THE CORRECTIONAL CONGLOMERATE

In private enterprise, a massive business corporation with far-reaching markets, numerous customers, and a vast array of different products and services would be called a *conglomerate*. Similarly, a government service composed of as many employees, clients, and diverse activities as corrections can also be considered a conglomerate. The difference between a business conglomerate and corrections is that *you* have a personal stake in the "profits" or "losses" of corrections—it is *your* tax dollars that support it, citizens in *your* community who are its "customers," and *your* safety that is involved in its success or failure. Moreover, it is through your elected and appointed government officials that the policies, procedures, and future directions of corrections are established. It is therefore in your interest to take a closer look at this correctional conglomerate.

The next "Close-up on Corrections" box describes a few of the thousands of scenarios occurring throughout the country every day that involve the correctional system. All of the offenders in these cases are correctional clients. All of the institutions constructed, programs developed, and services provided to accommodate them are part of the "conglomerate" of corrections.

As with any conglomerate, operating the correctional system requires a massive amount of fiscal and human resources:

- *How much does corrections cost?* Almost $25 billion annually. That is about $100 for every man, woman, and child in the United States.[2] Moreover, correctional costs have been increasing faster than expenditures for either police or the courts. If trends continue in the direction indicated in Figure 1.1, by the time you read this, spending on corrections may equal or even exceed the costs of law enforcement. In fact, a major national report has recently found that between 1986

---

[2]Sue A. Lindgren, "Justice Expenditure and Employment, 1990," *Bureau of Justice Statistics Bulletin* (Washington, DC: U.S. Department of Justice, 1992), p. 3.

Correctional Clientele

- Five college students are brutally slain, their bodies mutilated. The killer is awaiting execution on death row.
- Three gang members are seriously injured in a turf war with a rival gang. Their 18-year-old attackers are awaiting trial in jail.
- A woman's purse is snatched as she walks to her car. The thief is serving 10 months in a community-based correctional facility.
- A bank discovers $2000 missing from a teller's receipts. The embezzler agrees to provide restitution and is electronically monitored while confined at home.
- A young teenager runs away from home and turns to prostitution for financial support. She is placed in a juvenile detention facility.
- A prominent business leader uses cocaine at a party. He is sentenced to probation and required to complete a drug rehabilitation program.
- A former drug dealer has served 10 years in state prison. He is preparing for parole in a halfway house.

and 1991, corrections expenditures nearly doubled. During the same period, police expenditures increased at only half that rate. In other words, corrections has been receiving an increasingly larger share of total criminal justice resources.[3]

- *How many people does that employ?* The nation's 555,813 correctional employees[4] would populate the entire city of Denver with people in positions ranging from correctional officers to administrators, social workers, psychologists, psychiatrists, doctors, nurses, lawyers, teachers, counselors, secretaries, and maintenance personnel. In fact, just about every professional and support occupation you can name is probably employed somewhere in the correctional conglomerate!

- *Where do all of these employees work?* In the federal government (4%), the 50 states (62%), and the thousands of municipalities and counties (34%) throughout the United States[5]—in other words, in every governmental jurisdiction in the country.

- *How many clients does this conglomerate serve?* Picture the combined populations of Baltimore, Dallas, and San Diego. On any given day, an estimated 4.3 million adults are under some form of correctional care or custody.[6] Statistically, of every 46 adults you encounter, one is currently a correctional client.[7]

[3]"ABA Report Finds National Overemphasis on Drug Cases, Less on Violent Crime," *Crime Control Digest* (February 22, 1993), p. 2, citing a report released by the American Bar Association.
[4]Lindgren, p. 6. Full-time equivalent personnel: 547,166.
[5]Ibid., p. 7.
[6]Louis W. Jankowski, *Correctional Populations in the United States, 1990* (Washington, DC: U.S. Department of Justice, 1992), p. 5.
[7]*Bureau of Justice Statistics: National Update*, Vol. 1, No. 1 (July 1991), p. 9.

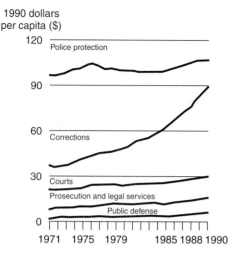

**Figure 1.1** Per capita spending for all levels of government in the justice system. *Source:* Sue A. Lindgren, "Justice Expenditure and Employment, 1990," *Bureau of Justice Statistics: Bulletin* (Washington, DC: U.S. Department of Justice, 1992), p. 5.

Of course, you would need to visit a prison or jail to "encounter" many of them. But do not mistakenly assume that the majority are confined to secure institutions. Most are not.

## Custodial Institutions

Corrections is easily stereotyped by its most visible physical structures—custodial institutions. For adults, these are prisons and jails. For juveniles, they are training schools and detention centers.

In fact, what do you picture when you hear the word "corrections"? Often, our first thought is of a forbidding-looking gray fortress surrounded by thick concrete walls with rifles protruding from guard towers, where expressionless inmates move in dull routines under the constant supervision of uniformed officers. That is generally the image of "corrections" portrayed in movies and on television. But of all adult inmates housed in correctional institutions throughout the United States, only about 15% are serving time in such *maximum-security* prisons.[8] Far more inmates are confined to *medium-security* institutions—where wire fencing replaces concrete walls, armed towers are nonexistent, and inmate supervision is less intense. The lowest-risk offenders, who can be trusted with more freedom, are serving their sentences or preparing for parole in *minimum-security* facilities such as halfway houses, which bear no more resemblance to a prison than does a college dormitory or apartment building.

In addition to being distinguished by their level of security, correctional institutions function within all three levels of government: *local, state,* and *federal.* The private sector also provides correctional services and has even begun operating custodial institutions, a topic discussed in greater detail in Chapter 15. But

[8]Compiled from figures presented in "Adult Inmate Population by Security and Age," *ACA Directory* (Laurel, MD: American Correctional Association, 1990), p. xxvii.

in practice, corrections is primarily a function of state government. States are responsible for the operation of *prisons,* where inmates serving time in excess of one year are confined.

Those convicted of federal crimes who are sentenced to a year or more serve their time in federal prisons. But there are far fewer federal (80) than state (957) prisons in the United States.[9]

In contrast to prisons, *jails* generally hold those serving sentences of less than one year, as well as unconvicted persons awaiting trial who either cannot make bail or are determined to be a potential threat to the community if released. Jails are a function of the local (county or city) level of government.

While the federal government also incarcerates those serving short sentences or awaiting trial, federal "jails" are usually called Metropolitan Correctional Centers. There are considerably more local jails (3316)[10] than state prisons (957). But ironically, there are fewer inmates confined in local jails (426,479)[11] than in state prisons (751,806).[12] Although jails are more numerous, they are smaller facilities designed to hold fewer offenders. (More information on both prisons and jails is provided in Chapters 6 and 7.)

## Noncustodial Alternatives

Most clients in the correctional "conglomerate" are not, however, serving time in either of these correctional institutions. Of all adults who are under some form of correctional care, custody, or supervision, *three out of four are not confined in prison or jail.*[13] As Figure 1.2 illustrates, the vast majority (74%) are actually serving their sentence in the community through such noncustodial alternatives as probation or parole. This certainly dispels any notion that corrections exclusively—or even typically—involves those serving time in secure confinement.

Clients under community supervision are predominately either on *probation* or *parole.* As the largest consumers of correctional services, probation and parole can be thought of as the "bookends" of corrections,[14] since they occur on either end of incarceration. That is, probation is a sentence provided as an alternative to *going to* an institution, whereas parole is early release provided as an alternative to *remaining in* an institution. Both enable the offender to serve time in the community rather than in a correctional facility. But probation is a *sentencing alternative* used by the courts instead of incarceration, whereas parole is an administrative decision to *conditionally release* an inmate from prison following a period of confinement.

[9]James Stephan, *Census of State and Federal Correctional Facilities, 1990* (Washington, DC: U.S. Department of Justice, 1992), p. 1.

[10]*Census of Local Jails, 1988* (Washington, DC: U.S. Department of Justice, 1991), p. v.

[11]Louis W. Jankowski, "Jail Inmates 1991," *Bureau of Justice Statistics Bulletin* (Washington, DC: U.S. Department of Justice, 1992), p. 1.

[12]Tracy L. Snell and Danielle C. Morton, "Prisoners in 1991," *Bureau of Justice Statistics Bulletin* (Washington, DC: U.S. Department of Justice, 1992), p. 2.

[13]Jankowski, *Correctional Populations,* cover page.

[14]Lawrence F. Travis, *Introduction to Criminal Justice* (Cincinnati, OH: Anderson Publishing Company, 1990), pp. 384–85.

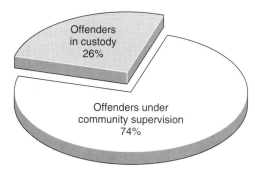

**Figure 1.2** Percentage of adult offenders in custody or under community supervision. *Source:* Compiled from Louis W. Jankowski, *Correctional Populations in the United States, 1990* (Washington, DC: U.S. Department of Justice, 1992), cover page.

Under probation, a convicted offender is sentenced to a period of supervision in the community. Certain conditions are imposed concerning what the probationer can and cannot do, violation of which could result in incarceration. Thus, probation is a community-based alternative to custodial confinement. Although parole also involves certain conditions and is also served in the community, it is awarded after some portion of the offender's sentence has already been served in a custodial institution. Violations of the conditions of parole can result in returning the offender to prison. (These concepts are described more extensively in Chapters 5 and 11.)

Despite the fact that such noncustodial alternatives as probation and parole are not the most visible part of corrections, they represent both the largest and fastest-growing component of the correctional conglomerate. Even though several states have abolished parole, the proportion of the total correctional population on parole increased by over 16% during 1990.[15] Much of this growth can be attributed to the prison crowding that has resulted from more punitive sentencing practices. Without engaging in massive new construction projects, at some point it is simply impossible to accommodate more inmates without releasing some of those currently confined. The increase in those on probation has been somewhat less (6%),[16] but probationers are already by far the largest component of the correctional conglomerate, as shown in Figure 1.3. It is difficult to appreciate how many clients are on probation without bringing these abstract numbers closer to home. How many adults do you think are on probation where you live? If you reside in a city of 100,000 people (excluding children), statistically speaking, over 1,400 of the adults in your community are on probation.[17]

Nor are noncustodial alternatives limited to probation and parole. There are also offenders who are paying fines, making restitution, or performing community service in lieu of sentencing who may be subject to the jurisdiction of corrections.

Corrections likewise encompasses criminal suspects who are released from jail after arrest on their "promise to appear" at trial. A small but growing number of these pretrial releasees are being electronically monitored while under

---

[15]Louis Jankowski, "Probation and Parole, 1990," *Bureau of Justice Statistics Bulletin* (Washington, DC: U.S. Department of Justice, 1991), p. 3.
[16]Ibid., p. 1.
[17]Ibid., p. 2.

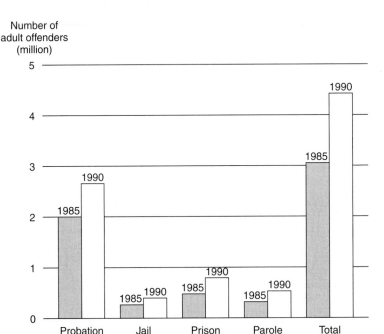

**Figure 1.3**  Distribution of the clients in the correctional conglomerate. *Source:* Louis Jankowski, "Probation and Parole 1990," *Bureau of Justice Statistics Bulletin* (Washington, DC: U.S. Department of Justice, 1991), p. 1.

"house arrest." That is, they are confined to their home for specified curfew hours, with their presence monitored by electronic transmitters and receivers. Although such alternatives to incarceration are sometimes criticized as being too lenient, they are generally reserved for less serious offenders,[18] and anyone who thinks that one's home cannot be "confining" should read a judge's account of his voluntary experiment with electronic monitoring![19]

### Juvenile Programs and Facilities

Nor is the correctional conglomerate limited to physical structures and noncustodial alternatives for adults. Also included are *juveniles* housed in detention or participating in the many residential and nonresidential treatment programs designed to meet their needs. Juvenile correctional services are provided at the local and state levels of government, along with considerable involvement on the part of the private sector.

Like their adult counterparts, most juveniles in the correctional system are not confined primarily in secure institutions. Of all facilities and programs designed to

[18]Annesley K. Schmidt, "Electronic Monitoring of Offenders Increases," *NIJ Reports* (Washington, DC: U.S. Department of Justice, 1989), p. 3.

[19]Alan Abrahamson, "Home Unpleasant during House Arrest, Judge Learns," *Corrections Today*, Vol. 53, No. 4 (July 1991), p. 76.

deal with juveniles, there are fewer custodial institutions and detention centers than such alternatives as diagnostic/reception centers, community-based facilities, medical/psychiatric units, group homes, camps, and other programs.[20]

This does not mean that many children are not dealt with as severely as adults, and in some cases, perhaps more severely. Unlike its adult counterpart, the juvenile correctional system embraces a wider clientele. It includes both *delinquents* (whose offenses would be considered crimes if they were older) and *status offenders* (whose activities are considered illegal only because of their age), as well as children voluntarily admitted by their parents and those who are dependent or neglected. The majority of those held in juvenile facilities (69%) are detained for a delinquent offense.[21] However, it is unfortunate but true that such institutions also house over 28,000 nondelinquents. Some of these children are status offenders (36%) whose conduct would not be against the law if they were adults. Most (63%) are simply nonoffenders[22]—that is, "voluntary" admissions or victims confined because they are dependent, neglected, or abused. Thus, although some serious delinquents may be treated more leniently within the juvenile system, there are also many children being confined for situations over which they have no control. Although corrections does not have jurisdiction over what dispositions juveniles receive by the courts, there is some movement toward dealing more harshly with serious delinquents involved in violent crime, while removing from secure confinement those whose behavior poses no particular threat to society (as discussed more thoroughly in Chapter 13).

### Corrections Defined

Figure 1.4 illustrates the basic components of the correctional conglomerate. Although the specific functions for which this conglomerate is responsible vary in different parts of the country, in general, corrections encompasses the following custodial institutions and noncustodial, community-based alternatives:

Custodial Institutions

- *Jails*: local correctional institutions for those awaiting trial or serving short sentences (usually medium security)
- *Prisons*: state or federal correctional institutions for those serving sentences of more than one year (usually, medium or maximum security)
- *Other (less secure) facilities:* local, state, or federal facilities for low-risk offenders serving sentences or preparing for parole, such as halfway houses
- *Juvenile detention centers:* local or state facilities confining juvenile defendants prior to adjudication

[20]*ACA Directory*, p. xx.
[21]Terence Thornberry, Stewart Tolnay, Timothy Flanagan, and Patty Glynn, *Children in Custody 1987: A Comparison of Public and Private Juvenile Custody Facilities* (Washington, DC: U.S. Department of Justice, Office of Juvenile Justice and Delinquency Prevention, 1991), p. 18.
[22]Ibid.

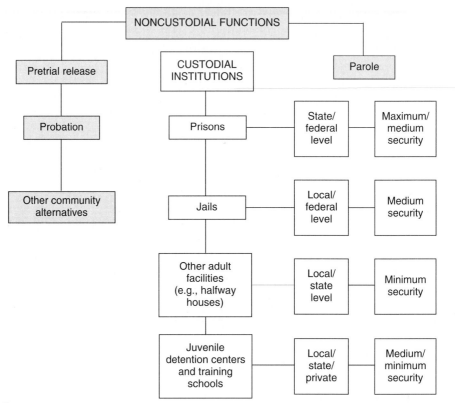

**Figure 1.4** Overview of the correctional conglomerate.

- *Training schools:* local, state, or private custodial facilities confining adjudicated juvenile offenders.

Noncustodial Alternatives

- *Pretrial release programs:* alternatives to incarceration for those awaiting trial
- *Probation:* a conditional sentence that enables the offender to remain free in the community
- *Parole* (or similarly, mandatory supervised release): conditional release for offenders serving time in prison
- *Other community-based programs:* restitution, community service, community treatment programs, and other noncustodial alternatives
- *Group homes and juvenile treatment programs:* residential and nonresidential alternatives to secure confinement for juveniles.

As we saw earlier in the "Close-up on Corrections," responsibilities of the correctional conglomerate extend from violent criminals in maximum security to far less serious offenders serving time in community-based facilities; from unconvicted suspects awaiting trial in jail to convicted offenders on probation or home confinement; from offenders on parole to children in juvenile detention. From these diverse, wide-ranging functions, it becomes apparent that corrections is essentially accountable for the *care, custody, and control* of offenders through either confinement or noninstitutional alternatives.

Looking at these terms more closely, corrections is responsible for the proper "care" of those entrusted to it, as well as the continual "custody" of those committed to its supervision. While the word "control" may appear to have an overly coercive or negative connotation, that is not the intent. Rather, control is meant to encompass not only discipline and incapacitation, but also the multitude of activities involved in treatment, rehabilitation, or otherwise changing behavior while under correctional jurisdiction—since the outcome of such efforts is, ideally, to replace *correctional* control with *self*-control.

In summary, corrections is *the combination of public and private services with legal authority to provide for the care, custody, and control of those accused or convicted of a criminal or status offense.* How effectively is that authority used? How well are care, custody, and control provided? Who are those accused or convicted of an offense? As in any human endeavor, there are no simple answers, but all of these topics will be addressed as we explore the correctional conglomerate in greater detail, discovering its fascinations as well as frustrations.

---

*LEARNING GOALS*

*Do you know:*

- *The three components of the criminal justice system?*
- *The factors which influence police discretion?*
- *The steps involved in processing criminals, from arrest through sentencing?*
- *What happens during booking and where it occurs?*
- *What a plea bargain is and why so many convictions are achieved through this procedure?*
- *The purpose of a presentence investigation report?*
- *What sentencing alternatives are available to judges and which is most frequently used?*

---

## ❖ THE CRIMINAL JUSTICE SYSTEM AND CORRECTIONS

Even the largest conglomerates do not operate in isolation, and corrections is no exception. As mentioned in the definition of corrections, responsibility for correctional care, custody, and control extends to adult criminals and juvenile delinquents who are either *accused* or *convicted* of violating the law. Corrections does not have the authority to intervene until a person is at least formally accused of a crime by the police, although in practice, most correctional services are provided after the accused offender is convicted and sentenced by the courts. This is why the National Commission on Criminal Justice Standards and Goals has noted that "[a] substantial obstacle to [the] development of effective corrections lies in its relationship to police and courts. . . . Corrections inherits any inefficiency, inequity, and improper discrimination that may have occurred in any earlier step of the criminal justice process."[23]

The components of the criminal justice system are traditionally listed in the order of *police* (arrest), *courts* (adjudication), and *corrections* (disposition), which reflects the general sequence through which offenders are processed. We will see, however, that corrections is involved at both the beginning and ending phases of processing in the system.

## Beginning the Process: Arrest

Dave, Bill, and Gary are celebrating the end of the week at a local bar. It is 1:00 A.M., and they are loud and boisterous after drinking for several hours. Gary shoves Bill aside to get to the bar, and Bill reacts with a punch. Dave tries to separate them, and all three become embroiled in a violent fistfight. Chairs are overturned; glasses break; customers scatter. Someone calls the police. The criminal justice process begins.

As with virtually every call they receive, the responding officers are faced with several decisions. They must determine:

- Whether a law has been violated.
- If so, whether there is probable cause to believe that the suspect(s) committed the violation.
- Whether to make an arrest, do something else to resolve the situation, or take no action at all.

In other words, they employ *discretion*. While the law distinguishes between legal and illegal behavior, as its enforcers, the police "make policy about what law to enforce, how much to enforce it, against whom, and on what occasions."[24]

A number of factors influence this discretionary decisionmaking: the seriousness of the offense; the officers' own attitudes, values, and beliefs; the suspect's appearance, behavior, and demeanor. This does not mean that the police will deliberately overlook a major criminal offense. But official action is more likely to be taken when a felony rather than a misdemeanor is involved, when the offense is personally repugnant to the officer, or when the suspect is uncooperative. Moreover, it is often the victim's decision whether to press charges or not, and "when faced with the responsibility to pursue matters as criminal, it is frequently

---

[23]National Advisory Commission on Criminal Justice Standards and Goals, *Corrections* (Washington, DC: U.S. Government Printing Office, 1973), p. 5.

[24]Kenneth Culp Davis, *Police Discretion* (St. Paul, MN: West Publishing Company, 1975), p. 1.

the citizen, not the police, who 'cops out.'"[25] Like the victim, the community at large exercises influence over police discretion. Widespread community support or lack of concern for enforcement of various forms of illegal activity put the police in a position of deciding what is an "appropriate level of enforcement."[26]

In this case, community sentiment, suspect demeanor, and victim cooperation all play a significant role in the officers' discretionary decisions. Numerous complaints have been made about noise, vandalism, and drunken driving in the area surrounding the bar, so the officers feel that they must take some action. Bill demands Gary's arrest, but both are so intoxicated that they engage in a heated argument with the officers about what happened. Witnesses confirm that Dave was involved innocently, and he answers questions respectfully. The officers decide to allow him to call a friend to arrange a ride home. They arrest Bill and Gary on assault, disorderly conduct, and public intoxication charges. Thus begins the lengthy process outlined in Figure 1.5.

## Next Stop: The Jail

The first contact that Bill and Gary have with the criminal justice system following arrest is the local jail, where they are transported to be booked.

The lobby of the jail is crowded with an assortment of prostitutes, vagrants, drug offenders, and drunk drivers. It is a confusing and overwhelming place. People are shouting orders back and forth. Arrestees are loudly protesting their innocence. Computers are churning out a steady stream of rap sheets. Typewriters are clicking furiously. The constant clanging of metal gates as cell doors open and close adds a continuous irritant. In the midst of this chaos, correctional officers begin the *booking process,* which includes:

- Officially recording the arrest.
- Obtaining personal identification information from the suspects.
- Determining whether the offense involved has a court-authorized bond that would enable the suspects to be released with some assurance that they will appear in court.

Bill and Gary answer a seemingly endless series of routine questions. They are searched and photographed. Their fingerprints are taken. They surrender their personal valuables for safekeeping. They are informed of their bond. Gary has several facial injuries that appear to need attention, so he is transported to the "jail ward" of the local hospital. Bill is escorted to the "drunk wing" of the jail to "sleep it off" under the watchful eye of correctional officers. Both are still too intoxicated to make the necessary arrangements to raise bond and bail-out, but they are becoming sober enough to wonder what they are doing in jail with "real criminals."

---

[25]Albert J. Reiss, Jr. *The Police and the Public* (New Haven, CT: Yale University Press, 1971), p. 82.
[26]Harry W. More, ed., *Critical Issues in Law Enforcement* (Cincinnati, OH: Anderson Publishing Company, 1972), p. 52.

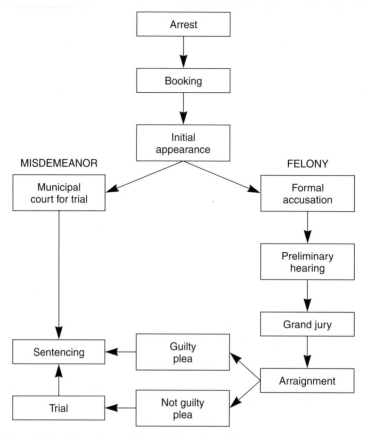

**Figure 1.5**   Overview of the criminal justice process. Source: James D. Stinchcomb, *Introduction to Criminal Justice: Instructor's Guide*, six audiovisual presentations (Washington, DC: Robert J. Brady Company, 1972), p. 27.

However, Bill and Gary are not unique among the jail's population. Suspects who cannot be released on bond, or who cannot raise the money required, are detained (at least temporarily) in jail. In conjunction with correctional officials, the courts may later determine that the individual is eligible for some other type of pretrial release program, such as release on one's own recognizance, or bail may be raised. If not, the suspect—who is still innocent in the eyes of the law—remains confined pending trial.

Such unconvicted offenders make up about half (51%) of the population of local jails.[27] This means that well over 100,000 technically innocent people are incarcerated throughout the country, and the longer their trials are delayed, the longer they remain incarcerated. That is not meant to imply that many such inmates are not of sufficient potential threat to the community to justify their confinement. But it does point out that (as illustrated in Figure 1.6) a sizable number of correctional

[27]Jankowski, "Jail Inmates," p. 2.

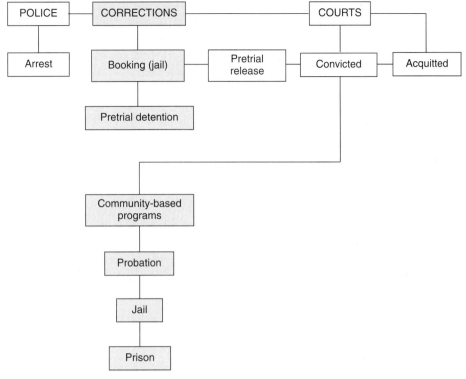

**Figure 1.6** Corrections in the criminal justice system.

clients at the local level enter the correctional system *after arrest* by the police but *before a formal finding of guilt or innocence* by the courts. Unlike the police, corrections does not have any discretion over whether or not to accept its clients.

### The Process Continues: Initial Appearance, Preliminary Hearing, and Arraignment

Under the American system of justice, a suspect is not supposed to languish in jail without formal notification of the charges. Whether confined or released after booking, the defendant is entitled to an *initial appearance* before a judge or magistrate "without unnecessary delay," which is generally interpreted as within 48 hours.[28] At this point, defendants are:

- Advised of their *legal rights*.
- Informed of the *charges* against them.
- Appointed an *attorney* if they are indigent.
- Provided with an opportunity to make *bail* or be released from confinement through some form of pretrial release program. (An example would be "release on recognizance," which frees the suspect from confinement upon a promise to appear at trial.)

[28]Frank Schmalleger, *Criminal Justice Today* (Englewood Cliffs, NJ: Prentice Hall, 1993), p. 279.

However, the judge may decide that the offense is so serious or the defendant considered so dangerous that bail is prohibited; if so, the suspect is returned to jail. On the other hand, very minor offenses may be settled at this point without penetrating further into the criminal justice process.

Fortunately for Bill and Gary, their offenses were not considered major crimes, and neither had prior criminal records, although Gary did have several encounters with the law while a teenager. (In most jurisdictions, juveniles are those under the age of 18. They are processed separately through the juvenile justice system, as described in Chapter 13.) Bill contacted an attorney and a bail bondsman. He was released following his initial appearance. Gary could not raise bail or afford an attorney. After 3 more days in jail, pretrial release was arranged, and a public defender was appointed to represent him.

Suspects facing more serious charges or remaining in detention are also entitled to a *preliminary hearing* before a judge to establish whether there is probable cause to continue the case. If there is not, the charges are dropped and the defendant is released, although charges can be refiled later if circumstances surrounding the case change. Unlike a trial, this preliminary review does not require proof beyond a reasonable doubt—only sufficient reason to believe that the suspect committed the offense. Basically, it is a testing of the evidence against the defendant.

Up to this point, the defendant has not been asked to enter a plea. That is reserved for the *arraignment*, where suspects are:

- Notified of the specific, formal charges against them.
- Allowed to enter a plea—guilty, not guilty, or *nolo contendere* (no contest).
- Informed of their trial date if they do not plead guilty.

At his arraignment, Gary pled guilty to the lesser charge of disorderly conduct, even though he did not believe he was "guilty" of anything. As with his pretrial incarceration, he was not unique. Over 90% of all criminal convictions are obtained through guilty pleas.[29]

Criminal trials are very costly and time consuming. When court dockets are crowded with serious felony cases, when prosecutors lack sufficient evidence to convict, or when defendants believe they will be convicted anyway, it is often in everyone's "best interest" to engage in plea bargaining. A *plea bargain* is a negotiation between the prosecutor and the defense in which the defendant agrees to plead guilty in exchange for reduced charges or a lesser sentence. It is essentially a "deal" between the prosecution and the defense, which is then presented to the judge for approval. The incentives for the defendant are avoiding trial, being convicted of a lesser offense (or fewer offenses in the case of multiple charges), and facing a less serious punishment. At the same time, the prosecutor avoids the time and expense of going to trial, particularly with cases where evidence is weak. But while plea bargaining may appear to be advantageous to

[29]N. Gary Holten and Lawson L. Lamar, *The Criminal Court: Structures, Personnel, and Processes* (New York: McGraw-Hill, 1991), p. 217, citing Milton Heumann, *Plea Bargaining: The Experiences of Prosecutors, Judges, and Defense Attorneys* (Chicago: University of Chicago Press, 1978), pp. 27–32.

everyone involved, it also raises a very dangerous possibility—that a defendant who is actually innocent may be pressured into pleading guilty.

In Gary's case, plea bargaining meant dropping the assault and public intoxication charges as well as the difference between a possible jail term and probation. Without the resources to hire his own attorney and having already taken off so much time from work that his job was in jeopardy, he did not want to face a criminal trial. Moreover, he was concerned that his prior juvenile record would become a factor and decided that he was better off accepting the prosecutor's offer to recommend a year's probation. The judge agreed with the plea and Gary became one of the almost 2 million correctional clients on probation.

### The Process Adjudicates: Trial

Given media attention to the drama of sensational trials, it is the *adjudication phase* of criminal justice processing that is the most visible to the public. Unseen are the hundreds of thousands of cases that are settled or dropped before reaching this point, as illustrated in Figure 1.7.

For those relatively few offenders who proceed this far into the system, trial is where the defendant's guilt or innocence is established. Generally, those accused of serious crimes or facing possible incarceration are entitled to a jury trial. Defendants can, however, waive their right to a jury trial, opting for a bench trial, where the outcome is decided by a judge. The trial itself is made up of:

- The *state*, represented by the prosecution.
- The *defendant*, represented by the defense attorney.
- The *public*, represented by the judge.

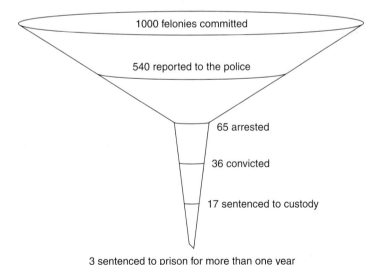

1000 felonies committed

540 reported to the police

65 arrested

36 convicted

17 sentenced to custody

3 sentenced to prison for more than one year

**Figure 1.7** Criminal justice funnel. *Source:* George F. Cole, *The American System of Criminal Justice* (Monterey, CA: Brooks/Cole Publishing, 1986), p. 122.

Trial is the mechanism whereby society determines whether it has the right to take responsibility for a person because he or she has harmed society. At trial, the state presents evidence against the defendant. The defense counsel then presents any contradictory evidence, and throughout the process, assures that the defendant is being treated fairly in the courtroom—that is, within the rules of *due process* of law.

In a democracy, government is committed to the proposition that the preservation of individual liberty is more important than the pursuit of justice. The due process procedures involved in the administration of justice in a democracy therefore emphasize—first and foremost—protection of its citizens. In contrast, the laws and legal process in a totalitarian society emphasize the security of the state over the welfare of the individual.

Thus, in a democratic system such as ours, there is sometimes a difference between "actual guilt" and "legal guilt" beyond a reasonable doubt. In order to protect due process rights, the courts recognize that at times there are some guilty defendants who will go free. For example, evidence obtained illegally by the police is not admissible, even if it is essential to establish guilt. It is only when legal guilt has been *proven within due process of law* that society is given the opportunity to intervene in the life of an offender through the correctional system.

During trial, the defense and the prosecution both present evidence and witnesses, hoping to convince the judge or jury of their side of the case. The judge referees this adversarial conflict, making sure that the rules of due process are followed. The ultimate aim is to uncover the truth within legally prescribed means. To achieve a conviction, the prosecutor must be able to prove that the defendant was guilty *beyond a reasonable doubt.* If the judge (or jury) does not believe that such a level of proof was demonstrated, the defendant is acquitted—found not guilty. In the case of a guilty verdict, the defendant may appeal for a new trial on certain procedural grounds. If the verdict is for acquittal, constitutional guarantees prevent a new trial on the same charge. In this respect, the state has no appeal.

Back to the case at hand. Gary is not willing to press charges of assault against his friend, so the prosecutor has decided to pursue only the public intoxication and disorderly conduct charges against Bill. It has been almost four months since the original incident, and the memories of witnesses are hazy. Bill's defense attorney tries to use the time lapse to question the credibility of the police officers' testimony. Failing that, he objects to their description of Bill as "intoxicated," since he was not subjected to any type of breath or blood analysis, and the bartender cannot remember how many drinks he served Bill that night. The judge agrees that there is reasonable doubt concerning Bill's level of intoxication, but convicts him on the disorderly conduct charge.

### The Process Concludes: Sentencing

Whether guilty by admission during arraignment or by conviction during trial, the offender must now be sentenced. Some would point out that sentencing is not the business of corrections—that corrections is responsible only for the implementation of sanctions imposed by the courts. Technically, that is true. But as a former president of the American Correctional Association has noted: "Sentencing defines the very nature of our work. To the extent that sentences are unjust, we who must carry them out become agents of injustice."[30]

It is, of course, the decisions of judges that ultimately determine how just or unjust the sentencing process is. Like the police in the arrest phase, judges have considerable discretion over the final disposition of a case. They can elect to impose:

- A *fine*.
- *Restitution* to the victim.
- Some type of *community service*.
- Supervision in the community through *probation*, which may be combined with a fine, restitution, community service, or even electronic monitoring at home.
- Short-term confinement in *jail* for a year or less.
- *Imprisonment* for a term up to life.
- *Capital punishment*—the death penalty.

As we have seen in terms of the number of correctional clients under community supervision as opposed to institutional confinement, judges are most likely to select *noncustodial* sentencing alternatives. Certainly, sentencing of felony offenders who have committed serious crimes of violence is quite likely to result in incarceration.[31] But particularly in less serious cases, probation is the sentencing option used most frequently.[32] Although probation, fines, and other community-based programs are sometimes viewed as too lenient by "letting offenders off" without "real punishment," they do impose conditions and intrusions on one's life that can appear to be quite punishing from the perspective of the offender. In fact, it is not unheard of for someone to opt for incarceration in the face of a highly restrictive community alternative. However, community-based correctional approaches are generally preferable for both the public and the nondangerous offender, since they offer a number of advantages by:

- Allowing the offender to remain employed, thereby enabling family support, payment of fines, or victim compensation.
- Avoiding the negative and stigmatizing effects of imprisonment.
- Providing some supervision without breaking ties to the community.
- Reducing costs to the public, since community-based approaches are far less expensive than incarceration.

The sentence imposed by the judge is determined by legal statutes. This means that judicial discretion is bound by limits imposed by the law. Such

[30]Perry Johnson, addressing the Midwinter Meeting of the American Correctional Association, Miami, FL (January 11, 1993).
[31]For example, 83 to 86% of homicide and robbery convictions result in incarceration. *Report to the Nation on Crime and Justice,* Second Edition (Washington, DC: U.S. Department of Justice, 1988), p. 97.
[32]Ibid., pp. 92 and 96.

boundaries have traditionally been quite flexible. But dissatisfaction with unequal sentences for similar offenses—along with public demands to "toughen up" on serious crime—have resulted in the enactment of *sentencing guidelines* by the federal government and numerous states.

Contrary to popular belief, these guidelines were not necessarily designed to be more punitive by imposing longer prison terms. Nor were they designed to create strict uniformity in sentencing by, for example, imposing the same sentence on all armed robbers. Given differences in the nature of the offense, the level of harm inflicted, and the offender's past criminal record, that would be just as unfair as more subjective sentencing. Rather, objective guidelines were meant to produce a more rational approach to arriving at a sentence—one that would allow for some variations within a consistently applied framework.[33]

As is shown by the matrix in Figure 1.8, sentencing guidelines generally take into account both the severity of the offense and the offender's prior criminal record. In some jurisdictions, minimum *mandatory* sentences are also prescribed for various crimes. Aside from such mandates, judges still have some discretion to deviate from sentencing guidelines, particularly when aggravating or mitigating circumstances are involved. Aggravating circumstances—such as a particularly heinous crime or complete lack of remorse by the offender—could justify a more severe penalty. On the other hand, mitigating circumstances— youthfulness of the offender or prior abuse by the victim—might call for a less serious penalty.

Sentencing guidelines have been developed by legislators presumably responding to the interests of the public. In addition, whether appointed or elected, the judge represents a type of politician and therefore must be in tune with the desires of the people. Citizens have varying views of what constitutes appropriate sentencing (i.e., punishment) for criminal behavior. Sometimes a judge is pressured to engage in "political sentencing" to meet the desires of the people of

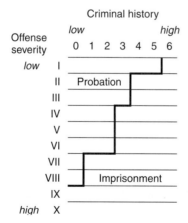

**Figure 1.8** Sentencing guideline matrix. *Source: Report to the Nation on Crime and Justice, Second Edition* (Washington, DC: U.S. Department of Justice, Bureau of Justice Statistics, 1988), p. 92. Adapted from "Preliminary Report on the Development and Impact of the Minnesota Sentencing Guidelines," Minnesota Sentencing Guidelines Commission, July 1982.

[33]Paul F. Cromwell, Jr., George G. Killinger, Hazel B. Kerper, and Charls Walker, *Probation and Parole in the Criminal Justice System*, Second Edition (St. Paul, MN: West Publishing Company, 1985), p. 189.

the community. To remain in office, judges must sentence in accordance with the opinions, emotions, values, fears, and concerns of their constituency.

In deciding what disposition to impose, judges often rely on probation officers to prepare a *presentence investigation* (PSI). This report outlines the offender's prior record (if any), family stability, employment, education, problems in such areas as substance abuse, and other relevant factors, along with a sentencing recommendation. The PSI report has been very influential in determining final disposition. Judges have been likely to follow its recommendations, particularly in cases that do not involve mandatory sentencing guidelines.

Bill's presentence investigation indicates that he is unmarried and has an erratic employment history. He has also received two prior speeding tickets, was convicted for driving-under-the-influence, and was arrested two years ago for public intoxication, with the charges eventually dropped. The judge is concerned about what appears to be a pattern of alcohol-related behavior problems. He sentences Bill to 10 days in jail to be served on weekends, along with mandatory participation in an alcohol treatment program.

## Corrections: First and Last Stop

We have already seen that a correctional institution—the jail—is the "first stop" for an offender after arrest. Corrections is also the "last stop" in the criminal justice process following sentencing. Pretrial detainees represent almost half of the jail's population. But all other correctional clients are those sentenced by the courts to community supervision, short-term confinement in jail, or longer-term imprisonment.

The workload of corrections is thus determined by other components of the justice system. The police can decide whether or not to make an arrest. Judges can decide whether or not to incarcerate an offender, and if so, for what period of time. But corrections cannot decide which clients to accept and has limited influence over how long they will remain under correctional supervision. The policies, procedures, and practices of the entire justice system have a significant impact on corrections. Like the assembly line that produces an inferior product when something goes wrong along the way, much of the success or failure of corrections is dependent on the entire criminal justice system as well as both the governmental structure within which it operates and the citizens who determine its policies.

---

*LEARNING GOALS*

*Do you know:*
- *The difference between the criminal justice functions of the legislative, judicial, and executive branches of government?*
- *What is meant by "jurisdictional separation" and "functional fragmentation" within the criminal justice system?*
- *How the effectiveness of the criminal justice system could be improved with a criminal justice policy impact assessment?*

Seeking freedom from the strong arm of centralized government control experienced in their homelands, early U.S. settlers brought to this country fierce sentiments favoring local government autonomy. The democratic form of government that they established through the U.S. Constitution reserves specific, limited powers for the federal level of government. All other governing authority is allocated to states and localities. By separating jurisdictions in this manner, local autonomy was created.

To further assure that no one branch became so powerful as to endanger the rights and freedoms guaranteed by the Constitution, government was further divided into legislative, judicial, and executive functions within each jurisdiction, as depicted in Figure 1.9.

• *Legislative.* Legislative branches of government operating at the local, state, and federal level have the power to make laws solely within their own jurisdiction. Local ordinances created by county or city commissions therefore apply only within that county or city. Laws enacted by state legislatures apply statewide. Federal legislation passed by the U.S. Congress applies nationwide.

• *Judicial.* Again within their jurisdiction, courts decide the guilt or innocence of defendants as well as the constitutionality of the law. When a local law is violated, a trial court of limited jurisdiction hears the case. If the violation involves a state law, the case is processed in a general trial court (sometimes called superior, district, or circuit court), with appeals made to the state supreme court. When a federal law is violated, the matter is referred to a federal district court. Cases involving a substantial constitutional issue may be appealed to the U.S. Supreme Court, which is the only court whose rulings apply throughout the country.

• *Executive.* Law enforcement and corrections are part of the executive branch of government. Just as an executive in private enterprise manages the

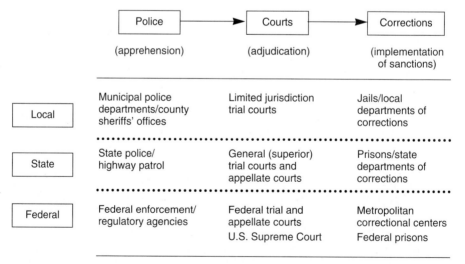

**Figure 1.9** Functions and jurisdiction of criminal justice agencies.

operations of a company, police and correctional officials manage the day-to-day operations of government that are related to crime and corrections. The police are entrusted with enforcing the laws created by the legislature. Corrections is charged primarily with implementing the sanctions decreed by the courts (although we have seen that the jail also confines some suspects prior to trial). County sheriffs combine both functions, since they have authority to enforce laws as well as administer the county jail.

Like their legislative and judicial counterparts, police and corrections operate only within their specific jurisdiction. Local municipal police and county sheriffs can enforce laws within their employing city, county, or town. State police or highway patrol officers have statewide jurisdiction. Federal agents enforce federal criminal statutes throughout the country. Similarly, jails represent the *local* branch of corrections; prisons operate at the *state* level; and the *federal* government maintains both jails (usually called "metropolitan correctional centers") and prisons for federal offenders.

## Jurisdictional Separation and Functional Fragmentation

As might be expected, these divisions of government by function and jurisdiction have both benefits and drawbacks. On the one hand, they bring government closer to the people and provide checks and balances to assure that no one agency becomes too powerful. But on the other hand, they foster *jurisdictional separation* and *functional fragmentation*—that is, lack of cooperation, insufficient coordination, and even territorial rivalries. Like the loyal employee of one company who views outside firms and competitors in other territories as potential rivals, employees of criminal justice agencies may tend to view others in the system with suspicion and mistrust.

As the first to arrive at the scene of a crime or disturbance, it is the police who "are exposed first-hand to the agony of victims, the danger of the streets, the violence of lawbreakers."[34] Law enforcement officers are therefore understandably frustrated when, practically before they have completed their paperwork, they see the offenders they arrest out on bail. Similarly, prosecutors are upset when inappropriate police procedures require them to reduce charges, omit evidence, or even lose cases. Corrections is equally frustrated when the police and the courts keep delivering clients who are in greater need of jobs, shelter, medical care, psychiatric treatment, or substance abuse programs than of confinement in secure institutions. And everyone is disillusioned when corrections fails to "correct." When the same people continue recycling through the system, it is apparent that the system is not working.

Fragmentation of the criminal justice system is not unlike the fragmentation that can occur within a family as parents and children pursue conflicting activities: when everyone is operating on different schedules; when no one takes

---

[34]National Commission on the Causes and Prevention of Violence, *Law and Order Reconsidered* (Washington, DC: U.S. Government Printing Office, 1969), p. 267.

time to listen to the others; when each believes that his or her interests are most important; when no one works to keep everyone together as a unit. Similarly, a system becomes fragmented when its parts function independently, becoming isolated from each other.[35] In criminal justice, each component serves different clients, performs different functions, and pursues different directions, often working at cross-purposes. Yet like a dysfunctional family, the actions of each affect those of the others.

### Interactions within Criminal Justice

In 1967, the President's Crime Commission introduced the concept of a "criminal justice system"[36] to illustrate the interrelated functions of what had previously been viewed as separate agencies. A "system," however, is generally envisioned as harmonious interaction between closely related functions, almost in an assembly-line manner. In criminal justice, nothing could be further from reality.

Even the traditional use of the word "system" is rather misleading when describing relationships among criminal justice agencies. Undoubtedly, the police, courts, and corrections are all interrelated, but only to the extent that what each component does has an impact throughout the system. Their individual policies, procedures, and practices "have not yet become so well-coordinated that they can be described as operating in unison."[37] The fact remains that while these agencies all share in the processing of offenders, they do not function in a systematically coordinated manner: "The American criminal justice system is not a single system, but rather, many separate systems and subsystems. . . . While they may appear similar in that they all apprehend, prosecute, convict, and attempt to rehabilitate law-breakers . . . few are linked together in any comprehensive manner."[38]

In large part, this lack of coordination results from the autonomy that was purposely built into each component of criminal justice. The police, courts, and corrections have separate and distinct missions, which are at times almost contradictory. Each component at each level of government has separate budgets, personnel, physical facilities, missions, and policies. They must often compete with each other for scarce fiscal and human resources. Yet the actions of each have ripple effects throughout the "system," as illustrated in the next "Close-up on Corrections." Although "Pleasantville" is a fictitous community, the scenario in this close-up illustrates the all-too-real domino effect of one component of the system on the others. Similar results are being experienced today in communities throughout the country.

[35]For an analysis of the organizational impediments to a systematic approach in criminal justice, see Don C. Gibbons, Florence Yospe, Joseph L. Thimm, and Gerald F. Blake, Jr., *Criminal Justice Planning: An Introduction* (Englewood Cliffs, NJ: Prentice Hall, 1977), pp. 46–58.

[36]President's Commission on the Administration of Justice, *The Challenge of Crime in a Free Society* (Washington, DC: U.S. Government Printing Office, 1967).

[37]Joseph J. Senna and Larry J. Siegel, *Introduction to Criminal Justice* (St. Paul, MN: West Publishing Company, 1978), p. 96.

[38]Harold J. Vetter and Clifford E. Simonsen, *Criminal Justice in America* (Philadelphia: W.B. Saunders, 1976), p. 2. See also Daniel K. Skoler, *Organizing the Non-System* (Lexington, MA: D. C. Heath and Company, 1977).

### Unanticipated Consequences

The citizens of Pleasantville were concerned about rising crime rates and no longer felt safe in their community. Demands for more police protection resulted in the city commission authorizing additional funds for the hiring of 25 more police officers. Dissatisfaction with what the public felt was lenient sentencing resulted in the election of judges who campaigned on the promise to "get tough" with criminals. To the public's surprise, crime did not decline, but in fact increased, and convicted offenders actually spent less time incarcerated. Why?

Perhaps more crime was being committed. More likely, more crimes were being detected by the newly authorized recruits. Although their average arrest rate remained about the same, the total number of arrests increased with the additional officers.

No extra funds were authorized for jail personnel. But bookings and admissions increased proportionately with the added arrests. Nor were more funds allocated for the prosecutor's office or public defender, both of whom worked under the burden of increasing caseloads. Everyone had less time to prepare for more cases, and prosecutors felt pressured to negotiate pleas to avoid further trial delays.

Judges kept their promise to increase the length of sentences. But the state prison, operating under a court-mandated population limit, simply could not admit any more offenders. Those sentenced to prison therefore backed-up in the already crowded jail, where exhausted staff—burned-out, overworked, and seeing no end in sight—began resigning.

To make room for more inmates, prison officials were authorized by the state legislature to initiate an early release program. Previously, offenders served an average of two-thirds of their court-imposed sentence before being eligible for release. The average dropped to one-third with early release measures.

One of the offenders released through the program returned to Pleasantville and engaged in a spree of robberies that resulted in the death of a prominent citizen. The community was outraged and once again called for more police protection and stiffer sentences.

## Criminal Justice Impact Assessment

When plans are made to construct a public building, it is mandatory to conduct an impact study to assess the potential damage to the environment. But no similar criminal justice *system impact assessment* is required to assess the potential systemwide disruption of new public policies.

Whenever police departments are expanded, new laws are created, sentencing practices are altered, or any other crime-related action is taken, the change will create a ripple effect throughout the criminal justice system. In many cases, the impact can be so severe that unanticipated consequences will result. In fact, as described in the last close-up, the long-term outcome may be completely contradictory to the initial intent. If no one anticipates how crowded jails and prisons will become with more punitive sentences, if no one provides the resources to expand the capacity of corrections to deal with more offenders, then no one will be satisfied when "longer" sentences actually translate into less time served.

The legislative branch of government has a tendency to increase prison sentences with great public fanfare. But when it becomes apparent that correctional facilities cannot accommodate the influx, lawmakers much more quietly authorize speeded-up formulas whereby inmates can amass credits toward early release. Such measures are short-term, shortsighted reactions to crisis conditions. If we truly wish to change and improve corrections in a proactive, long-term manner, "the criminal justice system must . . . interact,

When the resources are not provided to expand the capacity of corrections to deal with more offenders, short-term responses to overcrowding are improvised. Courtesy of the Michigan Department of Corrections.

share information, and develop a consistent . . . policy of handling criminals in America."[39]

Using statistical projection techniques, decision makers can estimate the impact of new policies on future correctional populations and associated costs. Some might argue that prison capacity or financial limitations should not determine criminal justice practices. But criminal justice policy does not operate in a vacuum and "must be held accountable for its effect on the allocation of human and fiscal resources. At some point we must ask whether we can afford to lock up everyone who offends us."[40]

In that respect, the American Bar Association's Criminal Justice Committee has called for a "rational sentencing policy" in response to the nation's drug crisis, which, among other things, recommends that "all legislative actions affecting sentencing should be accompanied by a prison impact statement."[41] See the next "Close-up on Corrections" for an account of what has happened in the "drug war" without such rational, proactive planning.

With the foresight of a systemwide impact assessment, new policies and programs could be implemented more sensibly. Citizens and elected officials could know in advance what effect would be created on the system, what level of staffing and physical facilities would be needed for effective implementation, and what the ultimate cost would be. The quick-fix, shortsighted "solutions" and fads that have characterized so much of the management of criminal justice agencies[42] could be replaced by long-term analysis. Independent decisions could be replaced by systemwide planning. Reacting to change could be replaced by proactively addressing challenges. Without such foresight, criminal justice agencies will continue to compete for limited resources, trying to do more with less, but in fact, doing more less effectively.

---

*LEARNING GOALS*

*Do you know:*

- *How the democratic process influences correctional practices?*
- *The difference between the medical model and the justice model of public policy?*
- *How corrections has been affected by society's change from the medical model to the justice model?*

---

[39]Tom L. Allison, "Jails beyond Walls," *American Jails,* Vol. V, No. 3 (July/August 1991), p. 10.

[40]Nola M. Joyce, "A View of the Future: The Effect of Policy on Prison Population Growth," *Crime and Delinquency,* Vol. 38, No. 3 (July 1992), p. 368.

[41]*Responding to the Problem of Drug Abuse: Strategies for the Criminal Justice System* (Washington, DC: Draft Report of Ad Hoc Committee, Criminal Justice Section, American Bar Association, 1992), p. 60.

[42]Paul Whisenand and Fred Ferguson, *The Managing of Police Organizations,* Third Edition (Englewood Cliffs, NJ: Prentice Hall, 1989), pp. 3–5. Although Whisenand and Ferguson are primarily describing law enforcement management, their critique is equally applicable throughout the system.

Systemwide planning through a criminal justice policy impact assessment would better coordinate the efforts of police, courts, and corrections. But it is not a panacea for resolving their differences. To function effectively, a "system" requires goals upon which all components mutually agree.

Even within criminal justice agencies themselves, goals can be contradictory. Some police administrators, for example, place greater emphasis on crime prevention and community relations; others focus on "by-the-book" enforcement and criminal apprehension. Some judges stress holding offenders fully

---

❖ *CLOSE-UP ON CORRECTIONS*

Why There's No Room in Our Prisons

Over the past decade, at least 50% of all new criminal justice expenditures were directed toward drug law enforcement. Because of aggressive federal policy, all jurisdictions now spend a much higher proportion of their criminal justice budgets on enforcing drug laws. Local and state law enforcement officials complain that federal assistance places too great an emphasis on drug crimes. Local departments thus find themselves restructuring priorities based on federal aid requirements.

That means less money, time and resources devoted to investigating homicides, rapes, domestic abuse, child molestation, etc. Government programs reevaluate their priorities to keep pace with social change. Within the context of criminal justice expenditures, reevaluation has led to huge increases in anti-drug spending. These increases do not occur in a vacuum, but rather, come at the expense of other justice programs. . . .

The result of such [a] policy emphasis has not been greater public safety. Take the case of Florida, for example. While [former] drug czar Bob Martinez was Governor there, the state embarked upon the largest prison expansion in Florida's history. At the same time, however, Martinez pressed for increased drug law enforcement and the enactment of mandatory minimums for drug offenders. The result was as unfortunate as it was predictable. New drug offenders serving mandatory minimums outpaced prison construction, and the state was forced to put many violent felons on early release.

At the beginning of Martinez's tenure as Governor, violent felons served an average of 52% of their sentences. When he left office, the average time served had plummeted to 30%. It is clear that the public's safety was not well served by locking up record numbers of drug offenders. . . .

The time has come to tell the bureaucrats in Washington that they can't have everything. They can't lock up record numbers of nonviolent drug offenders and then tell us there is no room in the prisons. . . .

*Source:* Gregory Y. Porter, "Why There's No Room in Our Prisons," *Law Enforcement News* (July/August 1992), p. 10.

---

accountable for their crimes; others are more likely to consider extenuating circumstances. Some correctional officials see their mission as incapacitation; others believe that corrections has a responsibility to promote behavioral change. In fact, within the correctional system itself, there are a wide variety of opinions about what constitutes "success": "The Correctional Officers think it is *no escapes*. The Teachers think it is a *GED* or an *educated person*. The Social Workers think it is a *rehabilitated person*. The Administrators think it is *someone who has successfully done their time.*"[43]

Although these are admittedly broad generalizations based on narrow occupational perspectives, they do illustrate the conflicting views reflected by differing community sentiments. In that regard it must be acknowledged that criminal justice decisionmakers do not function in isolation. They are responsible to elected officials, who, in turn, are responsible to the public.

### The Public's Role in Policymaking

Public attitudes about crime, criminals, and what should be done about both change over time. We will see in Chapter 4 how demands for harsh physical punishments for relatively minor misdeeds were replaced as a more humanitarian society called for more moderate punishments. These changes are reflected in the laws that are passed and the governing authorities who are elected.

Elected officials carry out the mandate of the public through the administrators they appoint. For example, politicians elected on a strong law-and-order platform are likely to express public opinion in the appointment of police chiefs and correctional administrators who share their philosophy. (In fact, the office of sheriff—responsible for both law enforcement and the jail—represents a direct expression of public attitudes, since it is typically an elected position.) If the public is dissatisfied with the outcome, the next election may find incumbents facing strong opposition from politicians with a different perspective. Thus, our democratic system of government assures that the opinions of the majority will be influential in the establishment of public policies. The difficulty for the criminal justice system is continuing to operate efficiently in the midst of such political and policy changes.

### Changing Public Policies

In the past several decades, criminal justice agencies have been required to adjust to dramatic shifts in public policies concerning crime and criminals. The public has changed its thinking about what causes people to commit crime, what types of sentences offenders should receive, and what corrections should be accomplishing.[44] Such changes are reflected in what has come to be known as the *medical model* and the *justice model* of criminal justice policymaking.

---

[43]Klaus P. Hilgers, "What Is Our Product? A New Perspective on Corrections," unpublished paper (Clearwater, FL: Epoch Consultants, 1991), p. 3.
[44]Much of this section is summarized from William G. Archambeault and Betty J. Archambeault, *Correctional Supervisory Management* (Englewood Cliffs, NJ: Prentice Hall, 1982), pp. 164–68.

Before exploring these policy models in greater detail, however, it is important to note that they do not necessarily represent clearly defined, distinct phases or an overnight transition from one to the other. Rather, each emerged gradually over time, and in fact, the "medical" and "justice" labels attached to them were coined in retrospect. It is only through the analysis of hindsight that their philosophies and resulting practices appear to be so unique and even contradictory today. Nor was the shift from the medical model to the justice model an immediate policy change that occurred through mutual agreement on a specified date. Rather, it was an evolutionary change driven by prevailing social opinion as expressed in the political arena and ultimately reflected in public policy. Nor are the concepts of these approaches completely mutually exclusive. As we will see much later (Chapter 15), elements of both can be combined operationally into an integrated justice/treatment model. But first, let us review the ingredients of each.

**The Medical Model.**   When you are ill, you see a doctor. You trust the doctor to diagnose your problem and prescribe medication to cure your illness. You do not expect the doctor to punish you for being sick. Similarly, the *medical model* of criminal justice, prevalent from the 1930s through the mid-1970s, views offenders as engaging in crime because of forces beyond their control. The forces shaping criminal behavior might be psychological (e.g., mental illness), sociological (e.g., disruptive family environment), economic (e.g., unemployment), or even physiological (e.g., improper diet). The point is that offenders are not held strictly accountable for their actions, any more than a patient suffering from an illness would be.

Because much of the burden for crime causation is placed on society in this line of reasoning, it is society that the medical model holds responsible for "diagnosing" the offender's "illness" and prescribing a "cure." In essence, the medical model views society as owing the offender "some sort of compensation."[45] In corrections, this philosophy translated into accountability for changing clients into law-abiding citizens and successfully returning them to the community— that is, rehabilitating and reintegrating.

It is not surprising that the medical model emerged in the 1930s, when exciting advances in psychology, psychiatry, and social work were demonstrating the potential for successful treatment of personal and social problems. It was also during this era that a worldwide economic depression changed the outlook of many who had previously believed that success and stability were solely the products of one's own initiative. The principles of the medical model clearly expressed public opinion at the time.

If offenders were to be effectively treated according to the medical model, it was essential that sentencing reflect their individual needs. Yet, social and psychological sciences are somewhat imprecise, making it difficult to determine how long a client would require treatment before being "cured." The object of sentencing under this model was therefore to "determine the conditions most conducive to rehabilitation,"[46] which translated into *indeterminate sentences*.

[45]Ibid., p. 164.
[46]Ibid., p. 165.

Under indeterminate sentencing practices, convicted offenders receive flexible terms, which can range anywhere between one year (or less) and life. Indeterminate sentencing was designed to enable a specific treatment plan to be prepared in which the offender participated for an indefinite period of time—until rehabilitated. When correctional officials, in conjunction with treatment personnel, determined that rehabilitation had occurred, the inmate was released on parole.

But while the medical model was so named because of its resemblance to the medical profession, it did not apply quite so precisely to corrections. Criminals convicted of the same offenses ended up serving widely differing lengths of time in correctional institutions, creating *sentencing disparities.*

Some inmates learned to manipulate the system to their advantage, essentially faking behavioral changes. Others were able to adjust their behavior while confined, but—unable to cope with freedom—reverted to criminal activities (i.e., recidivated) upon release. Nor did the taxpayers provide the full array of resources needed to adequately address the wide-ranging needs of correctional clientele, even assuming that their needs could be accurately identified.

Corrections may have been faced with an impossible mandate. But few took this into consideration as escalating crime rates, more conservative public attitudes, and high rates of recidivism created "get-tough-on-crime" demands by the mid-1970s. Perhaps the most devastating blow to the medical model came with the 1974 "Martinson report,"[47] which has often been cited to demonstrate the ineffectiveness of various forms of treatment programs: "Although the report merely confirmed the reality which correctional workers had been facing for years—namely, that some approaches work with some offenders under certain conditions and that nothing works with all offenders under all conditions—it had profound political and policy effects on corrections."[48]

Combined with other social forces that were challenging the assumptions of the medical model, the Martinson report was interpreted as evidence that the model was not working. As public confidence eroded in the ability of corrections to truly "rehabilitate," so too did faith in the principles of the medical model.

**The Justice Model.**   By the mid-1970s society had become increasingly frustrated with the system's inability to deal effectively with crime. No longer were people as eager to "excuse" criminal behavior as the product of forces outside the offender's control. A renewed emphasis on personal responsibility emerged, which eventually became known as the *justice* (or crime control) *model,* since its focus was on controlling crime and seeing justice served.

Under this new philosophy, people are viewed as capable of making rational choices—of deciding through their own free will whether or not to engage in crime. It therefore stands to reason that if one freely elects to commit a crime, punishment should follow to deter other potential criminals, achieve justice, and hold the person accountable for his or her actions.

---

[47]Robert Martinson, "What Works—Questions and Answers about Prison Reform," *The Public Interest,* Vol. 35 (Spring 1975), pp. 22–54.
[48]Archambeault and Archambeault, p. 3.

Unlike the indeterminate sentencing practices of the medical model, determinate sentences of "flat" or "fixed" length are called for in the justice model. Under this line of reasoning, "sanctions should be clear, explicit, and highly predictable."[49] The theory is that in this way, criminals know what punishment will be imposed for their actions, similar crimes will receive similar sentences, and projected release dates will not be subject to manipulation. With sentences that are proportional to the seriousness of the crime, the justice model maintains that offenders receive their *"just desserts,"* society obtains *retribution* for their criminal acts, and the community is *protected* during the period of their incarceration. Since this model is not based on the goal of rehabilitation, the length of the sentence is not determined by treatment effectiveness. Punishment is seen as being for the "good of society; treatment for the good of the offender."[50]

The justice model incorporates treatment only on a voluntary basis, in keeping with the belief that changing one's behavior cannot be forced, but rather, requires voluntary consent. As with the commission of crime, it holds that one must freely elect whether or not to seek personal change. Under the medical model, involvement in treatment was virtually required to become eligible for parole. However, the justice model would not penalize inmates who do not choose to participate in treatment, and in fact, advocates the abolishment of parole discretion to assure more uniformity in sentencing.

In contrast to the rehabilitation and reintegration goals of corrections under the medical model, the mission of corrections changed to a greater emphasis on incapacitation under the justice model. In more recent years, this approach has concentrated on *selectively* incapacitating those identified as a danger to the community because of the seriousness of their crimes and potential for recidivism. With mandatory treatment no longer required, the justice model defines the role of corrections as "legally and humanely" *controlling* the offender (either through community supervision or incarceration) and providing "voluntary treatment services."[51] In theory, corrections is therefore not accountable for changing behavior, but only for safe and secure control during the period in which the offender is under correctional supervision. (See Figure 1.10 for a summary of the differences between the medical model and the justice model.)

### Implications for Corrections

As every correctional official knows all too well, theory does not necessarily reflect reality. While a conservative society enthusiastically embraced the punitive sentencing, free will, and just desserts principles of the justice model, corrections has not escaped "blame" for the failures of its clients. When ex-offenders recidivate, the public still wants to know why corrections is not doing its job, while many correctional employees wonder just what that job is supposed to be.

[49]Dean J. Champion, *Corrections in the United States* (Englewood Cliffs, NJ: Prentice Hall, 1990), p. 24.

[50]Archambeault and Archambeault, p. 165.

[51]Ibid., p. 166.

|  | Medical Model | Justice Model |
|---|---|---|
| Crime is a result of . . . | Forces in society over which the offender has little or no control | The free will of the offender, who elects to engage in crime over law-abiding alternatives |
| Crime is best prevented by . . . | Changing the motivations which shape one's behavior | The deterrent effect of swift and certain punishment |
| Sentencing should be designed to . . . | Cure the offender through treatment, rehabilitation, and reintegration into the community | Punish the offender, protect society, and hold criminals accountable for their behavior through incarceration |
| The length of sentence should be . . . | Indeterminate (flexible) | Determinate (fixed) |
| Inmates should be released from confinement . . . | Through parole, when they are rehabilitated | Through mandatory release, after they have served their full term |

**Figure 1.10** Comparison of the medical model and the justice model.

Undoubtedly, there remains a "lack of agreement on the purpose of correctional agencies in our society."[52] Should corrections completely abandon the rehabilitative ideal, not concern itself with reintegration, and simply incapacitate or supervise offenders during the length of their sentence? Despite the advent of the justice model, in practice, corrections is still expected to, as the word itself implies, "correct": "The police are directed to arrest law breakers; prosecutors are expected to charge, try and convict offenders; and judges are empowered to punish those offenders. Correctional agencies, on the other hand, are usually *expressly charged* with the crime prevention function."[53]

Whether implicitly or explicitly responsible for crime prevention, corrections often becomes the scapegoat when the crimes of ex-offenders are not prevented. Public policies notwithstanding, it is corrections which remains accountable for its former clients. The fact that this situation is not officially recognized and endorsed by society only makes the mission of corrections all the more difficult and ambiguous. It is like telling a football coach to win games, then restricting the game plan and the equipment (not to mention draft choices)! Corrections was never well equipped to fulfill its rehabilitative function, and when that func-

[52]Lawrence F. Travis, Martin D. Schwartz, and Todd R. Clear, eds. *Corrections: An Issues Approach* (Cincinnati, OH: Anderson Publishing Company, 1980), p. xi.
[53]Ibid., p. 14.

tion became submerged with the justice model, it created a situation of *account-ability without authority*. Although corrections remains inherently "responsible" for its clients, it has neither the scope of authority nor sufficiency of resources to fulfill that responsibility successfully.

If there is such goal conflict within one component of the criminal justice system, it is not surprising that there is little agreement on what the system over-all requires to enhance its effectiveness. However, there appears to be at least one priority on which officials throughout the system appear to agree.

As more offenders were sentenced to longer periods of incarceration under the justice model during the 1980s, prison and jail capacities were strained to the limit. In 1989, correctional institutions in 36 of the 50 states were under court order.[54] Most of these orders related to reducing prison populations or improving conditions of confinement related to overcrowding. Although construction of new institutions was at an all-time high in the late 1980s and early 1990s, the availability of new beds has not kept pace with demand—a situation that has not gone unnoticed throughout the criminal justice system.

By the mid-1980s, in a survey of over 2000 state criminal justice administra-tors (representing corrections, police, prosecutors, public defenders, courts, and probation/parole), five of the six groups gave overcrowding in correctional institutions top priority. Crowded institutions were mentioned more often than any other topic when these officials throughout the criminal justice system were asked to identify the most pressing problem facing their state.[55] Nor have condi-tions improved since then. In a follow-up study conducted in 1992, institutional crowding—along with related staff and funding shortages—continued to rank as the key problems facing corrections in the immediate future.[56]

Thus, even if there is lack of agreement about what corrections should be accomplishing, there is some consensus among criminal justice colleagues that corrections can no longer attempt to absorb public policy changes without at least additional physical resources. How many new institutions are needed? How much will it cost the public? No one can answer these questions precisely, and correctional administrators themselves might well prefer other alternatives. But lacking such alternatives, construction will continue. As a society, we may not agree on what to do with offenders once they get there, but we are apparent-ly committed to making sure that there is somewhere for them to go. For as long as there is crime, there will be a need for corrections.

## ❖ SUMMARY

Developing a framework for the study of corrections is no easy task given the complexity of its services, the nature of its relationships with the rest of the crim-inal justice system, and the impact of public policies on its operations. At a cost

---

[54]*Vital Statistics in Corrections* (Laurel, MD: American Correctional Association, 1991), p. 52.

[55]Stephen Gettinger, "Assessing Criminal Justice Needs," *National Institute of Justice: Research in Brief* (Washington, DC: U.S. Department of Justice, 1984), p. 2.

[56]Charles B. DeWitt, "Assessing Criminal Justice Needs," *National Institute of Justice: Research in Brief* (Washington, DC: U.S. Department of Justice, 1992), p. 8.

of almost $25 billion, over 555,000 workers service the needs of 4.3 million clients in the correctional conglomerate. This conglomerate includes both custodial institutions and community-based alternatives. It assists adults as well as juveniles. It operates maximum, medium, and minimum security facilities and programs. It functions at the federal, state, and local level of government, and even within the private sector. In short, it provides care, custody, and control to those accused or convicted of a criminal offense. But it does not do so in a vacuum.

Every action taken, every policy formulated, every priority established by those within the criminal justice system has a potential impact on corrections. It is the "first stop" and the "last resort" for defendants processed through a system burdened by functional fragmentation and jurisdictional separation. It is affected by the laws created by the legislature, appointments made by elected officials, and decisions rendered by the judiciary. But perhaps above all, it is a reflection of the changing values, beliefs, and attitudes of society—which have variously directed corrections to treat, rehabilitate, and reintegrate offenders through the medical model, and more recently, simply to control those confined under the justice model. It is a complex, diverse, and often frustrating field of endeavor—which is exactly what makes it such a challenging, dynamic, and fascinating subject of study.

# chapter 2

# Crime and the Correctional Process

*Times Square, New York. . . . There, in stark relief, is the intrinsic tension between what adults do in pursuit of pleasure and the laws that define their behavior as criminal. Legal codes, enacted through the political process, may or may not reflect a broad consensus on good and evil. But they definitely represent the values of those who have the power to influence lawmaking.*[1]

*Georgette Bennett*

## ❖ CHAPTER OVERVIEW

Crime captivates public attention. Shocking criminal acts headlined in the media, televised accounts of courtroom drama, and personal fear of victimization all stimulate our interest in crime. Crime generates widespread concern, and coping with it presents an equally enormous challenge.

First, there is the basic issue of what should be considered criminal conduct. Since there is no universally accepted concept of "crime," society relies on the legislative process to define and sanction criminality. What is prohibited in the criminal statutes therefore becomes the legal definition of criminal behavior. But it is clear that merely legislating against something does not alleviate the problem. Moreover, there is sometimes basic disagreement over whether certain crimes should be addressed at all through the formal legal process. Then there is the difficulty of measuring crime. Existing procedures do not always provide a very reliable basis on which to determine whether we are any more or less successful in controlling criminal behavior. Finally, there is the challenge of seeking solutions, for it is rather futile to define and measure crime if we cannot develop appropriate responses to reduce its reoccurrence.

Each of these crime-related issues is addressed in this chapter since they play a significant role in the formation of public policy. Ultimately, it is the manner in which society responds to criminal behavior that will shape the nature of corrections.

[1]Georgette Bennett, *The Future of Crime in America* (New York: Anchor Books, 1989), pp. 209–10.

## ❖ DEVIANCE AND THE LAW

Legal restrictions are an integral part of everyday life—from the moment birth is certified until death is officially pronounced, virtually everything we do is governed to some extent by law. Food and drug laws regulate what we eat. Zoning ordinances determine where we can live. Compulsory education laws regulate the length of our schooling. Motor vehicle codes govern our driving practices. Tax laws establish how much we must pay to support the vast bureaucracy overseeing all of these regulations.

Most of us accept the need for such restrictions as a necessary individual sacrifice to support orderly group life. That is, we are willing to give up some degree of personal freedom in the overall interests of society. For example, while Americans cherish the right to free speech, yelling "fire!" in a crowded theater is not viewed as an acceptable expression of that right, because it jeopardizes the safety of others. Individual liberty extends only to the point where it does not interfere with the interests of society.

As the primary vehicle for maintaining social order, laws must attempt to balance individual rights and public interests (see Figure 2.1). Social order could be more efficiently achieved by tipping the balance in favor of the interests of society, as is the practice in totalitarian governments. We could, for example, substantially reduce crime by placing police officers on every corner, employing constant video surveillance, allowing the police free access to private homes, requiring personal identity checks at the border of each city or town, and so on. But in a democracy, we place a high value on the right of the individual to be free from unnecessary government intrusion. In exchange for more personal freedoms, we tolerate some amount of crime that could be prevented by more repressive measures.

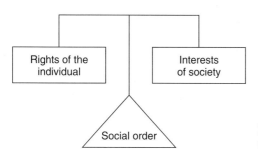

**Figure 2.1** Balancing individual rights and public interests.

At each stage in society's development, social patterns and the problems relating to them have become increasingly complex. The methods of social control, of enforcing the laws, and of punishing law violators have changed with the times. Early social systems were not governed by formal laws. On the other hand, modern American citizens endure the regulation of virtually all phases of life and living conditions.

When this country was composed of independent pioneers whose lifestyles seemingly affected no one, the need for rules governing personal conduct was minimal. But America is no longer a nation of spirited individualists conquering the hazards of undeveloped frontiers. The pressures of population growth, urbanization, and industrialization have forced us to take far more actions to regulate the conduct of the individual for the good of the community. From early times to modern days, controls grew as needed to fit the social conditions in which people lived. As described in the next "Close-up on Corrections," crime has evolved from the cultural values and social problems of society.

### Differing Perspectives on Crime

If everyone agreed on what type of conduct is socially acceptable, there would be less need for the creation of laws. But people differ in their perception of what is right and wrong, particularly in a society with as much cultural diversity as exists in the United States. As a result, the public does not necessarily agree on what should be considered "criminal."

> For example, citizens quarrel about whether induced abortion is a "right" or "murder." They debate whether keeping a bawdy house should or should not be criminal, and they disagree about whether "aiding and abetting" suicide should be the concern of the state. Arguments persist about whether crimes should be made out of driving without a seat belt, riding a bike without a helmet, spreading "hate literature" and pornography, having "too many" children, and selling "harmful" products.[2]

Because of such disagreements, crime is a rather loosely used word. We fear "crime in the streets," express concern over "rising crime rates," and seek to alleviate our fear and concern by legislating as "criminal" everything from first-degree murder to public intoxication. But just what *is* this behavior we so ambiguously refer to as "crime"?

Depending on one's perspective, crime can be interpreted as "an illegal act, behavior that is injurious to society, acts that deviate greatly from accepted norms," or even more basically, "sins" or "falsehoods."[3] But one can act illegally, injuriously, deviantly, sinfully, or untruthfully without being declared "criminal." Running a red traffic light is illegal. Abusing power is injurious. Wearing jeans to a formal dinner is deviant. Disobeying parents is sinful. Telling lies is

[2]Gwynn Nettler, *Responding to Crime* (Cincinnati, OH: Anderson Publishing Company, 1982), p. 25.

[3]Martin R. Haskell and Lewis Yablonsky, *Criminology: Crime and Criminality* (Chicago, IL: Rand McNally, 1974), p. 4.

The earliest behavioral norms were developed as *folkways* and *customs*—that is, habitual ways of doing things. For example, among the Plains Indians, it was taboo to scare away buffalo; while among the Eskimos, it was forbidden to harm seals. Even today, undeveloped groups in some parts of the world have no formal systems of political government, but rather, are governed by custom. As people developed more complex civilizations, emotional values were attached to some customs and they became institutionalized into cultural behavior as "right" and "wrong."

With the development of organized religion, creeds emerged to control interactions between people. These were more complex and refined than the early folkways and customs. After the development of writing, tribal taboos were set down in codes, such as the Code of Hammurabi in Babylon (about 1750 B.C.). One of the most influential codes was the Twelve Tables of wood on which were engraved the earliest codification of Roman law.

The Justinian Code was the last formulation of law between the ancient Roman Empire and the social chaos of the Middle Ages. Rome gave civilization the most refined practice of law known to that date. The common law as it is known today is basically derived from the code of the Justinian courts. From the fourth century A.D. until the late Middle Ages, the Roman Catholic Church was also an important agent of social control. Bishops were empowered to act as judges, and ecclesiastical courts eventually obtained jurisdiction over most issues, civil as well as criminal.

Parlimentary government began in England in the fourteenth and fifteenth centuries, when legislation was introduced to secure the social order. Laws forbidding war against the king, forbidding serfs to leave the land in search of work, and forbidding dogs from being kept by persons not owning property were invoked in an effort to maintain the status quo. During the sixteenth and seventeenth centuries, legislation was aimed at consolidation of church and state. Treason and heresy became capital crimes, as did swearing, adultery, and witchcraft.

In summary, it takes a long time to develop methods to control the behavior of groups. Primitive tribes used customs as a control mechanism. After a period of time, they attached emotional meaning to that custom, and it became "right" or "wrong." The next step in the development of social controls was the institutionalization of behavior in the culture. Then it became law. An example is the emergence of monogamous marriage. In early times, it was "customary" for one man and one woman to stay together. Then it became "right." After more time, it became a sacrament of the church. Then it became law. Primitive people lived by custom. Ancient people lived by mores and codes. Those in the Middle Ages lived by social institutions, primarily the church. Modern people live by law. The concept of law has taken a long time to come this far, changing dramatically with each passing century.

untruthful. But in and of themselves, none of these acts is *criminal*. In fact, it has been noted that "nothing is inherently criminal, it is only the response that makes it so."[4] In other words: "'crime' is not a concrete thing that can be easily measured. It is an idea, or a mental and social construct. In essence, it is a 'label' that is placed on some forms of behavior and not on others. . . . Official data of crimes serve . . . as an index of official reaction to deviant behavior."[5]

### Determining Criminality

When society becomes sufficiently disturbed by a particular type of behavior and responds by incorporating that act into the criminal code, it officially becomes a "crime." This does not, however, mean that everyone believes that it is equally harmful, such as in the case of many "vice" and "common decency" crimes. (It has only been within recent years, for example, that many states have eliminated homosexuality from criminal statutes.) Rather, it means that either enough people were in agreement to achieve *consensus,* or enough of those wielding power were able to exert their influence and resolve the *conflict* by having their views prevail. For a synopsis of the differences between these perspectives, see Figure 2.2.

**Consensus Model.**   According to the consensus point of view, criminal law originates—and behavior becomes defined as "criminal"—through various social processes:[6]

• *Group response to wrongful behavior.* One consensus-based theory views criminal law as evolving from *wrongs to individuals.* That is, all injuries were orig-

| Consensus | | Conflict |
|---|---|---|
| | Views criminal law as *based on* . . . | |
| Group agreement | | Group conflict |
| | *determined by* . . . | |
| Majority rule | | Powerful special interests |
| | *resulting in* . . . | |
| Development of a system of basic community standards | | Selective labeling of behavior according to social class |

**Figure 2.2**   Differences between consensus and conflict theories of criminal law.

[4]William J. Chambliss and Milton Mankoff, eds., *Whose Law? What Order?* (New York: Wiley, 1976), p. 102.
[5]Sue Titus Reid, *Crime and Criminology*, Second Edition (Hinsdale, IL: Dryden Press, 1979), p. 92.
[6]Much of the following material on consensus theory is summarized from Edwin H. Sutherland and Donald R. Cressey, *Criminology*, Tenth Edition (Philadelphia, J.B. Lippincott, 1978), pp. 9–11.

inally perceived as harmful to the individual victim, who then sought redress. When society began to assume responsibility for the transaction between victim and offender, these wrongs came to be regarded as harmful to the group or the state. According to this viewpoint, acts injurious to the individual take priority over those harmful to the entire group. There is presumed to be agreement over what acts should be legislated against.

- *Group consensus.* Another consensus-based theory perceives law as originating in the *rational processes of a unified society.* According to this assessment, law evolved from group determination that certain acts should be declared public wrongs in order to prevent their repetition. Criminal law is thus seen as a logical outgrowth of "public opinion," regardless of whether that opinion is based on an emotional expression (as in the case of prohibition against the sale of alcohol during the 1920s), or as a rational reaction to serious wrong-doing (as in the case of homicide).

- *Group mores.* One additional viewpoint based on consensual origin explains criminal law as the *product of group mores.* As customary patterns of behavior developed (mores), society reacted against infraction of these traditions by incorporating them into law. Law came to be a reflection of acceptable group behavior. But since behavioral patterns change more rapidly than legal definitions, some currently socially acceptable acts (such as purchasing restricted merchandise on a Sunday) remain legally forbidden in certain jurisdictions.

**Conflict Model.** The conflict version of criminal law focuses on the *resolution of differing group interests* through the enactment of laws. This theory maintains that both upper- and lower-class groups are involved in varying types of behavior which could be labeled "criminal," although upper-class deviant behavior is more likely to be discrete and less likely to be directly harmful than is that of the lower classes. But according to the *conflict model,* the political power of more privileged groups enables them to legislate against the activities of the lower classes to preserve their own special interests. For example, research indicates that the original purpose of vagrancy laws was "to keep cheap labor bound to the land"[7] and that they were enacted to provide wealthy landowners with manual labor needed in the fields after the Black Death in Europe.[8] Thus "whenever a law is created or interpreted, the values of some are . . . assured and the values of others either ignored or negated."[9]

Development and enforcement of criminal law is therefore viewed by conflict theorists as a reflection of the differential *distribution of power* in society. According to this perspective, the criteria for stigmatizing certain types of behavior as "criminal" are established by special-interest groups rather than widespread

[7]Shirley M. Hufstedler, "Should We Give Up Reform?" in Ralph A. Weisheit and Robert G. Culbertson, *Juvenile Delinquency: A Justice Perspective* (Prospect Heights, IL: Waveland Press, 1985), p. 193.

[8]Chambliss and Mankoff, p. 71.

[9]Richard Quinney, *The Social Reality of Crime* (Boston: Little, Brown, 1970), p. 37. See also Howard S. Becker, *Outsiders: Studies in the Sociology of Deviance* (New York: Free Press, 1963), p. 9, who maintains that "deviance is *not* a quality of the act the person commits, but rather, a consequence of the application by others of rules and sanctions. . . ."

consensus. In essence, conflict theory maintains that "we can have as much or as little crime as we please, depending on what we choose to count as criminal."[10]

Obviously, some criminal acts—murder, aggravated assault, armed robbery, rape—are so widely feared that their illegal status represents virtually universal consensus. But others—marijuana use, pornography, gambling—involve less widespread consensus. Some represent the ability of certain groups to impose their values on the majority. In still other cases, such as gun control, legislative action can be blocked by powerful interest groups. Not only does "crime" mean different things to different people, but its very existence depends to some extent on the differential ability to affect the legislative process.

---

*LEARNING GOALS*

*Do you know:*
- *The legal definition of crime?*
- *The conditions that must exist for an act to be considered criminal?*
- *What the "relativity" of crime is and how it affects who is labeled "criminal?"*

---

## ❖ DEFINITION OF CRIME

For those involved in the criminal justice system, it is, of course, the legal definition of crime that is of primary importance, regardless of whether that definition was achieved through consensus or conflict. The legal classification of crime makes a difference not only in the law enforcement process in terms of who will be arrested, but also in corrections, since correctional clients are those officially convicted of legally defined criminal acts. "Under the *legal definition* of crime, criminal behavior differs from other forms of social deviance in that it is in violation of the criminal laws promulgated by a political authority and subject to punishment administered by agents of the state."[11]

While many forms of behavior are deviant, they may or may not be criminal. For example, refusing to stand for the national anthem is certainly deviant, but not illegal. Parking in a restricted area is obviously illegal, but not criminal. On the other hand, criminal acts are—by their very definition—presumed to be both deviant and illegal.

### Necessary Conditions

For an act to be officially considered "criminal," a number of conditions must exist:[12]

---

[10]Herbert Packer, *The Limits of the Criminal Sanction* (Stanford, CA: Stanford University Press, 1968), p. 364.

[11]Elmer H. Johnson, *Crime, Correction, and Society,* Third Edition (Homewood, IL: Dorsey Press, 1974), p. 15.

[12]Several of the conditions outlined herein are summarized from Haskell and Yablonsky, pp. 5–7.

1. *There must be a prohibiting law.* No act can be labeled a crime if there is not a specific criminal code either restricting that behavior or requiring it (as in the case of an act of omission). Moreover, the law cannot be used *ex post facto*—sanctions cannot be applied to conduct committed prior to enactment of the law.

Criminal laws are classified into two major categories, *felonies* and *misdemeanors,* based on the seriousness of the offense. There is no uniform, nationwide distinction between these two types of offenses. What may be classified as a felony in one jurisdiction may be only a misdemeanor in another. But generally a felony is more serious, for which either death or confinement in the state or federal penal system can be invoked (although that does not prohibit a lesser punishment for a felony conviction). In contrast, misdemeanors are generally punishable by fines, probation, or incarceration in a local correctional facility. In some jurisdictions, misdemeanant incarceration is expressed in terms of months, with felony sentences expressed in terms of years.

2. *Punishment must be specified in the law.* In conjunction with the existence of a criminal code, the law must provide sanctions that can be imposed for the prohibited behavior. Punishments can range from the imposition of fines or probation to confinement for life, or even death in some states. But although one might argue that morally (and in accord with the justice model), punishment should "fit the crime," this is not necessarily a legal requirement. While the justice model has called attention to sentencing disparities, punishment for the same offense may still differ significantly, depending on individual circumstances and judicial discretion.

3. *There must be criminal intent (mens rea).* Literally translated, *mens rea* means "guilty mind." To be convicted of a crime, it must be determined that the offender had deliberately intended to commit the act and therefore could be held accountable for it. Small children and mental incompetents are not usually held responsible for criminal behavior because of the absence of *mens rea.*

4. *There must be an act or omission.* Mere intent to commit a crime is not sufficient. There must be action (or failure to act). Planning to commit murder, even to the point of arranging all of the preliminary details, does not constitute "murder" if the plans were not carried out. (However, the plotters may be arrested on conspiracy charges.) On the other hand, if the law requires performance of an act as a legal duty, failure to do so can constitute criminal negligence. For example, fleeing the scene of a fatal motor vehicle accident results in legally prohibited behavior which can be criminally prosecuted.

5. *Criminal intent and action must occur jointly.* In other words, what was intended must actually have been carried out. Intent without action, or vice versa—action without intent—does not constitute criminal violation.

Even given these very specific circumstances which must prevail before an act can be classified as a "crime," there is still considerable debate over who should be designated as a criminal. Is a criminal anyone who has *committed* a criminal act? Anyone who has been *arrested* in violation of a criminal law? Only those *convicted* of a crime? And how long should an offender be labeled "criminal?" Only while being *processed* through the system? Until one's probation, incarceration, or parole *term* is completed? For the remainder of one's *life?*

## Relativity of Crime

The difficulty in answering these questions relates to the public's basic perception of two distinct groups of people as being involved in crime: a minority of "criminals" and a majority of law-abiding citizens. Yet surveys have reported that the majority of the public at one time or another has committed an offense "for which they might have been sentenced if apprehended."[13] In other words, many of us simply have not been caught! This discrepancy may also be attributable to the "relativity" of crime. That is, what is defined as criminal in one place at one time and under one set of circumstances may not be so defined in another location, at a later date, under different circumstances.[14] Thus, "every time a new criminal law is passed, people whose behavior has previously been within the law become criminals by definition."[15]

Standards of law enforcement also change considerably over time. Although certain offenses, such as loitering, vagrancy, or adultery may still appear in the criminal code, they are not generally enforced. But regardless of the "relativity" of crime, it is apparent that crime is, in reality, more *normal* than *abnormal* in our society.

---

*LEARNING GOALS*

*Do you know:*

- *What crimes are included in the UCR's "crime index"?*
- *What factors affect the volume and type of reported crime in a community?*
- *The difference between the UCR and the National Crime Survey?*
- *Approximately what percentage of violent crimes known to victims are reported to the police?*

---

## ❖ EXTENT OF CRIME

Just how "normal" or prevalent is crime? No one knows for certain. Despite the fact that people have always been concerned over the amount of crime, a uniform, centralized crime-reporting system has been in existence in this country only since the 1930s. As early as 1829, England's Sir Robert Peel called for the

---

[13]President's Commission on Law Enforcement and Administration of Justice, *Task Force Report: Crime and Its Impact—An Assessment* (Washington, DC: U.S. Government Printing Office, 1967), p. 77.
    [14]Sutherland and Cressey, pp. 17–18.
    [15]Burton Wright and Vernon Fox, *Criminal Justice and the Social Sciences* (Philadelphia: W.B. Saunders, 1978), p. 135.

compilation and distribution of statistics in order to keep the citizenry informed of criminal activity, and the U.S. Congress mandated the collection of national crime statistics in this country some 40 years later. But initial efforts failed as a result of lack of cooperation from state and local law enforcement agencies.[16] Well over a half-century later, the lack of accurate, centrally collected, and comprehensive criminal statistics was criticized nationally by the Wickersham Commission, and in 1967, the President's Crime Commission noted with regard to crime reporting that "in some respects, the present system is not as good as that used in some European countries 100 years ago."[17]

## The *Uniform Crime Reports*

In conjunction with the Wickersham Commission's recommendations, a Committee on Uniform Crime Records was established by the International Association of Chiefs of Police, and in 1930, Congress authorized the Attorney General to gather crime information. The Attorney General designated the Federal Bureau of Investigation (FBI) to serve as the national clearinghouse for statistical information on crime.[18]

While the FBI collects, tabulates, and distributes the statistics contained in the annual *Uniform Crime Reports* (UCR), it is not solely responsible for the accuracy of the data. Previously, the UCR contained offense, arrest, and law enforcement information on local and state activities only (not federal). In 1988, Congress passed legislation mandating federal participation, which became effective with the 1991 reports. However, the FBI must still depend on the voluntary cooperation of several thousand independent local, state, and federal agencies throughout the country for the data published. Beyond the fundamental difficulty of obtaining the cooperation of such a multitude of agencies, the fact that each differs somewhat from the others in defining crime, enforcing the law, and maintaining criminal records restricts the reliability and comparability of UCR figures even further.[19]

The intent of the UCR is to enable comparisons of crime rates over time through creation of a *crime index*. Just as the index of a book gives an overview of its contents, the crime index is intended to provide an overview of fluctations in the amount and rate of crime.

The *amount* of crime is expressed by the number of reported offenses; the *rate* is the amount relative to the population. This permits comparison over time by both the number of offenses and the rate based on population figures. Thus, as reflected in Figure 2.3, the *number* of known offenses increased by 10% between 1987 and 1991. However, when the population during that time period is taken into account, we see that the crime *rate* increased by a slightly lower 6%. It would be misleading to report the number of offenses only, since a large population

[16]President's Commission on Law Enforcement and Administration of Justice, p. 124.
[17]Ibid., p. 123.
[18]Federal Bureau of Investigation, *Crime in the United States: Uniform Crime Reports* (Washington, DC: U.S. Government Printing Office, 1992), p. 1.
[19]Ronald H. Beattie, "Problems of Criminal Statistics in the United States," in Marvin E. Wolfgang, Leonard Savitz, and Norman Johnston, eds., *The Sociology of Crime and Delinquency* (New York: Wiley, 1962), p. 41.

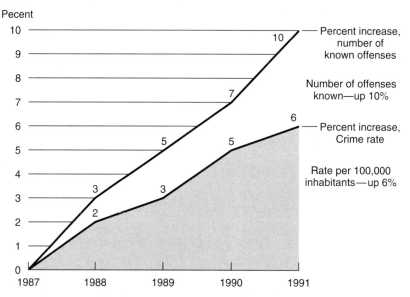

**Figure 2.3** Crime index changes, 1987–1991. *Source:* Federal Bureau of Investigation, *Crime in the United States: Uniform Crime Reports* (Washington, DC: U.S. Government Printing Office, 1992), p. 7.

with a large number of crimes would not be as much at risk of victimization as a smaller population with the same number of crimes. While Figure 2.3 points out that both are increasing, there is some comfort in observing that the *rate* of crime per 100,000 people is not increasing as rapidly as the absolute *number* of offenses.

UCR figures and rates are based on the "crime index," which is a summary of eight major offenses, involving both:

- *Personal violence:* murder, forcible rape, robbery, aggravated assault, and
- *Property crimes:* burglary, larceny-theft, motor vehicle theft, and arson.

The distribution of index offenses is illustrated in Figure 2.4, which indicates that although violent personal crimes are the most feared, it is actually *property crimes* that constitute the vast majority (87%) of index offenses.

Also demonstrating the greater prevalence of property crime is the FBI's "crime clock," which indicates how often offenses are committed—one violent crime every 17 seconds, in comparison with one property crime every 2 seconds. As noted in Figure 2.5, crime clocks should be viewed with care since they are calculated on the *absolute numbers* of offenses rather than on a *relative rate* based on population statistics. Moreover, when one's age, race, gender, and residence are taken into account, actual risk varies greatly, although the crime clocks could be interpreted erroneously as assuming that everyone stands the same chance of being victimized.[20]

[20]Harold J. Vetter and Ira J. Silverman, *The Nature of Crime* (Philadelphia: W.B. Saunders, 1978), pp. 35–36, citing Marvin E. Wolfgang, "Uniform Crime Reports: A Critical Appraisal," in *University of Pennsylvania Law Review*, Vol. 3 (1963), pp. 408–38.

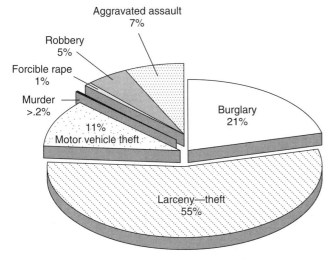

**Figure 2.4** Crime index offenses (percent distribution). *Note:* Arson data are included in reported trends, but sufficient data are not available to estimate totals for this offense. *Source:* Federal Bureau of Investigation, *Crime in the United States: Uniform Crime Reports* (Washington, DC: U.S. Government Printing Office, 1992), p. 8.

## Factors Affecting the Crime Rate

It is important to place such statistics in perspective. Crime figures may be a better measure of public policy than they are of criminal and delinquent behavior. A low crime rate or a high crime rate does not necessarily mean a healthy or an unhealthy community. A number of other factors must be consid-

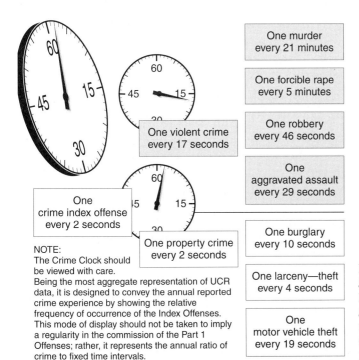

NOTE:
The Crime Clock should be viewed with care. Being the most aggregate representation of UCR data, it is designed to convey the annual reported crime experience by showing the relative frequency of occurrence of the Index Offenses. This mode of display should not be taken to imply a regularity in the commission of the Part 1 Offenses; rather, it represents the annual ratio of crime to fixed time intervals.

**Figure 2.5** Crime clock, 1991. *Source:* Federal Bureau of Investigation, *Crime in the United States: Uniform Crime Reports* (Washington, DC: U.S. Government Printing Office, 1992), p. 4.

ered before valid judgments can be made. Among them are various issues that affect the volume and type of reported crime:[21]

1. *Density, size, and stability of the population.* Metropolitan areas generally experience larger numbers of crimes per capita than less densely populated locations. This is not meant to imply that urban residents are more criminally inclined than their rural counterparts. The sheer numbers of people living in close proximity, their greater transiency, and the heterogeneous nature of metropolitan locations make them more vulnerable to crime.

2. *Composition of the population.* Younger persons, males, and certain minority groups are traditionally more likely to be arrested for criminal offenses. Thus, as the post–World War II baby boom reached its prime crime-involvement age, it was to be expected that considerable increases in the reported crime rate would occur. Similarly, communities with a large concentration of those most often apprehended for criminal offenses can anticipate higher crime rates.

3. *Economic status and cultural conditions.* A cause-and-effect relationship between economic conditions and crime cannot be proven with certainty. But it can be speculated that an economically secure community with strong informal rules of acceptable conduct will reflect lower crime rates than other areas.

4. *Climate.* Again, it is difficult to establish direct associations between the weather and crime. But crimes of personal violence appear to increase during warmer months, when people are outside and interacting more frequently, whereas property crimes are somewhat more prevalent during colder weather.[22]

5. *Effective strength of law enforcement agencies and public attitudes toward the police.* It may appear initially that a large per capita police force would be a factor in reducing crime. But as we saw in the "Pleasantville" experience (Chapter 1), exactly the opposite can occur. Larger numbers of enforcement personnel have some deterrent effect on preventing street crime. They are, however, also more likely to generate increased numbers of crimes merely by providing expanded observing and reporting capabilities. Moreover, in locations where the police are trusted and well respected by the citizenry, confidence in them and subsequent willingness to report crimes may well be enhanced. The resulting irony is that in areas with good police–community relations, crime rates may be higher as a reflection of public trust in the police.

6. *Policies of other components of the criminal justice system.* If citizens do not have confidence in the criminal justice system—if, for example, they believe that lenient practices will not result in more than perfunctory sanctioning of law violators—they may well feel that it is fruitless to report all but the most serious crimes.

7. *Crime-reporting practices of the citizenry.* Perhaps the greatest limitation of official statistics in the UCR is that they reflect only what is *known* to the police,

---

[21]The following categories are summarized from Federal Bureau of Investigation, *Crime in the United States*, p. v. This reference refers only to the listing of factors; explanatory comments are those of the authors.

[22]See John M. MacDonald, *The Murderer and His Victim* (Springfield, IL: Charles C Thomas, 1961), p. 10.

and in the case of crime, much more occurs than is known. There are many reasons why a victim might elect to avoid reporting crime—from lack of confidence in the system to unwillingness to become involved in the time-consuming process that follows when an arrest is made. Other common reasons involve a personal relationship with the offender (as in the case of spouse abuse), or the victim's belief that nothing could be done anyway.[23] The pedestrian whose wallet or purse is snatched is probably quite right in assuming that the money will not be recovered, even if the thief is identified. In cases where insurance coverage is involved, the likelihood of reporting is far greater, since that is usually a requirement for obtaining reimbursement. As a result, property crimes such as auto theft and burglary are more accurate indicators of criminal behavior than are personal crimes such as robbery and rape.

## The *National Crime Survey*

Because of variations in victim reporting practices, another major source of crime-related data has become the *National Crime Survey* (NCS). Initiated in 1972, the NCS measures both crimes reported to the police and unreported crimes, through household surveys asking whether respondents have been victimized.

While caution should be exercised in making comparisons between the UCR and the NCS because of differing methodologies,[24] it is not surprising to find that victim self-report studies have discovered that virtually all types of crimes occur more frequently than indicated in UCR statistics.

There are some crimes known only to the offender, which are obviously impossible to account for officially. But the NCS victimization studies reveal that even of those crimes known to the victims, *far less than half* (38%) were reported to the police. Nor is it just minor property crimes that are going unreported. Although *violent victimizations* are the most frequently reported crimes, even in this category, less than half (48%) were brought to the attention of the police in 1990.[25] As shown in Figure 2.6, such reporting trends have remained relatively stable over recent years.

## Implications for Corrections

Crime statistics are of concern to corrections because they generate the correctional caseload. Those persons represented in crime figures are not immediately correctional clients, since an extensive screening process occurs before an offender becomes part of the correctional system. Taking 1990 as an example, 4.3 million people were under some form of correctional care, custody, or supervi-

[23]For a review of the literature on nonreporting of crime and its relationship to self-help approaches of the victims, see Leslie W. Kennedy, "Going It Alone: Unreported Crime and Individual Self-Help," *Journal of Criminal Justice*, Vol. 16, No. 5 (1988), pp. 403–12.

[24]For a more extensive discussion of one approach to comparing these data bases, see Robert M. O'Brien, "Comparing Detrended UCR and NCS Crime Rates over Time: 1973–1986," *Journal of Criminal Justice*, Vol. 18, No. 3 (1990), pp. 229–38.

[25]Lisa D. Bastian and Marshall M. DeBerry, Jr., "Criminal Victimization 1990," *Bureau of Justice Statistics Bulletin* (Washington, DC: U.S. Department of Justice, 1991), p. 5.

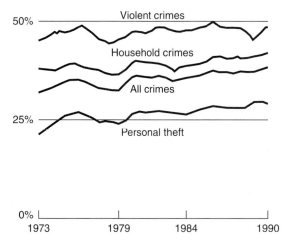

75% ───────────────────────────

50% ─── Violent crimes ───────

Household crimes

All crimes

25% ───────────────────────────

Personal theft

0% └──────┴──────┴──────┘
   1973    1979   1984    1990

**Figure 2.6** Percent of crimes reported to the police, 1973–1990. *Note:* Violent crimes include rape, robbery, and assault. Household crimes include home burglary and larceny, along with motor vehicle theft. *Source:* Lisa D. Bastiaan and Marshall M. DeBerry, Jr., "Criminal Victimization 1990," *Bureau of Justice Statistics Bulletin* (Washington, DC: U.S. Department of Justice, 1991), p. 5.

sion during that year.[26] Yet the National Crime Survey estimates that in the previous year (1989), over 35 million personal and household crimes were committed.[27] Moreover, 4 million of corrections' 4.3 million clients were *already* in the correctional system in 1989. Some offenders account for more than one crime, but it is difficult to imagine that 300,000 criminals were *each* responsible for an average of nearly 117 offenses.

This is admittedly an overly simplistic analysis, but the point is that many crimes are not reported, and of those that are, many are not solved. Additionally, even among offenses that are reported for which arrests are made, offenders will have been through a long screening process by the time they arrive in a correctional institution or caseload. During that process, a number will be "screened out." As shown in Figure 2.7, only a slight majority (54%) of felony law violators are ultimately convicted.

After the report of a crime, the police must determine whether the incident is serious enough to warrant a response. Even in those cases where the police do take action, the victim may choose not to press charges, or the event may not be classified as criminal. Of those felonies in Figure 2.7 that did generate an arrest, 45% of the cases were diverted, rejected, or dismissed. Of the remaining 54% who were convicted (predominately through guilty pleas), just over half (32) received the most severe

---

[26]Louis W. Jankowski, *Correctional Populations in the United States, 1990* (Washington, DC: U.S. Department of Justice, 1992), p. 5.
[27]Bastian and DeBerry, p. 3.

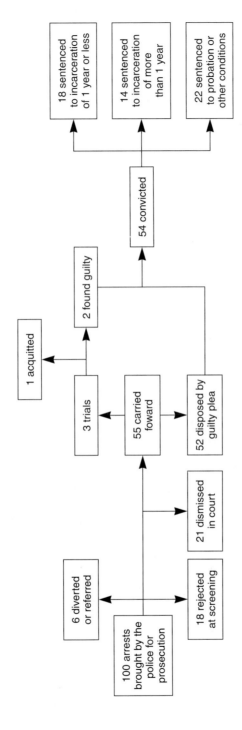

**Figure 2.7** Typical outcome of 100 felony arrests brought by the police for prosecution. *Source:* Barbara Boland, Paul Mahanna, and Ronald Sones, *The Prosecution of Felony Arrests, 1988* (Washington, DC: U.S. Department of Justice, 1992), cover page.

sanction of incarceration in prison or jail. Thus, as cases penetrate further and further into the criminal justice system, the number of offenders who remain in the system diminishes. As a result, corrections in general and custodial institutions in particular become the repository for those who were not able to "escape" at any prior stage.

---

*LEARNING GOALS*

*Do you know:*

- *What forms of retribution are used today?*
- *The difference between specific and general deterrence?*
- *What selective incapacitation is and what issues it raises?*
- *Whether collective incapacitation has reduced crime rates?*
- *Why rehabilitation is associated with indeterminate sentencing practices and what impact it has had?*
- *Why reintegration is necessary following release from correctional custody?*
- *Which correctional goals are reflected in the justice model and which are represented by the medical model?*

---

## ❖ SOCIETY'S RESPONSE TO CRIME

Just as society is not in agreement about what should be considered criminal behavior, there is little consensus about how to respond to it. In fact, there are many people who question why their tax dollars have to support "criminals" at all. The answer involves public policy, which is often a trade-off between economic goals and social values—a balance between what is *economically feasible* and what is *humanely desirable*. In fact, as the next "Close-up on Corrections" describes, during ancient and medieval times, society kept neither its serious offenders nor those who consumed more than they produced.

Public policy is a reflection of the prevailing views of society, which can differ widely when it comes to dealing with criminal behavior. It is public opinion concerning the appropriate response to crime which forms the basis for identifying the purpose of corrections—that is, what corrections is supposed to be accomplishing. Unfortunately, there is such a diversity of viewpoints over what should be "done with" law violators that it is impossible to identify any one mission or goal of corrections. At various times, corrections has been charged with fulfilling society's demand for retribution, deterrence, incapacitation, rehabilitation, and reintegration.

### Retribution

The belief that criminals deserve to be punished as repayment for their misdeeds is one of the oldest reactions to wrongdoing. The "law of retaliation" (*lex talionis*) traces its origins as far back as the Code of Hammurabi, as well as the Law of Moses, and the Old and New Testaments.

An Indian tribe in Labrador maintained a custom that the eldest son would kill his parents in a respectful and ritualistic manner when they began to consume more than they produced. Early Eskimo cultures had a practice in which the aging parents would kiss their families goodbye, go sit on the ice, and wait to die. Thousands of starving Romans threw themselves into the Tiber River during times of famine.

Primitive, ancient, and medieval people often did not have enough to eat and simply could not afford to keep nonproductive or dangerous people. In difficult economic situations, humanitarian values take second place. Even for modern society, the value system tends to lose its holding power when survival is threatened.

But with increased knowledge and improvements in technology, modern people have become more productive than their predecessors. Social programs began to appear in England with the Elizabethan Poor Law of 1601. Workhouses for minor offenders were built. At this point in society's economic development, people could begin to afford to keep those who were nonproductive, dangerous, or ill, and try to help them. Humanitarian values and social goals have thus become a part of public policy. In an affluent society, moral values can support "human rights," welfare payments, protection of children, and minimum standards for offenders. It is simply a matter of public policy choices.

In seeking retaliation, ancient and medieval punishments were violent and bloody—completely out of proportion to the seriousness of offenses. Common penalties were flogging, public boiling, mutilation, stocks and pillories, blinding, disemboweling alive, drawing and quartering, cutting out tongues, the rack (stretching a person by binding ankles and shoulders and pulling in opposite directions), and similar tortures.[28]

The modern-day concept of retribution is considerably more civilized than its early origins, although some still denounce it "because retribution invokes vengeance and sounds harsh."[29] In fact, it has been noted that retribution differs from revenge in that it is impersonally administered by "disinterested parties" through due process of law, which is designed to "balance the wrong done to the victim" rather than "incite retaliation."[30] As the public has become increasingly fearful of violent crime, frustrated over inability to control it, and concerned that criminals are not receiving their "just deserts," retribution has again

---

[28]Harry Elmer Barnes, *The Story of Punishment: A Record of Man's Inhumanity to Man* (New York: The Stratford Company, 1930), p. 63. Republished by Patterson Smith (Montclair, NJ, 1972). See also G. Abbott, *Tortures of the Tower of London* (London: David & Charles, 1986).

[29]Louis P. Carney, *Corrections: Treatment and Philosophy* (Englewood Cliffs, NJ: Prentice Hall, 1980), p. 6.

[30]Nettler, p. 11.

gained in popularity. Proponents of this view maintain that offenders freely elect to engage in criminal activities and should therefore be punished in order to "pay their debt" to society.

Punishment according to the modern view of retribution is generally in the form of some type of compensation or imprisonment. However, there are those who would argue for less humane conditions of confinement, even advocating a return to corporal punishment, and in fact, the death penalty remains an option in 36 states.[31]

*Capital punishment,* of course, is the ultimate retribution. As such, it has in recent years become a very controversial issue which provides an illustration of the divergence of opinions concerning correctional goals. The death sentence is reserved primarily for those convicted of homicide. If its purpose is vengeance or retribution, capital punishment serves a purpose. On the other hand, if it is designed to prevent such acts of violence, it is aimed at the wrong offenders. Murder is often a crime committed in the heat of passion or emotional strain, and its recidivism rate is low. Those convicted of homicide generally do not repeat their crime upon release from prison (and most are imprisoned and ultimately released). Thus, from a pragmatic point of view, retribution is the only goal truly achieved by imposition of the death penalty. (For a more extensive discussion of capital punishment, see Chapter 15.)

Punishment in the form of fines, restitution to the victim, community service, or other methods of "paying back" society are all types of retribution that have also recently received renewed emphasis. In fact, some are convinced that "punishment (insofar as it is justifiable at all) is justifiable only in terms of restitution. . . ."[32] In a capitalistic society, it is not surprising to find economics playing a significant role in the sanctioning of criminal behavior. Such sentences have been applauded as both holding offenders responsible for their actions and providing some relief to the victim to compensate at least partially for property loss, hospital bills, pain, or suffering. However, these sentencing practices have also been criticized as discriminating against the poor while allowing the rich simply to "write off" their wrongdoing with a check. There is no doubt that a $1000 fine is a severe imposition on a laborer receiving minimum hourly wages but only pocket change to a successful executive. To address this inequity, the Scandinavian system of *day fines* has been suggested, wherein the judge determines a number of "days" that the offender is to be fined (based on the seriousness of the offense and other related factors), with the amount paid per day based on the person's salary.[33]

While there is no valid evidence that the fear of punishment prevents crime, that is not actually the objective of retribution. Rather, the focus of retribution is on the satisfaction achieved by society in general and the victim in particular when criminals are required to "pay for their crimes"—whether in the form of economic compensation, loss of freedom, or even death.

[31]Lawrence A. Greenfeld, "Capital Punishment 1990," *Bureau of Justice Statistics Bulletin* (Washington, DC: U.S. Department of Justice, 1991), p. 1.

[32]Charles F. Abel and Frank H. Marsh, *Punishment and Restitution* (Westport, CT: Greenwood Press, 1984), p. 57.

[33]Hans Thornsted, "The Day Fine in Sweden," *Criminal Law Review* (June 1974), pp. 307–12.

## Deterrence

Unlike retribution, which reacts to past events, deterrence aims to prevent (i.e., deter) future criminal behavior. That is, retribution can be considered *reactive*, while deterrence is assumed to be *proactive*.

But despite the proactive emphasis of deterrence, it is not entirely unrelated to retribution. Both believe in holding offenders accountable for their behavior. Both see a relationship between increasing penalties and decreasing crime. In fact, it could be said that through retribution, deterrence can be achieved,[34] or put another way, "deterrence theory is used widely as a cloak for vengeance."[35] Whereas some would feel morally uncomfortable with demanding revenge, seeking to deter criminal behavior has a more socially acceptable connotation, even if the outcome is essentially the same for the offender.

The proactive nature of deterrence focuses on two approaches, specific and general:[36]

• *Specific deterrence* is directed toward the individual offender. The rationale is that by making the punishment sufficiently unpleasant, the offender will be discouraged from committing violations in the future. Just as a child is disciplined for inappropriate behavior to prevent its repetition, the idea is that criminals will avoid recidivism if punished properly .

• *General deterrence* is designed to use the offender to "set an example" for those who might otherwise consider engaging in similar criminal acts. The assumption is that crime will be reduced by "terrorizing bystanding citizens so much that they will be afraid to violate the law."[37] It requires punishment that is severe enough to have an impact, assurance that the sanction will be carried out, and enough examples to "remind people constantly of what lies ahead if they break the law."[38] Thus, both *certainty* and *severity* of punishment are essential ingredients in general deterrence.

This approach has been praised as necessary to "send a message" that crime will not be tolerated and that those involved in such activities will be dealt with firmly. On the other hand, general deterrence has been criticized because making an example of an offender "to discourage others from criminal acts is to make him suffer not for what he has done alone but because of *other* people's tendencies."[39] The issue posed by this line of reasoning is whether justice should

---

[34]See H. L. A. Hart, *Punishment and Responsibility: Essays in the Philosophy of Law* (Oxford: Clarendon Press, 1968).

[35]Karl Menninger, *The Crime of Punishment* (New York: Viking Press, 1968), p. 206.

[36]For a comprehensive review of deterrence literature and an assessment of its effectiveness, see Raymond Paternoster, "The Deterrent Effect of the Perceived Certainty and Severity of Punishment: A Review of the Evidence and Issues," *Justice Quarterly*, Vol. 4, No. 20 (June 1987), pp. 173–217.

[37]Donald R. Cressey, "Foreword," in Francis T. Cullen and Karen E. Gilbert, *Reaffirming Rehabilitation* (Cincinnati, OH: Anderson Publishing Company, 1982), p. xii.

[38]Todd R. Clear and George F. Cole, *American Corrections* (Monterey, CA: Brooks/Cole Publishing Company, 1986), p. 98.

[39]Menninger, p. 206.

be individualized to address specific deterrence, or generalized to serve as a warning to others.

In addition to this moral issue, generalized penalties also raise the question of *equity*, particularly when the punishment is out of proportion to the seriousness of the offense or the actual harm caused to society. Again, the death penalty is a good example.[40] The Federal Narcotic Act of 1956 was passed in the midst of what was then thought to be the "height" of the drug scare. It incorporated the death penalty for a second conviction of sale of drugs to a minor. "As could have been predicted—*because the penalty was inordinate*—no single individual was ever sentenced to death under this law. Nor did the sale of drugs abate."[41] But despite the historical ineffectiveness of this provision, there are demands today for the death penalty to deter major drug dealers.

On the other hand, individualized penalties present the dilemma of *applicability*, since what may be a deterrent to one may not be to another. People are motivated by different things: status, power, money, personal gratification, and so on. Likewise, they differ in terms of what is a deterrent to fulfilling their motivations. Some children, for example, can be reduced to tears simply by a parent's angry look, while others in the same family will test the extremes of their parents' tolerance, regardless of the penalties! In other words, what is a deterrent to one person is not necessarily equally productive with others. We cannot take it for granted that "penalty X will have the same influence, whether applied to transgressor A, B, C, or D."[42] To do so would also require assuming that (1) law violators believe they will be apprehended (which most do not), (2) criminals rationally plan their activities—that "burglars think like district attorneys," and (3) "the threat of punishment will result in an orderly process" whereby "the crime rate will diminish as the penalty scale increases. . . ."[43] However, many crimes are acts of passion or spontaneous responses, and many criminals are repeat offenders who have already experienced the presumably "deterrent" effect of punishment.

The extent to which either convicted or potential law violators are deterred by severe punishments is virtually impossible to determine accurately, because only those who are *not* deterred become clients of the criminal justice system. But that does not necessarily mean that the goal of deterrence is sought exclusively through harsh sentencing practices. More recently, "shock" incarceration and even "shock" parole have been experimented with to determine whether the shock of brief imprisonment (or unexpected release) might assist in deterring future law violations.

Whether deterrence is simply a more refined version of retribution or a distinct correctional goal in and of itself, with increased fear of crime, it has gained popular appeal as a result of its association (valid or not), with crime prevention.

[40]The following example is paraphrased from Carney, p. 7.
[41]Ibid.
[42]Ibid., p. 8.
[43]Franklin E. Zimring and Gordon J. Hawkins, *Deterrence* (Chicago: University of Chicago Press, 1973), pp. 19–20.

## Incapacitation

If retribution is viewed as reactive and deterrence as proactive, incapacitation could be characterized as something in between, or perhaps a combination of both. In its reactive sense, incapacitation in a correctional institution is to some degree a punishment for past behavior, although it is not technically "punishment" that is sought by incapacitation, but simply restraint. In a proactive sense, it is designed to prevent criminal activities—not so much in the future, as with deterrence—but more realistically, during the period when an offender is actually incarcerated. Certainly, specific deterrence can be achieved, at least temporarily, through incapacitation.

As such, incapacitation is probably the most pragmatic of the correctional goals. It does not specifically seek to prevent future crime, deter potential criminals, or change behavior. It simply focuses on *constraining* offenders in an effort to curtail their opportunities to commit additional crimes. That is not to say that criminal acts do not occur behind bars, although they are not predominately committed against those in free society.

Such constraint is traditionally (and many would maintain most effectively) accomplished through *isolation* from society in secure correctional facilities. The definition of incapacitation could, however, be extended to include the *community-based controls* imposed through probation, home confinement, or electronic monitoring. But it is incarceration which most closely reflects the fundamental intent of incapacitation—that is, rendering an offender incapable of preying further upon the public.

Theoretically, those who are most likely to be repeat offenders would represent the logical target for isolation in order to obtain the maximum benefit from

Incapacitation focuses on restraining offenders from committing additional crimes by isolating them from free society. Courtesy of the California Department of Corrections.

incapacitation. Research has demonstrated that among both juvenile delinquents and adult criminals, a relatively small number of "chronic offenders" are responsible for a large portion of offenses.[44] The idea is that if these chronic recidivists could be *selectively incapacitated,* the overall crime rate would be reduced.

Selective incapacitation is reflected in the recent movement toward habitual offender laws, which mandate specified sentences for those convicted of a certain number of prior offenses (usually three or more). In contrast, *collective incapacitation* refers to imposing the same sentence for all persons convicted of a designated offense.

While research points to the validity of such reasoning, selective incapacitation raises several operational and ethical difficulties. Foremost is how to accurately determine who should be confined extensively because of their potential threat to the community. Although detailed "prediction tables" have been formulated,[45] anticipating future behavior is never an exact science—creating the potential for selectively incapacitating some who would not actually pose any further threat to the community (or vice versa—overlooking those who would). In fact, it has been estimated that "for every offender correctly labelled dangerous, at least one offender will be erroneously labelled dangerous."[46]

Then there is the issue of the moral justice involved in sentencing on the basis of possible *future* actions. In a democratic system of due process, where defendants are innocent until proven guilty and punishment is presumably related to the offense *committed,* this presents a serious dilemma. Ethically, morally, and legally, can we extend incarceration to a longer term on the basis of what someone *might* do if released? Even if the answer is affirmative, on a more practical level, selective incapacitation of habitual offenders can be expected to further increase an already overburdened prison population. Thus, while the concept may have popular and political appeal, its implementation is not without drawbacks.[47]

Overall, the goals of incapacitation are quite basic and (apart from selectivity) relatively easy to achieve—*assuming* that the offender is properly identified. But since "many criminals remain undetected, unapprehended, and unrestrained . . . the . . . value of incarceration may be limited or overrated."[48] In addition, this concept presents a rather pessimistic and short-range outlook. Strong advocates of incapacitation would have society abdicate to a "lock-'em-up" philosophy, resigned to the belief that no other option will work as well. It is indeed

---

[44]Marvin Wolfgang, Robert Figlio, and Thorsten Sellin, *Delinquency in a Birth Cohort* (Chicago: University of Chicago Press, 1972). Peter Greenwood, "Controlling the Crime Rate through Imprisonment," in James Q. Wilson, ed., *Crime and Public Policy* (San Francisco: Institute for Contemporary Studies Press, 1983). Sholomo Shinnar and Reuel Shinnar, "The Effects of the Criminal Justice System on the Control of Crime: A Quantitative Approach," *Law and Society Review,* Vol. 9 (1975), pp. 581–611.

[45]Greenwood, p. 258.

[46]Lee S. Pershan, "Selective Imprisonment Should Not Be Used," in Bonnie Szumski, ed., *America's Prisons: Opposing Viewpoints,* Fourth Edition (St. Paul, MN: Greenhaven Press, 1985), p. 100.

[47]For a summary of the objections to selective incapacitation, see Jacqueline Cohen, "Incapacitating Criminals: Recent Research Findings," *National Institute of Justice Research in Brief* (Washington, DC: U.S. Department of Justice, 1983), p. 4.

[48]Dean Champion, *Corrections in the United States* (Englewood Cliffs, NJ: Prentice Hall, 1990), p. 17.

unfortunate to reach such a point of frustration that nothing more creative or imaginative than outright physical restraint can be envisioned as an appropriate response to crime.

But the more significant difficulty with incapacitation is its shortsighted perspective. Although it quite accurately maintains that crime is curtailed during the period of confinement, what happens upon release? With the exception of the relatively few inmates who die in jail or prison, all others will eventually return to the community. If "incapacation" is synonymous with "warehousing," and nothing productive was accomplished during the time they served, little can be expected in terms of long-range effectiveness.

As Figure 2.8 reveals, the impact of incarceration on crime may well be overrated. Among the three states depicted (California, Michigan, and Texas), increases in the violent crime rate appear to have steadily kept pace with increasing incarceration rates in the decade between 1980 and 1990. Similarly, a study conducted between 1985 and 1990 in Pennsylvania concluded that "putting more people behind bars has failed to make a dent" in that state's crime rate, and noted that "[u]sing incarceration as the primary sanction for the bulk of offenders does not appear to be justified. . . . The public should ask and deserves to be told what returns they are getting on their investment."[49]

In a summary of major published research projects addressing collective incapacitation, the most striking finding was that contrary to popular belief, incapacitation does not appear to achieve the large reductions in crime that might have been expected from a "lock-em-up" strategy. But "although the effects of collective incapacitation on crime reduction are low, the effects on prison populations are likely to be substantial."[50]

The obvious question, then, is why incapacitation is not producing the expected results. Some of the potential answers are contained in the next "Close-up on Corrections." As one observer has noted, "We assume that punishment deters crime, but it just might be the other way around. It just might be that crime deters punishment: that there is so much crime that it simply cannot be punished."[51]

## Rehabilitation

It is the belief that something positive should be accomplished during the period of incarceration that forms the basis of the rehabilitative approach. Rehabilitation advocates maintain that criminal sanctions should be used as an opportunity to make some type of positive change in the offender. As George Bernard Shaw once pointed out, "if you are going to punish a man retributively, you must injure him. If you are to reform him, you must improve him. And men are not improved by injuries."[52]

[49]"Study Finds Prison Not Cutting Crime," *Community Crime Prevention Digest* (October 1992), p. 3, quoting Darrell Steffensmeier.

[50]Cohen, p. 3.

[51]Richard Moran, "Punishment Does Not Work," in Szumski, p. 36.

[52]Cited in Louis P. Carney, *Probation and Parole: Legal and Social Dimensions* (New York: McGraw-Hill, 1977), p. 75.

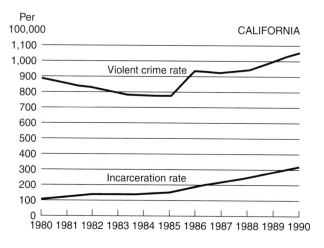

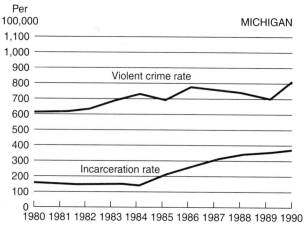

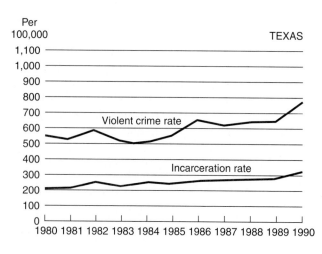

**Figure 2.8** Incarceration rates and crime rates in three states, 1980–1990. *Source:* Perry M. Johnson, "Methvin's Incarceration Argument Doesn't Hold Up under Scrutiny," *Corrections Today,* Vol. 54, No. 2 (April 1992), pp. 198–200.

Why Building More Prison Cells Won't Make a Safer Society

Why don't prisons do more to lower the crime rate? Californians certainly seem to believe that the greater the number of cells, the safer people are. Since 1980, the state's prison population has grown 300 percent. . . . Yet, violent crime in California jumped 4.3 percent [in 1991], according to the FBI.

The short answer to this puzzle is that we ask too much of prisons. . . . For it is one thing to say that a person will not commit a crime while incarcerated and quite another to say that society's overall crime rate will be affected. Put another way, more prison cells in California won't reduce crime. Here's why.

• A lot of predatory crime is committed by juveniles too young to be eligible for prison, or by young adults unlikely to be sent to prison for most first felony convictions. . . .

• Prison terms are usually imposed late in an offender's criminal career when criminal activity, on average, is tapering off. . . .

• Because the justice system only deals with an insignificant proportion of [total] crime, its ability to affect crime levels is minimal. Of the approximately 34 million serious felonies in 1990, 31 million never entered the criminal justice system, because they were either unreported or unsolved. This means that 90 percent of serious crime remains outside the purview of police, courts and prison officials. The remaining 10 percent is further eroded as a result of screening by prosecutors and dismissals or acquittals. . . .

• Studies have shown that much individual crime (particularly violent crime) is an impulsive response to an immediate stressful situation, often under the influence of drugs or alcohol. Rational-choice models require an offender to think clearly about the costs and benefits of committing crime, weigh those costs and determine that the costs outweigh the benefits. Yet more than half of all violent offenders are under the influence of drugs or alcohol at the time of their crime, a state of mind with little affinity for rational judgment.

• For imprisonment to deter offenders and potential offenders, it must be stigmatic and punishing. Prison is most likely to deter if the inmate's social standing is injured by punishment and if he or she feels in danger of being excluded from a group he or she cares about. But many of an offender's peers and relatives also have done time. . . . And estimates indicate that about one-quarter of all males living in inner cities will be jailed at some point in their lives, so the stigma attached to having a prison record in these neighborhoods may not be as great as it was when prison terms were relatively uncommon.

• Imprisonment may increase post-release criminal activity. RAND analysts recently studied a "matched sample" of California offenders convicted of similar crimes and with similar criminal records. The two groups differed only in their sentence—members of one group went to prison, the others received probation. After tracking the groups for three years, researchers found consistently higher re-arrest rates for offenders sentenced to prison. . . .

- Most important, for imprisonment to reduce crime, inmates must not be immediately replaced by new recruits. . . . In [some] instances, an arrest and a prison sentence create a vacancy. Typically, however, that vacancy is quickly filled. . . . In general, new recruits constantly refresh the ranks of active criminals. As a result, crime in the community continues unabated. . . .

Prisons, to be sure, are an important and necessary component of the criminal justice system. . . . But drug clinics do more to rehabilitate drug addicts than prison, job training does more to reduce recidivism than jails, and early childhood prevention programs do more than any other factor to reduce a propensity to crime. . . . Especially now, in the midst of [a national] recession . . . when every additional corrections officer may mean one fewer teacher, and every prison cell constructed may mean a gang-prevention program unfunded, public education is essential to meaningful change in our approach to the crime problem.

*Source:* Joan Petersilia, "Building More Prison Cells Won't Make a Safer Society," *Corrections Today,* Vol. 54, No. 8 (December 1992), pp. 168–70.

---

Since *re*habilitation literally means "to *restore* to good condition," some would maintain that the term is more properly "habilitation," as the condition of many offenders is not one to which corrections would wish to restore them. But regardless of semantics, the objective is to help offenders change their behavior so that they can reenter society as contributing citizens, or at least, not dangerous ones.

Just as retribution, deterrence, and incapacitation form the foundation of the justice model described earlier, rehabilitation is the hallmark of the medical model. Like deterrence, it has a somewhat proactive emphasis, but it differs in its more long-range focus on individual behavior. Like incapacitation, it seeks to reduce crime, but through "radically different means"—that is, by changing the "need or desire to commit crimes," not simply preventing the offender from "having an opportunity to do so."[53] Thus, the goals of rehabilitation are the most ambitious, and therefore, perhaps the most elusive of the various responses to crime.

Rehabilitative efforts can take many forms—from education and vocational training to detoxification and acupuncture. But most traditional approaches have centered on individual and group counseling, psychotherapy, and other clinical treatment procedures. Although these terms may imply very individualized treatment, such is not always the case, as is described in the next "Close-up on Corrections." The rehabilitative routine of "counseling for everyone" does not take into account one's personal motivation to change or willingness to participate in treatment. As the "close-up" describes, it has therefore been far from uniformly effective.

It is somewhat ironic that the rehabilitative approach has been denounced for its "rubber stamp" procedures, since it was originally designed to address

---

[53]Lawrence F. Travis, Martin D. Schwartz, and Todd R. Clear, *Corrections: An Issues Approach,* Second Edition (Cincinnati, OH: Anderson Publishing Company, 1983), p. 9.

### Fallacy of the Rehabilitative Routine

Though counseling may not have been equally effective with all offenders, it *was* seen as a "need" of all "clients." . . . It is this strategy of counseling-for-everyone which has proven consistently unsuccessful. . . .

A famous experiment reported by Stuart Adams . . . illustrates this point. In this case, the offenders were given intensive counseling while they were incarcerated. However, unbeknownst to the counselors, trained clinicians had already evaluated all of the subjects in advance to see if they were likely to benefit from counseling. Only a partial group of those amenable to therapy and a partial group of those not amenable to therapy were given counseling. The rest were just left alone and not given any sort of treatment.

The results of this experiment are important. As might be expected, the persons designated in advance as "amenables" did indeed fare better after receiving intensive counseling. However, those who were designated as "non-amenable" and were given counseling fared worse than that group of non-amenables who were not given counseling. In other words, counseling persons who were not amenable to therapy *decreased* their chances of success following treatment. As a group, they would have fared better if no treatment at all had been given.

*Source:* Lawrence F. Travis III, Martin D. Schwartz, and Todd R. Clear, *Corrections: An Issues Approach,* Second Edition (Cincinnati, OH: Anderson Publishing Company, 1983), p. 175, citing Stuart Adams, "Effectiveness of Interview Therapy with Older Youth Authority Wards: An Interim Evaluation of the PICO Project," Research Report 20 (Sacramento, CA: Youth Authority, 1961) (mimeographed).

specific needs of the individual. The intent was to assess the offender's problems, develop a personalized treatment plan, and provide an *indeterminate* (flexible) sentence whereby the length of confinement would largely be determined by one's progress toward rehabilitation. That was the theory. In reality, those incarcerated for similar offenses ended up serving widely different amounts of time, which raised the issue of sentencing *equity*. Moreover, the correctional officials, treatment personnel, and parole board members charged with determining when sufficient "rehabilitation" had occurred to justify release were not infallible. Since human nature cannot be precisely predicted, some were inevitably released before it was appropriate, while others were held longer than necessary.

Beyond these operational difficulties, to some extent, the rehabilitative concept was almost destined to flounder from the start because of the manner in which it was implemented. Given the long-term nature of clinical treatment approaches, they have been offered primarily in institutional settings. As a result, offenders must experience the negative impact of incarceration in order to receive the treatment necessary for their rehabilitation. The coercive nature of high-security correctional facilities is hardly the ideal environment for obtaining treatment and achieving rehabilitation. Nor are institutions equally well staffed and equipped to provide such services.

It is therefore not surprising to find that although some do make positive changes in their lives "in spite of the harmful influences of the prison culture . . . the occasions are so rare that the total effect is negligible," and in still other cases, the alleged "treatment" has been found to consist simply of confinement for so long that inmates have neither the "physical nor mental vigor to commit further crimes."[54] Although everyone might not view such outcomes as undesirable, there is little doubt that they are more reflective of incapacitation than rehabilitation in its true sense.

Even among more valid rehabilitative programs, results have been far from encouraging. In his comprehensive report of studies assessing attempts at rehabilitation from 1945 through 1967, Robert Martinson concludes that *"with few and isolated exceptions, the rehabilitative efforts that have been reported so far have had no appreciable effect on recidivism."*[55] The Martinson report has been widely cited as offering proof of the ineffectiveness of treatment. Its empirical evidence that "nothing works," has become a significant justification for movement from the medical model to the justice model, despite recent attempts to revitalize interest in rehabilitative concepts.[56]

Issues of sentencing inequities, untimely releases, and ineffective procedures have plagued the rehabilitative approach since its inception. By the 1980s, these concerns were combined with a more conservative political climate, rising crime rates, increasing recidivism, and the indictment of empirical research. Society seemed to have reached the limits of its tolerance for the unfulfilled promise of the rehabilitative ideal. In fact, the fundamental premise of rehabilitation was vocally attacked:

> To rehabilitate is to restore to a former constructive capacity or condition. *There is nothing to which to rehabilitate a criminal.* There is no earlier condition of being responsible to which to restore him. He never learned the ways of getting along in this world that most of us learned as children. Just as rehabilitation is a misconception, so too is the notion of "reintegrating the criminal into the community." It is absurd to speak of reintegrating him when he was never integrated in the first place. . . . [57]

As a result of this combination of forces, public policies began to be directed toward determinate (fixed) sentences, elimination of parole, and voluntary (versus mandatory) participation in rehabilitative programs. However, not everyone agrees that society is actually as opposed to rehabilitation as legislators and policymakers would like to think.

[54]Donald Clemmer, *The Prison Community* (New York: Holt, Rinehart and Winston, 1958), p. 313.

[55]Robert Martinson, "What Works? Questions and Answers about Prison Reform," *The Public Interest,* Vol. 35 (Spring 1975) p. 25. It should, however, be noted that Martinson's report did not specifically conclude that "nothing works," but rather, that the methodologies used to evaluate rehabilitative efforts were so inadequate that no effect could be validly measured—which points to the need for implementing more rigorous program evaluation techniques.

[56]Cullen and Gilbert.

[57]Stanton E. Samenow, "The Criminal Personality Exists before Prison," in Szumski, p. 63.

Recently, evidence has been offered demonstrating "the myth of the punitive public," which indicates that although support for punitive sanctions is widespread, there is also still considerable belief in rehabilitation as a legitimate correctional goal.[58] Moreover, there are others who argue against abandoning rehabilitation,[59] if for no other reason than because doing so would abandon the humanizing influence it has created in the correctional system.[60] Rehabilitation has played an important role in reforming not only the individual offender, but the system as well—perhaps not as effectively as its lofty goals intended, but not as ineffectively as its abolishment would justify. It is true that nothing works all the time with every inmate. Yet, that is not to say that we should reject all hope that anything ever works with anyone.

## Reintegration

To some extent, the demise of rehabilitation may also be related to the difficulty of reintegrating ex-offenders back into the community after long-term confinement. It has already been noted that much of what was pursued in the name of rehabilitation has occurred within the isolated institutional environment of secure correctional facilities. In prison, an inmate's every movement is under scrutiny. Strict compliance with rules is enforced. Established routines regulate everything from requesting an aspirin to eating and sleeping. In response to this "total institutional" climate,[61] an inmate subculture develops to socialize the population into such a "foreign" environment.[62] The negative effects of this regulation, routinization, and socialization into prison life can be intensive and long-lasting.

It is one thing to achieve behavioral change among those under such close supervision. It is quite another to assure that any improvements continue upon release—when ex-offenders are again faced with making their own decisions, regulating their own lives, and replacing institutional control with self-control. Reestablishing ties with the community is an essential ingredient in this process, and it is the focus of reintegration. If ex-offenders feel estranged from society, the chances are much greater that they will fall into old patterns of behavior and return to corrections as recidivists. Thus, reintegrative efforts such as parole are not simply a privilege for the offender, but also a protection for the community.

Successful reintegration can be difficult for all but the most motivated to achieve. Once convicted and incarcerated, offenders lose a number of privileges, such as eligibility for certain types of employment. They are also stigmatized or "labeled" as high risks for personal relationships and business transactions.

---

[58]Francis T. Cullen, John B. Cullen, and John F. Wozniak, "Is Rehabilitation Dead? The Myth of the Punitive Public," *Journal of Criminal Justice*, Vol. 16, No. 4 (1988), p. 303.

[59]Paul Gendreau and Robert R. Ross, "Revivification of Rehabilitation: Evidence from the 1980's," *Justice Quarterly*, Vol. 4, No. 3 (September 1987), pp. 349–408.

[60]Cullen and Gilbert, pp. 261–63.

[61]For a description of "total institutionalization," see Gresham Sykes, *The Society of Captives: A Study of Maximum Security Prison* (Princeton, NJ: Princeton University Press, 1958).

[62]For a detailed discussion of this topic, see Charles W. Thomas and David M. Petersen, "The Inmate Subculture," in David M. Petersen and Charles W. Thomas, eds. *Corrections: Problems and Prospects*, Second Edition (Englewood Cliffs, NJ: Prentice Hall, 1980), pp. 80–101.

Former friends and even family members may distance themselves. Potential employers may be reluctant to "take a chance" by hiring someone with a record. Apartment managers may seek excuses to avoid renting to a recent releasee. Banks may deny loans, without which it is difficult to find and keep employment when a car is needed for transportation. The overwhelming sense of frustration from experiencing such rejections can make the ex-offender a prime target for returning to crime.

While parole was in part designed to assist with such community reintegration, parole has a dual mandate of providing both support and continued supervision. When parole caseloads are high and public pressure is strong to detect recidivism among those released, it is not surprising to find parole officers' supervisory functions taking precedence over their supportive role. In addition, offenders serving full mandatory sentences without the possibility of parole leave the institution without either supervision or support.

Like parole, halfway houses have been established to help the offender phase gradually into community life. At a halfway house, staff are available to help with obtaining employment, transportation, permanent housing, and similar personal needs, such as continuing medication, outpatient therapy, or other postincarceration treatment.

Although halfway houses are most often associated with those who are "halfway out" of a correctional facility, they may also be provided as a community-based option instead of being confined in a secure institution. In the case of "halfway in" facilities, the goal is to avoid breaking family and social ties in the first place—that is, avoiding the need to *re*integrate by keeping offenders integrated within the community.

It has only been in relatively recent years that government agencies have invested resources in efforts designed to help with readjustment to the community. The reintegration approach has historically emphasized the role of private citizens in assisting ex-offenders. In fact, for many years, it was socially conscious private agencies that provided this community service (such as the Prisoners Aid Society, the John Howard Society, the Salvation Army, Volunteers of America, and others). No sooner had government begun to recognize the need for reintegrative support than public policies changed to embrace the justice model, again creating a greater need for private-sector involvement.

During the 1980s, both rehabilitation and reintegration were deemphasized in favor of retribution, deterrence, and incapacitation, as public policies moved from those reflecting the medical model to those of the justice model. The focus has thus become either deterring criminal behavior, or when prevention is unsuccessful, holding violators accountable for their actions. To the extent that "holding accountable" translates into lengthy prison sentences, there remains a need to address reintegration. The question is whether that need will again be officially recognized, or whether ex-offenders will be left to reestablish socially acceptable lifestyles as best they can. Those who can will disappear with the rest of us into the anonymity of law-abiding society. Those who cannot will continue to provide media headlines and correctional clientele.

Correctional clients are those against whom society has taken official action because their behavior is in violation of the criminal law. What is considered to be a crime will therefore determine who are identified as "criminals." The consensus perspective holds that crime is a violation against what we all hold in common as socially acceptable behavior. In contrast, conflict theory views crime as a product of the ability of influential people to promote legislation against behavior that endangers their special interests.

Just as we do not agree on what crime is or how it evolves, we do not have an accurate picture of how much of it occurs. Although data on criminal offenses are provided in the FBI's *Uniform Crime Reports,* their measurements are subject to a number of factors—not the least of which is the likelihood of crimes being reported to the police. According to victimization studies conducted through the *National Crime Survey,* a considerable amount of serious crime remains unreported. Even in those cases where the offense is reported, a suspect is apprehended, and official action is taken, a lengthy screening process eliminates many of the accused long before they reach the correctional system.

While there is disagreement about the definition and extensiveness of crime, there is even greater uncertainty over what should be done about it. Seeking repayment for the wrongdoing of criminal offenders, retribution guided the community's response to criminal behavior for centuries. As society accepted some responsibility for crime, experiments with rehabilitation occurred. Treatment programs were introduced to change one's motivation to commit crime, as well as to reintegrate the ex-offender more effectively into the community. But when the desired results were not forthcoming, the public became increasingly disenchanted with the ability of corrections to achieve lasting change. Thus, the popularity of retribution reemerged. Efforts were directed toward assuring that criminals receive their "just deserts." Offenders were incapacitated in correctional facilties—both to deter them specifically and to send a general deterrence message to the community. But apparently, everyone has not received the message. In the next chapter we explore why some have not.

# chapter 3

# The Correctional Client

*A skid row drunk lying in a gutter is crime. . . . Conspiracy to bribe public officials is crime. So is a strong-arm robbery. . . . These crimes can no more be lumped together for purposes of analysis than can measles and schizophrenia. . . . As with disease, so with crime: if causes are to be understood . . . and if preventive or remedial actions are to be taken, each kind must be looked at separately. Thinking of "crime" as a whole is futile.[1]*

*President's Commission on Law Enforcement and Administration of Justice*

## ❖ CHAPTER OVERVIEW

If you were asked to think of one explanation to describe motives for the behavior of everyone in your circle of family, friends, and acquaintances, you would undoubtedly find it impossible. It is equally difficult to generate one theory that satisfactorily explains why offenders from car thiefs to corporate executives engage in criminal activities. Just as there is no one type of person who can be identified as "criminal," there is no single explanation of why they commit crime. Nevertheless, theories of crime causation are important to correctional practitioners because theories influence public policies—that is, they shape the way we respond to crime. Theory is the rationale behind practice. Consequently, some knowledge of criminological theory is essential to the practice of corrections.

As long as there are crime and criminals, the search for what causes such behavior will continue. Explanations have ranged in sophistication from supernatural forces to biochemical imbalances. Many of these theories have been discarded as overly simplistic, and even those that have received some acclaim supply only fragmented portions of the enormous crime causation jigsaw puzzle. Given the diversity of crime itself, together with the wide-ranging nature of persons involved in criminal activities, it is hard to imagine that the puzzle will ever be assembled completely.

Searching for what is held in common among offenders displaying vastly different motives, circumstances, and criminal acts is a complicated task. Certain theories may explain one type of crime committed by one type of offender at one

---

[1]President's Commission on Law Enforcement and Administration of Justice, *The Challenge of Crime in a Free Society* (Washington, DC: U.S. Government Printing Office, 1967), p. 3.

particular point in time. But they have failed to account for why similarly situated persons have *not* been similarly involved in crime. A true causal explanation will be reached only when we can identify what is held in common by "rich and poor, blacks and whites, urban- and rural-dwellers, young and old, emotionally stable and emotionally unstable"[2]—a rather large order, to say the least!

Just as medical science is coming to the conclusion that there is no single cause of cancer, so are we realizing the futility of searching for a single cause of crime. This does not mean that efforts to explain criminal behavior are at a standstill. Nor does it mean that the theories developed thus far have no value simply because they lack universal application. However, explanations attempting to account for all types of criminal activity are too general to offer any practical solutions, and those focusing more specifically on one type of behavior are too narrow to address the wide variety of criminals. But as long as there is unexplained criminal behavior, the search for causes will continue—directed toward the common goal of crime reduction, and perhaps ultimately, even prevention.

---

*LEARNING GOALS*

*Do you know:*

- *What three types of criminal behavior generate the most arrests?*
- *Which component of criminology represents the major basis of correctional intervention?*

---

## ❖ NATURE OF CORRECTIONAL CLIENTELE

Criminal activity is portrayed in fiction as an exciting lifestyle. But in reality, many "criminals" are rather inconspicuous people whose involvement in crime is more an inability to cope with life than a search for excitement—the alcoholics, drug addicts, and social "misfits" who often can be more harmful to themselves than to others.

In 1991, law enforcement agencies throughout the country made over 14 million arrests.[3] The primary groups of offenders arrested were not murderers, armed robbers, or rapists. They were drunk drivers (1.8 million), thieves (1.6 million), and drug sellers or users (1 million).[4] Perhaps you know some of them. Many of these offenders are our friends, co-workers, classmates, neighbors, or even family members. The typical criminal is not a bizzare misfit with grotesque physical features. Crime is largely a feature of seemingly ordinary people. Some of them do very extraordinary things, but most of them do not. Anyone who has ever driven home after having too much to drink, taken something of value from

---

[2]Edwin Sutherland and Donald R. Cressey, "A Sociological Theory of Criminal Behavior," in Donald R. Cressey and David A. Ward, eds., *Delinquency, Crime, and Social Process* (New York: Harper & Row, 1969), p. 427.

[3]Federal Bureau of Investigation, *Crime in the United States: Uniform Crime Reports* (Washington, DC: U.S. Government Printing Office, 1992), p. 212.

[4]Ibid.

a store or office, or used illegal drugs has committed a crime for which Americans are arrested every day.

It is such ordinary people who compose a large portion of the clientele of corrections. They have violated the criminal law and therefore damaged the social order by their failure to conform to expected behavior. In addition, of course, they are the ones who got caught. They are different from the clients of other governmental agencies in that they have in some way damaged society and have been held legally responsible for their actions. Welfare clients may have been poor managers, physically disadvantaged, products of inadequate homes, or for many other reasons unable to deal effectively with their socioeconomic environment. Mental health clients may be mentally ill in a variety of ways, to the point of being dysfunctional. Clients of psychiatric clinics, marriage counselors, and family therapy services may display a high level of neurotic personality traits. But the correctional client differs from all other government clients, even though some of the others may be included in the correctional caseload. The criminal offender has damaged society by violation of the law.

### Identifying the Correctional Client

In many respects, correctional clients are quite similar to those who have not come into contact with the law. The only common denominator among all offenders is their conflict with social authority. The only common motivating force among them is to get out or remain out of correctional institutions and to be free from any sort of authoritative supervision.

Criminality and delinquency are products of a relationship between the individual and society. By definition, crime is a result of the way the law is created and applied socially and politically (as we saw in Chapter 2). Crime is a *social* problem to the extent that it concerns how the individual interacts with society, as well as society's response to the individual. Crime is also a *mental health* problem to the extent that it reflects psychological abnormalities. Crime could even be a *biological* problem to the extent that it involves physiological malfunctions. Whether social, psychological, or biological in nature, crime and delinquency represent a breakdown in adjustment of the individual to established social order.

Human behavior—including criminal behavior—is more complex than any one discipline can handle. In determining the cause of crime in any particular case, it is essential to assess the offender's personality, social relationships, cultural environment, and biological makeup.

*Personality* is the primary focus of psychology and psychiatry. Through these disciplines, information on the development of normal personalities can provide some clues as to what might have happened to cause the dysfunctional pattern of behavior defined as criminality. *Social relationships* are the primary focus of sociology. This discipline involves study of the interaction between individuals and groups of people, which can shed light on the group-related reasons for criminal behavior. *Culture* is a primary focus of anthropology, along with sociology and related disciplines of human endeavor. Culture is society's way of doing things, including how we distribute goods and services, operate government, structure occupations, and practice religion. It encompasses rules, regulations, customs, ethical patterns, and laws—the value of which correctional clients may have difficulty internalizing. *Physiology* is the primary focus of the physical and biological sciences. It is this discipline that looks at how behavior is affected by such physiological factors as genetics, body chemistry, and the food we eat. Crime and delinquency must be observed from all of these viewpoints.

## Responding to the Correctional Client

From a correctional perspective, personality and modification of individual behavior have been the major targets of intervention, for rather practical reasons. Moving offenders from one environment to another is the only way to change the impact of their cultural and social relationships. To some degree, incarceration in a correctional institution changes one's environment, but only for a temporary period of time and not necessarily in surroundings that would have a positive influence. While some institutions have experimented with dietary alterations designed to change behavior, more extensive biochemical or genetic manipulations are well beyond the scope of corrections because of their legal and ethical implications. Consequently, personality emerges as the most significant avenue of pursuit available to the correctional employee. Changes in attitude, self-concept, motivation, and goals—although not easy to achieve—are more manageable than attempting to change social relationships, cultural environment, or physiological features.

That does not mean that corrections can operate effectively without knowledge of criminological findings in disciplines other than psychology. As was discussed in Chapter 2, through public policies, society determines what correctional goals will be emphasized and what accompanying procedures will be used. Over the years, social policy has been influenced by prevailing explanations of criminal behavior. Thus, society's response to crime has been based on prevalent theories of the time. Because correctional agencies have a public mandate to implement the community's response to crime, it is necessary to understand the theories on which crime-related policies are based. In essence, corrections has become the agent responsible for putting *theory* into *practice*.

---

*LEARNING GOALS*

*Do you know:*

- *How Beccaria's mid-eighteenth century thinking affects our sentencing policies today?*
- *What the differences are between the Classical and Positive schools of thought in terms of how criminal behavior is motivated and how society should respond to it?*
- *How the Classical School has influenced the justice model, in contrast to the Positive School's influence on the medical model?*
- *Who is considered the father of the Positive School and the father of criminology (also noted for his theories on the "born criminal")?*

---

Criminal behavior and efforts to explain it are as old as civilization. Initially, *supernatural forces* were viewed as the source of all unexplainable events—from crime to floods and famines. Along with this line of thought, witch doctors were used to expel evil spirits, human sacrifices were made to appease the gods, and skull drilling was even practiced to rid the body of demons. But primitive reliance on demonology gave way to more rational reasoning as developments in physical science, philosophy, and religion began to demonstrate that the universe was actually governed by more orderly processes.[5]

### The Classical School

The classical languages—Greek and Latin—represented the first attempt to develop a system of more universal communication than regional dialects. Likewise, the *Classical School* of criminology derived its label because it was the first organized attempt to develop a theory of crime causation. The pioneer of classical thinking was *Cesare Beccaria*, whose *Essay on Crimes and Punishment* had a major impact on reform of the legal system in the mid-eighteenth century.

Beccaria was concerned over the inequity of extremely harsh punishments, which were applied even for relatively minor offenses. He argued for a more rational and formal system of sanctioning, based on the philosophy that has become the motto of the Clasical School—"Let the punishment fit the crime." This may now appear to be a very fundamental concept. But it was revolutionary at the time—when a man's hand could be cut off for stealing a loaf of bread to feed his starving family. Because of the logical and systematic reasoning that Beccaria employed, his writings enjoyed a landmark impact—becoming, in fact, the basis of sentencing policies in the United States.

Beccaria's work reflects a philosophy of *hedonism* and *free will*. That is, people tend to avoid pain and seek pleasure (hedonism), and they have the free will to make a rational choice between what will cause pain and what will result in pleasure. Thus, emphasis in the Classical School is on response to the *offense*. With swift and certain punishment for criminal behavior, it is assumed that people will be deterred from engaging in criminal activities. Sanctions are determined by the seriousness of the offense. Since the offender freely engages in crime over law-abiding alternatives, sanctions must be strong enough to deter without being excessive.

This line of thought certainly represented an improvement over earlier associations between supernatural powers and "evil" behavior. Moreover, it is a vivid illustration of the relationship between theory and practice. Beccaria's influence has surfaced again—over two centuries later—in the justice model's focus on the free will and rationality of offenders and the deterrent effect of punishment.

---

[5]For further details regarding these developments, see Vernon Fox, *Introduction to Criminology* Second Edition (Englewood Cliffs, NJ: Prentice Hall, 1985), pp. 7–13.

## The Positive School

The Classical School's exclusion of any factors beyond personal choice that might influence the offender's behavior gave rise to a second major development. The *Positive School* of criminology identified other variables that might predispose one to become involved in criminal activity, regardless of free will. From its emphasis on seeking more concrete explanations of behavior, this approach derived its identification as "positive" (or "positivistic"). Whereas the Classical School focused on responding to the offense, the Positive School emphasized responding to the needs of the *offender* (see Figure 3.1).

The Positive School maintains that people cannot always be held accountable for their behavior because of factors beyond their control. This is known as *determinism*—something beyond our power that is determining behavior. *Cesare Lombroso* is credited as the founder of the Positive School. A physician by training, his research into the physical characteristics associated with criminality established the groundwork for the methods of scientific inquiry on which the Positive School is based. (Because of his pioneering work in the area of biological explanations of crime, a detailed discussion of Lombroso's work is presented later when we look at physiological theories.)

Of course, methods of research and the factors being investigated have changed dramatically over the years since Lombroso's original works. But many modern criminological theories—as well as the medical model itself—are based on the positivist notion that intent and free will are modified by physical, psychological, or environmental conditions. On the other hand, much of the foundation of our existing legal system reflects the classical notion that punishment should fit the crime, with predisposing factors generally taken into account only in circumstances of insanity. As reflected in the following critique of the medical model versus free will, the resolution of these widely differing concepts is far from over: "The fallacy to the . . . talk about treating crime as a disease, about making a prison merely a hygienic environment like a hospital, of healing sin by slow scientific methods . . . is that evil is a matter of active choice, whereas disease is not."[6]

|  | Classical | Positive |
|---|---|---|
| Date | Mid-1700s | Mid-1800s |
| Founder | Beccaria | Lombroso |
| Focus | Offense; legality | Offender; predisposing factors |
| Methods | Conjecture | Scientific inquiry |
| Emphasis | Free will | Determinism |
| Philosophy | Let the punishment fit the crime | Let the treatment fit the criminal |

**Figure 3.1** Differences between the classical and positive schools of criminology.

[6]Allen C. Brownfeld, "Prisons Are for Society's Protection," in Bonnie Szumski, ed., *America's Prisons: Opposing Viewpoints*, Fourth Edition (St. Paul, MN: Greenhaven Press, 1985), p. 42.

Following in the footsteps of the Positive School of criminology, further advancements in the physical, psychological, and social sciences have resulted in numerous attempts to explain criminality. The resulting theories range from very specific focus on the individual's *biological characteristics* (physiology) or *personality traits* (psychology) to a broad-based view of the individual's *social relationships* and *cultural environmen,* (for purposes of this discussion, combined as sociology).

*Physiological* theories attempt to unlock the secrets of criminal behavior through study of genetic heredity, body chemistry, and physical characteristics. *Psychological* theories probe the mysteries of the mind—searching for criminal tendencies in personality development, emotional responses, and learning processes. *Sociological* theories explore the dynamics of how we interact with others, looking for the cause of crime in our immediate surroundings—family tension, economic conditions, group norms, and other features of our environment.

Each of these disciplines has made valuable contributions to the study of criminal behavior. Each has developed valid theories explaining one type of offender or one type of crime. Each has had an impact on how society deals with law-violating behavior. But none has fully accounted for all offenders or all types of crime. That remains a challenge for the future. To meet the challenges of the future, however, it is essential to understand the contributions of the past.

---

*LEARNING GOALS*

*Do you know:*

- *Of the three body types identified by Sheldon, which is considered more likely to become criminal and what factors beyond physique might contribute to such findings?*
- *How the impact of physical or biological characteristics on criminal behavior is also influenced by social factors?*
- *How what we eat can affect our behavior?*

---

## ❖ PHYSIOLOGICAL APPROACHES

Searches for biological causes of criminal behavior are among both the oldest and most modern attempts to explain criminality. Begun by what now seems a rather crude effort to identify criminals by their physical traits, physiological theories later regained brief popularity when it was discovered that some offenders were the unknowing victims of chromosome abnormalities. More recently, nutritional deficiencies resulting in chemical imbalances in the body have been cited as playing a role in aggressive, hyperactive, and acting-out behavior. Some ridicule the notion that "what we are" has anything to do with what we eat. But others point to the origin of biochemical theories in the widely respected medical sciences as evidence of their validity.

## Physical Abnormalities

*Cesare Lombroso,* founder of the Positive School of criminology, is credited with being the first to relate biological characteristics to criminality. His physical measurements of criminals and the mentally insane led to the conclusion that certain people were simply *born criminals,* as a result of congenital defects. Among them, Lombroso observed what he noted were some of the characteristics of savages—excessive jaw, prominent cheekbones, drooping eyelids, long arms, and fleshy lips.[7] From this evidence, he determined that criminals are "atavistic"—throwbacks to earlier forms of evolution.

Lombroso's findings were considered revolutionary at the time. They contributed significantly to the application of scientific inquiry to criminal behavior, earning him tribute as the "father of criminology." But not everyone agreed with his findings or methods. Prominent among the skeptics was *Charles Goring,* who, early in the twentieth century, set out to refute Lombroso.[8] In a 12-year study of 3000 prisoners, along with a control group of nonoffenders, Goring found no basis for the physical distinctions claimed by Lombroso.

The popularity of biological determinism was revived again several years later with the work of *Ernest Hooten.*[9] On the basis of his examination of over 100 physical traits among thousands of criminals and control groups, Hooten concluded that criminals are organically inferior as a result of heredity. He even recommended that the "physically, mentally, and morally unfit" should be segregated from society.[10]

## Body Types

At about the same time that Hooten was conducting his studies, *Ernest Kretschmer* found a relationship between one's body type (i.e., "constitution") and varieties of behavior. *William Sheldon* expanded on this work, identifying three basic "body types" in distinguishing between criminals and noncriminals:[11]

- *Endomorph:* short and fat, with an easy-going personality, and therefore not likely to be criminal material.
- *Ectomorph:* just the opposite—tall, thin, and fragile, with a sensitive and introverted temperament. Again, not a probable candidate for criminality.
- *Mesomorph:* muscular and athletic—more inclined to be aggressive, and therefore more likely to become a criminal than the other two.

But social as well as physical factors must be taken into account when considering the mesomorph's deviant activities. For example, it is obviously unlikely that a very fat or very thin person would be recruited into delinquent subcul-

---

[7]Gina Lombroso-Ferrero, *Criminal Man according to the Classification of Cesare Lombroso* (Montclair, NJ: Patterson Smith, 1972), pp. 10–16.

[8]Charles Goring, *The English Convict* (London: H.M. Stationery Office, 1919), p. 16.

[9]Ernest A. Hooten, *Crime and Man* (Cambridge, MA: Harvard University Press, 1939).

[10]Edwin M. Schur, *Our Criminal Society* (Englewood Cliffs, NJ: Prentice Hall, 1969), p. 57.

[11]W. H. Sheldon, *The Varieties of Human Physique: An Introduction to Constitutional Psychology* (New York: Harper & Row, 1940).

tures.[12] The question then becomes whether physique truly determines behavior, or rather, whether it influences social interaction, which in turn, affects individual conduct.

Even before these scientific findings, body build has been associated with behavior. As Shakespeare wrote in *Julius Caesar*, "Let me have men about me that are fat; . . . Cassius has a lean and hungry look; he thinks too much: such men are dangerous." In more contemporary times, it has become known that some endocrine conditions will affect temperament. For example, someone with a *hypo*thyroid is obese and lethargic. On the other hand, those with *hyper*thyroids are thin and nervous. Although these conditions present adjustment problems, that does not necessarily mean that the adjustment is predestined to result in criminal or delinquent behavior.

Similarly, physical handicaps and disfigurements have been viewed as predisposing factors in crime. Again, the social and self-concept problems caused by disfigurement are greater for people with such handicaps. To compensate for their physical appearance or disability, some may turn to crime. But in such cases, the causal explanation is more likely in the social reaction to one's physical condition than the disfigurement itself. In light of this, some correctional programs in the past have included cosmetic surgery: straightening crossed eyes, removing tattoos or facial scars, and the like. While some view such treatment as frivolous, the long-term results can be effective when the lack of self-esteem caused by disfigurement is generating antisocial behavior. For a unique perspective on the influence of social reactions to physical "abnormalities," see the next "Close-up on Corrections."

For these and other reasons, the studies of body types never gained much acceptance.[13] With their contributions, the era of belief in external physical characteristics as the source of criminal tendencies largely came to a close.

## Chromosome Abnormalities

More recent research into physiological foundations of behavior established a potential link between crime and sex *chromosomes*. Normal males have a chromosome balance of XY; females XX. When it was discovered in the early 1960s that some males had an extra Y chromosome ("super" males), studies were undertaken to determine whether aggressiveness could be accounted for by this biological factor. Some found that a significant portion of prisoners did possess this faulty genetic composition (3.5%) in contrast to the general population (1.3%).[14] Popular attention was drawn to this theory in the mid-1950s, when

[12]Don C. Gibbons, *Society, Crime and Criminal Careers* (Englewood Cliffs, NJ: Prentice Hall, 1968), p. 134.

[13]The many criticisms of the body-type approach are summarized by George Vold in *Theoretical Criminology* (New York: Oxford University Press, 1958), p. 74, in which he states: "There is no such present evidence at all of physical type, as such, having any consistent relationship to legal and sociologically defined crime."

[14]Walter C. Reckless, *American Criminology: New Directions* (New York: Meredith Corporation, 1973), p. 18, citing Ashley Montagu's investigation. See also Johannes Nielsen, Takayuki Tsubsi, Georg Sturup, and David Romano, "XYY Chromosomal Constitution in Criminal Psychopaths," *Lancet*, Vol. 2 (1968), p. 576.

The Eye of the Beholder

". . . beauty is in the eye of the beholder." Every time I hear that phrase, I think of the *Twilight Zone* episode called "The Eye of the Beholder." A heavily bandaged woman is being operated on in an attempt to become beautiful. During the operation, she's in constant conversation with the sympathetic doctors and nurses. When they pull off the bandages and put a mirror to her face, the woman screams in horror. The camera zooms in for a close-up. She is beautiful. Then the camera pans out again. For the first time, we see the misshapen, deformed faces of the doctors and nurses, and we understand that the operation has been a failure—she is still a freak in that society.

*Source:* David J. Neal, "Can't Live Without 'em: Eye of the Beholder," *Tropic Magazine* (*The Miami Herald,* September 15, 1991), p. 25.

Richard Speck, convicted of murdering eight nurses in Chicago, was identified as having an XYY imbalance.[15]

But this field of inquiry has studied small samples, and there is no solid proof of a link between the XYY chromosome and crime.[16] As in the case of hyper- or hypothyroids, it may be that abnormal chromosome structure results in more difficult social adjustment—creating an interactive effect between one's physical condition and the environment. For example, epilepsy is found more frequently in prison populations than among the general public. Periodic irritability preceding an epilepsy seizure may explain some quarrelsome behavior. In addition, it is harder for an epileptic to find a job if the disease is acknowledged on an employment application. In general, social adaptation is more difficult. The side effects of these adjustment problems may be more responsible for criminal behavior than the epilepsy itself. Even if a relationship between chromosomes and crime could be established, what practical solutions would be available? Although perhaps genetic manipulation will become biologically possible, it is never likely to be morally, legally, or ethically feasible.

## Biochemical Theories

Among the most current physiological approaches to criminology are recent explorations into the association between body chemistry and behavioral reactions.

Advanced first by *Linus Pauling* (famous for his controversial discovery of the relationship between vitamin C and the common cold), biochemical theories

---

[15]Richard Speck died in prison in 1991 at the age of 49. Further studies have not conclusively determined a relationship between chromosome imbalance and criminal acts, and much of the research on this issue may have died with him.

[16]"Link between XYY Syndrome and Criminality Not Clear," *Public Health Reports,* Vol. 89, No. 10 (October 1969), p. 914.

maintain that certain types of behavior can be activated by imbalances among chemicals in the brain.

Nutritional disorders are viewed as the basis of such imbalances. They have been associated with food allergies, hypoglycemia (low blood sugar), vitamin deficiencies (in which essential vitamins are lacking in the diet), and vitamin dependencies (where more excessive amounts of a particular vitamin are required than are normally present in the diet). These disorders can then be reflected in behavior, primarily through perceptual problems or hyperactivity.[17] As a result of perceptual disorders, for example, children can become restless, experience learning difficulties, and seem to ignore the positive and negative sanctioning of their behavior. Did you ever try to calm down a hyperactive child who had consumed too much sugar? Have you ever felt jittery and restless after drinking too much coffee? These are examples of how what we eat can affect how we act.

Physiologists examine body chemistry to determine whether basic dietary changes can be made to alter one's behavior. Success in this direction has been reported at rates of up to 80% in the treatment of children, alcoholics, and drug addicts through such approaches as megavitamin therapy.[18] However, acceptance of the biochemical approach has suffered from a number of drawbacks, among them the costs of diagnosis and treatment, as well as the foundation of biochemical theories in the medical sciences. The field of criminology is largely dominated by sociology in terms of research and by psychology in terms of offender treatment. The social science literature has not widely embraced advances in medicine and biochemistry. In addition, such theories appear to be somewhat simplistic in their support for the age-old saying, "You are what you eat!" Treatment of this nature also raises several ethical questions. We might entertain manipulating the environment, and even the mind, in an effort to reduce criminality, but manipulation of the body for social purposes is another issue entirely.

## Biology and the Environment

The major question posed by physiological theories is the extent to which one's *biological attributes* determine behavior (i.e., biological determinism). Are we fully governed by what we inherit at birth, or is our biological predestination modified by the environment in which we are raised? Studies of twins and children adopted at birth have attempted to address this issue. Much of the evidence points toward a significant biological impact. For example, the criminal behavior of identical twins appears to be more similar than that of nonidentical (fraternal) twins.[19] Moreover, children adopted at birth have a tendency to reflect the criminality of their biological parents, regardless of the environment in which they were raised.[20]

[17]See Leonard J. Hippchen, ed., *Ecologic–Biochemical Approaches to Treatment of Delinquents and Criminals* (New York: Van Nostrand Reinhold, 1978); and Leonard J. Hippchen, "Biochemical Approaches to Offender Rehabilitation," *Offender Rehabilitation*, Vol. 1, No. 1 (Fall 1976), pp. 117–18.

[18]Hippchen, "Biochemical Approaches," p. 117.

[19]Karl Christiansen, "A Preliminary Study of Criminality among Twins," in Sarnoff Mednick and Karl O. Christiansen, eds., *Biosocial Bases of Criminal Behavior* (New York: Gardner Press, 1977).

[20]R. B. Cattell, *The Inheritance of Personality and Ability: Research Methods and Findings* (New York: Academic Press, 1982).

But such findings do not mean that the effects of the environment can be completely dismissed. More recently, *James Q. Wilson* and *Richard Herrnstein*[21] have made a substantial case for the *interactive effect* between biological inheritance and environmental influence. Although they agree that certain inherited traits may create a predisposition toward criminal involvement, they maintain that variables in one's environment either reinforce or reduce the impact of biology. Thus, one's criminally prone inheritance (such as aggressiveness, a mesomorphic body type, or limited intelligence) can be reinforced by inadequate schools or a dysfunctional family life. On the other hand, the negative influence of biological inheritance can be substantially reduced by nurturing schools and a secure family life in which a healthy conscience is developed. Wilson and Herrnstein's theory has been criticized for its exclusive focus on explaining street crimes, which are more characteristic of lower- than of upper-class criminality. But it is also one of the few explanations of crime that has crossed disciplinary boundaries to explore how different perspectives may be equally valid if we view them interactively rather than in isolation.

---

*LEARNING GOALS*

*Do you know:*

- *The three personality components described by Freud and how they create internal tension within us?*
- *How life in prison is similar to the childhood state and what relationship that has to motives for criminal behavior?*
- *What types of defense mechanisms criminals use most often?*
- *How reinforcement theory is applied through behavior modification and why the results are not always maintained upon release from prison?*

---

## ❖ PSYCHOLOGICAL APPROACHES

The fields of psychology and psychiatry (generally combined as "psychology" in this section) are not totally unrelated to the physiological approaches discussed above. While psychologists maintain that behavior is determined primarily by experience and learning, psychiatrists place more significance on biological determinism. That is, they maintain that some of our behavior is attributable to basic instincts with which we are born, as illustrated in the next "Close-up on Corrections."

### Psychoanalytic Theory

Introduced by *Sigmund Freud* over a century ago, *psychiatry* attempts to relate behavior to certain mental conditions by exploring early developmental processes.

---

[21]James Q. Wilson and Richard J. Herrnstein, *Crime and Human Nature* (New York: Simon and Schuster, 1985).

Nature versus Nurture

Honeybees construct a honeycomb in a perfect hexagon, not because they were trained to do so, but because they cannot help it—they were "built" to act this way. In one of Kinsey's early experiments with wasps, he crushed a female wasp on a board and brushed the remains away. The male wasps still elicited sexual responses in that area in the complete absence of the female. This suggests reflex or "instinctual" behavior. Dogs retain many characteristics that are apparently biologically determined, although they can be trained within limits. When you take away a bone from a basset hound, the dog reacts with a sad-eyed hope that the bone will be given back. When a bone is removed from a pit bull, however, it had best be done with extreme caution! German shepherds are used for sentry training because their temperament is appropriate for it. Similarly, some dogs are more easily trained for shepherding and hunting than others. Nobody has ever heard of a poodle shepherding a herd of cattle.

Regarding human beings, the question raised is how much biological determinism is left in people and how much of our behavior is learned by experience or conditioning. This issue has become known as the nature/nurture debate. That is, how much of our behavior is inherited (nature) and how much is a product of the environment (nurture)? Most social and behavioral sciences base their interpretations of behavior on the process through which we learn, are conditioned, and interact with others. However, others (such as those in the field of psychiatry) still include instincts as motivating forces in human behavior. What do you think?

---

Freud believed that all human beings are inherently (or instinctively) assertive and aggressive. Because of the constraints toward conformity imposed by society, mental conflict develops between these *basic instincts* and *social approval.*[22]

> Beginning in infancy, we all have basic desires which we want to have fulfilled. But at some point in childhood, the individual discovers that all such desires cannot be met, because they come into conflict with the needs and desires of others. Thus, the person develops some mechanism of either internally controlling, repressing, or acting-out instinctual behavior. The alternative chosen determines what type of adjustment and behavior will result.

According to Freud, the personality contains three components:

---

[22]For a more detailed discussion of Freud's concepts and the relationship of psychoanalysis to crime, see Seymour L. Halleck, *Psychiatry and the Dilemmas of Crime* (New York: Harper & Row, 1967).

- *Id:* source of the *drives, impulses,* and *instincts* motivating our behavior—the part of us that seeks pleasure at all costs. Someone "experimenting" with drugs to get a "quick high" could be responding to the pressures of the id.
- *Superego:* contrasting pressures toward conformity, norms, and values; that is, our *conscience*—the "police officer" of our personality. Those who avoid drug use because they fear the consequences (even though they think the effects might be pleasurable) could be viewed as responding to their superego.
- *Ego:* That part of our conscious personality trying to *balance* the forces of the *id* (which is telling us "do it; you'll like it!") and the forces of the *superego* (which is telling us "don't you dare; it's wrong!").

Freudian psychiatrists maintain that we are in this constant state of internal tension—with the id striving for satisfaction of our fundamental instincts, the superego "policing" these unconscious drives, and the ego trying to achieve stability between these two conflicts.

During early childhood development, behavior is almost always governed by the *id,* which is present from birth. The infant is virtually helpless and demands satisfaction of basic physical needs from parents. Later, the child discovers that this parental source of nurturing is also the source of restrictions. The child encounters the "do's" and "don'ts" that confront the instincts of the id. As the normally developing person matures later in life, the *superego* internalizes these social expectations and modifies demands of the id. The *ego* serves to keep the two in proper balance. Both the father and the mother play key roles in this developmental process.

When the individual is not *properly socialized* or has not adequately *internalized values,* antisocial behavior can result. If, for example, the drives of the id have not been controlled properly by the superego, a person can act-out aggressiveness without regard for its consequences. This is the type of offender who simply cannot keep basic instincts under control—who strikes out physically with the slightest provocation.

Basic to the psychoanalytic approach is the discovery that motives underlying deviant behavior are not always readily apparent. What may appear on the surface to be completely irrational, unexplainable behavior may be related to developmental problems that occurred many years before, creating deep-rooted personality maladjustments. The habitual car thief who merely abandons the vehicle, for example, may be seeking attention, acting-out frustrations, or demonstrating any number of other problems that have nothing to do with the acquisition of cars.

*Karl Menninger* also provides a unique perspective on why offenders not only commit crimes, but sometimes may actually *want* to get caught. His comparison of prison life with the childhood state points out some interesting similarities. Both provide the necessities of food, clothing, and shelter, as well as continual supervision—which eliminates choices of where to go, what to do, and how to act.[23] This presents a subconscious motivational possibility: Are many

---

[23]Karl Menninger, *The Crime of Punishment* (New York: Viking Press, 1968), p. 176.

habitual offenders simply seeking the more "secure" environment of confinement in an effort to revert to childhood and avoid facing the demands of adult life in free society? Or could some offenders actually be seeking punishment because of subconscious guilt complexes? As *David Abrahamsen* has noted, strong feelings of guilt over things which happened many years in the past may become so severe that they transform people into criminals "because they unconsciously want to be punished."[24]

Psychoanalytic theory holds that criminals—as well as ordinary citizens—are unaware of their motivations and rarely know completely the reason for their conduct.[25] All behavior therefore is viewed as a product of one's past. Consequently, one can determine true motives only by tracing into the past through psychoanalysis to identify what caused breakdown of the normal personality development process. It becomes the psychiatrist's task to explore the client's background, discover when and how the breakdown occurred, and assist in either *resolving* the problem or helping the individual *adjust* to it in a socially acceptable manner. This is not a short-term process, which is why such in-depth treatment is often reserved for more serious cases.

## Clinical Psychology

While psychiatrists are engaged in the search for deep-rooted causes of behavior, psychologists deal with the ways in which behavior is expressed *externally*. The goal is to help the offender better manage conflict (rather than completely resolve it), without resorting to a time-consuming search for its origins.

Stress is viewed by clinical psychologists as the primary motivation for deviant behavior. Unlike psychiatrists, who search for the *causes* of stress, psychology focuses on *reactions* to it. The most aggressive reaction to stress—attack—occurs when one's anger and hostility are directed outward. An opposite method for dealing with stress is withdrawal, either physically or psychologically. In this reaction, the person avoids stress-inducing situations by developing a protective shell, as in the case of alcoholics or drug addicts who are seeking to "escape" from the real world.

Basic to psychological reasoning are the methods used to preserve one's ego or sense of worth—that is, *defense mechanisms*, such as rationalization.

All of us have rationalized our behavior at some time, seeking to justify what we do. Whether this defense mechanism is socially harmful or not depends upon what is being rationalized—the shoplifter's theft of merchandise because "that store is ripping off customers anyway," or the student's inability to remember historical dates because "they don't really matter."

Criminals are often noted for the defense called *projection*—transferring the blame for one's own shortcomings to others. Such projections are essentially excuses to avoid accepting responsibility. A common pattern among correctional clients, for example, is the projection of blame on society or "the system." Using this line of thinking, offenders can convince themselves that they are not in trou-

[24]David Abrahamsen, *Who Are the Guilty?* (New York: Grove Press, 1972), p. 95.
[25]Ibid., p. 21.

ble because of their own fault, but rather, because of cops who were "out to get" them, judges who were "corrupt," a victim who "asked for it," or a lawyer who was "incompetent." The reality or unreality of these attitudes does not matter— the fact remains that they exist.

In treating criminal behavior, clinical psychologists attempt to divert the offender from socially unacceptable activities. This is done by channeling aggressions, frustrations, and other stress and tensions into more *socially acceptable* ego defense mechanisms. However, deviant behavior usually occurs well before treatment personnel enter the person's life, and changing long-established patterns of behavior is a far-from-easy task.

## Behavioralism

The concept of behavior being determined by its *rewards* and *punishments* was first introduced with the Classical School of criminology. But it was not operationalized until advancements were made in the behavioral sciences in the early part of this century. In his laboratory experiments with dogs, *Irving Pavlov* revolutionized thinking with the discovery of *conditioning*.

Repeatedly ringing a bell and subsequently presenting food to his dogs, Pavlov found that they could be conditioned to expect food merely with the ringing of the bell. *B. F. Skinner* carried this thought further with his development of *reinforcement theory*, which maintains that behavior is learned from sources of reinforcement in a person's environment.[26] That is, behaviors could be elicited or maintained on the basis of the rewards (positive reinforcement) or punishments (negative reinforcement) which are associated with that conduct.

Operant conditioning principles have been incorporated into the treatment of offenders through techniques known as *behavior modification*. Correctional institutions are ideal settings for behavior modification because they are a closed environment, where punishments and rewards can be closely controlled by the staff. Institutional applications of behavior modification are often based on a token economy, where inmates can earn or lose tokens based on their willingness to comply with rules and regulations. Tokens represent the ability to purchase desired goods and services, such as movie privileges, weekend passes, candy, or cigarettes. They are awarded or withheld by staff according to whether or not the client demonstrates approved behavior: performing assigned tasks, maintaining clean quarters, participating in required activities, and so on. Through this system, inmates can earn privileges through behavioral compliance with a treatment system that gradually attempts to reduce their antisocial tendencies.

Unlike psychoanalysis and clinical psychology, behavior modification has the advantage of being able to be implemented by nonprofessional staff with appropriate supervision and training.[27] But staff can be "conned" by crafty inmates who appear superficially to be complying with the system, but have not

[26]For a further discussion of Skinnerian principles and reinforcement, see Charles G. Morris, *Psychology*, Second Edition (Englewood Cliffs, NJ: Prentice Hall, 1976), pp. 134–50.
[27]Ralph Wetzel, "Use of Behavioral Techniques in a Case of Compulsive Stealing," *Journal of Consulting Psychology*, Vol. 30 (October 1966), pp. 367–74.

in fact altered their basic behavioral patterns. Moreover, the controlled conditions that exist in institutions do not resemble the freedom of choice which exists on the outside. When the continual reinforcements provided by the institution are not forthcoming, even those whose behavior was changed temporarily may resume previous patterns of response upon release.

## Intelligence and Education

While not a separate discipline in itself, the relationship between *intelligence* and *behavior* has been explored within the field of psychology. Again, intelligence involves the nature/nurture debate. Although it may have a physiological base, it is also greatly affected by environmental factors. Adding to the dilemmas surrounding intelligence is the difficulty of measuring it. Traditional IQ tests have been criticized for their cultural bias toward the white middle class. Such tests often identified those from certain cultural, racial, or social classes (and criminals in particular) as intellectually inferior to the general population.[28] But these differences have largely disappeared as IQ tests became less bound to a specific culture or vocabulary and were refined by incorporating more nonverbal and performance testing.[29] Research has also failed to establish a connection between intelligence and the seriousness of an offense or the likelihood of recidivism.[30] It does not now appear that intelligence differs significantly between offenders and the general population from which they are drawn.

However, there is a considerable distinction between *intelligence* (inherent ability) and *education* (formal schooling). Substantial differences are apparent between offenders and the general population with regard to schooling. For example, more than half (53%) of those in prison are high school dropouts, in comparison with 29% of the overall population.[31] School attendance has also been linked with criminality. Many inmates first came to the attention of authorities for truancy violations,[32] and relationships have been demonstrated between academic performance and delinquency.[33] Moreover, research has shown that

[28]See such early efforts as Maud A. Merrill, *Problems of Child Delinquency* (Boston: Houghton Mifflin, 1947), p. 338, and Sheldon and Eleanor Glueck, *Unraveling Juvenile Delinquency* (New York: The Commonwealth Fund, 1950).

[29]See, for example, Leonard Blank, "The Intellectual Functioning of Delinquents," *Journal of Social Psychology*, Vol. 47 (1958), pp. 9–14.

[30]B. Marcus, "Intelligence, Criminality, and the Expectation of Recidivism," *British Journal of Delinquency*, Vol. 6, No. 2 (September 1965), pp. 147–51.

[31]National School Safety Center, *School Safety Checkbook* (Malibu, CA: National School Safety Center, 1990), pp. 66, 69. The 53% dropout figure is found in *Sourcebook of Criminal Justice Statistics—1991* (Washington, DC: U.S. Department of Justice, 1992), p. 648. See also G. Ross Bell, "Of Dropouts and Pushouts," *Bulletin*, National Association of Secondary School Principals, Vol. 60 (May 1976), pp. 48–49.

[32]*Justice and the Child in New Jersey*, Report of the New Jersey Juvenile Delinquency Commission (1939), p. 110, cited in Paul H. Hahn, *The Juvenile Offender and the Law* (Cincinnati, OH: Anderson Publishing Company, 1975), p. 201. Of 2021 inmates in New Jersey's correctional institutions, two out of five had been first committed because of truancy.

[33]See, for example, President's Commission on Law Enforcement and Administration of Justice, *Task Force Report: Juvenile Delinquency and Youth Crime* (Washington, DC: U.S. Government Printing Office, 1967), p. 51; Alexander Liazos, "Schools, Alienation, and Delinquency," *Crime and Delinquency*, Vol. 24 (1978), pp. 355–61; Lamar T. Empey and Steven G. Lubeck, *Explaining Delinquency* (Lexington, MA: D.C. Heath, 1971), pp. 92–93.

while the offenders studied had, on average, completed schooling through the eighth grade, their performance on standardized tests was only at the 4.9 grade level.[34] This means that grade completion does not necessarily accurately reflect ability. Thus, many within the institutional population of corrections may be *functionally illiterate* (generally defined as functioning at the fifth-grade level or less). Many of these correctional clients have failed in school for a variety of reasons and have dropped out, therefore limiting their future opportunities, and creating a downward spiral of further failures.

Nor are the difficulties resulting from lack of adequate education restricted to employment limitations. Formal education is relatively simple to measure. More illusive is what those lacking in formal education have also missed in terms of socialization, since the school is one of our primary socializing institutions. Those who have insufficient schooling have probably also missed the social values and cultural conditioning that are equally important functions of the school. Education is not just learning knowledge or skills, but also the development of work habits, a feeling of achievement, self-respect, and the self-discipline it takes to succeed.

Poor work habits and lack of motivation appear to characterize the correctional client. The job-holding ability of gang members, school dropouts, and the educationally unprepared is generally poor in relation to that of the regular work force.[35] They lack the staying power needed for participation in remedial or training programs, preferring a job *now*, with money to spend *immediately*. In other words, their expectations are unrealistic in terms of their background. Corrections has responded to this problem through the development of educational programs and prison industries. But not all of the skills taught are transferrable to the outside world, and many occupations remain restricted for ex-offenders.

---

*LEARNING GOALS*

*Do you know:*

- *What links the Chicago School found between crime and transitional neighborhoods, economic insecurity, and institutional instability?*
- *How criminal behavior can be learned through differential association?*
- *According to opportunity theory, why people from lower socioeconomic classes engage in crime?*
- *How containment theory explains why everyone from lower socioeconomic classes does not become involved in crime, while some of those from upper classes do?*
- *How the stigmatizing effect of labeling can shape one's self-concept and contribute further to criminal behavior through a self-fulfilling prophecy?*

---

[34]*Special Labor Force Report 100,* U.S. Department of Labor, Bureau of Labor Statistics (Washington, DC: U.S. Government Printing Office, 1969).

[35]Samuel M. Burt and Herbert E. Striner, *Toward Greater Industry and Government Involvement in Manpower Development* (Kalamazoo, MI: W.E. Upjohn Institute, 1968).

In this discussion of the socializing role of education, we have made the transition from psychological to sociological perspectives. Sociological theories of crime causation have been the focus of much of the research that has been conducted on criminality. Researchers have noted the large proportion of criminal and delinquent activities that have been committed by the lower classes, leading them to seek associations between social conditions and crime. More recently, however, reasoning in this field has expanded to include upper-class criminality. The very process through which behavior is identified as "criminal" has been subject to scrutiny as well.

For a humorous story illustrating the differences between those who believe that criminality is an inherent feature of the individual and those who maintain that it is a product of the social environment, see the next "Close-up on Corrections."

### The Chicago School—Ecological Theory

The first comprehensive study in the United States to address the problem of crime was conducted in Chicago during the 1920s. Those associated with the *Chicago School* (Clifford Shaw, Henry McKay, Ernest Burgess, and Robert Park) were convinced that the *physical environment* of certain sections of the city was more conducive to criminal involvement than other areas. They searched for a relationship between the environment and criminal behavior—hence the description of their theory as *ecological*.

Drawing a series of "concentric circles" around Chicago and plotting delinquency rates within them, they found that the greatest amount of delinquent

❖ *CLOSE-UP ON CORRECTIONS*

Criminality: A Product of the Person or the Situation?

During the nineteenth century in Italy, public officials were concerned because people kept urinating in the street. Public urination was illegal and people guilty of it were punished. A famous criminologist of that period, Cesare Lombroso, suggested that such criminals be confined for their actions. Reflecting his own conclusions about crime, Lombroso logically argued that people who commit crimes are inherently different from others and there is little that one can do to change these innate characteristics. Therefore, society should simply confine those who commit criminal acts. However, a young student of Lombroso, Enrico Ferri, who was to become a famous criminologist in his own right, suggested an alternative: public urinals.

*Source:* James C. Hackler, "The Need to Do Something," in Ralph A. Weisheit and Robert G. Culbertson, *Juvenile Delinquency: A Justice Perspective* (Prospect Heights, IL: Waveland Press, 1985), p. 183.

activity occurred in locations close to the central business district.[36] As distance from the inner city increased, they noted that crime decreased (see Figure 3.2) and concluded that environmental factors produce criminality.

In places where extensive delinquency was found, a very transitory and heterogeneous population resided. When these studies were conducted—from 1900 to 1933—U.S. urban areas were experiencing sizable growth from foreign immigrants, whose lack of financial resources forced them to locate in the least desirable parts of the city. As their economic status improved, better housing was sought, making room for additional newcomers in a constantly changing section of the city, called the *zone of transition.*

In this transitional area, two widespread problems were evident: *economic insecurity* and *institutional instability.* If they could find employment at all, immigrants in the transitional zone could expect to obtain only the most menial labor at the lowest wage—creating economic insecurity. But the instability of social institutions in this zone could be just as devastating. With such a mixed population, there was little basis for social cohesiveness.

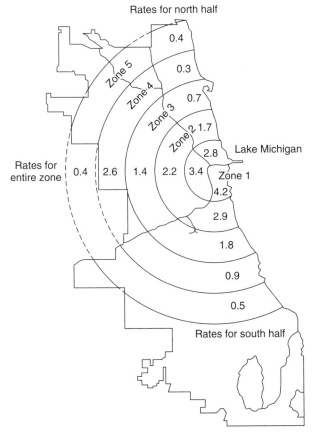

**Figure 3.2** Concentric circles of the Chicago school's ecological theory. *Source:* Clifford R. Shaw and Henry D. McKay, *Juvenile Delinquency and Urban Areas,* rev. ed. (Chicago: University of Chicago Press, 1969), p. 78.

[36]Clifford R. Shaw and Henry D. McKay, *Juvenile Delinquency and Urban Areas,* rev. ed. (Chicago: University of Chicago Press, 1969), p. 55.

The impact of disorganized family life, inadequate schools, lack of recreation, and the absence of social service agencies all contributed to institutional instability. It is hardly surprising to have found fertile grounds for the breeding of crime. Nor have inner-city conditions improved much in this respect over the past half-century, as we see in the story of one young man's continuing frustrations in the next "Close-up on Corrections."

The unanswered question remaining from the Chicago studies is whether such conditions actually *cause* crime or whether crime is merely associated with them. For example, some rural areas also experience high levels of poverty, unemployment, and institutional instability, but are not equally crime ridden. From this point of view, the concentric circle theories are more descriptive than explanatory, although even today, numerous projects operate in high-crime areas of urban communities in an attempt to deal with the problems uncovered by these studies. These days, however, many such programs address the disruptive impact of drugs—a problem virtually unheard of at the time of the Chicago studies.

## Differential Association

*Edwin Sutherland* also looked for the source of delinquency in external associations. But whereas the Chicago School focused on geographic location and community ties, Sutherland emphasized the influence of social contacts in his theory of *differential association*.

According to Sutherland, criminal behavior is *learned*—just as is law-abiding behavior—from interaction with others in intimate personal groups. Patterns of behavior therefore vary on the basis of the types of associations to which one is exposed. This should not be interpreted to mean that merely becoming involved with the "wrong crowd" will result in deviance. But as one is exposed more *frequently, consistently,* and *intensively* to criminal behavior, it is more likely that the individual will learn and accept it. Since such learning occurs within intimate personal groups, Sutherland explains why those only casually associating with criminals—such as the police—do not develop criminal traits. Differential association may provide an explanation of delinquent gangs and organized criminal activities. But it falls somewhat short in cases of isolated criminality among those who have not previously been exposed to such behavior. Nor does it explain why everyone who maintains intimate contact with antisocial behavior does not ultimately succumb to that type of lifestyle. In any event, the concepts underlying differential association are reflected in efforts to establish positive *role models* for those who are otherwise predominately exposed to negative behavior.

## Alienation, Adaptation, and Opportunity Theory

With urbanization and industrialization, modern society has become very complex. Technological progress has taken its toll on our values and lifestyles. The importance of the individual has diminished, creating feelings of powerlessness, mess, impotence, and personal insignificance. As people become more *alienated* from society, lose touch with cultural standards, or find the means for achieving their goals blocked, some will resort to deviant behavior.

Transitional Zones Today

[M]ost prisoners are poorly educated young men raised in slum neighborhoods by low income parents, often a single mother who is underemployed or unemployed. These young men have virtually no job skills or job experience, and no hope of ever getting a stable and adequate job. Most of them grow up in the streets where they live from day-to-day, engaging in ill-planned and unskilled crimes in order to obtain money for their daily needs. The case of Eddie Turner exemplifies this type of offender.

Turner, shirtless and muscular, his body tattoed and scarred . . . [returned] from an unsuccessful morning's search for work. "They say, `Sorry, there are no openings, but if you take a seat and fill out an application, we will get back to you when there is.' They never do," he said. . . . At least three times a week . . . he was making a journey in search of work. "I go by bus, my mother's car, sometimes a friend drops me off," he said. "Sometimes it gets frustrating. I feel bad about being rejected. I feel like I'm not accepted; they don't want me. But I can't let one job stop me. If they don't call me back, I can't sweat it. There are jobs there—I know it. You got to get out and get them. So every day, I think about getting a job. . . . I need one real bad."

There is another dilemma, a hidden penalty. Because Turner and his two brothers are over 18 and out of school, their mother's welfare check has been cut, even though they continue to rely on her for support. [She] winds up struggling to raise her four children with money meant for her and her 17-year-old daughter. So Turner's mother pressures him to move out and his need for a job, money and independence grow, [but he is] stymied by meager qualifications—high school dropout and former street gang member. It was not supposed to be this way. He used to dream of becoming a plumber, carpenter, or mechanic. He wanted to move to the mountains where a teacher once took him to spend a few weeks away from the inner city, and where he vowed to return. For a brief while, his ambitions seemed to have a chance. Turner worked as a plumber's assistant. But he was injured on the job and replaced. Now ambition labors against the lure of "the streets"—alcoholism, welfare, broken homes—and the pull of an underground economy in which a career can be had selling drugs.

It was eight days ago that Eddie Turner talked about the pain of trying to find a job. It was three days later that [his mother] talked about her worst fears that "the streets" would capture her son. And it was a day later that the streets did just that. Eddie Turner was arrested on suspicion of robbing a man at gunpoint. . . . He faces at least two years in prison if convicted.

Turner, a typical first-termer, is very different from the popular image of a vicious criminal. As a matter of fact, so are the vast majority of those sent to prison. . . .

*Source:* John Irwin and James Austin, "It's about Time: Solving America's Prison Crowding Crisis," in Lawrence F. Travis, Martin D. Schwartz, and Todd R. Clear, *Corrections: An Issues Approach* (Cincinnati, OH: Anderson Publishing Company, 1992).

Most of us—law-violating and law-abiding alike—share similar goals. We want to achieve success. Particularly in a capitalistic culture, success is measured primarily by money, status, and prestige. However, the means to fulfill our goals are not always equally accessible to everyone. *Robert Merton* recognized this in describing how people adapt differently to goals and the means of achieving them. *Goals* and *means* are established by the dominant groups in society.[37] They therefore reflect standards and conduct that are often not available to the lower social classes. Through the mass media, however, everyone is rather painfully aware of what they are "missing."

According to Merton, those from lower socioeconomic classes are denied access to *conventional goals* because they do not have *legitimate means* of achieving them. In their resulting frustration, they may adapt such "innovative" alternatives as crime. The wealthy and middle classes can achieve conventional goals through conventional means: going to college, obtaining a good job, and so on. Lower-class members with less access to these advantages will seek the means available to them, which may well involve socially unacceptable behavior, such as drug dealing. *Richard Cloward* and *Lloyd Ohlin* carry this line of thinking further to note that even *illegitimate* opportunities are not accessible in some neighborhoods, creating the potential for retreating into alcohol or drugs, as well as gang membership.[38] Thus, some people become so detached that they abandon both established goals and efforts to achieve them by any means.[39]

Such theories are valuable contributions toward understanding deviant behavior resulting from group conflict. But they do not explain why only certain persons in similar circumstances lose contact with cultural goals. Nor do they address why those to whom legitimate means are available may elect illegitimate alternatives (i.e., the white-collar criminal). To explore these questions of individual differences, we turn to a *social-psychological* theory that combines the perspectives of these two disciplines.

## Containment Theory

Initiated by *Walter Reckless,* the theory of *containment* is based on a system of "inner" and "outer" restraints. *Outer* containment is represented by those social forces in our environment—family, friends, organizations, community standards—which exert an influence on keeping behavior within bounds. *Inner* containment is one's internal capacity for self-control. For example, a favorable self-image contributes to one's ability to act responsibly, keep within limits, tolerate frustration, set realistic goals, and follow approved standards of behavior.

This combination of external and internal containments represents our *buffers* against deviance. But just as there are external and internal containments keeping our behavior within limits, there are external and internal *pressures* toward nonconformity. Pressures exerted from the outside—poverty, unemploy-

[37]See Robert K. Merton, *Social Theory and Social Structure* (New York: Free Press, 1957), pp. 131–60.
[38]Richard Cloward and Lloyd Ohlin, *Delinquency and Opportunity* (New York: Free Press, 1960).
[39]Ibid., p. 186.

ment, inequality, and so on—can break through containment buffers. Internal drives can also provide their own source of "push" toward nonconformity. If external pressures or internal drives are too strong (or, on the other hand, if inner and outer containments are too weak), a person may succumb to deviant behavior.

Containment theory has the advantage of being able to account for many types of criminal behavior, since it includes both environmental factors and individual differences. It explains why everyone exposed to the inequity of a lower-class lifestyle does not become involved in crime (strong inner containments), as well as why some of those enjoying greater status and prestige do (strong pressures; weak containments). Its practical limitations result largely from the very breadth of the theory. Obviously, it is impossible for society to attempt to control all of the external forces, much less the internal variables, associated with containment. But like the interactive theory of Wilson and Herrnstein, it is a significant contribution for embracing both psychological forces and sociological factors in an interdisciplinary perspective.

## Labeling Theory

Labeling theory differs from the more traditional perspectives described thus far in that it does not specifically address the causes of crime. Rather, it directs attention to society's *reaction* to criminal behavior.

During the 1960s and 1970s, society witnessed for the first time widespread challenges to the traditional authority of established social institutions. The Vietnam war protests, civil rights demonstrations, and the aftermath of Watergate caused many to question the practices of government officials—from local police officers to the president of the United States. It was in this turbulent environment of disputing the "status quo" that the legitimacy of our laws and system of criminal justice came under fire with the emergence of *labeling theory.*

Based on the conflict perspective of how criminal law is developed (see Chapter 2), labeling is concerned with society's role in creating deviance by "making the rules whose infraction constitutes deviance."[40] When laws are developed and enforced, certain interests are preserved and others are subverted. As *Richard Quinney* has noted, "whenever a law is created or interpreted, the values of some are necessarily assured and the values of others either ignored or negated."[41]

Labeling particularly focuses on what occurs when the criminal law is applied by those *with power* to those *without power. Howard Becker's* study of those we isolate as "outsiders" maintains that "deviance is *not* a quality of the act the person commits, but rather, a consequence of the application by others of rules and sanctions. . . . "[42] That "consequence" is the label which society attach-

---

[40]Howard Becker, *Outsiders: Studies in the Sociology of Deviance* (New York: Free Press, 1963), p. 9.
[41]Richard Quinney, *The Social Reality of Crime* (Boston: Little, Brown, 1970), p. 37.
[42]Becker, p. 9.

es to those who have engaged in behavior that reflects what has been officially identified as "criminal." For a unique insight into labeling from the perspective of an anonymous inmate's poetic verse, see the next "Close-up on Corrections."

We have already seen that many employment opportunities, housing choices, and financial transactions are limited for those who have broken the law. As a result, "rule-breakers become entrenched in deviant roles because they are labeled 'deviant' by others and are consequently excluded from resuming normal roles in the community."[43]

Moreover, advocates of this perspective maintain that the label becomes a *self-fulfilling prophecy*. As society increasingly identifies someone as a "loser," an "addict," or an "ex-con," the individual begins to internalize that same belief. The label becomes one's identity, shaping self-concept. Thus, it is self-reinforcing—affecting not only how society reacts to the individual but how the individual feels about himself or herself.

Because labeling deals with the *consequences* rather than the *causes* of criminal behavior, it cannot technically be considered a theory of crime causation. It is

---

### ❖ CLOSE-UP ON CORRECTIONS

The Saints Who've Never Been Caught

When some fellow yields to temptation
And breaks a conventional law,
We look for no good in his makeup,
But, Lord, how we look for the flaw.

No one asks, "Who did the tempting?"
Nor allows for the battles he's fought;
His name becomes food for the jackals,
The Saints who've never been caught.

I'm a sinner, O Lord, and I know it,
I am weak, and I blunder and fail;
I am tossed on life's stormy ocean,
Like a ship that is caught in a gale.

I am willing to trust in Thy mercy,
To keep the commandments taught,
But deliver me, Lord, from the judging
Of Saints who've never been caught.

*Anonymous Convict*

*Source:* Louis P. Carney, *Probation and Parole: Legal and Social Dimensions* (New York: McGraw-Hill, 1977), p. 203.

---

[43]Milton Mankoff, "Societal Reaction and Career Deviance: A Critical Analysis," in William J. Chambliss and Milton Mankoff, eds., *Whose Law? What Order?* (New York: Wiley, 1976), p. 240.

of greater value in explaining why criminals recidivate than how they become involved in crime originally. Nor does it recognize that some may overcome the negative effects of labeling and go on to lead productive lives. Moreover, it would appear to give the impression that crime could be eliminated simply by eliminating criminal laws, or at least not processing law violators through the system.

Yet, labeling has had an impact on practices in recent years, particularly in the juvenile justice system. Efforts have been directed toward diverting first-time offenders out of the system, focusing on treatment rather than incarceration, removing juveniles from adult jails, and deinstitutionalizing juvenile facilities (topics that are covered in Chapter 13). All of these approaches are based on avoiding the stigmatizing effects of labeling.

## ❖ SUMMARY

The elusive search for one satisfactory theory of crime causation is virtually as old as civilization—originating with demonology and primitive superstitions that later gave way to the Classical School's concept of free will and individual responsibility. Since then we have embraced the Postitive School's philosophy of physical and environmental determinism, reflected from the 1930s to the 1970s in the medical model's emphasis on identifying the causes of and treatment for criminal behavior.

In searching for causes, the social, psychological, and physical sciences have all made significant contributions. The scientific experiments of biologists and physicians have pointed to the importance of *genetics* and *chemical functions* within the body—stimulating the nature/nurture debate. Psychologists and psychiatrists have explored the *mind, personality,* and associated behavior of the individual—looking at early childhood nurturing, the development of defense mechanisms, and conditioning through punishments and rewards. Sociologists have emphasized external, *environmental factors* related to our interactions with society—focusing on causes ranging from economic insecurity and institutional instability to differential association. Some sociologists have even questioned the legitimacy of the criminal law itself and placed considerable responsibility on society's *reactions* to what is defined as "law-violating" behavior.

Each of these disciplines has been useful in explaining certain types of criminals under certain types of conditions. But none has yet developed a comprehensive theory with broad applications. Until then we will continue to put together the crime causation puzzle piece by piece. In the meantime, a public increasingly frustrated with the inability to diagnose and effectively treat criminal behavior has reverted to the "punishment fitting the crime" philosophy of the Classical School. In that sense we have come back to where we began.

# chapter 4

# The Development of Corrections

> In the years to come, it is hoped that . . . citizens will direct a new genera-
> tion of correctional workers to create more positive chapters in corrections'
> history. For the harm done through their wrongdoings, offenders are respon-
> sible. But for using inappropriate methods for treating offenders, when bet-
> ter methods are known, we are all guilty.[1]
>
> American Correctional Association

## ❖ CHAPTER OVERVIEW

If it is true that society is judged by how it treats its prisoners, the methods
employed in the past are harsh indictments indeed. For those of us living in the
twentieth century, it may be difficult to envision the savage treatment of offenders in the past. Life without prisons and jails, or even courts and trials, may be
incomprehensible to us—yet these have been relatively recent "inventions." But
while there have not always been correctional institutions and justice as we
know it today, there *has* always been criminal behavior—and our predecessors
were rather ingenious at devising brutal methods of responding to it. It was not
without reason that America's forefathers established a constitutional guarantee
against "cruel and unusual punishment."

As everything from clothing to child-rearing has changed with the times,
so has our concept of "cruel and unusual," and along with it, our correctional
practices. The tortures, floggings, and public humiliations that characterized
"corrections" of the past conflict with today's concept of the worth of life and
human dignity. Although there are still countries in which severe physical punishment is employed in response to criminal behavior, the humanitarian values
upon which democracy in the United States is based preclude such practices.

Undoubtedly, there are times when, in extreme frustration with our inability to deal with crime, demands arise for a return to the "good old days"—when
offenders were more likely than not assumed to be guilty, and harsh punishment

---

[1] *The American Prison: From the Beginning . . . A Pictorial History* (College Park, MD: American
Correctional Association, 1983), p. 261.

could be bestowed by the victim. (In fact, it is in part for this reason that occasionally graphic descriptions of those times have been retained herein—to enable the reader to view them in the light of rationality rather than the emotion of nostalgia.) With every social advancement come trade-offs. Just as we sacrifice some amount of crime for the right to be free of overly restrictive government intrusions, we have traded the barbarity of vengeance for the civilization of due process and respect for human rights.

---

*LEARNING GOALS*

*Do you know:*

- *What role the victim played in achieving justice during primitive times and why this often led to "blood feuds"?*
- *What is meant by the concept of* lex talionis?
- *How religion influenced early forms of punishment?*

---

## ❖ PRIMITIVE LAW

Every society has various methods of social control—ranging from public disapproval to death—that hold individuals to expected standards of behavior. Early primitive tribes were no exception.

As primitive people gathered together to form tribes, group living created certain customs that everyone was expected to observe. There was no concept of "crime" or "private property" as we know it today. Deviations from folkways and customs were not illegal. But they did produce concern among other persons in the group whose anticipations of expected behavior had been violated. When a serious offense such as murder was committed, guilt was not determined by expert witnesses or rational proof.[2] In case of doubt, *oaths* and *ordeals* were used—severe tests of endurance, survival of which demonstrated "innocence." Guilt, however, was often assumed.

### Blood Feuds

Ancient cultures developed the idea of justice based on vengeance, retribution, and compensation. When a crime was committed, the victim was expected to dole out justice with his own hands. Punishment was carried out by the victim personally, along with help provided by one's family. The offender also sought refuge through family and friends. As a result of this system, *blood feuds* developed[3] in which the victim's family avenged the wrongs against its members by assaulting or killing the offender or members of the offender's family.

[2]See Bronislaw Malinowski, *Crime and Custom in Savage Society* (New York: Harcourt, Brace & World, 1932).
[3]For information on the role of the blood feud in the development of law, see William Seagle, *The History of Law* (New York: Tudor, 1946), p. 36.

"Justice" was a very personal matter. It was also a brutal process. If a person stole game from his neighbor's traps, he could expect to pay for the crime in a pot of boiling oil or a cage of wild beasts.[4]

Inevitably, communities which stood behind their members became embroiled in blood feuds with other tribes. Primitive society intervened in the feud when too many persons were involved in it and the practice threatened the group's very existence. Even though murder and theft (along with other behaviors that we now define as criminal) were not considered to be as important as they are today, the resulting blood feuds carried vengeance beyond the welfare of the tribes. Looking for less violent ways to settle disputes, the tribe assumed more and more responsibility for individual crimes as civilization progressed. There was a shift from the idea that the political community was based on blood kinship to the idea that a local community could serve as the basis of common political action. The unity of kindred groups for the welfare of all among several tribes resulted in agreements, not unlike the treaties common among the American Indians in the United States.

## Written Codes

With the development of writing, prohibitions against tribal customs were set down in written form. The first such document was the *Code of Hammurabi* in Babylon, which dealt with legal questions ranging from marriage contracts to the treatment of slaves. The Sermon on the Mount by Jesus was probably the epitome of these early formulations, which were really refinements of social experience in a society growing increasingly civilized. Many of these codes were unified by Emperor Justinian of the Byzantine Empire (A.D. 529–565) into what became known as the *Justinian Code.*

### *Lex Talionis*

It is important to remember that these formulations were codes, not laws. Functionally, the system of social control was still quite simple. On a practical basis, personal retribution by the victim was still the dominant method of control. In fact, the law of retaliation (*lex talionis*) against the offender was reflected in the Code of Hammurabi and the Law of Moses, as well as the Old Testament:

- *Deuteronomy 19:21* (650 B.C.): "And thine eye shall not pity; but life shall go for life, eye for eye, tooth for tooth, hand for hand, foot for foot."
- *Leviticus 24:20* (570 B.C.): "Breach for breach, eye for eye, tooth for tooth, as he has caused a blemish in a man, so shall it be done to him again."

However, the New Testament spoke in opposition to retribution:

- *Matthew 5:38, 39* (A.D. 65): "Ye have heard that it hath been said, An eye for an eye, and a tooth for a tooth: But I say unto you, That ye resist not evil: but whosoever shall smite thee on thy right cheek, turn to him the other also."

[4]James D. Stinchcomb, *Introduction to Criminal Justice: Instructor's Guide,* six audiovisual presentations (Washington, DC: Robert J. Brady Company, 1972), p. 6.

Despite the above-cited Biblical constraint, retribution remained the primary form of social control. The influence of Christian teachings on everyday practice was not to occur for many years.

## The Roman Empire

About the time of Christ, the Roman Emperor Augustus selected men from his military legions to form the Praetorian guard to protect the palace. Augustus also established the first civilian police force, called the Vigiles of Rome (from which the term *vigilante* derived). Although they sometimes kept peace with a heavy hand, they also performed such important public services as firefighting. But most offenses were still dealt with through private redress. When public authority intervened, "it did so because an offender refused to make restitution."[5]

As civilized people moved into agriculture, land became valuable. When agriculture became established as the basis of an economy, it required permanent residence. The ancient feudal system began to emerge. The best organizer in an area claimed the land, and other people worked for him in exchange for economic security. As these feudal lords grew, they expanded their holdings by waging war and capturing land in neighboring domains. The ancient empires were thus developed.

By this time, the disastrous consequences of the blood feuds (sometimes resulting in all-out wars) forced society to create a more orderly system of social control, making a judicial process necessary. Ancient feudal lords therefore established *arbitration courts.* The decisions of the court generally involved an indemnity (bondage) to the victim's family for two or three years, but this form of "restitution" could continue through life until the debt was paid. Other dispositions of these courts included forced labor in public works projects (which virtually amounted to slavery), exile, or death. This system developed a society of free people and slaves that remained intact for centuries. At the time of Plato, for example, only about one out of ten citizens was free.

## The Rise of Religions and Confinement

In a somewhat ironic development, retributive punishments became even more severe with the rise of the major religions. It was believed that sin and crime were offenses against God, and thus became infractions of divine law and God's will, as well as damaging to society.

The many references to "prison" in the Old and New Testaments and other religious books were there long before the modern concept of prison evolved. At that time, they referred to confinement in rooms and facilities not originally designed for punishment—such as old cellars, dens for animals, and other makeshift resources. They were used in a manner not unlike sending an errant child to his or her room for detention. In fact, according to ancient codes, long-term confinement was not to be used as punishment for crime. Although

---

[5]Charles F. Abel and Frank H. Marsh, *Punishment and Restitution* (Westport, CT: Greenwood Press, 1984), p. 28.

Jerusalem had places of detention as early as the sixth century B.C., the concept of jails and prisons in the modern sense was still centuries away.

---

*LEARNING GOALS*

*Do you know:*

- *How some offenders were protected in medieval times by benefit of clergy and the right of sanctuary?*
- *What purposes were served by the* hue and cry *and* posse comitatus?
- *How jails were first used, in contrast to their functions today?*
- *What impact the breakdown of the feudal system had on the development of debtors' prisons and workhouses?*
- *Why banishment and exile were used extensively following the Industrial Revolution?*

---

## ❖ MEDIEVAL PRACTICES

As the feudal fiefs developed into empires, all subjects and slaves were forced to go to the courts for redress of wrongs. Noblemen were "above the law" and did not need to use the courts. In many areas, free citizens could manage their own affairs through *trial by combat*. If one could conquer an opponent in a pitched battle, his neighbors were satisfied to let him go free. Trials by ordeal were also still common. An accused murderer, for example, could prove innocence by surviving a plunge into boiling water or a walk across hot coals.

### Church Influence

During this period of time, the Roman Catholic Church emerged as an organized political entity, maintaining control of considerable territory and punishing those who violated canon law. Ecclesiastical prisons were constructed to supplement places of confinement, which were mainly the gatehouses of the abbeys. By the eleventh century, tribunals (or courts) were church operated, and a class of church lawyers had emerged.

Although the feudal and spiritual courts were kept separate, the influence of the church was unmistakable. *Benefit of clergy* was afforded to anyone (not merely clergy) who was able to read and write. According to this tradition, those who were literate were relatively safe from serious penalties for almost any crime, at least for the first offense. The *right of sanctuary* was also recognized, through which certain locations (often churches or holy places) were designated as places where an offender might go to escape punishment.

### Anglo-Saxon England

With the downfall of the Roman Empire, Europe was in chaos. Germanic tribes invaded the old Roman territory of Britain, mixing their blood with the conquered English to form an independent race called Anglo-Saxons. For purposes of security and mutual economic benefit, tribes and clans were replaced by "tuns" and "hundreds." Ten families made up a tun (town). Casual agreements among villagers eventually became a formal legal arrangement called the *tithing system*. A tithing was a community of 10 families, each responsible for its neighbor's behavior. This type of cooperation among villagers gradually led to the consolidation of tuns into hundreds—groups of 10 tithings. A group of 100 was roughly equivalent to a shire (or county) and was led by the political head of the shire—the *shire-reeve*. This office was the origin of our modern-day county sheriff.

The shire-reeve was responsible for collecting taxes, keeping the peace, and operating the *gaol* (pronounced "jail"). He also had the power of *posse comitatus*, which called all men of the shire together when assistance was needed—the forerunner of the sheriff's "posse." Even though shire-reeves were full-time appointments, their job was to call on the residents to respond to law violators. Enforcement of the law was still very much in the hands of local citizens. When an offense was committed, the night watchmen (often called "bailiffs") raised a *hue and cry*. Citizens were expected to respond and pursue the offender. Because of the reluctance of some to heed the "hue and cry," the Statute of Winchester in 1285 made this civic duty a requirement, and criminal penalties were established for failure to respond.

## Medieval Punishments

Like their ancient forerunners, medieval Europeans were very brutal in the exercise of punishment. Knives, axes, whips, barnacles, collars, and cuffs were commonly used to inflict punishment, along with confinement in cold, dark, damp, vermin-infested dungeons. "Man's primitive fear of being confined in the darkness" was used "as both torture and punishment."[6]

The death penalty was invoked frequently—not in the quick, almost sterile manner in which it is carried out today, but through methods designed to extract as much pain and suffering as possible. Several ingenious devices were designed for this purpose. Among the most grotesque was the "iron maiden"—which was a boxlike device, with the front half hinged like a door so that a person could be placed inside. When the door was shut, protruding spikes, both back and front, entered the body of the victim. Equally barbaric was the "rack"—a device for dragging apart the joints by the feet and hands. The Tower of London (originally built as a fortress for defense of the city) was infamous for such cruelty. It was there that an even more torturous contraption was developed. Whereas the rack stretched its victims, this machine compressed the body: "more dreadful and more complete than the rack . . . the whole body is so bent that with some, the blood exudes from the tips of the hands and feet; with others, the box of the chest being burst, a quantity of blood is expelled from the mouth and nostrils."[7]

Executions by burning, beheading, and hanging were also employed liberally. These were public events, attended by crowds of gleeful onlookers, as evidenced in the English poem in the next "Close-up on Corrections." Perhaps most

[6]G. Abbott, *Tortures of the Tower of London* (London: David & Charles, 1986), p. 9.
[7]Ibid., p. 25.

Poor John Goose, poor John Goose

For him not the speed of the hangman's noose
But the crackle and spit of the ghastly fire
As inch by inch the flames grow higher.
Burn him merrily, cry the crowd,
So he hath no need of a burial shroud.

*Source:* Shelagh Abbott (in G. Abbott), *Tortures of the Tower of London* (London: David & Charles, 1986), p. 60.

reprehensible was the "widespread practice of taking children to see hangings and gibbetted corpses and whipping them soundly on the site."[8] For more than 200 years, England used capital punishment extensively. During the reign of Queen Elizabeth alone, for example, there were some 72,000 executions.

Following the signing of the *Magna Carta* by King John in 1215, the crown could no longer imprison or execute subjects unless they were first tried by a jury of fellow citizens. The Magna Carta was also significant in a number of other respects, reducing much of the king's power and returning it to the local community.

But if found guilty of a capital offense, the offender "would not only lose his life, but also forfeit his lands and property . . . leaving his family destitute."[9] It was therefore to a defendant's advantage to refuse to plead guilty. However, those who did so were subjected to brutal techniques of "persuasion," which often led to death. Despite the torture of such interrogations, if death resulted, it would occur before a trial was conducted and a verdict was reached. The state therefore would have no claim to the defendant's properties, and his family could inherit them. As a result, many still subjected themselves to the horrors of the iron maiden, the rack, and similar torture devices to retain an inheritance for their families.

Those fortunate enough to escape the gallows or the tortures inflicted in castles and dungeons might find themselves confined to the galleys of convict ships that sailed the seas aimlessly with a cargo of felons. These vessels may have been offshoots of the "hulks" or nonseaworthy vessels that had been anchored in the Thames River in London and elsewhere as places of confinement. Like the slave galleys of ancient Rome and Greece, floggings were common and conditions were extremely harsh: "chained to their crowded benches, often for six months at a time and perhaps for longer . . . [t]he rowers were exposed to all weathers and were fed on hard fare, and frequently much sinted in water-supply."[10] In addition, many of these vessels also contained their own torture devices.

[8]Keith Baker and Robert J. Rubel, *Violence and Crime in the Schools* (Lexington, MA: D.C. Heath, 1980), p. 5.
[9]Abbott, p. 12.
[10]George Ives, *History of Penal Methods* (Montclair, NJ: Patterson Smith, 1970), pp. 104–105.

## Confinement Practices

Originally, incarceration was used only until a confession was obtained or the death penalty was imposed. It was the church that first made use of long-term confinement of offenders by locking them into the gatehouse of the abbey during the Middle Ages as a humane gesture to replace execution. In the twelfth century, some private prisons were constructed by wealthy landowners. This enabled those with sufficient power and influence to build their own prisons and incarcerate anyone who interfered with their political ambitions or personal inclinations.[11] Among the more famous private prisons were the Castle of Spielberg, the Bastille in Paris, the wells of the Ducal Palace in Venice, and the Seven Towers of Constantinople.

It was not until the *Assize of Clarendon* (Constitutions of Clarendon) in A.D. 1166 that construction of the first facility designed solely for public incarceration was authorized—the *gaol* (or, as it is now spelled, "jail"). The Assize of Clarendon also formalized court procedure, establishing the jury system essentially as it remains today. The shire-reeve was recognized as an officer of the law, and among his responsibilities was operation of the gaol. Certain offenses against the "king's peace" were defined, including arson, robbery, murder, false coinage, and crimes of violence. The beginnings of classification of crimes as felonies and misdemeanors appeared. Since an offender who committed a felony was disturbing the king's peace, he was punished by the state rather than the victim's family or village.

Along with the Magna Carta in 1215 and the Statutes of Westminster (1275–1285), a growing philosophy of government by the consent of the governed was emerging. It included provisions for courts, free elections, greater local government control, elimination of certain abuses, and theoretically treating all persons alike before the law, whether rich or poor. During this period, the security of the state was being consolidated. Methods of social control were becoming legitimized and formalized. The origins of civil and constitutional rights as we know them were emerging. However, these were very rudimentary beginnings, and in reality, the "justice" one received was still very much determined by social class.

## Early English Jails

With the development of trials, a place was needed to confine offenders until the king's court could be convened in the county where the crime occurred. That place became the *gaol*. In contrast to its use today, one did not serve time as punishment in jail. Rather, the jail was employed to confine those awaiting either *trial* or the imposition of *punishment* (functions that are still performed by modern jails). However, the punishment being awaited was more often than not death during this period of time. Nor was it uncommon for untried prisoners to wait years to appear before the court.[12]

---

[11]Leslie Fairweather, "The Evolution of the Prison," in Guiseppe de Gennaro and Sergio Lenci, eds., *Prison Architecture* (London: United Nations Social Defence Research Institute, Architectural Press, 1975), pp. 13–14.

[12]Linda L. Zupan, *Jails: Reform and the New Generation Philosophy* (Cincinnati, OH: Anderson Publishing Company, 1991), p. 12. (Much of the material on conditions in early jails is paraphrased from this source, pp. 10–14.)

The shire-reeves were responsible for the jails, but the crown provided no funds for their operation. As a result, sheriffs contracted with "keepers" to assure that inmates did not escape. Although the keeper was paid no salary, such contracts were actually quite lucrative. They generated income from *fees* charged to inmates, since prisoners were required "to pay for every service and good provided by the keeper."[13] For example, fees were charged to be booked, to eat, to sleep on a mattress, to obtain a bed, and to be released (even with a judicial order). Because the physical structures were so insecure and prone to easy escape, prisoners were often weighted down by "manacles, shackles, and iron collars, which they also paid the keeper a fee for the privilege of wearing."[14] To pay for their keep, inmates could beg or accept charitable donations, and profit was also made by selling inmate labor. Essentially, offenders were required to "pay for the privilege of being in jail"[15] through a system that basically amounted to extortion. For a vivid account of physical conditions and the fee system in a famous London gaol, see the next "Close-up on Corrections."

Wealthy offenders could pay for the privilege of living in plush quarters within or outside the jail. But those who could not afford this "higher-rent district" faced virtually intolerable living conditions. Everyone was literally dumped together. Children and adults, men and women, felons and debtors, healthy and sick (including lepers)—all were forced to live communally.[16] Given the extreme crowding, the filthy, rat-infested environment, and the lack of proper nutrition, it was not surprising that the strong preyed on the weak. Rape was common. Illnesses abounded. Many died of starvation or disease. The hopelessness of people confined in such conditions is perhaps best illustrated in the words scrawled on a cell wall by one desperate inmate: *To the builders of this nitemare though you may never get to read these words. I pity you; for the cruelity [sic] of your minds have designed this hell; if men's buildings are a reflection of what they are, this one portraits the ugliness of all humanity. IF ONLY YOU HAD SOME COMPASSION.*"[17]

## Breakdown of the Feudal System

As long as people were tied to the land and obliged to landowners through systems of serfdom and tithings, their behavior was relatively easy to control. But with the breakdown of the feudal system and the decline of craft guilds came mass unemployment and poverty. People moved about from county to city, dissolving their ties to neighbors, family, and the land that had held them in bounds for centuries. The hungry and jobless migrated en masse from rural areas to the cities, bringing with them a rise in crime that society was ill equipped to cope with. Added to this social disruption was the invention of gin in the early eighteenth century, which provided an inexpensive means for the poor to drown their troubles.[18]

---

[13]Ibid., p. 10.

[14]Ibid., p. 11.

[15]Henry Burns, *Corrections: Organization and Administration* (St. Paul, MN: West Publishing Company, 1975), p. 148.

[16]Zupan, pp. 11 and 13.

[17]William G. Nagel, *The New Red Barn: A Critical Look at the Modern Prison* (New York: Walker and Company, 1973), p. 188.

[18]Frank Schmalleger, *Criminal Justice Today* (Englewood Cliffs, NJ: Prentice Hall, 1991), p. 143.

London's famous Newgate Gaol was not a prison in the modern sense. There were no programs or discipline inside until well into the nineteenth century. Courtesy of Sir John Soane's Museum, London.

Massive drinking resulted in "gin riots"—huge crowds roaming the streets in drunken binges, destroying property and endangering the safety of citizens.

To deal with the social outcasts of society, *debtors' prisons* were established

## ❖ CLOSE-UP ON CORRECTIONS

### London's Famous Newgate Gaol

The outside had a nice appearance, but the inside was another matter. The dark and gloomy cells were poorly ventilated, the water supply inadequate, and the stench appalling. These conditions gave rise to outbreaks of gaol fever, which was a form of typhus. The gaol fumes help[ed] spread the disease to many prisoners. . . .

There seems to have been very little, if any, segregation of the Newgaters, with the exception of those cast into the lower dungeons. . . . According to an inmate placed there in 1724, it was "a terrible stinking dark and dismal place situated underground into which no daylight can come. It was paved with stone; the prisoners had no beds and lay on the pavement whereby they endured great misery and hardship."

Those prisoners who could afford to do so had their food and clothing sent to them from the outside. The alternative was to purchase such items from the keeper and his turnkeys, which resulted in tidy profits. . . . The gaol workers also made sums of money from the sale of spirits, candles, food, and even water. Gaolers also charged for the privilege of being released from irons and for allowing prisoners to approach the warming fire.

*Source:* J. M. Moynahan and Troy R. Bunke, "London's Famous Newgate Gaol (1188–1902)," *American Jails*, Vol. 5, No. 2 (May/June 1991), pp. 76–77.

in addition to jails and workhouses.[19] In fact, it has been noted that "the earliest candidates for incarceration in institutions for purposes other than awaiting some bodily punishment were largely the poor and the insane."[20] With the scarcity of laborers following the Black Death, workhouses were used as sources of cheap, forced labor. The city of London established a workhouse at St. Brigit's Well—called Bridewell—in 1557. The use of workhouses became widespread throughout Europe to house the insane and to "reform" minor offenders (such as beggars and pickpockets) by hard work and discipline. Debtor's prisons housed the indigent, who were incarcerated until family, friends, or charitable sources paid their monetary obligations—or until death.

### Banishment and Exile

Serious offenders were transported to banishment or exile. *Banishment* was considered an appropriate response to misbehavior, even, in modified form, for small children. In the Coventry area of England, for example, an errant child could be punished by cutting off all communication with everyone for extended periods of time. When this practice spread throughout England, it was popularly known as being placed "in Coventry." For criminal offenders, banishment presented a means of ridding civilized society of its nuisances through a sentence to the wilds of the unknown, as reflected in the following decree: "I sentence you . . . but to what I know not—perhaps to storm and shipwreck, perhaps to infectious disorders, perhaps to famine, perhaps to be massacred by savages, perhaps to be devoured by wild beasts. Anyway, take your chance, perish or prosper, suffer or enjoy; I rid myself of the sight of you; . . . I shall give myself no more trouble over you."[21]

Banishment was also a reflection of the economic conditions of the time. Replacement of the feudal system with a developing capitalistic economy occurred with the Industrial Revolution in the mid-eighteenth century. The mechanization provided by the Industrial Revolution no longer made slavery profitable, either on land or in the galleys at sea. Consequently, criminals had to be exported. Russia sent hers to Siberia. Spain and Portugal sent theirs to Africa. France sent hers to South America. England sent her criminals to Australia and America. As one historian has noted, "wilderness was the first penal colony."[22]

In 1717, the British Parliament formally designated America as England's penal colony (although prisoners had been shipped there as early as 1650). By the time of the American Revolution, there had been an estimated 100,000 criminals transported in chains to America. Because the exiled prisoners provided a free source of labor for the mother country in the developing colonies, there was

---

[19]For a description of the emergence of correctional institutions as tools of social control, see John Irwin, *The Jail: Managing the Underclass in American Society* (Berkeley, CA: University of California Press, 1985), p. 4.

[20]Richard Hawkins and Geoffrey P. Alpert, *American Prison Systems: Punishment and Justice* (Englewood Cliffs, NJ: Prentice Hall, 1989), p. 13.

[21]Leonard P. Liggio, "The Transportation of Criminals: A Brief Political–Economic History," in Randy E. Barnett and John Hagel III, eds., *Assessing the Criminal* (Cambridge: Ballinger, 1977), p. 282, citing the works of Jeremy Bentham.

[22]Ives, p. 97.

a considerable economic advantage to this practice. In fact, convicts were later assigned to private contractors who sold them as *indentured servants*. They could then work off their debt to society by providing services for a specified period of time to wealthy colonists. At the beginning of the American Revolution in 1776, however, America was closed to British prisoners because the government did not want to risk shipping more able-bodied Englishmen who would take up arms against the mother country. Subsequently, convicted offenders were sent to Australia until 1879, when that practice was terminated. Prisons eventually substituted for banishment.

---

*LEARNING GOALS*

*Do you know:*

- *What types of punishment were first employed in the American colonies?*
- *When and where the first U.S. prison was established?*

---

### ❖ EARLY AMERICAN CORRECTIONS

The origins of corrections in America had a harsh beginning. Although the Spanish explored Florida and established the city of St. Augustine in 1564, most of the early development of the United States centered on the northeastern seaboard, where the English came in search of freedom from religious persecution in their homeland. The Puritans who settled there, however, were equally intolerant of religious views that conflicted with their own. (In fact, what is now Rhode Island was founded by a minister, Roger Williams, who was forced to leave the original colony in 1636.)

### Colonial Punishments

The colonists brought with them extremely severe criminal codes from England, which, combined with the Puritans' strict concepts of sin, created a rigid system of social control. The famous witchcraft trials in 1692 were prompted by this religious fervor. Even the celebration of Christmas was considered sacrilegious and outlawed in 1659, and the Connecticut Code of 1650 "stipulated the death penalty for children who disobeyed their parents."[23]

Infractions were dealt with severely. Reflecting the colonists' British heritage, *corporal* and *capital punishment* were used frequently and carried out publicly. Branding and various forms of mutilation were employed, both as punishment and to mark the lawbreaker with identification. "The removal of a hand or finger, the slitting of the nostrils, the severing of an ear, or branding usually made it impossible for the marked individual to find honest employment."[24] Minor

---

[23]Alexis M. Durham III, "Social Control and Imprisonment during the American Revolution: Newgate of Connecticut," *Justice Quarterly*, Vol. 7, No. 2 (June 1990), pp. 315–16.

[24]Todd R. Clear and George F. Cole, *American Corrections* (Monterey, CA: Brooks/Cole Publishing Company, 1986), p. 64.

During colonial times, minor offenders could find themselves in a revolving pillory, subjected to public humiliation in the town square. Courtesy of the U.S. Bureau of Prisons.

offenders such as gossips might find themselves subjected to public humiliation through the ducking stool (submerged in water until near-drowning).

Stocks and pillories secured the offender's head and hands within wooden frames that were located in the town square. These devices were not just passive measures. In addition to provoking verbal ridicule, they enabled passers-by to pelt the constrained offender with stones and various other missiles. "The victim might also be whipped or branded while in the stocks or pillory," and when released, "compelled either to tear his ears loose from the nails or have them cut away carelessly by the officer in charge."[25] For more serious crimes, capital punishment was imposed—by hanging, burning at the stake, or breaking on the rack.[26]

## Colonial Correctional Institutions

Along with England's laws and punishments, early settlers brought with them the English system of jails, which became the first correctional institutions in this country. Like British gaols, early American jails housed defendants waiting trial or convicted offenders waiting the imposition of their sentence. The concept of "serving time" in jail was still unknown. Also like their British counterparts, Americans adopted the *fee system* for operating jails, along with the resulting abuses and corruption. The first U.S. jails, established in Virginia

[25]Burns, p. 82.
[26]American Correctional Association, p. 28.

during the early seventeenth century, charged "two pounds of tobacco" as the fee for admission or release.[27]

Despite the democratic ideals on which this country was founded, the British practice of enabling the rich to avoid jail or live in comfortable quarters was adopted. In contrast to the privileges afforded the wealthy, the poor were confined in gruesome conditions of hunger, filth, and disease spread by communal living. Food was minimal, sanitary conditions deplorable, and discipline nonexistent. Similar to their jailed English counterparts, "it was not uncommon for individuals with no resources to die of starvation."[28]

The first institution intended for long-term punishment rather than pretrial detention was *Newgate* prison, established in Simsbury, Connecticut, just prior to the American Revolution (1773). Actually, Newgate was an abandoned copper mine, with administrative buildings constructed over the mine's shaft. Three excavated caverns with one pool of fresh water constituted the prison. Offenders were confined underground, in the dripping water, foul air, and "horrid gloom" of what has been described as essentially a "dungeon."[29] Men and women, adults and children, sick and well, criminals and political prisoners (Tory sympathizers) were all placed together. Escapes were frequent, since "existence in the dungeon was so unbearable that getting out was the one incentive that kept its inmates alive."[30]

---

*LEARNING GOALS*

*Do you know:*

- *What contributions John Howard made to correctional developments in the eighteenth century?*
- *Why the U.S. Constitution is important to American corrections?*
- *What constitutional rights are protected under the first 10 amendments to the U.S. Constitution?*

---

## ❖ FROM VENGEANCE TO JUSTICE

By the mid-eighteenth century, conditions were ripe for major changes in both Europe and the United States. Punishments had become excessively violent and bloody, totally out of proportion to the seriousness of the offense. At the same time, Europe was experiencing the impact of the *Enlightenment* (also known as the "Age of Reasoning"). Traditional assumptions were challenged, greater worth was placed on the equality of the individual, and the barbarity of punishment practices was called into question.

---

[27]Burns, p. 149.
[28]Ibid., p. 153.
[29]Durham, pp. 308–09.
[30]Durham, p. 309, quoting W. Storrs Lee, "Stone Walls Do Not a Prison Make," *American Heritage*, Vol. 18, No. 2 (1967), p. 90.

### John Howard's Prison Reforms

Among the pioneers insisting on changes in penal practices of the time was the sheriff of Bedfordshire, *John Howard.* A former prisoner himself, the next "Close-up on Corrections" features an account of Howard's personal experiences, which inspired his demands for change.

Struck by the deplorable conditions that he found when he became responsible for the local gaol, Howard embarked on visits to prisons throughout both England and the Continent, documenting what he found and pressing for reform. His blistering essay on *The State of the Prisons in England and Wales* (1777) for the first time called public attention to the plight of incarcerated offenders. Among the improvements that he advocated were:[31]

- Segregation of prisoners by age, sex, and severity of their offense.
- Cells for prisoners, to reduce moral and physical contamination.

### ❖ CLOSE-UP ON CORRECTIONS

#### John Howard (1726–1790)

John Howard's interest in prisons began when he was on his way to Portugal in 1754. His ship was captured by a French privateer, and those on board were treated with great severity. While confined, he gained sufficient evidence to show that hundreds of English prisoners had perished because of poor treatment. He was permitted to return to England on parole to negotiate an exchange, and in 1773, he became the high sheriff of Bedfordshire. In that capacity he visited the jail which he was in charge of and found people detained for months until they paid fees for their own release. His first act was to apply for a salary for the jailer in order to reduce the reliance on fees. From that time on, he devoted himself to penal reform.

In 1774, he helped obtain passage of legislation liberating all prisoners whom the grand jury had failed to indict, and compensating the jailer for his fees. He also worked for another act requiring justices of the peace to see that the walls and ceilings of jails were scraped and whitewashed once a year, that rooms were regularly cleaned and ventilated, that underground dungeons should be used as little as possible, and that measures be taken to preserve the health of the prisoners. Howard printed the new legislation and distributed it at his own cost. While he was not an advocate of luxury in prison, he felt that every prisoner should have a pound and a half of good household bread a day and a quart of good beer.[a]

[a]D.L. Howard, *John Howard: Prison Reformer* (London: Christopher Johnson, 1958), p. 25.

[31]Zupan, p. 14, quoting D. L. Howard, *The English Prisons: Their Past and Their Future* (London: Methuen & Company, 1960).

- Salaried staff to prevent the extortion of prisoners.
- Appointment of chaplains and medical officers to address the spiritual and physical needs of inmates.
- Prohibitions against the sale of liquor to prisoners.
- Provision of adequate clothing and food to ensure continued good health.

While these may seem to be fundamental essentials of decency in the twentieth century, they were far from popular perspectives in the early stages of the Enlightenment. But because of the factual manner in which Howard presented the findings of his investigation, they captured public attention and became the basis for the Penitentiary Act passed by Parliament in 1779. The act provided for "secure and sanitary structures, systematic inspection, abolition of fees for basic services, and a reformatory regime."[32] Rejecting hard labor, Howard coined the term "penitentiary" to indicate that such institutions should be designed according to the Quaker philosophy of penance and contrition by reflecting on one's sins. But Howard did not live to see the implementation of his reforms, for it was not until years after his death in 1790 that improvements were made in jail conditions.[33] The impact of his legacy, however, lives on even today, through prison reform groups that commemorate his name—the John Howard Societies.

### Bentham, Beccaria, and Blackstone

It was also during this period of time that the *Classical School* emerged (see Chapter 3), with its emphasis on rationality, free will, and punishment in proportion to the offense. Based on the works of *Jeremy Bentham* and *Cesare Beccaria*, the Classical School of thought was a reaction against the harsh penalties of the time. These enlightened thinkers supported fair and speedy trials, imprisonment, and deterrence. They maintained that the basis of all action should be "utilitarian"—that is, crime should be considered an injury to society, and prevention should be considered more important than punishment. Punishment should thus be sufficient to deter, but not excessive.

An important result of these ideas was that crimes became codified and well defined in statutes. Before this, there was no criminal law as it is known today. Wrongs were heard on their own merit, with punishments meted out according to the judgment of the court. *William Blackstone* recodified English criminal law, defined specific crimes, and identified resulting punishments. For the first time, definitions of crime and criminal procedure were formulated in law. It was also under the influence of this age of reasoning that the American Constitution was written and adopted in 1789.

### The U.S. Constitution

Having thrown off the rule of England, American colonists were concerned with protecting their hard-won liberties. Rejecting Europe's class-based aristoc-

[32]American Correctional Association, p. 16.
[33]Ibid.

racy and monarchy rule, they embraced equality and a democratic system of government. Moreover, the Constitution of the United States was developed during the period of enlightenment, reflecting many of its humanitarian principles. The colonists followed this line of thinking, introducing a new concept in government—that rights which belonged to them were "inherent and inalienable."[34]

The Constitution is of prime importance to the field of corrections, because it provides the framework for the American system of administering justice. Citizens (including criminal offenders) may lose some of their civil rights but never their constitutional guarantees. While the Constitution itself establishes our democratic system of government, it is the first 10 Amendments to the Constitution that are of particular importance—the *Bill of Rights*. See the next "Close-up on Corrections" for a discussion of the rights and privileges afforded to all U.S. citizens through this document.

Firmly preserved in the Constitution, the American philosophy of crime control, law enforcement, and punishment is based on the principle that our greatest concern is the preservation of individual liberty—over and above the pursuit of justice. Articulated by such signers of the Declaration of Independence as Patrick Henry ("Give me liberty or give me death!"), this emphasis on the worth of human life, along with the liberty to enjoy it, was in stark contrast to the arbitrary and inhumane practices of the past. Today, some may complain about offenders "getting off" on technicalities. Nevertheless, we preserve the belief that even if some who are guilty go free, that is preferable to convicting an innocent person. For if we are to uphold the ideals on which the Constitution is based, we must do so consistently, not just when it suits our purpose. In short, "the Constitution is not designed to protect society—it is designed to protect the individual."[35] Nor are such safeguards limited to law-abiding citizens—"the law must serve everyone, those it protects as well as those it punishes."[36]

---

*LEARNING GOALS*

*Do you know:*

- *What group established the Walnut Street Jail and what significance it is to corrections?*
- *The differences between the Pennsylvania and the Auburn systems?*
- *Why the Auburn system was adopted in the United States?*

---

[34]See Edward Elliott, *Biographical Story of the Constitution: A Study of the Growth of the American Union* (New York: G.P. Putnam's Sons, 1910), pp. 1–26.

[35]Former Attorney General Richard Kleindienst, in response to questioning by the famed committee headed by Senator Sam Ervin which investigated the Watergate scandal in July 1973.

[36]David Fogel, *We Are the Living Proof: The Justice Model for Corrections* (Cincinnati, OH: Anderson Publishing Company, 1975), p. iii, quoting Article VI, *Declaration of the Rights of Man*, 1789.

Even before such protections were established in the Constitution, Pennsylvania had a reform-minded governor, *William Penn*. He replaced existing regulations governing conduct in that colony with the Quaker criminal code. Quite humane in comparison to the extremely severe criminal codes in effect at the time, it called for:

- Abolishing capital punishment for crimes other than homicide.
- Substituting imprisonment at hard labor for bloody punishments.
- Providing free food and lodging to inmates.
- Replacing the pillory and stocks with houses of detention.[37]

Penn's humanitarian principles were repealed at the time of his death in 1718. But they were later revived by one of the original signers of the Declaration of Independence, *Dr. Benjamin Rush*, who headed the "Philadelphia Society for Alleviating the Miseries of the Public Prisons" (which also counted Benjamin Franklin among its members). Under Rush's leadership, the society protested both capital punishment and excessive displays of harsh public reprisals, maintaining that they only served to harden criminals.

### The Walnut Street Jail

If the widespread use of corporal and capital punishments was to be abandoned, it was necessary to develop an alternative sanction. It was for this purpose that the Philadelphia Society established the first penitentiary in 1790 at the *Walnut Street Jail*. "Unlike the workhouses, prisons, and jails already in existence, the Walnut Street Jail was used exclusively for the correction of convicted felons."[38] In stark contrast to Newgate, it was the first institution designed for reform—that is, to make the offender penitent (hence the term "penitentiary").

Following many of the concepts advocated by John Howard, men and women were housed in separate facilities. Liquor was prohibited. Inmates were classified by the seriousness of their offense. During the day, they worked on handicrafts in their cells under strict rules of silence. A small exercise yard was attached to each cell. Cells were constructed to provide solitary confinement in order to eliminate moral contamination from other prisoners. This also served to encourage inmates to meditate at night on the evils of their ways. The Quaker's religious motivation created a more humane prison aimed at treatment by solitary confinement, hard work, religious instruction, and Bible reading. "Nothing was to detract the penitent prisoner from the path toward reform."[39] Despite its relative progressiveness, however, imposed silence and lack of personal contact over extended periods of time took a toll on the inmates' mental health—generating both suicides and mental illness.

[37]American Correctional Association, p. 24.
[38]Ibid., p. 29.
[39]Clear and Cole, p. 76.

The Bill of Rights

## AMENDMENT 1

The First Amendment establishes our right to freedom of religion, freedom of speech, and freedom of the press, along with the right to peaceably assemble and "petition government for a redress of grievances." Thus, anyone who is dissatisfied with the manner in which he or she is being treated by government can file a petition to request a review. Prisoners can now use their First Amendment privileges to challenge the conditions of their confinement.

## AMENDMENT 2

Along with establishing a "well-regulated militia," the Second Amendment prohibits infringements on the "right to keep and bear arms," an issue that has come under considerable debate in recent years as gun-control advocates have called for restrictions on the purchase of weapons in an effort to reduce firearms-related crimes.

## AMENDMENT 3

This amendment was added in response to the hated British practice of taking over private residences for housing soldiers during the American Revolution. It prohibits the quartering of soldiers in any house "without consent of the owner" in times of peace, and only "in a manner prescribed by law" during time of war.

## AMENDMENT 4

Again with concern for maintaining the privacy of one's home, "unreasonable searches and seizures" are prohibited. Search warrants are provided for only "upon probable cause," with the warrant describing "the place to be searched and the persons or things to be seized." Police officers therefore cannot arbitrarily enter a private dwelling in order to look for evidence without first obtaining a warrant.

## AMENDMENT 5

A defendant's refusal to testify in court has become known as "pleading the fifth," because of the provision in this amendment against compelling someone to be a "witness against himself." That is why police officers read suspects their "Miranda rights" prior to interrogation—to remind them of their constitutional right to remain silent. In addition, this amendment:

- Requires indictment by a grand jury before one can be "held to answer for a capital or otherwise infamous crime." In other words, it is not just the police and the prosecutor who must be convinced that there is probable cause to suspect that the defendant committed such a crime. A grand jury made up of citizens must find probable cause as well.
- Prohibits double jeopardy. Thus, a defendant cannot be held accountable in a court of law twice for the same offense.
- Requires "due process of law" before anyone can be deprived of "life, liberty, or property." This means that the criminal justice procedures outlined in Chapter 1 must be followed before a defendant can be convicted.

## AMENDMENT 6

The Sixth Amendment protects citizens against arbitrary practices of government, particularly with regard to procedures involved in the trial phase of the criminal justice process. It guarantees a "speedy and public trial by an impartial jury," as well as the right to be "informed of the accusations," "confront witnesses" (which is becoming a controversal issue in the era of videotaped testimony), and obtain "assistance of counsel" for one's defense (which has been interpreted to mean that those who cannot afford legal assistance have the right to an attorney provided by the state).

## AMENDMENT 7

Not directly related to criminal justice, the Seventh Amendment addresses "common law" suits, preserving the right of trial by jury "where the value in controversy shall exceed twenty dollars."

## AMENDMENT 8

It is this provision that is often invoked by inmates challenging the constitutionality of their confinement, since it prohibits the infliction of "cruel and unusual punishment" as well as "excessive bail and fines."

## AMENDMENT 9

Essentially, the Ninth Amendment states that simply because a particular right is not "enumerated in the Constitution" should not be interpreted to mean that it is intended to be denied.

## AMENDMENT 10

The final provision of the Bill of Rights delegates to the individual states those powers not reserved for the federal government by the Constitution "nor prohibited by it to the states." Except for the authority specifically outlined in the Constitution as reserved for the federal government, all other power is delegated to the 50 states.

These first 10 Amendments to the Constitution are what is known as the Bill of Rights. However, the framers of our government realized that additional amendments might also be necessary to accommodate future needs. They therefore included provisions for changing the Constitution further. One of these additional amendments which we will see later has had a considerable impact on inmate litigation is the Fourteenth Amendment.

## AMENDMENT 14

This addition assured that "all persons born or naturalized in the United States" are citizens and that "no state shall make or enforce any law which shall abridge the privileges or immunities of citizens of the United States." In essense, states cannot exceed the authority of the U.S. Constitution. Further applying constitutional guarantees to the states, the Fourteenth Amendment assures all citizens that no state shall "deprive any person of life, liberty, or property without due process of law; nor deny to any person . . . the equal protection of the laws."

The Walnut Street Jail served as the model for what became known as the *Pennsylvania system*. It was adopted at Eastern State Penitentiary (outside Philadelphia), the Western State Penitentiary in Pittsburgh, and in prisons throughout a number of other northeastern states. While we will see that the Pennsylvania system did not survive in this country, it did make a permanent impact on the public's response to criminal behavior and the nature of correctional practices from that point forward.

## The Auburn System

It is somewhat ironic that the major competition to the Pennsylvania system came from Auburn, New York, since the facility constructed there in 1815 was originally based on many of the principles of the Walnut Street Jail. In fact, both systems included solitary confinement in separate cells and enforced silence at all times to prevent inmates from communicating. But while prisoners at Auburn were locked in their cells at night, during the day, they participated together in congregate work. Although the mental distraction of work may appear to create a more humane system, Auburn was far from a humanitarian environment. As described in the next "Close-up on Corrections," inside accounts reveal rigid routines and harsh discipline to control inmate behavior. Adding further to their humiliation, although inmates were not permitted to receive visitors, "citizens who paid admission could come into the prison and look them over," as if they were in a zoo.[40]

Unlike Auburn, the Pennsylvania system incorporated work within one's cell only as a limited diversion from its major emphasis on seeking penance through required Bible reading and reflection on one's sins. Complete solitary confinement was considered essential at all times in order to maintain discipline, prevent contamination, and more effectively manipulate the inmate's will. In contrast, the Auburn system could confine inmates in smaller units—since they did not need cell space in which to work, and discipline could be assured with on-the-spot lashings for rule violations. But more important, Auburn "could generate productive labor by groups of men working at the same task and by setting up factory areas where machines could be employed."[41] Thus, it became a more profitable system to operate.

For a number of years, intense and spirited debate raged in both the United States and in Europe over the relative merits of each system:

> Advocates of both [sides] . . . agreed that the prisoner must be isolated from society and subjected to a disciplined routine. . . . What divided the two camps was the way in which reformation was to be brought about. The Auburn proponents maintained that inmates first had to be "broken" and then socialized by means of a rigid discipline of congregate but silent labor. Those who pushed for the separate system of Pennsylvania rejected such harshness and, following Howard, renounced physical punishments and

[40]Clemens Bartollas, "The Prison: Disorder Personified," in John W. Murphy and Jack E. Dison, eds., *Are Prisons Any Better? Twenty Years of Correctional Reform* (Newbury Park, CA: Sage Publications, 1990), p. 14.
[41]Hawkins and Alpert, p. 45.

### Discipline in the Auburn System

The rule of absolute silence and noncommunication was maintained and enforced by the immediate use of the lash for the slightest infraction. Flogging was advocated . . . as the most effective way to maintain order. . . . Another bizarre form of discipline that was developed at Auburn was the lockstep formation. Prisoners were required to line up in close formation with their hands on the shoulders or under the arms of the prisoner in front. The line then moved rapidly toward its destination as the prisoners shuffled their feet in unison, without lifting them from the ground. Because this nonstop shuffle was "encouraged" by the use of the lash, any prisoner who fell out of lockstep risked a broken ankle or other serious injury from the steadily moving formation.

*Source:* Harry E. Allen and Clifford E. Simonsen, *Corrections in America,* Sixth Edition (New York: Macmillan, 1992), pp. 42–43.

The prisoners are obliged to obey instantly all orders issued by the foremen, to work quickly and efficiently without pause, in silence, and with downcast eyes. When they approach their superiors, they must show deep respect, and when they speak to such persons, they must do so in the politest terms. They may not speak to one another except when ordered to do so by their supervisors. They are obliged to avoid everything that could cause the least distraction or unrest. . . . They are expressly forbidden to converse with visitors, to destroy or damage their tools or other objects they use, and to speak to their guards about matters that do not concern their work or their needs. The least breach of these rules is punished immediately and sternly. Any misdeed shall be penalized instantly and without mercy by flogging with a whip or a cane on the shoulders or the naked back. Every supervisor has the right to mete out punishment, and there is no fixed limit to the number of stripes that may be given. All that is required of the one who administers the flogging is that he report the name of the prisoner to the Governor, as well as the reason for the punishment and the number of stripes given.

*Source:* Torsten Eriksson, *The Reformers: An Historical Survey of Pioneer Experiments in the Treatment of Criminals* (New York: Elsevier, 1976), pp. 56–57.

any other form of human degradation. The New Yorkers countered that [their] system cost less, was an efficient use of convict labor, and developed individuals . . . imbued with the discipline necessary for the industrial age. Pennsylvania supporters countered that New York had sacrificed the principal goal of the penitentiary (reformation) to the accessory goal (cost-effectiveness). . . . [42]

[42]Clear and Cole, pp. 77–78.

The Auburn system's introduction of striped uniforms and lock-step marching still prevailed in American prisons through the turn of the century. Courtesy of the Illinois Department of Corrections. Used with permission of the American Correctional Association.

While Europeans eventually opted for the more humane and treatment-oriented philosophy of the Pennsylvania system, most American states adopted the economical Auburn plan. The Pennsylvania system was geared toward small crafts that were rapidly becoming outdated, whereas Auburn's methods were adaptable to the emerging factory-oriented methods of industrial production. In fact, vestiges of the Auburn system can still be seen in large penitentiaries, and the degrading "prison stripes" uniforms introduced there over 150 years ago have been discarded only within the past several decades.

---

*LEARNING GOALS*

*Do you know:*

- *How Alexander Maconochie, Walter Crofton, and Zebulon Brockway influenced correctional developments?*
- *What caused the downfall of the industrial era of corrections?*
- *The three general types of prison labor still in use?*

---

Along with Auburn's philosophy of congregate work, U.S. prisons adopted its stern discipline and degrading practices. Emphasizing strict rules and obedient compliance, infractions were dealt with swiftly and harshly. Staff were relatively free to respond to misbehavior and "disrespect" as they saw fit. This promoted efficiency in terms of administrative operations, but it did little in terms of constructive change for the offenders. Prisons were judged by their "production record and number of escapes, not by the number of inmates rehabilitated," and during much of the nineteenth century, "silence characterized not only prisoners, but the public" as well.[43] There were no John Howards, William Penns, or Benjamin Rushes pressing for prison reforms. We will see later that hope for improvement appeared on the horizon by 1870. In the meantime, there were only more and more severe prisons being constructed to confine more and more subservient inmates.

### Regional Developments

Most of the significant prisons during this period were established in the more densely populated areas of the northeast, midwest, and California. Generally, these were large, industrial, gothic-style "fortresses," designed to hold as many as 4000 to 6000 prisoners in conditions of tight security. (By contrast, the average large prison today would hold only about half that number.)

In the less-populated western states, most of the prisons developed from old territorial jails (a pattern similar to that in Canada). The former territorial jails at Walla Walla, Washington, and Calgary, Alberta, for example, are now prisons. The major exception was in California, where the resources were available to construct large industrial prisons in the eastern style.

The southern states developed in still a different pattern. The agricultural economy there was based on a semifeudal system in which the plantation owners maintained hired help and slaves on large tracts of land. As a result, people tended to assume personal responsibility for law and order within their own jurisidiction. Consequently, there was little need for large, central prisons. The Civil War changed not only the economy but the penal system as well. The postwar South was impoverished, with landowners selling their plantations at panic prices for U.S. currency. Slaves, previously worth about $2000 each, were required to be freed without compensation to their "owners." In short, the southern ruling class or power structure was destroyed. It was the occupation armies from the North who established the first real prisons in most southern states during the Reconstruction. For an interesting account of the part in history played by two southern correctional institutions, see the next "Close-up on Corrections."

In the postwar south, there were not enough tax funds to support adequate schools, so it is not surprising that correctional institutions received low priority. Thus, arrangements were made in most southern states to *lease* prisoners to the highest bidder. The bidders were generally large landowners, railroad compa-

---

[43]American Correctional Association, p. 55.

nies, or turpentine operators. Unfortunately, such enterprises were more concerned with making profits than with providing humane conditions for their laborers. The abuses, exploitation, and atrocities that resulted from this system have created a sordid chapter not just in the history of corrections, but in the overall saga of man's inhumanity to man:[44] "In retrospect, the most that can be said for this period of American prison history is that . . . it was better than a return to the barbarities of capital and corporal punishment."[45]

---

### ❖ CLOSE-UP ON CORRECTIONS

Andersonville Prison

Throughout the Civil War, prisons arose in the north and south to confine enemies captured from the other side. One of these, Andersonville, Georgia, probably holds the record as the worst prison in American history. Rampant disease, outright starvation, and basic cruelty flourished at levels unknown since medieval times. In one year, from February 1864 to March 1865, nearly 1000 Union soldiers died each month.[46] The commander of the prison was executed after the war. Andersonville is now preserved as a national park and cemetery, in honor of those who lost their lives there.

Fort Jefferson

One of the most remote of America's prisons was Fort Jefferson (now a national monument), located on Garden Key in the Dry Tortugas of the Gulf of Mexico, 69 miles west of Key West, Florida.[47] Begun in 1846, Fort Jefferson was built by slaves, but it was a long process, for there is no fresh water on the island. Water had to be shipped in, rain caught, or obtained through desalinization of ocean water.

Finally opened 15 years later, in 1861, among the many prisoners held there were such famous names as Geronimo, the Apache Indian leader, and Dr. Samuel A. Mudd, who set the broken leg of John Wilkes Booth, assassinator of Abraham Lincoln. Dr. Mudd was released in 1869 and went back to his hometown in Maryland. Hoping to renew his life, he was instead rejected by all of his former friends and neighbors, giving rise to the expression, "His name is mud"—one of numerous ex-offenders who have experienced the difficulties of reintegration.

---

[44]For a documentary on this era, see J. C. Powell, *The American Siberia*, 1891 (reprinted, Montclair, NJ: Patterson Smith, 1970).

[45]American Correctional Association, p. 63.

[46]See *Andersonville: The Story of a Civil War Prison Camp* (Washington, DC: U.S. Government Printing Office, 1975). Also, Peggy Sheppard, *Andersonville, Georgia, U.S.A.* (Leslie, GA: Sheppard Publications, 1973); and Ovid L. Futch, *History of Andersonville Prison* (Gainesville, FL: University of Florida Press, 1968).

[47]See Charles J. Eichman, "Florida's Historic Prison Fortress," *American Journal of Correction*, Vol. 29, No. 4 (July/August, 1967), pp. 24–26.

## The Reform Era

With attention no longer diverted or distorted by war, the sorry plight of American prisons finally recaptured public notice by 1870. Reform-minded prison administrators, members of Congress, and prominent citizens gathered in Cincinnati that year to form the National Prison Association, conducting the first meeting of what has now become the American Correctional Association (ACA). The long tradition of ACA as a national advocate for correctional improvements was firmly established by the foresighted principles adopted at the 1870 meeting, described in the next "Close-up on Corrections." Among the leaders influencing deliberations in Cincinnati, and later, developments throughout the country, were:

• *Rutherford B. Hayes*, former president of the United States, who was elected as the first president of the National Prison Association in Cincinnati, serving until his death in 1893. A progressive social reformer, Hayes pressed for jail reform, separation of offenders by age, indeterminate sentences, and improved academic and vocational education for inmates.[48]

• Captain *Alexander Maconochie*, an Englishman in charge of the British penal colony on Norfolk Island in the South Pacific. When Maconochie arrived at his post in 1840, conditions were so bad that "men reprieved from the death penalty wept, and those who were to die thanked God."[49] While he did not totally aban-

Emphasis on work and exercise continued in reformatories for youthful offenders through World War II, when "victory gardens" were a common sight. Courtesy of Anthony W. Zumpetta.

---

[48] American Correctional Association, p. 75.
[49] Harry E. Allen and Clifford E. Simonsen, *Corrections in America*, Sixth Edition (New York: Macmillan, 1992), p. 46, citing John V. Barry, "Captain Alexander Maconochie," *Victorian Historical Magazine*, Vol. 27 (June 1975), p. 5.

Principles of the 1870 National Prison Association

1. Reformation, not the vindictive infliction of suffering, should be the purpose of penal treatment.
2. Prisoners should be classified on the basis of a mark system patterned after the Irish system.
3. Rewards should be provided for good conduct.
4. Prisoners should be made to realize that their futures rest in their own hands.
5. Indeterminate sentences should be substituted for fixed sentences, and disparities in sentences removed.
6. Religion and education are the most important agencies of reformation.
7. Discipline should be administered so that it gains the cooperation of the inmate and maintains his self-respect.
8. The goal of the prison should be to make industrious free citizens, not orderly and obedient prisoners.
9. Industrial training should be fully provided.
10. Prisons should be small; separate institutions should be provided for different types of offenders.
11. The social training of prisoners should be facilitated; silence rules should be abolished.
12. Society at large must realize that it is responsible for the conditions that breed crime.

*Source:* Todd R. Clear and George F. Cole, *American Corrections* (Monterey, CA: Brooks/Cole Publishing Company, 1986), p. 82, citing E. C. Wines, ed., *Transactions of the National Congress on Penitentiary and Reformatory Discipline* (Albany, NY: Argus, 1871).

don the concept of punishment for one's crimes, he maintained that an attempt should also be made to reform offenders by providing incentives to encourage good behavior and some measure of hope for early release. The practice of determinate sentencing offered no chance for release until the full term was served. Maconochie therefore implemented the first form of *indeterminate sentencing*—a "mark system," whereby freedom could be earned through hard work and proper behavior. An elaborate process of earning "marks" through labor and good conduct was developed, with discipline gradually diminished as inmates progressed through the system. The idea was to reward inmates with greater privileges obtained by "marks," thereby providing incentives to reform and better preparation for release. Unfortunately, Maconochie's practices were not well received among the British business enterprises dependent on inmate labor, and he was eventually removed from office. His visionary concepts, however, lived on.

- Sir *Walter Crofton*, chairman of the board of directors of the Irish Convicts Prisons. Influenced by Maconochie's efforts, Crofton also believed that the amount of time served should be related to the prisoner's reformation. Based on that theory, in 1854 he established the Irish *ticket-of-leave* system—essentially, the first form of *parole*. Offenders could earn their release by progression through a series of stages. In the first stage, inmates were held in solitary confinement and performed dull, monotonous work. The next stage consisted of assignment to various public works projects. As offenders moved through various later stages, both discipline and the length of their sentences were reduced. During the final stage, they worked without supervision, moving freely between the prison and the community. Those who proceeded successfully through all stages were awarded a final "ticket of leave." This was a conditional release that could be revoked any time before the original sentence expired if the offender violated established standards—in much the same manner as parole can be revoked today.

- *Zebulon Brockway*, superintendent of the Elmira Reformatory in New York, which opened in 1876 for young offenders 16 to 30 years of age. In the United States, it was Brockway who first experimented with these enlightened approaches. While still maintaining strong discipline, he implemented a number of reforms designed to improve both body and mind. These included *classification* according to behavior and achievements, regular *exercise, vocational training*, and academic *education*. Emphasis was placed on reform of the offender and preparation for eventual release. Because education was viewed as Elmira's most important mission, industrial production and profit making were secondary concerns. With approval of the New York legislature to permit indeterminate sentencing, release was earned through a modified version of the "mark system," combined with the Irish ticket-of-leave.

The successes claimed by Elmira encouraged similar experiments elsewhere. Through the early part of the twentieth century, it became the model for reformatories across the country. Given its emphasis on education, it is not surprising that the reformatory movement was gaining strength at a time that society was turning to public education as a solution to many social problems.

But improvements of the Reform Era were largely directed toward institutions for youthful offenders. They were slow to make an impact on the adult correctional system. Moreover, the promise of original intentions was diminished by a combination of two drawbacks: (1) the lack of qualified staff (who were better prepared to promote discipline than provide education); and (2) the introduction of probation (which diverted the most promising offenders from reformatories).

That is not to say that the visions of these reformers were fruitless. Quite the contrary, their foresight and influence are still apparent in correctional practices ranging from basic education to parole and indeterminate sentencing. Perhaps most important is the debt they are owed for stimulating faith in the potential for positive change. Their ideals not only made major contributions to the improvement of American corrections at the time, but continue to inspire progressive administrators today.

## The Industrial Era

Inmate labor has been central to the development of prisons since the first workhouses were opened in Europe during the sixteenth century. Even in the penitence-minded Walnut Street Jail, private contractors furnished raw material that prisoners turned into finished products in their cells for an agreed price. More profitable industrial production has been a feature of corrections since the Auburn Penitentiary and, as we have seen, played a major role in the Auburn versus Pennsylvania debate. Self-supporting prisons have always been popular with taxpayers. As early as 1828, prisons at Auburn and Sing Sing were paying for themselves.

But it was not until the twentieth century that inmate industries flourished on a large scale. Although the leasing of inmates outside the prison continued, it was at this time that a new system of *contract labor* emerged.

Prison factories were constructed within the walls of the institution, and administrators contracted with firms either for wages or for the sale of finished products. In rural areas, offenders worked at manual labor in prison-owned farms. Many of these operations were justified under the guise of achieving reform through disciplined work. But the underlying motive was monetary profit—or more explicitly, achieving the greatest return for the least investment.

As railroads expanded and new roads were needed for the automobile, there was a general trend away from the leasing of prisoners toward employing them to build and maintain highways and railroads. Under this system, inmates were often virtual slaves of the state, working long hours under harsh conditions with minimal subsistence. The infamous chain gangs of this era attest to the brutality of conditions. Chained together, offenders swung sledgehammers in monotonous unison under the watchful eye of shotgun-toting supervisors, who administered lashes to those who could not keep up with the line. Nor did they hesitate to shoot anyone attempting to escape. In fact, it has been noted that during this period, the exploitation of inmate labor "embittered the hearts of prisoners" to the extent that they came out "more vindictive and more ready to injure society than they were when first placed within prison walls."[50]

The chain gangs continued working on road projects and prison construction in some states for many years. However, the peak year for prison production in the United States was 1923, when $74 million worth of material was made in U.S. prisons. The late 1920s marked the beginning of the end for large-scale prison industries. This time it was not the progressive views of humanitarian reformers that altered prison practices, but rather, the political realities of the labor market. As organized labor emerged in the industrial northeast, paid workers complained about competing with free inmate labor, which dramatically reduced the price at which their goods could be sold. In response to these concerns, Congress passed the *Hawes-Cooper Act* of 1929, which subjected prison products to the laws of the state to which they were shipped. This was the first of a number of restrictions on inmate products.

[50]American Correctional Association, p. 95, quoting Louis N. Robinson, *Penology in the United States*, 1921.

Prison production of marketable goods reached its height during the Industrial Era of corrections. Courtesy of the Washington Department of Corrections, Olympia, Washington.

With the severe unemployment of the Great Depression in the 1930s, even more momentum was gained to prohibit the interference of inmate labor with free markets. Additional legislation was passed to limit prison industries further through such measures as requiring use of a "prison-made" label and, ultimately, prohibiting the shipment of prison goods across state lines. By 1940, every state had passed similar restrictions on prison-made products as the power and influence of organized labor increased. These restrictions largely remain in force today. In some states, there are expanded statutes preventing the use of inmate labor on highways or other public works projects.

Such developments have curtailed the profit motive and dramatically altered the shape of prison industry. But they have not abolished it completely. There are generally three types of prison labor currently in use by various correctional departments throughout the country:

1. *State account system.* Goods are produced in prison and sold on a restricted market within the state.
2. *State use system.* Goods produced are restricted to items that can be used by other state agencies, such as schools, and mental health institutions.
3. *Public works system.* Inmates provide labor for construction and maintenance of roads, parks, conservation projects, and other public facilities.

From World War I until relatively recent years, large prison farms also continued as another work option. While farming has long been the most insulated from restrictions by special-interest groups, many prisons began to phase-out farm operations by the 1970s. In part, this move was related to the theory that prison work is justified as preparation for employment upon release, and few ex-offenders can now find jobs in agriculture. At the same time, prison farms were becoming increasingly expensive to operate, and many institutions found it cheaper to purchase food on the open market.

The most common forms of prison labor today are the state use system and the public works system. Neither is an ideal solution, particularly in light of the primary goals of prison industry to:

- Provide useful and meaningful work.
- Offer trade training and practice.
- Instill self-discipline and develop work habits.
- Prepare a person for release back to the community as a self-respecting, wage-earning citizen.[51]

In addition to being prohibited in some states, public works projects do not generally equip inmates with the types of job skills that are in wide demand. Under the state use form of labor, some marketable skills—such as cabinetmaking, printing, and machinery-repair—can be developed. But there are other prison enterprises—such as the production of license plates—which serve no useful purpose on the outside. Effectiveness of the state use system is therefore inhibited by limitations on the goods it can produce.

Certainly, the widespread abuse and exploitation of inmate labor prevalent during the Industrial Era called for change. But unfortunately, change came in the form of political restrictions rather than practical reforms. For years, corrections struggled to cope with the complete reversal from forced labor to forced leisure. Although inmate idleness is a problem that still faces correctional administrators, there has been renewed effort to provide offenders with meaningful labor.

By the mid-1970s, a resurgence of support for prison industries emerged. This re-emphasis gained an advocate in 1983 when former Chief Justice Warren Burger called for prisons to be "factories with fences,"[52] to provide relief from the boredom of prison life, equip inmates with marketable skills, and create a prison environment more reflective of the real world.[53] Since then, leaders in the field have been pressing to sell the merits of correctional industries to the public in a more proactive fashion.[54] In fact, it has been predicted that by the year 2000, with the help of private corporations and community businesses, new prison industries

---

[51]*Correctional Industries Association Newsletter*, Vol. 1, No. 2 (October 1968), p. 4.

[52]"Burger Again Calls for More Prison Industries," *Corrections Digest*, Vol. 14, No. 13 (June 15, 1983), p. 1.

[53]In 1985, retired Chief Justice Burger's National Task Force on Prison Industries published a report through the National Center for Innovation in Corrections (Washington, DC), outlining 50 recommendations for modernizing, expanding, and strengthening prison industries.

[54]Anthony P. Travisano, "On the Offensive! Correctional Industries," *Corrections Today*, Vol. 48, No. 7 (October 1986), p. 4.

will have been created that closely reflect job opportunities in the free world.[55] Some examples of how industries have developed in recent years are described in the next "Close-up on Corrections," and as we will see in Chapter 15, the private sector is again becoming increasingly involved in modern-day corrections.

---

*LEARNING GOALS*

*Do you know:*

- *What factors stimulated the rehabilitative era of corrections?*
- *Why the courts for many years maintained a "hands-off" approach to corrections?*
- *What basic constitutional rights the Supreme Court recognized on the part of inmates during the 1960s?*
- *What social forces during the 1980s generated the move from indeterminate to determinate sentencing and what major correctional problem resulted?*
- *Why "gain time" was needed during the 1980s and how it has compromised the original goals of the justice model?*

---

### ❖ CORRECTIONS TODAY

By the late 1930s, the seeds were being planted for a dramatic shift that is still influential in modern correctional practices. As punitive punishments became less and less acceptable, a new emphasis on *treatment* and *rehabilitation* emerged. Concerns were raised about the negative effects of imprisonment. Sentencing options other than incarceration became more attractive alternatives. Society began to display a greater awareness of and interest in what was happening behind prison walls. Institutions became more open to public scrutiny. In general, there was excitement and optimism about the possibility of salvaging offenders through treatment—of accomplishing what the term "corrections" is meant to imply.

But improvements did not occur quickly or uniformly. Some institutions were considerably more progressive than others, and looking back in retrospect, it is apparent that corrections overall was never well equipped to achieve rehabilitative ideals. Nor was the extensive idleness imposed by drastic reductions in prison industries fully offset by therapeutic, educational, or training programs. Through it all, administrators were forced to accommodate greater numbers of inmates in often antiquated facilities. At the same time, the courts were beginning to recognize the rights of inmates to challenge conditions and procedures that violated constitutional protections. All of these events—positive and negative—have had an impact on the roles and realities of corrections today.

---

[55]Louie L. Wainwright, "Corrections in the Year 2000," *Corrections Today*, Vol. 48, No. 7 (October 1986), p. 28.

Developments in Prison Industries

In 1975, the federal Law Enforcement Assistance Administration promoted the transformation of traditional prison industries into profit-making businesses that benefit both the correctional system and participating inmates.[a] Since then, a number of states, including Colorado, Connecticut, Illinois, Iowa, South Carolina, and Washington, have participated in this effort. Kansas began a metal fabrication shop (Zephyr Industries) in 1981 to make cabinets, carts, and other metal products.[b] Arizona began Resident Operated Business Enterprises (ROBE), in which inmates have become entrepreneurs in a bakery, autobody repair shop, photocopying, designing belt buckles, and other enterprises. Utah has operated a graphics program in which inmate employees have been considered "employees of the state." Nevada generated projects that manufacture brooms, brushes, and mops, as well as fiberglass disk antennas.

By the mid-1980s, inmates in Wisconsin were manufacturing modular furniture—a skill highly sought in the labor market. Illinois Correctional Industries were manufacturing some 235 different products annually. The Springfield, Massachusetts, Chamber of Commerce teamed up with a local correctional facility to create a joint industrial program to produce office chairs. Florida turned its statewide inmate industries over to private-sector management through a nonprofit corporation called PRIDE (Prison Rehabilitative Industries and Diversified Enterprises, Inc.). In 1988 the Federal Bureau of Prisons Industries (UNICOR) provided employment for over 15,000 inmates in the production of a wide range of items, from executive furniture to electronics, textiles, and graphics, along with such services as computer data entry, printing, and furniture refinishing.[c]

Perhaps most important for the future of correctional industries, by 1986, Congress had authorized that a select group of federally certified state prison industry projects be exempt from the provisions of legislation that, until then, restricted inmate goods from interstate commerce. The resulting enterprises involve joint ventures with the private sector, including such examples as an airline reservation center in California, a sign shop in Utah, computer software development in Minnesota, and even a factory producing rubber mattresses for water beds in Nevada. In addition to providing wages to the inmate workers, these projects have generated tax revenues, room and board payments to correctional agencies, financial support to families, and restitution payments to victims.[d]

[a]*Improved Prison Work Programs Will Benefit Correctional Institutions and Inmates—Report to the Attorney General* (Washington, DC: General Accounting Office, June 29, 1982), p. 39.
[b]Ron Bertothy, "Prison Industries: Taking a Closer Look at the Seven State Pilot Project," *Corrections Digest,* Vol. 14, No. 11 (May 18, 1983), p. 5.
[c]*State of the Bureau of Prisons, January 1988* (Washington, DC: U.S. Bureau of Prisons, 1988), p. 5.
[d]Nicholas L. Demos and Louise S. Lucas, "Industries Initiative," *Corrections Today,* Vol. 48, No. 7 (October 1986), pp. 64–65, 73.

Although their uniforms resemble police officers, these early twenti-eth-century correctional officers were part of the custodial staff at the Pennsylvania Industrial School during the 1920s. Courtesy of Anthony W. Zumpetta.

## The Rehabilitative Era

With the stock market crash and resulting Great Depression of the 1930s came economic disaster. The security previously enjoyed by society was destroyed. Savings were wiped out virtually overnight. Unemployment skyrock-eted to all-time record highs. Hunger reduced distinctions between social class-es. Many who had been economically comfortable—even wealthy—were reduced to living in poverty. The most desperate committed suicide. Others turned to crime for survival. All of this was due to events which they had no ability to influence. The long-held explanations of crime as "sins" or personal weaknesses of the offender no longer seemed as valid. Society began to realize that perhaps it was through no fault of their own that some engage in crime, but rather, that it may be a reaction to forces beyond their control.

At the same time, major advancements were unfolding in the psychological and social sciences. Freud's theories of *psychoanalytic treatment* offered potential for "curing" criminal behavior. The field of *social work* provided legitimate recog-nition to attending to the needs of the underprivileged. With these develop-ments, more attention was being focused on corrections, and a new role was cre-ated for offenders as psychiatric and social work clients.

Along with changing perspectives on crime and such promising new hope for dealing with it came a new philosophy of corrections—the *medical model*. Emphasis moved from retribution through incapacitation to improvement through rehabilitation. Chain gangs, lockstep marching, and striped uniforms gave way to psychological diagnosis, individual counseling, and group therapy.

Determining inmates' needs began to take priority over punishing their deeds. By the 1950s, indeterminate sentences and the widespread use of parole held out the possibility of early release for progress in treatment programs. Society had finally begun to accept some degree of responsibility for the offender.

That does not mean that all abuses had vanished. Although shifts in ideology pointed the field in a new direction, progress was relative to the dismal conditions of the past. Eventually, it would take the outside attention brought on by inmate riots and court intervention to improve the substandard physical conditions and dehumanizing supervisory techniques to which prisoners were still subjected. In the meantime, with each major turning point in society— Prohibition, the Depression, post–World War II—came a fresh wave of crime and corresponding increases in the prison population. Crowded correctional institutions may be receiving considerable attention today, but the problem is far from a recent occurrence.

## Impact of the 1960s

The medical model reached its height in the midst of the turbulent 1960s— a period marked not only by "hippies," psychedelic drugs, student uprisings, and the Vietnam War, but also by liberal social attitudes, extensive federal funding, "wars" on poverty and crime, and massive civil rights demonstrations. The nation was swept up in vocal and sometimes violent protests against the status quo. No longer were traditional practices accepted routinely. Pressure mounted for change. The assumed authority of social institutions was open to challenge on a widespread, nationwide basis, and corrections was no exception.

In keeping with the euphoria of the 1960s and its advocacy on behalf of the powerless in society, the Supreme Court intervened in the previously sacrosanct world of correctional administrators. Prior to that time, the courts had generally maintained a "hands-off" approach toward corrections.

In light of government's separation of powers, the judiciary had been reluctant to interfere with the duties of the executive branch. In addition, judges tended to defer to the presumed "expertise" of correctional administrators in managing their institutions. That perspective changed dramatically as inmates gained a powerful advocate in the Supreme Court. By the mid-1960s, the Court had recognized the constitutional right of those incarcerated to *maintain access to the judicial process,* and specifically, to *challenge the conditions* under which they are confined.[56] Even more important, the Court later prohibited correctional administrators from *denying or obstructing* that fundamental right.[57] It became the duty of correctional officials to assure that the constitutional protections of inmates under their charge were not violated—opening a floodgate of litigation holding correctional personnel accountable for their actions.

In this climate it was rapidly becoming apparent that if corrections did not take proactive steps to address its own deficiencies, the courts would. It was also at this point in time that the public was becoming increasingly concerned about

[56]*Coleman v. Peyton,* 302 2nd 904 (4th Cir. 1966).
[57]*Johnson v. Avery,* 89 S. Ct. 747 (1969).

crime and the ability of the criminal justice system to deal with it. Thus, it is not surprising that in 1965, President Lyndon Johnson convened the *President's Commission on Law Enforcement and Administration of Justice,* a prestigious group of national experts, to address the nation's crime problem and make recommendations for improved functioning of the police, courts, and corrections. The Crime Commission's Task Force on Corrections was assisted by hundreds of academicians and practitioners from all levels of government as well as the private sector. Since so little was known about corrections on a nationwide basis, the resulting *Task Force Report on Corrections* represented the first comprehensive survey of correctional practices in this country. Additionally, it included recommendations for "a greatly improved correctional system of the future."[58]

The task force firmly believed that "above all else" the effectiveness of corrections relies on "a sufficient number of qualified staff."[59] Many of its recommendations therefore called for major improvements in the selection, training, supervision, and accountability of correctional personnel. The farsighted visions of the task force were also evident in its suggested changes for the inmate population, such as:

- Expanded community-based correctional programs as alternatives to institutionalization.
- New methods to reintegrate offenders by mobilizing community resources.
- Upgrading educational and vocational training.
- Improving prison industries.
- Expanding graduated release and furlough programs.
- Separate treatment for special offender groups.

Moreover, the task force established the first *correctional standards* for operating institutions and programs. These served as forerunners of the standards currently in use by the American Correctional Association's Commission on Accreditation, which now evaluates correctional institutions for voluntary accreditation in much the same way as colleges and hospitals are accredited. Concern for the proper treatment and well-being of inmates is illustrated in the standards that the task force devised for custodial supervision and discipline, several of which are highlighted in the next "Close-up on Corrections."

While the President's Task Force was conducting its study, the federal government was also becoming active in providing funds to support new correctional philosophies and innovative approaches. For example, the federal Prisoner Rehabilitation Act of 1965 offered grants to stimulate model projects. Many of these focused on alternatives to institutionalization—thus for the first time giving official recognition and status to *community-based corrections.* Programs such as VISTA (Volunteers in Service to America), Head Start, and Model Cities addressed prevention by focusing on such underlying causes of

[58]President's Commission on Law Enforcement and Administration of Justice, *Task Force Report: Corrections* (Washington, DC: U.S. Government Printing Office, 1967), p. ix.
[59]Ibid., p. 93.

## Task Force on Corrections: Standards for Custodial Supervision and Discipline

- Correctional institutions should have facilities for diversification of custody and program by age, sex, custodial requirements, types of inmates, and program needs.
- Every institution should have predetermined and well-defined plans for civil defense and for coping with emergencies such as fire, disorder, escape, and power failure.
- The types of disciplinary measures authorized should be set forth in writing and strictly controlled by the central office or governing body of the correctional system.
- Hearings on discipline should be conducted and disciplinary measures should be imposed not by a single official but by a disciplinary committee.
- Confinement to disciplinary quarters should be for short periods and should not exceed 30 days. Inmates in disciplinary confinement should be visited daily by a supervisory officer of the institution and by the medical officer. They should be given a daily exercise period and a regular diet with a minimum of 2,100 calories per day. No inmate should be placed on a restricted diet without the approval of the medical officer.
- Corporal punishment should never be used under any circumstances. Physical force may be used only when necessary to protect one's self or others from injury, to prevent escape, and to prevent serious injury to property. Officers should not be permitted to carry clubs.
- Useless "make-work" for purposes of punishment or humiliation should be prohibited.

*Source:* President's Commission on Law Enforcement and Administration of Justice, *Task Force Report: Corrections* (Washington, DC: U.S. Government Printing Office, 1967), p. 210.

crime as poverty, hunger, inadequate schooling, and substandard housing. Within the Model Cities program, the need for closer ties with local communities was addressed, in order to "redirect the lifestyles of potential, actual, and ex-offenders in Model Neighborhood Areas . . . by working in cooperation with local correctional agencies."[60] The Joint Commission on Correctional Manpower and Training, composed of 95 private and public organizations, conducted a three-year study of the entire correctional system. The resulting report—appropriately entitled *A Time to Act*—called for greater representation of minority

[60]Community Planning and Evaluation Institute, *Planning Approaches for Police and Corrections Projects in the Community* (Washington, DC: U.S. Department of Housing and Urban Development, 1972), p. 20.

groups and young people in the correctional work force, along with removal of restraints preventing the employment of ex-offenders. Moreover, in terms of the ability of corrections to achieve its rehabilitative goals, the Joint Commission report issued a warning (outlined in the next "Close-up on Corrections") that essentially predicted why the medical model was doomed to failure.

Even though national studies, presidentially appointed commissions, and federally funded projects could not change conditions overnight, their impact was certainly felt. By the 1970s, the public had become much more aware of and concerned about the state of corrections. Minimum-security community-based approaches were used far more commonly. Within institutions, inmates were classified and separated by age, offense, and special needs. Specialized treatment facilities emerged. The Commission on Accreditation for Corrections was established to set and monitor standards for everything from cell size to health care, food, recreation, and staff training. "Guards" were becoming correctional officers, with job descriptions that focused as much on relating to offenders as restricting their behavior. The 1978 *National Manpower Study* called attention to the need for "significant staffing and personnel upgrading."[61] In places that were slow to adapt, reforms were stimulated by the courts. Inmates, no longer viewed as "slaves of the state," began to exercise their newly defined constitutional rights to challenge the conditions of their confinement. But despite improvements, crime was still increasing, much of it committed by repeat offenders who had presumably been rehabilitated.

---

❖ CLOSE-UP ON CORRECTIONS

A Time To Act

"[T]here can be no solution to the problem of recidivism as long as harsh laws, huge isolated prisons, token program resources, and discriminatory practices which deprive offenders of employment, education, and other opportunities are tolerated. . . . [A]s long as there is a predominance of low-paid, dead-end jobs in corrections, the field will continue to be burdened with a poor performance record. . . .

Little will be accomplished by increasing agency budgets and staffs without simultaneously providing the means for changing community attitudes toward offenders. To be concerned about the incidence of crime is not enough. . . . The whole community and its social institutions must become involved in reshaping correctional rehabilitative methods."

*Source: A Time to Act* (Washington, DC: Joint Commission on Correctional Manpower and Training, 1969), p. 2.

---

[61]*The National Manpower Survey of the Criminal Justice System, Vol. 3, Corrections* (Washington, DC: U.S. Department of Justice, Law Enforcement Assistance Administration, 1978), p. 5.

## The Past as Prologue

Belief that "the past is prologue to the future" is perhaps nowhere better illustrated than in the retreat from rehabilitation toward a renewed emphasis on punishment by the 1980s. As the liberal attitudes of the 1960s gave way to conservative politics of the 1980s, the public became increasingly disenchanted with the unfulfilled promises of the medical model. As concerns were voiced that rehabilitation was not working, the Martinson report[62] appeared to confirm the worst suspicions. As the crime rate continued steadily upward, society became increasingly frustrated with the system's ineffectiveness as well as impatient with the offender's ability to change.

In retrospect, it is possible that the extent to which public policies or correctional practices were to blame was overstated, in light of the fact that the post–World War II "baby boom" had reached its primary crime-risk age (late teens to young adulthood). It is possible that demographic patterns alone might have produced rising crime regardless of sentencing procedures or correctional approaches. But the timing was ripe for reassessing America's response to crime. Pressures to "get tough" and assure that offenders receive their "just deserts" mounted, resulting in changes in both the length and nature of sentencing. Indeterminate sentences and the hope they held out for early release were replaced by determinate (flat, fixed) sentences, and in some jurisdictions, the abolishment of discretionary parole. Judicial discretion was also dramatically reduced by: (1) *mandatory sentencing* legislation requiring specific minimum terms for certain types of crimes or habitual offenders, and (2) *sentencing guidelines* requiring judges to select sentences from a narrowly defined range, based on such factors as the seriousness of the offense and the offender's prior record.

As we have seen in Chapter 1, the shift from rehabilitation to retribution did not necessarily produce the intended effects. Without the advance planning needed to accommodate longer and more punitive sentencing, the justice model was no more equipped to achieve its goals than its predecessor. Just as the funds were never forthcoming to implement the medical model effectively, the facilities needed to incarcerate greater numbers of inmates for longer periods of time were not provided. Correctional institutions were unprepared for the massive influx of offenders into already strained facilities. Nor were the courts willing to tolerate vastly overcrowded institutions.

When facilities began drastically exceeding their designed capacity, the courts intervened, requiring that corrections keep the number of inmates being confined within mandated *population caps*.[63]

At the same time, correctional officials were becoming concerned about their ability to control inmates in the absence of the incentive that parole provided for good behavior. The answer to both crowding and control came in the

---

[62]Robert Martinson, "What Works—Questions and Answers about Prison Reform," *The Public Interest*, Vol. 35 (Spring 1975), pp. 22–54.

[63]As of 1989, the entire state adult corrections department or one or more institutions were under court order in 32 states, primarily for overcrowding. *ACA Directory* (Laurel, MD: American Correctional Association, 1990), p. xvi.

form of *gain time,* whereby a specified number of days is automatically deducted from an offender's sentence for every month served without disciplinary infractions. This modification was certainly essential to reduce prison populations to somewhat more manageable levels. As we have seen in Chapter l, however, gain time defeats the original purpose of the justice model to deter crime, incapacitate offenders, and assure that one's "debt to society" is paid by serving a full term without the possibility of early release.

If the past is, in fact, prologue to the future, it is possible that the philosophy of corrections will again be reevaluated in the face of disenchantment with the justice model. In the meantime, corrections is faced with the challenge of accommodating demands for punishment without totally abandoning directions toward positive change. Admittedly, the field is in short supply of both the physical facilities and program resources necessary to fulfill such a mission.

But it is difficult to appreciate the present without an understanding of the past. Undoubtedly, corrections faces numerous challenges today—from overcrowding to underfunding—and a public largely indifferent to it all. An enterprise that deals with the disenfranchised of society will never be likely to attain the priority it deserves. Yet when viewed in comparison to the conditions faced by reformers from William Penn to Zebulon Brockway, corrections has made great strides. To those entrenched in day-to-day operational realities, there may not appear to be a great deal of hope on the horizon. This field may not in our lifetime reach the lofty heights in the dreams of today's visionary correctional administrators. But that is probably what our predecessors thought as well. They would indeed be surprised to see the progress achieved today, and we may well be in their place tomorrow.

## ❖ SUMMARY

While the victim's role in the criminal justice system has become more active today, it is far removed from the primitive practice in which the victim sought harsh retribution directly against the offender—often leading families to become embroiled in "blood feuds." With the rise of religion, crime was viewed as a sin that violated divine law and God's will, as well as socially unacceptable behavior. As a result, punishments in medieval times were brutal. Those suspected of violating society's standards were subjected to extreme pain, suffering, and often, death. The more "fortunate" were confined to convict ships or banished.

As the concepts of trials and courts developed, *gaols* were used to confine suspects until the king's court could convene or until punishment could be carried out. Despite the fact that their occupants were still technically innocent, these early jails maintained virtually intolerable living conditions. Men and women, young and old, healthy and sick were forced to live together and pay fees for even the most minor necessities—a system later copied in American jails.

Adhering to strict Puritan religious beliefs, the first American colonists likewise employed extremely severe punishments for criminal offenses. Mutilation, branding, stocks, and pillories were all commonly used. Just prior to the American Revolution, the first U.S. prison—Newgate—was established in an abandoned copper mine, where conditions were as abysmal as those of the English gaols.

With the Age of Enlightenment, the pioneering work of John Howard, and the emergence of the Classical School of thought, public attention was called to the plight of law violators. Emphasis was placed on punishment in proportion to the offense. The fundamental rights of the individual were formally recognized in the U.S. Constitution. The first U.S. penitentiary was established by the Quakers at the Walnut Street Jail. But the penitence-oriented philosophy of the Pennsylvania system was challenged by the greater economic benefit of congregate work in the Auburn system. Adopting the stern discipline, imposed silence, and hard work practiced at Auburn, corrections in the United States entered a period marked by abuses and exploitations that were not to be challenged until the beginning of the Reform Era in 1870.

Such reform-minded men as Alexander Maconochie, Walter Crofton, and Zebulon Brockway promoted innovations ranging from indeterminate sentencing to parole and inmate education. Despite their forward thinking, throughout much of the early twentieth century, corrections focused predominately on the generation of profits through inmate leasing, contract labor, and prison farms and factories. With the Great Depression of the 1930s, society could no longer afford competition from free inmate labor. The Industrial Era thus ended with legislative action restricting the sale of inmate products. Although interest in inmate industries is reviving, the focus today is more on providing meaningful work and career training than on strictly economic gains.

Following the introduction of psychoanalytic and social work techniques, corrections moved into the Rehabilitative Era. The offender treatment and counseling of the medical model reached its peak during the 1960s, with national studies of the correctional system, massive federal funding for social projects, and judicial recognition of inmates' rights. Eventually, the liberal politics of the 1960s gave way to the conservative agenda of the 1980s. Society became increasingly disillusioned with rising crime, recidivism, and the ineffectiveness of rehabilitation. The medical model was replaced by the justice model. Offenders were held responsible for their actions. Sentencing guidelines restricted judicial discretion. Fixed, determinate sentences were imposed.

But correctional facilities were no more equipped to implement the justice model than its predecessor. As institutions filled well beyond capacity, court-ordered population caps forced early release through gain time, thereby defeating the purpose of assuring that offenders receive their "just deserts." These often contradictory historical fluctuations make it difficult to forecast just where corrections will be tomorrow, as society again reevaluates priorities. In the meantime, the challenge is to adapt to more punitive sanctions without abandoning more positive solutions.

# part II

# Correctional Services, Practices, and Institutions

*While recognizing that offenders are responsible for their own actions, we must also recognize our responsibility for providing the best possible correctional services.[1]*

Correctional Service of Canada

Courtesy of the American Jail Association.

[1]*Mission of the Correctional Service of Canada* (Ottawa, Ontario: Correctional Service of Canada, 1991), p. 7.

One of the greatest difficulties in the field of corrections is that the general public is not aware of what goes on behind prison walls, inside jails, or within the caseloads of probation and parole. The law enforcement component of the criminal justice system has far more visibility, and therefore, greater support. Police officers—working directly with the public and easily identifiable by uniforms and marked cars—apprehend and arrest offenders, beginning the process of "putting them away." What happens after that is frequently left to the dark recesses of correctional institutions, caseloads, and routines in which low visibility is to some extent desirable for effective treatment. The correctional process is long, sometimes tedious, and often not very rewarding in terms of public acclaim.

Moreover, society's clamor for punishment appears to give little support to community-based sentencing alternatives that do not involve institutional confinement. Outside the correctional system, few may recognize the merits of such options as diversion, probation, or electronically monitored home confinement. Nor do most appreciate how restrictive community supervision can actually be. Demands for more punitive sanctions may well be related to this fundamental lack of understanding, but in any event, the focus today is on secure confinement.

That does not mean, however, that the public is clear about what correctional institutions should be accomplishing. Although everyone is concerned when prisons and jails fail to "rehabilitate" offenders, society has recognized the futility of achieving long-term behavioral changes. Consequently, it has left correctional institutions with a basic incapacitation mandate. Such a social compromise creates a more realistic mission for corrections but a less optimistic outlook for its clients.

Throughout the next three chapters, these issues are explored as we look at both community-based and institutional corrections—from the types of offenders involved to the types of services provided to them. Beginning with community-based alternatives in Chapter 5, we see how the least visible component of corrections works. The advantages and disadvantages of diverting offenders out of the justice system are discussed, along with how electronically monitored home confinement can serve as an intermediate option for those who would otherwise be sent to jail or prison. Even in the midst of the justice model's emphasis on punishment, institutional crowding has, if nothing else, necessitated continual use, and even expansion, of such alternatives.

As the oldest and most frequently used sentencing alternative, we next turn our attention to probation—looking at who is eligible for probation, what restrictions probationers are subject to, what services they are provided, and how they are supervised. Of course, not everyone functions effectively under community supervision, so we must also consider under what circumstances this privilege can be revoked. The unsuccessful termination of probation brings us to Chapter 6 and the next level on the sentencing scale: short-term confinement in jail.

Just as the public is not often aware of what actually occurs within community corrections, there is equal uncertainty about the function of jails. Yet, there are far more jails than prisons in the United States and, as a unit of local government, jails are closer to the communities they serve. Because there are so many of them, we will see the wide variations among these local correctional institutions —from small, rural facilities to the megajails of major metropolitan areas; from the antiquated, unsanitary facilities built in the past century to the modern "new generation" jails constructed in the past few years.

Looking at the population of jails, we will find similar disparities. Jail inmates range from those who are convicted to those still awaiting trial; from those serving short sentences for minor offenses to those awaiting transfer to prison for major violations; from alcoholics and drug addicts to juveniles, vagrants, and the mentally ill. In the midst of such diversity, we will see how jails cope administratively with everything from classification to crowding.

This portrait of the jail is naturally followed by a description of those institutions reserved for offenders with longer-term sentences—state and federal prisons. Since they are less numerous than jails, there is more standardization among prisons. But as we see in Chapter 7, they too can vary widely—ranging from minimum-security farms, ranches, or work-release centers to the maximum-security custodial institutions that we traditionally tend to associate with the term "prison."

After exploring their various security classifications, we encounter the problems created by the continually escalating prison population in recent years. A review of overcrowding leads us to examine just who is in prison and why they are there. From this perspective, we begin to see that prisons, like jails, may not always be housing those who most need to be kept in secure confinement. Again, this raises the question of what society expects its correctional institutions to accomplish. Finally, we look inside the prison compound to see how the institution is organized, how the warden influences its operations, and to what extent the inmates rather than staff are actually in control.

In summary, whether the topic is community-based or institutional corrections, the bottom line is that a society concerned with crime and recidivism basically has two choices. We can attempt to prepare inmates for a law-abiding lifestyle during confinement, or we can avoid the debilitating effects of institutional life by retaining offenders under control in the community. Both approaches are explored in the following chapters, beginning with community-based treatment alternatives, moving to short-term confinement in jail, and concluding with incarceration in prison. Both options have their advocates as well as opponents; benefits as well as drawbacks. But without an understanding of community-based as well as institutional corrections, it is impossible to make informed public policy choices.

# chapter 5

# Community-Based Alternatives

*From the very beginning, the direction of the correctional process must be back toward the community. It is in the community that crime will be committed or a useful life lived.*[1]

*Ramsey Clark*

## ❖ CHAPTER OVERVIEW

Over the past two decades, community-based alternatives have come to imply excessive leniency—"coddling criminals," "wrist slapping," "being soft on crime"—quite the opposite of the public's demands for "just deserts." In fact, it has been noted that programs which used to be called "alternatives to incarceration" are now labeled "intermediate *sanctions* or *punishments*," presumably because society does not interpret "alternatives to incarceration" as sufficiently punitive.[2]

But renewed emphasis on the harsher sentencing practices of the justice model has provided a false sense of security. On the one hand, it was anticipated that potential offenders would think twice before engaging in crime if they knew the severity with which they would be punished. Moreover, even if would-be offenders were not deterred by the threat of punishment (and most were not), there was satisfaction in knowing that incapacitation would prevent further involvement in crime during the period of confinement. Quite true; also quite shortsighted. Upon release, offenders are returning to the very place they came from—free society. How secure are we in the belief that, having been exposed to the debilitating effects of prison life and now stigmatized as ex-offenders, they will make the dramatic changes necessary to become law-abiding citizens? If the answer is "not very," then community-based approaches assume greater signifi-

---

[1]Ramsey Clark, *Crime in America* (New York: Simon and Schuster, 1970), p. 220.
[2]Ken Kerle, "Jails and Intermediate Punishment," *American Jails*, Vol. 5, No. 1 (March/April 1991), p. 4.

cance in achieving the goals of the justice system. That does not mean that community corrections is a panacea for solving the crime problem. But even if a community-based approach does not do anything to improve offenders, at least it is not doing anything to worsen them. It is highly unlikely that the same could be said of incarceration.

Certainly, there is a small proportion of offenders whose crimes are so violent and whose behavior is so uncontrollable that prison or jail is the only feasible option. Nevertheless, there are many others who are harmed more than helped by incarceration. Even in the midst of the punitive sentencing practices of the "get-tough-on-crime" era, community-based alternatives to secure confinement were never abandoned. In part, this was a result of the inability of new prison construction to keep pace with demand. Overcrowding has forced a reconsideration of priorities, calling attention to the need to reserve costly prison beds for truly violent, hard-core, chronic offenders. Apparently, "out of crisis sometimes comes opportunity."[3] But beyond the practical limitations of space in secure confinement, there remains a fundamental ray of hope in the ability to sanction behavior properly without severing bonds with the community.

Everyone benefits if selected, low-risk offenders can pay their debt to society through community-based alternatives such as diversion, home confinement, community-based treatment, victim restitution, community service, or probation. The offender avoids the social isolation and stigmatizing impact of imprisonment. Society avoids the economic impact of unproductive confinement in high-cost facilities. However, without awareness of its benefits, community corrections can easily be dismissed as a disagreeable economic compromise rather than a directed effort to control behavior cost-effectively. Consider the following scenario: "When hundreds of Alabama residents were asked how they would sentence 20 convicted offenders, virtually all thought prison appropriate. After some explanation of costs and alternatives, the same people 'resentenced' most of these cases to intermediate sanctions. This demonstrates that an educated public will support alternative sanctions."[4]

To what extent community-based alternatives will be "sold" to the public and maintained in the face of pressure for stiffer sentences will largely determine the shape of future public policy. In that regard, such programs can not afford to be viewed as "freedom without responsibility" or "sanctions without accountability." Rather, they must be seen as involving real penalties that are as stringent as incarceration would have been.[5] While community-based corrections has suffered from image problems, there is some evidence that society may not be as unsupportive as we might think. A recent national survey, for example, found that four out of five people favor community corrections programs over prison

---

[3]Thomas J. Quinn, "Delaware—A Structural Response to Correctional Overcrowding," *American Jails*, Vol. 5, No. 1 (March/April 1991), p. 14.

[4]Michael N. Castle, "Alternative Sentencing: Selling It to the Public," *Research in Action Monograph* (Washington, DC: U.S. Department of Justice, 1991), p. 2, citing a study conducted by the Edna McConnell Clark Foundation.

[5]Perry Johnson, addressing the Midwinter Meeting of the American Correctional Association, Miami, FL (January 11, 1993).

for nondangerous offenders, leading to the conclusion that "Americans are beginning to reformulate their thinking that prison is the only way to punish convicted offenders. It is becoming increasingly clear that America cannot build its way out of the prison crowding crisis. Intermediate sanctions are a viable option to imprisonment and are more cost-effective and beneficial to society in the long run."[6] Even if for economic rather than egalitarian reasons, it appears that community-based approaches will continue to represent a significant function in the correctional system.

---

*LEARNING GOALS*

*Do you know:*

- *How pretrial intervention differs from other forms of community-based corrections?*
- *Why clients of diversion cannot technically be considered "offenders"?*
- *The difference between formal and informal diversion?*
- *How the process of alternative dispute resolution operates?*
- *The advantages and disadvantages of diversion?*
- *What net widening is, and how it relates to diversion and home confinement?*

---

## ❖ PRETRIAL INTERVENTION

Whereas most of the programs discussed in this chapter involve options for keeping offenders out of correctional institutions after adjudication,[7] *pretrial intervention* is significantly different. It diverts the entire case out of the criminal justice system *before* adjudication. When first time offenders or those acting under mitigating circumstances are viewed as good risks, they may be eligible for a program of voluntary supervision in the community without being convicted. Eligibility means that the person does not present a clear or present danger to society and that no constructive purpose would be served by conviction and sentencing.

As the term *pretrial* implies, the system has intervened to remove the case from the criminal justice process *before trial*. In essence, the alleged offender is being offered a second chance to avoid either arrest or prosecution in exchange for voluntary participation in some treatment, counseling, training, or educational program in the community. This type of diversion has been practiced extensively for many years in juvenile court, and various forms of diversion have also been used in the adult system. However, its application to adult offenders did

---

[6]"Community Corrections Survey: Public Indicates Strong Support," *Corrections Today*, Vol. 53, No. 7 (December 1991), p. 134, citing Neil Tilow, president of the International Association of Residential and Community Alternatives.

[7]It should be noted that this chapter is focused exclusively on nonresidential community-based alternatives. Community residential centers are included in the discussion of minimum-security facilities in Chapter 7.

not begin in earnest until the 1960s (following recommendations proposed by the President's Crime Commission)[8] and became an integral part of the justice system in the mid 1970s. By 1973, the National Advisory Commission on Criminal Justice Standards and Goals had recognized diversion as an appropriate alternative when "there is a substantial likelihood that conviction could be obtained and the benefits to society from channeling an offender into an available noncriminal diversion program outweigh any harm done to society by abandoning criminal prosecution."[9]

We tend to think of corrections as the last phase of the criminal justice system. It may therefore appear contradictory to include diversion within the correctional caseload. But recall Chapter 1, where we saw that corrections (specifically, the local jail) is also responsible for pretrial detention—confining those awaiting trial who are not released pending adjudication. Similarly, alleged offenders who have been diverted out of the system before trial can be considered correctional clients. Although they have been accused of criminal behavior, it has been determined that their needs can best be met without official processing, through programs offered in the community. The idea is to treat criminal behavior "at its source"—that is, where crime originates, "ideally, treatment ought to originate."[10]

### The Diversion Process

Pretrial intervention is commonly referred to as *diversion*, since the suspect is diverted from official processing, thereby minimizing penetration into the justice system. As Figure 5.1 illustrates, it occurs in the absence of any finding of guilt or innocence—in other words, without subjecting the defendant to trial. Clients of diversion therefore cannot technically be considered "offenders," since they have not actually been convicted.

Pretrial intervention represents the system's first opportunity to make a positive change in the defendant's lifestyle, at a point before more serious criminal behavior patterns become firmly established. By providing individual treat-

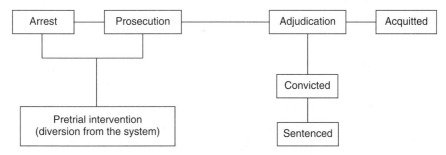

**Figure 5.1** Pretrial intervention in the criminal justice process.

[8]President's Commission on Law Enforcement and Administration of Justice, *Task Force Report: The Courts* (Washington, DC: U.S. Government Printing Office, 1967), pp. 97–107.
[9]National Advisory Commission on Criminal Justice Standards and Goals, *Courts* (Washington, DC: U.S. Government Printing Office, 1973), p. 32.
[10]Louis P. Carney, *Corrections and the Community* (Englewood Cliffs, NJ: Prentice Hall, 1977), p. 54.

ment in the community, the intent is to help resolve whatever problems led the client to come to the attention of criminal justice authorities.

Diversion is invoked whenever authorities elect to informally respond to apparent criminal activity. Thus, diversion basically involves the use of police and prosecutorial *discretion*. As discussed in Chapter 1, law enforcement officers have considerable discretion in deciding whether or not to make an arrest. In Chapter 2 we also pointed out the public's ambivalence about just what should be considered "criminal" and what official action should be taken in response to it. To some extent, such subjective judgments are purposely built into the system to provide flexibility in the administration of justice. In this way, justice can be more individualized. That is, "criminal statutes may be interpreted in terms of the problems and needs of the individual offender, the impact of [the] offense, or the expectations of the community. . . ."[11] When the needs of the client can be better served through community programs than official processing, when the offense is not overly harmful to society, or when significant social standards have not been violated, officials may use their discretionary judgment to divert the case out of the system.

## Formal and Informal Diversion

Diversion can occur at any phase of processing prior to adjudication. In fact, whenever officials decide not to invoke the criminal justice process, they are "diverting the individual from the criminal justice system."[12] Much of the willingness to employ diversion is based on the availability of accessible options. In the absence of options, the process simply becomes diversion *from* the system rather than *to* a more appropriate alternative.

As the defendant's first point of contact in the system, the police represent the earliest point at which intervention can occur. The police can make an arrest (thereby continuing the case for further processing) or they can elect to dispose of the situation informally through a verbal warning, referral to a social service agency, or some other form of unofficial action. Such practices are considered *informal diversion* because while they remove the case from the justice system, the police do not have authority to require any enforceable conditions of the defendant.

For example, an officer confronting someone mildly intoxicated with no permanent address might issue a verbal reprimand, recommend obtaining treatment, and even provide transportation to an alcohol rehabilitation clinic. But no official action was taken. No report was filed. No one was taken into custody. No record of the incident was created. As a result, the person is not a criminal justice client and therefore not legally obliged to follow the officer's suggestions. If the police suspect that voluntary compliance will not be forthcoming, they are more likely to bypass their option for informal diversion and make an arrest.

Even after the defendant is officially taken into custody, the prosecutor can decide to withhold the filing of charges (or offer to dismiss charges) in favor of an alternative means of resolving the situation. Particularly if the victim is more

---

[11]Belinda Rodgers McCarthy and Bernard J. McCarthy, Jr., *Community-Based Corrections*, Second Edition (Pacific Grove, CA: Brooks/Cole Publishing Company, 1991), p. 21.
[12]Ibid.

concerned with being compensated for losses than seeking a criminal conviction, the prosecutor may arrange an agreement whereby the alleged offender repays the victim in exchange for dropping the charges. In recent years, such approaches have become officially accepted, standardized practices known in many jurisdictions as *alternative dispute resolution.*

In Canada, where this concept is called *victim–offender reconciliation*, the resolution of minor complaints can range from victim compensation to simply offering an apology, in order to "personalize and humanize the criminal justice system."[13] Dispute resolution programs in the United States are similar in some respects to the arbitration of labor–management conflicts. Negotiation between the victim and the alleged offender is mediated by an impartial third party, and an effort is made to reach a satisfactory resolution for all involved.

While dispute resolution is often handled by arbitrators outside the criminal justice system, the case has still been officially entered for processing. Intervention at this point therefore represents more *formal diversion* (sometimes called *deferred prosecution* or probation without adjudication).

In contrast to informal diversion, the defendant is now accountable for assuring that the conditions established are actually fulfilled. Should compensation to the victim or the requirements of dispute resolution not be completed as agreed, the prosecutor can consider proceeding with the original charges.

Even if the case comes to court, the judge has a number of discretionary options available. For example, judges can choose to *withhold adjudication*, diverting the defendant into any of a variety of community treatment, education, training, or counseling programs. They can also *suspend sentencing* following an adjudication of guilt, opting for an alternative to incarceration. However, since the defendant has been found guilty at this point, a suspended sentence would represent a form of posttrial rather than pretrial intervention.

With the escalation of drug abuse cases currently flooding the criminal justice system, a popular diversionary program in many jurisdictions has emerged in the form of *treatment alternatives to street crimes (TASC)*. Such programs are based on the assumption that drug users benefit more from being treated for their addiction than from being adjudicated and incarcerated. They diagnose drug problems, make treatment referrals, and monitor the client's progress. Similar options also exist in many communities for alcohol detoxification, family crisis intervention, and other common problems that are more effectively addressed outside the criminal justice arena. Again, a defendant's failure to comply successfully with program requirements can result in reactivating the case by proceeding with adjudication or lifting the sentencing suspension.

## Advantages and Disadvantages of Diversion

To both the defendant and the system, pretrial diversion offers substantial benefits. Several of these advantages are outlined in Figure 5.2, which compares community-based with institutional corrections.

[13]Gordon Perry and John Walker, "Intermediate Sanctions in Canada," *American Jails*, Vol. 5, No. 1 (March/April 1991), p. 124.

| Characteristic | Community-Based | Institution-Based |
|---|---|---|
| Monetary cost | Less costly | More costly |
| Environmental conditions | Natural: promotes normal social and community relationships | Artificial: promotes abnormal social relationships |
| Location | Treatment is based in the community | Treatment is based in an institutional/custodial setting |
| Effectiveness as an instrument of rehabilitation | Questionable effectiveness; at least as effective as institution-based corrections | Clearly not effective |
| Philosophical basis | Reintegration | Incapacitation/retribution/ deterrence/rehabilitation |

**Figure 5.2**  Comparison of institutional and community-based corrections. *Source:* Stephen E. Doeren and Mary J. Hageman, *Community Corrrections* (Cincinnati, OH: Anderson Publishing Company, 1982), p. 18.

Untried offenders who truly are committed to making positive changes in their lives may appreciate this "second chance," as well as the opportunity it presents to obtain help with their problems. At the same time, greater advantage is taken of resources available in the community—thereby supplementing the limited capabilities of the criminal justice system to deal with the vast array of personal problems generating criminal activities. However, that does not mean that all diversionary options are necessarily treatment-oriented. Victim compensation, for example, while a form of repaying one's debt to society, does not necessarily address any underlying causes of shoplifting, purse snatching, embezzlement, or whatever crime was involved.

**Stigma.**  Even pretrial interventions that do not address the root causes of behavior at least do no further harm to the defendant. By providing an option to official processing through the system, the stigma of being labeled "criminal" is avoided. Having a criminal record has long been acknowledged as a serious obstacle to employment, social relationships, and even family stability. To defendants facing the prospect of conviction and possible jail or prison time, it is certainly advantageous to elect to participate in a diversionary program. Otherwise, they risk being labeled throughout life as "convicts" or "ex-offenders," along with all of the limitations and restrictions which that entails.

**Leniency and Effectiveness.**  On the other hand, the fact that diversion reduces the consequences of criminal behavior raises the criticism that it is too lenient, doing little to hold offenders accountable for their actions or to deter future crime. But some diversionary programs are actually harsher than the consequences that would probably follow conviction. For example, in one state: "few defendants invoke the . . . diversion statute for first-offense [drug] possession charges. The anticipated result of prosecution on such charges is a conditional dismissal, largely unsupervised, or a lenient sentence. Diversion, on the other hand, imposes a lengthy treatment period, requires an admission of drug dependency or addiction, and forces the defendant to accept a selected treatment program."[14]

Also overlooked is the fact that community corrections has "significant sanction value" that is both "compatible with the demand for retribution" and useful, particularly in terms of retribution.[15] To be taken more seriously as a form of punishment, however, community-based alternatives must demonstrate that they are "tough with the enforcement of court orders—most of all, in quick, decisive and uncompromising reaction to non-compliance."[16] When community corrections takes its mission seriously—firmly supervising its clients and holding them accountable for compliance with established conditions—concern that it is too lenient is considerably diminished.

The perception that diversion is excessively permissive also raises the issue of whether recidivism rates are higher for those diverted than for those officially processed. That is a difficult, if not impossible question to answer. Some evidence of successful programs tends to refute such thinking. But for a number of reasons, it is "extremely difficult to assess the overall effectiveness of diversion," as a result of the wide variety of programs that have been promoted as "diversionary," coupled with the "low quality" of evaluations and the "mixed findings" that have been reported.[17] Moreover, even positive results may not necessarily provide evidence of diversion's success, since some clients may do well because they probably did not need any intervention in the first place.

**Normal Environment.** Although the effectiveness of diversion remains debatable, the effects of prison are all too well known. In the restrictive, closed environment of prisons and jails, primary emphasis is placed on security. Treatment of the inmates' problems is a secondary concern (to the extent that it is addressed at all). In contrast, the open environment of the community "encourages offenders to try to live as they would if they were free,"[18] with minimal restrictions guiding their behavior. Thus, diversion has been commended for offering an alternative to the counterproductiveness of incarceration, substituting "a normal environment for an abnormal one, and at a substantially reduced cost."[19]

**Costs.** In comparison with the expense of going to trial, the skyrocketing costs of prison construction, and the sophisticated technology needed to maintain

[14]Raymond T. Nimmer, *Diversion: The Search for Alternative Forms of Prosecution* (Chicago: American Bar Foundation, 1974), p. 99.

[15]David E. Duffee, "Community Corrections: Its Presumed Characteristics and an Argument for a New Approach," in David E. Duffee and Edmund F. McGarrell, eds., *Community Corrections: A Community Field Approach* (Cincinnati, OH: Anderson Publishing Company, 1990), p. 4.

[16]Benjamin F. Baer, "Good PR Programs Enhance Public Acceptance," in *Intermediate Punishment: Community-Based Sanctions* (Laurel, MD: American Correctional Association, 1990), p. 16, quoting Barry J. Nidorf, chief probation officer of Los Angeles County, California.

[17]Stephen E. Doeren and Mary J. Hageman, *Community Corrections* (Cincinnati, OH: Anderson Publishing Company, 1982), p. 40.

[18]Herbert G. Callison, *Introduction* to *Community-Based Corrections* (New York: McGraw-Hill, 1983), p. 15.

[19]Carney, p. 58.

institutional security, diversion is significantly less expensive. Cost-effectiveness is particularly attractive when funds are limited. Of course, economic considerations alone should not determine how extensively pretrial intervention is used. The fact remains that imprisonment is notoriously destructive. If more beneficial results can be achieved in the community, lower costs represent an added incentive to experiment with such options.

**Efficiency and Flexibility.**   Beyond lower costs, diversion presents an opportunity to enhance the efficiency of the criminal justice system. Given the fact that the courts are already overburdened with serious violent crimes, the system would probably crush under its own weight if all previously diverted, less serious offenses were suddenly added to its official workload. As with plea bargaining, some may advocate abolishing diversion. But that is neither a realistic nor a feasible option in terms of current staffing or funding.

Moreover, diversion allows the system some flexibility. As we saw in Chapter 2, the law changes much more slowly than public opinion. Discretion allows the system to adjust its response to law-violating behavior during the transition. Society would not want all laws strictly enforced at all times in all situations. Nor is it likely that we would truly support a justice process that operated routinely by the book, without consideration of either the circumstances of the individual or the management capability of the system. It has been argued that "many offenders' crimes are caused by special problems—vagrancy, alcoholism, emotional distress—that cannot be managed effectively through the criminal justice system."[20] Without the opportunity for diversion and the expanded community resources which it embraces, such cases would probably be dealt with through rather limited, generally punitive, and often inappropriate responses.

**Discretion.**   On the other hand, too much unregulated discretion can produce coercion—forcing treatment on those who have committed no crime or for whom there is "insufficient evidence to obtain a conviction."[21] Avoiding a conviction is not the objective of diversion. Rather, it is a tool to facilitate "effective treatment of the social, psychological, or interpersonal problems underlying the deviant act."[22] Pressuring defendants into pretrial diversion programs not only raises ethical questions but also creates a situation wherein defendants may involuntarily abdicate many of their due process rights—most significantly, the right to trial and protection against self-incrimination. "Even though an overwhelming majority of programs do not require an admission of guilt, there is presumption of guilt inherent in the system."[23]

The effects of coercion may also include the potential that those unwillingly

---

[20]Todd R. Clear and George F. Cole, *American Corrections* (Monterey, CA: Brooks/Cole Publishing Company, 1986), p. 214.

[21]McCarthy and McCarthy, p. 48.

[22]Nimmer, p. 47.

[23]Doeren and Hageman, p. 37. See also Bruce Bullington, James Sprowls, Daniel Katkin, and Mark Phillips, "A Critique of Diversionary Juvenile Justice," *Crime and Delinquency,* Vol. 24, No. 1 (January 1978), pp. 59–71, who express concern that "voluntary participation" may actually be "a result of plea bargaining away constitutional rights to minimize the chances of institutional confinement."

diverted may not be motivated to complete the program to which they were referred, and are therefore more likely to drop out or fail. This presents the possibility that they will subsequently be prosecuted and punished more vigorously because they appear "uncooperative." For example, one study has found that those not successfully completing a job training and employment diversionary program often received harsher sentences upon their return to court than would otherwise have been expected.[24] It is for such reasons that regulation of the diversionary process has been advocated by more closely controlling discretion through such procedures as contracts outlining terms and conditions. To achieve greater equity and uniformity, it is necessary that "pre-judicial diversion . . . not remain a random and inconsistent event, but become a clear, conscious policy and procedure."[25]

**Net widening.** Finally, the extent to which diversionary options are available is itself a source of concern. If, for example, the defendant would have been subjected to less interference or less supervision in the absence of diversionary options, are these programs truly serving the purpose for which they were intended? In this regard it has been noted that "innovations designed to reduce the overall intrusiveness of the system, no matter how well-intentioned, often backfire and instead add to its capacity for social control."[26]

When police, prosecutors, and judges are aware that offenders can obtain help for their problems rather than simply serve time, there is some danger that the system will extend its reach into borderline behavior that would otherwise have been overlooked. For example, when they are aware that the court's options are limited, police officers might ignore a situation involving possession of a small amount of drugs by a young person—concerned that it would be unproductive to see this person incarcerated for such an offense. But when drug treatment is well-known as an available diversionary program, the police may be more likely to make an arrest in order to get the offender help. This illustrates the concept of *net widening*—when a new program broadens official intervention rather than improving the shortcomings of the existing system.

If diversion results in bringing more clients into the system and/or dealing with them more harshly, it becomes a form of net widening. In this respect, "true diversion is possible only when less costly, more humane, and less severe programs are applied to defendants whose destinies would otherwise be the harsh realities of jail."[27] On the other hand, it could be argued that the system's initial reluctance to interfere with obvious law-violating behavior before the availability of diversionary options was equally inappropriate and could not be justified simply because effective response alternatives were lacking. In any case, debates surrounding the effectiveness and equity of pretrial interventions continue. Nevertheless, they remain useful alternatives that are often more benevolent to the offender as well as more beneficial to the victim, the system, or both.

---

[24]Franklin Zimring, "Measuring the Impact of Pretrial Diversion from the Criminal Justice System," *University of Chicago Law Review*, Vol. 94 (1974), p. 241.

[25]Carney, p. 55.

[26]Clear and Cole, p. 215.

[27]Ibid.

## ❖ HOME CONFINEMENT AND ELECTRONIC MONITORING

Home confinement through *electronic monitoring* is a recent innovation that has considerable potential for reducing prison populations, but at the same time, for "widening the net" as well.

When diversion was originally developed, the restrictions it imposed did not tend to interfere with freedom of movement. With technological advances in recent years, however, it has become possible to combine diversion with confinement in one's residence, as verified by electronic monitors. In fact, as illustrated in Figure 5.3, home confinement under electronic monitoring can be employed at virtually any point in the criminal justice process following arrest—from pretrial to postsentencing, and even postincarceration. In other words, it can be used:

- With pretrial diversion.
- After a period of pretrial detention.
- Following conviction as:
  —A form of sentencing
  —A condition of probation
  —An option for probation violators
  —A "front-end" alternative to going to prison.
- Following a prison sentence as:
  —A "back-end" alternative to staying in prison
  —Preparation for release from prison
  —A condition of parole
  —An option for parole violators.

During the period of confinement, participants are placed on a form of curfew, restricted from leaving their place of residence. Exceptions are made during work hours if the client is employed, or for such legitimate reasons as performing community service, grocery shopping, or attending authorized activities (e.g., training or treatment programs, church services, medical appointments). Otherwise, the client is expected to remain at home.

Surveillance of the person's whereabouts is maintained by one of two systems that are either "programmed-contact" or "continuously signaling"

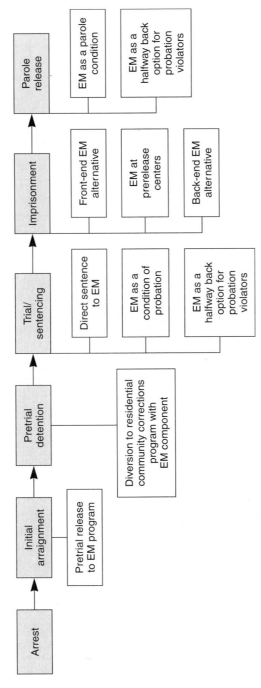

**Figure 5.3** Key decision points in the criminal justice system where electronic monitoring (EM) is being used. *Source:* Bureau of Justice Assistance, *Electronic Monitoring in Intensive Probation and Parole Programs* (Washington, DC: U.S. Department of Justice, 1989), p. 2.

devices.[28] Programmed-contact systems use a computer to dial the client's telephone number randomly during the hours of the curfew. Upon answering the phone, the participant inserts a transmitter into special equipment attached to the phone, which electronically verifies his or her presence. To avoid the possibility of someone else responding, the transmitter inserted is often in the form of a tamperproof bracelet, worn to ensure that the person answering is indeed the client. On the other hand, continuously signaling systems operate with a device that constantly monitors one's presence at a particular location. If participants are not where they are supposed to be when they are supposed to be there, the signal is broken, and a computer alerts correctional personnel. In either case, those whose presence is not properly verified are subject to rearrest and revocation of home confinement.

## Electronically Monitored Clients

Because of its diverse uses and flexibility, it is not surprising to find that electronically monitored home confinement is being employed with more and more offenders. In fact, the number of people being supervised through electronic monitoring has been virtually tripling each year since 1987.[29] As Figure 5.4 indicates, 37 states were using such monitoring programs by 1989, with Florida and Michigan accounting for the largest portion of clients.

Because eligibility criteria vary among states, the thousands of offenders being monitored represent a wide range of criminal behavior. Most have been either convicted or accused of *major traffic offenses* (usually DUI—driving under the influence), *property crimes,* or *drug offenses* (possession or distribution).[30] In 1987, the typical participant was a male convicted of DUI. But by 1989, the typical person being monitored was a burglar, and drug offenders had become increasingly common.[31]

## Advantages

Certainly, much of the recent popularity of this approach has resulted from the combination of increasingly punitive public attitudes toward crime and decreasingly available space in correctional institutions. With society not in a mood to "coddle criminals," alternatives to prison crowding must be tough, not compromising public safety. Home confinement is viewed as meeting these criteria.[32] Unlike institutional incapacitation, it also provides greater opportunity for treatment. (In reality, however, that opportunity is rarely fulfilled, since treatment is not often a component of such programs.) When enforced by elec-

---

[28]For more information on the differences between various types of electronic monitoring equipment, see Annesley K. Schmidt, "Electronic Monitoring of Offenders Increases," *National Institute of Justice Reports* (January/February 1989), p. 4.

[29]Marc Renzema and David Skelton, "Use of Electronic Monitoring in the United States: 1989 Update," *National Institute of Justice Reports* (November/December 1990), p. 9.

[30]Ibid., p. 11.

[31]Ibid., p. 12.

[32]Joan Petersilia, "House Arrest," *National Institute of Justice; Crime File Study Guide* (Washington, DC: U.S. Department of Justice, 1988), p. 1.

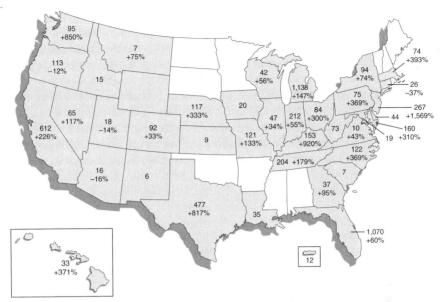

**Figure 5.4**  Number of offenders being electronically monitored on February 12, 1989, and percent change from 1988. *Note:* If no percent change is noted, the state had no electronically monitored offenders on the survey date in 1988. There were no programs in Alaska. Not shown: An additional 669 offenders were monitored under programs serving more than one state. *Source:* Marc Renzema and David T. Skelton, "Use of Electronic Monitoring in the United States: 1989 Update," *National Institute of Justice Reports* (November/December 1990), p. 10.

tronic monitoring, home confinement satisfies the public's demand for retribution and protection without abandoning the system's desire for more productive offender processing. It has thus produced a reasonable alternative that can simultaneously "satisfy punishment, public safety, and treatment objectives" by:

- "Providing a cost-effective community supervision tool;
- Administering sanctions which are appropriate to the seriousness of the offense;
- Providing surveillance and risk control strategies. . . . "[33]

Particularly in times of fiscal shortages, home confinement is especially attractive. In comparison to the $10,000 to $20,000 required to maintain an offender in prison (not to mention the investment in new prison construction), the costs of home confinement range from $1500 to $7000 annually.[34] When coupled with electronic monitoring, the price tag jumps to between $2500 and

---

[33]Bureau of Justice Assistance, *Electronic Monitoring in Intensive Probation and Parole Programs* (Washington, DC: U.S. Department of Justice, 1989), p. 3.

[34]Petersilia, p. 2.

$8000,[35] although that is still well below prison costs, and many programs charge the participants fees to offset expenses.[36]

Beyond monetary considerations, social benefits represent other advantages. The offender can remain employed, continue any treatment initiated in the community, avert family breakup, and, of course, avoid the negative effects of prison. In addition, home confinement is well suited to dealing with special-needs offenders who might be particularly vulnerable in prison or jail settings (e.g., those who are mentally retarded, pregnant, youthful, or terminally ill). In contrast to correctional institutions, it represents a speedier and more flexible response to handling vast numbers of clients than would ever be possible through new facility construction. In fact, it has also been used in conjunction with early release to reduce jail and prison crowding.

## Disadvantages

Despite its appealing features, however, home confinement through electronic monitoring is not without drawbacks. To the extent that it becomes a "cheap panacea" for prison, a number of disturbing questions are raised,[37] among them the net-widening potential mentioned earlier. In that regard, it has been observed that "non-violent and low-risk offenders are prime candidates for house arrest; [yet] these offenders are least likely to have been sentenced to prison in the first place."[38] Net widening provokes concern about the appropriate use of such sanctions. If they are not reserved for the truly prison bound, cost-effectiveness is dramatically reduced. Moreover, the "widened net" in this case can extend beyond the individual offender to his or her family as well, particularly when home confinement is combined with electronic monitoring and calls come in at any time of the day or night.

In that regard, the intrusiveness of electronic monitoring into private residences has also been criticized. With this alternative to incarceration, one's home in essence becomes a prison. Opponents of these Orwellian, "big brother" aspects have suggested that "we may well be extending discipline from prisons into the larger society."[39] In response, some maintain that home confinement certainly provides greater privacy than prison or jail, and that in any event, participation is voluntary. As one advocate of its use maintains, "so long as criminals are the ones imprisoned in their homes to prevent crime, rather than citizens from fear of crime, society will be well served."[40] But others ask "what's next?," predicting such frightening pictures of electronic excesses as the following: "In the future, people . . . won't be confined to their homes or to . . . short

[35]Ibid.

[36]Renzema and Skelton, pp. 4–5.

[37]See, for example, Ronald Corbett and Gary T. Marx, "No Soul in the New Machine: Technofallacies in the Electronic Monitoring Movement," *Justice Quarterly*, Vol. 8, No. 3 (September 1991), pp. 399–414.

[38]Petersilia, p. 3.

[39]Georgette Bennett, *Crimewarps: The Future of Crime in America* (New York; Anchor Books, 1987), p. 356, quoting Thomas Blomberg.

[40]Perry Johnson, "Electronically Monitored Home Confinement," in *Intermediate Punishment: Community-based Sanctions*, p. 59.

distances. Voice identification, visual verification, and tracking by satellite are all in the works. Surgically implanted, nuclear-powered, electronic devices will allow them to move freely, but a monitor will know where they are every second. . . . Except for the worst offenders, the prisons of the future will be prisons without walls."[41]

While these hypothetical scenarios might seem farfetched, consider the fact that by 1991 community corrections programs in Kansas were already using telemonitoring—"a form of house arrest in which visual contacts with offenders are produced via telephone from the offender's home," with a breath-alcohol monitor attached to the video to ensure abstinence of alcohol use.[42] In addition, some correctional practitioners have expressed concerns with "Robo-cop" implications for drastically changing the traditionally people-oriented practice of community corrections into a computer-driven emphasis on surveillance.[43]

Not everyone who disagrees with home confinement/electronic monitoring is opposed to the severity of its intrusiveness. Quite the contrary, there are those who do not believe that it is *sufficiently* harsh, particularly advocates of tougher drunk-driving penalties. At the same time, offenders who are not eligible because of the fees involved and the necessity to have a telephone at home have raised the issue of discrimination, since "persons without these resources may have no alternative but prison."[44] Nor is electronic monitoring a failproof means of preventing criminal activity on the part of those being monitored.

These are but a few among the many issues that must be addressed in the future of electronic monitoring and home confinement, keeping in mind that "it is all too tempting to employ the equipment simply because the means are available to do so."[45] In the meantime, just as home confinement was originally created as an alternative to incarceration, prison remains as an alternative to home confinement.

---

*LEARNING GOALS*

*Do you know:*

- *The definition of probation?*
- *How frequently probation is used in contrast to other sentencing options?*
- *Why probation is often combined with a suspended sentence?*

---

[41]Bennett, pp. 356–57.

[42]Gail Townsend, "Kansas Community Corrections Programs," *American Jails,* Vol 5, No. 1 (March/April 1991), p. 30.

[43]Ronald Corbett, "Electronic Monitoring," and Gary Graham, "High-Tech Monitoring: Are We Losing the Human Element?" in *Intermediate Punishment: Community-Based Sanctions,* pp. 21–25, 35–39.

[44]Petersilia, p. 3.

[45]Ray Wahl, "Is Electronic Home Monitoring a Viable Option?" in *Intermediate Punishment: Community-Based Sanctions,* p. 27.

For the vast majority of offenders, incarceration is not necessary. As a community-based approach, probation has the advantage of dealing with problems in the social environment where they originated. It avoids the breakdown of ties with home, family, and relationships that occurs with being institutionalized in a closed environment. By working with the individual in the community (including his or her family), an offender's total situation can better be handled—thus preventing the "social surgery" of complete removal from free society. When the objective is to assist with adjustment to the environment, it is more effective to work with social relationships than to sever them. In short, it is easier and more efficient to maintain the offender's integration as a part of society than to attempt to reintegrate upon release from secure confinement. It is also less expensive, since it costs 10 to 15 times more to maintain a person in an institution than it does to supervise someone in the community.

The courts have recognized these advantages in their sentencing practices, making probation the most widely used correctional disposition in the United States.[46] Of all adults under correctional care or custody on any given day in 1989, almost *two out of three* (over 62%) were on probation, representing more than 2.3 million clients[47] (see Figure 5.5). By 1990, the number of probationers had increased to more than 2.6 million,[48] and there are undoubtedly even more on probation today.

In contrast to diversion, which is intervention *before* trial, *probation* is an actual sentence for a *convicted* offender. In other words, "it *is* a sentence and not simply a dismissal of the case."[49] As we have seen in the preceding section, probation can also be combined with home confinement and electronic monitoring. In addition, it is often combined with a *suspended sentence,* whereby the judge sentences a defendant to prison or jail time and then suspends the sentence in

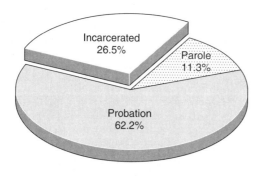

**Figure 5.5**   Percentage of adult offenders on probation. *Source:* "Probation and Parole 1989," *Bureau of Justice Statistics Bulletin* (Washington, DC: U.S. Department of Justice, 1990), p. 2.

---

[46]*Report to the Nation on Crime and Justice,* Second Edition (Washington, DC: U.S. Department of Justice, 1988), p. 96.

[47]Louis Jankowski, "Probation and Parole 1989," *Bureau of Justice Statistics Bulletin* (Washington, DC: U.S. Department of Justice, 1990), p. 2.

[48]Louis Jankowski, "Probation and Parole 1990," *Bureau of Justice Statistics Bulletin* (Washington, DC: U.S. Department of Justice, 1991), p. 1.

[49]Donald J. Newman, *Introduction to Criminal Justice,* Second Edition (Philadelphia: J.B. Lippincott, 1978), p. 281.

favor of probation. In this way, offenders are presumed to be more motivated to comply with the conditions of probation by knowing what awaits should they fail to do so. If the conditions imposed by the court during the probationary period are violated, the suspension can be lifted, resulting in confinement. Thus, probation is *a conditional sentence served under supervision in the community.*

Among the conditions that may be imposed on probationers are such restrictions as keeping reasonable hours, remaining employed, and supporting one's family, along with rules that apply to a particular case, such as abstaining from alcohol and drugs. Mandatory participation in training, education, or treatment programs can also be added to meet specific needs of the offender. Community service work or other forms of restitution can likewise be required as a condition of probation. Generally, there is a wider variation among probation rules than among parole regulations, since the conditions of probation are generally set by individual judges rather than by a single state agency as in the case of parole. In light of the restrictions imposed, probation has been described as a "trial period" during which one is expected to prove one's "ability to meet certain required standards."[50]

Although probation is commonly considered a part of the correctional system because it is a post-conviction sanction, it is technically a judicial function, in which convicted offenders are formally placed under supervision of the court. In practice, however, probation officers are usually employed by the state department of corrections, although in a number of jurisdictions, they remain attached to the court system.[51]

---

*LEARNING GOALS*

*Do you know:*

- *How probation as we know it today originated?*
- *Who is considered the "father of probation"?*

---

### History of Probation

Probation and suspended sentences have been practiced since ancient times, although not according to the modern meaning of these terms. Historically, probably the oldest form of a mitigated sentence was the *right to sanctuary,* used to designate certain places where an offender might go to escape punishment from the victim. Holy sanctuaries were frequently used for this purpose. A related concept that emerged during the middle ages was the *benefit of clergy,* which first applied only to members of the clergy. Later it was extended to those who could prove their literacy by reading a "test" verse in Psalms 51 (appropriately, the passage that begins with the words "Have mercy on me").

[50]Harold B. Trester, *Supervision of the Offender* (Englewood Cliffs, NJ: Prentice Hall, 1981), p. 39.
[51]For a more detailed description of the providers of probation services, see *Vital Statistics in Corrections* (Laurel, MD: American Correctional Association, 1991), p. 38.

However, as those who were illiterate began to memorize this psalm, the practice gradually ended.[52]

The beginning of probation as we now know it in the U.S. originated in 1841 when a Boston cobbler, *John Augustus,* began visiting the courts. As a temperance crusader, he was both interested in the potential of rehabilitating alcoholics and "disturbed by the fact that common drunks were often forced to remain in jail because they had no money . . . to pay their fines."[53] Convinced that he could help such offenders, Augustus would provide their bail or pay their fines, asking the judge to place them under his supervision. He would assist them with remaining sober, finding work, and staying out of trouble. As more and more petty criminals were released to his supervision, his house was "literally filled with people he had bailed."[54] By 1858 he had supervised nearly 2000 clients—1152 men and 794 women and girls—almost none of whom violated his trust.

As the next "Close-up on Corrections" describes, Augustus was responsible for reporting back to the court on their progress, which the judge usually took into account in deciding a disposition. Reformed offenders were thereforE spared incarceration in a correctional facility. Because of his pioneering efforts, John Augustus is considered the "father of probation." That does not mean that probation was any more popular with the public in his day than it is now. Quite the contrary, Augustus was denounced for his efforts. But upon his death in 1859, supporters continued his work. As a result, the first probation statute was passed in Massachusetts in 1878, enabling the city of Boston to establish a salaried probation officer. By 1954, all states had some form of probation.

---

*LEARNING GOALS* ▬▬▬▬▬▬▬▬▬▬▬▬▬▬▬▬▬▬▬▬▬▬▬▬▬▬

*Do you know:*

- *How probation is organized administratively?*
- *What training and education are required for employment in probation today?*

---

## Probation Today

Probation is a function of various governmental jurisdictions. Therefore, staff size, organizational structure, and availability of services vary widely throughout the country. Probation services are now provided in all states and the federal government. But in terms of size, the number of state and county probation officers ranges from 3176 in California to 1 in Wyoming (although Wyoming has another 48 officers who serve as combined probation/parole agents).[55]

---

[52]Louis P. Carney, *Probation and Parole: Legal and Social Dimensions* (New York: McGraw-Hill, 1977), p. 76.
[53]Harry E. Allen and Clifford Simonsen, *Corrections in America,* Sixth Edition (New York: Macmillan, 1992), p. 193.
[54]Howard Abadinsky, *Probation and Parole: Theory and Practice* (Englewood Cliffs, NJ: Prentice Hall, 1977), p. 23.
[55]*Vital Statistics in Corrections,* p. 39.

### The Work of John Augustus

In the month of August, 1841, I was in court one morning, when . . . an officer entered, followed by a ragged and wretched looking man, who took his seat upon the bench allotted to prisoners. I imagined from the man's appearance that his offense was that of yielding to his appetite for intoxicating drinks, and in a few moments, I found that my suspicions were correct, for the clerk read the complaint, in which the man was charged with being a common drunkard. . . . I conversed with him for a few moments, and found that he was not yet past all hope for reformation. . . . He told me that if he could be saved from the House of Correction, he never again would taste intoxicating liquors, [and] there was such an earnestness in that tone, and a look of firm resolve, that I determined to aid him. I bailed him, by permission of the court. He was ordered to appear for sentence in three weeks from that time. He signed the pledge and became a sober man; at the expiration of this period of probation, I accompanied him into the court room. . . . The judge expressed himself much pleased with the account we gave of the man, and instead of the usual penalty—imprisonment in the House of Corrections—he fined him one cent and costs amounting in all to $3.76, which was immediately paid. The man continued industrious and sober, and without doubt has been by his treatment, saved from a drunkard's grave.

*Source:* John Augustus, *A Report of the Labors of John Augustus, for the Last Ten Years, in Aid of the Unfortunate* (Boston: Wright and Hasty, 1852), reprinted as *John Augustus, First Probation Officer* (New York: Probation Association, 1939), pp. 4–5.

In terms of organizational structure, most jurisdictions administer probation through the state department of corrections. But in others, probation is the responsibility of independent boards, separate departments, the courts, county government, or various combinations thereof. Many states have centralized probation at the state level in order to make service more uniform and assure that it is available in those counties that cannot afford a probation staff. In these states, the pattern is often to have parole agents also assume the functions of probation. But large counties and metropolitan areas generally maintain their own probation staffs, as does the federal government.

In terms of services, some probation offices have their own diagnostic clinics with a full-time psychiatric staff. Others contract with private vendors. Still others are limited to what can be accomplished through their often-overburdened employees. As a result of these differences, it is obvious that there is little uniformity with regard to the quality and quantity of probation throughout the country.

In contrast to these administrative factors, staff educational requirements are somewhat more standardized among jurisdictions. Following the lead of the federal probation services in 1930, most jurisdictions now require a minimum of a bachelor's degree for entry-level probation or parole officers.[56] However, that does not necessarily mean that the degree must be related to the job. (In fact, as recently as the mid-1980s, someone with a bachelor of fine arts degree in fashion design was hired as a probation officer and placed on the job with no additional classroom training.) Although higher education broadens one's perspective and develops advanced reasoning capabilities, it does not provide job-specific skills or knowledge of rules, regulations, and operational procedures that training is designed to achieve. It is for this reason that both entry-level training and subsequent in-service updating are essential to effective job performance. But states have generally required very little mandatory training before job assignment as a probation officer. Although there are some exceptions (such as Oklahoma, where a 520-hour curriculum is required, and Florida, which mandates 345 hours), the minimum preservice requirement is commonly 40 hours of training.[57] Unfortunately, as with training for institutional employees, the minimum required often becomes the maximum provided.

If there is one qualification that probation officers do have in common virtually everywhere, it is the personal ability and ingenuity to make good use of community resources. In addition to their counseling and casework functions, officers usually know the community as well as anyone. They are aware of employers who can offer jobs for probationers, as well as providers of many other services needed by their clients, from temporary shelter to drug treatment. It is likely because of conscientious and creative personnel that—while probation is often unsupported, understaffed, and undergoing criticism—it is also acknowledged as a relatively effective alternative to imprisonment.

---

*LEARNING GOALS*

*Do you know:*

- *The difference between general and specific conditions of probation?*
- *Why some jurisdictions require probationers to pay supervision fees?*

---

## Conditions of Probation

Among the reasons that the public has not been overly enthusiastic about probation is the common misperception that it involves unrestricted freedom. Quite the contrary, probationers lose a considerable measure of privacy and liberty. Moreover, they are required to meet a number of conditions. At a minimum, these conditions usually include:

---

[56]Although states vary from 33% to 100% in terms of the percentage of their jurisdictions minimally requiring a bachelor's degree for probation or parole officers, the vast majority of locations in most states maintain this requirement for entry. *Vital Statistics in Corrections*, p. 40.

[57]Diane Carter, "The Status of Education and Training," *Journal of Correctional Training* (Spring 1992), p. 6.

- Remaining within the geographic jurisdiction of the court.
- Reporting to a probation officer on a prescribed schedule (e.g., once a month; once a week).
- Refraining from association with certain types of people (e.g., known criminals) or places (e.g., bars).
- Not possessing a firearm or committing a new offense.
- Cooperating with the probation staff.

The judge can also mandate such further requirements as maintaining a curfew, fulfilling financial obligations, and remaining employed or seeking employment. These *general* conditions of probation are directed toward controlling the offender's behavior. In addition, *specific* conditions tailored to the client's particular situation or needs may be added that are more individualized or treatment oriented.

For example, family support and/or victim compensation can be required, along with participation in various training, educational, drug treatment, alcohol detoxification, or psychological counseling programs. As detailed in the next "Close-up on Corrections," offenders are also increasingly being required to pay fees that offset at least some of the cost of their supervision. Probationers can additionally be subjected to periodic or random drug and alcohol tests to assure that they have not lapsed back into previous patterns of behavior. Many offenders faithfully fulfill the conditions of their probation, taking advantage of this opportunity to avoid incarceration. On the other hand, there are those who attempt to take advantage of the system by violating the trust placed in them.

---

*LEARNING GOALS*

*Do you know:*

- *What types of offenders are eligible for probation?*
- *What category of offenses represents the bulk of probation clients?*

---

## Probation Eligibility

The fact that probation does not appear to work equally well with all clients raises the issue of who should be eligible for it, as well as for whom it would be most beneficial. Because probation is a less harsh sentence than incarceration, it might be assumed erroneously that it is reserved for those convicted of misdemeanors rather than felonies. Such is not the case. In fact, not only is probation an available option for sentencing felony offenders, there are actually *more felons than misdemeanants* on probation. Of the total number of adults on probation in 1990, for example, approximately 37% were felons, compared with only 24% who were misdemeanants. (The status of the remaining 39% was either unknown or involved some other type of offense, primarily driving while intoxi-

Probationers Paying Their Own Way

With correctional costs skyrocketing in recent years, more and more government officials have decided that offenders should help pay for the cost of their own supervision. Of course, judges have long imposed court costs on defendants, and most jail and prison work programs already require inmates to contribute a portion of their earnings to their own upkeep.

In the past decade, the offender population on probation and parole has risen at a more rapid rate than the prison population. . . . However, spending for probation and parole has increased at a lesser rate than spending for prisons, forcing probation and parole officials to provide more intensive supervision and a wider range of services, while drawing on increasingly limited resources.

Faced with this problem, policymakers and professionals have explored offender fees as a new revenue source to defray some of their expenses. . . . With over 2.6 million offenders on probation in 1990, even a fee of $20 a month for 6 months would generate more than $300 million annually. And despite a common perception of the criminal as penniless and unemployable, most offenders on probation who have committed misdemeanors—and even many who have committed felonies—can afford reasonable monthly supervision fees.

Already, more than half the states allow local probation departments to charge fees to probationers, and many states have raised substantial amounts of money from these assessments. . . . [For example], Texas has been highly successful in generating probation fees. In 1990, Texas collected fees from approximately 90% of all misdemeanor offenders on probation and approximately 65% of all felony offenders on probation. Texas spent more than $106 million to supervise probationers, but collected more than $57 million in fees—about one-half the cost of basic probation supervision.

*Source:* Peter Finn and Dale Parent, "Making the Offender Foot the Bill: A Texas Program," *National Institute of Justice: Program Focus* (Washington, DC: U.S. Department of Justice, 1992), pp. 2, 12.

cated.[58]) This may be because pretrial intervention or intermediate sanctions such as fines and community service are used more often in misdemeanor cases. Additionally, felons who receive probation are those assessed as having a low probability of recidivism (although we will see later that such predictions are not always accurate). But whatever the reason, the fact remains that a sizable proportion of probationers have felony convictions.

In deciding whether to impose probation or incarceration, judges obviously take a number of factors into consideration in addition to the classification of the offense. For example, a Rand Corporation study of felons sentenced to probation found that a defendant is more likely to receive a prison term than probation if he or she:

[58]*Correctional Populations in the United States, 1990* (Washington, DC: U.S. Department of Justice, 1992), p. 33.

- Is convicted of multiple charges.
- Has a record of prior convictions.
- Is a drug addict.
- Used a weapon during commission of the offense or seriously injured the victim.[59]

But while such factors predicted about three out of four (75%) of the sentencing decisions in the Rand study, they did not explain the remainder. Thus, in 25% of the cases, those sent to prison could not be effectively distinguished from those receiving probation. Even among less serious offenders on probation, recidivism occurred "at rather high rates," often involving more serious crimes than their original convictions.[60] As a result, the Rand report called for better risk prediction prior to sentencing, as well as expanded alternatives directed toward more intensive supervision and greater control of offenders in the community.

As was discussed in Chapter 2 with regard to selective incapacitation, anticipating future behavior is never an exact science. Even sophisticated "prediction tables" cannot always anticipate the risk an offender poses to society. With the exception of cases in which sentencing guidelines strictly preclude a judge from issuing probation for certain crimes, determination of whether an offender receives probation or incarceration is largely a function of judicial discretion. In the past, some states have made efforts to further limit discretion through, for example, legislation mandating that probation may be granted only if:

- A new offense is not likely to be committed.
- Public interest does not require that the defendant receive a (harsher) penalty.
- Offender rehabilitation does not require penalty imposition.[61]

But how does a judge determine the likelihood of committing a new offense? How is "public interest" interpreted? What types of "offender rehabilitation" would and would not require imprisonment? The answers still involve value judgments and the use of discretion.

---

*LEARNING GOALS*

*Do you know:*

- *What information is contained in a presentence investigation?*
- *How a PSI is used?*
- *What issues are involved in disclosure of information from the PSI?*

---

[59]Joan Petersilia, Susan Turner, James Kahan, and Joyce Peterson, *Granting Felons Probation: Public Risks and Alternatives* (Santa Monica, CA: Rand Corporation, 1985), pp. 30–31.
[60]Ibid., p. 63.
[61]*Illinois Revised Statutes, 1969,* Chapter 28, Article 117-1.

## Presentence Investigations

To assist in their decision making, judges have traditionally relied on a *presentence investigation* (PSI). Although plea bargaining, mandatory minimum terms, and sentencing guidelines have reduced the need for PSIs today, they still play an important role in sentencing decisions in many jurisdictions.

The presentence investigation is a report generally prepared by a probation officer after interviewing the offender and assessing his or her social situation. (However, some jurisdictions contract with the private sector for preparation of PSIs.[62]) The investigator probes family, educational, and social background and evaluates the defendant's strengths and weaknesses, with a view toward working out an effective treatment program. The presentence investigation is then presented to the judge after the offender has been convicted but before sentencing, in order to guide the judge's disposition of the case. It generally includes an evaluation of family background, social relationships, occupational strengths and weaknesses, employment history, school background, criminal involvement, and any other pertinent factors.[63]

The presentence investigation can be a significant tool in helping a judge address these issues. In addition to aiding the court in determining the appropriate sentence, a PSI can also later help the probation officer with identifying rehabilitative options during probationary supervision. Even if the defendant is eventually sentenced to prison, the PSI can assist correctional institutions in planning classification and treatment programs, and ultimately, it can furnish the parole board with information pertinent to the offender's possible release.

Several states have laws making the presentence investigation mandatory, but the majority of states leave it to the judge's discretion. In practice, a wide variety of patterns occurs, and as mentioned above, the PSI is declining in importance with the movement toward minimum mandatory sentences and sentencing guidelines. Many judges like having a PSI report because it provides them with some information they would not otherwise have, enabling them to feel more confident that they have made the best judgment possible. When making a decision that involves life and liberty, judges naturally tend to feel more secure when they have all available information at hand. However, a few judges who possess a stern legalistic philosophy want no part of the presentence investigation, because they do not want to be influenced by anything other than "the merits of the case" as it was heard in court. Some judges of this type have gone so far as to tell the probation officer to prepare a PSI report, but they do not want to see it until after the sentence has been pronounced. On the other hand, it has been noted that some judges "lean on them too heavily, and routinely sentence in accordance with the recommendations contained in the reports; hence, in many cases, the probation officer is really the person determining the sentence."[64]

---

[62]See C. J. Kulis, "Profit in the Private Presentence Report," *Federal Probation*, Vol. 47, No. 4 (1983); J. S. Granelli, "Presentence Reports Go Private," *National Law Review*, Vol. 2 (1983).

[63]A detailed discussion of the presentence investigation is contained in Paul W. Keve, *The Probation Officer Investigates* (Minneapolis, MN: University of Minnesota Press, 1960).

[64]N. Gary Holten and Lawson L. Lamar, *The Criminal Courts: Structures, Personnel, and Processes* (New York: McGraw-Hill, 1991), pp. 308–9.

**Preparation and Disclosure of PSI Reports.**   Along with the supervision of clients on probation, the preparation of presentence investigations represents one of the two primary functions of probation officers. As a result of the extensive material contained in PSIs, they represent a substantial part of the probation officer's workload.

Ideally, PSIs are based on information gained by interviewing the offender, family members, and those who have had contact with the offender, such as previous employers, teachers or school administrators, and personnel in other social agencies (including the courts and police). But as a result of overworked staff and insufficient time, many presentence investigations are based primarily on interviews with the offender, along with whatever documents might be available as corroborating evidence. Consequently, the value and validity of PSI reports vary widely from court to court, and for that matter, from probation officer to probation officer.

It is largely for this reason that defendants have pressured the courts for access to their PSI. Like a person's credit report, the PSI can contain subjective material—hearsay statements, personal impressions, undocumented accusations, or outright inaccuracies. Historically, the presentence investigation has been considered confidential, to be used only by the judge in determining disposition of the case. The rationale for confidentiality is based on "reluctance to divulge the names of those individuals who gave the information," as well as the belief that "unfavorable comments would damage rehabilitative efforts."[65] In other words, after reading negative comments in the PSI, the offender could become further embittered or less likely to engage in voluntary treatment. But others have argued that restricting access "denies due process"; that the defendant (and/or one's attorney) "should be able to examine and refute inaccuracies"; and that "it is much better that an offender know the facts behind a sentencing decision," since understanding why the judge selected a particular sentence could enhance acceptance of it.[66] Moreover, knowing that the contents can be disclosed is more likely to assure that probation officers are conscientious about what information is included in the PSI and relied on for recommendations.

Thus, in Canada and many jurisdictions in the United States, the PSI report is now available to defense counsel and the defendant (with the exception of any information that the sources were promised would be kept confidential or which would endanger other persons). Since its recommendation may well influence the future freedom of the person involved, there is considerable movement in the United States toward stripping the report of its confidentiality.

**Contents of PSI Reports.**   The format of the PSI report generally starts with the standard identifying information—the offender's name, birth date, offense, date of arrest and conviction, race, sex, and similar information. Most PSIs then address the facts surrounding the offense, including both the offender's version and the official version. The extent to which these agree or conflict may reflect

[65]Merlin Lewis, Warren Bundy, and James L. Hague, *An Introduction to the Courts and Judicial Process* (Englewood Cliffs, NJ: Prentice Hall, 1978) pp. 221–22.
[66]Ibid., p. 222.

the defendant's attitude or could be viewed as a measure of one's contact with reality. A brief social history usually follows, including significant family members, education, employment history, and general behavior patterns in terms of work habits and leisure pursuits.

A criminal history section encompasses any previous contacts with the juvenile justice system, the police, and adult courts. This information presents the individual's record as developed from the FBI's National Crime Information Center, which documents each time a person has been fingerprinted after an arrest.

An assessment of community attitudes toward the offender is generally provided, particularly if there is some doubt about how society would react to a noninstitutional alternative. Whether the offender would be accepted in the community on probation or should be placed in secure confinement because of public outcry is a consideration of the justice process in a democratic society. In addition, for those offenders denied probation, a record of the intensity of community attitudes might be used in future planning when parole from prison is being debated.

The closing paragraph of the presentence investigation report contains a rough diagnosis of the problem—for example, whether it is a result of chemical addition, poor family relationships, gang involvement, or whatever. In this section the probation officer outlines what are believed to be the significant factors contributing to the crime. An assessment of the strengths available within the family, the individual, the community, or elsewhere is also included, along with any prescriptions for developing a treatment plan.

In the last section of the PSI, a recommendation as to the suggested disposition is usually made to the judge. In making this recommendation, it appears that relatively few items actually enter into the decision-making process. In terms of the basis on which they recommend probation or imprisonment, one study of probation officers found that only the offense and prior record were consistently cited as taken into consideration.[67] (The defendant's statement, attitude, family history, psychological/psychiatric diagnosis, and age were also mentioned by a majority of those surveyed, but minimal consideration of other factors was reported.)

If previous criminal history indicates that stronger controls provided by prison or jail are required, an institutional sentence will be recommended. In other cases, intense community attitudes hostile to the offender may prevent an otherwise eligible person from being placed on probation. Sometimes the probation officer's caseload is already too heavy to work with another offender. On the other hand, the state prison may be so crowded that officers feel pressured to recommend probation for all but the most obviously unfit. But often, the decision is simply based on whether probation officers believe they can effectively work with the offender in the community. In the final analysis, there are no truly objective criteria for suggesting probation.

Whatever the recommendation, presentence investigation reports have been significant in the sentencing process, since judges have tended to follow

[67]Robert M. Carter, "The Presentence Report and the Decision Making Process," *Journal of Crime and Delinquency* (July 1967), p. 205.

their recommendations. On the relatively rare occasions when a judge does not accept the recommendations of the probation officer, it may well be a matter of differences in perspective. For example, the probation officer may place heavier emphasis on the rehabilitative potential of the offender than on community attitudes. The judge, on the other hand, is generally an elected official, who may place more weight on the potential response of the community. In most cases, however, the judge accepts the recommendations of the probation officer.

An informative PSI report can also be extremely helpful for a long period of time in the correctional process. It can subsequently be used in the prison system, by parole decision makers, and by the supervising parole officer. It is therefore important that the information it contains be accurate and complete. An inadequate report can be a persistent impediment to dealing appropriately with the client's problems in terms of proper classification, treatment, and eventual release.

---

*LEARNING GOALS*

*Do you know:*

- *How the job functions of probation officers can create role conflict?*
- *The difference between "brokerage" and "casework" models of probation services?*
- *With what types of clients and under what circumstances probation is most successful?*
- *The two ways that a probationer can be released from supervision?*
- *The due process rights of probationers facing revocation?*
- *On what grounds certain conditions of probation have been overruled by the courts?*

---

## The Role of Probation Officers

As outlined in Figure 5.6, the probation officer's job involves elements of investigation, counseling, service coordination, and rule enforcement. In addition to developing the presentence investigation, probation officers are responsible for the supervision of clients on their caseload. Unfortunately, as a result of the extensive amount of time required to research and prepare thorough PSIs, the time available for client supervision is often less than is necessary to do this complex portion of the job effectively.

Probation supervision includes not only casework and counseling, employment assistance, and personal planning, but also enforcement of the rules and regulations that constitute the conditions of probation.[68] Thus, the role of probation officers involves both *support* and *surveillance*—a combination of social worker and

---

[68]See Charles L. Newman, "Concepts of Treatment in Probation and Parole Supervision," *Federal Probation*, Vol. 25 (March 1961), pp. 11–18; Robert M. Carter and Leslie T. Wilkens, eds., *Probation and Parole: Selected Readings* (New York: Wiley, 1970), pp. 279–89.

Investigation
    Presentence investigation reports
    Case documentation
    Violation reports

Counseling
    Initial interview
    Individual supervision
    Family counseling
    Personal counseling
    Financial planning

Service coordination
    Job training
    Educational opportunities
    Employment assistance
    Transportation
    Shelter and subsistence
    Treatment programs

Enforcement
    Probation violation
    Probation revocation recommendation
    Individual enforcement

**Figure 5.6** Major components of the probation officer's job.

law enforcer. The police department can provide surveillance to assure that rules are not being broken. But probation is designed to offer more in terms of casework, counseling, and community assistance. However, it is difficult for one person to fulfill such demands equally effectively. For example, an officer who becomes overly empathetic toward the offender's problems and devotes considerable effort to help resolve them might well be tempted to "look the other way" in the face of minor rule violations. On the other hand, strict rule-enforcing officers may be less inclined to offer much assistance, perhaps even waiting for a chance to "catch" the offender "messing up." Balancing these two contradictory expectations is a challenging task that can lead to *role conflict* for probation officers.

It is for this reason that a "team concept" has been advocated, with services as well as surveillance provided by teams of officers, each specializing in a particular aspect of the probation function.[69] For a look at how such a team approach works, see the next "Close-up on Corrections." Although most probation agencies are not organized around specialized teams of officers, some do separate responsibility for client supervision from presentence investigation. This enables certain officers to prepare PSI reports exclusively, whereas others deal only with the supervision of probationers.

**Supervision of Probationers.** Regardless of how the task is organized administratively, supervising probationers must be done on the basis of mutual trust,

[69]See Walter L. Barkdull, "Probation: Call It Control—and Mean It," in Lawrence F. Travis, Martin D. Schwartz, and Todd R. Clear, eds. *Corrections: An Issues Approach,* Second Edition (Cincinnati, OH: Anderson Publishing Company, 1980), pp. 154–55.

The Team Concept in Probation

[B]ecause of the complexities involved, [there is] an argument for the team concept of supervision. One officer or aide may specialize in surveillance. Working closely with local law enforcement units, [this officer] can determine whether the probationer is living where he says he does, working where he is supposed to (and regularly), how he spends his leisure hours and with whom, and whether he's out at odd hours, if he's drinking, and in some instances, whether he's taking . . . required medication. This officer can also administer anti-narcotic examinations and tests in appropriate cases, [and] also ought to have a pretty good idea where to find the client if he goes AWOL. . . .

Another team officer may specialize in finding employment or other placement, continuing education or job training; helping the client get necessary licenses [or] credit; locating housing; and providing any necessary temporary assistance. . . .

Still a third officer may provide help with marital or family problems, counseling to help the client deal with everyday adversities, and other highly-professional casework services. One thing to keep in mind is that one officer has got to be in charge, or no one will be responsible for the probationer's behavior.

*Source:* Walter L. Barkdull, "Probation: Call It Control—and Mean It," in Lawrence F. Travis, Martin D. Schwartz, and Todd R. Clear, eds., *Corrections: An Issues Approach,* Second Edition (Cincinnati, OH: Anderson Publishing Company, 1983), pp. 154–55.

cooperation, and responsibility between the officer and the client. The probation staff must find the proper balance between control and treatment that best meets the needs of the offender. This balance may well shift over time—initially emphasizing greater control, which can be reduced gradually as the probationer responds favorably. However, the most important objectives are to help clients understand themselves, gain independence, and ultimately, control their own behavior. There are several guiding principles for achieving this:

- Change comes from within the person; therefore, a probationer must be an active participant in any treatment program.
- The needs, problems, capacities, and limitations of the individual must be considered in planning a program.
- Legally binding conditions of probation are essential and in the best interests of the offender and the community.
- The goal of supervision is to help offenders understand their own problems and deal adequately with them.[70]

[70]*Manual of Correctional Standards* (Laurel, MD: American Correctional Association, 1966), p. 107.

Personal counseling for the offender is particularly important in cases of alcoholism, drug addiction, mental illness, or similar problems. The need to involve family members in supervising the probationer is likewise indisputable. An interested family offers the social ties that assist in providing necessary controls. On occasion, the probationer simply needs security or the implied presence of a supporting authority figure.

Employment counseling and assistance in finding jobs are major portions of the probation officer's supervisory work. Locating a job is a significant challenge, especially for clients who do not have good work habits or prior employment records. Probation officers must use the resources of the community skillfully in the process of job placement.

In fact, it is essential for probation staff to be knowledgeable about and take maximum advantage of all resources available in the community. Various employment services, treatment programs, family counseling services, welfare agencies, guidance clinics, mental health facilities, and social work services are all of potential auxiliary help. This reflects what has been called the *brokerage* or *resource management approach*—where the "supervising officer is not concerned primarily with understanding or changing the behavior of the offender, but rather, with assessing the concrete needs of the individual" and arranging for the receipt of "services which directly address those needs."[71]

In contrast, a *clinical, casework approach* focuses more on diagnosis and treatment, toward the goal of changing the offender's law-violating behavior. Based on the original philosophy and humanitarian efforts of John Augustus, the casework method shaped the delivery of probation services for many years. Informal counseling skills are still used by the probation officer in day-to-day work. But in terms of more formal or long-term counseling, most officers are too burdened by heavy caseloads and paperwork to do more than immediate crisis intervention. Moreover, while clients may benefit equally from linking their needs with community resources, there is often a tendency to undervalue the practical services delivered by the officer in favor of more "therapeutic" casework. In fact, some would maintain that the authoritative setting of probation is inappropriate to the practice of casework techniques, which again raises the issue discussed earlier of separating probationary functions through teamwork. (For a summary of the differences between casework and brokerage/resource management models of probation, see Figure 5.7.)

**Assessing Effectiveness.**  The effectiveness of probation can be evaluated from two perspectives—the quality of services provided by staff and the success rates of their clientele. Measuring the diverse services rendered by a probation department is a challenging task. Presentence investigation reports are tangible—they can be read and evaluated. Constructively improving their quality is usually not a difficult task. But casework, treatment, and community coordination are much less tangible and therefore more difficult to evaluate. Supervising these functions

[71]Edward J. Latessa, "Community Supervision: Research, Trends, and Innovations," in Travis et al., p. 163. See also Paul F. Cromwell et al., *Probation and Parole in the Criminal Justice System* (St. Paul, MN: West Publishing Company, 1985), pp. 109–10.

|  | Brokerage | Casework |
|---|---|---|
| Goal | (Re)integration | Rehabilitation |
| Focus | Practical services | Treatment assistance |
| Approach | Addressing specific, immediate ("survival") needs of the client | Diagnosing/treating problems causing the client's behavioral difficulties |
| Method | Linking needs of clients with available resources in the community (e.g., training, education, employment, health care) | Clinical, therapeutic services (e.g., counseling, group work, other psychiatric, psychological, or social work techniques) |
| Role of the officer | Coordinating community resources | Establishing a one-on-one relationship with the client |
| Skills needed | Administrative, organizational, managerial | Counseling, treatment, casework |
| Relationship to clients | Advocate | Counselor |

**Figure 5.7** Brokerage (resource management) and casework models of probation.

involves reading the progress reports of the cases handled to get a general factual background of what is happening, along with professional conferences with each probation officer concerning the use of appropriate techniques (although what is considered "appropriate" is in itself a personal value judgment). In the absence of more objective criteria, observing the success or failure of clients over a period of time has been one method used to evaluate the officer's work, assuming that difficult cases are relatively uniformly distributed among the staff.

But personnel cannot be held responsible for the nature of clients assigned to their caseload. In that regard, it has been found that those with several prior felony convictions are "less successful on probation than other offenders."[72] Of felons assigned to probation, 43% were rearrested for another felony violation within three years of sentencing in one national study.[73] Similarly, research indicates that the percentage of revocations varies directly with predicted risk—ranging from a revocation rate of 3% for *low-risk* clients to 37% in the *high-risk* category.[74] Given such data, it is not surprising to find one researcher noting that "probation officials are under fire to explain why they have not been able to curb the criminal behavior of the felons placed under their care. [Yet], our study shows that they do not lack either commitment or energy. Rather their efforts are hampered by inadequate resources and the lack

[72]McCarthy and McCarthy, p. 120.

[73]Patrick A. Langan and Mark A. Cuniff, "Recidivism of Felons on Probation, 1986–1989," *Bureau of Justice Statistics Special Report* (Washington, DC: U.S. Department of Justice, 1992), p. 1.

[74]S. Christopher Baird, "Probation and Parole Classification: The Wisconsin Model," *Corrections Today*, Vol. 43, No. 3 (May/June 1981), p. 38.

of a clear mandate that would help them make the best use of the resources they have."[75]

Along with the need for more definitive direction, appropriately matching styles and capabilities of probation officers with the personalities and needs of clients may well contribute to both better job performance and improved success. Studies have shown that probation can produce impressive results and a positive impact, particularly when the offender's problem is well defined and the intervention strategy is directly related to the offender's criminal behavior.[76]

**Rule Enforcement and Investigation.** In addition to their counseling and supportive functions, probation officers are authority figures responsible for ensuring that the offender complies with the conditions established when the judge awarded probation. Probation is a privilege, not a right. Violation of the conditions required to maintain that privilege can result in its revocation. In other words, what the courts giveth, the courts can taketh away. As mentioned previously, a suspended sentence is often issued along with the probation, and upon revocation, it is common practice for the judge to order the original sentence to be carried out.

It is the probation officer's function to determine that whatever restrictions and mandates the court required are, in fact, being upheld. In this respect, the officer's *implied presence* is sometimes more influential than actual supervision. Implied presence is the implication that the officer could appear at any time, thereby subtly restraining behavior and discouraging rule violation. Conversely, it also means that the client has supportive authority available. Thus, it is helpful in either respect.

Along with rule enforcement, the investigation and information-gathering role of probation officers cannot be overlooked. It is important to know what relationships are being developed and discarded. For example, a client breaking contact with employment and family can signal the beginning of a deteriorating social relationship. Ultimately, it may mean that the person should be incarcerated for a short time, or in extreme cases, that probation should be revoked.

**Discharge and Revocation.** There are two ways in which a probationer can be released from supervision: through *discharge* or *revocation*. Discharge generally means that the client has successfully completed the period of probation to which he or she was sentenced. However, some jurisdictions have developed the practice of discharging persons "not amenable to probation" rather than sending them to prison, which is somewhat similar to the difference between a "dishonorable" and an "undesirable" discharge from the military services. In case of a subsequent conviction, those discharged as "not amenable" are not again placed on probation in that jurisdiction. In contrast, revocation means that the privilege of probation has been withdrawn and that another disposition must be made of the case, such as incarceration.

After the period of probation has expired, the officer can recommend discharge, which (like PSI recommendations) the court must then act upon. Sometimes

[75]Joan Petersilia, "Probation Can Work" in Bonnie Szumski, ed., *America's Prisons: Opposing Viewpoints,* Fourth Edition (St. Paul, MN: Greenhaven Press, 1985), p. 117.
[76]McCarthy and McCarthy, p. 120, citing Harry Allen, Eric Carlson, and Evalyn Parks, *Critical Issues in Adult Probation: Summary* (Washington, DC: National Institute of Law Enforcement and Criminal Justice, 1979), pp. 37, 144-59, as well as several other studies.

the client is considered a good risk for discharge prior to official expiration of the probation term, which is within the discretion of the judge to do. On the other hand, an extension could be made for certain minor violations, thereby requiring the offender to complete a longer term under supervision than was originally imposed.

Generally, there are two reasons for recommending probation revocation: commission of a new crime, or a *technical violation* of the rules. In most jurisdictions, revocation is relatively automatic with the commission of another offense, although there may be limited exceptions in minor cases. Technical violations involve breaking one or more of the conditions of probation. Whatever the general and specific conditions are for a particular person, violation of them can result in a recommendation of revocation by the probation officer. In practice, the enthusiasm with which officers enforce these regulations varies considerably, as mentioned earlier in the discussion of role conflicts surrounding this occupation. However, it is a rare officer who will overlook very many technical violations before taking action.

But that does not mean that probation will automatically be terminated upon the officer's recommendation. In recent years, both probationers and parolees facing revocation have been extended a number of due process rights, among them, a formal hearing. The revocation hearing is usually held in the courtroom or judge's chambers. The judge and the probationer hear the probation officer's recommendation for revocation (based on detailed information in the violation report), and the judge makes a decision. In 1967, the U.S. Supreme Court determined in the *Mempa v. Rhay* case[77] that the probationer is entitled to representation by an attorney. With this ruling, the court began to emphasize the revocation process as a "critical phase" in the justice system, which falls within the due process protections of the 14th Amendment. The criticality of the hearing, of course, refers to the fact that, potentially, it involves the loss of liberty, since having one's probation revoked may well result in a jail or prison sentence.

Due process protections were extended further in the 1973 *Gagnon v. Scarpelli*[78] case, which initiated a two-stage hearing process. In addition to the actual revocation hearing, this case established a *preliminary hearing,* in order to determine whether there is probable cause to revoke probation (similar to the function of a preliminary hearing when the defendant is originally accused of a crime). At both the preliminary hearing and subsequent revocation hearing, this case also provided the probationer with certain minimum due process rights, including:

- Prior notice of the hearing.
- Written notice of the alleged violation.
- The right to:
  —Be present at the hearing
  —Present evidence and witnesses
  —Be judged before a neutral and detached official.

But despite these protections, just as disparities occur in sentencing, they also appear in probation revocation. Petty or unrealistic conditions invite viola-

---

[77]*Mempa v. Rhay*, 389 U.S. 128 (1967).
[78]*Gagnon v. Scarpelli*, 411 U.S. 778 (1973).

tions, which do not necessarily reflect poor probation adjustment. In some cases, revocations have been overly routine, rather than being tempered by the use of discretion and judgment. It is in such instances that appellate courts have begun to intervene, particularly when the conditions established do not specifically address the needs of the client. For example, consider the following California case involving a female convicted of robbery, who

> was ordered as a condition of probation not to become pregnant until she was married. After she violated this condition, she was sent to prison. But the revocation of probation was overturned by the appellate court, which then prohibited trial court judges from imposing conditions for probation that have *no relationship to the offender's original crime,* that relate to conduct that is *not in itself criminal,* or that forbid conduct *not reasonably related to future criminal conduct* by the offender[79] [emphasis added].

On the other hand, some rather unusual conditions have been upheld when they related directly to the client's offense. Examples include "requiring a rapist to undergo a vasectomy, forbidding a bookie to have a telephone in his home, . . . and forbidding a person convicted for offenses arising out of an antiwar demonstration from participating in future demonstrations."[80] In essence, the courts are apparently overruling conditions that are irrelevant to the case while upholding those that have a direct bearing on the original conviction.

Even the general conditions of probation have been subject to challenge, especially when they are vague or ambiguous. How, for instance, does one objectively determine whether the client is "cooperating" with the probation officer? How strictly should "regular church attendance" be enforced? What about the client who lives on a state border and "travels out of state" to seek employment in the nearest city, which happens to be across the state line? When such questions are raised, they can provide the basis for legal challenges regarding fairness and practicality, as well as denial of due process, since the conditions are not necessarily related to the offender's circumstances.[81] In response, the courts have tended to dismiss the enforcement of conditions that "are unreasonable," "endanger the offender's welfare," or prohibit the client from "engaging in an innocuous activity."[82] Thus, it appears that the courts are agreeing that revocation and imprisonment should not be for punishment or arbitrary reasons, but rather, for a constructive purpose.[83]

---

[79]Holten and Lamar, p. 304, citing Hazel B. Kerper and Jansen Kerper, *Legal Rights of the Convicted* (St. Paul, MN: West Publishing Company, 1974), p. 250.

[80]Ibid., citing Kerper and Kerper, p. 257.

[81]"Serve or Surveil?" in Travis et al., p. 119.

[82]David A. Jones, *The Law of Criminal Procedure: An Analysis and Critique* (Boston: Little, Brown, 1981), p. 540.

[83]Eugene C. DiCerbo, "When Should Probation Be Revoked?" *Federal Probation,* Vol. 30, No. 2 (June 1966), pp. 11–16.

LEARNING GOALS

*Do you know:*

- *How classification helps probation officers manage large caseloads?*
- *The difference between "traditional" and "intensive supervision" probation?*
- *What a probation subsidy is and how it works?*
- *The purpose and limitations of "shock" probation?*

## Probation Caseloads

One of the primary difficulties in the field of probation is heavy caseloads. In some places the situation has deteriorated to the extent that officers have so many people on their caseloads that they cannot keep their files in alphabetical order, much less provide necessary services. The average size of caseloads in 1989 was over 120, ranging from a low of 31 in Washington, DC, to a high of 346 in North Dakota.[84] These figures are likely to be even higher today. With caseloads of "100–200 in many urban areas, close supervision and helping services are too often the exception" rather than the rule.[85] Such heavy workloads, combined with unrealistic expectations of continual surveillance, can result in focusing the efforts of probation more on "reactive supervision"[86] than on proactive support.

**Classification.** One of the ways that strained probation staffs are attempting to cope with ever-increasing caseloads in the absence of accompanying fiscal increases is through classifying cases according to the level of supervision needed.

Clients vary in terms of the number and types of contacts that they should have because of such factors as the nature of their offense, their prior record, the variety and intensity of their problems, and the potential risk they pose. Classification recognizes these distinctions, providing differing levels of services according to the requirements of the client. For example:

- Wisconsin introduced a system ranging from "maximum, medium, or minimum" to "mail-in" supervision.[87]
- Hamilton County, Ohio, has experimented with an "intake screening tool" which enables low-risk cases (representing 40% of the total), to be diverted into "non-reporting probation status."[88]

[84]Compiled from figures presented in *Sourcebook of Criminal Justice Statistics—1991* (Washington, DC: U.S. Department of Justice, 1992), pp. 97–98. (However, it should be noted that statistics for seven states were missing from this survey, including one of the most populated—New York.)

[85]Norval Morris and Michael Tonry, "Between Prison and Probation—Intermediate Punishments in a Rational Sentencing System," *National Institute of Justice Reports* (January/February 1990), p. 8.

[86]Donald Cochrane, "Corrections' Catch 22," *Corrections Today*, Vol. 51, No. 6 (October 1989), p. 16.

[87]Callison, p. 104.

[88]Nora Harlow and E. Kim Nelson, "Probation's Responses to Fiscal Restraints," in Duffee and McGarrell, p. 170.

- Connecticut developed a three-level system that separates those who can be supervised by "telephone and written correspondence" from those who either need surveillance or are more amenable to change. To reduce role conflict, officers' caseloads are generally composed exclusively of either the cases identified for surveillance or those classified as capable of being helped. In fact, the director of adult probation in Connecticut has noted that "there is no way that we could continue to be described as a service-providing agency . . . concerned with protecting the community if we did not have this system. We have had no new positions assigned to this agency by the legislature since 1977, and the caseload since that time has increased by 6,500 cases."[89]

In addition to obviously providing some relief in the face of budgetary shortages, efficiency and productivity are improved with better caseload management resulting from such classification procedures. Although there is no direct evidence to prove that lower caseloads reduce recidivism, the amount of time in supervision does appear to have a positive effect, along with how that time was spent (i.e., on surveillance that would increase technical violations, or counseling that would improve adjustment).[90] Workload reduction alone is not sufficient to achieve maximum effectiveness unless there is a commitment to specific treatment programs. But it is apparent that officers laboring under excessively high caseloads simply cannot provide the necessary time and attention to deserving clients.

**Intensive Supervision Probation.**   Many of the first efforts designed to classify and manage probation caseloads actually contained early versions of what has now become known as *intensive supervision probation* (ISP). Florida, for instance, passed legislation in 1983 to slow down prison admissions through "community control"—a "punishment-oriented program of intensive supervision" that combines home confinement with strong surveillance.[91]

Today, ISP programs have become recognized as a "response to pressures created by a demand for incarceration which exceeds prison capacity.[92] (Figure 5.8 illustrates where intensive probation fits into the range of sentencing options.) Public policy toward crime has become increasingly punitive without accompanying expansion of prison space. The need has therefore emerged for another type of intermediate sanction—something stronger than traditional probation but not as harsh as incarceration. For selected offenders, the solution has come in the form of more intensively supervised probation, which is designed to:

- Provide a cost-effective community option for offenders who would otherwise be incarcerated.

---

[89]Ibid., p. 169.

[90]M. G. Neithercutt and D. M. Gottfredson, *Case Load Size Variation and Differences in Probation/Parole Performance* (Pittsburgh, PA: National Center for Juvenile Justice, 1974).

[91]Harry T. Dodd, "Florida's Experience with Electronic Monitoring," in *Intermediate Punishment: Community-Based Sanctions*, p. 41.

[92]Bureau of Justice Assistance, *Intensive Supervision Probation and Parole (ISP): Program Brief* (Washington, DC: U.S. Department of Justice, 1988), p. 7.

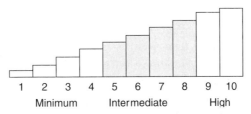

**Figure 5.8** Range of sentencing options (from minimum to high levels of punishment). 1. Restitution; 2. fine (plus restitution); 3. community service; 4. active probation; 5. intensive probation; 6. house arrest; 7. residential community corrections; 8. split sentence; 9. jail; 10. prison. *Source*: James M. Byrne, "The Future of Intensive Probation Supervision and the New Intermediate Sanctions," *Crime and Delinquency*, Vol. 36, No. 1 (1990), p. 39.

- Administer sanctions appropriate to the offense.
- Promote public safety by providing surveillance and risk control strategies.
- Increase the availability of treatment resources to meet offender needs.
- Promote a crime-free lifestyle by requiring ISP offenders to be employed, perform community service, make restitution, and remain substance-free.[93]

To meet these objectives, ISP programs differ from more traditional probation in a number of respects. As its name implies, ISP requires a more intense level of supervision, which is achieved through such measures as:

- Manageable caseloads.
- Frequent face-to-face contacts.
- Home confinement and electronic monitoring.
- Regular visits to the client's home and workplace.
- Verification of treatment program participation.
- Drug and alcohol screening.
- Clear revocation guidelines that are consistently administered.

In addition, those on ISP may also be required to make restitution payments, perform some type of community service, and pay supervision fees. See the next "Close-up on Corrections" for an inside view of how one ISP program operates.

Although ISP is relatively recent, studies of programs operating in Georgia, New York, Texas, and New Jersey have been quite positive, indicating lower recidivism rates for serious crimes, high rates of successful completion, and greater cost-effectiveness.[94]

[93]Ibid., p. 9.
[94]Ibid., pp. 17–20. See also Frank S. Pearson, "Evaluation of New Jersey's Intensive Supervision Program," *Crime and Delinquency*, Vol. 34, No. 4 (1988), pp. 437–48.

### Intensive Supervision Probation (ISP): The Georgia Experience

In Georgia, the target group for ISP was defined as the nonviolent yet serious offender who—without the ISP option—would be sentenced to prison. . . .

Georgia's program is tough relative to regular probation, as well as other ISP programs. It keeps the offender under curfew, employed, drug- and alcohol-free, and performing community services while under close surveillance. Standards call for:

- Five face-to-face contacts per week . . . ;
- Mandatory curfew;
- Mandatory employment;
- Weekly check of local arrest records . . . ;
- Routine drug and alcohol screens.

These standards are enforced by a team consisting of a probation officer and a surveillance officer assigned to a caseload of 25 clients. . . . The design places the probation officer in charge of case management, treatment and counseling services, and court-related activities. Surveillance officers, usually from lawenforcement or correctional officer backgrounds, are given primary responsibility for:

- Home visits at frequent and unannounced intervals;
- Checking curfews;
- Performing drug and alcohol screens . . . ;
- Weekly checks of arrest records.

In actual practice, the surveillance officer gets to know the family and becomes keenly aware of the home situation. Both officer types report a great deal of overlap in their roles. An interesting discovery is the fact that it is almost impossible to separate the treatment and surveillance functions.

*Source:* Bureau of Justice Assistance, *Intensive Supervision, Probation and Parole (ISP)* (Washington, DC: U.S. Department of Justice, 1988), p. 17.

However, ISP programs have also been noted for often limiting participation to low-risk, property offenders[95]—thus potentially inflating their success rate. In fact, research indicates that "offender selection is one of the most problematic areas of ISP."[96] When ISP becomes a form of net widening, many of its

[95]See, for example, Todd R. Clear and Patricia L. Hardyman, "The New Intensive Supervision Movement," *Crime and Delinquency,* Vol. 36, No. 1 (1990), p. 49, who maintain that "there are almost certainly numerous persons on regular probation who represent a considerably higher public safety problem than the ISP client."

[96]Betsy Fulton and Susan Stone, "Evaluating the Effectiveness of Intensive Supervision," *Corrections Today,* Vol. 54, No. 8 (December 1992), p. 82.

objectives are defeated. It has also been noted that when recidivism does occur, it is not necessarily a reflection of the fact that the public is not being protected. Given the stringent conditions of ISP, there is more opportunity for technical violations to occur. In that respect it has been argued that removing offenders from the streets because of technical violations precludes further criminal behavior, thereby enhancing public safety.[97]

On the other hand, ISP's heavy emphasis on surveillance functions might be generating an underestimate of its potential if the proper clients were selected and focus on treatment was expanded. This issue was addressed in a study examining ISP programs for serious offenders with prior records at three locations in California. The results revealed that at all sites, offenders who participated in treatment programs had lower recidivism rates than those who did not, and it was concluded that ISP provided "a useful intermediate sanction between prison and routine probation."[98] Others agree that although ISP should be continued, its emphasis should shift from "exclusive incapacitative and punitive measures to a more integrated approach," since the current conditions of ISP provide short-range crime control, "while rehabilitation has been associated with long-term behavioral change."[99]

**Defraying the Costs of Probation.** The personalized aspects of ISP make it more costly than traditional probation.[100] But both are obviously less expensive than incarceration. Additionally, as we saw earlier, some states are making efforts to get probationers more involved in subsidizing their own supervision in order to offset some of the expense. By 1991, offenders in 28 states were being charged probation supervision fees averaging between $10 and $30 per month (although probationers in Louisiana paid as much as $100).[101] Such fees can have a major impact on agency staffing and services. For example: "The Travis County [Texas] Adult Probation Department faced a severe budget shortfall. . . . In order to balance their budget, they terminated a large percent of the probation staff. Caseloads for remaining staff tripled to more than 300. The Department launched an aggressive program to increase fee collection, and later was able to re-fill most of those positions, in large measure due to their success in raising fee revenues."[102]

Taxpayers applaud such efforts, and they also assist with teaching offenders a measure of personal responsibility. But this practice has caused problems with collecting the fees, as well as dilemmas concerning whether to revoke pro-

---

[97]Ibid., citing Barry Nidorf.

[98]Joan Petersilia and Susan Turner,"Objectively Evaluating ISPs," *Corrections Today*, Vol. 53, No. 3 (June 1991), p. 28.

[99]Fulton and Stone, p. 85.

[100]Ibid. In the California study, estimated program and court costs for ISP averaged $7240 to $8902, compared with $4923 to $7123 for routine probation.

[101]"Probation and Parole Fee Programs Surveyed," *On the Line*, Vol. 15, No. 1 (January 1992), American Correctional Association), p. 5. See also Christopher Baird, Douglas Holien and Audrey Bakke, *Fees for Probation Services* (Madison, WI: National Council on Crime and Delinquency, 1986); Gerald Wheeler, Therese Macan, Rodney Hissong, and Morgan Slusher, "The Effects of Probation Service Fees on Case Management Strategy and Sanctions," *Journal of Criminal Justice*, Vol. 17, No. 1 (1989), pp. 15–24.

[102]Dale Parent, *Recovering Correctional Costs through Offender Fees* (Washington, DC: U.S. Department of Justice, 1990), p. 21.

bation for nonpayment. Depending on the circumstances involved, the courts may or may not uphold revocation for nonpayment. If, for example, the offender is indigent, it is not likely that revocation would be upheld, based on the *Bearden v. Georgia* case, in which the Supreme Court ruled that probation could not be revoked when an indigent client had not paid fines or made restitution.[103]

Other efforts to reduce expenses as well as workloads in probation departments have included the use of volunteers and paraprofessional aides. Los Angeles, for example, developed a program called VISTO—Volunteers in Service to Offenders—to assist with client supervision. In one year alone, citizens contributed over 37,000 hours of service, providing everything from job placement and temporary housing to tutorial assistance, remedial education, transportation, and baby-sitting.[104] Other successful programs have been reported in Michigan as well as Philadelphia, where carefully screened female volunteers have assisted with the supervision of delinquent girls.[105] A number of jurisdictions are also using volunteers to counsel, tutor, and serve as big brothers or big sisters to juvenile probationers.[106] Aides and student interns can likewise perform semiprofessional work and many routine administrative duties, freeing the probation officer from some of the seemingly endless reams of paperwork associated with the job.[107]

A rather unique approach to defraying the costs of probation is the concept of a *probation subsidy*, in which the state provides financial payment to a county for *not* increasing the number of defendants committed to state correctional institutions. These funds, which would otherwise have gone to support offenders in prison, can then be used to subsidize probation services. Under this arrangement, both the county and the state benefit. While the county obtains additional funds needed to finance probation, the state is still paying far less than it would have for incarceration. For a description of how probation subsidy has operated in California (which originated the program in 1965), along with related advantages as well as drawbacks, see the next "Close-up on Corrections."

**Shock Probation.**   In contrast to probation subsidies that provide an economic incentive for keeping offenders out of prison, *shock probation* combines a brief exposure to incarceration with subsequent release on probation. The idea is that the "shock" of a short stay in prison will make such an indelible impression that offenders will be deterred from future crime. With shock probation, the negative effects of lengthy imprisonment can be avoided, while still giving the offender a "taste" of institutional life, and still maintaining postrelease control through pro-

---

[103]*Bearden v. Georgia*, 461 U.S. 660 (1983).

[104]Philip Stein, "I'm Only One Person—What Can I Do?" *Federal Probation*, Vol. 34, No. 2 (June 1970), pp. 7–11.

[105]Cromwell et al., p. 198.

[106]John T. Whitehead and Steven P. Lab, *Juvenile Justice: An Introduction* (Cincinnati, OH: Anderson Publishing Company, 1990), p. 387.

[107]Donald E. Loughery, Jr., "Innovations in Probation Management," *Crime and Delinquency*, Vol. 15, No. 2 (April 1969), pp. 247–58.

### California's Probation Subsidy Program

[If a county] sent 100 offenders to prison annually (on average over the past five years), the norm for this county would be set at 100. In future years, for every offender under 100 sent to prison from this county, local officials would receive approximately $4,000 from state funds, to be spent to assist the people in the community. For instance, if ten less persons were sent to prison from this county in a given year, the county would receive $40,000 for community crime control efforts. In turn, the state would save about $80,000, for if these ten had gone to prison, the annual cost would come to roughly $120,000 or $12,000 per inmate.

This type of subsidy program builds economic incentives for judges and other county officials to retain offenders in the community. However, the California subsidy program had a flaw. While the money returned to the counties was to go solely to development of probation services, the retaining of inmates in the community put strains on other resources, including the police and local jails. It would have been better and much more effective if the monies returned to the county had been apportioned among all agencies in the local criminal justice system to better enable them to absorb these offenders.

*Source:* Donald J. Newman, "A Critique of Prison Building," in Lawrence F. Travis, Martin D. Schwartz, and Todd R. Clear, *Corrections: An Issues Approach,* Second Edition (Cincinnati, OH: Anderson Publishing Company, 1983), p. 92.

bation supervision.[108] The advantages of probation are therefore combined with the use of an institution.

Although Ohio was the first state to experiment with shock probation as early as 1965, only a handful of states (about 16) have enacted such programs in the years since it was originated. Reluctance to embrace this approach may be based on concern that "*any* institutional stay interferes with therapeutic efforts," and even limited prison exposure can produce negative attitudes and promote resentment.[109] In fact, such a detrimental effect has been suggested in some of the research on shock probation. For example, one study focusing on the length of incarceration reported that those spending 3 months in prison were as likely to recidivate as those serving 7 to 12 months.[110] On the other hand, it was found that offenders confined for 30 days or less had a lower reincarceration rate than those serving more than 30 days.[111] Such findings have resulted in the conclusion that

---

[108]Diane Vaughan, "Shock Probation and Shock Parole: The Impact of Changing Correctional Ideology," in David M. Petersen and Charles W. Thomas, eds., *Corrections: Problems and Prospects,* Second Edition (Englewood Cliffs, NJ: Prentice Hall, 1980), p. 216.

[109]Ibid., p. 217.

[110]Joseph A. Waldron and Henry R. Angelino, "Shock Probation: A Natural Experiment on the Effect of a Short Period of Incarceration," *Prison Journal,* Vol. 57 (1977), pp. 45–52.

[111]G. F. Vito and H. E. Allen, "Shock Probation in Ohio: A Comparison of Outcomes," *International Journal of Offender Therapy and Comparative Criminology,* Vol. 3 (1978), pp. 123–32.

"the negative effects of exposure to prison begin to occur very quickly—much sooner than shock probation programs are designed to release offenders."[112]

Moreover, shock probation is not always implemented as originally intended. If the true value of "shock" is to be maximized, it is logical to presume that these programs would be reserved for first-time offenders, or at least those who have not previously served time. However, judges are not necessarily bound by shock probation guidelines. In one state, for instance, it has been noted that although the intent was to "deny shock probation to potentially violent and narcotics offenders . . . slightly more than one-third of those granted early release had committed offenses in these categories.[113] As might be expected, higher success rates have been reported among groups for which the program was intended—"young adults who commit non-violent probation-eligible offenses."[114] On the other hand, it may be that such offenders would have done equally well with standard probation. In short, studies of the effectiveness of shock probation "suggest great caution in exposing persons to confinement who can be safely supervised in the community."[115] As we will see in upcoming chapters on jails, prisons, and their effect on the inmate population, that is sound advice.

## ❖ SUMMARY

Community-based alternatives to incarceration were developed in an effort to deal more effectively with the offender's problems where they originated, to avoid breaking social ties, and to prevent exposure to the negative effects of secure confinement. As prison crowding provided additional incentives to retain offenders under community supervision, much of what had previously been called "community-based alternatives" became known as intermediate sanctions, reflecting more punitive attitudes and concerns that such programs assure the safety and protection of society.

Pretrial intervention represents the least intrusive community-based intervention, since it diverts the case out of the criminal justice system prior to adjudication. In addition to providing a "second chance," diversion avoids the stigma of a criminal record. It also takes advantage of resources available in the community and enhances the efficiency, flexibility, and cost-effectiveness of the criminal justice system. However, it has been criticized as, on the one hand, being too lenient, and on the other hand, entailing the potential for improper use of discretion through net widening.

One form of community-based supervision that has become popular in both pre- and postadjudication phases of the justice system is home confinement, which is often combined with electronic monitoring to assure compliance with curfew restrictions. Use of this alternative is increasing dramatically as an alternative to prison crowding, since it enables community-based treatment without compro-

[112]Wayne Logan, "Description of Shock Probation and Parole," in Dale G. Parent, *Shock Incarceration: An Overview of Existing Programs* (Washington, DC: U.S. Department of Justice, 1989), p. 53.
[113]Vaughan, p. 223.
[114]Logan, p. 52, citing P. C. Friday and D. M. Peterson, "Shock Probation: A New Approach to Crime Control," Ohio State University Program for the Study of Crime and Delinquency, 1973.
[115]Logan, p. 53.

mising public safety, at a cost considerably less than incarceration. But it has also raised questions with regard to net widening, and the intrusiveness of electronic monitoring has been especially vulnerable to the criticism that government is now invading one's private residence. At the same time, there are those who do not believe that home confinement is a sufficiently serious penalty, as well as those who fear that it discriminates against clients without financial resources.

While home confinement and electronic monitoring have been very recent developments, probation originated over 150 years ago with the work of John Augustus. It is now the most frequently used sentencing option. Since probationers are *convicted* offenders, they represent felons or misdemeanants, in contrast to the unconvicted status of those diverted through pretrial intervention. Probation is actually a conditional sentence, served under supervision in the community. In many cases it is combined with an institutional sentence that is suspended during the probationary period.

In determining whether to sentence someone to probation or incarceration, judges often rely on a presentence investigation report, which contains information on the offense and the offender's background, along with a recommended disposition. In addition to preparing such reports, the probation officer is responsible for supervising clients, which involves both support and surveillance functions. Officers vary in terms of their supervisory styles, with some focusing on casework/counseling, while others act more as "brokers," linking the needs of clients with resources in the community.

Probationers can be released from supervision either through discharge (successful completion) or by revoking probation and making another disposition of the case (usually incarceration). Those facing revocation have certain due process rights, including a two-stage hearing. Revocations involving technical violations have tended to be upheld by the courts if the conditions established were related directly to the offender's circumstances.

As probation officers struggle with high caseloads, efforts have begun to classify cases according to the level of supervision needed. For example, intensive supervision probation has emerged as a more punishment-oriented alternative to traditional probation. Sometimes combined with home confinement and electronic monitoring, ISP provides more frequent face-to-face contacts, regular home visits, verification of treatment, and consistently enforced rules. Shock probation combines a brief exposure to incarceration with subsequent release on probation.

Although community-based approaches are less expensive than correctional institutions, they are not without cost. To defray expenses, some jurisdictions assess fees, others use volunteers, and still others provide a probation subsidy from the state.

The alternatives described herein are among the varieties of programs that serve as intermediate sanctions between fines or community service and correctional institutions. They are becoming increasingly attractive as society continues to explore mechanisms for dealing with prison overflow, keeping costs in line with what taxpayers will support, and providing help to those who can remain in the community without endangering public safety. For those who cannot, there will always be prisons and jails—as explored in the next chapters on institutional corrections.

# chapter 6

# Jails: Pretrial Detention and Short-term Confinement

*[T]he "jail problem" is a complex collection of problems, including jurisdictional authority and responsibility, Constitutional rights, sociological and medical opinion, basic public safety, and perhaps most difficult, the allotment of increasingly scarce resources for the benefit of an exceedingly unpopular constituency."[1]*

*Advisory Commission on Intergovernmental Relations*

## ❖ CHAPTER OVERVIEW

Before society had police officers, judges, courts, or prisons, there were local jails. But because jails are the oldest component of the criminal justice system, they have also in many respects been the most neglected. Tracing their origins back to the absymal conditions and corrupt fee system of the English *gaols* described in Chapter 4, American jails have endured a legacy of insufficient funding, inappropriate facilities, idle inmates, inadequate staffing, and a public largely indifferent to it all.

Modern, reform-minded jail administrators have faced the extraordinary challenge of overcoming these historical obstacles and bringing today's jails into the twentieth century. It has not been an easy task, for despite how long they have been with us and how many people they incarcerate, jails are not highly visible. Listen to a news broadcast the next time a well-publicized case results in a jail sentence—you may well hear that the defendant will be spending "three months in prison" (a virtual impossibility). Nor are you likely to hear anything in the news about the many inmates in jail who have not even been convicted. And although the public has now become aware of prison crowding, how often do you hear of jail crowding?

Just as corrections is the least known function of the criminal justice system, jails represent the "silent majority" of the correctional system—"silent" because of their low profile; "majority" because they actually process more clients than any other correctional institutions. Although the average stay in jail

[1]*Jails: Intergovernmental Dimensions of a Local Problem* (Washington, DC: Advisory Commission on Intergovernmental Relations, 1984), pp. 5–6.

is much shorter than in prison, jails admit *20 times* more inmates than prisons.[2] Moreover, all jail inmates do not necessarily go on to prison, but practically all prison inmates have experienced time in jail.

Beyond their lack of visibility, jails must struggle with a role that has never been well defined. If society is uncertain about whether corrections should be a symbol of deterrence, a place of incapacitation, or a method of rehabilitation, the role of the jail is even more unclear. With a mixture of sentenced/unsentenced, convicted/unconvicted, and felon/misdemeanant populations, jails must balance multiple missions. Their functions range from the first stop for the police after making an arrest to the last resort for a community when no other resources exist to deal with the problem. As a result, anyone from homeless hitchhikers to homicide offenders can be found in jail.

But where challenges seem endless, the potential for change is equally limitless. With obstacles also come opportunities. Creative administrators have begun to seize these opportunities to make a positive impact on the status of the nation's jails. Particularly in major metropolitan areas, the dirty, dark, decrepit jails lingering from the past century have begun to be replaced by clean, well-lighted, modern facilities that no more resemble the traditional image of jails than today's computers resemble yesterday's typewriters. Under the "new generation" approach, jails are structured to produce a normal environment. They are secured by doors rather than bars. They are staffed by officers trained in direct supervision techniques. But most of all, they confirm that there is, indeed, hope on the horizon for turning jails from virtual dungeons into viable detention centers.

Admittedly, there is still a long way to go toward securing the public attention, funding, and support that jails need and deserve to fulfill their potential. The day may come when society realizes that more effectively dealing with those in jail may well reduce the demand for so many prisons. But until that time, there is reassurance in knowing that no matter what the future holds for jails, it will inevitably be an improvement on the past.

---

*LEARNING GOALS*

*Do you know:*

- *How many jails there are in the United States and why the number has been decreasing?*
- *The definition of a jail?*
- *How many U.S. jails are 100 years old or more?*
- *What size of facility makes up the majority of the nation's jails?*
- *In what size of jail the majority of inmates are confined?*
- *What problems are experienced by very small jails?*
- *What regional jail consolidation is and what impact it has had?*

---

[2]For example, in 1990, prisons admitted 474,128 inmates in comparison to the 10,064,927 admitted to jails. *Sourcebook of Criminal Justice Statistics—1991* (Washington, DC: U.S. Department of Justice, 1992), pp. 617, 638.

No one knows exactly how many jails operate in the United States. As surprising as this may seem, it relates to society's uncertainty about the function of jails. Because we do not agree on what jails should be *doing*, it is difficult to determine what types of facilities are performing whatever that role is. Definitions of what a jail is vary throughout the country, ranging from massive detention centers operating in large urban counties to small "lockups," "holdovers," or "drunk tanks" in police stations. In this chapter, the term *jail* will be limited to *locally administered confinement facilities that hold persons awaiting trial (for more than 48 hours) or those committed after adjudication, usually for sentences of a year or less.*[3]

Using that definition, there were 3316 jails in the United States during 1988.[4] As Figure 6.1 indicates, this actually represents a *decrease* over the previous ten-year period. Does that mean that fewer people are going to jail? No. Does it mean that there is less need for jails? No. Does it mean that many jails are not seriously crowded? No. The declining number of jails is not a reflection of jails being closed for lack of use. Rather, it reflects two trends: (1) the number of extremely old jails that are being phased out of service, and (2) the number of small jails that are being consolidated into large detention centers.

### Eliminating Old Jails

There is no doubt that antiquated, 100-year-old facilities must be replaced. The structures that were built in the past century, even if still physically sound (which most are not), simply do not meet the needs or address the goals of modern jail administration. However, there are still over 700 jails in the United States that are more than 50 years old, including 140 that are 100 years old or more.[5] Consider the fact that these jails were constructed prior to the turn of the century—before people rode in "horseless carriages" or had such "modern conveniences" as indoor plumbing, electricity, or air conditioning. Needless to say, such facilities have long outlived their usefulness. Nevertheless, they still confine over 12,000 inmates,[6] representing those who are innocent as well as guilty. The public certainly need not be concerned that these inmates are being "cod-

| Year | Number | Percent Change Since 1978 |
|------|--------|---------------------------|
| 1978 | 3,493  |                           |
| 1983 | 3,336  | − 4.5%                    |
| 1988 | 3,316  | − 5.1%                    |

**Figure 6.1**  Decreasing number of jails: 1978–1988. *Source:* Adapted from *Sourcebook of Criminal Justice Statistics—1990* (Washington, DC: U.S. Department of Justice, 1991), p. 582.

[3]Paraphrased from Allen J. Beck, "Profile of Jail Inmates, 1989," *Bureau of Justice Statistics Special Report* (April 1991), p. 2.
[4]*Sourcebook,* p. 612.
[5]*Sourcebook of Criminal Justice Statistics—1990* (Washington, DC: U.S. Department of Justice, 1991), p. 584.
[6]Ibid.

dled!" For several inside accounts of the deplorable conditions that have been experienced in aging jails, see the next "Close-up on Corrections."

### Accounting for the Jail Population

While phasing out such obsolete facilities is essential to correctional progress, another obstacle in the path of modernization is the *large number* of relatively *small jails*. As Figure 6.2 illustrates, facilities housing fewer than 50 inmates actually make up the majority (67%) of the nation's jails. There are some *2219* of these small jails, compared to only *51* large jails holding 1000 inmates or more. That might create the assumption that most of the people in jail are confined in small facilities. But they are not. Despite their dramatically fewer numbers, large jails actually account for more than double the number of inmates as small jails—96,054 are in jails of 1,000 or more, compared with only 40,004 in jails of 50 or less.[7] In other words, less than 2 percent of the nation's jails—the largest facilities—house more than a quarter of the total inmates (28%). As a result, there is one problem that small jails generally do not appear to have—crowding.

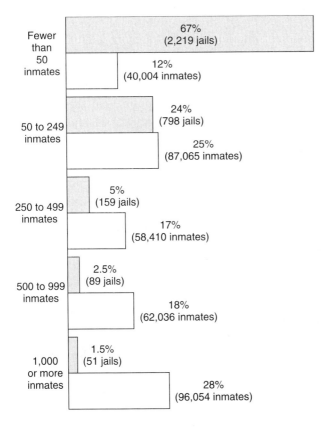

**Figure 6.2** Number of jails in the United States by size. *Source:* Adapted from *Sourcebook of Criminal Justice Statistics—1990* (Washington, DC: U.S. Department of Justice, 1991), pp. 580, 582.

[7]Ibid., p. 579.

### Conditions in Aging Jails

In some older facilities, cells are not equipped with either toilets or sinks. Still in existence in some jails is the "honey bucket" system wherein a bucket serves as a toilet. The plumbing is so antiquated in other[s] . . . that toilets may not flush or may occasionally back up. In these cases, persistent and unpleasant smells permeate the cells. . . . In many facilities, the lack of light gives a dark, dreary and depressing appearance. . . . Many . . . have antiquated ventilation and heating/cooling systems. While the jail is hot in the summer, it is inevitably cold in the winter. . . . A typical problem in aging facilities is plumbing that leaks water onto the floor. In a number of these facilities, overcrowding forces inmates to sleep on floors, and, consequently, in puddles of water.

*Source:* Linda L. Zupan, *Jails: Reform and the New Genration Philosophy* (Cincinnati, OH: Anderson Publishing Company, 1991), pp. 40–42.

Bobby Taylor, the young director of . . . Legal Aid collected his mail one morning in 1972 and spotted a strange, lumpy envelope. Tearing it open, he pulled out a twisted, dry piece of beef and a short note. "This is what we had for dinner today at the jail," it read. "See that green spot in the center? Guess what that is?" . . . Tossing the moldy piece of beef in the trash, he decided to investigate. What he saw at the jail shocked him. The building was overflowing with inmates. Dozens of them were packed in small, dungeon-like "tanks"; at least 30 slept without mattresses or blankets on the floor, sweltering in the hot, foul air. . . . Standing there listening, Taylor would shake first one leg, then the other, trying in vain to keep the cockroaches from crawling up his pants.

*Source:* Philip B. Taft, Jr., "Jail Litigation: Winning in Court Is Only Half the Battle," *Corrections Magazine*, Vol. IX, No. 3 (June 1983), p. 23.

Extensive cleaning is not possible in some old jails because the ironwork is rusted, the cement floors are broken, and the walls would disintegrate. Such jails are havens for rodents, body lice, and other vermin that can successfully survive sporadic attempts at extermination. . . . If cleanliness is next to godliness . . . [these] jails lie securely in the province of hell.

*Source:* Hans W. Mattick, "The Contemporary Jails of the United States: An Unknown and Neglected Area of Justice," in Daniel Glaser, ed., *Handbook of Criminology* (Chicago: Rand McNally, 1974), p. 802.

For the 85 inmates locked in cells on the eighth floor . . . the first few minutes after 5 a.m. were a hell some will never get the chance to comprehend. A yell of "Fire!" first shook them awake. Then their nostrils registered the stink of smoke. Sounds of panic overtook the floor. . . . Dense smoke made it impossible to see, but inmates heard the sound of breaking glass as men crowded in front of windows, fighting for air. . . . Only after firemen arrived was anyone on the eighth floor removed from his cell. . . . Seven occupants were found huddled together on the floor, dead of smoke inhalation and third-degree burns. . . . The jail, built in 1926, is not unlike many of the country's municipal and county jails . . . it is antiquated and overcrowded . . . it did not have sprinklers [or] smoke detectors. . . .

*Source:* Mary Jo Patterson, "Jail Fires: The Price of Neglect Is Tragedy," *Corrections Magazine*, Vol. IX, No. 1 (February 1983), p. 7.

Although their limited size might create the expectation that small jails would be more crowded than those with much greater capacity, data indicate that exactly the opposite is the case. Particularly among small jails opened within the last several decades, the typical pattern has been 28 beds for an average daily population of less than 17 inmates.[8] Moreover, spatial density varies directly in proportion to jail size. Jails housing fewer than 50 inmates provide the most space per resident—an average of 61 square feet. Those confining 1000 or more inmates provide the least space—only 46 square feet per resident. (This is below the standard established by the American Correctional Association, which suggests that each inmate have 60 square feet of floorspace.[9]) Overall, in terms of the percentage of their capacity that is occupied, very small jails tend to have space to spare, occupying only 64% of their capacity. In contrast, megajails are at 126% occupancy—well over their capacity.[10]

On the other hand, in very small, rural jails, it is virtually impossible to provide the facility design, training, range of services, and varieties of personnel that are available in larger, urban jails. The most pressing issues facing small jails include staff shortages, lack of round-the-clock coverage, maintenance difficulties, and inability to provide adequate physical separation of special inmates (e.g., juveniles, females, mentally ill, etc.)[11] Moreover, the lack of ability to properly classify and separate inmates accelerates other operational problems such as attacks, assaults, and the introduction of weapons and other unauthorized items.[12] Even segregating only the most obvious groups (male/female; young/old; felons/misdemeanants) can create crowded conditions in small jails, despite the fact that the total population is well within the facility's overall capacity.

### Consolidating Small Jails

For many of these reasons, there has been considerable movement in recent years toward the *consolidation* of small jails into larger regional detention centers. Just as the centralization of purchasing reduces the cost of items to each department involved, regional jail consolidation enhances cost-effectiveness, along with providing more and better services.

[8]Dennis A. Kimme et al., *The Nature of New Small Jails: Report and Analysis* (Champaign, IL: KIMME Planning and Architecture, 1985), p. 4.

[9]Christopher A. Innes, "Population Density in Local Jails, 1988," *Bureau of Justice Statistics Special Report* (Washington, DC: U.S. Department of Justice, 1990), pp. 1, 4.

[10]*Sourcebook—1990*, p. 579.

[11]Kimme et al., pp. 4–5, 13.

[12]Ibid., p. 6.

Some states are even taking the lead by encouraging local jails to regionalize. In Virginia, for example, the state will reimburse up to half of the new construction or renovation costs when three or more jurisdictions consolidate. As a result, by 1991, there were 12 regional jails in Virginia. Considering that these 12 jails represent a total of 24 counties and 11 cities that otherwise would have had to maintain their own small jails, the savings in construction and operating costs alone have been cited as "economically staggering."[13] In addition to Virginia, both West Virginia and a number of states in the midwest have or are developing regionalized jail systems.

Such cooperative efforts also enable a jail to offer programs that jurisdictions functioning independently could not afford to staff or operate. In addition, through regionalization, it is possible to assure that minimally acceptable standards are met. Variations in staffing patterns, training programs, operational procedures, and inmate services can be eliminated or at least reduced significantly.

Thus, it is not surprising to find that, as shown in Figure 6.3, the type of jail that has been declining the most since 1978 is the jail housing fewer than 50 inmates. At the other extreme, megajails confining 1000 or more inmates represent the type of facilities that are rapidly increasing. In short, while we still have far more very small jails, they are dropping in number. By the same token, while we still have few very large jails, they are increasing in number. In the meantime, most inmates are actually incarcerated in the more sizable facilities, particularly the largest megajails.

---

*LEARNING GOALS*

*Do you know:*

- *What functions are performed by jails?*
- *What percentage of the jail population is pretrial (versus convicted)?*
- *For what types of offenses most people are in jail?*
- *To what extent alcohol and drug abuse affect the jail population?*
- *What the maximum sentence is that one can generally serve in jail?*

---

| Jail Size (Inmates) | Year | Number | Percent Change Since 1978 |
|---|---|---|---|
| Small jails (fewer than 50 inmates) | 1978 | 2844 | |
| | 1983 | 2471 | – 13.1% |
| | 1988 | 2219 | – 22.0% |
| Large jails (1000 or more inmates) | 1978 | 10 | |
| | 1983 | 19 | + 90.0% |
| | 1988 | 51 | + 410.0% |

**Figure 6.3** Changes in types of jails: 1978–1988. *Source:* Adapted from *Sourcebook of Criminal Justice Statistics—1990* (Washington, DC: U.S. Department of Justice, 1991), p. 582.

---

[13]Morton J. Leibowitz, "Regionalization in Virginia Jails," *American Jails,* Vol. 5, No. 5 (November/December 1991), pp. 42–43.

Facilities confining 1,000 or more inmates represent the types of jails that are increasing in number throughout the United States. Courtesy of the American Jail Association.

## ❖ FUNCTIONS OF THE JAIL

As noted in Chapter 4, the first English *gaols* originated as places to confine those awaiting either trial or imposition of the death penalty. (In contrast to today, at that time, the defendant could expect to wait longer for the former than the latter.) Those on death row are now housed in state prisons. But local jails have retained their pretrial function to this day. In terms of their conviction status, the bulk of the jail population breaks down into two general groups:

1. *Accused* defendants *awaiting trial.*
2. *Convicted* offenders who are *serving short-term sentences* (usually one year or less).

### Pretrial Detention and Convicted Offenders

Since incarceration is considered a form of punishment, it would be logical to expect that jails would house more *convicted* offenders serving sentences than *accused* suspects waiting for trial. That is not the case. Of the total jail population, those who have been *convicted* are actually in the *minority* (49%). The remaining 51% are unconvicted, confined in pretrial detention.[14]

Over the past several decades, jail populations have generally represented this distribution—approximately half awaiting trial and half serving sentences. In recent years, jails, like prisons, have faced serious crowding problems. Obviously, jail personnel have little control over the sentences of those convicted. But many jail administrators have made concerted attempts to respond to overcrowding by reducing their pretrial population through such alternatives as release on recognizance (discussed in Chapter 1). Also, the courts have become more active in keeping unconvicted defendants out of jail through various pretrial interventions (discussed in Chapter 5).

As a result, it might be anticipated that the number (or at least the percentage) of pretrial inmates in jail would be declining. Not so. While the numbers of pretrial detainees would undoubtedly be much greater without such measures, they still continue to increase steadily each year. In fact, it is interesting to note that the percentage of the total jail population that is *unconvicted* has remained stable at 51 to 53% for nine consecutive years between 1983 and 1991 (see Figure 6.4). What this means is that despite efforts to reserve jail for those who have been found guilty in a court of law, over 200,000 jail inmates are technically innocent in the eyes of the law.

| Year | Convicted | Unconvicted |
|------|-----------|-------------|
| 1983 | 107,660 (49%) | 113,984 (51%) |
| 1984 | 113,491 (49%) | 116,331 (51%) |
| 1985 | 123,409 (49%) | 127,059 (51%) |
| 1986 | 127,067 (47%) | 142,112 (53%) |
| 1987 | 139,394 (48%) | 150,101 (52%) |
| 1988 | 166,224 (49%) | 175,669 (51%) |
| 1989 | 189,012 (48%) | 204,291 (52%) |
| 1990 | 195,661 (49%) | 207,358 (51%) |
| 1991 | 206,458 (49%) | 217,671 (51%) |

**Figure 6.4** Conviction status of inmates in jail. *Note:* Figures reflect the total number of adults with a known conviction status. *Source:* Adapted from *Sourcebook of Criminal Justice Statistics—1991* (Washington, DC: U.S. Department of Justice, 1992), p. 623.

[14]Louis W. Jankowski, "Jail Inmates 1991," *Bureau of Justice Statistics Bulletin* (Washington, DC: U.S. Department of Justice, 1992), p. 1.

## Other Jail Inmates

Beyond confining pretrial detainees and those serving short sentences, as illustrated in Figure 6.5, jails also maintain several other significant responsibilities:

1. *Booking* those arrested.
2. Holding convicted offenders *awaiting sentencing*.
3. Holding sentenced offenders *awaiting transfer* to other correctional facilities.
4. *Readmitting* probation, parole, and bail/bond violators or absconders.

Of these functions, holding inmates waiting to be transferred to prison is the most controversial. Lately, it has become a source of conflict between some local and state jurisdictions. As prisons fill above capacity, an overflow of sentenced inmates can quickly back up in already crowded jails. For example, in 1991, there were over 23,000 prisoners in jails as a result of overcrowded state facilities.[15]

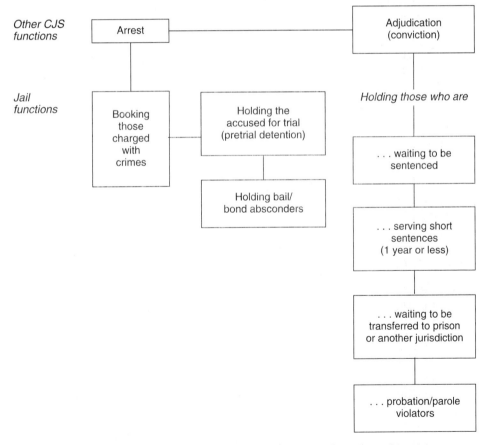

**Figure 6.5** Major functions of the jail in relation to the criminal justice system.

[15]Ibid.

When the state refuses to accept such inmates in a timely manner, it can generate antagonism between the local jail and state prison officials. In fact, in one case that would be humorous if it were not a reflection of a serious problem, a local jail administrator became so frustrated that when the state would not admit its inmates being transferred from jail, they were left handcuffed to the prison fence! Some counties have pursued a more genteel approach—suing the state to force the removal of prisoners in a timely manner. In other locations, somewhat more amenable compromises are attempted, such as state payments to local jurisdictions for the maintenance of inmates intended for institutions that cannot accept new admissions because of crowding. But fiscal reimbursement is not a strong incentive in locations where the jail itself is operating well beyond capacity. Moreover, those awaiting transfer to state prison are primarily felony offenders, in contrast to the bulk of jail inmates, who tend to be either pretrial defendants or convicted misdemeanants. Thus, keeping those intended for state prison in local jails compounds the "already serious problems faced by jail administrators attempting to deal with disparate populations . . . by mixing serious offenders with petty criminals."[16]

The diversity of the jail's population can even extend to such other "miscellaneous" categories of people as *material witnesses* and those needing *protective custody* because they have been threatened if they testify in court. The jail also serves other purposes for which it was not intended. For example, jails can hold *juveniles*—pending their trial in adult court or transfer to other correctional facilities; *probation and parole violators*—pending their revocation hearings; the *mentally ill*—pending their transfer to mental health facilities (when such resources are available); and *indigent transients*—who, unfortunately, are usually not pending transfer anywhere but back on the streets, since the jail is often the only facility open 24 hours a day to house them.

### Offenses of Jail Inmates

From this wide assortment of people, it is apparent that the jail serves many purposes and confines many different varieties of inmates. Although the public may be under the impression that local jails are incarcerating primarily hardened, violent offenders, such is not always the case. One study, for example, maintains that most jails hold "only a very few persons who fit the popular conception of a criminal—a predator who seriously threatens the lives and property of ordinary citizens."[17] However, another study refutes the claim that jails primarily confine "detached and disreputable persons whose real problem is offensiveness" rather than serious criminality—citing evidence that over 90% of the jail bookings in one urban county were for charges of a serious nature (although 85% of the bookings in a rural county were for misdemeanor charges).[18] Of course, the profile of book-

[16]*Jails: Intergovernmental Dimensions of a Local Problem,* p. 169.
[17]John Irwin, *The Jail: Managing the Underclass in American Society* (Berkeley, CA: University of California Press, 1985), p. 1.
[18]John A. Backstrand, Don C. Gibbons, and Joseph F. Jones, "Who Is in Jail? An Examination of the Rabble Hypothesis," *Crime and Delinquency,* Vol. 38, No. 2 (April 1992), p. 226.

ings may differ from that of those ultimately serving time in jail (in contrast to those who are "passing through" enroute to a longer term in prison).

While the types of offenses for which people are confined in jail are likely to vary with local policies, a national picture of the jail population presents some interesting findings. Considering everyone in jail throughout the country—both convicted and pretrial inmates—less than *one-fourth* (22.5%) of the population is confined for such *violent offenses* as murder, kidnapping, rape, robbery, or assault.[19] Of these, most are in *pretrial* status, partly because those suspected of such violent crimes are less likely to qualify for bail or release on recognizance. In addition, once someone is convicted and incarcerated for a very serious offense, the sentence received may well exceed the amount of time that one is lawfully permitted to serve in jail.

Thus, as Figure 6.6 illustrates, the *majority* of inmates are *not* in jail for the types of violent personal crimes most feared by society—but rather, for:

- *Property* crimes (30%).
- *Drug-related* offenses (23%).
- *Public order* offenses (22.8%), such as traffic violations, obstruction of justice, weapons charges, or—most commonly—driving while intoxicated.[20]

In fact, of all the offenses for which people find themselves confined in jail, only burglary and possession or trafficking of drugs exceeds driving while intoxicated. This is not meant to imply that jail crowding should be reduced by legalizing drugs or that drunk driving is not a significant threat to public safety. But it does point out that the public's perception of the "typical" jail inmate may not conform with who is actually in jail.

**Alcohol and Drug Abusers.**   It is apparent from this inmate profile that the bulk of the jail's population is experiencing some type of difficulty with either alcohol

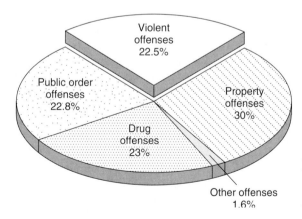

**Figure 6.6**   Most serious offenses of jail inmates. *Source:* Allen J. Beck, "Profile of Jail Inmates, 1989," *Bureau of Justice Statistics Special Report* (April 1991), p. 4.

[19]Beck, p. 4.
[20]Ibid.

or drugs. Many of the jail's residents are homeless, drifters, vagrants, or "skid row"[21] inhabitants. Since public intoxication remains an offense in most jurisdictions, a sizable number of these people find themselves incarcerated for drunkenness, vagrancy, or disorderly conduct.[22] Some chronic drinkers have been arrested more than 100 times and have served 10 to 20 years in jail on short-term sentences. They may or may not be clinical alcoholics, but they are unable to assume responsibility or function in a stable capacity. In fact, there is evidence that jail provides some alcoholics with a stable environment, a substitute social system, and a quasi-family setting.[23]

During the mid-1960s, two federal court decisions held that conviction of alcoholics on charges of public intoxication was tantamount to the conviction of sick persons for displaying symptoms of a disease and was unconstitutional (although a subsequent Supreme Court ruling brought these decisions into question).[24] In another case, a law making narcotic addiction illegal was struck down by the Supreme Court as cruel and unusual, since it punished a condition beyond the control of the offender.[25] Even police chiefs are acknowledging that law enforcement is not the solution to the drug problem and that the underlying social causes must be addressed.[26] Moreover, in studying mandatory minimum sentences for drug-related crimes, the American Bar Association called such penalties unfair, distorted, and requiring "expenditures disproportionate to any deterrent or rehabilitative effect they might have."[27] Closer partnerships between the jail and community services have been cited as potentially reducing the jail population in the long run by providing assistance in solving the fundamental problems of jail inmates.[28]

But in the meantime, both alcohol and drug abuse continue to produce inmates who constitute different problems than the jail was designed to handle. Those with such difficulties place a heavy burden on both the court system and local jails, few of which are equipped with the treatment facilities necessary to

[21]The term "skid row" originated in Seattle in the late nineteenth century, when that city was a shipping point for lumber from logging operations in the northwest. Logs were skidded down Seattle's steep landscape into the bay for sawing and processing. The loggers would come into town on Saturday night and frequently get drunk, leading to that area of the city becoming known as "skid row."

[22]In 1991, for example, there were 1,257,695 arrests for these offenses. Federal Bureau of Investigation, *Crime in the United States: Uniform Crime Reports* (Washington, DC: U.S. Government Printing Office, 1992), p. 214.

[23]S. Sidlofsky, "The Role of the Prison Community in the Behavior of the Chronic Drunkenness Offender," Master's thesis, University of Toronto, 1961.

[24]See Criminal Justice Coordinating Council of New York City and Vera Institute of Justice, *In Lieu of Arrest—The Manhattan Bowery Project—Treatment for Homeless Alcoholics* (New York: Vera Institute of Justice, 1969).

[25]Henry W. Wrobleski and Karen M. Hess, *Introduction to Law Enforcement and Criminal Justice* (St. Paul, MN: West Publishing Company, 1990), p. 85.

[26]Robert Reinhold, "Police, Hard Pressed in Drug War, Are Turning to Preventive Efforts," in John J. Sullivan and Joseph L. Victor, eds., *Annual Editions: Criminal Justice 91/92* (Guilford, CT: Dushkin Publishing Group, 1991), p. 99.

[27]"Emphasis on Enforcement Not the Answer to the Drug Crisis, ABA Report Says," *Narcotics Control Digest* (January 29, 1992), p. 4.

[28]Charles L. Newman, Barbara R. Price, Jacqueline B. Sobel, Sheldon Adelberg, Marque Bagshaw, and Dean Phillips, *Local Jails and Drug Treatment* (University Park, PA: Pennsylvania State University, College of Human Development, 1976), p. 300.

respond to their needs. "Detoxification centers" have begun to replace "drunk tanks" in the jails of larger cities. But the system's overall effort is still in many respects directed more toward punitive than productive responses. In short, "the common drunk remains a headache for jails, despite [trends toward] the decriminalization of public drunkenness."[29] As long as society continues to focus more on building jails than developing treatment programs, the cycle of drug- and alcohol-related crime can be expected to continue.

## Length of Time Served

Regardless of their offense, in most jurisdictions, the jail is not authorized to hold inmates serving longer than one year. Thus, as a general rule, those with a sentence of a year or less will serve it in jail, while those with longer terms will serve their time in prison. As with most general statements, however, there are exceptions. Some counties enable inmates to serve up to five years in jail. Others have *no* maximum length on jail sentences.[30] But since there are about as many *admissions to* as *releases from* jails on an annual basis (10,266,267 admissions; 9,929,347 releases),[31] it is apparent that there is a high turnover among the jail population—in other words, few stay there very long.

Although it might be anticipated that pretrial detainees would spend considerably less time in jail than convicted offenders, figures do not exactly confirm this expectation. Actually, those *not yet convicted* appear to be serving almost as much time (3.2 months) as *sentenced inmates* (5.4 months).[32]

On the one hand, there are valid arguments that pretrial detention is necessary in some cases to protect the safety of the community or to prevent the suspect from fleeing before being brought to justice.[33] "Speedy trial" legislation also has assured that cases get to court much more quickly today than in the jail's early origins. (Most jurisdictions now require trial between 90 and 120 days following arrest, not counting delays initiated by the defense). Moreover, some defendants may be held very briefly until they can raise bail or qualify for various pretrial release programs.

But regardless of reasons or qualifiers, the fact remains that the majority of jail inmates are unconvicted. In the eyes of the law they are innocent. Yet, on average, they are held nearly as long as their convicted counterparts—potentially looking "more and more guilty with each passing day in confinement."[34]

---

[29]Kenneth E. Kerle, "Introduction," in Joel A. Thompson and G. Larry Mays, eds., *American Jails: Public Policy Issues* (Chicago: Nelson-Hall, 1991), p. xiv.

[30]Kenneth E. Kerle and Francis R. Ford, *The State of Our Nation's Jails* (Washington, DC: National Sheriff's Association, 1982), p. 157.

[31]Jankowski, p. 2.

[32]Kerle and Ford, p. 157. A more recent study using different procedures reveals similar findings—an average of 5 months for those serving time, in comparison with a mean of 3.4 months for those awaiting trial or sentencing. Beck, p. 7.

[33]For example, one study found that "among felony defendants granted pretrial release, 24% failed to appear for a scheduled court hearing, and 18% were rearrested while on release." "Most Felony Defendants Released before Trial," *Crime Control Digest*, Vol. 26, No. 49 (December 7, 1992), quoting Steven D. Dillingham, Director, Bureau of Justice Statistics.

[34]Harry E. Allen and Clifford E. Simonsen, *Corrections in America*, Sixth Edition (New York: Macmillan, 1992), p. 507.

Beyond questions of justice and equity, if nothing else, this raises issues concerning what conditions the 51% who are unconvicted should be subject to while spending their 3.2 months in jail.

---

*LEARNING GOALS*

*Do you know:*

- *What the differences are between first-, second-, and third (new)-generation jails?*
- *How architecture and management style shape behavior in direct-supervision facilities?*
- *Why the greater amenities of direct-supervision jails do not result in higher construction or operating costs?*
- *The difference between direct-supervision facilities and traditional jails in terms of violent incidents, escapes, vandalism, and property damage?*
- *What impact direct supervison has on the need for staff training?*
- *Why direct-supervision/new-generation jails cannot be run with "old-generation" management?*

---

## ❖ DIRECT-SUPERVISION (NEW-GENERATION) JAILS

If you bought a computer several years ago, you have probably already found that it is obsolete. Newer, faster, more sophisticated models are constantly replacing each previous "generation" of computers. As society progresses and new advancements are made, one might expect that similar changes would be reflected in our jails. But if you visited a jail within the past several years, you probably found a new meaning for what is truly "obsolete." Even facilities constructed as recently as 25 to 30 years ago "are not radically different, in most respects, from the nation's first penitentiary—the Walnut Street Jail of 1790."[35] They may be cleaner. They may be better lighted. They may include more high-tech security. But their basic features have remained essentially the same.

### Philosophy

In response to the need for a "new generation" of correctional facilities, several jails were constructed during the mid-1970s that no more resemble traditional jails than manual typewriters resemble today's computers. The rationale behind this new-generation movement is based on several fundamental principles:

- The majority of those in jail have *not yet been convicted*. It is therefore questionable whether pretrial inmates should be punished by subjecting them to conditions that are actually worse than what they would find if convicted and sentenced to prison.

[35]Stephen H. Gettinger, *New Generation Jails: An Innovative Approach to an Age-Old Problem* (Washington, DC: U.S. Department of Justice, 1984), p. 2.

- The *physical design* of a correctional facility shapes inmate as well as staff behavior. When people are degraded to the point of putting them in cages otherwise reserved for animals, it should not be surprising if their reactions more closely resemble animal than human behavior. When staff are overstressed by the noise, confusion, and depressing environment of the jail, it should not be surprising if they become frustrated, quit, or act in an unprofessional manner.
- The *control of behavior* within a correctional facility should be a function of staff rather than inmates. When jail personnel cannot adequately observe what all inmates are doing at all times, gaps are created. Inmates will be quick to fill such a leadership vacuum, with the strong preying on the weak.
- The fundamental purpose of jails is to *maintain custody* of those who have been deprived of their liberty. In other words, the role of the jail is not to inflict greater punishment than the loss of freedom. Exposure to substandard living conditions, sexual attacks, demeaning treatment, inmate dominance, and the like are not what the courts have authorized as part of an inmate's "sentence."

In recognition of these problems, the courts have intervened to improve jail conditions. As successful cases challenged the constitutionality of the jail environment on grounds of "cruel and unusual punishment," many localities were, in essense, forced to upgrade their jails. Rather than waiting to react to court decisions, the new generation philosophy assumes a *proactive* approach—creating facilities that not only meet basic standards of human decency, but come as close to replicating a "normal" environment as can be achieved in confinement.

### Architecture and Inmate Supervision

The two major features that set new-generation facilities apart from traditional jails—and to which much of their success in behavioral control can be attributed—are *architecture* and *management style*. These features work hand in hand to shape behavior and are reflected in the three generations through which jails have progressed:[36]

1. *First-generation* jails are those we would most typically think of if asked to describe a jail. Inmates are confined in multiple-housing cells that are lined in rows along a corridor. The end of each row comes together toward a central control area, similar to the spokes on a wheel (see Figure 6.7). Officers patrol the corridors (or "catwalks") on an intermittent, infrequent basis. They cannot observe everyone in all cells at any one time. Their interaction with inmates is generally through bars as they pass by. As a result, activities often occur in the cells without staff knowledge or control. Because of the linear layout of the cells and the lack of constant supervision, the inmate management style of first-generation jails is known as *linear remote (or intermittent) surveillance*.

---

[36]Much of the following architectural descriptions are summarized from Lois Spears and Donald Taylor, "Coping with Our Jam-Packed Jails," *Corrections Today*, Vol. 52 (June 1990), p. 20; and W. Raymond Nelson, "Cost Savings in New Generation Jails: The Direct Supervision Approach," *National Institute of Justice Construction Bulletin* (July 1988), p. 2.

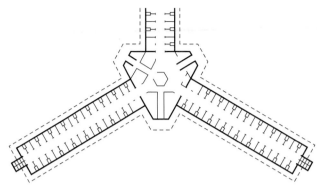

**Figure 6.7** Linear remote (intermittent) surveillance. *Source:* W. Raymond Nelson, "Cost Savings in New Generation Jails: The Direct Supervision Approach," *National Institute of Justice Construction Bulletin* (July 1988), p. 2.

2. In the next, *second generation* of jails to be developed, inmate housing surrounds a secure control booth (see Figure 6.8). Officers can see directly into the housing units. Thus, rather than physically patrolling corridors, staff can observe inmates directly from their glass-enclosed booth. Although this design increases visual surveillance, the officer's isolation in the booth reduces verbal interaction with the residents. Communication with inmates is accomplished through an intercom. Because of the lack of personal contact, the inmate management style of second-generation jails is known as *indirect* (or *remote*) *surveillance.*

3. The *third (or new) generation* of jails combines the principles of continual surveillance with personal interaction. That is, individual housing units are located around an open area, where an officer is stationed permanently (see Figure 6.9). No barrier separates personnel from residents. Inmates freely move throughout the unit, under the continual supervision of the officer in charge. It is for this reason that new-generation jails are known as *direct-supervision* facilities. When residents do not elect to remain in their rooms, they can combat boredom by watching television, playing cards, and engaging in recreational activities in the open area (or the adjoining outside recreation yard), all under the constant supervision of the officer in the unit. To reduce the need for unnecessary movement throughout the facility, all services are provided directly in the unit— meals, telephones, shower rooms, laundry facilities, counseling services, visits,

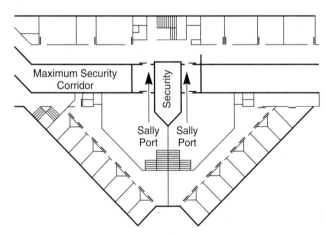

**Figure 6.8** Indirect (remote) surveillance. *Source:* W. Raymond Nelson, "Cost Savings in New Generation Jails: The Direct Supervision Approach," *National Institute of Justice Construction Bulletin* (July 1988), p. 2.

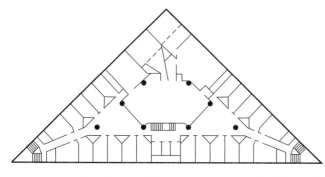

**Figure 6.9** Direct supervision. *Source:* W. Raymond Nelson, "Cost Savings in New Generation Jails: The Direct Supervision Approach," *National Institute of Justice Construction Bulletin* (July 1988), p. 3.

consultations with attorneys, and the like. Although the relative freedom may give the impression that security is lacking, new-generation jails concentrate security on the outside perimeter. Internal security devices are designed to be as unobtrusive as possible.

### Physical Features

Visitors to a direct-supervision facility are almost immediately struck by how unlike a "jail" it looks. The atmosphere is calm. You can practically feel the lack of tension. In fact, it is so quiet that some visitors have thought the inmates were "tranquilized."[37] The floors are carpeted. Windows provide natural light. There are no communal cells with bars. Instead, there are individual rooms with doors. As the next "Close-up on Corrections" describes, the atmosphere is similar to what you might find in a college dorm.

The initial reaction to direct-supervision facilities is how totally contrary they are to our traditional concept of what a jail has been (and to some people, what jails should still be today). In fact, the greatest criticism of new-generation jails has come from those who believe that such facilities are too "plush"—that they are "coddling" criminals. But in addition to the fact that most of the jail's residents are accused citizens rather than convicted criminals, there are actually operational reasons for the amenities provided. For example:

- *Carpeting, acoustical tile,* and *open spaces* are designed to reduce noise and the tension it creates by absorbing sounds.
- *Solid walls and doors* instead of gates and bars are used to eliminate the constant irritation of metal clanging against metal.
- *Natural lighting* and *soft color* schemes are employed to create a soothing behavioral effect and reduce the impression of being in an institutional environment.[38]

[37]Richard Werner, F. W. Frazier, and Jay Farbstein, "Direct Supervision of Correctional Institutions," in *Podular, Direct Supervision Jails* (Boulder, CO: National Institute of Corrections Jail Center, 1991), p. 3.

[38]For more information on the relationship between color schemes and inmate behavior, see I. S. K. Reeves V, "Soothing Shades: Color and Its Effect on Inmate Behavior," *Corrections Today*, Vol. 54, No. 2 (April 1992), pp. 128–130.

The scene resembles a college dormitory with a student union lounge attached. At one end of a large, colorful room, a handful of young men is watching television; in another area, a second group watches a different set. Two inmates are playing ping-pong. A group of inmates goes up to the uniformed deputy, who is chatting amiably with someone, and asks him for the volleyball. He gives it to them, and they rush out the door to the recreation yard. Another man pads from the shower room to his private room, where he closes the door for privacy.

The area is bright, sunny, and clean. The furniture—sofas and chairs—is comfortable and clean. The carpet on the floor is unstained. No one has scratched his initials in the paint or on the butcher-block tables and desks. Windows allow a view of the outside. Despite all the activity, the room is relatively quiet. The television volume is low, and no one is shouting.

This is not the scene at most jails, old or new, in the United States today. It is, however, typical of daily activity in . . . facilities known as "New Generation" jails, and they are generally regarded as the state of the art in jail design.

*Source:* Stephen H. Gettinger, *New Generation Jails: An Innovative Approach to an Age-Old Problem* (Washington, DC: U.S. Department of Justice, 1984), p. l.

Through such measures, the new-generation jail attempts to provide more natural surroundings, based on the belief that the environment in which we live is self-reinforcing. In other words, the conditions to which people are exposed have a significant effect on their behavior—with normal conditions producing more normal behavior.

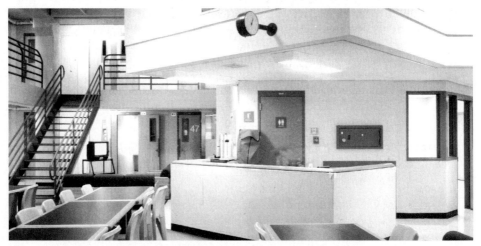

Carpeting, acoustical tile, open spaces, solid doors, and natural lighting combine to create a soothing behavioral effect in direct supervision facilities. Courtesy of the American Jail Association.

## Costs and Effectiveness

The amenities provided in direct-supervision jails may give the impression that such facilities are more expensive to construct and operate than traditional jails. But evidence indicates that exactly the opposite is the case. Cost savings are achieved in a number of ways, including:[39]

- The use of *standard, commercial-grade* fixtures rather than high-security, vandal-proof materials.
- The efficiency resulting from the *need for fewer staff,* since personnel are in constant contact with the inmates and are not required to transport them as often because most services are offered directly in the housing unit.
- The *reduced* use of *sick leave* by personnel;
- The *lower maintenance* costs resulting from the absence of vandalism and graffiti.

For just one unit housing 48 inmates, it has been estimated that direct-supervision jails save over $200,000 in terms of construction costs alone.[40] Moreover, annual operating costs are significantly reduced as well. For example, one jurisdiction debating whether to construct a second- or third-generation jail compiled figures estimating that by the time a new-generation jail is in operation for 20 years, the county will have saved over $97,000,000.[41]

Although cost savings are certainly a high priority for any responsible government official, they usually come only at the expense of reducing the quality of service. But again, new-generation jails represent an exception to this rule of thumb. As noted previously, direct-supervision facilities provide a more natural environment, with the anticipation that inmate behavior, in turn, will be modified. Evidence of this self-reinforcing effect is quite dramatic. It has been found that in these jails:

- *Violent incidents* overall are reduced by 30 to 90%.[42]
- *Homosexual rape* virtually disappears.[43]
- *Aggravated assaults* are substantially reduced.[44]
- Inmates experience fewer symptoms of *stress*.[45]
- The numbers of *suicides* and *escapes* are considerably lower.[46]

---

[39]Summarized from Nelson, pp. 4–6.

[40]Ibid., p. 6.

[41]Dade County Stockade Expansion, "Comparative Analysis of Design Schemes," in *Podular, Direct Supervision Jails*, p. 71.

[42]Richard Werner, William Frazier, and Jay Farbstein, "Building Better Jails," *Psychology Today*, Vol. 21, No. 6 (June 1987), p. 42.

[43]Ibid.

[44]Michael O'Toole, "New Generation Jail Survey: Comparative Data from 1981 and 1982 on Assaults and Escapes," in *Podular, Direct Supervision Jails*, p. 62.

[45]Linda L. Zupan, *Jails: Reform and the New Generation Philosophy* (Cincinnati, OH: Anderson Publishing Company, 1991), p. 160.

[46]W. Raymond Nelson and Michael O'Toole, *New Generation Jails* (Boulder, CO: National Institute of Corrections Jail Center, 1983).

Direct-supervision jails are based on the concept that inmates will behave more normally when they are confined in a more normal environment. Courtesy of the Nassau County Sheriff's Department, East Meadow, New York.

- The introduction of *contraband* (unauthorized items) is practically nonexistent.[47]
- *Vandalism* and *destruction of property* are almost completely eliminated. For example, in one facility "the number of damaged mattresses dropped from 150 per year to none in two years"; the number of TV sets needing repair dropped from "two per week to two in two years."[48]

These positive results do not mean that direct-supervision jails are intentionally designed for the purpose of treating or rehabilitating inmates. Rather, they are simply designed to prevent those incarcerated from deteriorating further as a result of their jail exposure. But they can promote rehabilitation by providing a setting in which any treatment programs that are offered have a better chance to work.[49] By creating a more normal environment, it is expected that those confined will behave more normally, and research thus far has confirmed this expectation.

[47]Herbert R. Sigurdson, *Pima County Detention Center: A Study of Podular Direct Supervision* (Washington, DC: National Institute of Corrections, 1987); Herbert R. Sigurdson, *Larimer County Detention Center: A Study of Podular Direct Supervision* (Washington, DC: National Institute of Corrections, 1987).

[48]Werner et al., "Building Better Jails," p. 42. For a more detailed comparison of traditional and direct-supervision jails in terms of rule violations resulting in incident reports, see Jeffrey D. Senese, Joe Wilson, Authur O. Evans, Robert Aguirre, and David B. Kalinich, "Evaluating Jail Reform: Inmate Infractions and Disciplinary Response in a Traditional and a Podular/Direct Supervision Jail," *American Jails,* Vol. 6, No. 4 (September/October 1992), pp. 14–23.

[49]Werner et al., "Direct Supervision," p. 6.

## Training and Management

The residents, of course, are quite receptive to direct-supervision jails. Beyond their basic comforts, they are much safer facilities in which to be confined. No longer do inmates constantly have to fear for their safety or make weapons for their own defense. Officers, however, sometimes experience difficulties with the transition to a new-generation jail. Those who have become accustomed to being physically separated from the inmates quite naturally feel safer being on the "other side of the bars." As a result, they may initially resist being placed directly into a housing unit which "seemingly places officers at the mercy of inmates."[50] Personnel are not permitted to carry weapons on the inside of any type of correctional facility, because of the potential that weapons would encourage attacks on staff and fall into the wrong hands. When officers are separated from inmates by secure metal bars, this is not viewed as a major disadvantage. But it is an entirely different situation when removing the bars requires staff to interact face to face with inmates continuously, relying only on verbal skills to control their behavior.

It is for these reasons that training is so critical to the effective implementation of direct-supervision jails. Such training focuses on the underlying principles of new-generation jailing, the significance of staff to its success, and the interpersonal skills needed to deal properly with inmates in such an environment. Upon completion of training, officers gain greater confidence in their ability to handle this new role. Some will still be skeptical. However, most soon come to realize that although their job may in some respects be more demanding, it is also considerably easier and more satisfying because staff rather than inmates are in control. With direct supervision, officers can respond *proactively* to minor issues before they become major problems, rather than dealing *reactively* with the consequences.

By being in constant contact with inmates, officers "get to know them well. They learn to recognize and respond to trouble before it escalates into violence; . . . negotiation and communication become more important than brute strength."[51] In fact, after staff have experienced the relative tranquility, reduced tension, and improved inmate behavior of such jails, they are usually reluctant to work in any other type of facility.

Just as officers must be appropriately prepared for their new role in new-generation jailing, supervisors must also become familiar with a new management style. In traditional jails, lower-level staff tend to have routine assignments, management is centralized, and upper-level administrators make all important decisions. In contrast, new-generation jailing will only be effective when management adopts a more *decentralized approach.*

As the personnel in charge of the units, officers require much more autonomy to carry out their job. Thus, they must be granted more authority to participate in jail management, make their own decisions, and provide leadership within their unit. In other words, "you can't run a new generation jail with old generation management."[52] The physical design is only half of the formula for

[50]Werner et al., "Building Better Jails," p. 42.
[51]Ibid.
[52]Gettinger, p. 20. See also Jerry W. Fuqua, "New Generation Jails—Old Generation Management," *American Jails,* Vol. 5, No. 1 (March/April 1991), pp. 80–83.

the success of direct-supervision jails—as in any correctional facility, it is staffing and training which are really the key ingredients.

---

*LEARNING GOALS* ▰▰▰▰▰▰▰▰▰▰▰▰▰▰▰▰▰▰▰▰▰▰▰▰▰▰▰▰▰▰

*Do you know:*

- *At what level of government most jails function, and where the exceptions are?*
- *How the "elected sheriff" model of jail management differs from the "appointed administrator" model?*
- *How intake affects one's adjustment to jail?*
- *In contrast to prison, why jails are particularly vulnerable to suicides?*
- *How public policy changes resulted in more of the mentally ill being confined in jails?*
- *How inmates are separated through classification?*
- *What the difference is between "design" and "rated" capacity of jails?*
- *What size of jail is the most crowded?*

---

## ❖ JAIL ADMINISTRATION AND OPERATIONS

While the number of direct-supervision facilities increases each year, they represent only about 100 of the more than 3000 jails currently in existence. The vast majority of jails still reflect varieties of first- and second-generation architecture. The major reason that there is so little consistency in terms of everything from size to facility design is that jails are financed, operated, and controlled primarily by *local governments.*

Although there are federal jails for inmates serving short sentences or awaiting trial on federal charges, they represent less than a half dozen of the nation's 3316 jails.[53] For many years there were so few federal inmates that it was more economical for the federal government to contract with local jails to house them. But by the late 1960s, local jail crowding was making it increasingly difficult to do so. The federal government therefore began a major construction effort to provide its own jails. Since these facilities were newly constructed rather than renovations of existing structures, an opportunity was provided to create jails that were substantially different from those already in existence. The result was the first direct-supervision jails, which at the federal level are called *metropolitan correctional centers (MCCs).*

New-generation jailing was particularly appropriate to MCCs because many federal jail inmates are in pretrial status (since sentences for more serious federal offenses tend to exceed the amount of time that one can legally spend in jail). It was therefore the federal government that provided the impetus for direct-supervision jails.

---

[53] *Who's Who in American Jails* (Hagerstown, MD: American Jail Association, 1991), p. 431.

An innovative concept in detention emerged with the opening of the Metropolitan Correctional Center in San Diego, California. Based on the architectural and management concepts of direct supervision, MCCs have ushered in a new generation of jailing. Courtesy of the United States Bureau of Prisons.

But the fact remains that both direct-supervision jails and federal jails are in the vast minority. The *majority* of jails function at the *local level* of government. Because most jails are local facilities housing a relatively short-term, transient population, they have not received much attention or priority. As a result, they have frequently been referred to as the "stepchild of the criminal justice system."[54]

Counties and municipalities are relatively free to set their own policies and procedures with regard to jail operations. Again, however, there are exceptions. In most states, jails are a function of local government. But in six states—Alaska, Connecticut, Delaware, Hawaii, Rhode Island, and Vermont—jails are a responsibility of the *state level* of government. In addition, even when the jail is locally

[54]Belinda R. McCarthy, "The Use of Jail Confinement in the Disposition of Felony Arrests," *Journal of Criminal Justice*, Vol. 17, No. 4 (1989), p. 241.

controlled, states may intervene in jail operations. Some, for example, require that jails adhere to state-mandated standards; others provide fiscal incentives to improve jail conditions.

## Two Models of Administration

Despite these exceptions, however, over 90% of the nation's jails are administered at the *county level* of government.[55] As a result of its English origins, the typical jail today is run by the *county sheriff*, who (like the early shire-reeve) is generally responsible for both *enforcing the law* and *running the jail*. Again, however, there are the inevitable exceptions. In some counties, the sheriff's functions do not include law enforcement, but rather, are limited to jail administration, court security, and the serving of legal documents.

As an elected official, the sheriff is ultimately accountable to the citizens. This can be advantageous to the jail if the public is concerned about maintaining safe and sanitary conditions in its local correctional facilities. But more often, voters place a higher priority on reducing crime than improving jails—and the sheriff who does not respond to public pressures is not likely to be reelected. Since the sheriff's budget can only stretch so far, it may therefore be more politically expedient to devote scarce resources to battling crime than to bettering conditions for "criminals." There are certainly many professional sheriffs who take their responsibilities for jail administration as seriously as their law enforcement duties. But there are also others who neglect the needs of the jail in favor of higher-visibility enforcement activities that are more likely to generate votes.

As a result of these political realities, the needs of local corrections can become subservient to the demands for local law enforcement. When a sheriff must choose between the two, it is apparent which is likely to suffer. In fact, the low priority of the jail is perhaps nowhere as obvious as in those locations that have assigned deputies to the jail as disciplinary punishment or as duty for those who cannot interact effectively with the public on the street. Fortunately, such practices are much less prevalent today. But even where the jail is not used as a personnel "dumping ground," deputies working in detention have traditionally not been paid as much as those assigned to road patrol—sending a subtle but significant message that corrections is not as important as crime fighting. Although national organizations and some states have addressed the situation by encouraging pay parity,[56] there is usually little the state can do to correct such practices at the local level of government.

In an effort to balance law enforcement and correctional responsibilities more equitably, some counties have either created separate budgets for law enforcement and correctional functions or actually abolished the office of sheriff. In Florida, for example, a growing number of jurisdictions have, like Metropolitan Dade County (Miami), established a local department of corrections that is independent from the county's police department. Under this arrange-

[55]Kerle and Ford, p. 33.
[56]As early as 1984, the National Sheriffs' Association passed a resolution in favor of pay parity, but police or road patrol officers are still paid more than local correctional officers in many jurisdictions.

ment, both the police chief and the corrections director are *appointed* by the county administrator rather than elected by the public as in the case of the sheriff. In this type of management system, the jail may well be more likely to receive its "fair share" of fiscal resources, since it has a separate administrator advocating its needs and is not as subject to the pressures of varying political climates. On the other hand, it is then up to elected county commissioners to assure that both the police and the jail are responsive and accountable to the public. (For an illustration of these two models of jail management, see Figure 6.10.)

## The Administrator's Role: Setting the Tone for Staff

Regardless of whether the person in charge of the jail is appointed or elected, it is that individual who sets the tone for how the facility will operate. As public servants, jail administrators must remember that they serve the general public—especially that part of the public under their custody in jail. A manager who excuses intolerable conditions with such remarks as, "This ain't no hotel we're runnin' here!" is obviously not one who takes a great deal of pride in the job. Even such "minor" indiscretions as allowing employees to report to work late; tolerating wrinkled, unkempt uniforms; or letting trash accumulate on the floors all send a message of unconcern. It is the administrator who makes it clear—by actions as well as inactions—just what will and will not be acceptable.

When the facility's leadership is indifferent to what is going on, staff members get the message that their work is unimportant, and inmates will be quick

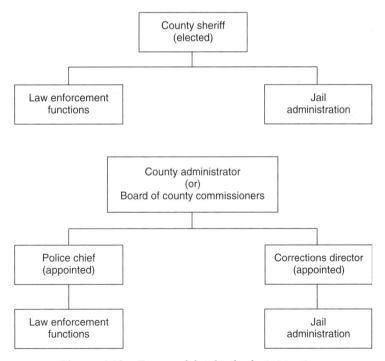

**Figure 6.10** Two models of jail administration.

to take advantage of the situation. For example, institutions with poor morale generally have more escape attempts than those with good morale. Such an administrative style can make even the most modern, well-designed jail an unpleasant place to be—for both inmates *and* staff.

On the other hand, jail managers who pay attention to details, take an active interest in daily operations, and assure that rules and regulations are firmly enforced can create a positive climate, even in a less than desirable physical facility. This does not mean that jail administrators should be authoritarian or maintain a highly centralized organizational structure—quite the contrary. As we have seen with new generation jailing, although humane physical conditions are essential, operational staff are actually the key ingredient to managing any correctional facility effectively (a theme explored in greater detail in Chapter 14).

Administrators are beginning to recognize the importance of staff to jail operations. In a survey by the National Sheriffs' Association, personnel issues were cited as the leading problem confronting jails throughout the country.[57] As this study noted, "too often, there are no standards for recruitment, and warm bodies are taken off the street, put into uniform, given a set of keys, and told to go to work."[58] Such practices hardly convey the importance of a jail assignment. Even the terminology often used to refer to jail personnel (and for that matter, those working in prisons as well) is demeaning to the significance of the job: "Far too many people in corrections and journalism who should know better still refer to jail officers as guards. They are not guards! This is something a person does when he [or she] patrols a warehouse or department store. Jail officers are supervisors of inmates, and good supervision requires initiative, intelligence, tact, and diplomacy."[59]

In recognition of the demands placed on jail officers and their key role in facility operations, recommendations have been made calling for such improvements as:

- Higher salaries
- More and better training
- Higher educational requirements
- In-depth selection screening
- Job enrichment
- Greater involvement in establishing overall policy and procedure[60]

Because of their tremendous diversity, however, jails vary considerably with regard to how extensively they have implemented these recommendations. Some jails continue to pay virtually minimum wage. Others compensate on a scale equivalent to police officers. Some jails continue to hire "warm bodies." Others select personnel through such sophisticated techniques as assessment centers.[61]

[57]Kerle and Ford, p. 230.
[58]Ibid., p. 231.
[59]Ibid., pp. 230–231.
[60]Ibid., p. 232.
[61]See Jeanne B. Stinchcomb, "Why Not the Best? Using Assessment Centers for Officer Selection," *Corrections Today*, Vol. 47, No. 3 (June 1985), pp. 120–124.

Some jails continue to provide little if any training. Others offer as much as 640 hours of classroom preparation before job assignment.[62]

Admittedly, sparing personnel for training and development can be difficult when jails are struggling with severe staff shortages. But even chronically understaffed facilities no longer have an excuse for not providing at least some training with such flexible options now available as the American Jail Association's *Jail Operations/Management Bulletins* (brief handouts and videotapes for use in roll-call and supervisory/management training), and the American Correctional Association's correspondence courses (through which officers can complete self-paced study at home or work). While videotapes, roll-call training, and correspondence programs cannot substitute for mandated classroom training, they can provide useful supplements and current updates. Many of the issues related to personnel selection and training are addressed further in Chapter 14. But the bottom line is simply that physical facilities notwithstanding, any jail will be only as good as the people staffing it.

## Staff Roles: Setting the Tone for Inmates

Just as the jail administrator creates an operating environment for staff, it is operational personnel who, in turn, establish the climate for inmates. They are the people who are in day-to-day, continuous interaction with the jail's population. Inmates are completely dependent upon them—for everything from the time they eat, to what they can keep in their cells, to whether they can obtain an aspirin for a headache. In other words, staff control virtually every aspect of an inmate's life during confinement, in accordance with the rules and regulations of the facility.

When inmates do not elect to conform to the rules and regulations, it is also operational personnel who must initiate *formal disciplinary procedures* (described in further detail in Chapter 8). Unfortunately, in some less progressive prisons and jails, discipline may be informally administered by staff, or even by inmates. Needless to say, it is dangerous and unacceptable practice to permit inmates to supervise other inmates. This does not necessarily mean that the use of trusties who may be supervising inmates on work details is inappropriate. In fact, many misdemeanants are "steady customers" at the jail, well known by staff, and frequently used to help maintain the facility or handle routine administrative procedures. But when staff abdicate much of their control function to inmates, ruthless and aggressive offenders can extort money and services from those who are weaker, often leading to homosexual encounters. In situations of isolation and deprivation, it is almost inevitable that some will try to influence and exploit others to improve their standard of life.

It is therefore particularly important that jail personnel enforce simple and reasonable disciplinary rules. Such rules can be used as tools by sensitive and intelligent staff to achieve control and modify of behavior. In this regard, it is notable that discipline is not a negative concept. Discipline means group order,

---

[62]See Jeanne B. Stinchcomb, "Moving toward Professionalism: A Pre-service Approach to Entry-Level Training," *Journal of Correctional Training* (Summer 1990), pp. 9–10.

which can be better accomplished by good relationships with clients than coercive techniques. Regardless of the specific rules and regulations established, when invoking the disciplinary process, officers must do so in a manner that is:

- *Firm.* Inmates should be fully advised of what is and is not acceptable and held accountable for their behavior. Only when rules are steadfastly enforced will everyone get the message that violations will not be tolerated.
- *Fair.* Arbitrary, meaningless, or discriminatory practices soon degrade the entire disciplinary process, as well as both officer and inmate respect for it. By treating inmates equitably and impartially, greater overall compliance is likely to be achieved. Even among those who do not comply, there is less likely to be the type of resentment that occurs when one is "singled out" inappropriately.
- *Consistent.* There is always some personal judgment and discretion involved in enforcing rules. But staff must take precautions to ensure that there is a degree of uniformity in terms of how discipline is handled among various officers, between shifts, and at diffferent periods of time. If inmates perceive that some officers are more lenient than others, some shifts are unconcerned with infractions, or some periods of time are too hectic to pay attention to discipline, they will quickly take advantage of such patterns.

To the extent that first impressions are lasting, it is during initial intake that the jail has the greatest potential for making a positive or negative impression. The attitudes of staff, the way inmates are handled, and the level of professionalism displayed during the receiving process do much to establish the frame of mind for the inmate's adjustment to jail. An offender who is rough-handled physically, demeaned verbally, or simply treated discourteously during intake is likely to form lasting impressions of distrust and disrespect that will influence subsequent interactions with the jail's personnel. On the other hand, when new arrivals are treated with dignity, courtesy, and respect, the effect can often be reinforcing in terms of how they, in turn, interact with staff.

### Intake Procedures

Inmates are usually received by way of an outside enclosure called a "sallyport," through which the police or sheriff's car transporting the offender passes. To accommodate those coming directly from court, many jails have an enclosed walkway connected to the courtrooms. This reduces the security risks involved during outside transportation. But one's first contact with the jail will be through the sallyport upon arrest. Once the police vehicle is inside and the gate secured, the suspect is removed to the receiving area of the jail. The arrest form must be checked carefully during the intake and booking process, since legal problems can arise when a person is deprived of liberty without adequate and completely legal documentation. Assuming that immediate medical attention is not needed, most jails then conduct a *pat-down* or *frisk search* (often followed later by a full strip search).

All valuables confiscated are carefully recorded, placed in an envelope, and signed for on a property receipt. Since cash and expensive jewelry are not permitted in most jails, these items are placed in a property storage room, to be collected upon release. Needless to say, the proper handling of money and valuables is very important.

Basic information is then taken—such as name, address, physical description, occupation, specific charges, name and phone number of anyone to be notified in case of emergency, attorney's name and address, and name/address of those who may be expected to visit the inmate. In addition, some jails record a particularly personal item of information that only the person being admitted would be likely to know, such as mother's maiden name. The purpose of this procedure is to ensure that upon release, the correct inmate is being discharged, since several inmates may share exactly the same name and even bear a physical resemblance, especially in very large jails.

*Photographing* and *fingerprinting* follow next, with a complete set of prints sent to the FBI to check on outstanding warrants and file with the National Crime Information Center. The FBI, in turn, sends back a "rap sheet," which is a criminal record history based on the times the person has been fingerprinted. This gives jail personnel a more complete picture of whom they are dealing with in order to determine whether the person poses any identifiable security or safety risks.

The inmate is then given a shower to eliminate body lice and vermin and is checked regarding such items as dentures, artificial limbs, and braces. Some facilities issue jail uniforms; others enable inmates to remain in their civilian clothes.

## Operational Considerations

Because no one can be held "incommunicado" in jail, inmates must also be given opportunities to make arrangements for bail (or release on recognizance) and to contact their attorney. Visits must be carefully controlled, with a record made of who visits and when. No person can be denied access to counsel at any time. Care must be taken not to delay visits from attorneys, since this could be interpreted as a denial of access to counsel, and thus serve as a basis for a lawsuit. Incoming packages have to be inspected to prevent the introduction of drugs, alcohol, weapons, or other contraband items. Medicines must be carefully controlled—issued by qualified medical staff and taken in their presence.

These are but a few of the legal and security-oriented operational considerations that must be handled effectively by jail personnel. Since most operational practices of jails also pertain to prisons, more detailed discussion of these procedures is contained in Chapter 8. But it is noteworthy that in some respects, jails incur greater security risks than prisons. Not only is there a constant flow of inmates into and out of the jail, but the sizable pretrial population must be transported to all of their preliminary court appearances, as well as to and from the courtroom during each day of their trials. Such continuous movement presents a significant security challenge, requiring jail personnel to be alert at all times to the potential for escape.

## Treatment and Industrial Programs

In the past, most inmates lingered unproductively in jails, making security matters even more difficult as residents sought "creative" outlets for their boredom. In part, this is a reflection of the jail's early history as a holding facility, which did not include reform or rehabilitation among its goals.[63] Moreover, both treatment and constructive employment are particularly difficult in jails because of the high turnover of the population as a result of their short-term confinement. But "without appropriate programs that focus on changing the criminal behavior of inmates, the jail becomes a 'revolving door,' releasing individuals into the community simply to re-admit them in a few months, weeks, days, or even hours, when they are arrested for another crime."[64] Progressive administrators today are therefore attempting to provide activities that offer personal help, promote job skills, occupy time, and in some cases, even reduce the cost of jail management.

Most jails now at least have reading materials available in a library, recreational opportunities, arts and crafts, and organized religious programs. Many have also added various forms of educational classes, correspondence courses, group counseling sessions, and even self-paced, computer-assisted instruction. In addition, productive labor is expanding under the federally sponsored Jail Industries Initiative, through which "[m]any inmates in American jails are getting away from television sets and are, literally, getting *into* productive work. Some are simply earning privileges; some are earning wages that go toward repayment of custodial costs and compensation to crime victims. Some are honing new job skills that improve their chances for successful employment following release."[65]

Beyond reducing idleness, such programs are designed to improve work habits, develop new skills, and generate revenues or reduce costs for the county.[66] Activities in which inmates are engaged range from landscaping to assembling electronics components. Thus, mutually beneficial inmate labor is beginning to expand beyond the routine facility maintenance functions to which jail inmates had largely been limited in the past.

### Medical Services

At some point early in the admission process, it is important that a medical examination be administered. People have died in jails for lack of proper medical attention. Court cases resulting from such tragedies, as well as increasing pressure for adequate medical standards, have recently focused more attention on health care in jails.[67] Conducting an initial medical exam is not a frivolous luxury but a minimal necessity. For example, some suspects who have

---

[63] Calvin A. Lightfoot, Linda L. Zupan, and Mary K. Stohr, "Jails and the Community: Modeling the Future in Local Detention Facilities," *American Jails*, Vol. 5, No. 4 (September/October 1991), p. 50.

[64] Ibid.

[65] Rod Miller, George E. Sexton, and Victor J. Jacobsen, "Making Jails Productive," *National Institute of Justice: Research in Brief* (Washington, DC: U.S. Department of Justice, 1991), p. 1.

[66] Ibid., p. 2. For an example of how industries work in one jail setting, see Marilyn Allen, "Strafford County, New Hampshire, Jail Industry," *American Jails*, Vol. 4, No. 1 (May/June 1990), pp. 48–49.

[67] See, for example, Ken Kerle, "Jail Health Care" and John Clark, "Correctional Health Care Issues in the Nineties—Forecast and Recommendations," *American Jails*, Vol. 5, No. 4 (September/October 1991), pp. 5, 22–23.

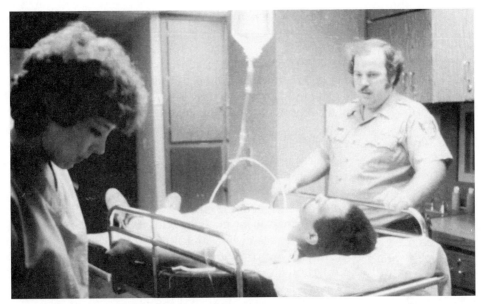

Providing for routine health care, as well as emergency medical services, is an essential feature of modern jails. Courtesy of the Dade County Department of Corrections and Rehabilitation, Miami, Florida.

been arrested for apparent drunkenness were later found to have had a fractured skull, diabetes, or other illnesses or injuries which actually caused physical behavior that could easily be misinterpreted as intoxication, particularly with alcohol on the breath.

Moreover, infectious diseases (such as hepatitis, tuberculosis, and more recently, AIDS) are not uncommon among those most frequently brought into jail, and treatment is often unavailable to them in the community. While society has these people in custody, it has an opportunity to provide diagnosis and as much medical treatment as possible—not only for the benefit of the individual client, but for the ultimate benefit of the entire community by reducing the spread of infection.

### Suicide Vulnerability

Another critical element of the intake process is identifying those who may be displaying signs and symptoms that indicate they are intent on taking their own life. This is a particularly significant problem, since *suicide* outranks *all other causes of deaths* in jail. In contrast, most deaths in prisons are a result of illness or natural causes.[68] Nor do statistics on jail suicides reflect the many additional but unsuccessful attempts that were prevented by alert personnel.

Those in jail are especially vulnerable to the potential for suicide. To begin with, many jail inmates are suffering from various forms of mental illness (dis-

---

[68]In 1988, 43% of deaths in jails were attributable to suicide, in comparison to only 7% of deaths in prisons during 1989. *Sourcebook—1990,* pp. 599, 673.

cussed further in the next section), which can be aggravated further by exposure to jail.[69] But even among otherwise mentally healthy inmates, the jail includes more of the types of people most prone to suicide than are found among the general population in free society—such as young, unemployed, unmarried males.

Moreover, admission to jail can be a traumatic experience, particularly for someone who has never been incarcerated before. By the time offenders go through the full legal process and are sentenced to prison, they have more or less accepted and adjusted to the fact that they are facing a period of confinement. But the uncertainty of how long they will be kept in jail—combined with the sense of loss, hopelessness, and personal embarrassment accompanying one's first exposure to jail—can promote suicidal thoughts.

Added to this is the fact that a sizable percentage of inmates arrive in jail intoxicated or under the influence of drugs.[70] When the effects of the alcohol or drugs wear off, depression can set in, along with realization of the seriousness of one's situation. In fact, it has been found that 60% of jail suicide victims were intoxicated at the time of incarceration.[71]

To deal properly with such inmates, it is essential that intake staff as well as custodial officers be familiar with warning signs and suicidal "profiles."[72] The role of intake is especially important, since most suicide attempts in holding areas occur within the first 3 hours of incarceration.[73] Moreover, research on jail suicides reveals that the vast majority (89 to 97%) did not undergo any form of intake screening as part of their booking process.[74]

Even after inmates have completed intake and been assigned to a cell, officers must be able to "tune in" to obvious as well as subtle signals and remain alert to any sudden behavioral changes. How well they do so will largely be determined by how well they listen and observe.[75] In this regard, direct supervision presents obvious advantages over remote, intermittent suveillance, as illustrated by the inside accounts of suicide attempts in the next "Close-up on Corrections." It is therefore not surprising to find fewer suicides in direct-supervision jails.

[69]See Rob Wilson, "Who Will Care for the 'Mad and Bad'?" *Corrections Magazine* (February 1980), pp. 5–17.
[70]For example, one study revealed that "more than half of all convicted jail inmates said they were under the influence of drugs or alcohol at the time of their current offense." Beck, p. 8. It has also been found that jail inmates are "7 times more likely than the general population to be current users of drugs." Caroline Wolf Harlow, "Drugs and Jail Inmates, 1989," *Bureau of Justice Statistics Special Report* (1991), p. 4.
[71]Ronald Jemelka, "The Mentally Ill in Local Jails: Issues in Admission and Booking," in Henry J. Steadman, ed., *Jail Diversion for the Mentally Ill* (Washington, DC: National Institute of Corrections, n.d.), p. 42, citing L. Hayes, "National Study of Jail Suicides: Seven Years Later," *Psychiatric Quarterly,* Vol. 60 (1989), pp. 7–29.
[72]However, it should be noted that since some maintain that it is not "reasonable or possible" to develop accurate suicide profiles, a more realistic goal may be to improve environmental security by, for example, eliminating "points of attachment" that could be used in hangings. See William E. Stone, "Means of the Cause of Death in Texas Jail Suicides, 1986–1988," *American Jails,* Vol. 4, No. 1 (May/June 1990), pp. 50–53.
[73]Jemelka, p. 42.
[74]Ibid., p. 43.
[75]Joseph R. Rowan and Lindsay M. Hayes, *Training Curriculum on Suicide Detection and Prevention in Jails and Lockups* (Washington, DC: National Center on Institutions and Alternatives, 1988), pp. 13-1, 13-2.

### Suicide Prevention in Direct-Supervision/New-Generation Jails

[A] particular inmate was despondent and possibly suicidal. . . . [T]he unit officer who reported the inmate was keeping an eye on [him]. This was a direct supervision unit. I think it is fair to say that in a traditional style facility, the officer would have no idea [that] an inmate's behavior had changed until it was too late. . . .

In another case, an inmate told officers that he would have most certainly killed himself were it not for the interest shown him by a unit officer when he was at his lowest point. These cases generally are not reported, so there is no way of knowing how often they occur. . . .

The units themselves . . . have a great effect on a person's outlook in custody. The main jail is well-lighted, with a window in each room. It is brightly painted and nicely furnished. The inmate presently has his own room that he may retreat to when things are tense, or he may join the others in the dayroom. This offers far less tension than traditional jail living units. Officers working in the direct supervision units are more likely to know their inmates better than officers in traditional jails. The officer will be more sensitive to inmate behavior changes, an important factor in detecting and preventing suicide. General conditions in most jails promote isolation through loss of control over one's environment. A rigid, authoritarian structure can increase feelings of anomie, hopelessness, and depression, which are ingredients in consideration of committing suicide.

*Source:* Robert Conroy, "Direct Supervision and Suicide," *Direct Supervision Jails: Proceedings of the 5th Annual Symposium* (Hagerstown, MD: American Jail Association, 1990), pp. 102–3.

When the possibility of suicide is suspected, personnel must take immediate action. Unfortunately, the ability of many jails to deal with mentally disturbed suicidal inmates may be limited to isolating them from the general population. But this approach can be counterproductive, since isolation "tends to create fear and suspicion . . . further undermining their mental state" and increasing the potential for suicide.[76]

Precautions taken to respond adequately to suicide risks will depend on the situation. Based on the seriousness of the symptoms, responses can range from simply talking with the inmate, to removing any items that could be used for self-destruction, to arranging for more frequent or even constant monitoring, to reassignment in special management units or "suicide-proof" cells. The most serious cases, of course, should also be referred for psychiatric evaluation. But no matter how trivial they may seem, no suicidal threats should be taken lightly in the vulnerable atmosphere of the jail.

[76]*Jails: Intergovernmental Dimensions of a Local Problem*, p. 179.

## The Mentally Ill

Beyond its role in identifying those prone to suicide, intake screening has been described as "one of the most significant mental health services that a jail can offer."[77] That is because for a number of reasons, the mentally ill are "over-represented in the jail population."[78] Even if the resources are not available to properly treat them (as is often the case), it is important that they be identified to better assure their safety during confinement. But determining who is mentally ill among jail inmates does not answer the question of why they represent such a sizable portion of the jail population.

For many years, mental patients were warehoused in substandard mental health institutions. In response, there was a major move throughout the country during the 1960s to close down these large institutions and replace them with community-based mental health facilities. This process of *deinstitutionalization* did, in fact, result in the closing of many of the worst mental hospitals. But the community outpatient treatment services envisioned to replace them were not as readily forthcoming.

As communities closed their mental health institutions without providing other alternatives, many former patients were found wandering the streets, vulnerable to arrest. In addition, closer restrictions designed to ensure that only the truly ill are confined to mental hospitals have made commitment procedures more difficult. As a result of these circumstances, "people whose bizzare behavior might have landed them in a hospital bed a few years ago, are now being arrested and are ending up in jail."[79]

In other words, while most are no longer being warehoused in substandard mental health institutions, many are still being warehoused in jails—"the only place left to 'put' them and the only institution that cannot say 'no.'"[80] That is not meant to imply that correctional institutions are simply ignoring this unwanted responsibility. To the contrary, some are making substantial efforts to cope with the needs of the mentally ill.[81] But it does raise the serious public policy question of whether jails are the appropriate entity of government for responding to those with such problems.[82] To see how one mentally disturbed client landed in jail as the last stop in a series of efforts to get him help, read the next "Close-up on Corrections." As that case illustrates, "obviously, an adequate response cannot be expected if mental health service needs are defined simply as the jail's problem."[83]

---

[77]H. J. Steadman, D. W. McCarty, and J. P. Morrisey, *The Mentally Ill in Jail: Planning for Essential Services* (New York: Guilford Press, 1989), p. 34.

[78]Zupan, p. 31.

[79]Wilson, p. 14. For an innovative approach used by one state to remove the mentally ill from jail, see Don Wesely, "Jailing of the Mentally Ill in Nebraska," *American Jails*, Vol. 3, No. 3 (Fall 1989), pp. 12–15.

[80]*Jails: Intergovernmental Dimensions of a Local Problem*, p. 180.

[81]See, for example, Valerie Hildebeitel, "Addressing the Needs of the Mentally Ill Inmate," *American Jails*, Vol. 6, No. 5 (November/December 1992), pp. 60–61.

[82]See *Criminalizing the Seriously Mentally Ill: The Abuse of Jails as Mental Hospitals* (Washington, DC: Joint Report of the National Alliance for the Mentally Ill and the Public Citizen's Health Research Group, 1992).

[83]Steadman et al., p. 126.

## The Mentally Ill in Jail

[A]n ambulance was stopping in back of a parked bus. . . . They [ambulance personnel] ran inside the bus and brought out a large burly black man. The officers exclaimed, "Charlie, what are you doing?" Charlie greeted them with equal friendliness. Evidently, Charlie was the neighborhood character. . . . The bus driver, not realizing Charlie was drunk, was afraid he was ill and had called for an ambulance. The paramedics, seeing that Charlie was only drunk, left him in our charge. The officers asked Charlie if he wanted to go to detox and he said "sure." . . . The people [at detox] took one look at Charlie and would not accept him. Evidently, he was potentially violent and disruptive. . . . The officers asked if they would sign a complaint. They said yes. Evidently, he had been [to the jail] so often that they already had a sheet on him, so it was easy to get him into a cell. The officer complained to me that Charlie was a problem because he wasn't crazy enough to go to the mental hospital. The people [at the mental hospital] wouldn't accept him because he was potentially violent and often drunk. The detox people didn't want him, even though he was an alcoholic, because he was potentially violent and bothered other patients with his crazy ways. So that left the jail. They would put him in lock-up overnight; he would go to court in the morning and then would be released. In the meantime, they would get him off the street. Charlie was booked for disorderly conduct. The detox facility was the complainant, although he had done nothing disorderly.

*Source:* Linda A. Teplin, "Policing the Mentally Ill: Styles, Strategies, and Implications," in Henry J. Steadman, ed., *Jail Diversion for the Mentally Ill* (Washington, DC: National Institute of Corrections, n.d.), p. 14.

## Classification

Just as certain inmates may need to be handled separately because they are suicidal or mentally ill, there are other groups who also need to be housed separately to provide them with needed services, as well as to promote the safety of all inmates and the security of the institution. This is what is meant by *classification*—the "systematic grouping of inmates into categories based on shared characteristics and/or behavioral patterns."[84] Classification is used to "ensure the safety and security of the individual inmate, as well as the smooth operation of the facility."[85]

Correctional facilities did not always group inmates separately. As we saw in the early origins of the jail, men and women, young and old, and even sick and healthy inmates were all housed together. In the history of correctional insti-

[84]The following list, as well as much of the remaining information on classification, is summarized from School of Justice and Safety Administration, "Classification" (Miami, FL: Miami-Dade Community College: unpublished lesson plan, n.d.), p. 1.
[85]Ibid.

tutions, "separation by sex came first, then separation by age, followed by separation by problems."[86]

In today's jails, classification functions to segregate:

- *Pretrial* defendants from *convicted* inmates
- *Sentenced* from *un*sentenced inmates
- *Males* from *females*
- *Adults* from *juveniles*
- *Violent* from *non*violent inmates
- *General* population from *special-need* inmates (e.g., drug/alcohol abusers, emotionally disturbed, mentally handicapped, sexual predators, elderly, physically handicapped)[87]

Jail personnel determine an inmate's housing assignment on the basis of classification procedures. The information used to classify inmates comes from a number of sources, including observations and interviews, along with review of available court reports (e.g., the presentence investigation), the inmate's personal history, and medical or psychological screening records. Staff look at such things as the offense committed (or charged), and the offender's legal status, background, attitude, education, and desire for self-improvement. In doing so, jail personnel get a better picture of whom they are dealing with and how best to handle them in terms of everything from housing assignment to degree of supervision needed and eligibility for various work release, educational, or treatment programs.

## Crowding

Even the best intentioned and most sophisticated classification programs cannot achieve their objectives in institutions that are seriously crowded. When space is limited, just having enough room for initial screening, booking, and classification becomes a "luxury."[88] Moreover, when space is severely restricted, inmates must be "fit in" wherever a spare bed can be found (or added). Under such conditions, the integrity of the classification system is compromised.

Many people use the term *over*crowding to describe such conditions. But it has been noted that "overcrowding is a misnomer"—that is, it "implies that there is an acceptable level of crowding, [and] when you exceed that level, you are then overcrowded."[89] In reality, there is no "acceptable" level of crowding. Any jail that is operating beyond its capacity is, plainly and simply, *crowded*. Regardless of the terms used, the fact remains that many jails are struggling to cope with too many inmates in too little space. Although the seriousness of this situation is apparent, the next "Close-up on Corrections" offers a humorous comparison of

[86]Vernon Fox, *Correctional Institutions* (Englewood Cliffs, NJ: Prentice Hall, 1983), p. 61.
[87]School of Justice and Safety Administration, p. l.
[88]Jemelka, p. 38.
[89]Russell Davis, "After All This, We Are Still Overcrowded!! A Guideline for Managing the Overcrowded Facility," *Direct Supervision Jails: Proceedings of the 5th Annual Symposium* (Hagerstown, MD: American Jail Association, 1990), p. 40.

Jail Crowding

It was a beautiful Saturday morning—the birds were singing, the sky was blue, and a blessed event was just about to be bestowed on a friend of mine. Most new fathers would probably worry at this point, but not him—he [had] thoroughly planned ahead. . . .

Two months after marrying his lovely wife, they decided to have their first child . . . they bought an affordable new two-bedroom house. Next, they spent a fortune on the furnishings for the baby's room, but it was worth it. A real oak crib, a real oak two-drawer dresser, a wind-up swing set to rock the little tyke to sleep. You should see the cute little baby bath—it's one of a kind. The wallpaper, the new paint, the new carpet, the new clothes, and, let us not forget, the oak rocker for mom to rock and feed the child. Finally, they knew that their 1971 Volkswagen certainly was good enough for them, but not for this child. They bought a new Ford Festiva, small, but efficient and safe. . . .

I only mention this because they performed some pretty steady planning. Unfortunately, like all well-planned events, [Murphy's Law] paid my friends a visit . . . they had triplets. That's right, not one, not two, but three adorable babies. . . . Mother and babies are doing fine. Dad is on the brink of despair. Why, you ask? For the same reason that most administrators of overcrowded . . . facilities are on the brink of despair. Too many people requiring services which were designed for the . . . amount of people that a well-thought-out and planned budget allowed for.

*Source:* James Myers and Michael Kramer, "The Effect of Overcrowding on Direct Supervision: The Experiences of Washoe County," *Direct Supervision Jails: Proceedings of the 5th Annual Symposium* (Hagerstown, MD: American Jail Association, 1990), p. 47.

jail crowding to a family planning scenario that most everyone can appreciate.

A correctional facility is generally considered to be crowded when it exceeds either:

- *Design capacity:* the number of inmates that it was originally constructed to confine; or
- *Rated capacity:* the number of inmates that an acknowledged expert (such as a state prison inspector) estimates the jail can safely hold, which is generally a less conservative figure.

When jails are assessed in terms of the percentage of rated capacity occupied, it is apparent that they have become increasingly crowded in recent years—moving from an average 85% occupancy in 1983 to 101% in 1991.[90] If the smaller (design capacity) figure were used, the extent of crowding would undoubtedly be even greater.

[90]*Sourcebook—1991*, p. 611.

Overall averages, however, do not give the full picture, since, as was mentioned earlier, very small jails do not tend to have severe crowding problems. In fact, it has been noted that there is a direct relationship between jail size and the percentage of space that is occupied, with the smallest jails occupying 64% of capacity in contrast to the 126% occupancy rate of mega-jails.[91] But overlooked in these generalities is the fact that the need for classification can quickly create crowded conditions in small jails—when, for instance, males have to be double-bunked to accommodate a newlyarriving female or juvenile inmate.

At some point, such a severe level of crowding is reached that the jail's resources are strained beyond further ability to cope. That point has not been specifically defined, but it is apparent that the courts are not oblivious to the problem. As inmates have begun to challenge crowded conditions, the courts are becoming increasingly active in correcting the situation. By 1988, over 300 jails were either under *court order* to reduce crowding or were operating under a mandatory *consent decree*,[92] whereby they agreed to lower their inmate population.

Undoubtedly, even more are functioning under such restrictions today. Several hundred may not seem like a large number (given the more than 3000 jails in operation). But many more jails are under court order or consent decree for a number of conditions that may well be related to crowding—such as fire hazards or lack of sufficient recreational facilities, medical services, staffing patterns, visiting practices, library services, or inmate classification.[93]

The basic fact that the judicial branch of government has determined that the situation is so serious as to warrant court action is itself illustrative of the severity of the problem. New construction, expansion of existing facilities, and early release are among the many options that have been used to reduce crowding. However, while everyone agrees that additional space is needed, no one wants a jail in their neighborhood. Such public opposition has forced some jurisdictions to become impressively creative in finding sites for new facilities.

For example, Norfolk County (Massachusetts) solved this problem by building their new jail on a federal highway's right-of-way, between the north and southbound lanes of a major divided highway. Although this unusual site "presented some significant challenges in programming and design," it did make good use of an available location with minimal impact on the surrounding community.[94] A similarly creative option has been employed in New York City, where the nation's first floating jail—a refurbished Staten Island Ferry—was opened in 1987 on the East River. In addition to avoiding negative public reaction, it has been found that floating facilities are much faster to build. Whereas "permanent land-based jails take up to five years to construct in New York City," barges and ferries can be refurbished into a jail within an average of six months.[95]

---

[91] Ibid., p. 612.

[92] Ibid., p. 100.

[93] Ibid.

[94] "Direct Supervision in the Fast Lane," *Direct Supervision Network,* Vol. 2 (July/September 1991), p. 7 (a publication of the Direct Supervision Institute, Denver, CO).

[95] Hedvig Chappell, "New York City's Floating Jails: `Waving' Away Overcrowding," *The National Sheriff,* Vol. 41, No. 6 (December 1989/January 1990), p. 19.

This maritime facility is an 800-bed floating detention center that is completely self-contained. The largest of five floating jails in New York City, it joins two decommissioned Staten Island Ferry boats and two modified barges. Courtesy of the New York City Department of Correction.

Creative as they are, many of these innovations are short-term, stop-gap measures, and new facilities often fill to capacity quickly. The issue cannot truly be addressed effectively without systemwide attention to everything from public policies and sentencing practices to consideration of the community-based alternatives described in Chapter 5. Jail administrators cannot be the only personnel who take responsiblity for the crowding crisis. To the contrary, "virtually every decision-maker in the local justice system exercises discretion that can affect the jail population."[96] Throughout the justice system, there are a "lot of little ways" that can add up to reduce the jail population without releasing serious offenders. Several examples from throughout the country are highlighted in the next "Close-up on Corrections."

While these illustrations are indicative of the significant steps being taken, it must be recognized that jail crowding is a complex challenge that cannot be adequately addressed by one or two isolated changes. The long-term plight of crowded jails will only be resolved when jails are reserved for those who actually need to be confined behind bars—who are not there simply because the system is slow in processing them, or because there is no other resource in the community to deal with their problems. Moreover, as long as society continues to respond to the symptoms rather than the causes of behavior for which people are confined, the public will continue to be disenchanted with the performance of its jails. As long as jails remain the primary vehicle for responding to such social problems as mental illness, alcoholism, and drug abuse, their role will continue to be unclear; their performance will continue to be unsatisfactory; and

[96]Andy Hall, "Systemwide Strategies to Alleviate Jail Crowding," *National Institute of Justice Research in Brief* (Washington, DC: U.S. Department of Justice, 1987), p. 2. See also Alvin W. Cohn, "National Overview of Innovative Options to Relieve Jail Overcrowding," unpublished paper (Longmont, CO: National Institute of Corrections, 1989).

### Systemwide Strategies to Alleviate Jail Crowding

#### LAW ENFORCEMENT

Decisions surrounding local arrest practices—whether to arrest, transport to jail, book, or detain for bail—are critical determinants of jail population size.

- San Diego (California) has been successful in reducing crowding through the use of a privately operated detoxification reception program, where inebriates must remain for a minimum 4-hour period.
- Law enforcement officials in Galveston County (Texas) have instituted practices to divert the mentally ill. A team of deputies receives special training to assist in meeting the emergency needs of the mentally ill, thereby allowing them to be taken directly to a mental health facility.
- Prearrest diversion programs are in effect for homeless persons in a number of jurisdictions throughout the United States.

#### JAIL ADMINISTRATORS

Elected sheriffs or appointed jail executives are often viewed as the managers most affected but least powerful in dealing with jail crowding. While having little direct control over admissions and length of confinement, jail administrators nevertheless can help reduce crowding by assuring ready access to pretrial release screening and bail review.

- The Bexar County (Texas) jail administrator provides data to help judges monitor the court status of prisoners and prevent length of confinement from being extended through oversight or inattention.
- In some jurisdictions, jail administrators are delegated authority to release defendants prior to trial or to divert drunk drivers to treatment centers.
- Other administrators have worked with neighboring jurisdictions to alleviate crowding on a cooperative, multicounty basis.

#### PROSECUTORS

Early case screening by prosecutors reduces unnecessary length of confinement by eliminating or downgrading weak cases as soon as possible.

- Assistant prosecutors in Milwaukee County (Wisconsin) review arrests around the clock, enabling them to decide on the appropriate charge within 24 to 36 hours after arrest.
- Prosecutors in a number of jurisdictions have taken an active role by chairing jail population reduction boards.

#### PRETRIAL SERVICES

Providing background information on defendants, release recommendations, and other pretrial assistance can be an important component of solutions to crowding.

- In Mecklenburg County (North Carolina), pretrial services and magistrate bail setting are available 24 hours a day, 7 days a week.

- In San Mateo County (California), pretrial staff are authorized to release misdemeanor suspects prior to their first court appearance.
- A National Institute of Justice study found that supervised release programs in Miami (Florida), Portland (Oregon), and Milwaukee (Wisconsin) significantly reduced the . . . population without significantly increasing the risk to public safety.

## JUDICIARY

Judges make more decisions affecting jail populations than anyone else. This often makes them leaders in seeking jail-crowding solutions.

- The King County (Washington) District Court has a "three-tier" release policy that reduces court time, jail admissions, and length of confinement. Guidelines specify the charges for which pretrial services staff may (1) release without consulting the court, (2) release after phoning a duty judge, or (3) make recommendations to the court.
- In Bexar County (Texas), each judge receives a weekly list of inmates awaiting indictment, trial, sentencing, or revocation in that judge's court.
- Many judges have worked to extend the range of nonjail sentencing options, including suspended sentences, fines, community service, restitution, halfway house placements, and other alternatives.
- When the jail is at capacity, a growing number of courts defer the serving of sentences in cases where jail is believed to be an appropriate sentence, but immediate jailing is not essential for the community's safety.

## DEFENSE

Early screening for indigency and public defender appointment can decrease length of confinement, and thus yield substantial savings of jail space.

- In Mecklenburg County (North Carolina), pretrial conferences between defense and prosecution help identify, eliminate, or downgrade marginal cases and facilitate plea negotiation.
- In St. Louis (Missouri), appointing private attorneys in felony cases has reduced staggering public defender caseloads and resulted in shorter pretrial confinement.

## PROBATION AND PAROLE

Probation and parole agencies can enhance case-processing efficiency by streamlining presentence investigation procedures and expediting revocation decisions, which helps cut the length of confinement.

- In Brevard County (Florida), the jail population oversight committee worked with probation and parole officers to cut PSI preparation time from 90 days to 30 to 35 days for jail cases.
- This same county also cut to 24 hours the time required for decisions on probation revocation, thus decreasing the use of jail beds for persons on probation "hold" orders.

*Source:* Paraphrased from Andy Hall, "Systemwide Strategies to Alleviate Jail Crowding," *National Institute of Justice Research in Brief* (Washington, DC: U.S. Department of Justice, 1987), pp. 2–4.

their space will continue to be filled beyond capacity. Direct-supervision/new-generation jails can change living conditions for those confined, but only a new generation of public policies can challenge long-held considerations of who should *be* confined.

## ❖ SUMMARY

As the oldest component of the criminal justice system, jails have historical legacies which remain evident today in antiquated facilities that have long outlived their usefulness. With the closing of such jails (along with the consolidation of small jails into larger, more economical regional detention centers), the number of jails in existence today actually represents a decline. Although there are still far more jails housing 50 inmates or less than megajails confining 1000 or more inmates, the largest facilities hold the greatest percentage of the overall inmate population.

Of those in jail, approximately half are convicted offenders, while the remaining half are accused defendants awaiting trial. Jails also book arrestees, hold those awaiting sentencing or transfer, and readmit probation, parole, or bail/bond violators. Many inmates confined in jail have not been involved in violent crimes, but rather, are being held for drug-related, public order, or property offenses. In fact, alcohol and drug abusers represent a sizable portion of the jail's clients, despite the lack of adequate resources to address their problems while incarcerated.

In most jurisdictions, jails do not have authority to confine offenders with sentences of more than one year. As a result, there is a high turnover among the jail's population. But on average, those who have been sentenced spend only slightly more time in jail than do their unconvicted cellmates. This raises the issue of whether pretrial inmates—technically innocent in the eyes of the law—should be subjected to worse conditions than they would encounter if convicted and sentenced to prison. Additionally, it has been noted that the physical features of a correctional facility have a considerable influence on inmate behavior.

These are among the reasons that some jurisdictions have embraced a new generation of jailing, which attempts to create as "normal" an environment as can be achieved in confinement. Architecture, physical amenities, and management style all work together to shape behavior in such jails. In contrast to the intermittent or remote style of surveillance in traditional facilities, these jails rely on direct supervision. Officers interact directly with inmates, unobstructed by bars or glass enclosures. While such facilities have been criticized as too "plush," their basic intent is not to promote comfort but to provide a safe and secure environment wherein staff rather than inmates are in control. Consequently, they tend to experience lower rates of violent incidents, suicides, escapes, and vandalism. Despite their effectiveness and pleasant appearance, direct supervision facilities are actually less costly to build, operate, and maintain.

Because jails are administered primarily at the local level of government, they represent considerable diversity with regard to everything from size to facility design and management style. Most jails are under the supervision of an elected sheriff, although in some jurisdictions, jails are run by an appointed director of corrections. It is the jail administrator who sets the tone for how the jail will operate—just as staff, in turn, establish the climate for inmates. Because proper staffing is so important to the jail's functions, increasing attention is being given to improving the compensation, training, selection, and use of personnel. Qualified personnel are essential to enforcing the facility's rules and regulations through disciplinary procedures that are firm, fair, and consistent.

Inmates are admitted to jail through the process of intake, which includes such tasks as booking, taking information, searching, photographing, and fingerprinting. Once admitted, many jails now provide recreational, educational, and counseling services, and some have even initiated jail industries to enable inmates to engage in productive work.

The availability of medical services is a critical necessity in jails, not only to provide appropriate treatment to the inmate, but also to curtail the spread of infectious diseases. Because suicide is the primary cause of death in jail, personnel must be especially alert to its signs and symptoms, taking immediate precautions whenever the potential for suicide is suspected. Like those vulnerable to suicide, the mentally ill are overrepresented among the jail population, largely as a result of the deinstitutionalization of mental health facilities. Because of the lack of resources to deal with them in the community, the mentally ill are often confined in jails, which are poorly suited to address their problems.

To better ensure safety and security of all inmates, the jail population is classified according to their conviction/sentencing status, sex, age, offense, and needs. Inmates are then assigned to housing according to their classification. But it is difficult to provide proper classification in crowded facilities, where limited space does not always enable the appropriate separation of inmates. Jails are considered crowded when the number of persons they are holding exceeds either the facility's design or rated capacity. A number of severely crowded jails are operating under court order or consent decree to reduce their population. Although new construction, renovations, and early release have been employed to address the crowding problem, those measures have generally proven insufficient. Nor is the situation much better in prisons, as we will see in the following chapters.

# chapter 7

# Prisons and Other Correctional Facilities

*[T]he "jail problem" is a complex collection of problems, including jurisdictional authority and responsibility, Constitutional rights, sociological and medical opinion, basic public safety, and perhaps most difficult, the allotment of increasingly scarce resources for the benefit of an exceedingly unpopular constituency."[1]*

*Advisory Commission on Intergovernmental Relations*

## ❖ CHAPTER OVERVIEW

If jails are the last resort for a community that has no other alternatives to deal with its social problems, prisons presumably represent the last resort for a criminal justice system which has exhausted all other alternatives. Although a first-time offender may be sent to prison for a serious offense, the majority of prison inmates have had previous experience with the criminal justice system. Some had been afforded a "second chance" through probation; others had served prior time. But whatever their prior experience, it was obviously unsuccessful in changing long-term behavior—leaving the prison to attempt to accomplish what other sanctions failed to achieve. In most cases, however, it is equally unable to do so. About the only thing that prisons are able to accomplish with consistent success is suppressing further involvement in street crime during the period of incarceration. Whether the offender becomes better or worse as a result of prison experience is no longer the issue. Society has apparently settled for this compromise.

Even as community-based alternatives to incarceration have expanded, prison populations have steadily increased. As the most visible image of corrections, it is prisons that first come to mind when the public considers responses to crime. Like anything else that is not easily comprehended, isolation behind thick walls, barbed-wire fencing, and high-powered rifles protruding from guard towers creates an aura of mystique. The public is at the same time both fearful of and fascinated by its prisons.

[1]National Advisory Commission on Criminal Justice Standards and Goals, *Corrections* (Washington, DC: U.S. Government Printing Office, 1973), pp. 342–43.

As such, prisons are the central focus—the hard-core base—of the correctional process. They provide the direct, external control demanded when such indirect social controls as norms, values, and even laws proved ineffective. Because of their significance and their impact on the historical development of corrections, prisons tend to disproportionately influence the philosophy of the entire correctional system.

As a matter of fact, many other correctional components evolved from or were added to the prison. For example, as described in Chapter 4, indeterminate sentencing originated in the Norfolk Island penal colony. Parole developed from the Irish prison practice of releasing inmates through gradual reduction of security and "tickets of leave." Probation evolved as an alternative to prevent people who could be reformed in the community from going to prison or jail unnecessarily. Juvenile institutions split off from prisons in the nineteenth century as a result of the "child-saving" movement. More recently, electronic monitoring emerged as an option to incarceration for those needing more restrictions than traditional probation. As we have seen in Chapter 6, prison crowding can have a detrimental impact on local jails. Moreover, many wardens and prison staff make recommendations to parole boards supporting or opposing the release of inmates, thereby influencing other phases of corrections. Even where parole has been abolished, prison personnel to some extent control the "time off for good behavior" that enables early release, which has an impact on the fundamental goals of the sentencing process. As a result of these current trends and historical developments, prisons have been and continue to be a very influential segment of the criminal justice system.

---

*LEARNING GOALS*

*Do you know:*

- *What levels of government are responsible for the operation of prisons?*
- *How many prisons there are in the United States?*
- *How much per bed it costs to build a prison?*
- *How much per year it costs to confine an inmate in prison?*
- *Which level of government carries the burden for the bulk of correctional expenditures?*
- *What percentage of an average inmate's sentence will actually be served?*

---

## ❖ NUMBER AND TYPES OF INSTITUTIONS

As we have seen in the historical development of corrections, prisons range from large, high-security complexes to small, rural road camps. Like jails, some date to the turn of the century, whereas others are much more modern. But because they do not trace their history as far back as jails, prisons overall have been more recently constructed. Conditions in the worst jails are therefore likely to be inferior to the worst prisons. But on the other hand, conditions in the best jails may surpass those in the best prisons, since the new generation philosophy has yet to influence prison construction.

### Federal, State, and Military Facilities

Beyond their more recent development, prisons are also far less numerous than jails, thereby enabling greater uniformity. Since jails are a function of the local level of government, every county and municipality potentially has the authority to operate a jail. Prisons, however, are a responsibility of the *state* and *federal* levels of government, which represent only 51 jurisdictions. Thus, in contrast to the more than 3000 jails spread throughout the country, there are only 957 state prisons in the United States,[2] ranging from 1 in North Dakota to 57 in New York.[3] Adding the 80 federal institutions[4] brings the total number of prisons to 1037.

While prisons are fewer in number and therefore likely to be more standardized than jails, there is still considerable diversity among them. Moreover, not included in these figures are an additional 250 state-administered correctional facilities that are not technically considered "prisons"—such as prerelease centers, work release centers, halfway houses, and educational/training facilities.[5]

In addition, the U.S. Army, Navy, Air Force, and Marine Corps maintain correctional facilities for military personnel. Some of these prisoners have been turned over to the military for trial, sentencing, and imprisonment after committing crimes in civilian jurisdictions. Others have been convicted of violations of the Uniform Code of Military Conduct [e.g., desertion, disrespect for a superior officer, or being AWOL (absent without official leave)]. In this respect, military corrections differs somewhat from its civilian counterparts, since the primary objective is restoration of the offender to active duty.

### The Costs of Imprisonment

How expensive any particular correctional institution is to build and operate will depend on a number of factors—where it is located, the number of inmates it confines, the number of personnel needed to adequately staff it, how secure it is designed to be, the extensiveness of inmate programs and treatment offered, and so on. In general, the larger and more secure a prison is, the more expensive it will be. Construction costs range from:

- Over $70,000 *per bed* for maximum security state prisons, to
- Just under $30,000 *per bed* for minimum security facilities, to
- Some $26,000 *per bed* for juvenile institutions,[6] and that is just initial construction. Annual operating costs vary from almost $6000 to over $23,000

[2]James Stephan, *Census of State and Federal Correctional Facilities, 1990* (Washington, DC: U.S. Department of Justice, 1992), p. 1.
[3]Compiled from figures presented in "Number of Adult Facilities and Programs," *ACA Directory* (Laurel, MD: American Correctional Association, 1990), p. xviii.
[4]Ibid.
[5]Ibid.
[6]*Report to the Nation on Crime and Justice,* Second Edition (Washington, DC: U.S. Department of Justice, Bureau of Justice Statistics, 1988), p. 124.

*per inmate.*[7] A recent analysis indicates that the average yearly cost of keeping someone in prison has increased to about $14,000,[8] (although other estimates are much higher—ranging from $30,000 to $60,000).[9] In an effort to offset the escalating costs of prison construction, some of the money from the U.S. Justice Department's Asset Forfeiture Fund has been directed toward prison building needs.[10]

Because the majority of prisons operate at the state level of government, it is not surprising to find that as shown in Figure 7.1, it is the states that are bearing the primary brunt of this fiscal burden. Moreover, the burden is ever increas-

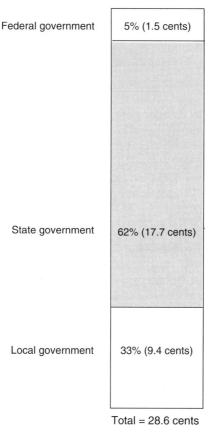

Federal government — 5% (1.5 cents)

State government — 62% (17.7 cents)

Local government — 33% (9.4 cents)

Total = 28.6 cents

**Figure 7.1** Responsibility for correctional expenditures. *Note:* 28.6 cents of every "justice" dollar is spent on corrections, largely at the state level of government. *Source:* Calculated from statistics presented in *Report to the Nation on Crime and Justice* (Washington, DC: U.S. Department of Justice, Bureau of Justice Statistics, 1988), p. 117.

[7]Ibid., pp. 123–24.

[8]"Study Shows Prison Cheaper Than Having Criminals on the Street," *Community Crime Prevention Digest* (January 1991), p. 4, citing John J. DiIulio's study of prison inmates, conducted for the Wisconsin Policy Research Institute.

[9]"The Cost of Criminal Justice," *CJ International,* Vol. 8, No. 3 (May/June 1992), p. 8.

[10]Between 1985 and 1991, almost $500 million has gone to prison construction from this fund. See "Justice Department Forfeitures Turn Drug Profits into Prison Funding," *On the Line,* Vol. 14, No. 3 (May 1991), p. 2.

ing. State and local spending for corrections has been climbing more rapidly in recent years than spending for such other government functions as education, welfare, health care, highways, and police protection (see Figure 7.2).

Undoubtedly, imprisonment is an expensive option. For what it costs to keep a prisoner in maximum custody for a year, a student could attend one of the best universities in the country; 20 to 25 offenders could be supervised on probation or parole in the community; hot meals could be provided to thousands of needy people. It is for such reasons that this country's extensive use of incarceration frequently comes under fire.

But others argue that the costs of prison must be balanced against the costs of crime. At least one study indicates that an average crime costs society $2300 in losses to victims, court costs, and police expenditures. Given a yearly median crime rate of 12 offenses per criminal, this research estimates that it actually costs *less* to keep someone in prison (12 times $2,300 = $27,600, versus $14,000 for incarceration).[11] Whether or not such sizable fiscal savings are achieved by incarceration, the costs of imprisonment must be weighed against the alternatives.

## Offender Fees

Despite the economic arguments pro and con, the fact remains that current public policies place considerable emphasis on the use of imprisonment. As correctional costs have skyrocketed in recent years, some jurisdictions have turned to the private sector to attempt to operate prisons more cost-effectively (a topic discussed further in Chapter 15). In addition, "the notion that offenders should contribute to their own supervision costs has gained widespread political support" in recent years.[12] In an effort to offset expenses, certain institutions are beginning to charge offenders fees. By 1988, some 36 states had authorized inmate fees for items ranging from special health services to room and board for those on work release.[13] In fact, as described in the next "Close-up on Corrections," even the federal government has become involved in collecting "rent" from its residents.

To some, charging offenders for their confinement brings back memories of the inequities involved in the fee system that was common during the early history

| | Percent Change |
|---|---|
| Education | +56% |
| Public welfare | +216% |
| Hospitals and health care | +119% |
| Highways | -21% |
| Police protection | +73% |
| Corrections | +218% |

**Figure 7.2** Changes in per capita spending by state and local governments for corrections, in comparison to other public services between 1960 and 1985. *Source: Report to the Nation on Crime and Justice* (Washington, DC: U.S. Department of Justice, Bureau of Justice Statistics, 1988), p. 120.

[11]"Study Shows Prison Cheaper," p. 4.
[12]Dale Parent, *Recovering Correctional Costs through Offender Fees* (Washington, DC: U.S. Department of Justice, 1990), p. 1.
[13]Ibid., pp. 3, 7.

**"Say, Warden, Could I Pay More for a Room with a View?"**

*. . . $27.20 per night (single rate). Secure blocks, diverse clientele, meal plan. Free exercise room and safe for valuables*

[W]hen [former] Washington [DC] Mayor Marion Barry was sentenced for cocaine possession, he suffered one more humiliation . . . pay[ing] for his stay in the pokey.

Actually, [the] . . . order that Barry pay $9,653 for jail time and one year of supervision—on top of a $5,000 fine—was fully in accord with the law. Since U.S. sentencing guidelines took effect in late 1987, all federal prisoners are supposed to ante up for their confinement. "Why should the taxpayers have to cover an inmate's room and board and medical services when the defendant can afford it?" asks William Wilkins, the federal appeals judge who is chairman of the U.S. Sentencing Commission. Judges are supposed to waive the rule for inmates who are indigent or have dependents needing subsistence money; inmates with limited funds also make restitution for their crimes first. Thus, officials estimate that only 10 percent of inmates wind up paying for their time. . . .

Critics attack the novel pay-for-jail provision as "unseemly," in light of the less than four-star-prison conditions. Sam Buffone, former chair of an American Bar Association sentencing committee, says, "It's a lot of show," given the lack of money collected. But "show" has a place in criminal law. Barry's $9,653 tab may help deter the next high roller who decides to party in a hotel room.

*Source:* "Say, Warden, Could I Pay More for a View?" *Newsweek* (November 12, 1990), p. 87.

---

of corrections. Thus, it is not surprising to find that there is significant debate surrounding these practices, which have been criticized as being "impractical, unprofessional, or inherently unfair."[14] But when government revenues are increasingly limited while demands continue to escalate, there is also considerable support for requiring users to pay for the services they receive—even if the "users" are inmates and the "services" are food, clothing, and shelter in a prison cell.

### Time Served

Regardless of whether they are paying "rent" for being there, prison inmates face longer periods of confinement than their jail counterparts. State and federal correctional institutions generally confine those sentenced to minimum terms that are *longer than one year*.[15] The maximum, of course, can extend to life

---

[14]Ibid., p. 1.

[15]The federal level of government, as described in Chapter 6, operates both institutions for pretrial detention or short-term confinement (i.e., metropolitan correctional centers, the equivalent of local jails), and institutions for long-term confinement (federal prisons).

imprisonment, and states that provide for capital punishment also hold inmates awaiting execution on death row.

But the sentence *received* is often not the same as the sentence that is, in fact, *served*. As we have already seen in Chapters 1 and 4, options such as gain time and parole have reduced the time one serves. Even as the popularity of parole has diminished with the justice model's emphasis on "tightening-up" sentences, prison crowding has forced many states to supplement parole with some other form of early release. As a result, inmates are really serving only about *one-third* (34%) of the maximum that they could have been required to serve under their sentence.[16] For example, in 1988, the average maximum sentence length of those in state prisons was 82 months—almost seven years.[17] Yet, they were being released after spending an average of only 28 months behind bars—just over two years.[18] To the extent that the public has been misled into believing that the sentence awarded by a judge approximates that which the offender actually serves in prison, society is sadly mistaken.

In terms of *where* they are confined, there may also be a misperception that those serving longer sentences or convicted of more serious offenses are incarcerated in federal prisons. In fact, whether one's time is served in a federal or a state facility depends not on the length of sentence or the seriousness of the offense, but rather, on whether it was a *federal* or a *state* law that was violated. Murder, for example—considered the most serious violent offense—is typically a violation of a state statute, resulting in state imprisonment. On the other hand, federal prisons hold offenders guilty of such federal offenses as interstate commerce violations, tax fraud, or drug trafficking, as well as crimes involving federal property (e.g., post offices or banks covered by the Federal Deposit Insurance Corporation).

---

*LEARNING GOALS*

*Do you know:*

- *The difference between maximum-, medium-, and minimum-security correctional institutions?*
- *At what level of security classification most inmates are assigned?*
- *How an inmate's custody classification is determined?*

---

## ❖ SECURITY CLASSIFICATIONS

Beyond their jurisdictional differences, prisons also operate at varying levels of *custody classification*. For security purposes, correctional institutions are classified into three general categories—maximum, medium, and minimum—depending on the level of control they exert.

---

[16]Craig Perkins and Darrell K. Gilliard, *National Corrections Reporting Program, 1988* (Washington, DC: U.S. Department of Justice, 1992), p. 29.
[17]Ibid., based on statistics for first releases from prisons in 35 states.
[18]Ibid.

The security level of a particular institution is based on such factors as how heavily the outside perimeter is controlled, the presence or absence of "guard" towers, the extent of external patrols, the number of detection devices, the security of housing areas, and the level of staffing.[19] An entire facility may be classified at one level (e.g., maximum), or various levels of security may be established for different units within an institution. Thus, within the same compound might be found sections designated as maximum, medium, or even minimum security.

## Maximum Security

A *maximum-security* facility is characterized by a walled outside perimeter, armed guard towers, searchlights, alarms, electronic detection devices, and similar high-security measures. Often located in remote rural areas, these institutions have been characterized as "fortresses" that are placed "out in the country as if they were for lepers or for people with contagious diseases."[20]

In such facilities, cells are generally found inside large cellblocks or constructed back to back, with each unit facing a wall. *External* security is physically obvious, and *internal* security is tight as well. Movement within the institution is closely restricted. Visits are limited and carefully controlled. Inmate counts are conducted frequently (as often as every two hours). Because surveillance is so continuous, privacy is essentially eliminated. Certainly, maximum custody is where the hard-core offender is found.

Layers of barbed wire and imposing guard towers are features of high-security institutions. Courtesy of the Nassau County Sheriff's Department, East Meadow, New York.

[19]Paraphrased from *Federal Bureau of Prisons: Facilities* (Washington, DC: U.S. Department of Justice, n.d.), p. 3.

[20]Prison Research Education Action Project, "Prisons Cannot Protect Society," in Bonnie Szumski, ed., *America's Prisons: Opposing Viewpoints*, Fourth Edition (St. Paul, MN: Greenhaven Press, 1985), p. 46.

Larger, more populated states usually have one or more maximum-security prisons. In states with fewer institutions, a portion of a medium-security compound might be designated for maximum internal security. In still other locations, an additional category of *close security* has been added, which is not quite as restrictive as maximum but more closely supervised than medium. For a look inside two maximum-security institutions, see the next "Close-up on Corrections."

## Medium Security

A *medium-custody* institution usually has a wire fence, along with a strong perimeter that can include guard towers or booths. (Walls prevent outside visibility, but fences do not.) From the exterior, some medium-security physical plants may not be noticeably different from maximum prisons. But they contain less restriction inside the fences or compound—fewer counts, more privileges, greater freedom of movement, and more interaction with other inmates. However, all of these "liberties" are relative to the virtual isolation of those in maximum confinement. There will still be such controls as alarms, closed-circuit television, and locked gates, with the flow of traffic restricted to certain specified areas.

These types of institutions house a wide variety of offenders—virtually anyone who is not dangerous enough to require maximum security but not a sufficiently low risk to be entrusted to a minimum level of security. Because they are viewed as more "salvageable" than the hardened offenders in maximum custody, medium-security prisons tend to offer more training, treatment, and work programs.

## Minimum Security

In contrast, a *minimum-custody* facility has extremely little external control or regimentation. It frequently possesses only a single fence or no exterior obstruction at all. There are no towers, outside patrols, or the like. Inside, there are no cells, bars, or other obvious security measures. Housing is generally arranged in dormitory fashion. The physical structure itself may look like a farm, ranch, or college campus.

In fact, minimum-security facilities are rarely referred to as "prisons." More likely, they are called halfway houses, work release centers, or prerelease centers. Especially in urban areas, where minimum-security facilities are located directly in the community, they have recently come to be known by the generic term *community residential centers:* "Community residential centers represent a promising, yet underutilized, resource. . . . [They] may be used as a pretrial detention option, as a condition of probation, as part of a sentence of confinement, as a transitional setting for offenders about to be released into the community from jail or prison, and as an intermediate sanction for violations of community supervision requirements."[21]

In this type of setting, "custody is a function of classification rather than of prison hardware."[22] In other words, only those sufficiently trustworthy are

[21]Bernard J. McCarthy, "Community Residential Centers: An Intermediate Sanction for the 1990s," in Peter J. Benekos and Alida V. Merlo, eds., *Corrections: Dilemmas and Directions* (Cincinnati, OH: Anderson Publishing Company, 1992), p. 190.

[22]National Advisory Commission, p. 345.

## The "Hole"

Since Pelican Bay opened [in 1990] . . . it has obtained a reputation as perhaps the most modern and secure penal facility in the country. Built to isolate and punish the state's most troublesome convicts, the quiet, high-tech complex is almost Orwellian in its cold efficiency. . . .

SHU [security housing unit] inmates are locked in windowless eight-by-ten cells for 22 1/2 hours a day. Whenever they are outside their cells, they are in waist restraints and handcuffs with a double escort and under the gun, except when showering or exercising alone in a tiny courtyard. They eat in their cells on trays passed through narrow openings.

Inmates are not allowed to take classes, do not work, and cannot earn time off for good behavior.

No smoking is allowed, nor are matches. Prison-issue jumpsuits have ties in place of buttons and zippers, which might be converted into weapons. Prisoners are permitted 10 books or magazines, but all staples are removed. Every object that enters the building is searched by hand and X-rayed. . . .

The grounds are surrounded by a double 14-foot cyclone fence, wired with an alarm and topped with coils of razor ribbon. Officers with rifles stand in . . . watchtowers overlooking a "no-man's land" between the fence and the prison and keep watch 24 hours a day. The no-man's land is studded with sensors that sound an alarm when stepped on.

No one has tried to skip.

There are few visitors.

*Source:* Kevin Leary, "A Prisoner's Nightmare," *San Francisco Chronicle* (July 5, 1991), p. A1.

## Maximum Security

In theory, each new inmate was evaluated and assigned to a cell block according to his behavior and future prospects; in practice, he was sent to wherever there was an empty cell. . . .

If an inmate feared for his life . . . he had an option, albeit an extreme one. He could request "protective custody," thereby effecting his removal from the regular blocks to an area specifically set aside. . . . There he would spend his time in solitary confinement with very limited time out of his cell each week for individual exercise, visits, or showers. . . .

In addition to the standard barred cell door, half the cells had solid metal doors with one tiny window in them. The cells themselves had no windows, and once the metal door was closed, the cell's occupant was effectively sealed off from the rest of the world.

[1]Source: Kelsey Kauffman, *Prison Officers and Their World* (Cambridge, MA: Harvard University Press, 1988), pp. 26–30.

assigned to minimum custody, so there is little need for elaborate physical security systems. Administrators concerned with quelling the public's fears about being neighbors to a community-based facility are sensitive to the need for both careful screening and proper supervision of the residents.[23] In that regard, one review of community residential centers indicated that "residential programming is strict, intensive, and accountability-oriented."[24] Verifying the strict supervision, one offender who was fulfilling the last months of his sentence at a community residential center stated on national television that serving time there was harder than in prison![25] Quite likely, that observation was a reflection of the fact that in minimum security, the stern imposition of external control is replaced by the firm expectation of self-control.

Inmates in such institutions may hold jobs or attend classes in the community by day, returning to the facility after work or school. Most commonly, the programs offered are a combination of work release and drug treatment.[26] Although those returning from outside assignments are likely to be searched, much of the facility's security depends on the "honor system," which most tend to respect in order to avoid losing the greater freedoms and privileges of minimum security. Because considerable trust is placed in minimum-security inmates, these institutions "are most likely to promote greater self-confidence and self-esteem."[27] As the name implies, both internal and external security involve the least restrictions necessary.

Those confined in minimum security tend to be nonviolent, first-time offenders serving short sentences, those who have earned a lower custody classification through good behavior in higher-security facilities, or inmates preparing for release or parole. Placing "novice" prisoners in such facilities avoids many of the harmful effects of long-term association with hardened offenders. By the same token, phasing-out inmates through minimum security near the end of their sentence enables them to resume life in free society while still under some supervision and lessens the trauma of their readjustment. See the next "Close-up on Corrections" for an inside view of a unique minimum security facility.

### Security Distribution

Maximum-security prisons undoubtedly have the greatest notoriety among the public. Institutions such as San Quentin, Alcatraz (now closed), and Attica have been the subject of numerous books, songs, television programs, and movies. But despite this publicity, there are actually fewer inmates serving time in maximum (253,664) than medium custody (351,900), although the fewest of all are housed in minimum security (93,006)[28] (see Figure 7.3).

[23]Anthony M. Scillia, "Winning the 'Not-in-My-Neighborhood' Game: Security Systems Play Major Role in Allaying Public Fear about Community Corrections Centers," *Corrections Today*, Vol. 51, No. 4 (July 1989), pp. 114–17.

[24]Bobbie L. Huskey, "The Expanding Use of CRCs," *Corrections Today*, Vol. 54, No. 8 (December 1992), p. 73.

[25]Ibid., p. 72.

[26]Ibid.

[27]Dean J. Champion, *Corrections in the United States* (Englewood Cliffs, NJ: Prentice Hall, 1990), p. 215.

[28]Stephan, p. 8.

### Minimum Security

One remarkable minimum security correctional center was opened in 1972 at Vienna, IL, as a branch of the Illinois State Penitentiary. Although a large facility, it approaches the quality of [a] non-penal institution. Buildings resembling garden apartments are built around a "town square," complete with churches, schools, shops, and [a] library. Paths lead off to "neighborhoods" where "homes" provide private rooms in small clusters. Extensive provision has been made for both indoor and outdoor recreation. Academic, commercial, and vocational education facilities equal or surpass those of many technical high schools. . . . The non-prisonlike design permits it to be adapted for a variety of educational, mental health, or other human service functions.

*Source:* National Advisory Commission on Criminal Justice Standards and Goals, *Corrections* (Washington, DC: U.S. Government Printing Office, 1973), p. 345.

## Classification Procedures

Custody classification relates to the level of *externally imposed* control needed by those whose law-violating behavior indicates that they have not developed sufficiently strong *internal* controls. As we saw in Chapter 6, classification refers to the separation of inmates into groups according to characteristics they share in common. In jails, there is less need for minimum-, medium-, and maximum-security classifications because offenders are (among other things) separated according to their pretrial versus convicted status. Those who are convicted and sentenced to shorter-term confinement in jail would not be expected to be the most serious violent criminals. In contrast, those sentenced to serve their time in prison represent a much wider range of seriousness in terms of both their current offense and prior criminal history—from check forgery to mass murder. Prison inmates are therefore classified according to the degree of security they require.

The processing of new arrivals in the system is essentially similar in all prisons, although the quality, extensiveness, and effectiveness of the process can vary widely. When a prisoner arrives at the institution, a file is set up in the

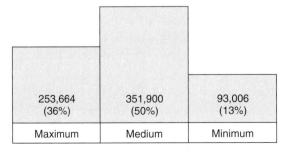

**Figure 7.3** Security classification of adult inmates in state and federal confinement facilities. *Source:* James Stephan, *Census of State and Federal Correctional Facilities, 1990* (Washington, DC: U.S. Department of Justice, 1992), p. 8.

| 253,664 (36%) | 351,900 (50%) | 93,006 (13%) |
|---|---|---|
| Maximum | Medium | Minimum |

records office. All departments are notified—such as the control room (for operational custody), the deputy warden's office, the classification department, the identification unit (for pictures and fingerprints), and all others whose services and procedures are affected by the presence of a new inmate.

During initial intake, an evaluation assessment is conducted. In larger systems, this screening is conducted at a central reception or diagnostic center, where all new inmates are transferred upon arrival into the system. In smaller systems, initial assessment might take place in a separate area of a particular institution.

The reception process itself ranges considerably in terms of sophistication. Some systems may simply review the official documents accompanying the inmate's transfer (e.g., court papers, arrest forms, the presentence investigation report, etc.). Others may conduct an in-depth interview with the offender, as well as an extensive battery of psychological evaluations, intelligence tests, medical exams, aptitude tests, and vocational interest measures. On the basis of intake processing, information concerning the inmate is recorded in a permanent file.

After this information is gathered, the classification unit makes determinations with regard to custodial classification, housing assignment, and what (if any) types of educational, treatment, or work programs the inmate will be offered. Throughout this process, efforts are made to predict both security risk and treatment potential. Greatest emphasis, however, is on determining the level of risk or dangerousness of the offender, both to protect other inmates and to better assure the order and safety of the total institution. For example, in deciding one's custody classification, the U.S. Bureau of Prisons ranks offenders on such factors as "severity of current offense, expected length of incarceration, type of prior commitments, history of escape attempts, and history of violence," along with additional internal management considerations, such as racial balance and degree of crowding in various facilities.[29] (More detailed information on how classification decisions are made and subsequently used is contained in Chapter 9.)

Initial classification does not preclude a change in status at a later time. The process is not foolproof, and it may turn out that someone was either overclassified or inappropriately classified at too low a level of security. Additionally, as inmates prove themselves worthy of greater trust over the years, their custodial classification could be reduced. Moreover, it is in the institution's interest to lower one's security classification. The less custody, the less expensive the supervision, and simultaneously, the closer the correctional process is to reintegrating the offender into society. Thus, during the period of their incarceration, prisoners may be reclassified and assigned to new housing, jobs, or programs any number of times.

As we have seen in terms of how classification operates in jails, the process does not always work effectively, particularly when a system is faced with such severe crowding that inmates must be placed where there is room rather than where they can function best. Nevertheless, the basic concept of classification is to match the security needs of the inmate with the appropriate custody level of the institution.

---

[29]*Federal Bureau of Prisons: Facilities*, p. 3.

## ❖ THE PRISON POPULATION

Just as there are concerns that people such as vagrants, alcoholics, and the mentally ill are being detained in jails inappropriately, the question has been raised as to whether prisons are being reserved for those who truly need or deserve to be behind bars.[30] For example, the perception that only serious, dangerous offenders are going to prison was challenged by one study which found that only 18% of new admissions could be ranked "serious" or "severe" on the basis of the offense for which they were committed.[31] Others cite similar evidence indicating that a substantial majority of new inmates are classified as minimum custody upon intake, although limited space in such facilities may not necessarily enable them to be confined there.

But other points of view maintain that crime victimization rates appear to be *decreasing* as prison rates *increase*, and that some inmates are entering prison with a long criminal history, (even though the offense they are being admitted for may be nonviolent).[32] These issues came under considerable debate by the early 1990s, when it became apparent that the United States was entering a third decade of continually increasing prison populations, with no end in sight.

### Number of Inmates

As Figure 7.4 illustrates, the number of inmates in state and federal prisons has been rather dramatically increasing at a steady pace since the 1970s. By the end of 1991, the total number of state and federal prisoners had reached a record high of 823,414—representing a 150% increase over the previous 11-year period.[33] It is therefore not surprising to find that during that same year, over 12,000

---

[30]During a National Teleconference on the subject of "Who Goes to Prison?", broadcast throughout the country on December 4, 1991, there was considerable debate over whether or not those in prison are predominately violent offenders.

[31]Quoted by Dr. James Austin, Executive Vice President, National Council on Crime and Delinquency, during the December 4, 1991, National Teleconference, "Who Goes to Prison?".

[32]Comments made by Larry Greenfeld, Chief, Correctional Statistics Program, Bureau of Justice Statistics, at the December 4, 1991, National Teleconference, "Who Goes to Prison?".

[33]Tracy L. Snell, "Prisoners in 1991," *Bureau of Justice Statistics: Bulletin* (Washington, DC: U.S. Department of Justice, 1992), p. 1.

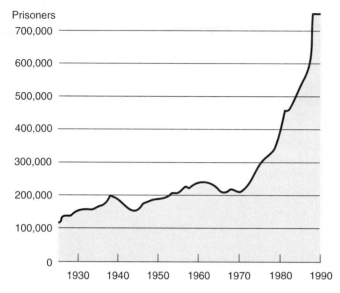

**Figure 7.4** Sentenced prisoners in state and federal institutions, 1925–1990. *Source: Sourcebook of Criminal Justice Statistics—1991* (Washington, DC: U.S. Department of Justice, 1992), p. 634.

state inmates were being held in local jails because of prison crowding. Even so, prisons were still estimated to be operating at 116% of their "highest capacities."[34] As of 1990, one of every seven state correctional facilities was under court order or consent decree for "specific conditions related to crowding."[35]

Raw numbers do not, of course, tell the whole story, since an area with a rapidly expanding population might well be expected to be experiencing more crime, and hence more people being imprisoned. But as Figure 7.5 shows, even when incarceration rates are calculated on the basis of population data, the *rate* of imprisonment has likewise been continuing steadily upward in recent years— reflecting a 123% increase in the years between 1980 and 1991.[36] In fact, it has been noted that the United States has the "dubious distinction" of having the highest incarceration rate of any country in the world,[37] (as illustrated in Figure 7.6).

## Prison Crowding

Numbers and charts do not, of course, begin to portray the misery of living conditions to which inmates are subjected in overflowing prisons. The consequence of housing too many people in too little space means that "offenders are doubled-up in cells meant for one; packed into makeshift dormitories; and bunked in the basements, corridors, and converted hospital facilities, tents, trailers, ware-

---

[34]Ibid., pp. 5 and 7.

[35]Stephan, p. 1.

[36]Snell, p. 2. For additional information on more precise and specific methods of calculating prison populations by "faction in prison," "chance of imprisonment," "prevalence of imprisonment," and "duration of imprisonment," see James Garofalo, "Measuring the Use of Imprisonment," *National Institute of Justice: Research in Action* (Washington, DC: U.S. Department of Justice, n.d.).

[37]*Responding to the Problem of Drug Abuse: Strategies for the Criminal Justice System* (Washington, DC: American Bar Association, 1992), p. 60.

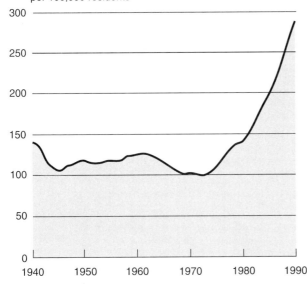

Number of sentenced prisoners per 100,000 residents

**Figure 7.5** Rate (per 100,000 resident population) of sentenced prisoners in state and federal institutions, 1940–1990. *Source: Sourcebook of Criminal Justice Statistics—1991* (Washington, DC: U.S. Department of Justice, 1992), p. 635.

houses, and program activity areas of the nation's prisons."[38] Under such conditions, it is not surprising to find that inmates have fewer opportunities for everything from visits to recreation or treatment programs. But even more importantly,

Double-bunking is one measure that both jails and prisons use to address the crowding issue. Courtesy of the American Jail Association.

[38]Harry E. Allen and Clifford E. Simonsen, *Corrections in America*, Sixth Edition (New York: Macmillan, 1992), p. 219.

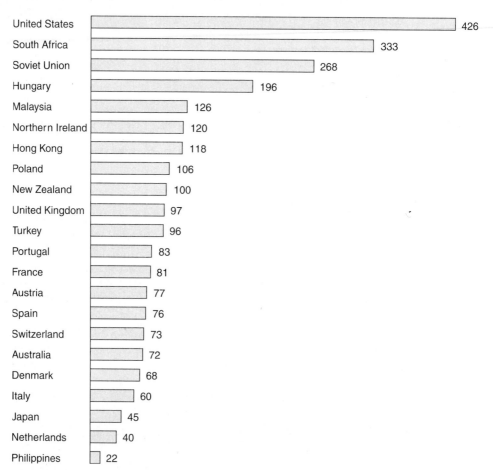

| | |
|---|---|
| United States | 426 |
| South Africa | 333 |
| Soviet Union | 268 |
| Hungary | 196 |
| Malaysia | 126 |
| Northern Ireland | 120 |
| Hong Kong | 118 |
| Poland | 106 |
| New Zealand | 100 |
| United Kingdom | 97 |
| Turkey | 96 |
| Portugal | 83 |
| France | 81 |
| Austria | 77 |
| Spain | 76 |
| Switzerland | 73 |
| Australia | 72 |
| Denmark | 68 |
| Italy | 60 |
| Japan | 45 |
| Netherlands | 40 |
| Philippines | 22 |

**Figure 7.6** International incarceration rates. *Source:* Reprinted from "Americans behind Bars," by Marc Mauer, assistant director of The Sentencing Project, American Bar Association, Washington, DC; *Criminal Justice,* Vol. 6, No. 4 (Winter 1992), p. 15.

there are serious health and safety risks associated with packing more inmates into less space: "The rates of death, suicide, homicide, inmate assault, and disturbance increase as prison population density increases. . . . The incidence of colds, infectious diseases, tuberculosis, sexually-communicable diseases, psychological disturbances, and psychiatric crises also is related to overcrowding. The more overcrowded the institution, the higher the incidence of medical problems."[39]

Nor are prison staff able to exert as much managerial control over the population of excessively crowded facilities:

As the numbers of prisoners increase, the space normally used for recreation or education is diverted to dormitory use. Incidents of violence

[39]Ibid., p. 223.

between prisoners increase, and control of the institution gradually slips to the most aggressive groups. . . . The exhaustion of services and the limitation on recreational activities further lead to tension, boredom, and conflict. . . . Eventually, there is a degradation of morale among the staff, greater staff turnover, and a vicious cycle of diminished control.[40]

Unfortunately, as mentioned in Chapter 1, the need for additional prison space was not taken into account by policymakers advocating longer sentences and greater certainty of confinement for law violators. In the absence of any meaningful proactive planning, prison administrators have been thrust into playing reactive catch-up.

Reactions to the crowding crisis have naturally included both the expansion of existing facilities and the construction of new institutions. But these responses have been insufficient to meet the needs. New and expanded prisons have been filling up as quickly as they are opened. Moreover, reliance on increasing physical capacity has not only been costly, but has also been criticized by those who maintain that "expanding a failure will only create a more expensive failure."[41]

In recognition of the futility and expense of this approach, a range of additional options has been advocated—from a *front-end reduction* in the number of people *going into* prisons to a *back-end increase* in the number *coming out*. The intent of front-end solutions is to keep more people from being incarcerated, through the use of community-based alternatives (diversion, electronic monitoring, probation, etc.) discussed in Chapter 5. Back-end approaches are designed to release more of those already confined, through such options as time off for good behavior, parole, weekend confinement, and other forms of early or temporary release.[42] Some would argue that neither front- nor back-end solutions have been pursued very vigorously. But in any event, these approaches have not thus far made a significant impact on the continually escalating size of the prison population.

## Characteristics of Inmates

With so many people incarcerated, it is reasonable to ask just who exactly *is* in all these prison cells—or, if trends continue in the same direction, the more pertinent question may become who is *not*. As the data in Figure 7.7 indicate, the typical profile of a state prison inmate is a relatively young, white (Anglo) male. However, blacks are disproportionately represented, since they comprise only about 12% of the general population in free society, in contrast to almost 48% of the inmate population.[43] The average inmate is unmarried (either single, separat-

[40]Alfred Blumstein, "Prison Crowding," *National Institute of Justice: Crime File Study Guide* (Washington, DC: U.S. Department of Justice, n.d.), p. 1.

[41]Lawrence F. Travis, Martin D. Schwartz, and Todd R. Clear, eds., *Corrections: An Issues Approach,* Second Edition (Cincinnati, OH: Anderson Publishing Company, 1980), p. 60.

[42]For further discussion of these approaches, see Blumstein, p. 3.

[43]Moreover, it has been noted that one out of every four black men in America is under some form of correctional control. Harry E. Allen, "Prison Overcrowding and the Conservative Ideology Revisited," paper presented at the Academy of Criminal Justice Sciences meeting in Pittsburgh, PA, March 11, 1992, citing Marc Mauer, *Young Black Men and the Criminal Justice System: A Growing National Problem* (Washington, DC: The Sentencing Project, 1990).

| Sex | Male | 96.0% |
| Race | White | 49.6% |
| | Black | 47.8% |
| Ethnicity | Non-Hispanic | 90.1% |
| Age | Under 25 | 36.4% |
| | Under 35 | 78.8% |
| Marital status | Unmarried (or separated) | 77.6% |
| Education | Less than high school | 52.7% |
| Prearrest employment | Employed full-time | 60.5% |
| Income prior to arrest | Less than $10,000 | 64.0% |

**Figure 7.7** Characteristics of state prison inmates. *Source:* Compiled from *Sourcebook of Criminal Justice Statistics—1991* (Washington, DC: U.S. Department of Justice, 1992), p. 648.

ed, divorced, or widowed), educated at less than the high school level, and prior to being incarcerated, was employed at a low-paying job.

Prisoners are generally familiar with the criminal justice system—the vast majority (81.5%) are recidivists, as opposed to first-time offenders.[44] Nor is prison a new experience for many of them. More than three out of five have been incarcerated before, either as an adult, a juvenile, or both.[45] This may be a reflection of their involvement in serious crime—a similar proportion (65.7%) are either currently serving time for, or have previously committed, a violent offense.[46]

### Offenses of Inmates

In terms of the type of violation for which they are presently incarcerated, a slight majority (54.6%) are serving time for violent offenses—predominately robbery.[47] However, a sizable percentage (31%) are in prison for property crimes—primarily burglary. While some of these crimes are undoubtedly drug-related, there is a relatively small percentage of inmates (8.6%) incarcerated for possession, trafficking, or other drug offenses. For a detailed summary of the current offenses of state prison inmates, see Figure 7.8.

Given this offender background and current offense information, there appears to be some discrepancy between these figures and the research cited previously indicating that very few new admissions are being incarcerated for crimes that could be rated "serious" or "severe." In part, this contrast may relate to different measurement techniques. But it is also to some extent accounted for by the difference between looking at *new* inmates and those already serving time. As the effects of mandatory minimum sentencing guidelines begin to be reflected in new prison admissions, it appears that less serious offenders are being incarcerated.

In contrast, the data quoted throughout this section are based on a national profile of those incarcerated in state prisons during 1986. Although some effect

[44]Christopher A. Innes, "Profile of State Prison Inmates, 1986," *Bureau of Justice Statistics Special Report* (Washington, DC: U.S. Department of Justice, 1988), p. 2.
[45]Ibid., pp. 3–4.
[46]Ibid., p. 2.
[47]Ibid., p. 3.

| | | |
|---|---|---|
| Violent offenses | | 54.6% |
| Murder | 11.2% | |
| Manslaughter | 3.2% | |
| Kidnapping | 1.7% | |
| Rape | 4.2% | |
| Other sexual assault | 4.5% | |
| Robbery | 20.9% | |
| Assault | 8.0% | |
| Other violent crime | .8% | |
| Property offenses | | 31.0% |
| Burglary | 16.5% | |
| Larceny–theft | 6.0% | |
| Motor vehicle theft | 1.4% | |
| Arson | .8% | |
| Fraud | 3.8% | |
| Stolen property | 2.0% | |
| Other property crimes | .5% | |
| Drug offenses | | 8.6% |
| Possession | 2.9% | |
| Trafficking | 5.4% | |
| Other drug offenses | .3% | |
| Public order offenses | | 5.1% |
| Weapons offenses | 1.4% | |
| Other public order offenses | 3.7% | |
| Other offenses | | .7% |

**Figure 7.8** Current offenses of state prison inmates, 1986. *Source:* Christopher A. Innes, "Profile of State Prison Inmates, 1986," *Bureau of Justice Statistics Special Report* (Washington, DC: U.S. Department of Justice, 1988), p. 3.

of stricter mandatory sentencing guidelines could have been reflected among the prison population by that year, these figures also include those incarcerated earlier for lengthy sentences that had not yet expired. Looking at the total prison population in 1986 may therefore present a portrait of more serious offenders than looking at those just coming into the system more recently.

In fact, one analysis has found that the sharp rise in the prison population since 1973 is not the result of offenders serving longer sentences, but rather, the greater likelihood of receiving a prison sentence.[48] Apparently, prosecutors are obtaining more felony convictions and judges are giving more prison sentences. For example, it was found that "a person arrested for robbery had a 28% chance of going to prison in 1986, compared with a 19% chance in 1974 . . . for burglary, a 15% chance of a prison term in 1984, compared with a 9% chance in 1974."[49] At least some evidence therefore indicates that there is, indeed, a trend toward greater use of imprisonment. The question then becomes what return society expects for the costly investment it is making in institutional confinement.

[48]"Crowding Attributed to Increased Likelihood of Incarceration," *Corrections Today* Vol. 53, No. 3 (June 1991), p. 14, citing research reported by Patrick A. Langan in *Science* (March 29, 1991).
[49]Ibid. See also Edwin W. Zedlewski, "The Economics of Disincarceration," *National Institute of Justice Reports* (May 1984), pp. 4–8.

## ❖ THE PURPOSE OF PRISONS

What society achieves through its prisons has much to do with what it expects them to accomplish. But it is difficult to obtain consensus on what the actual objectives of a prison should be. As a result, we cannot evaluate how effective our prisons are, because we are not entirely sure what they should be doing—as the saying goes, "If you don't know where you're going, how will you know when you get there?"

As described in Chapter 4, correctional institutions were first developed to provide a more humane alternative to corporal or capital punishment. In line with their Quaker-initiated origins, the first prisons were viewed as a place where one could read the Bible, reflect upon past wrong-doings, and ultimately, repent for one's sins. As one historian puts it, "the founders of the American prison were idealists who believed that prisons and other total institutions could be used to change human beings for the better."[50] With the advent of the Industrial Era, achieving penitance gave way to attaining profits. Then, as the promise of the medical model renewed hope for rehabilitation, the purpose of prisons shifted again. The degrading pictures of chain gangs, forced labor, and physical punishment gave way to the uplifting potential of counseling, therapy, and treatment. There are probably few who would advocate a return to the barbaric practices of the past. But society's frustrations with the apparent inability to accomplish long-term behavioral changes in prison, coupled with the fears generated by increasing crime rates, again called for a new prison agenda. In summary, "each generation has criticized the prisons and penal philosophies of its predecessor and has offered new rationales and management theories. . . . Time and again in American history, men and women have looked to penal institutions for solutions to individual and social problems. Time and again, they have been disappointed."[51]

### Social Compromise

By the early 1980s, the justice model's concern for retribution, deterrence, and certainty of punishment had found a receptive public audience. From the unfulfilled promises of the medical model came an unconditional plan for

---

[50]James B. Jacobs, "Inside Prisons," *National Institute of Justice: Crime File Study Guide* (Washington, DC: U.S. Department of Justice, n.d.), p. 1, quoting historian David Rothman.
[51]Ibid.

change. If it was too much to hope that prisons could improve people, at least they could incapacitate them. If rehabilitation was an impossible expectation, at least retribution would ensure that "justice was served." If criminals were not mindful of penalties, at least they would be reminded through punishment. And if this did not deter them, at least they would pay their debt.

When society came to the conclusion that the situation was out of control, it settled for these compromises. Essentially, we elected to "pull drowning people out of the river without going upstream to find out why they are drowning in the first place."[52] The problem is that they are "drowning" for many complicated reasons that we cannot comprehend, cannot respond to effectively, or simply do not wish to address. Thus, we continue to pull offenders out of the social mainstream and put them into secure institutions. There they find a fertile environment to nourish isolation, frustration, and antisocial behavior—as we see in the next "Close-up on Corrections."

But if nothing else, changing to the justice model's approach has lowered the public's unrealistic expectations of prisons. No longer are correctional institutions necessarily expected to rehabilitate. No longer are they charged with "forcing" treatment upon an unwilling client—and then criticized when it does

❖ *CLOSE-UP ON CORRECTIONS*

### Prison Life and Human Worth

There is a slang phrase which probably originated far from prison but which applies better to prison life than do any other two words in the English language—"put down." It eloquently describes the emotional effect of being squelched, and . . . it tells sadly, bitterly just what prison is. To the person who never has served time, it is hard to realize just how much of a daily humiliating "put-down" prison life can be even in a well-run institution.

It is not necessary to look for a venal warden, or even a merely inept one. It is not necessary to look for sadistic guards, political chicanery from the governor's office, inadequate food, or stingy budgets from an uncaring legislature. . . . When we look for such factors, we are missing the real guts of the problem, which is that in the best of prisons with the nicest of custodians and the most generous of kitchens, the necessary minutiae of management tend to deny and even insult the basic needs of individuals. . . . Sooner or later, the prisoner must lose his spirit, or he must rebel.

*Source:* Paul W. Keve, *Prison Life and Human Worth* (Minneapolis, MN: University of Minnesota Press, 1974), pp. 15, 41–42.

[52]Paraphrased from Dennis Rosenbaum's analogy comparing reactive to proactive policing in Andrew H. Malcolm, "New Strategies to Fight Crime Go Far beyond Stiffer Terms and More Cells," in John J. Sullivan and Joseph L. Victor, eds. *Annual Editions: Criminal Justice 91/92* (Guilford, CT: Dushkin Publishing Group, 1991), p. 27.

not work. Rather, treatment under the justice model is provided only on a voluntary basis, not as an incentive for obtaining parole or early release. It would appear that all that is expected under this approach is incapacitation—restraining the offender from further involvement in crime, with the hope that strict and sure sentences will discourage would-be offenders, and if not, that "just deserts" will have been achieved.

## Public Opinion

However, as mentioned in Chapter 2, there is some doubt that the public in general is truly as punitive as advocates of the justice model would like to believe. Although there is certainly considerable support for strict sentencing practices, society has not completely lost faith in the potential of rehabilitation.[53] For example, as recently as 1989, a Gallup Poll asked the following question of people throughout the country: "In dealing with those who are in prison, do you think it is more important to punish them for their crimes, or more important to get them started 'on the right road'?"

Given the presumed popularity of the justice model, it would be reasonable to assume that the response was overwhelmingly in favor of punishment. Not so. Overall, only 38% supported punishment, in comparison to the 48% favoring rehabilitation (14% had no opinion one way or the other).[54] Certain groups were more staunch advocates of rehabilitation than others—such as college graduates and those over 50 years of age, earning higher incomes, or residing in large cities. But even among Democrats and Republicans, it is interesting to note that approximately equal percentages supported rehabilitation (Republicans, 49%; Democrats, 51%).[55] Moreover, in virtually *all* sex, age, race, educational, political, income, and residency categories, those *favoring rehabilitation* surpassed those favoring punishment.

Of course, it is impossible to tell how the respondents were interpreting "punishment," and it may be that visions of harsh discipline or severe corporal punishment affected their answers. Perhaps the outcome would have differed if the question had substituted "social protection" for rehabilitation. In other words, as far as society is concerned, the goal of prisons may be public protection rather than *either* punishment *or* rehabilitation. Nor is it possible to determine what was in the minds of respondents in terms of getting inmates started "on the right road." It may be that the public is favorably disposed to more pragmatic forms of rehabilitation—education or vocational training, for example—but maintains little consensus about anything else. In any event, it appears from at least this national opinion poll that society may envision somewhat different goals for its prisons than do public policymakers.

[53]See Francis T. Cullen, John B. Cullen, and John F. Wozniak, "Is Rehabilitation Dead? The Myth of the Punitive Public," *Journal of Criminal Justice*, Vol. 16, No. 4 (1988), p. 303.

[54]*Sourcebook of Criminal Justice Statistics—1991* (Washington, DC: U.S. Department of Justice, 1992), p. 210.

[55]However, Republicans were slightly more likely to favor punishment (41%) than were their Democratic counterparts (35%). Ibid.

## ❖ PRISON ORGANIZATION

The fact that society's true sentiments may not be accurately represented in the principles of the justice model does not necessarily mean that public opinions are not reflected in the way prisons are operated. Quite the contrary, the attitude of the public influences the political leadership, which, in turn, is responsible for appointing correctional leadership. In most states, for example, the state director (or commissioner) of corrections is appointed by the governor—some for fixed terms, some serving "at the pleasure" of the governor.[56] Thus, the type of administration that prevails at any institution is ultimately a reflection of public preferences, as expressed through the political process. Similarly, prison directors themselves develop a reputation for having a certain operational "style" and are attracted to locations where public sentiments are consistent with their approach.

### Political Influence

This system of political influence can be a positive benefit when it works to the advantage of the public constituency. However, it can also be a negative factor when "politics" unduly interfere with correctional practices. For example, following a highly visible escape or institutional disturbance, the correctional administrator or warden may be fired, serving as a "political scapegoat" for public disenchantment with the system. Moreover, when a new governor is elected, it is almost certain that new cabinet appointments will be made, including the director of corrections. This is a legacy dating back to the time when states were small, the correctional "system" consisted of one prison, and the warden was the sole correctional administrator, appointed by and responsible to the governor:

> Under such conditions, it was inevitable that the position should be used for political patronage, and so the early history of prisons—with a few stellar exceptions—was a history of mediocre administration by men who brought no specialized skill to their job, often were no more than mildly interested in the work, and always were ready to move casually to something else if the state government changed hands at the next election. There were some [who] . . . administered with intelligent dedication, but part of the reason for their outstanding leadership was the wasteland of mediocrity around them.[57]

[56]*Vital Statistics in Corrections* (Laurel, MD: American Correctional Association, 1991), p. 8.
[57]Paul W. Keve, *Prison Life and Human Worth* (Minneapolis, MN: University of Minnesota Press, 1974), pp. 63–64.

Today, some appointments are still politically motivated, which can result in appointing a director with little knowledge of or experience in corrections. But even when more qualified candidates are appointed, it is essential for them to know the political system and be able to work adeptly within it. When a career correctional expert is placed in a turbulent political environment and does not understand the political maneuvering required, the outcome can be disastrous—resulting, potentially, in being dismissed under fire. It is for such reasons that those in charge of state correctional systems generally experience relatively short tenures, often regardless of their talents or effectiveness.

> In the four years between 1986 and 1990, there were 52 changes in the heads of state adult corrections programs. . . . [O]n average, there [is] a 25% turnover of administrators annually. (In sharp contrast . . . Canada [has] only a 3% annual change.) . . . [T]he average tenure of [U.S] political appointees is about three years—hardly long enough for the inexperienced appointee to learn the job and assess the adequacy and competence of staff available, let alone weigh the need for change."[58]

As a result, it is not uncommon to find directors who have experienced a virtual career of "musical chairs," having been in charge of corrections in any number of states. Even where there is more stability in the upper ranks, it may be attained at the cost of continually adjusting to the changing political climate. And without any consistency in the managerial philosophy of corrections, it is of little surprise to find researchers concluding that "nothing works." Needless to say, such instability is neither personally desirable nor organizationally productive.

## Institutional Organization

Relatively frequent leadership turnover is one of the few organizational features that many correctional facilities have in common. The specific manner in which prisons and other correctional institutions are organized and operated varies according to their size, purpose, and degree of custody. For example, the California Institution for Men—housing more than 6000 inmates in various security classifications[59]—will have an entirely different managerial structure than the Red Eagle Honor Farm that serves 219 minimum-security inmates in Montgomery, Alabama.[60] Correctional institutions range from large, sprawling prison complexes to road camps or halfway houses that hold as few as 10 or 20 people. The manner in which they are organized varies likewise.

In medium-sized to large facilities, the administrative structure of the organization is typically divided into three general components:

- *Operations* (also called *custody* or *security*)

[58]Joseph Rowan, "Politics and Corrections in America: A Good System Goes Bad in Wisconsin," *CJ: The Americas*, Vol. 5, No. 3 (June/July 1992), p. 7.
[59]*ACA Directory*, p. 34.
[60]Ibid., p. 5.

- *Program services* (also called *treatment* or *inmate programs)*
- Support services (also called *administrative or staff services)*.

In those larger institutions that provide their own in-house medical staff (rather than contracting with an outside provider), there may also be a separate unit for health services. A general overview of the table of organization for a typical prison housing about 2000 residents is shown in Figure 7.9.

**Operations.** The *operational* division includes all of the custodial staff and activities directly related to providing both internal and external *security,* as well as *inmate supervision.* Within operations, staff authority is assigned on the basis of rank—starting with officers (or "line" staff), and moving up the supervisory hierarchy to corporals (where this intermediate rank exists), sergeants, lieutenants, and captains. Ultimately, all sworn personnel report to a deputy or assistant warden for operations. However, it is expected that they will do so through the "chain of command," starting with their immediate supervisor and working upward if the issue cannot be resolved.

The number of operational staff will, of course, vary with the size of the facility, as will the officer/inmate ratio (number of officers in comparison to the number of inmates). Throughout the country, the average officer/inmate ratio is 4.70—that is, one correctional officer for every 4.70 inmates.[61] However, the ratio ranges from a high of 33 in Indiana to a low of 1.89 in Hawaii.[62]

**Program Services.** Within the *program services* division are found all of the units providing inmate programs and treatment: for example, vocational training, education, prison industries, the library, recreation, casework, counseling, and the like. Other responsibilities related to the welfare of the residents are also likely to fall within this division, such as the maintenance of inmate records, the chaplain's office, and the classification unit. In contrast to the operational division, personnel in program services tend to be nonsworn civilians (although sworn staff on specialized assignments may be included).

Because of differences in backgrounds, job classifications, and the nature of their work, there is considerable potential for conflict between operational and program personnel. The goals of custody and treatment differ substantially, and each needs to understand the other if mistrust and divisiveness are to be avoided. It is essential for the prison administrator to assure that security and treatment staff develop and maintain effective and productive relationships. In other words, they must interact with some degree of harmony and mutual cooperation if the overall interests of the total institution are to be served.

**Administrative (Support) Services.** Generally speaking, *administrative (or support) services* encompass the many activities ongoing within a prison that support the treatment and custody functions. In some prisons, this unit may be further

[61]*Vital Statistics,* p. 30.
[62]Ibid.

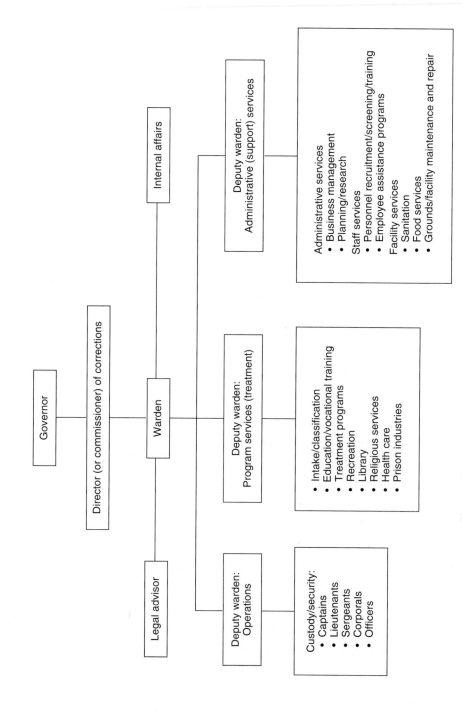

**Figure 7.9** Organization chart for an average-sized prison.

divided into two separate sections: one addressing *facility maintenance* and one focusing on *staff support.* Within facility support are such services as physical plant maintenance (e.g., electricity, water, heat, sanitation, etc.), clothing issue and laundry, food preparation, fire protection, locksmithing, and anything else related to the proper functioning of the physical complex. Business management, accounting, purchasing, planning, research, and new construction may be considered support services, or these functions may be provided through a separate administrative unit. Support services related to staff include the recruitment, screening, and training of personnel (described in Chapter 14), as well as various employee assistance programs.

**Career Opportunities.** Regardless of how the prison is organized administratively, the overall compound of a large institution functions as a community within itself. Because of their self-contained nature, correctional institutions offer a wide variety of career opportunities. To operate independently, they need everyone from such obvious occupations as teachers, medical personnel, psychologists, social workers, and correctional officers to the less visible people working behind the scenes, such as clerical staff, cooks, barbers, electricians, and maintenance personnel. As a result, wide varieties of career opportunities are available, even for those who do not desire security-related work. In fact, corrections tops the list of the fastest-growing jobs in American cities.[63]

---

*LEARNING GOALS* ▬▬▬▬▬▬▬▬▬▬▬▬▬▬▬▬▬▬

*Do you know:*

- *What the responsibilities of a prison warden are and how the warden's style influences prison operations?*
- *To what extent inmates exert control in prisons?*
- *How informal social control works among the inmate population?*
- *How participatory management has been used in prison settings?*
- *How inmate self-governance relates to Maslow's hierarchy of needs and why it has often been ineffective?*

---

❖ PRISON ADMINISTRATION

Just as the organization of a prison differs according to the size and complexity of the institution, so do the demands on the person in charge. Each correctional institution within a state is headed by an administrator, whose title is typically *warden* or *superintendent.* Generally career civil servants, they are appointed by the director (or commissioner) of corrections. Among their major responsibilities are:

---

[63]James D. Stinchcomb, *Opportunities in Law Enforcement and Criminal Justice* (Lincolnwood, IL: VGM Career Horizons, 1990), p. 111, citing the U.S. Census Bureau.

- *Coordination* of the various administrative divisions, to assure that all are working in relative unison toward common goals.
- Establishment of the institution's *policies and procedures,* which guide the work of staff on a day-to-day basis.
- Authority for *personnel decision making* (e.g., hiring, promotions, demotions, terminations).
- Preparation and presentation of the facility's *budget.*
- Development of *external relationships* with civic groups, professional associations, and the like—ranging from "image-building" public relations to substantive discussions of problems and needs.

It is the warden or superintendent who is ultimately in charge of all internal operations and external interactions. With authority over all staff and final decisions, it is this person who is ultimately responsible for the institution. Thus, it is also the warden who establishes the priorities and sets the tone for the entire facility.

## Administrative Styles

While the leadership styles of wardens vary widely, their fundamental principles are generally in line with the director who appointed them. Whatever their administrative style, it is reflected throughout the prison. For example, there are some prison administrators who seek to exert complete control, to be "on top" of any situation. This type of warden leaves no doubt as to who is in charge. But demands for tight control can also result in rigidly regimented prisons with strict rules and stern discipline. In such a highly controlled setting, the institution is generally well known as a "tough" prison in which to do time—one where tensions and apprehensions prevail.[64]

Other correctional administrators are more treatment oriented. Those whose careers began with work in inmate programs and remained committed to rehabilitative ideals throughout their career generally represent a treatment orientation. The type of treatment emphasized may vary widely—from programs directed toward education and vocational training to sophisticated therapy based on group living, guided group interaction, and other clinical approaches.

This is not meant to imply that administrative styles are exclusively "treatment" or "punishment" oriented. Some have made efforts to combine elements of both. Others emphasize neither—but rather, simply focus on custody, or what might be termed "warehousing." Still other administrators may try to simplify procedures so that prison life is as nearly "normal" as possible. The result is an institution in which discipline is used sparingly and only when necessary, but adequate treatment or inmate programs may not be a high priority. In such an environment, the prime objective is to run the facility as quietly as possible—that is, to "keep the lid on."

Nor is the administrator always personally aware of his or her own style. When asked what their objective is, most wardens and superintendents are like-

---

[64]See Joseph Ragen and Charles Finston, *Inside the World's Toughest Prison* (Springfield, IL: Charles C Thomas, 1962). The title refers to Stateville Correctional Center in Illinois.

ly to focus on rehabilitation. Despite the advent of the justice model, this remains the perspective that to a considerable extent still permeates the field of corrections. But what may be "rehabilitation" to one may mean a strict emphasis on discipline and work in order to instill greater personal responsibility, while another would restrict the term to therapeutic treatment.

## Operational Impact

Regardless of what particular administrative style is established by upper-level management, there is little doubt that it will affect policies and procedures throughout the entire system—which, in turn, will have an impact on both operational practices and inmate behavior. As a result, even the same institution can vary dramatically over the years, depending on who is in charge, as described in the next "Close-up on Corrections."

The potent influence of leadership style on inmate behavior is perhaps best illustrated in a major study of the "quality of prison life" in three states with widely varying administrative styles.[65] The states in the study included:

- Texas, which at the time had highly centralized, no-nonsense controls that placed considerable emphasis on inmate obedience.
- Michigan, where inmates were given substantially more autonomy and responsibility.
- California, which represented a form of compromise, in essence, a middle course between the extremes of other two.

Because of the sometimes rather heavy-handed manner in which discipline was carried out in the Texas system, it might be expected that inmates would react violently against their "oppressors," generating high rates of homicides, assaults, injuries, escape attempts, and riots. To the contrary, "infractions in Texas were not only less frequent, but less severe than those in Michigan and California. . . . In most states, a person is more likely to be murdered inside of prison than on the streets. In Texas, however, the reverse has been true."[66]

Admittedly, other factors beyond administrative style might logically explain such differences. But it was found, for example, that Texas did not have newer facilities or a smaller percentage of "violence-prone" inmates. Nor was more money spent on its prisoners. (In fact, Texas spent far less.) Nor were its institutions less crowded. (In fact, they were more crowded.) Nor was more staff training provided. (In fact, there was less.)[67] What, then, could account for the lower level of violence in Texas?

Critics (and supporters) of the Texas prison system have claimed that [it] was so orderly for so long because it used repressive administrative tac-

[65]The study described herein is summarized from John J. DiIulio, *Governing Prisons: A Comparative Study of Correctional Management* (New York: Free Press, 1987).

[66]Ibid., p. 53, citing data from Joan Petersilia et al., *The Prison Experience of Career Criminals* (Santa Monica, CA: Rand Corporation, 1980).

[67]DiIulio, pp. 69–86.

Stateville: Fifty Years of Frustrations

### PARTISAN POLITICS, 1925–1936

From its opening in 1925, the Stateville Penitentiary in Illinois began a dismal legacy that lasted for over a decade. This was the era of the "spoils system"—when influential politicians gathered in smoke-filled back rooms to reward those who had supported their election with government appointments. Corrections was no exception. The warden and many staff members at Stateville owed their positions to political patronage. With neither prior correctional experience nor any particular commitment to the field, it is not surprising that they were motivated by little more than pleasing their political sponsors. "Job security was nonexistent. Wages were barely above subsistence. Rules were made on the spot. Discipline was arbitrary and capricious." For inmates with political connections, favoritism and corruption flourished, while those in solitary were "handcuffed to the bars for eight hours a day," living on "one glass of water and one slice of bread."

### CHARISMATIC DOMINANCE, 1936–1961

Realizing the seriousness of the situation by 1936, a reform governor appointed a no-nonsense administrator who came to be known as "Mr. Prison"—Joseph E. Ragen. Sure enough, Ragen drastically changed things. But not everyone would agree with the manner in which he did so. In a complete turnaround from the chaotic conditions he found, Ragen implemented an authoritarian system that he personally dominated. "His daily inspection of the prison, accompanied only by his two dogs, symbolized his highly personalistic rule. He alone managed all contacts with the outside, thereby reinforcing his personal power. From his staff, he demanded absolute loyalty. . . . " For the inmates as well as the staff, discipline was rigid. Punishments were severe. Criticism was not tolerated. Inmate leaders were coopted to support the system by good jobs. Ragen's totalitarian rule and charismatic leadership left no doubt about who was in charge or how Stateville should be run—a system of dominance that survived for a quarter-century.

### DRIFT, 1961–1970

For most of the next decade, the institution would drift between control and chaos. Although Ragen's successor was a hand-picked assistant warden who had risen through the ranks under "Mr. Prison's" leadership, he had neither the charismatic style nor the formal authority of his predecessor. In part, this was because his former boss had left Stateville to become director of public safety in Illinois, and from his position, still exercised considerable control over the prison. Ragen's eventual replacement continued this practice of direct external influence over the institution, liberalizing many aspects of the prison environment, from dress codes to rules restricting communication with other inmates. Education, recreation, and rehabilitative programs were implemented. But at the same time, the euphoria of the mass demonstrations of the 1960s was being felt inside the walls. Black Muslims organized to challenge the authority of the system—a move that was met with massive administrative resistance and repression. As the courts intervened, the Illinois legislature was also changing sentencing and parole policies. Old-time "con's" who had been inmate leaders were suddenly released, creating a power vacuum. The inmates were no longer in control. But neither was the traditional system of authority. The timing was ripe for a crisis.

## CRISIS, 1970–1975

Stateville had come a long way from the abuses of the spoils system and the autocracy of "Mr. Prison." The next two wardens were "well-educated professionals" who believed in rehabilitation and the "human relations model of management." In place of the authoritarian regime, they attempted to establish a system based on the consent of subordinates. But many who had been groomed under Ragen saw these changes as too "permissive." Among the staff, treatment personnel lined up against custodial personnel. Among the inmates, gangs lined up against other gangs. And everyone lined up against the administration. "Inmates simply refused to follow orders, refused to work, and refused to follow the rules." Strikes and riots erupted. Hostages were taken. Gang fights broke out. As confrontations escalated, crack-downs ensued. "Having no other strategy to maintain control, the reform regimes periodically reverted to measures even more repressive than those of previous decades." Conditions "deteriorated to a level of violence and destruction beyond anything previously seen in Illinois."

## RESTORATION, 1975–

The next administrator had no where to go but up, and he met the challenge with determination and enthusiasm. Beginning with sweeping upper-level management changes, he completely reorganized the facility. Improvements were made in everything from the disciplinary process to institutional security and inmate services. The human relations model of management was replaced with a "highly-rational, problem-oriented" strategy. Administration resembled "corporate" more than correctional management in its emphasis on professionalism, detachment, and cost-consciousness.

## EPILOGUE

The study on which this synopsis is based did not continue long enough to assess the results of these alterations, and in the ensuing years, leadership has changed hands again. It will be up to a future generation of researchers to document the administrative styles of subsequent wardens. But those of the past have certainly left their mark on Stateville. The political patronage of the spoils system. The paragon of toughness. The "puppet" of Regan. The human relations of the participatory managers. The objective professionalism of the rational businessman. Each has had his own style. Each has shaped the prison, the people within it, and the public's perception of both.

*Source:* With the exception of the epilogue, this material is paraphrased along with direct citations (in quotes) from James B. Jacobs, *Stateville* (Chicago: University of Chicago Press, 1977).

tics. . . . [I]f it were true that order in Texas prisons was achieved mainly or solely through brutal tactics, then one would suppose that similar measures employed elsewhere would have similar effects. . . . [I]n Texas and elsewhere, prison order has been achieved only where managers have employed a mix of legal and duly-authorized carrots and sticks. Merely repressive correctional measures simply do not work. . . . [T]he quality of prison life varies according to the quality of prison management.[68]

In fact, it was when management in Texas changed hands that the level of violence in the state's prisons escalated dramatically.[69] However, this result could also be explained by the tendency of those without power to band together to challenge authority when there is a "change in the status quo and a period of rising expectations, followed by disappointment."[70] If the inmates put faith in the ability of new leadership to exert positive changes that were not forthcoming, the resulting disillusionment could well have sparked the flames of discontent.

In addition, the administrative style of the prison manager has much to do with establishing the level of inmate morale. Thus, another explanation of the seemingly contradictory findings in Texas may be related to the fact that prison disturbances do not tend to occur in prisons with either very *high* or very *low* morale.[71] While the former makes sense, the latter may not. However, in institutions where morale is exceedingly low, the residents tend to endure oppression in a docile manner. In short, they become so demoralized (or subservient) that violent reaction against the system is simply not a consideration.[72]

Institutions with some level of disorder may not, therefore, necessarily be inferior to those with a calmer appearance. Just as society "tolerates" some amount of crime to ensure the preservation of individual freedoms, prisons must seek a compromise between total chaos and complete control.

## Inmate Control

The question then becomes: Just who *is* in control of prisons? Some correctional administrators have noted that most institutions are actually run by inmates—if not officially, at least unofficially. It is, of course, the inmates who outnumber officers and civilian staff. But the extent to which inmates rather than staff are in charge of a prison depends primarily on the capacity in which inmates are used within the institution.

In previous years, it was common for many of the clerical and technical jobs in prisons to be assigned to inmates, particularly when budgets were too limited to hire enough staff. In fact, well into the twentieth century, some south-

[68]Ibid., pp. 94–95.
[69]It should be noted that during this same period of time, federal court intervention dismantled the "building tender" system whereby selected inmates used strong-arm techniques to keep other inmates in line.
[70]Lee G. Bolman and Terrance E. Deal, *Modern Approaches to Understanding and Managing Organizations* (San Francisco, CA: Jossey-Bass, 1989), p. 137.
[71]Vernon Fox, *Correctional Institutions* (Englewood Cliffs, NJ: Prentice Hall, 1983), p. 124.
[72]Paraphrased from Fox, p. 124.

ern and southwestern states went so far as to rely on "inmate guards" to maintain order among the prison population. For an inside account of how brutal these unofficial "staff" could be in dealing with fellow inmates as recently as 1981, see the next "Close-up on Corrections." (Interestingly, the events described took place in Texas following the change in administration discussed earlier.)

Even in prisons where inmates were prohibited from using physical force against other inmates, they might be used for such sensitive assignments as meeting visitors at the airport, delivering and picking up supplies or equipment, and bookkeeping or accounting. Needless to say, these practices were open to considerable abuse. Freedom to travel outside the compound made the introduction of contraband quite tempting. Moreover, even "trusties" in clerical jobs often used their positions to personal advantage—as a basis for gaining authority over other inmates by extending favors to them.

As the corruption resulting from such practices captured administrative attention, strong arguments were made to provide sufficient fiscal support to enable prisons to function without extensive dependence on inmate skills. As a result, inmates now tend to work in much less sensitive areas and have generally

---

❖ *CLOSE-UP ON CORRECTIONS*

## Inmate Control over Inmates

Inside the prison, a general alarm sounded. . . . While the guards milled about, testing the heft of their three-foot black batons . . . another group [was] forming in the gym. About 150 inmate trusties, known in Texas prisons as building tenders, plus 150 of their aides and chums were also preparing to restore order. They were the inmates who really ran the asylum: the meanest characters the administration could co-opt into doing the state's bidding. While rocks smashed against the gym's barred windows . . . the boss tender ordered *his* troops to tie white bandannas on their heads so they wouldn't be confused with the rioters. . . . "They're carrying trash-can lids, pipes, clubs, weight-lifting bars," he recalls, "The adrenaline's really flowing, flowing so much it's spooky. . . . "

The rioters [were] fleeing toward one corner of the yard. And pursuing them were the building tenders. One of the tenders, who calls himself Tommy B., remembers what happened next: "We had clubs, bats, chains, knives, everything, and we formed what we called a 'whupping' line." The only way to the safety of the gym was down that gantlet, and the rioters, now edging toward panic, began running through. . . . Inmate Ronnie . . . was inside the main building as the "whupped" staggered in. "Some of the guys you couldn't recognize, and a lot were unconscious. I wasn't sure if they was alive or dead." The inmates who could walk staggered back to the cell blocks; the others were carried inside to wait for ambulances. . . .

*Source:* "Inside America's Toughest Prison," *Newsweek* (October 6, 1986), pp. 46–48.

---

been absolved of any custodial supervision over other prisoners. But even today, many institutions rely extensively on residents for carpentry, plumbing, general maintenance, and other non-security-related tasks.

Eliminating inappropriate job assignments has not, however, eliminated inmate influence. Particularly in those institutions that assign new correctional officers to work without any basic recruit training, security personnel may well find themselves relying on "friendly" inmates to teach them their job. The American Correctional Association now has training standards that call for the provision of a minimum of 40 hours of training prior to job assignment.[73] But in addition to the fact that this is a clearly minimum requirement, as we will see in later chapters, compliance with ACA standards is voluntary. Until training standards are mandated, there are potentially places where the bizzare situations reflected in the next "Close-up on Corrections" can occur.

## ❖ CLOSE-UP ON CORRECTIONS

### Inmates Training Officers

Most who entered the prison service prior to 1972, when a training academy was established, reported that they were simply issued "a badge, a club and a hat," shown the yard, and told to go to work. . . .

[W]ith reluctance on the part of the experienced officers to instruct the rookie correction officers, new men were in many cases forced to turn for advice to the inmates over whom they had authority. . . . Many officers reported that when a rookie officer was sent to an area of the institution with which he was unfamiliar, there always seemed to be an inmate there who knew what was supposed to happen. . . . [T]he new officer had virtually nowhere else to turn to discover what was going on in the prison but to the inmates. . . . "The guy that broke me in[to] the mess hall was a murderer. You couldn't work for a nicer guy. . . . Inmates trained officers. Really! He told me to stand back, and he showed me how and where to frisk. He hit the table top to sound it out. Rap the bars to see if they were solid. Many times . . . there's an inmate that shows you the right way." . . .

Such an experience must have made the new officer wonder about the primacy of the security aspect of his job. How important can security be if the instruction concerning security comes from those over whom one is to maintain security? . . . This . . . might lead an officer to place more trust in the inmate than in the administration or in his fellow officers, both of whom failed to provide him with much guidance.

*Source:* Lucien X. Lombardo, *Guards Imprisoned: Correctional Officers at Work,* Second Edition (Cincinnati, OH: Anderson Publishing Company, 1989), pp. 35, 39–40.

[73]*Standards for Adult Correctional Institutions* (Laurel, MD: American Correctional Association, 1990), p. 79. The standards also call for an additional 120 hours of training during the first year of employment (p. 81).

But regardless of how inmates are officially or unofficially used in prisons, there is a balance between inmate control and staff control. While the extent of inmate authority and influence will differ according to institutional practices, there are few places where the residents do not possess some degree of power.

### Informal Social Control

In every prison there is informal control among the inmates that enables the institution to run smoothly. Some have a personal stake in a trouble-free prison—whether they are in positions of responsibility or simply want to "do their own time" as quietly as possible. Because of this personal investment, they will take steps to preserve the system and will help to keep other inmates in control. Naturally, administrators must be alert to ensure that the "peace-keepers" themselves do not become disorderly by physically taking authority into their own hands (as we saw earlier in the case of the building tenders).

But even if it is not formally endorsed by the administration, this type of *informal social control* is imposed by the inmate body upon itself and can help to run the prison without disturbance. In return for healthy self-government, the administration may extend certain privileges to the inmate population, ranging from work release to conjugal visits. Participants in such programs will carefully guard these benefits and informally pressure others to conform when their behavior threatens the system. Everyone knows, for example, that if those on work release take advantage of this liberty by attempting to escape, the privilege will be revoked for everyone. Similarly, engaging in disruptive behavior results in additional supervision, restriction, and scrutiny that inmates do not want forced upon them.

### Participatory Management

There have been efforts to formalize such inmate self-control through various forms of official recognition—from simple "suggestion boxes" to full-fledged "inmate councils" with decision-making power. The idea behind increased involvement of inmates in institutional procedures is based on the principles of *participatory management.*

According to participatory management, people are more likely to be *committed* to decisions or policies which they were *involved* in making. If, for example, the warden determines that there will be a nonsmoking policy throughout the institution, it will probably meet with considerable resistance. If, on the other hand, inmates become sufficiently dissatisfied with stale air and concerned about the ill effects of smoking on everyone that they propose a smoking ban, it will probably encounter less resistance. The idea is that people inherently resist being *told* what to do (often regardless of whether or not they actually favor doing it). But when the idea is *theirs*, they have "ownership" of it and are therefore more likely to support it. As one former prison warden noted, "If inmates are allowed to participate in decision-making, they will tend to act more responsibly toward themselves, others, and prison society."[74]

[74]Thomas O. Murton, "Prison Management: The Past, the Present, and the Possible Future," in Marvin E. Wolfgang, ed., *Prisons: Present and Possible* (Lexington, MA: Lexington Books, 1979), p. 24.

Because of the need for security-related restrictions, prisons are obviously not the ideal environment for inmate participation in facility management. Quite the contrary, correctional institutions are usually well noted for exercising "total control" over everything from the movement of inmates to the timing of meals.

But prison administrators have also recognized that such impotence can produce disastrous consequences when resulting frustrations explode into violence. Moreover, officers dealing with inmates on a day-to-day basis experience their frustrations firsthand as they attempt to resolve a series of seemingly endless complaints before situations escalate into serious disruptions. In addition, the courts have become more active with regard to intervening on behalf of inmates when prison conditions fall below constitutionally acceptable levels of safety, sanitation, or security.

From this perspective, the advantage underlying some form of inmate participation is that it enables the administration to respond *proactively* to concerns before they get out of hand. Otherwise, staff are in a position of continually *reacting* to the consequences of imposed constraints.

### Inmate Self-Governance

Recognizing the benefits of involving inmates in prison management is not a new concept. The first formal effort in this direction occurred at Michigan State Prison (now the State Prison of Southern Michigan) as early as 1885.[75] Called the "Mutual Aid League," this initial effort at *inmate self-government* did not last long for a variety of reasons, some of them political. Following World War I, a similar program was established at New York's Auburn Correctional Facility, which worked well for a few years. Failure to install sufficient protections and controls resulted in its abolition about 1928, when a few powerful inmate leaders were using it for their own purposes.

As the Auburn experience illustrates, adequate administrative controls are essential in any inmate self-governance experiment. Caution must be exercised in determining to what extent and in what areas the governing body will be able to exercise authority, with care taken to assure that established limits are not exceeded. Inmate self-governance is a form of *sharing* power and decision-making with inmates, not *abdicating* authority to them. In other words, it is a "system of control over prisoners that is not based on arbitrary decision-making . . . a formal system of decision-making in which all diverse parties . . . have some input . . . in which the conditions of work and confinement, the rules of the institution, and the special problems and grievances of different parties . . . are negotiated."[76]

Inmate governing councils have existed in varying forms in a number of institutions. One of the most widely used has been the inmate council system in which elected inmates discuss policies and complaints with management staff. In this form of inmate involvement, elected representatives do not have the power or authority to change policies or implement new procedures. Rather,

---

[75]Harold M. Helfman, "Antecedents of Thomas Mott Osborn's Mutual Welfare League in Michigan," *Journal of Law and Criminology,* Vol. 40, No. 5 (January/February 1950), pp. 597–600.
[76]John Irwin, *Prisons in Turmoil* (Boston: Little, Brown, 1980), p. 241.

they simply bring to administrative attention issues that are of concern to the resident population. For example, they might forward inmate grievances, make suggestions, identify problem areas, help work out unnecessary conflicts, and interpret administrative decisions to the general population.

The results can be quite favorable to all involved when proactive adjustments are made in response to the inmates' concerns. In doing so, not only can potential disruptions be curtailed, but inmates also begin to see that the administration cares about their welfare, potentially resulting in improved relationships between inmates and staff.

### Self-Governance Critique

Of course, not all forms of inmate self-governance are equally effective. In fact, as illustrated in the next "Close-up on Corrections," some would maintain that most are virtually destined to fail.

---

### ❖ CLOSE-UP ON CORRECTIONS

Inmate Self-Governance

[H]ere was the recipe for an ostensibly new and better form of prison government . . . invest responsibility in inmate leaders . . . and everything from inmate–staff relations to recidivism rates will improve. In essence, this was the recipe for participative prison management. To many . . . it seemed like a recipe for disaster. As one veteran of two experiments with participative prison management recalled:

> Boil it down, and the thing was to be nice to the inmates, to let them have a real hand in running the show. Some so-called experts discovered that these men had never had enough responsibility for themselves and that was why they had killed people, beat up teachers, raped, and so forth. So that was the main thing now . . . let them organize themselves. We used to say 'do your own time.' Now we said 'do time in your own way'—you organize the place, you run it. Just don't try to escape or get too crazy on us. . . .

[O]ne of the most forthright experiments in inmate self-government was made . . . in response to inmate strikes and threats to riot. The formal prison administration abdicated in favor of inmate leaders. Among those who came to rule the prison were the "Bikers," a prison gang which, when not terrorizing other inmates or the staff, extended [to] its members the privilege of racing their motorcycles on the prison yard. The experiment ended when the internal situation became so thoroughly chaotic that public pressure mounted to regain control of the institution. . . .

*Source:* John J. DiIulio, Jr., *Governing Prisons* (New York: Free Press, 1987), pp. 36–38.

---

The question then becomes why it is that so many experiments with inmate involvement in institutional management have not succeeded. One might assume that those institutions where inmates have a greater "say" in rules and regulations affecting them would tend to be less disruptive. To the contrary, as the research reflected in the last "Close-up on Corrections" concludes, there is "little evidence . . . to support the belief that prisons where inmates enjoy more self-government are better than prisons where they enjoy less."[77] The reasons for this apparent contradiction are as varied as the types of inmate self-governance that have been implemented. But they may well relate to such issues as timing, authority, relationships, and inmate maturity.

- *Timing.* As mentioned in the previous close-up, it is not uncommon for inmate governance to be implemented as a result of the threat of a riot or a strike. In such a situation, the population has apparently reached such a high level of frustration with existing administrative procedures or institutional conditions that they believe these are the only tactics that will get the attention of those in charge. In other words, they are *re*acting (or at least threatening reaction) to the lack of an administrative climate that *proactively* seeks to address grievances before they build up to the point of violence. If inmates are to be involved in facility management, the time to do so is *before* complaints escalate to such a dangerous point. Otherwise, the perception is created that the administration is abandoning its responsibilities by "giving in" to demands, thereby opening the door for exploiting such signs of "weakness."

- *Authority.* Particularly if the expansion of inmate participation is seen as a concession by management, inmates may tend to get somewhat carried away with their newfound source of power and authority. Those who have been docilely subservient for many years may well find it difficult to cope with any amount of power without abusing it. In fact, one survey noted that the main objection to inmate councils by correctional administrators is that they permit "one inmate to have authority over another."[78] Obviously, it must be emphasized in both written policy and unwritten practice that inmate involvement is *advisory* only (unlike the "Bikers" example in the last "Close-up on Corrections"). It must be clear that inmates are not *running* the facility, but rather, simply making suggestions for how it *could be run* better. Reducing inmate roles to an advisory capacity still involves some risks, however, since those representing the population have the power to bring forth or withhold issues for administrative consideration.

- *Relationships.* Even the most clear-cut guidelines restricting the authority of the inmate governing body will produce ineffective results if the system is nothing more than a public relations "gimmick." If the primary concern is *improving the image* of administration instead of *making fundamental changes* in response to legitimate concerns, the effort will be self-defeating. When communication consists of one-way, inmate-to-staff "gripe sessions," trust and confidence in the process quickly disap-

[77]DiIulio, p. 38.
[78]J.E. Baker, *The Right to Participate: Inmate Involvement in Prison Administration* (Metuchen, NJ: Scarecrow Press, 1974), p. 246, although he goes on to state that a properly prepared implementation plan "can easily and effectively rule out any possibility of this occurring."

pear. Not only are two-way dialogue and feedback needed, but staff must also take inmate concerns seriously and make good-faith efforts to act on those that can reasonably be changed without jeopardizing institutional safety or security.

• *Inmate maturity.* Needless to say, those inmates selected to represent the prison population in any form of participatory government will play a crucial role in whether or not the process works. Especially when inmate representatives are given too much authority, the process can break down as a result of their lack of experience with power, resulting in their inability to use it responsibly. Many of those in prison are simply not accustomed to making their own decisions or taking personal responsibility for their actions. In fact (as mentioned in Chapter 3), it could be argued that some may actually be subconsciously seeking the secure environment of an institution to avoid facing the demands of adult life in free society.[79]

In this regard, Maslow's *hierarchy of needs*[80] is a useful tool for assessing the motivation of inmates to participate in and benefit from self-governance. As illustrated in Figure 7.10, Maslow maintains that our behavior is determined by our personal motives or needs, which can be arranged on a hierarchy. *Physiological* (or physical) needs—food, clothing, shelter—dominate initially. These are our most powerful motivators until they are at least somewhat satis-

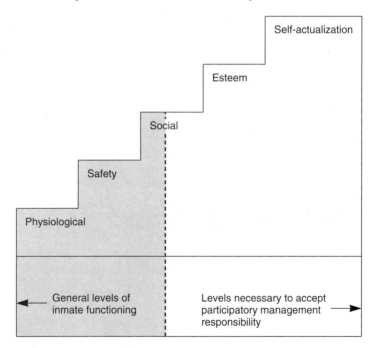

**Figure 7.10** Maslow's hierarchy of needs related to inmates and participatory management.

[79]See Karl Menninger, *The Crime of Punishment* (New York: Viking Press, 1968), p. 176.
[80]Abraham H. Maslow, *Motivation and Personality* (New York: Harper & Row, 1954).

fied. Once our needs for physical well-being are gratified, *safety* dominates—the need to be secure, free of risk, danger, or concern for our physical needs. When both physiological and safety needs are relatively well met, we are motivated by the need for *social* affiliation—to belong to various groups and to be accepted by them. But once we belong to a group, we often want to be more than a member—perhaps a leader, trusted advisor, or at least someone held in respect—reflecting our need for *esteem.* Finally, it is no longer sufficient to be recognized by others, leading to our desire for *self-actualization*—that is, to become everything within our capability—to be "all that we can be."

Very few people reach the top of Maslow's hierarchy (self-actualization), and prison is certainly not the ideal environment for achieving one's full potential. Nor are the majority of inmates likely to be functioning on the level of self-esteem, since many characterize themselves as "losers," "dropouts," "failures," and the like—some going so far as to tattoo themselves with the message "born to lose." In essence, "the hierarchy of needs attainment stops at the safety and security level in the correctional setting."[81] It is therefore likely that the bulk of the inmate population is functioning at the physiological, safety, or at most, social levels of Maslow's hierarchy.

However, participatory management will be effective only insofar as the participants are sufficiently emotionally mature—that is, motivated at the upper levels of Maslow's hierarchy.[82] Only when the participants are mature enough to accept the responsibilities of being involved in making their own decisions will true participatory management work effectively. Otherwise, it is similar to parents involving their children in making daily decisions about what to eat, when to go to bed, or anything else concerning their welfare. They are simply not mature enough to make such decisions in a responsible manner.

This, of course, does not negate the need to be responsive to complaints. But it is perhaps for this reason more than any other that the ideals of actual participation in management have met with so much failure when implemented in the reality of the prison environment. Nor, as the next chapter reveals, is the nature of the environment itself conducive to the rationality of behavior that we associate with life in free society. Prisoners may or may not be substantially "different" from the rest of society. But they are imprisoned, and that, if nothing else, distinguishes them from everyone else.

## ❖ SUMMARY

As a responsibility of the state and federal levels of government, prisons are considerably less numerous than local jails. But while prisons are typically more standardized than jails, they still reflect considerable diversity—from high-security custodial institutions to minimum-security community residential centers.

[81]David B. Kalinich and Terry Pitcher, *Surviving in Corrections* (Springfield, IL: Charles C Thomas, 1984), p. 12.
[82]See Paul Hersey and Ken Blanchard, *Management of Organizational Behavior: Utilizing Human Resources,* Fourth Edition (Englewood Cliffs, NJ: Prentice Hall, 1982), pp. 168–69.

In addition, the military operates correctional facilities confining enlisted personnel and officers.

Compared to other alternatives, prisons are the most expensive component of the correctional system. Beyond the $26,000 to $70,000 per bed cost of construction, annual operating costs run from $6000 to $23,000 per inmate. Most of these expenses are paid by the state level of government, although some jurisdictions have begun to collect fees from inmates to offset costs.

Generally, prisons confine those serving sentences of longer than one year. But the time served by prison inmates is significantly less than the maximum allowed under their sentence. The type of institution in which an inmate will serve time is determined by the person's security (or custody) classification. Those requiring the greatest amount of control are assigned to maximum security, which imposes a high level of both external and internal restrictions. At the other extreme, the most trustworthy offenders are assigned to minimum security, which provides far greater freedoms and privileges. However, most inmates are serving time in the intermediate level of custody—medium security.

The offender's custody level is determined through the classification process, which identifies the person's level of risk or dangerousness. During classification, the inmate is received into the system, processed, and assigned to housing. Prisoners may be reclassified at any time during their confinement.

In recent years, the number of inmates sentenced to state and federal correctional institutions has been increasing at a steady and alarming pace, causing many facilities to become severely crowded. The effects of crowding not only reduce the availability and quality of inmate programs and services, but they also pose serious health and safety risks. Responses to the crowding issue have ranged from expansion and new construction to "front-end" alternatives designed to keep people out of prison, and "back-end" approaches to release more of those already confined. Despite such efforts, the prison population continues to escalate.

The typical profile of a state prison inmate is a relatively young, white (Anglo) male (although blacks are disproportionately represented), who is unmarried, has not graduated from high school, and was employed at a low-paying job before confinement. The majority are recidivists, and many have been incarcerated previously. Most are in prison for violent crimes, although almost one-third are serving time for property offenses. More recently, the profile of inmates may be changing as the chance of being imprisoned for a wide range of crimes increases. While society has not clearly expressed what it expects its prisons to accomplish with these offenders, changing from the medical model to the justice model has reduced the emphasis on rehabilitation. However, a majority of the public still appears to support rehabilitation over punishment for those in prison.

Organizationally, state departments of corrections are headed by a director (or commissioner), who, in most states is appointed by the governor. As a result, there is potential for political influence, and directors are often replaced with the election of a new governor. The state director appoints the warden (or superintendent) of each facility, who is responsible for internal coordination, institutional policies and procedures, personnel decision making, and the development of external relationships. It is the warden's job to assure that the organizational units within the prison (operations, program services, and support services) are working together toward mutually compatible goals. The administrative style of the warden has an impact on the prison itself, the people within it, and the public's perception of both. In fact, it has been said that the quality of life in prison is largely dependent on the quality of its management.

But while the management of prisons is formally in the hands of the warden, the inmate population has considerable formal and informal control as well. The extent of the inmates' influence depends largely on how they are used within the institution. To prevent inmates from exercising too much unofficial authority, efforts have been made to restrict them to less sensitive work assignments and to remove them from direct supervision over other inmates. However, prisoners still exert significant informal social control, which in some institutions has been formalized through participatory management. Where participatory management has expanded into inmate self-governance, some difficulties have arisen— particularly when officials abdicate authority *to* the inmates rather than share power *with* them. Many offenders simply may not be sufficiently emotionally mature to accept the responsibilities of self-governance in a responsible manner. Moreover, the security-conscious nature of the prison environment is not conducive to the types of rational behavior associated with life in free society.

# part III

# Correctional Institutions: Custody, Treatment, Confinement, and Release

*Only those who have been incarcerated in a prison are able to realize what it means to be deprived of freedom. To have to get up in the morning at a certain time, have meals at a certain time, go to bed at a certain time [are things] the average citizen does every day. But he can, if he chooses, stay home from work or take his family out for dinner one evening, or go to a movie. That the prisoner cannot do, and that is the difference.[1]*

*David Abrahamsen*

Courtesy of Correctional Services of Canada.

[1]David Abrahamsen, *Who Are the Guilty? A Study of Education and Crime* (New York: Grove Press, 1952), p. 206.

To a society fearful of crime, it is undoubtedly reassuring to know that convicted offenders are confined behind bars. In the short term at least, the public can take some comfort in knowing that an offender cannot continue to victimize society while serving time in a correctional facility. But a short-term sense of safety does little to address long-term solutions. Very few offenders die in prison (actually, fewer than one-half of 1%)[2]—which is another way of saying that almost all inmates are eventually released to society—replacing our sense of comfort today with a renewed concern for our safety tomorrow.

In the upcoming chapters, we explore this issue by looking at just what does happen when an offender is incarcerated. Since much of society's emphasis under the justice model has moved toward incapacitation, the logical starting point is an inside view of prisons and their custodial procedures. If nothing else, correctional institutions are expected to retain inmates in custody. In Chapter 8 we will see how this is accomplished—from the formal controls achieved through physical restrictions, rules, and regulations to the informal controls encouraged through interpersonal relationships between staff and inmates.

In the process of maintaining control, it is apparent that a rather "artificial" environment is created, where even the most seemingly insignificant details can quickly escalate into major disputes. If, in such a closed environment, big resentments are made out of little ones, offenders themselves can become "victims of the system"—worse when they come out than they were upon arrival. Punishment through imprisonment does serve a social function by enabling the criminal "outgroup" to absorb the hostility of the "normal" citizenry, thereby permitting a general draining of aggression by the public. However, punishment can also intensify the person's maladjustment by adding frustration to frustration and reinforcing failure. In any case, it does not address the offender's basic problem.

It therefore stands to reason that the overall objective of protecting society is better served in the long run by treatment than exclusive reliance on incapacitation or punishment. Thus, in Chapter 9, we turn our attention to the various clinical, educational, and training approaches that have been provided within correctional institutions. Some of these efforts focus on improved behavioral adjustment. Others emphasize developing self-respect and social responsibility. Still others target the need for marketable job skills. But regardless of their specific approach, all have in common the goal of better preparing the offender for a law-abiding lifestyle upon release.

However, as we will see in Chapter 10, the ability to accomplish this far-reaching goal is constrained by the very environment within which such training or treatment programs are offered. Correctional institutions are notorious for the negative impact they have upon those confined. Even the most humane, progressive institutions are, in the final analysis, just that—institutions. They are not rehabilitation centers. They are not job training facilities. They are not personal

---

[2]Compiled from figures presented in Louis W. Jankowski, *Correctional Populations in the United States, 1990* (Washington, DC: U.S. Department of Justice, 1991), pp. 78 and 97, which report that of the 774,375 prisoners under state or federal jurisdiction in 1990, only 1597 died before the completion of their sentence.

treatment programs. They are, first and foremost, institutions—where residents are closed off from normal relationships, unable to make even the most minor personal decisions, and pressured by others to fit into the inmate society and conform to its "informal code" of conduct.

Some of those incarcerated are more negatively affected by this total institutional environment than others, and in Chapter 10 we also address various factors that influence individual adaptations—from psychological defense mechanisms to the powerful inducement of gangs. We likewise discover how frustrations are expressed in the ultimate form of collective violence—institutional riots. After observing their devastating impact in terms of loss of life, injuries, and widespread property damage, we explore what *pro*active measures can be taken to prevent the need for *re*active responses following such violent disturbances.

While all inmates do not participate in prison riots, everyone *is* affected in some way by the dehumanizing impact of the institutional environment, which inherently generates a steady, debilitating effect on those confined. For many, prison reinforces rather than reduces antisocial tendencies. As a result, it is perhaps not surprising that so many offenders return to a life of crime, but rather, more surprising why some do not.

It is to this issue of life after institutional confinement that Chapter 11 is devoted—considering such issues as how well institutional regimentation prepares one for success upon release; how likely former inmates are to recidivate, and how reasonable is it to expect that an ex-offender can take responsibility for functioning in a socially acceptable manner. Just as the movement from the medical model to the justice model has influenced sentencing practices, we will see how this shift has changed the very nature of parole. As determinate, flat-time sentencing has replaced the flexibility of indeterminate sentences, we will review the impact on release criteria, time served, and postrelease supervision practices.

Exploring this transition from confinement to community, we will see that the public's acceptance of ex-offenders has much to do with their ultimate success or failure. A society reassured by the confinement of offenders behind bars is unlikely to welcome the reintegration of those same offenders back into the community. But that is exactly where over 99% are eventually coming. And it is when they are released that the public must confront the issue of how prudent it is to dismiss long-term solutions for a short-term sense of safety.

# chapter 8

# Institutional Procedures: Custody

*The clanging of the metal doors to the main entrance . . . is unlike any sound you have ever heard. It is loud, heavy, and harsh. An exclamation point hammering home the fact that you are now inside a prison.*[1]

Grace L. Wojda et al.

## ❖ CHAPTER OVERVIEW

Correctional institutions are designed to receive, house, care for, and release offenders committed to their care. During confinement, maintaining custody is a primary concern. Keeping the institution *safe and secure* and *preventing escapes* are the major custodial functions. Quite simply, the institution cannot treat inmates if it does not have them in custody. Although the most appropriate type of treatment is very much subject to debate, security is not considered debatable.

Traditional security involves well-known, routine practices—such as counting, controlling movement, conducting searches, staffing tower observation points, regulating contact with the outside, and managing inmate behavior. Some inherent restrictions are built into the physical plant itself. Others result from custodial procedures implemented by staff. All emphasize maintaining compliance with the rules and regulations of the institution. When such compliance is not achieved, the results can be disastrous—escapes, violence, riots, and other disturbances that jeopardize the safety and security of inmates, staff, and/or facility. But these custodial features represent only one aspect of maintaining institutional control. Often overlooked are the more informal, noncoercive controls emerging from the relationship established between correctional officers and the inmate population.

The nature of that relationship has changed considerably over time. Prior to the 1960s, the role of those "guarding" inmates had changed little since its ori-

---

[1]Grace L. Wojda, Raymond G. Wojda, Norman Erik Smith, and Richard K. Jones, *Behind Bars* (Laurel, MD: American Correctional Association, 1991), p. 3.

gin in the Auburn Penitentiary. Primary attention was focused on enforcing institutional regulations and supervising custodial procedures. Given the limited scope of their duties and what was expected of them, operational staff were commonly referred to as "guards" or "turnkeys." But during the height of the medical model, it became apparent that line correctional personnel could play an important role beyond custodial supervision.

Until this point, the fact that those dealing directly with the inmates have significant potential for achieving a positive impact on their behavior was largely overlooked. But it has now become clear that operational staff are perhaps even more influential than treatment staff because of their continuous interaction through day-to-day contact with those incarcerated. Like the teachers a child encounters at school, treatment personnel play a major role in shaping values and attitudes. But teachers cannot completely replace the impact of the family, with whom the child interacts more intimately on a daily basis. In a correctional institution, it is the operational staff who are to some extent the inmate's surrogate "family"—whose empathy and understanding can go far toward making time in a correctional institution more tolerable and treatment more effective.

This recognition of a broader role for line staff began the translation from the punitive, rule-enforcement "guard" to the modern concept of a "correctional officer," whose responsibilities extend beyond custody toward establishing a genuine relationship based on mutual respect. That does not, however, mean that enforcing traditional security measures is overlooked in an effort to avoid destroying relationships. Inmate respect is not earned by "looking the other way" when rules are violated. On the other hand, officers who demonstrate a caring concern and empathetic understanding are more likely to obtain a level of voluntary compliance that can reduce the need to rely exclusively on coercive techniques. With even the most efficient custodial procedures, it is difficult to control those who do not voluntarily consent to be controlled. Thus in the long term, developing effective working relationships not only promotes treatment but serves security objectives as well. It is this combination of conventional controls and informal influence through relationship building that best enables an institution to achieve its custodial mandate.

---

*LEARNING GOALS*

*Do you know:*
- *The primary function of custody?*
- *The operational objectives of custody?*
- *Why custodial security is necessary to achieve effective treatment?*

---

## ❖ FUNCTIONS OF CUSTODY

Every prison has custody at its central core. The primary function of custody is to provide *external controls* for those who do not have sufficient internal controls to function effectively in free society. Ideally, custody should provide only that amount of external control which is immediately necessary. It is for this reason that, as we saw in Chapter 7, correctional institutions function at various levels of security—from minimum to maximum. Even for those who are initially assigned to a high level of security classification, the system is designed to reduce the level of control gradually for those who increasingly demonstrate the ability to function on their own as they better internalize self-control.

While correctional facilities represent the ultimate form of control, less restrictive social controls are also maintained by many other institutions in society: the family, schools, churches, civic organizations, and so on. It is through these institutions that we learn morals, values, and socially acceptable behavior. It is when the socializing influences of these other institutions have failed with a particular person that correctional control takes over. Custody in corrections, of course, is more direct and better organized, because it deals with people in a closed environment—where behavior must be more strictly controlled to prevent inmates from disturbing others or harming themselves.

## Purposes of Custody

Custodial procedures in correctional facilities are designed to control individual behavior for the well-being of the total institution. More specifically, the immediate operational *objectives of custody* are to:

1. Prevent *escape.*
2. Maintain *order and safety.*
3. Promote the *efficient functioning* of the overall institution.

In the long term, the types of behavioral restraints involved in maintaining custody are also designed to shape the offender's behavior in a manner that better enables reentry into society as a contributing, law-abiding citizen (or at least, not a dangerous one). Undoubtedly, other programs offered during the period of confinement—counseling, vocational training, work release, and the like—contribute significantly to this long-term goal. But it is custody that permits such programs to function.

## Custody/Treatment Relationships

Referring back to the discussion of Maslow's hierarchy of needs in Chapter 7, it is apparent that at least some minimal level of physiological well-being, safety, and security must be established before higher-level motivations can be fulfilled. In more practical terms, it is difficult, if not impossible, to develop meaningful programs when work schedules are "frequently interrupted by violence" or classrooms become "battlegrounds."[2] If one is constantly concerned about self-protection and institutional disruption, the appropriate environment

[2]John J. DiIulio, *Governing Prisons: A Comparative Study of Correctional Management* (New York: Free Press, 1987), p. 92.

for working, learning, or changing behavior is simply lacking. As one officer put it:" Security doesn't mean keep them from going over the wall. It means you try to make the guy feel secure, that he's not going to get killed or hurt. . . . So he doesn't have to worry about something happening. . . . If they want to go out, they'll find a way. It's not that kind of security."[3]

There is, in fact, a "correlation between good security and good inmate programming," and blending the two creates a system that is "responsive to the needs of both inmates and staff."[4] In other words, custody and treatment go hand in hand: "Most program staff realize that effective programs cannot exist in a disorderly, dangerous institution. Most correctional staff understand that offering a variety of institutional programs actually helps them manage the institution more effectively. In short, these two main segments of the institutional community need each other."[5]

Even under the best of conditions, correctional institutions are far from the ideal environment for the implementation of meaningful treatment programs. But in those facilities where basic control is absent, treatment faces a formidable obstacle. On the other hand, the most secure institution might be one that keeps the inmates in their cells at all times. But it would be next to impossible to provide education, training, or any other programs under those conditions. Nor does such restriction prepare the inmate for the interaction with others that is inevitably encountered upon release. Consequently, the institution is faced with finding the appropriate balance between program operations and security needs.

## Security Techniques

Different correctional institutions seek to achieve this balance in different ways. In part, the extent to which service versus custody is emphasized will depend on the security classification of the institution. Certainly, more freedoms and opportunities for program participation are available in minimum-security facilities. However, that does not mean that services must be sacrificed to achieve custody. Quite the contrary, *custody* is a necessary condition for *treatment*.[6]

Maintaining custody is achieved in part through the architectural features and security hardware of the *physical plant* itself. But even the most architecturally sound institution designed for the highest level of security also requires such *control procedures* as separation, restricted movement, counts, searches, and the regulation of everything from visiting and correspondence to tools and property. Throughout the remainder of this chapter, we will see how physical features, combined with security techniques, function together to maintain custodial security.

---

[3]Lucien X. Lombardo, *Guards Imprisoned: Correctional Officers at Work,* Second Edition (Cincinnati, OH: Anderson Publishing Company, 1989), p. 64.

[4]Anthony Travisono, "Editorial," *On the Line,* Vol. 13, No. 2 (March 1990), p.1.

[5]*Correctional Officer Resource Guide* (Laurel, MD: American Correctional Association, 1989), p. 108.

[6]Paraphrased from DiIulio, p. 41.

*LEARNING GOALS* ▐▬▬▬▬▬▬▬▬▬▬▬▬▬▬▬▬▬▬▬▬▬▬▬▬▬▬▬▬▬▬▬▬▬

*Do you know:*

- *How security is incorporated into the physical design of a correctional institution?*
- *What external security features are used to prevent unauthorized prison entrance or exit?*
- *What "double door" security is?*

## ❖ ARCHITECTURAL DESIGN

To a considerable extent, the physical design of a correctional facility reflects its philosophy. As an example, one only needs to look at the forbidding prison "fortresses" surrounded by thick, impenetrable concrete walls that were built before the turn of the century. The cold, uninviting atmosphere of such a sternly institutional structure immediately communicates a harsh, morbid impression of the prison as a symbol of punishment.

Although prison architecture has progressed through various changes throughout this century, the need to incorporate *security* into physical design remains a primary consideration in prison construction. The challenge more recently has become integrating the "dual mission" of treatment and security into facility design.[7] In addition, the American Correctional Association has established certain minimum standards that institutions seeking the endorsement of ACA accreditation are required to meet. (See Chapter 15 for more details on the accreditation process.) Although the internal and external security measures built into prisons today may be somewhat more subtle, upon entering a prison, there is little doubt about where you are. For an inside account of the impact of prison security on a newly arriving visitor, see the next "Close-up on Corrections."

### External Security

Simply by looking at the external physical plant, it is often possible to determine the security classification of a correctional institution. The higher the security classification, the more accute "reminders" there will be of the institution's custodial function.

As was noted in Chapter 7, maximum-security institutions have traditionally had a perimeter composed of high walls. Building miles and miles of walls around a prison compound has, however, become extremely expensive. More recently, walls have tended to be replaced by the type of fencing common in medium-custody facilities, topped with row upon row of razor wire for added security. Beyond keeping prisoners inside, a wall or fence also serves to prevent the passage of contraband into the institution. A general principle of wall and

---

[7]Scarlett V. Carp and Joyce A. Davis, "Planning and Designing a Facility for a Special Needs Population," *Corrections Today,* Vol. 53, No. 2 (April 1991), p. 102.

Towering fortress-like walls traditionally formed the perimeter of high-security prisons constructed during the early twentieth century. Courtesy of the Iowa Department of Social Services.

fence construction is that there should be a minimum of openings, combined with remote control of the entrance gate.

At various points throughout the perimeter, guard towers are located, sometimes surrounded by bulletproof glass and equipped with search lights. From these towers, armed officers with binoculars constantly survey the area for signs of disturbances, escapes, or anything else that is out of the ordinary. In fact, it has been said that: "if there is any doubt as to the nature of the institution or . . . the purpose of the custodial staff, the inmate may merely glance at the walls. The tower guard symbolizes the stern hand of the community that has placed him in exile. . . . The guard always has the inmate under surveillance, while the inmate always must take the tower guard into account."[8]

In addition, ground posts may be situated between towers on the outside perimeter. These are staffed during times when there is low visibility from the towers, such as during fogs or storms. In some very high-security facilities, ground sensors—designed to sound an alarm or alert personnel when activated—may also be installed in areas inside the perimeter fences that are off-limits.

[8]James B. Jacobs and Harold G. Retsky, "Prison Guard," *Urban Life*, Vol. 4, No. 1 (April 1975) p. 19.

### Welcome to Lebanon

More than the miles of razor-sharp concertina wire that surround the institution, more than the guard towers that loom over the compound, it is the clanging of the three-inch thick steel doors that defines what life is like inside the prison.

In some respects, your first view of Lebanon is disappointing. There's no shoving and pushing going on. Nobody is manacled. The inmates don't march in lock step; the officers don't even carry guns. In fact, it all seems pretty tame.

But a senior correctional officer quickly puts things into focus. "This is not a boys' camp," he says, "You never forget what they're here for." Adds another officer, "You can't totally relax in here. If you do, you're a fool." . . .

Tuesday is laundry day. . . . In the space of 35 minutes, all 2,000 inmates walk the length of the prison, deposit their old sheets and pillowcases in large hampers, pickup clean linen, and head back to their cells. It is the single biggest mass movement among the inmates that takes place at Lebanon, and it presents . . . security problems.

During the exchange, inmates are required—as always—to walk along the right-hand wall. . . . The sheets are . . . folded and placed over the left shoulder, allowing the officer to watch the inmates' hands and ensure that no weapons or contraband are being transported.

The most obvious security problem, however, is the simple fact that 2,000 inmates are in one place at one time. That's a lot of men to watch. . . .

*Source:* Grace L. Wojda, Raymond, G. Wojda, Norman Erik Smith, and Richard K. Jones, *Behind Bars* (Laurel, MD: American Correctional Association, 1990), pp. 3–4, 11.

## Internal Security

The entrance to a correctional facility (sometimes called the *sallyport*) is generally equipped with a ground post and sometimes with a tower as well. In this way, the entrance gates can be manipulated by the correctional officer in the tower, while the officer in the ground post can conduct any necessary vehicle searches and inspection of passes. The main gates are secured by locks, with passage in and out controlled by the officer on duty.

Search procedures for those entering the compound will vary according to the security classification of the prison. However, even prisons with the same security level may vary the intensity of searches according to the particular administrative policy of the institution. Procedures range from a superficial "frisk" to the use of a metal detector or even the inspectroscope equipment used to screen baggage for airline security. The difficulty with the metal detector is, of course, that a belt buckle, a money clip, or a pocket full of change can set it off. But the greater limitation in terms of its use in corrections is that while it can detect metal weapons, it does not identify plastics or such nonmetallic contraband items as drugs.

Once inside, the physical plant is constructed to limit and monitor movement throughout the compound. In addition to the ground posts and guard towers, this can be accomplished through closed-circuit TV monitors, centralized locking devices, control booths, alarms, and even computer-controlled door access.[9]

Not all facilities have highly sophisticated security equipment, but virtually every maximum or medium institution will have a system of *double-door security* monitored from control booths, whereby no two consecutive doors or gates can be opened at the same time. Movement therefore occurs sequentially, from one security post to the next, with the rear gate always closing behind you before the upcoming gate is opened. In this way, if a disturbance occurs during movement, it can be separated from the rest of the population, or one entire area of the compound can be closed off to keep an uprising from spreading further.

All of these security features—from external fences and towers to internal gates and alarms—function together to promote the custodial security of the institution. They help to assure that those who are not authorized to do so neither come in nor get out.

---

*LEARNING GOALS* ▰▰▰▰▰▰▰▰▰▰▰▰▰▰▰▰▰▰▰▰▰

*Do you know:*

- *The purpose of segregating inmates?*
- *The difference between protective custody and administrative segregation?*
- *In what ways movement is controlled within a correctional institution?*
- *How and why periodic counts are conducted?*
- *In contrast to media portrayals, how most prison escapes occur?*

---

## ❖ CONTROL PROCEDURES

Even the best and most modern physical plant represents only part of what is needed for secure custodial control. The structure and hardware of the prison must work hand in hand with the people and procedures used to ensure institutional security. Architectural design and electronic gadgetry cannot replace the need for operational procedures that provide further controls within the confines of the physical structure. As correctional administrators have phrased it, "We all know that closed-circuit cameras do not catch escapees, just as towers didn't catch them a century ago."[10] "The best video monitoring system in the world never broke up a fight in an exercise yard." We need to remember that

---

[9]See, for example, Duncan C. McCulloch, "Achieving Maximum Security with the Help of Computers," *Corrections Today*, Vol. 50, No. 4 (July 1988), pp. 122, 128–30.

[10]James E. Murphy, "Combining Technology and Staff to Achieve Fail-Safe Security, *Corrections Today*, Vol. 53, No. 4 (July 1991), p. 6. See also O. Lane McCotter, "Vulnerability of a High-Tech Prison: Relying on Hardware Is a Dangerous Mistake," *Corrections Today*, Vol. 51, No. 4 (July 1989), pp. 64–65.

Even with the most sophisticated electronic devices, security is primarily dependent upon the men and women who make the system work. Courtesy of the International Association of Correctional Officers.

"behind every good security system stand the people who make it work."[11] In the end, security is primarily dependent on personnel.

Prisons differ considerably with regard to the degree of operational restrictions imposed and how rigorously they are enforced. Obviously, institutions with high-security classifications will have the most severe restrictions and will be less tolerant about infractions. But again, even within prisons of similar custodial classifications, there will be variations in terms of how extensively inmates are segregated, how strictly movement is controlled, how frequently counts and searches are conducted, how much effort is devoted to property and tool control, how often visits are permitted, and the like. Moreover, the specific rules and regulations governing inmate behavior will vary in terms of content, enforcement,

[11]Susan B. Cohen, "Never Forget . . . Behind Every Good Security System Stand the People Who Make it Work," *Corrections Today*, Vol. 53, No. 4 (July 1991), pp. 86–88.

and resulting penalties. But regardless of the implementation differences among various prisons, there are certain general techniques that serve as control procedures in most secure correctional institutions.

### Segregation

Just as the prison itself is physically separated from the outside world, *segregation* within the institution functions to isolate inmates from each other. It is based on the premise that *minimizing interaction* between inmates also minimizes their opportunity for disruptive behavior—everything from planning escapes and dealing in contraband to engaging in fights and assaults.

Within a correctional institution, segregation can be employed either *proactively* (to prevent such behavior) or *reactively* (in response to inappropriate behavior). For example, in most secure prisons, a proactive strategy may be used, whereby each inmate is confined in a separate cell. Unlike the individual living units of new-generation jails, however, the cells do not open into a dayroom to which inmates have free access. Rather, movement in and out of the cell is strictly regulated—often confined to brief periods of recreation or visiting—and always under the close supervision of a correctional officer. Such an approach obviously serves the security interests of the institution. But there are also trade-offs in terms of the psychological effects of isolation, as well as the limitations it imposes on the development of social skills or participation in institutional programs.

Additionally, with the pressures of crowding in recent years, more and more inmates are being doubled-up in cells that may have been originally intended for single occupancy. Among the factors involved in determining whether or not single cells can be converted into double occupancy are size, ventilation, and the amount of time inmates are in their cells. For example, if the inmates primarily spend only sleeping hours confined to their cells, doubling-up is much less a problem than if they must spend the bulk of the day in extremely close quarters.

As a result of such considerations, many facilities have two or more inmates in a cell, while other institutions use the dormitory concept. Group living has definite social and psychological advantages over single-cell isolation. But here, too, there are trade-offs, since it is far more difficult to control group behavior, particularly when observation is limited to an officer occasionally passing by the cellblock on routine "patrol." It is for such reasons that new-generation jailing combines group interaction with individual living units and direct supervision by officers.

Of course, not everyone is equally capable of living amicably in a dormitory, and the weak are easy prey for the strong in such an environment. Thus, segregation can also be used reactively to respond to problems created by group living. For instance, an inmate who fears for his safety in a group dormitory can request isolation for personal protection. Some inmates are also administratively assigned to protective custody, as in high-profile cases or those involving former judges, police, or correctional officers whose safety in the general population would be in jeopardy.

Once someone is assigned or moved to *protective custody,* it is very difficult to assimilate into (or return to) the population, since that person now has a reputation for being unable to stand up for himself. It is therefore more likely that an inmate will be isolated for administrative reasons than upon personal request.

*Administrative segregation* refers to any number of reasons for which an inmate may be separated other than disciplinary infractions. Examples might include those experiencing deteriorating mental health, undergoing "mood swings," or requiring gradual reentry following hospitalization. In essence, any circumstances that call for greater attention and supervision than would be available in the general population could result in administrative segregation. In such cases, the inmate has not necessarily done anything that would be a violation of institutional rules.

In contrast, *disciplinary segregation* is used for punitive purposes in response to rule infractions. Disciplinary segregation may include various levels of supervision (ranging from "close" to "maximum"). But it is most often associated with solitary confinement. Under solitary conditions, inmates spend all but a few recreational hours in their cells. Additional privileges such as commissary and visiting may also be restricted. Such isolation is reserved for those who committed serious institutional violations. Inmates are confined to such conditions for a specified length of time following a disciplinary hearing (unlike administrative segregation, which is more subject to staff discretion). The function of disciplinary segregation is to isolate and control those whose behavior presents a problem for others or for the overall security of the facility.

All prisons have their troublemakers, agitators, or quarrelsome people who cannot get along in the general population. Some prisons segregate all of these disruptive inmates in a single unit. Others distribute them throughout the population, allowing the informal inmate control system to handle the problems, and reserving isolation for those few who cannot be controlled by the other inmates. Neither approach is an ideal solution.

Without violating constitutional protections, there are a relatively limited number of benefits and privileges that can be withdrawn through disciplinary action in prisons. When these have been exhausted, there may be no other alternative but to separate the offender physically. Segregation is therefore used as the ultimate disciplinary procedure for those who have seriously violated institutional rules and regulations. In this way it also serves to protect others from assaults, homosexual attacks, strong-arm tactics, and the like. Thus, segregation can be used to confine those who are threatening to others, dangerous to themselves, or in need of protective custody from other inmates.[12]

## Controlled Movement

Another primary way in which inmates are physically restricted is through closely *controlled movement* within the institution. This is an important feature of custody, since every time inmates are moved—particularly in groups—there is a

---

[12]Robert E. Doran, *A Study of California Prison Adjustment Centers* (Washington, D.C.: U.S. Department of Justice, Law Enforcement Assistance Administration, 1973), pp. 39–44.

potential *security risk* (as noted in the laundry situation described in the last close-up). In addition, it is essential to know where all inmates are at all times, which becomes increasingly difficult with frequent movements.

The amount of movement allowed within a facility will largely depend on the institution's security classification. In minimum-security facilities, there are few restraints—inmates are permitted to go relatively freely from their living quarters to work assignments, recreation areas, and dining halls. In Chapter 6 we also saw how direct-supervision jails reduce the need for movement by arranging for visiting, feeding, recreation, and other services directly within the living unit.

But maximum-security prisons reduce the potential for escapes by (among other things) closely supervising and very strictly limiting the amount of movement. Particularly in a maximum institution, all persons and articles going into and out of prison must be controlled. The next "Close-up on Corrections" describes these movement controls, along with the segregation and other restrictions imposed within one of the highest-security U.S. prisons.

In such extremely secure institutions, where inmates are isolated in individual cells, movement is often restricted further by in-cell feeding. However, crowding has reduced the supply of single cells, and many institutions were designed with group dining halls and recreation areas that require movement to a centralized area. In most prisons, some movement is therefore almost inevitable several times each day. In addition, inmates participating in various institutional programs need to be escorted to those locations. The basic concept is that the *less* inmates need to be moved, the easier it is for an institution to maintain security. But the security advantages of restricted movement must be weighed against the disadvantages of excessive boredom accompanying prolonged confinement.

**Individual Passes and Group Movement.** A *system of passes* is often used to control movement within the prison. For example, if an individual prisoner is to go from a work assignment to a counselor, the correctional officer writes and signs a pass, which includes the time of departure and designated location. The pass is then similarly signed by the correctional officer at the identified destination. When the inmate returns, the correctional officer notes the time. All such passes are submitted to the control room or the deputy warden's office at the end of the shift, to be filed for further reference in case they are needed.

This manual method of recording movement is "time-consuming, subject to error," and potentially dangerous, since each time officers log one person's transfer, they are "temporarily unable to keep a close watch on other inmates."[13] Recently, a modern high-tech approach that automatically records all transfers has become available as an alternative to the pass system. Each inmate wears a bracelet which contains a bar code that is scanned at various locations throughout the facility whenever the inmate is moved. Like the bar code system used at the supermarket checkout, an electronic scanning device produces a printout that records precisely when and where the inmate was moved throughout the

---

[13]Warren Rohn and Trish Ostroski, "Advances in Technology Make It Easier to Monitor Inmates," *Corrections Today*, Vol. 53, No. 4 (July 1991), p. 144.

Inside the Nation's Most Secure Prison

A black box over his handcuffs keeps the inmate from picking the locks. Chains lead through it, wrapped and padlocked around his waist. Shackles hobble his feet. But even so, three (officers) surround him as he walks. . . .

This (is) the U.S. Penitentiary at Marion, Ill. . . . the most rigidly controlled prison in the United States. . . .

The first lesson any prisoner learns at Marion is about movement. If an inmate refuses to move, a specially trained five-man unit in riot helmets and flack jackets enters his cell. Each is assigned a body part: an arm, a leg, the waist. They take him down, chain him and carry him out. But most of the 430 inmates don't move very much at all. They are confined to their cells 22 hours a day. . . .

Until recently, their food came in cellophane wrappers, but those . . . have now been banned. . . . [S]ome inmates melted cellophane [and] . . . fashioned it into crude blades. . . . [A] prisoner managed to fashion a bomb . . . sewn meticulously into the rolled-up cardboard backing of a legal pad. So cardboard is contraband. . . . By trial and error, and this long process of elimination, nearly everything has been taken from the prisoners. . . .

|  | GENERAL POPULATION AT OTHER U.S. PENITENTIARIES | AT MARION |
|---|---|---|
| Food service | Buffet style in central mess hall; seconds | Prepackaged ration in cell; no seconds |
| Out-of-cell time | 14–16 hours/day | 2 hours/day |
| Recreation | 5 hours/day, minimum | 2 hours/day |
| Commissary | Convenience-store inventory | Limited goods . . . |
| Restraints when moved inside | No | Yes, handcuffs |

*Source:* Christopher Dickey, "A New Home for Noriega?" *Newsweek* (January 15, 1990), pp. 66–69.

day. In fact, the same system can be used to obtain books from the library or charge items purchased at the commissary to an inmate's account.[14]

There are also times when inmates must be moved in groups. Prisoners of the past were marched in silence through lock-step, military-type formations, (as we saw in previous descriptions of the disciplinary system used in the early years of the Auburn Penitentiary). Such rigidity has been replaced today by movement through less regimented lines, accompanied by correc-

[14]Ibid. Another equally high-tech system—retina scanning—uses an "eyeprint" to determine positive identification at any point from initial intake to eventual release. See David S. Pemberton, Jim Rentiers, and Joe Schneider, "Eyeprint Identification: The High-Tech Alternative," *Corrections Today*, Vol. 50, No. 4 (July 1988), pp. 118–120.

tional officers who keep a careful count of those involved and are watchful for signs of misbehavior.

When inmates are to be moved together to work or educational assignments, they may be required to meet at a specified time and location. At this predetermined staging area, they are then checked off by their supervisor, frisk searched, and prepared for movement. Separate groups are then escorted to their designated locations. A similar system is used to return inmates to their assigned housing area.

Anyone failing to show for pickup from the staging area without an excused absence may incur a disciplinary infraction. Depending on the circumstances, a latecomer may be escorted individually or sent with a written pass. But efforts are made to keep such disruptions to a minimum in order to preserve the integrity of the security system. Once authorized to participate in a particular program or work detail, the inmate is expected to be there during specified times. Failure to attend an assigned activity can result in a disciplinary infraction and/or removal from the program.

**External Transportation.**    To limit the need for transportation outside of the prison, most large institutions provide as many services as possible within the compound. For example, some facilities contract with medical specialists to provide clinics within the institution on a regular basis. In other cases, judges may

Specially-designed buses are used when a sizeable number of inmates must be transported to locations outside of the facility where they are housed. Courtesy of the Dade County Department of Corrections and Rehabilitation, Miami, Florida.

even conduct various types of proceedings inside institutional walls or through two-way video monitoring. However, there will always be a need for *external movement* in order to transport inmates to other correctional facilities, hospitals, court appearances, funerals, and so on.[15] In fact, such outside movement has become so extensive in some locations that a corrections administrator once complained that he had a population of 2000 in institutions and another 1000 on the road at any given time. While that may be an overstatement reflecting the frustration of maintaining security during transit, there is considerable need in some facilities to transport inmates outside.

Security procedures are obviously much tighter for external transportation than for internal movement within the prison walls. For example, although staff are not permitted to carry weapons while supervising inmates within the facility, those transporting inmates to the outside are almost always armed. The inmates themselves are restrained by handcuffs, which are sometimes attached to waist chains. Leg irons may also be used to control a prisoner's stride and eliminate a foot race. When several are being transported together, the cuffs are chained together, linking each inmate to the others in groups of six (commonly referred to as a "six-pack").

All outside trips must be well planned. If, for instance, an inmate is being transported to a hospital or funeral parlor, the local police should be contacted in advance to verify the relative's illness or death. The precise route should be carefully determined and scheduled, with law enforcement officials notified if additional police protection is needed. In particularly dangerous situations, a "chase" vehicle may also follow the transporting vehicle to provide backup assistance in case an escape is attempted. Needless to say, the prisoner should be taken only to the places specified, and contact with the public should be avoided as much as possible.

### Conducting Counts

The purpose of restrictions on inmate movement is naturally to keep track of where everyone is. The precise location of all inmates is also determined periodically through *headcounts.* Most counts are done physically by correctional officers. But here, too, technology now exists in terms of a sensor device worn like a wristwatch that not only has an automated headcount feature but can also be used by the inmate to signal for help in a dangerous situation.[16] Such sophisticated devices are still, however, a long way from replacing the counting functions of correctional personnel.

As the central headquarters of custodial operations, the control room is usually where the count is coordinated. The officers in the control room should know the location of all inmates and be responsible for the count. Direct tele-

---

[15]Within the Federal Bureau of Prisons alone, some 50,000 people are transported for "court appearances, medical care, and long-term housing" every year. Laurie Vaught, "New Transfer Center to Streamline BOP Inmates' Movement across U.S.," *Corrections Today,* Vol. 54, No. 2 (April 1992), p. 125.

[16]Philip J. Boyle and James G. Ricketts, "Using Technology to Achieve Higher Efficiency in Correctional Facilities," *Corrections Today,* Vol. 54, No. 5 (July 1992), pp. 78–80.

phone lines from each tower and cellblock connect to the control room. Over these lines, the cellblocks report the counts, and the towers identify any unusual occurrences (although more recently, this can be done by computer). Correctional officers report any inmates who are absent for work or other assignments, and the control room checks passes to determine whether the inmate is somewhere else legitimately. In the case of towers and posts, correctional officers report periodically, as often as every hour.

Counts are one of the most important functions of custody. Correctional officers are always counting inmates as a routine part of their duties. In addition, at certain specified times, an overall count is taken. Because the count is so significant, other activities stop when it is conducted. Inmates may be required to stand in order to be properly identified. But regardless of the specific procedures employed, officers must be extremely careful to identify each inmate personally. Assuming, for instance, that a bulky form under blankets on a bed is actually the cell's occupant gives an escaping inmate valuable time until the next count is conducted. On the other hand, inefficient counting which erroneously indicates that an inmate is missing can cause serious disruption of normal institutional operations while a needless recount or search is mounted.

In maximum security, counts may occur as often as every two hours. While counts are not as frequent in minimum-security facilities, they are still conducted, usually at mealtime and before inmates retire for the evening. All counts are called in to central control and verified by written documentation. Any count that does not match the number on the official roster (whether over or under), results in everyone being "locked down" in the living units while a rapid recheck is made and another full count is conducted. If the discrepancy still exists, emergency search procedures are activated.

## Escapes

Having exactly the right number of inmates in custody at any given time is most important to any correctional institution. Any fewer than there should be results in activating an escape alarm, notifying appropriate law enforcement agencies, and closing down normal operations while an extensive search is mounted. Generally, if the escapee is not located within a certain period of time, fingerprints are forwarded to the FBI with a notification that the offender is wanted. For a firsthand account of the adrenalin-pumping response to a missing inmate, see the next "Close-up on Corrections."

The overdramatized television and movie accounts of prison breakouts would have us believe that escapes are accompanied by elaborate plotting, high suspense, and violent outcomes. But in real life, escape attempts take many forms. In one case, a telephone call from a "probation officer" requested the release of a prisoner, but a return call to the officer indicated that no such request had been made. The prisoner himself was discovered telephoning from the institution's pay phone!

Many escape attempts are simply "walk-aways," often in conjunction with visiting, outside work assignments, or a low level of institutional security. While there are few escapes from inside the walls of high-security facilities, those are

Inmate's Escaped!

"It's been another long, slow day at work, which is routine around here. The inmates are mostly out on one of many laborious details; picking up litter along the roadsides, paving new streets, or doing maintenance jobs in and around the institution. Pretty soon, they'll trickle in, go down to the mess hall to eat and then prepare for the evening's activities. I am getting antsy, looking forward to a long weekend. . . .

[T]he daywatch supervisor bursts into the control center where I am assigned. 'Owens!' he cries, 'I think David . . . is missing! Let's do a quick count and make sure!' Although I'm alarmed, I'm hardly surprised. Several weeks of excruciating boredom drift by, and now suddenly, it is time to act, to remember procedure, to try to keep a cool head while all hell breaks loose around me. I run down the hall to alert the others, then head back to the Control Room. Mr. D. comes running back in, agitated, 'O.K. men, I think we have an escape, let's do it!' He then starts barking orders, and everyone scrambles to lock down the institution and commence the search. . . .

"I grab a loaded .357 and jump into the van to search outside the perimeter. The neighborhood consists mostly of ramshackle houses and ancient trailers, many of which are abandoned. As I begin looking around, several of the residents nearby peer out from their homes, their eyes filled with fear and wonderment. My nerves are acting out; I keep hearing sounds inside this one trailer, so I draw my weapon and creep back. I know who this guy is, but I don't know what he'll do if cornered. . . .

"It is getting late now, and he has yet to be found. The dragnet has widened over several counties. I have an official from the central office who is riding with me, so I am careful to follow procedure closely. I call in my position to the command post, and am told to return. I am disappointed that I'm unable to return with him as my prisoner, but that feeling is routine. 'Next time,' I say to myself. I think of the looks on the people's faces as they saw me invade their neighborhood, and I hope for them there won't be a next time. But I know there will, when I least expect it."

*Source:* Doug Owens, "In Search of Dignity," *Keeper's Voice,* Vol. 13, No. 1 (January 1992), pp. 23–24.

the ones that make the headlines—such as the first helicopter escape, accomplished when an inmate was plucked from the yard of the State Prison of Southern Michigan at Jackson in 1975. But of the more than 7000 escapes in 1990, the vast majority were from minimum security facilities or in conjunction with furloughs, outside work, or educational release.[17]

[17]*Sourcebook of Criminal Justice Statistics—1991* (Washington, DC: U.S. Department of Justice, 1992), p. 691.

Most are eventually apprehended—in 1990 alone, over 6200 former escapees were returned to custody.[18] (In fact, the inmate involved in Michigan's helicopter escape was located just 30 hours later.) Experience indicates that few escapees stay away for very long. Moreover, with the "electronic bulletin boards" available in recent years through such nationally broadcast television programs as *America's Most Wanted,* the high visibility given to dangerous escapees assists in their recapture.

In the rare instances where an absconder is never heard from again, it generally means that he is either deceased or getting along somewhere without incident (which, of course, was the original objective of incarceration in the first place). This raises the question of whether a person should be brought back to prison after a long period of time has elapsed. In one case, for example, an inmate who had escaped in 1923 from the Nevada State Prison at Carson City was located in 1969—some 46 years later. At the age of 77, a judge ordered his return to Nevada authorities. The issue in such cases is finding the optimum balance between legalistic objectives and correctional or rehabilitative objectives. In an effort to satisfy both and not uproot people, many states have worked out informal arrangements with other jurisdictions where long-term escapees have been found to reside.

---

*LEARNING GOALS*

*Do you know:*

- *What types of searches are conducted in a correctional institution?*
- *The definition of contraband?*
- *Under what conditions cells can be searched?*
- *The differences between frisk, strip, and body cavity searches?*
- *What procedures are used to control tools and keys in correctional institutions?*
- *How inmates are supervised during daily prison operations?*

---

## ❖ CONTRABAND, SEARCHES, AND EQUIPMENT CONTROL

The type of search resulting from an escape extends throughout the institution as well as to the outside community. But other more restricted searches are also conducted within the facility on a daily basis. These can include both *cell searches* and *personal (body) searches.*

Searches of cells or dormitories (generally referred to as "shakedowns"), are routine in security-minded institutions. A maximum-custody institution might have a regular shakedown once or twice a month and even more frequently on an irregular basis, depending on need. The purpose of conducting cell searches is to detect contraband. It therefore stands to reason that the searches should not be so routinely scheduled that inmates are well aware of when they will be conducted.

[18]Ibid.

## Contraband

*Contraband* consists of any item (or quantity of item) that is *not authorized within the institution* or an authorized item that is *altered from its original state.* For example, a certain amount of food may be permitted in one's cell, but hoarding large amounts would exceed the quantity allowed. A normally authorized item that has been altered could be something as simple as a pen or a plastic eating utensil that is melted down and sharpened into a "shank" (weapon). Some unauthorized items are universally forbidden in all correctional institutions, such as liquor, drugs, knives, guns, or other items that could be used as weapons.

Facilities vary widely, however, in terms of what is and is not considered contraband. Some go so far as to prohibit such seemingly innocent things as family photos. Some permit inmates to keep a specified amount of money (although it would be a violation to be in possession of a quantity greater than the authorized amount). Others use a token or paper-script fiscal system in place of cash. (But even nonmonetary contraband is valuable, since it is used as currency to barter for other items or services.) At the opposite extreme, a number of facilities do not permit any money at all in order to discourage theft and gambling. When inmates wish to make purchases from the commissary (inmate

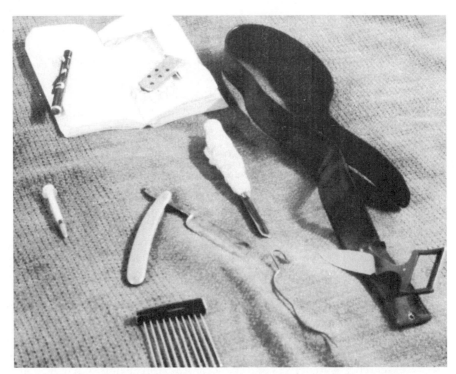

Samples of contraband items located during searches. Note how the interior is carved out of the book to form a convenient hiding place. Courtesy of the Dade County Department of Corrections and Rehabilitation, Miami, Florida.

store), the transaction is made by computerized account system through which no actual cash changes hands.

By removing contraband from the facility, the intent is to reduce the potential for escapes, fights, threats, and assaults that it creates, thereby promoting the safety and security of both inmates and staff. Moreover, dealing in contraband allows some inmates to have power over others by being the distributors of illicit resources that are in wide demand.[19] Contraband can never be eliminated completely. There are simply too many sources through which it can pass into the institution—from a kiss or embrace during visiting, to interaction with the vendor on a food delivery truck, to contact with a staff member in need of extra money.

## Cell Searches (Shakedowns)

Of course, the longer the list of restricted items, the more difficult it is for officers to confiscate everything that is prohibited. Some amount of contraband-related behavior among inmates may also be tolerated as a "trade-off" in an effort to maintain institutional order.[20] Nevertheless, it is for the purpose of detecting contraband that *cell searches* or *shakedowns* are conducted.

In free society, it would not be legal for a police officer to search your home without a court-issued warrant based on probable cause. As we saw in Chapter 4, the right to be free from illicit searches is protected under the Fourth Amendment. But it is entirely different in a correctional facility. Inmates do not enjoy as much privacy because of the overriding need to maintain institutional security. Within a correctional institution, general searches can be "authorized at any time without specific cause" unless there is "abuse or wanton conduct during the search."[21] In other words, correctional officers do not need a warrant or probable cause to justify a search. But they cannot recklessly destroy property in the process of the search.

Searches may be conducted:

- *Routinely*, at certain predetermined—but unannounced—times;
- *Randomly*, at undetermined, unannounced times; or
- Based on *reasonable suspicion*, such as information received from a reliable informant.

Searches cannot, however, be used to single-out any particular person for harassment by, for example, continuously focusing searches on one person's cell to the exclusion of all others for no particular reason.

To the inmate, of course, any intrusion into the minuscule amount of privacy afforded in a correctional institution can be viewed as "harassing." To enable the officers to work without interference and to avoid confrontations with the cell's occupants, searches are often conducted during the day, when prisoners are at

[19]Stan Stojkovic, "Social Bases of Power and Control Mechanisms among Prisoners in a Prison Organization," *Justice Quarterly*, Vol. 1, No. 4 (1984), p. 526.

[20]David B. Kalinich, The Inmate Economy (Lexington, MA: D. C. Heath, 1980), p. 77.

[21]Vernon Fox, *Correctional Institutions* (Englewood Cliffs, NJ: Prentice Hall, 1983), pp. 47–48.

work or participating in institutional programs. On the other hand, at some institutions, cell searches are conducted in the presence of the inmates, so they have a chance to see everything that is done and cannot later make accusations that anything was stolen or damaged (or that contraband was planted).

Inmates can be ingenious at finding unsuspected hiding places, particularly in the many cracks and crevices of older institutions. Conducting a thorough cell search can therefore become quite physically disruptive. Tearing apart what is for all practical purposes an inmate's "home" will create further animosity if the contents are not replaced in an order similar to that in which they were found. Moreover, it is particularly irritating if one's personal possessions were disturbed only to confiscate some insignificant item on the contraband list. Shakedowns are therefore more likely to be effective and inmates are more likely to observe contraband prohibitions if the focus is on items that are obvious security risks, rather than every minor thing that could be confiscated.

Another method that has been used on occasion to uncover contraband without disrupting individual cells is to deceive inmates into discarding their own contraband. For example, sometimes an institution-wide shakedown is announced by officials, who actually begin the search but abandon it shortly thereafter. Once the search procedures start and the word spreads, inmates will often take actions to avoid being caught with contraband. They may flush homemade liquor, drugs, illegally obtained food, and the like down the toilets, while throwing "shanks" or other nonflushable items out of their cells. Staff then collect the items and discontinue their effort. Needless to say, however, a pattern of fake shakedowns can create animosity. Full searches should be conducted in the face of concerns about potential escapes, riots, or resulting hostilities.

### Personal Searches

Searches within correctional institutions are not limited to cell shakedowns. Ultimately, contraband must be personally transported to one's cell. It is therefore inevitable that personal *body searches* are also routine features of prison life, particularly when an inmate enters or leaves the facility.

The intrusiveness of personal searches ranges from a simple frisk (or "pat down), to an unclothed strip search, to a body-cavity search. As illustrated in Figure 8.1, a *frisk search* is an external inspection of a fully clothed person. It is the least intrusive, since the officer only feels exterior surfaces to determine if any items are being concealed within one's clothing, hair, shoes, and so on.

Much more intrusive is the *strip search,* wherein the naked body and its cavities are visually inspected from all angles. Especially for those who are not accustomed to such procedures, strip searches can be very personally degrading. They must therefore be conducted in a manner that retains as much dignity as possible.

As inmates became increasingly creative in their efforts to conceal contraband, the need for *internal body-cavity searches* emerged. In fact, body-cavity searches have yielded items ranging from drugs to ammunition, weapons, and tools. Because they are the most intrusive type of search, they demand justification based on reasonable suspicion. Special permission from a higher authority

#1 The officer should begin the search by:

• Running the prisoner's shirt collar between his fingers carefully, feeling for small hidden wires, hacksaw blades, etc.

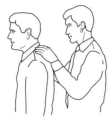

#2 Then the officer should:

• Move his hands downward, running them over the shoulders, down the *outside* of the prisoner's arms to the shirt cuffs. Then the officer should move his hands up the *insides* of the arms to the armpits.(During this part of the search, such items as small knives and razor blades have often been found taped to prisoner's arms.)

#3 After carefully checking the armpits, the officer should:

• Run his hands down the shirt front, checking the pocket and stopping at the prisoner's beltline.

#4 The officer should then check the waistline in this manner:

• Run his fingures around the inside of the waistband, feeling for any small articles hidden there or hidden behind the belt.

#5

• From the waistline, the officer should run his hands down the prisoner's buttocks (all the time he should be feeling for places which might contain illegal articles).

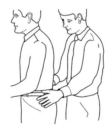

#6

• Then the officer should move both hands to one leg and run them carefully down the leg, checking all around it for concealed articles. At the end of the leg, the officer should make a point of checking the trouser cuff for concealed articles. Repeat the process on the other leg.

#7 As the last step to frisk search, the officer should:

• Run his hands over the prisoner's lower abdomen and crotch carefully, looking for concealed articles that may be taped to these areas.

**Figure 8.1**   Steps in a frisk search. *Source:* Alice Howard Blummer, *Jail Operations: A Training Course for Jail Officers* (Washington, DC: U.S. Bureau of Prisons, n.d.), pp. 117–23.

(such as the prison warden) is generally required, along with a written explanation for the reasons. Moreover, there is potential for injury, infection, or the spread of disease if such searches are not conducted properly. As a result, they can only be performed by appropriate medical staff.

The procedures discussed thus far have focused exclusively on searches of prisoners. There are also circumstances in which employees are suspected of transporting contraband. Staff searches, however, will require a higher due process standard, since correctional personnel retain considerably greater Fourth Amendment rights than inmates. For example, although pat-down frisks of employees are permitted on the basis of reasonable suspicion,[22] a search warrant would be required to conduct a body-cavity search of prison staff.[23]

## Tool Control

It should be apparent by now that the major purpose of searches is to detect contraband. But even within the same institution, certain items may generally be regarded as contraband yet permitted under some circumstances. For example, scissors or tire irons would normally be considered weapons and therefore prohibited. However, it would be difficult to offer a sewing or auto repair course without such tools.

The proper control of tools is essential because of their potential use as weapons. The basic premise of a tool control program is a rigid check system, with receipts kept for the tools available in shops, and a classification system used to store different types of tools. For example, tools that can cut steel (such as welding torches), must be stored in a secure area overnight and personally distributed by the maintenance supervisor or vocational school instructor each morning. Other less powerful tools may be stored in the machine shop, under close scrutiny. But even such routine tools as pliers and screwdrivers should be maintained under some type of observation.

In accounting for industrial or vocational training tools, a *shadow board* is helpful. This is a sort of bulletin-board on which tools are physically stored. The outline of each tool is painted on the board so that the supervisor can determine what pieces are missing. When tools are checked out, each inmate using any particular piece of equipment surrenders a chit with his assigned number on it and signs a receipt for the tool. If the tool is not returned, the "chit" indicates who last checked it out.

## Key Control

Because keys provide the most direct access to escape, key control is of primary importance in correctional institutions. Key rings are stored in the control room and arranged according to the tour of duty of each correctional officer. An officer's ring may contain as many as 20 to 25 keys or as few as one or two,

---

[22]William C. Collins, *Correctional Law 1986: An Analysis and Discussion of the Key Issues and Developments in Correctional Law over the Past Year* (Olympia, WA: W. C. Collins, 1986), pp. 60–61.
[23]*Security and Law Enforcement Employees District Council #82 v. Carey* 737 F. 2d 187 (1984).

depending on the duties involved. These key rings must be checked out appropriately, with very accurate records kept.

Anyone who inadvertently takes a key ring home should be required to bring it back immediately to assure institutional security as well as to emphasize the necessity to return keys properly. Keys inadvertently left unattended for even a few brief moments have been pressed into a bar of soap for models. Inmates have even been known to observe keys and manufacture replicas from visual recall. When a key is lost, there is no recourse but to change the locks and issue new keys to the affected areas—a time-consuming and expensive process.

## Inmate Supervision

It may seem somewhat unreasonable to discuss careful tool and key control in order to avoid their use as weapons when, at the same time, items such as knives and industrial scissors are available to trusties working in the prison kitchen or sewing shop. These implements must also be controlled carefully to assure that they do not leave the area. Nevertheless, they could potentially be used in a stabbing attempt while in the hands of inmate workers. For many institutions, the expense of operating a large kitchen or tailor's shop using only civilian staff would be prohibitive. Naturally, when determining such work assignments, every effort is made to screen out quarrelsome prisoners with a reputation for trouble-making. Moreover, as we will see in Chapter 9, effective programming is a method of inmate management. It is next to impossible to maintain any real sense of control over a cellblock of idle inmates.

When making job assignments in such areas as food services, the inmate worker (foreground) is carefully screened and closely supervised. Courtesy of the Dade County Department of Corrections and Rehabilitation, Miami, Florida.

In addition to careful selection, those on various work details must also be closely supervised. Although a civilian supervisor may be on-site to oversee the production process, it is the correctional officer's responsibility to provide *custodial supervision* and security. Particularly when assignments involve work outside the prison compound, it is the correctional officer's duty to prevent unauthorized contacts with other people and the acquisition of contraband. Otherwise, those on external work details can be used as a "trafficking service" in contraband items or an underground "messenger service" between the outside and other inmates.

Even within the prison, certain work details can provide opportunities for graft, corruption, and contraband trading if officers do not maintain close oversight of the activities. For example, many institutions have traditionally used inmates as barbers. If a prisoner wants a good haircut, it may be customary to give the barber a pack of cigarettes or another item of value. While every inmate is entitled to a "state haircut" at certain intervals, the inferior cuts resulting when such "tips" are not forthcoming can often be clearly identified. Barbers also have access to lotions that could be used for drinking, as well as razors that are obviously contraband, and their location makes them an ideal contact point for inmates who would otherwise be kept apart. It takes close watching and detailed supervision to prevent related problems from occurring.

The correctional officer's responsibility is not, however, limited to those engaged in work assignments. Throughout the day, the inside of the institution is supervised by operational personnel, with at least one officer generally assigned to each school, factory, or shop, as well as such other areas of the prison as the infirmary, counseling offices, and recreation yard. During these assignments, officers are responsible for constantly observing all activities to detect signs of danger. It is largely through training and experience that operational staff develop the insights and intuition that alert them to potential problems. Even when inmates are not misbehaving, there may be certain warning signs of imminent danger, as described in the next "Close-up on Corrections."

Particularly in large institutions, the system of passes described earlier may be used. Passes are issued by the officer when inmates have a legitimate need to go to another location beyond that to which they are assigned. When groups of inmates or especially dangerous offenders are being moved within the prison, they are escorted by correctional officers to assure that they get to and from the designated location without incident. During certain times of the day (e.g., 8:00 A.M. to 4:30 P.M.), inmates may have a wider range of unescorted movement, after which certain areas are closed off to the population. This is what is referred to as *custodial zoning*—identifying where inmates are authorized to be at specified times. For example, the recreation yard may be available until sundown, after which only the cellblocks may be open to inmate movement.

All of the search techniques and regulatory procedures described herein serve to maintain secure custody. But in the final analysis, it is not so much the explicit control of staff as the implicit cooperation of inmates that enables the system to operate effectively. The observations of a former director of corrections in the "Close-up on Corrections" on page 300 vividly portray this fact of institutional life.

Never Stop Observing

[A]n officer supervising a recreation period in the gymnasium notices that two basketball games are going on, one at each end of the court. On one end, the game consists of eight black inmates. On the other end, the players are six white inmates. An inexperienced person might *observe* the make-up of the two teams, watching carefully that neither game gets out of hand. Another, more experienced officer observes that same scene, however, couples that observation with his knowledge of other circumstances, and makes conclusions. He knows that for the past three months, the fourteen players have been playing together, both black and white, in the same basketball game. The officer is sensitive to any racial problems in [the] prison and is uneasy about his current observation. He also recalled reading the log from the last shift, which noted an unusual amount of racial segregation at the chow line the same day. He records his observation and notifies his shift commander. He then continues to carefully observe the inmates and their moods and interactions with each other, being extremely sensitive to any racial provocation on anyone's part.

*Source:* David B. Kalinich and Terry Pitcher, *Surviving in Corrections* (Springfield, IL: Charles C Thomas, 1984), pp. 51–52.

---

*LEARNING GOALS*

*Do you know:*

- *Why inmate contact with the outside must be restricted but not eliminated?*
- *How correctional institutions limit outside contacts by phone and mail?*
- *What restrictions are imposed on visits to inmates?*
- *The difference between "contact" and "conjugal" visits?*
- *The advantages and disadvantages of conjugal visiting?*
- *What furloughs are designed to accomplish?*

## ❖ CONTACTS WITH THE OUTSIDE

Beyond those controls that restrict freedom within the compound, everyone confined within a correctional institution is subject to isolation from the rest of society. As a result, it is largely through visits, phone calls, and letters that inmates maintain ties with the community.

On the one hand, it is important to retain such communication with the outside because of its constructive influence in terms of inmate behavior and morale. External contacts help to reduce the negative impact of socializing only

### Control through Cooperation

[N]o matter how unobtrusive the process, there is no real doubt that the inmate body does have its share in the [institution's] control. It is only a question of degree. . . . [T]he custodians are vastly outnumbered. Inmates are out of their cells during the day, working in shops and offices throughout a vast complex where the opportunities for mischief are enormous. Inmates carry out duties in the kitchen where there are knives and cleavers. Mechanically skilled inmates are employed in shops where metal-working machinery offers daily opportunity to fashion weapons. Ingenious inmates have also found ways to brew liquor, print counterfeit securities or documents, and enjoy an astonishing variety of surreptitious enterprises. But the prison is utterly dependent upon the willingness of all prisoners to leave their daytime activities and return at night to their cells for lockup. It is equally dependent upon their willingness to keep their activities reasonably and delicately balanced between licit and illicit behavior.

*Source:* Paul W. Keve, *Prison Life and Human Worth* (Minneapolis, MN: University of Minnesota Press, 1974), p. 67.

---

with other criminals day after day. They promote a more civilizing atmosphere, serve as a reminder of what life is like on the outside, and assist with eventual readjustment to society.

On the other hand, interactions between the prison and the public present security risks. They can facilitate both escapes and the introduction of contraband. The key is to find the proper balance between overly restricting outside contacts and overly jeopardizing institutional security. As a result, limits have been placed on phone calls, written correspondence, and visiting.

### Telephone

Although all correctional institutions permit inmates to use the telephone, the number of calls authorized is generally limited according to one's security classification. Minimum-security facilities might have a centrally located telephone for all to use with few restrictions. In contrast, medium and maximum custody are more likely to involve individual arrangements for telephone access, such as using modular outlets to enable a phone to be moved into cells during designated times.

Since many of the calls inmates make are long-distance, it is essential for the institution to avoid being held accountable for individual phone bills. Some facilities employ a process of placing phone charges on the inmate's commissary account. In others, phones are designed to accommodate only collect calls. But those in prison often demonstrate a great deal of creative ingenuity in circumventing even the most sophisticated systems.

## Mail

In the free world outside prisons, much of our written communication has been replaced by the telephone. But since prisoners do not have the immediate convenience of picking up the phone that the rest of us enjoy, written correspondence is of great importance to them. Anyone who has ever been away from home in an unfamiliar environment for an extended period of time can appreciate how much letters from family help to ease loneliness, tension, and anxiety. In fact, it is not uncommon for an inmate who is usually quite orderly to strike out against another inmate, staff member, or even himself as an expression of frustration over hearing bad news—or no news—from home.

In the past, all incoming mail and packages were very closely scrutinized—to the point of censorship. Rejected articles were returned to the sender. As we will see in Chapter 15, legal challenges in more recent years have resulted in arbitrary censorship giving way to practices that can be justified on the basis of institutional security, such as inspection for contraband. As prison populations have expanded, it has also become increasingly difficult and labor-intensive to read and censor all correspondence. In some institutions, the inspection of mail may be limited to a spot-check for the few inmates from whom there is reason to expect trouble. Of course, letters to attorneys, judges, or other government officials cannot be either censored or read. However, inmates may be required to open such correspondence in the presence of a correctional officer if transmission of contraband is suspected. Whereas incoming mail may be opened and checked for contraband (without being read), outgoing mail is not ordinarily opened or checked in any way.

## Visiting

During the initial intake process, approved visiting and correspondence lists are made up for each inmate. Visiting lists will generally be more limited than those approved for written correspondence. Immediate family members are almost always approved automatically, and one's attorney can visit at any time. Other relatives and friends may need further justification, particularly in maximum-security institutions.

In addition to who can visit, prisons regulate how often they can come. Again, the number of visits allowed may depend on custody classification. Moreover, a severely crowded facility may need to further restrict the frequency of visits simply because of operational inability to manage the necessary movements.

Beyond the obstacles presented by institutional regulations, it may be difficult for an inmate's family to visit when the prison is located in a rural area far from home and not accessible to public transportation. Contacts between legally married wives and first-term male inmates have been found to grow fewer in the second year of incarceration and beyond, indicating that the marriage gradually erodes with the length of incarceration.[24] It is indeed a dedicated family member who will

---

[24]Norman Holt and Donald Miller, *Explorations in Inmate–Family Relationships* (Sacramento, CA: California Department of Corrections, January 1972), p. vi.

Outside visits may be supervised from a number of vantage points within the walls of secure institutions. Courtesy of Anthony W. Zumpetta.

go to the expense, take the time, and suffer the humiliation often involved in visiting someone in prison. As a result, the typical inmate may be fortunate to receive one visit a month—hardly conducive to maintaining family stability.

Part of the reluctance to visit those in prison relates to the abnormal atmosphere surrounding the conditions under which outside contact takes place. Privacy is virtually nonexistent. Visits are supervised and carefully monitored by uniformed correctional officers to reduce the introduction of contraband. Inmates are also generally searched before and after each visit, and the visitors themselves may be subject to frisk searches as well.

In very high-security situations, visitors and residents are placed in two different rooms. They are separated by a window of plate glass, with a telephone device used for communication.[25] Visits in a lower-security environment may be conducted around long tables, with inmates sitting on one side and visitors on the other, sometimes monitored by video surveillance cameras. The least restrictive are *contact visits,* which permit physical contact between inmates and visitors (within specified rules). Except in very secure facilities, contact visits are often permitted. Even within the same institution, however, greater restrictions may be reserved for certain inmates, such as those in disciplinary segregation.

In minimum security, the visiting process is considerably more relaxed and casual, sometimes conducted on the outside lawns around picnic tables. Although there are rules prohibiting excessive open affection, inmates and their visitors may sit side by side with arms around each other or holding hands. Of course, with greater visiting freedom also comes greater potential for the introduction of contraband.

[25]The following material on visiting is summarized from Fox, pp. 142–43.

## Conjugal Visits

Even the most liberal and informal visiting procedures cannot replace the intimacy of heterosexual relationships. Confinement in prison can severely strain a marriage and has actually represented grounds for divorce in a number of states. Some believe that sexual deprivations are to be expected as an inherent part of the punishment function of incarceration. Others express concern about the promotion of homosexual activities when the legitimate expression of basic sexual drives is denied.

In response to such concerns, several states have authorized inmates to participate in *conjugal visits*. Unsupervised visits from members of the opposite sex have been common in a number of South American and Scandinavian countries. But the more conservative nature of North American sexual and social attitudes has restrained their development in the United States.

Although it was not openly admitted, conjugal visiting has actually been available in American prisons from time to time on an informal basis. South Carolina initiated such visits in the late nineteenth century, and Mississippi started the practice informally at the state penitentiary in Parchman early in the twentieth century. California began family visiting on an experimental basis in 1968, adopting it throughout the state by 1972, and several other states have followed suit. By 1991, New York, Minnesota, Connecticut, and Washington had joined South Carolina, Mississippi, and California in making conjugal visits available.[26]

An evaluation of the program at Parchman was quite positive,[27] and subsequent research has shown that such programs contribute to rehabilitation as well as reduced recidivism rates.[28] Advantages of conjugal visits include fewer pressures to engage in homosexuality and improved morale, along with a strengthening of family bonds. The potential loss of conjugal visiting privileges is also a strong restraint upon behavior. But they are not without drawbacks. For one thing, if visits are limited to married inmates, everyone will not qualify, and "there is some evidence that the provocation of seeing others participate actually drives ineligible residents to homosexuality."[29] Additionally, some wives may not participate for a variety of reasons, particularly if the process is viewed as degrading. Even if it is handled in a sensitive manner, the pain of subsequent separation may override any immediate benefits.[30] Participants also are faced with issues surrounding pregnancies and sexually transmitted disease.

For the correctional institution, both administrative and operational issues are involved. Administratively, there are concerns surrounding the verification of marriages and the question of whether or not to accept common-law relationships. Operationally, potential problems include the difficulty of controlling con-

---

[26]Donald Schneller, "The Conjugal Visit: A Tool for Rehabilitation," *Network News*, Vol. 3, No. 2 (July 1991), p. 4.

[27]Columbus B. Hopper, *Sex in Prison* (Baton Route, LA: Louisiana State University Press, 1968).

[28]Schneller, p. 2, citing Norman Holt and Donald Miller, "Explorations in Inmate–Family Relationships," *Criminal Justice Newsletter*, Vol. 19 (1988), pp. 2–3.

[29]Fox, p. 147.

[30]A. Crosthwaite, "Punishment for Whom, the Prisoner or His Wife?" *International Journal of Offender Therapy and Comparative Criminology*, Vol. 19, No. 3 (1975), pp. 275–84.

traband and enforcing appropriate behavior, along with resentment on the part of those who do not have access to conjugal visits.[31] Thus, the question becomes whether the benefits outweigh the risks.

## Furloughs

Many correctional administrators who are opposed to conjugal visits favor the use of *furloughs* instead. Essentially, furloughs involve a brief period of *temporary release*—often over a weekend—with the understanding that the prisoner will return to the institution at a specified time. Because a large portion of those incarcerated are single or divorced, more inmates will qualify for furloughs. Moreover, the emphasis with furloughs is on broader social reintegration rather than the exclusive sexual focus of conjugal visits. Another benefit is that rather than seeing their parent in a prison setting, children can interact with mom or dad at home during furloughs.

Offering inmates temporary freedom does, however, entail obvious dangers. Although efforts are made to select those awarded furloughs carefully, there is always the possibility that the desire to live on the outside again will be too great to resist. Absconding is generally not as great a problem as might be expected, since there is considerable pressure from other inmates to abide by the rules of the program so that the privilege is not revoked for everyone. In fact, a recent study indicates that seven states report 100% success rates, with most others ranging between 95 and 99.9%.[32] But there is always the potential of awarding a furlough to someone who does not have sufficient self-control to avoid becoming involved in crime. This concern was propelled into a major national issue that affected the 1988 presidential election—when an inmate granted a weekend pass in Massachusetts (Willie Horton) engaged in a series of violent crimes that ultimately reflected upon the campaign of former Governor Michael Dukakis.[33]

As a result of the public outcry following the Horton case, a number of correctional administrators implemented much more restrictive measures governing furlough eligibility. In that regard, one correctional practitioner commented that the tightening of furloughs following this public backlash was creating a situation of "zero tolerance"—similar to reducing the driving speed limit to 10 mph to prevent traffic crashes. The number of eligible inmates is often so limited that furloughs cannot in reality be considered a practical alternative to conjugal visiting. Yet the use of furloughs has begun to increase in a number of states.[34] Furthermore, research indicates that participation in furloughs "appears to have a pronounced

[31]"Family Visitation," *Corrections Compendium*, Vol 4, No. 7 (January, 1980), pp. 2–5.

[32]"Number of Prison Furloughs Increases," *On the Line*, Vol. 15, No. 2 (March 1992), p. 5, citing *Corrections Compendium*.

[33]In fact, as recently as 1992 (by which time Willie Horton was confined in a Maryland prison), he was still being widely referred to in conjunction with presidential campaigning, having been cited on 420 occasions in newspapers and magazines throughout the country—prompting a *Wall Street Journal* editorial which called for "a furlough" of the Willie Horton issue. See Paul A. Gigot, "Willie Horton: The Mother of All Diversions," *The Wall Street Journal* (April 17, 1992), p. A-10.

[34]"Number of Prison Furloughs Increases," p. 5.

and consistent positive impact on lowered recidivism."[35] Like conjugal visits, the use of furloughs is not without risks. A reasonable compromise must be found between an excessively liberal furlough policy that completely disregards public safety and overly restrictive practices that deny the benefits of social interaction to virtually everyone except a handful of the most model prisoners.

---

**LEARNING GOALS**

*Do you know:*

- *What the functions, constructive factors, and irritating aspects of prison discipline are?*
- *What types of rules and regulations govern inmate conduct?*
- *What disciplinary procedures are employed when an inmate violates the rules?*
- *What rights inmates have when facing severe disciplinary action?*
- *What sanctions can be imposed for rule violations?*

---

## ❖ INSTITUTIONAL RULES AND DISCIPLINE

All of the procedures discussed thus far—from segregating prisoners within the institution to restricting their contacts with the outside—are designed to control inmate behavior. In a tightly controlled prison, "everyone knows his place;" roles and relationships are "clearly defined . . . certain areas of the building are off limits . . . lines are drawn on the floor to dictate where inmates will walk and where staff will walk . . . all inmates dress in the same state-issue[d] clothing. . . ."[36]

Not all prisons are so rigidly controlled. All do, however, have provisions for shaping individual behavior for the benefit of the overall population. As we saw with movement, counts, and outside contacts, these provisions will be fewer and more relaxed in minimum-security facilities. But inmates in higher-custody classifications presumably lack the self-control necessary to constrain their own behavior. They must therefore be constrained by external restrictions.

The purpose of institutional rules and regulations is to provide the *guidelines regulating conduct* through which an effort is made to achieve *orderly group life.* While institutional regulations compel compliance within the prison, resulting frustrations can be counterproductive to reintegration. If one's prison experience was embittering and degrading, bottled-up hostilities may be unleashed as soon as institutional controls are removed. Recognition of these drawbacks,

---

[35]Daniel P. LeClair and Susan Guarino-Ghezzi, "Does Incapacitation Guarantee Public Safety? Lessons from the Massachusetts Furlough and Prerelease Programs," *Justice Quarterly,* Vol. 8, No. 1 (March 1991), p. 9.

[36]Ben M. Crouch, "The Guard in a Changing Prison World," in Ben M. Crouch, ed., *The Keepers: Prison Guards and Contemporary Corrections* (Springfield, IL: Charles C Thomas, 1980), p. 28.

however, does not negate the need for correctional facilities to control behavior through rules and regulations during confinement.

## Rules and Regulations

One of the first things that a newly arriving inmate receives upon initial reception is the rulebook outlining the "do's" and "don'ts" that are expected during the period of confinement. Rules are designed to promote one's adjustment to the institutional routine and thereby maintain order. It is, of course, essential that all inmates fully understand what is required and prohibited, as well as their due process rights when facing disciplinary action. Thus, institutions with sizable non-English-speaking populations often publish rules and regulations in other languages. Some have even produced detailed videotapes explaining these requirements.

The length and nature of inmate rules will vary depending on the size and security classification of the facility. More rigorous and extensive regulations will naturally be found in settings with higher custodial classifications. But virtually all institutions will have at least some number of general rules governing such things as:

- *Inmate–officer relationships* (e.g., addressing employees respectfully; immediately obeying orders issued by officers)
- *Relationships with other inmates* (e.g., no fighting, assaults, homosexual behavior, or conspiring with other inmates)
- *Prohibited activities* (e.g., no profanity, gambling, trafficking, bartering, trading, attempting escape, running, etc.)
- *Prohibited items* (e.g., no unauthorized items that are designated as contraband)
- *Personal hygiene/grooming* (e.g., requirements regarding personal attire and cleanliness)
- *Outside contacts* (e.g., mail, phone, and visiting restrictions)
- *Overall institutional regulations* (e.g., prohibited areas of the compound; personal property limitations within cells; disciplinary and grievance procedures; the schedule of daily routines governing eating, sleeping, etc.)

In addition to these general rules, some institutions extend regulations to very precise details—such as prohibiting catcalls, whistling, hissing, or derisive shouting. As noted previously with regard to the control of contraband, the longer and more complex the list of rules, the more difficult they are to enforce. Additionally, the more rules are viewed as petty harassments, the more likely they are to be violated. On the one hand, too much rigidity can promote resistance. On the other hand, too little regulation can produce chaos, confusion, and lack of control.

## Disciplinary Procedures

Whatever the institution's specific rules are, it is up to the operational staff to assure that they are being observed, and if not, to deal with infractions. How

Major violations are recorded on disciplinary action reports and forwarded through the agency's chain of command. Courtesy of the Nassau County Sheriff's Department, East Meadow, New York.

firmly regulations are enforced will vary considerably, depending on the institution, the situation, and the particular officer involved. Ultimately, it is through both formal disciplinary measures (i.e., rule enforcement) and informal communication that a process for managing inmate behavior develops.

Correctional officers have the day-to-day authority to enforce rules. That does not mean that they have the power to inflict formal punishment for disciplinary infractions. Operational staff may have limited authority to handle minor misconduct informally. But major violations are "written up" on official *disciplinary action reports* and submitted through the organizational chain of command.

Typically, major violations in prisons involve gambling, sexual activities, group fighting, and personal assaults. Stealing and refusing to work or obey an officer's orders can also occur with frequency. Anything involving physical harm or a major security violation is most likely to be officially referred for formal disciplinary action. However, as the employee guidelines of one prison state, "Minor matters of discipline, where no danger to life, security or property exists, shall be handled quietly and routinely."[37]

When a major infraction is reported, upper-level command staff must then determine if further action is warranted. If so, the inmate is afforded a hearing before either a *hearing examiner* or a *disciplinary (or hearing) committee*. Generally, a committee contains from three to five members, drawn from the custodial, treatment, and/or classification staff. In some institutions, the classification committee or the treatment team has handled disciplinary proceedings, although operational staff have usually been represented.

[37]Lombardo, p. 100.

The trend today, however, is to invoke the services of an outside hearing examiner. This has developed in response to concerns that using staff in disciplinary proceedings is inherently biased against the inmate, tending to favor institutional concerns. The outside hearing examiner is viewed as capable of conducting a more impartial tribunal. Additionally, committees can also take up an inordinate amount of staff time. Since the hearing examiner is only one person, the process is more cost-effective. It also enables the examiner to concentrate on the cases at hand, rather than viewing the hearing as an inconvenience added to one's regularly scheduled job.

In the past, inmates had no universally recognized due process rights during disciplinary hearings. In fact, correctional administrators were free to impose penalties without a hearing. Needless to say, this widespread discretion was open to potential abuse, particularly within closed institutions with little public oversight or administrative restraints. In an effort to assure more objective and impartial proceedings, the Supreme Court ruled that inmates are entitled to certain due process protections when facing severe disciplinary action, (e.g., that which would further restrict their freedom or extend their confinement). Thus, since the Wolff v. McDonnell[38] case in 1974, inmates facing such penalties now are entitled to:

1. Advance written notice of the charges.
2. The right to a fair and impartial hearing.
3. The right to present evidence and call witnesses on their behalf (when permission to do so "will not be unduly hazardous to institutional safety or correctional goals").
4. Use of counsel or counsel substitute for illiterate accused persons or those who otherwise cannot understand the proceedings.
5. Written statement of the decision reached and the reasons for it.

Inmates are not entitled to appeal the outcome of disciplinary hearings in a court of law. Nevertheless, many institutions provide for an appeal to the prison warden, and some allow appeals beyond the institution to the state director of corrections.

Aside from solitary confinement or disciplinary segregation, the most severe penalty an inmate can receive is loss of credits reducing the length of their sentence (e.g., good time or gain time, which are described further in Chapter 11). As we have seen earlier, the fact that those in prison are serving considerably less than the sentence they received indicates that many are being released early through the accumulation of time reductions from their sentences. No inmate wants to jeopardize that release date. Time credits therefore represent both a major incentive to maintain good behavior and the ultimate penalty for misconduct.

Moreover, many of the harsh punishments used in the past (such as bread-and-water diets and corporal punishment) have been ruled unconstitutional.[39]

[38] *Wolff v. McDonnell*, 418 U.S. 539 (1974).

[39] For example, in *Landman v. Royster*, 333 F. Supp. 621 (E.D. Va. 1971) bread and water diets, as well as other conditions that constituted cruel and unusual punishment, were held to be unconstitutional. In *Holt v. Sarver*, 300 F. Supp. 825 (E.D. Ark. 1969), mental abuse and corporal punishment were held in violation of the cruel and unusual punishment clause of the Eighth Amendment.

Restricting visits, commissary privileges, recreation, and the like must also be done within legal limits. As a result, the loss of time credit is the one primary behavioral control mechanism that correctional personnel still have to induce compliance with institutional rules and regulations.

---

*LEARNING GOALS*

*Do you know:*

- *How officers exercise formal and informal controls to regulate inmate behavior?*
- *What results occur when officers either over- or underenforce institutional rules?*
- *Why the relationship between officers and inmates has been called a "corrupt alliance"?*
- *Why formal disciplinary action must be balanced with some degree of informality?*
- *How officers can use interpersonal communication skills to manage inmate behavior proactively?*

---

## ❖ INMATE MANAGEMENT

Some inmates recognize that the rules exist largely for their own protection and therefore tend to support their enforcement. Older, long-timers who simply want to "do their time" as quietly as possible are particularly likely to hold such cooperative attitudes. Those who are younger, recent arrivals, and more militant, however, are more likely to view institutional regulations as a form of repression and a personal challenge.[40] The extent to which inmates respect authority and realize that the rules exist for their own benefit will have much to do with the level of their compliance.

When voluntary compliance is not forthcoming, it is the correctional officer's job to initiate the disciplinary process. In fact, it has been noted that "whatever else they may be," correctional officers are "primarily agents of social control."[41] Although officers must be observant to detect violations, the responsibility of managing inmates is certainly not restricted to simple visual surveillance. If that were the case, closed-circuit television could largely replace the need for human supervision in correctional facilities. This point was vividly made in one minimum-security institution when a perimeter fence was installed: "Staff were taken from interacting

---

[40]It has been found that "adolescents who have unresolved resentments against parental figures, for example, may feel unable to cope . . . with the presence of prison guards. Other [inmates] expect rejection . . . and invite it by behaving in obnoxious, challenging ways. Still others . . . feel that no one has a right to tell them what to do," angrily reacting to any "perceived infringements of their autonomy." Hans Toch and J. Douglas Grant, "Noncoping and Maladaptation in Confinement," in Lynne Goodstein and Doris Layton MacKenzie, eds., *The American Prison: Issues in Research and Policy* (New York: Plenum Press, 1989), pp. 214–215.

[41]John R. Hepburn, "Prison Guards as Agents of Social Control," in Goodstein and MacKenzie, p. 204.

with inmates and committed to operating and monitoring a fence. Perhaps it was not surprising that the fence did not reduce the number of escapes."[42] It is the officer's ability to *communicate verbally* that is of greatest importance—a skill that is not confined to issuing orders, but rather, one which, when used properly, establishes an *effective working relationship* with the inmate population.

Just as the rules themselves must be properly balanced between too much rigidity and too little regulation, officers also find that they must steer a middle course between severity and laxity in enforcing them. Institutional regulations represent the "tools of discipline." It takes experience, sensitivity, and training to learn how to use them properly, as it takes practice and instruction to use any other kind of tool.

The extent to which regulations are enforced varies from institution to institution. As we saw in Chapter 7, some differences reflect the administrative style of the warden. But even within the same institution, enforcement styles can vary from one shift to another and from one officer to another. It is the administrator's job to assure that there is general enforcement consistency, which cannot be achieved simply by telling operational staff that they are expected to "fully enforce all rules at all times." Like police officers enforcing society's laws on the street, correctional officers find that it is neither possible nor practical to do so. Faced with a wide variety of regulations, many of which are ambiguous, they have a great deal of discretion in deciding what rules will be enforced, against whom, and under what circumstances.[43]

## Rules and Relationships

It is not only through institutional regulations that inmates are managed. As in free society, institutional behavior is controlled through both *rules* and *relationships*. Parents, for example, establish certain boundaries (rules) governing their children's actions. At one extreme, an excessively stern parent might immediately resort to punishment whenever a child crosses the established boundaries. At the other extreme, an overly lenient parent might totally avoid any type of punishment, trying instead to reason, bribe, or coax the child into compliance. In-between these extremes are those who attempt to find a reasonable compromise—developing a nurturing relationship that communicates care and support, guiding the child toward self-restraint but resorting to some form of discipline when these informal controls do not work.

Correctional officers likewise employ a great deal of discretion in the management of inmate behavior. Faced with choices between relying on rules or developing relationships, the actions they take can be directed toward:

1. *Formal controls:* initiating the disciplinary action process by officially "writing up" the offender through a disciplinary action report, or

---

[42]Adria Lynn Libolt, "Technology Cannot Be a Replacement for Creative Planning and Programming," *Corrections Today*, Vol. 53, No. 4 (July 1991), p. 21.

[43]The discussion of discretion and police decision making in Kenneth Culp Davis, *Police Discretion* (St. Paul, MN: West Publishing Company, 1975), is equally pertinent to corrections.

2. *Informal controls:* using informal verbal communication to either prevent or deal with a situation, in an effort to foster voluntary compliance without the need to resort to official action.

Within a correctional institution, neither excessive reliance on formal disciplinary action procedures (overenforcement) nor too much informality (underenforcement) is an effective approach to managing inmate behavior. As we will see in the following sections, the key is to find the proper balance between these two extremes.

## Overenforcement

Some officers enforce the rules strictly "by the book," writing up every inmate for even the most minor infractions. Such practices are obviously resented by inmates. That can create a dangerous process of retribution, as illustrated in the following scenario: "At approximately 5:15 P.M., the officer on duty in C cellhouse was standing just inside the office door when an iron weight of about five pounds was dropped from an upper range. It landed on the metal screen covering the office. It is believed this was a measure of retaliation against the officer, who was performing his job in a manner seen as 'overzealous' by inmates."[44]

Nor do inmates have to resort to physical attacks to avenge an officer's heavy-handed rule enforcement. Simply by being uncooperative, they can cast a negative light on the officer's supervisory abilities. For example: "They may attempt to elude the counting officer by hiding in their cell or by shuffling back and forth if the count is taken while the inmates are in line. . . . In either case, the delay and disruption of the prison routine will be attributed to the [officer] who is responsible . . . [who may] earn both formal censure and informal derision from his colleagues."[45]

Such tactics vividly point out the difference between rule enforcement within correctional institutions and law enforcement in free society. Outside a court of law, police officers may never again encounter those against whom they take action. But it is entirely different in the enclosed environment of corrections, where officers must continue to interact on a daily basis with those against whom they enforce the rules. As a result, one's safety and even job security may be jeopardized by a "hard-line" approach.

In addition, the activities of law enforcement officers are rarely witnessed by other co-workers, whereas in corrections, officers are closely scrutinized by their colleagues. Hard-liners do not earn much respect from their operational peers or supervisors. They are generally viewed by other staff members as being too weak to manage inmate behavior without using the rulebook as a crutch. In other words, "writing formal complaints in minor cases degrade[s] the officer and demonstrate[s] that he [is] incapable of handling such offenses without resorting to 'authority.'"[46] Moreover, because of the resentment and retaliation

[44]Anthony L. Guenther and Mary Quinn Guenther, "Screws vs. Thugs," in Crouch, p. 171.
[45]Jacobs and Retsky, p. 15.
[46]Lombardo, p. 110.

that their actions may create among the inmates, those who rely excessively on the formal disciplinary process can place their co-workers in danger as well. For a look at the ineffectiveness of overreliance on formal sanctions in one institution, see the next "Close-up on Corrections."

## Underenforcement

On the other hand, there are those who rarely take any formal action at all. Such "laissez-faire" officers may simply be intimidated by fear. Or they may be overly sympathetic to the plight of those incarcerated. Or they may be trying to avoid ill will by deemphasizing their enforcement role. For whatever reasons, they attempt to remain in the good graces of the population simply by "looking the other way" when rules are violated.

Even those who may not be concerned about how they are viewed by the inmates can fall into a laid-back supervisory style if they come to the conclusion that their disciplinary actions will not be supported by upper-level management. Consider, for example, how you would react after experiencing the following situation:

> On one occasion, I witnessed an officer break up a fight between two inmates. He waded in among some 25 spectators and separated the two combatants. He informed each that they were to be reported for fighting and ordered them to return to their cells. At this point, he was accosted by the spectators, who argued that there was no apparent reason for reporting them, as it had merely been a friendly argument. Nonetheless, the officer stood his ground, reported the inmates, and returned them to their cells. Later that day, he learned that the captain had returned them to normal status, and that no Disciplinary Board was recommended, as there had been no animosity involved.[47]

When officers are confronted continually with situations in which they feel that their efforts were not backed up by the chain of command, it can become very frustrating. In some cases, lack of further action may be justified on the basis of mitigating circumstances that the officer had no knowledge of, making such perceptions inaccurate. But to the person holding them, perceptions *are* reality, and officers who believe that the administration "doesn't care anyway" are likely to be considerably less enthusiastic about taking action in the future.

Some prisoners use the greater freedoms they are afforded under a laissez-faire approach to manipulate staff and see how much they can "get away with." Others find themselves victimized as strong inmate leaders emerge within the vacuum created when rules are not enforced. Officers likewise come to resent the additional burden placed on them when some are not carrying out their full responsibilities. Needless to say, neither inmates nor staff members respect those who actively avoid rule enforcement on a continuous basis.

---

[47]Leo Carroll, *Hacks, Blacks, and Cons: Race Relations in a Maximum Security Prison* (Lexington, MA: Lexington Books/D. C.Heath, 1974), p. 55.

Power in a Prison

A formal disciplinary procedure existed at all Massachusetts state prisons which consisted in essence of the following. When an inmate broke a rule, the officer in charge could "write-up" the incident in a Disciplinary Report ("D-Report" or "ticket"). The case would then be heard by the prison Disciplinary Board ("D-Board"). If the inmate was found guilty, the Disciplinary Board was empowered to impose sanctions.

Two problems undermined this system. First, frequent recourse by an officer to writing D-Reports was not deemed an acceptable means of maintaining control. Although a few officers "didn't let a sneeze go by without writing a ticket," such behavior typically led to derision from fellow officers, threats of reprisal from inmates, and routine reversal of tickets by the D-Board. ([One] officer who resorted too often to writing tickets was reportedly pulled from the yard by his supervisors and placed for months in the towers). "They lose respect when a person writes a lot of tickets," for he indicates thereby that he cannot otherwise maintain control. . . . Most officers reported that they rarely, if ever, resorted to ticket writing except for obvious and major transgressions: stabbings, contraband found during a major shakedown, and the like. . . .

Second, the sanctions the D-Board could impose were few in number. . . .an inmate could lose "good time" (thereby making his stay in prison longer); he could be locked in his own cell for a few days or weeks ("isolation time" or "ice time"); he could be removed from the minimum end to the more restrictive maximum end or from either [the] minimum or maximum end to Block 10. . . . Each step involved more of the same: more restraint, more isolation, more deprivation. [In addition], Block 10 . . .was often not viewed as punishment at all. Despite confinement to one's cell twenty-three hours a day or more in squalid conditions, . . .many inmates *preferred* to be in Block 10. It was often safer than the maximum or minimum blocks. . . .By committing an obvious offense, (preferably assault on an officer), and being "sentenced" to Block 10, an inmate could effect his withdrawal from the prison population without losing his standing among fellow inmates.

*Source:* Kelsey Kauffman, *Prison Officers and Their World* (Cambridge, MA: Harvard University Press, 1988), pp. 62–63.

## Corrupt Alliance

To a certain extent, almost all officers will overlook some things. In fact, one study found that "experienced and effective officers" never went completely "by the book," for several reasons: "First, the many complex human situations that must be dealt with could not be adequately covered by any set of rules, so that flexibility in rule enforcement was necessary. Moreover . . . bending correctional rules is necessary to secure compliance from inmates so that control can be maintained. . . . In this way, negotiation secures compliance in a situation where coercive enforcement . . . would produce resentment and hostility. . . . "[48]

In other words, a willingness to tolerate violations of "minor" rules and regulations enables the officer to obtain compliance with the "major" areas of the custodial regime.[49] The resulting system of informal compromises has been cited as usurping official authority by developing a *corrupt alliance* between the inmates and custodial staff. In this respect, "corrupt" is not used in the sinister sense of exploitation for illicit gain, but rather, in the more benign sense of seeking a workable accommodation.

In normal settings it is in the subordinate's best interests to comply with the orders issued by those in charge. Whether the order is issued by a parent or an office manager, there is a certain "sense of duty" that motivates compliance. But correctional institutions are not normal settings, and inmates are primarily confined to their custody because they have not demonstrated such internal moral controls in the past. In prison, "the custodians find themselves confronting men who must be forced, bribed, or cajoled into compliance."[50]

Needless to say, submission through physical force is no longer permissible. Nor, as we have seen earlier, are there many incentives left with which to "bribe" inmates into compliance: "Mail and visiting privileges, recreational privileges, the supply of personal possessions—all are given to the inmate at the time of his arrival. . . . The prisoner, then, finds himself unable to win any significant gains by means of compliance, for there are no gains left to be won."[51]

Beyond this lack of incentives, the close working relationships established between officers and inmates throughout the course of weeks, months, and (in some cases) years can serve to inhibit stern reactions to misbehavior. Moreover, we have seen that those writing too many disciplinary reports are often frowned upon by their supervisors. As a result, a situation can be created in which the officer, "under pressure to achieve a smoothly running tour of duty not with the stick but with the carrot . . . finds that one of the most meaningful rewards he can offer is to ignore certain offenses or make sure that he never places himself in a position where he will discover them. . . . In effect . . . buy[ing] compliance or obedience in certain areas at the cost of tolerating disobedience elsewhere."[52]

Of course, it must be kept in mind that the disobedience tolerated represents relatively minor rule infractions, the excessive enforcement of which could be viewed as unnecessary harassment. In addition, officers who find themselves chronically overworked in overcrowded prisons with an overwhelming number of rules must develop some system of prioritizing simply to survive. Whether the

[48]Frances E. Cheek and Marie Di Stefano Miller, "A New Look at Officers' Role Ambiguity," *Correctional Officers: Power, Pressure and Responsibility* (Laurel, MD: American Correctional Association, 1983), p. 12

[49]Gresham M. Sykes, *Society of Captives: A Study of a Maximum Security Prison* (Princeton, NJ: Princeton University Press, 1958), p. 58. The following discussion of the "corrupt alliance" between inmates and officers is based on Chapter 3, "The Defects of Total Power" of this reference.

[50]Ibid., p. 47.

[51]Ibid., p. 51.

[52]Ibid., pp. 56–57.

result is considered a "corrupt alliance" achieved by implicit bargaining or a "calculated arrangement" accomplished by impartially balancing priorities is largely a matter of perspective. In the end, the result may be less a planned maneuver designed to secure cooperation than simply the "human" thing to do.[53]

## Changing Supervisory Styles

Maintaining a proper balance between formally enforcing rules through disciplinary action and informally encouraging compliance through interpersonal relationships takes some time to develop. Thus, it is not surprising to find that even the same person varies his or her supervisory style with greater experience. For example, officers have been found to employ a somewhat idealistic *by the book* approach during their early days of uncertainty as new recruits. As they realize the futility of attempting to achieve full enforcement, they may later progress to a *firm but fair* style that reflects an effort to enforce the rules with predictability and uniformity.[54]

Throughout the course of a career, there are also officers who totally *tune out*—avoiding rule enforcement entirely (such as those who become frustrated with the system or are on a "downhill slide" toward retirement). Others can become *co-opted*—allowing inmates to accumulate so many favors that they "actually have control over the officer's job."[55] While officers are generally noted for one particular supervisory style, they can occasionally "drift" from one form of control to another. That is not meant to imply that such changing adaptations are necessarily inappropriate. To the contrary, as we will see shortly, alteration of one's style in a manner that fits the situation can be a most effective technique.

## Balanced Enforcement

By now it should be apparent that the enforcement of discipline must be reasonable, steering a middle course between severity and laxity. As a veteran of San Quentin stated: "If you come in here and feel a man is worthless because he's a killer . . . or if you start feeling sorry for these guys, you've lost all your perspective. . . .You can't come in here and be one extreme or another. You've got to walk right down the middle of the road."[56] The same theme is echoed by an officer in Rhode Island, who cautions that staff cannot gain respect either by "being an easy mark" or through "bully tactics."[57] The most effective officers seek a reasonable compromise between these two extremes—neither ignoring nor overenforcing the rules.

Officers must be aware of the institution's disciplinary standards. They must know their limits and act within them. But the development of a uniform and reasonable approach to discipline does not result from the rulebook alone. As

[53]Lombardo, p. 63.
[54]Barry D. Smith, "Styles of Control and Supervision," in *Correctional Officers*, pp. 26–27.
[55]Ibid., p. 28.
[56]Edgar May, "Prison Guards in America—The Inside Story, *Corrections Magazine*, Vol. 2, No. 6 (December 1976), p. 36.
[57]Ibid.

one Massachusetts officer observed, "If you run this institution [strictly] by the book they give you, you'd have a riot. You can't do it. It's impossible."[58] Another agrees that "none of the rules are enforced all the time. . . . They have to be ignored at times. Rules aren't absolutes."[59] Thus, it is essential to employ a common sense approach to discipline in which "regulations are subject to interpretation."[60] Beyond the rules themselves, such factors as individual personality, formal training, and administrative policy all affect the development of one's disciplinary style.

## Consistency

There are some who would maintain that a consistent inmate management style means treating everyone exactly alike. But such an approach is no more effective with inmates than it would be if parents responded to all of their children in precisely the same manner, or if employers used the same tactics in supervising all their employees. Like everyone else, the needs and behavioral motives of inmates differ widely. Some will respond promptly to a mild verbal warning. Others will openly defy even a direct order. The key is to remain fair and objective without showing favoritism.[61] This requires the type of "professional judgment," that calls for more adaptability than mere adherence to hard and fast rules.[62] In other words, "[t]he officer who is flexible, who adapts to various situations, who can change from authority figure to counselor, depending on the type of interaction required, who has the good judgment to realize which rules and regulations need to be rigidly enforced and which ones can be bent . . . approximates the image of a professional."[63]

In addition to variations among inmates, the particular circumstances involved may also call for considerably different responses. An emergency situation obviously requires immediate take-charge action, whereas a minor infraction could be handled on a more informal basis. Developing a *consistent management style* means responding to a similar circumstance or type of behavior in a similar manner whenever it occurs, as opposed to treating all inmates and situations alike. In other words, "consistency is using the same style for all similar situations and varying the style appropriately as the situation changes."[64]

---

[58]Edgar May, "A Day on the Job—In Prison," *Corrections Magazine,* Vol. 2, No. 6 (December 1976), p. 11

[59]G. L. Webb and David G. Morris, "Prison Guard Conceptions," in Crouch, p. 151.

[60]Ibid.

[61]David B. Kalinich and Terry Pitcher, *Surviving in Corrections* (Springfield, IL: Charles C Thomas, 1984), p. 39.

[62]Jacobs and Retsky, pp. 7–8.

[63]Robert Blair and Peter C. Kratcoski, "Professionalism among Correctional Officers: A Longitudinal Analysis of Individual and Structural Determinants," in Peter J. Benekos and Alida V. Merlo, *Corrections: Dilemmas and Directions* (Cincinnati, OH: Anderson Publishing Company, 1992), p. 117.

[64]Paul Hersey and Kenneth H. Blanchard, *Management of Organizational Behavior: Utilizing Human Resources,* Fourth Edition (Englewood Cliffs, NJ: Prentice Hall, 1982), p. 100. Although this citation is taken from employer–employee management literature, it is equally applicable to officer–inmate supervision.

## Informal Controls

Thus far, our discussion has focused largely on the extent to which formal disciplinary action is taken in an effort to obtain compliance with institutional rules. It has become apparent that both over- and underenforcement are equally inappropriate. Nor can officers "rely upon the authority of [the] uniform alone"; they must "add the weight of [their] personal authority."[65]

To be effective, the correctional officer must therefore appreciate the ultimate objective of discipline—that is, *developing control from within*—rather than focusing on the narrow concept of discipline as what is imposed through rules and regimentation.[66] In other words, it is both a last resort and only one component of the overall view of discipline as a means of "teaching self-control and correcting improper behavior consistently and fairly."[67] The question then becomes how order can be promoted without either ignoring or excessively writing-up violations of the rules and regulations. The answer involves how officers use both informal disciplinary action and verbal communication.

Just as police discretion may result in taking such unofficial action as issuing a verbal warning, correctional officers have similar options available to them. Simply because an infraction is not officially recorded on a disciplinary action form does not necessarily mean that it was ignored. In addition to a verbal warning, officers may be able to reduce television privileges, remove an inmate from a work detail, or initiate similar informal responses to misconduct. Although the range of privileges that can be restricted is somewhat limited and temporary in nature, there are means short of official action that can be used to achieve compliance.

But it is obviously far more effective to prevent violations *proactively* than to deal *reactively* with misbehavior after if occurs. In other words, it is best to encourage *voluntary compliance* in order to reduce the need to resort to official action. Needless to say, this is quite a challenge when dealing with those whose lack of internal restraints can have much to do with why they are incarcerated. It calls for developing appropriate interpersonal working relationships that are neither too close nor too distant.

## Social Distance

Naturally, there must be some social distance between officers and inmates. There is a fine line between properly displaying some degree of empathy and improperly becoming overly sympathetic. Those who become sympathetic and emotionally involved with prisoners are inevitably vulnerable to deception and manipulation.[68] Inmates are inherently quick to identify staff

---

[65]Ben M. Crouch, "The Book vs. the Boot," in Crouch, p. 221.

[66]Cornelius D. Hogan, Jr., "A Training Design: Discipline in the Correctional Institution," *American Journal of Correction*, Vol. 32, No. 1 (January/February, 1970), pp. 14–15.

[67]*Jail Operations: A Training Course for Jail Officers*, Book 5, *Discipline* (Washington, DC: U.S. Bureau of Prisons, n.d.), p. 1.

[68]See, for example, Bud Allen and Diana Bosta, *Games Criminals Play and How You Can Profit by Knowing Them* (Laurel, MD: American Correctional Association, 1981); and Gary Cornelius, "Keys to Effective Inmate Management," in *The Effective Correctional Officer* (Laurel, MD: American Correctional Association, 1992).

weaknesses and prey upon them. It is for such reasons that officers have been encouraged to avoid such things as using nicknames to address inmates, making "deals," discussing the personal life of staff, giving advice about inmates' legal or family matters, and the like.[69]

At the other extreme, there are those who are coldly detached from the inmates—performing their duties in a routine, bureaucratic manner, and making it clear that they are unapproachable, regardless of the inmate's personal needs. Like the physician who must maintain a caring but clinical relationship with patients, correctional officers must balance personal concern with professional caution. Those who are successful in doing so develop a style of *detached commitment*, whereby their professional commitment to the well-being of the inmate is tempered with a degree of personal detachment that promotes objective judgments and rational decision making.

## Interpersonal Communications

Since so much of an officer's time is spent interacting with inmates, the development of effective *interpersonal communication skills* is an essential ingredient of the job. The manner in which officers build and maintain relationships with inmates will have much to do with their success or failure in managing behavior. It will also largely determine whether they can proactively control inmates or whether they must rely on reactive measures.

Some officers are by nature better at dealing with people than others. But there are certain basic skills that can be taught through training to improve one's capability to communicate. As identified by the National Institute of Corrections, these include:[70]

1. *Positioning*
   —Being close enough to hear but far enough away to be safe
   —Facing the inmate squarely
   —Staying alert
   —Changing position occasionally so that movements cannot be predicted easily
2. *Posturing*
   —Standing erect
   —Inclining slightly forward
   —Maintaining direct eye contact
   —Avoiding distractive mannerisms (e.g., hand waving, foot tapping, etc.)
3. *Observing*
   —Seeing, hearing, and interpreting what is occurring
   —Watching both verbal and nonverbal clues
   —Making inferences based on observed facts (e.g., determining whether what is being observed is a break in usual patterns)

[69]Kalinich and Pitcher, pp. 45–53.

[70]The principles of Interpersonal Communications (IPC) skills described herein are summarized from "The Basics: Sizing Up the Situation," *Interpersonal Communications in the Correctional Setting* (Boulder, CO: National Institute of Corrections, 1983), pp. 2.1–7.1.

Simply being there to listen is often the "safety valve" that is need-
ed to prevent frustrations from exploding into violence. Courtesy of
Michael Dersin. Used with permission of the American Correctional
Association.

4. *Listening*
   —Suspending judgment (e.g., hearing the inmate out before making a
   judgment about what is being said)
   —Picking out key words (e.g., concentrating on what is being said rather
   than mentally planning a response)
   —Identifying mood or intensity (e.g., determining the feelings and level

of emotion being expressed, particularly when signs of potential trouble or danger are involved).

It may on the surface appear that listening is a simple task. After all, we spend an average of 40% of our time presumably doing it every day.[71] But there is a distinct difference between actively *listening* and passively *hearing*. True listening takes place through the mind, not the ears. Listening that is *active* (versus passive) and *nonevaluative* (versus judgmental) is both hard work and a well-refined skill.

In corrections, staff are sometimes so inundated with "requests, complaints, and stories from inmates on a daily basis that listening skills become tainted and weakened as time goes by."[72] Like the narrator on a guided tour, it is difficult to maintain the same enthusiasm with the last group in the evening as the first group in the morning. Day after day, correctional officers hear the same troubles, gripes, and pleas—often from the same inmates, and many times concerning things that the staff can do nothing about. But simply being there to listen is often just the "safety valve" that is needed to prevent an inmate's frustration from exploding into violence. See the next "Close-up on Corrections" for some examples in the words of officers themselves.

As a result, "one of the greatest talents any staff person can possess is the ability to listen."[73] As noted earlier, verbal communication is not limited to a one-way issuing of orders and commands. Rather, it involves engaging in a two-way dialogue that establishes an effective working relationship with the inmate population. Proactively listening can be a far more powerful management tool than reactively responding. Quite simply, a good inmate manager is a good inmate listener.

## ❖ SUMMARY

Because many of those in prison have not displayed sufficient internal controls to function effectively in society, an elaborate system of external controls is imposed to maintain security. The operational objectives of custody are to prevent escape, maintain order and safety, and promote efficient functioning of the institution. Moreover, custody is a necessary condition for effectively implementing treatment programs.

Institutional custody is achieved through the architectural design and security hardware of the physical plant, as well as the control procedures enacted by prison staff. Externally, high-security institutions maintain custody through such features as perimeter walls, fences, and razorwire, along with guard towers, ground posts, locks and alarms, double-door security, and the like. Internally, control procedures include inmate segregation, controlled movement, periodic counts, cell searches, personal searches, and control of tools, keys, and equip-

---

[71]Madelyn Burley-Allen, *Listening: The Forgotten Skill* (New York: Wiley, 1982), p. 2.
[72]Kalinich and Pitcher, p. 55.
[73]Ibid.

The Importance of Listening

"I listen. You find out you gain more respect if you listen. Give them your attention. It's appreciated. I spent half my career listening to personal problems" (p. 81). "On my job in the school, guys come up to you with personal problems like sickness, a death in the family, and want to see a counselor. It might take three to five days before he does. You have to deal with this then and there . . . " (p. 54).

One guy was shaking and upset. He said he was in a big jam. . . . He gave me a check he'd gotten in the mail; (correspondence had overlooked it). I took the check, gave the guy a receipt and put it in his account. It's not a big thing, just little things to take the edge off. Sometimes if you're helpful, you can correct things and save trouble. When they can't handle it, they just swing out" (p. 62).

"They've got problems. They get bad-news letters, they stay in and brood about it. I call the service unit and get a 'it's none of your business.' . . . I had a guy working for me, a good worker . . . . Everybody was down on him. They said he'd be a bum. I said let's see what he does. I asked what his problem was and he said that he got a bad letter. His little girl had had an operation. He didn't know how serious it was, but he was worried. I tried to make arrangements for him to make a phone call. . . . He got his phone call and perked up" (p. 63).

"I went by a guy's cell and he was crying. He says for me to go, but if he tips, he might hurt six or seven people. I opened his cell, walked in and started talking and got him calmed down. . . . Other inmates asked me what was happening when I went by. I told them 'Nothing's going on.' You don't spread the word on a thing like that. If the inmate knows this, it takes the edge off and he feels better" (p. 82).

*Source:*Lucien X. Lombardo, *Guards Imprisoned: Correctional Officers at Work,* Second Edition (Cincinnati, OH: Anderson Publishing Company, 1989), pp. 54, 62, 63, 81, 82.

ment. Because both external and internal security provisions are less rigid in minimum-security and community-based facilities, they are the most vulnerable to escapes. Most inmates who abscond are, however, eventually apprehended.

To detect and remove contraband items from the institution, cell searches are conducted either routinely, randomly, or for reasonable suspicion. Especially following visits or outside work assignments, inmates are also subject to personal searches. In terms of intrusiveness, body searches range from a simple frisk, to a full strip search, to a body-cavity examination. Whenever inmates are engaged in activities outside their cells, they are also supervised by correctional officers for signs of misconduct or impending danger.

To further reduce the risk of escape or the introduction of contraband, correctional institutions control inmate contact with the outside. Use of the telephone is restricted, mail is checked, and the number of visits is limited. In high-security prisons, visitors are separated from inmates by plate glass. Less secure institutions may conduct visits along two sides of a long table, and minimum-security facilities normally allow contact visits. Some states permit conjugal visits to reduce homosexual activities, improve morale, and strengthen family bonds. But not all inmates qualify for conjugal visits, which can create resentment. Some institutions therefore favor the use of furloughs, through which inmates can better maintain social integration and interaction with their children. However, furloughs present the obvious risk of absconding or committing new crimes during the period of freedom.

In an effort to achieve orderly group life, a number of rules and regulations govern individual conduct within correctional institutions. Officers are responsible for enforcing the rules, and they possess considerable discretion in this regard. Although minor infractions may not be fully enforced, major violations are written up through official disciplinary action reports. If it is determined that further action is necessary, the inmate is afforded a hearing before a disciplinary committee, which has the authority to impose sanctions when a penalty is warranted. Solitary confinement and the loss of time credits are the most severe sanctions that an inmate can receive.

In addition to formal controls imposed through official disciplinary action, officers can use informal verbal communication to proactively encourage voluntary compliance with the rules. Obtaining compliance without taking official action can create an accommodation between officers and prisoners, whereby officers accept some degree of minor misconduct as a trade-off for the observance of major rules. To some extent, this is the result of an effort to avoid either over- or under-enforcing the rules. Overly strict enforcement is viewed by the inmates as unnecessary harassment, whereas nonenforcement diminishes respect for both the officer and the rules. The volume of rules as well as the number of people being supervised necessitates some system of prioritizing. Ultimately, the purpose of discipline is developing internal self-control, rather than forcing involuntary submission through rigid regimentation.

Encouraging voluntary compliance involves the need to develop an appropriate interpersonal working relationship with the inmates. But officers must be careful to maintain a certain social distance—balancing personal concern with professional caution. In terms of interpersonal communication skills, an officer's greatest attribute is the ability to be an active, nonevaluative listener. Much of an inmate's frustration, anxiety, and tension can be reduced simply by having someone who is willing to listen without passing judgment. Establishing a two-way dialogue rather than a one-way dictation of commands not only lessens potential hostility but creates an atmosphere more conducive to proactive inmate management.

# chapter 9

# Institutional Procedures: Treatment

*When a sheriff or a marshal takes a man from a courthouse in a prison van and transports him to confinement for two or three or ten years, this is our act. We have tolled the bell for him. And whether we like it or not, we have made him our collective responsibility. We are free to do something about him; he is not.*[1]

*Former Chief Justice Warren Burger*

## ❖ CHAPTER OVERVIEW

Treatment in correctional institutions involves all of the programs and services that bring socializing influences to bear on the inmate. Thus, it encompasses much more than a narrow focus on in-depth diagnosis and therapeutic intervention. Viewed more comprehensively, treatment refers to all of the processes that ordinarily promote the normal socialization of people in the free community—such as schools, religion, recreation, and medical care—as well as the psychological, psychiatric, and social work services that are traditionally associated with the term *treatment.* In fact, to some degree, corrections replaces the original functions of the family, peer groups, and other social institutions during the inmate's confinement. To accomplish the dual treatment/custody mission of correctional institutions, an accepting but firmly controlled environment is necessary—where external controls are applied in conjunction with the treatment process. To the extent that they contribute to the inmate's socialization, a wide variety of factors can be broadly viewed as treatment—from the work habits learned in prison industries, to the high school equivalency diplomas earned in GED classes, to the discipline instilled by compliance with regulations.

Despite society's shift from the specific rehabilitative emphasis of the medical model to the more punitive focus of the justice model, corrections has not abandoned the broad scope of treatment. In part, this may be a reflection of practical considerations. A prison in which training, education, work, or religious

[1]Warren Burger, quoted in Charles E. Silberman, *Criminal Violence, Criminal Justice* (New York: Vintage Books, 1978), p. 502.

activities are lacking is one in which boredom and idleness prevail, compounding the already difficult task of maintaining custody and control. Institutional programs not only enable better supervision than custodial staff alone can provide, but they also focus the inmate in a positive direction and help neutralize feelings of frustration.

In addition, despite the presumably voluntary nature of treatment under the justice model, it is inevitably the corrections component of the criminal justice system which is criticized when ex-offenders become recidivists. Even if the public views the mission of corrections as restricted to incapacitation, it may not be willing to absolve prisons of at least some blame when they fail to make positive changes among those confined. The *legal* responsibility of the prison may be limited to the court's demand for humane custody and security. But the public's *protective* demand is ultimately to return the offender to society as a law-abiding citizen. In that regard, "education, mental health, substance abuse, and other rehabilitative programs . . . are not a bleeding heart coddling of inmates, but rather, are directly related to public safety and are cost beneficial."[2]

Moreover, correctional administrators themselves continue to express a belief in rehabilitation. As one warden expresssed it, "although society's concern in recent years has been to get tough on crime, most corrections professionals never really gave up on program interventions."[3] A national survey of federal and state prison wardens in 1991 found that while "maintaining custody and institutional order are dominant concerns," there was also clear "support for rehabilitation as a secondary but fundamental goal." Not only did wardens feel that rehabilitation programs have an important place in their institutions, they also expressed a desire to expand inmate treatment opportunities.[4] As we will see in this chapter, that is a legitimate concern, since treatment in the traditional clinical or casework sense is sadly lacking in most correctional facilities.

Although wardens may not view rehabilitation as their primary objective, they apparently recognize that (as discussed in Chapter 8), security and control provide the fundamental basis for meaningful treatment programs. In fact, to some extent, the custodial rules and regulations described earlier could be considered a part of the overall treatment process—by promoting the safe and secure environment necessary for effective treatment as well as the internal self-control necessary to function appropriately on the outside. The drawback of a broad-based view of treatment is that professionally oriented approaches such as counseling, therapy, and the like may not be afforded the priority they deserve. Treatment is not necessarily limited to these procedures. It is not confined to a single program or service. But neither is it merely a process for helping the inmate adapt to the institutional environment with a minimum of irritation and anxiety. Rather, it is related to what every officer, counselor, work supervi-

[2]Richard G. Kiekbusch, "Leadership Roles: How Are We Doing?" *American Jails*, Vol. 6, No. 5 (November/December 1992), p. 6.
[3]Margaret C. Hambrick, "Intervention Programs: Setting Change in Motion," *Corrections Today*, Vol. 53, No. 5 (August 1991), p. 6.
[4]Francis T. Cullen, Edward J. Latessa, Velmer S. Burton, and Lucien X. Lombardo, "The Correctional Orientation of Prison Wardens: Is the Rehabilitative Ideal Supported?" *Criminology*, Vol. 31, No. 1 (1993), pp. 84–85.

sor, chaplain, or other institutional employee does that has a positive impact on the inmate's long-term social adjustment.

The process begins immediately upon admission, during the period of reception and diagnosis that is designed to determine the offender's level of risk, individual needs, and potential for change. Through this classification process, inmates are assigned to different institutions and programs in order to provide the best available services to fit their requirements. Decisions are made regarding what (if any) job an inmate should have, what level of security should be imposed, what medical attention is required, what training, education, or therapy should be provided, and the like.

Although not all institutions have the luxury of being able to offer the full range of services that a particular inmate may need, most do make an effort to assure that available resources are allocated appropriately. Even in those facilities lacking sophisticated clinical or therapeutic programs, much can be done on a routine day-to-day basis to promote the overall treatment effort by introducing socializing influences into lives that have often been characterized by personal disorganization and social dysfunction. In other words, the correctional process must be directed toward *"changing behavior,* rather than just *containing behavior."*[5]

---

*LEARNING GOALS*

*Do you know:*

- *For what purposes inmates are classified?*
- *How the emphasis of classification has changed over time?*
- *What the role of a reception and diagnostic center is in the classification process?*
- *On what basis classification decisions are made and how they affect the offender?*
- *The phases through which classification has progressed historically?*
- *What team treatment and functional unit management are?*
- *The advantages and disadvantages of using objective prediction models in classification decision making?*

---

## ❖ INMATE CLASSIFICATION

We may not think of classification as a part of life in free society, but there are many ways in which it functions outside prisons as well as within institutions. For example, every time that you go to the "express" line in the supermarket, the "cash-only" checkout in a department store, or the "self-service" pump at a gas station, classification is being used to expedite your transactions. Similarly, the public schools group students according to academic levels. Even within the same grade, classification techniques such as reading level, performance on stan-

---

[5]W. Ray Nelson, "The First International Symposium on the Future of Law Enforcement," *Direct Supervision Network,* Vol. 1 (April/June 1991), p. 4.

dardized tests, and teacher assessments are used to subdivide students further according to their specific educational needs.

Within corrections, classification refers to the *separation of inmates according to characteristics that they share in common* (as described in Chapter 6). It is therefore a helpful tool in managing large numbers of cases more efficiently than they could be handled on an individual basis. By identifying general patterns of problems and grouping services to match them, the unique requirements of large numbers of people can better be met. Thus, classification permits homogeneous grouping of offenders for the purpose of focusing on specific targets and goals. The goals can range from learning auto mechanics through vocational training, to becoming functionally literate through computer-assisted instruction, to achieving social adjustment through group therapy. As noted in the next "Close-up on Corrections," classification serves a number of objectives that are related to both institutional concerns and inmate considerations.

## Historical Developments

As we saw in the history of corrections, there was originally no attempt to separate prisoners in correctional institutions. But gradually, classification on the basis of individual characteristics emerged. Initially, classification was based on custodial considerations, but later expanded to separation based on treatment potential. As we will see later, the field has come full cycle, with more recent classification techniques reemphasizing levels of institutional security.

### ❖ CLOSE-UP ON CORRECTIONS

Purposes of Offender Classification

1. To systematically identify types of inmates who are distinguishable on the basis of program needs, security needs, and/or treatment needs. . . .
2. To allocate such correctional resources as staff, treatment options, and bed space in a rational manner. . . .
3. To assign offenders to minimum, medium, or maximum security institutions or supervision levels on the basis of their predicted likelihood of recidivism, escape, or disciplinary infraction. . . .
4. To assign offenders to living units within a correctional setting on the basis of psychological screening or security criteria. . . .
5. To match offenders to appropriate treatment approaches on the basis of psychological, developmental, or personality characteristics. . . .
6. To identify and prioritize offender needs. . . .

*Source:* Patricia Van Voorhis, "An Overview of Offender Classification Systems," in David Lester, Michael Braswell, and Patricia Van Voorhis, eds., *Correctional Counseling,* Second Edition (Cincinnati, OH: Anderson Publishing Company, 1992), pp. 74–75.

Probably the earliest example of classification was Spain's separation of men and women in 1519. In the United States, the Quakers separated the sexes in the Walnut Street Jail of 1790. Children began to be segregated from adults around 1825 with New York's establishment of private Houses of Refuge, followed by public juvenile training schools in Massachusetts (1847) and educational programs for juveniles at the Elmira Reformatory (1876). Following emphasis on gender and age, inmates were later separated on the basis of severity of offense. These early beginnings represented the *segregation period* of classification[6]—when offenders were isolated from one another primarily for safety and security, to promote the orderly functioning of correctional institutions.

Separation for treatment purposes began to appear in France when Binet and Simon were commissioned in 1904 to develop an intelligence test to determine which problem children could be educated and which should be sent to work. Their efforts resulted in the first intelligence (IQ) test, which was translated into English and brought to New Jersey's Vineland Training School in 1911. These developments stimulated the period in which classification was used for *diagnosis and planning*, which shifted the focus from institutional security considerations to identification of offender needs.

With the emergence of the medical model and psychoanalytic techniques in the 1930s, many state correctional systems in the United States adopted the classification concept, since diagnosis of individual needs was considered essential to proper treatment and rehabilitation. This ushered in the *classification for treatment* era, based on the concept that the outcome of classification procedures would be used to determine appropriate treatment interventions. During the 1930s, the Federal Bureau of Prisons was organized, introducing programs of individual treatment using classification procedures, and in 1938, the American Correctional Association appointed a committee to develop the first handbook on classification procedures. Many of the treatment developments discussed in this chapter—from counseling, to group therapy, to the role-playing of psychodrama—were initiated in the 1950s during this period.

By the 1980s, the rehabilitative goals and virtually mandated treatment of the medical model gave way to the emphasis on confinement and voluntary treatment of the justice model. This resulted in the use of classification for *security and custody*, as opposed to rehabilitative purposes.[7] Identifying treatment needs is not necessarily excluded from current classification decision making. But neither is it any longer the exclusive objective.

---

[6]The titles of classification periods used throughout this section on historical developments generally reflect those identified by Leonard J. Hippchen, "Trends in Classification Philosophy and Practice," in Leonard J. Hippchen, Edith E. Flynn, Chester D. Owens, and Alfred C. Schnur, eds., *Handbook on Correctional Classification: Programming for Treatment and Reintegration* (Cincinnati, OH: Anderson Publishing Company, 1978).

[7]Michael W. Forcier, "The Development of the Modern Classification System," in Bruce I. Wolford and Pam Lawrenz, eds., *Classification: Innovative Correctional Programs* (Richmond, KY: Department of Correctional Services, 1988), p. l.

## Reception and Diagnosis

The initial step in classifying inmates is the diagnostic process that occurs during reception and intake, which often takes place at a location specifically designed for this purpose. The first such facility was the Diagnostic Depot at Joliet, Illinois. Several states subsequently opened *reception or diagnostic centers,* and the trend spread throughout much of the country.

Before the adoption of classification on a statewide basis, judges could sentence offenders to any of a series of prisons within the state. Thus classification was essentially a function of the court. In contrast to the court-controlled system of inmate assignment, state-controlled classification places everyone sentenced by the courts under the central authority of the state department of corrections rather than under the authority of any single institution. While inmates are physically confined in any of a number of institutions throughout the state, the overall responsibility for their custody rests with the department of corrections.

At diagnostic centers, incoming inmates are thoroughly interviewed, tested, examined, and evaluated by a team of doctors, psychologists, psychiatrists, and similar professionals. The detailed contents of presentence investigation reports are also reviewed. If further background information is needed, additional contacts may be made with family members, previous employers, schools attended, and other social service agencies with which the inmate had prior contact.

## Classification Decisions

After all of the necessary information is gathered, a report is prepared outlining the person's past background, present needs, and future potential. On the basis of that information, decisions are made concerning housing and program assignments (e.g., education, training, work, etc.). In addition, an estimation is made of the inmate's custody requirements (as described in Chapter 7) along with any special programs that would be advisable, such as group therapy, alcohol/drug rehabilitation, psychiatric referral, or other specialized treatment alternatives. Classification therefore can serve both placement and planning functions.[8]

This is how classification is designed to operate, but the process is far from being foolproof or completely objective. Subjective opinions of a classification committee can override clinical assessments, and stereotyped thinking can distort diagnostic perceptions.[9] The sheer volume of cases being reviewed can create routinized decisions that are based more on efficient processing than effective prognosis. One study, for example, found that although staff "talk a great deal about individual attention," inmates spend an average of only ten minutes before the classification committee, and decisions are often the product of placing inmates in preconceived stereotyped categories.[10] As several staff members commented, "For half the inmates

---

[8]See Carl B. Clements, "The Measurement and Evaluation of Correctional Resource Management," in Wolford and Lawrenz, p. 5.

[9]See, for example, Robert E. Doran, "Organizational Stereotyping: The Case of the Adjustment Center Classification Committee," in David F. Greenberg, ed., *Corrections and Punishment* (Beverly Hills, CA: Sage Publications, 1977), pp. 41–68.

[10]Ibid., pp. 45–46.

Classification decisions have a substantial impact on the offender. Among many other things, the classification process determines an inmate's housing assignment. Courtesy of the Nassau County Sheriff's Department, East Meadow, New York.

appearing, we already know what we are going to do. The inmate knows, too," so the process is basically one of going through the motions in order "to meet the *Manual* requirements. . . . "[11] It is in part for such reasons that more clearly defined, objective criteria are now being used in many correctional classification systems.

However they are made, classification decisions can have a long-term impact on the offender. Everything from job placement, to educational programming, to parole eligibility is tied to classification outcomes. Moreover, inmates identified as potential troublemakers, high security risks, and the like may well attempt to live up to the label placed on them. In essence, classifying people "channels destinies and determines fate,"[12] at times becoming a self-fulfilling prophecy.

### Relationship to the Medical Model

The reception and diagnostic process was not only compatible with, but actually a critical ingredient of the medical model's focus on the physical, psychological and/or social "illness" of the offender. Since the medical model viewed criminal acts as a "cry for help," early and accurate diagnosis was essential, "followed by prompt and effective therapeutic intervention," as outlined in the treatment plan during classification.[13]

[11]Ibid., p. 47.

[12]Hans Toch, "The Care and Feeding of Typologies and Labels," *Federal Probation*, Vol. 34, No. 3 (September 1970), pp. 15–19.

[13]Donal E. J. MacNamara, "The Medical Model in Corrections: Requiesat in Pace," *Criminology*, Vol. 14, No. 4 (February 1977), pp. 439–40.

Whether or not the inmate desired treatment was not the point. The offender's own motivation to seek help—or lack thereof—was largely ignored. Rather, the treatment plan was based on the classification committee's view of inmate *needs*, as opposed to what the person *wanted* or had the motivation to *do*. Realizing that "going along with the system" would provide the only avenue to freedom naturally created a strong incentive for doing what was prescribed, even if that might mean simply going through the motions to demonstrate eligibility for release. Although there is some evidence that court-ordered treatment can be even more effective than voluntary treatment,[14] the move from the medical model to the justice model was, in part, intended to deemphasize mandated treatment in favor of voluntary participation.

## Institutional Implications

There are both advantages and disadvantages of a centralized diagnostic and reception center. The strength of the reception center is that, by concentrating diagnostic resources in one location, a thorough individual analysis and appropriate treatment plan can theoretically be developed for each case. In this way, administrators can also "make more efficient use of limited resources and . . . avoid providing resources for offenders who do not require them."[15]

One of its weaknesses, however, is that a centralized diagnostic and reception center may tend to drain the institutions themselves of professional treatment personnel. If treatment specialists are largely concentrated at the diagnostic center, fewer are available to provide services at the institutional level, thereby placing a premium on initial analysis rather than subsequent application of the findings. In other words, the process may raise aspirations "above the level of possible achievement."[16]

Moreover, as correctional facilities have become increasingly crowded, it is not always feasible to place inmates in the institutions and programs that have been identified as best suited for them.[17] It has, for instance, been noted that "[a] state with 75% maximum security spaces will tend to classify 75% of its intake population as maximum security."[18] Studies have indicated that subjective classification systems tend to violate "one of the cardinal rules of classification by 'overclassifying'"—that is, "unnecessarily placing many inmates in higher levels of security than required, given the risks they pose."[19] Classification has also

---

[14]In one alcohol/drug treatment program, for example, it was found that court-ordered referrals had better success rates than did voluntary entrants. Marie Ragghianti and Toni Glenn, *Reducing Recidivism: Treating the Addicted Inmate* (Center City, MN: Hazelden, 1991), p. 12.

[15]National Advisory Commission on Criminal Justice Standards and Goals, *Corrections* (Washington, DC: U.S. Government Printing Office, 1973), p. 201.

[16]Harry E. Allen and Clifford E. Simonsen, *Corrections in America: An Introduction*, Sixth Edition (New York: Macmillan, 1992), p. 226.

[17]See Stephen H. Gettinger, "Objective Classification," *Corrections Magazine*, Vol. 8, No. 3 (June 1982), pp. 24–29, 32–37.

[18]Hans Toch, "Inmate Classification as a Transaction," *Criminal Justice and Behavior*, Vol. 8, No. 1 (March 1981), p. 4.

[19]Forcier, p. 2, citing James Austin, "Assessing the New Generation of Prison Classification Models," *Crime and Delinquency*, Vol. 29, No. 4 (October 1983), pp. 561–76.

been criticized for being unrelated in any meaningful way to treatment, and therefore, often irrelevant to the rehabilitative process.[20] While the process may not always work as intended, the aim of a properly implemented classification system is to match the security and treatment needs of the inmate with the resources available within the correctional system.

## Classification Developments

As correctional classification procedures have moved from the very rudimentary separation of inmates on the basis of age and sex to the sophisticated diagnostic procedures available today, the process itself has progressed through the following phases:

1. Preprofessional
2. Traditional
3. Integrated
4. Professional
5. Team treatment
6. Functional unit management
7. Objective prediction models

**Preprofessional.**   The earliest, *preprofessional stage* characterized classification procedures when the process first began. At this time, classification committees were large groups that generally included the warden, deputy warden, and significant department heads.

The practice was usually to meet twice a week for half a day to classify the inmates who had come in approximately a month before. Each member of the committee would, in turn, take a file and give a brief history of the case, along with a recommendation, usually directed more toward the needs of the institution than the benefit of the prisoner. When the inmate came in to meet with the committee, the member with that file would tell the inmate what the committee had decided.

**Traditional.**   With the addition of sociologists, psychologists, and other professional staff to prepare a more detailed analysis of the case, the social history report was introduced. This provided an initial recommendation that could be accepted or changed by the rest of the classification committee. In this *traditional approach,* everything remained essentially the same as in the preprofessional stage, with the exception that professional staff had been added to prepare the inmate's social history.

**Integrated.**   In the next phase, classification moved toward being more *integrated* into the total prison program. Before this, the classification committee's recommendations were simply that—recommendations. It was up to the deputy

---

[20]Edith E. Flynn, "Problems of Reception and Diagnostic Centers," in Leonard J. Hippchen, ed., *Correctional Classification and Treatment* (Cincinnati, OH: Anderson Publishing Company, 1975), p. 29.

warden of each institution to implement them. Implementation was hampered by, among other things, the need for controlled movement. For example, custodial personnel did not want prisoners coming from all directions of the institution to the kitchen at 4:30 in the morning to prepare breakfast. Consequently, everyone who worked in the kitchen would be confined within one cellblock, everyone who worked in the laundry in another, and so on. Beyond the issue of security considerations, many custodial administrators thought that they could tell more about a prisoner than the classification personnel, and some outright ignored the committee's recommendations.

At the same time that awareness was growing with regard to how the process was being subverted at the institutional level, classification systems were gaining credibility, strength, and influence. As a result, their recommendations essentially became an order. This represented a significant move toward the integration of classification into the actual prison program. The deputy warden could still request that the committee reconsider a case for the safety and security of the institution. If such requests were made too frequently, however, the warden would be asked to send a new representative to the classification committee in whom there was greater confidence, since custody was already represented in the membership of the committee.

**Professional.**   Up to this point, the classification committee was made up of 10 to 12 department heads and significant personnel from the institutions. Consequently, well-paid institutional staff were tied up for two half-days each week. Reducing these large and unwieldy groups to a three-person *professional classification committee* was seen as a step toward greater efficiency and economy. Under this system, the committee was composed of the director of classification, a high-ranking custodial officer, and the counselor who prepared the inmate's social history report. This streamling presented obvious benefit. But one drawback was that the committee lost the function of educating and involving the department heads in the correctional classification process.

**Team Treatment.**   In a further step to integrate classification and subsequent treatment more fully into the daily institutional routine, the *treatment team concept* emerged in the late 1950s. In this approach, three people—generally, a counselor, a custodial officer, and an educational instructor—function as a team to address the needs of individual inmates. Anyone can serve on this treatment-oriented team, but a counselor and custodial officer must be included.

For greater administrative efficiency, the same team may be assigned to all residents of a specific dormitory or cellblock. The team then determines all of the actions formerly decided by the classification committee. In fact, where fully implemented, the team may also handle any disciplinary problems that arise during the inmate's confinement. In addition to reducing the isolation between classification and institutional personnel, among the benefits of a team approach is that correctional officers and other facility staff come to better appreciate the treatment process.

**Functional Unit Management.**   A further refinement of the treatment team concept, *functional unit management* was introduced into the Federal Bureau of

Prisons and several states during the mid-1970s in an effort to decentralize treatment services.[21] Each living unit (such as a dormitory or cellblock) has a unit manager, one or two caseworkers, counselors, and an administrative assistant. The unit manager serves as a "subwarden," and each unit is, in a sense, a "subinstitution." All decisions and problems concerning the inmates are handled in the unit, with the unit manager in charge. The idea is to decentralize authority by dividing the prison into smaller, more manageable components.[22] "The arrangement is analogous to neighborhoods in a city. Each neighborhood can be intimate, but is part of and has access to the amenities of the city. . . . Autonomy lets units develop their own cultures and identities. But the unit still functions as part of the whole prison."[23] Unit management is not a particular form of treatment program. Rather, it is a system whereby custody and treatment work hand in hand within a setting that promotes their close cooperation.

In some cases, counselors in the unit management system also approve visitors and correspondence lists, process requests for job assignments, and review requests for program changes. In other places, each inmate is assigned a counselor upon arrival, and the counselor keeps that person on the caseload throughout the entire incarceration period. One of the major advantages of functional unit management is that it "works as well in high security institutions as it does in low or medium security facilities."[24] But its success is perhaps best indicated by the fact that, thus far, no correctional system which has adopted this approach has later abandoned it.[25]

**Objective Prediction Models.** As early as 1967, the President's Task Force on Corrections expressed a desire for a more objective and easily administered classification tool, noting that

> it would be of great help to have some relatively simple screening process, capable of administration in general day-to-day correctional intake procedures, that would group offenders according to their management and treatment needs. To the extent that such screening procedures could be regularized, the errors attendant upon having a wide variety of persons make decisions on the basis of different kinds of information and presumptions would be reduced.[26]

---

[21]Martin J. Bohn, Richard A. Wazak, and Bill R. Storey, *Transition to Functional Unit, 1973–1974* (Tallahassee, FL: Federal Correctional Institution Notes, Vol. 4, No. 1, 1974).

[22]See Robert B. Levinson and Roy E. Gerard, "Functional Units: A Different Correctional Approach," *Federal Probation*, Vol. 37, No. 4 (December 1973), pp. 8–16.

[23]Hans Toch, "Functional Unit Management: An Unsung Achievement," *Federal Prisons Journal*, Vol. 2, No. 4 (Winter 1992), p. 15–16.

[24]James H. Webster, "Designing Facilities for Effective Unit Management," *Corrections Today*, Vol. 53, No. 2 (April 1991), p. 38.

[25]Robert B. Levinson, "The Future of Unit Management," *Corrections Today*, Vol. 53, No. 2 (April 1991), p. 46.

[26]President's Commission on Law Enforcement and Administration of Justice, *Task Force Report: Corrections* (Washington, DC: U.S. Government Printing Office, 1967), p. 20.

Shortly thereafter, the Federal Bureau of Prisons in 1969 implemented a classification procedure that could be computerized.[27] The system produced a code that could be translated into three treatment categories, depending on whether there should be a great, moderate, or no expenditure of resources above the essential levels of service. Called the *RAPS system*, the "R" represented one's rehabilitative potential code, based on the staff's professional opinion regarding prospects for change. The "A" referred to age, "P" the number of prior sentences, and "S" the nature of the sentence in terms of length or special classification (e.g., juveniles, addicts, etc.). The combinations of these codes, when fed into a computer, elicited categories of treatment—from highest to lowest priority.

The RAPS system represented the early beginnings of computerized classification. Throughout the history of classification progress (with the exception of the first preprofessional stage), all of the phases described thus far required some type of professional treatment personnel to make the initial diagnosis and develop the related custody and treatment plans. As noted earlier, this is not only costly, but also vulnerable to subjective opinions.

To streamline the process and make it more objective, there has been a move in recent years toward more empirically valid classification measures.[28] As described in the objective classification guidelines developed by the National Institute of Justice, improved classification of inmates is an essential component of the response to prison crowding:

> With proper classification . . . only those inmates requiring high levels of security are placed in costly, tight custody facilities, while those evidencing less threat can be assigned to lower security institutions. Appropriate classification also can assist in determining which inmates can be considered for early release or for retention in the community with appropriate supervision. Most importantly, effective classification helps assure the safety of the public, agency staff, and prisoner population."[29]

By removing personal opinions and subjective judgments, these prediction models are designed to be more fair and equitable to all inmates. Methods used to classify for treatment purposes are directed toward understanding causes of criminal behavior and identifying specific targets for change. In contrast, objective systems use "standardized decision-making criteria"[30] that are focused more on classification for institutional management or inmate adjustment to confinement.

[27]*United States Bureau of Prisons Policy Statement on the Case Management System* (Washington, DC: U.S. Bureau of Prisons, 1969).

[28]In addition, it has been noted that primary reasons for developing objective classification systems were to address overclassification and respond to or prevent court litigation. See Robert A. Buchanan, Karen L. Whitlow, and James Austin, "National Evaluation of Objective Prison Classification Systems: The Current State-of-the-Art," *Crime and Delinquency*, Vol. 32, No. 3 (July 1986), p. 275.

[29]Robert A. Buchanan and Karen L. Whitlow, *Guidelines for Developing, Implementing, and Revising an Objective Prison Classification System* (Washington, DC: National Institute of Justice, 1987), p. 1

[30]Doris Layton MacKenzie, "Prison Classification: The Management and Psychological Perspectives," in Lynne Goodstein and Doris Layton MacKenzie, eds. *The American Prison: Issues in Research and Policy* (New York: Plenum Press, 1989), pp. 168, 184.

It is not surprising that *objective classification models* have gained support during the period of time when sentencing guidelines and selective incapacitation prediction formulas have also become popular. All of these numerical formulas, models, and prediction devices may also owe much of their prominence to fascination with the capabilities of computers and mathematical problem solving. If decisions are numerically derived, there is a tendency to view them as more valid and trustworthy, despite the fact that the variables being analyzed are still a product of human choice.

Certainly, the variables taken into consideration in objective prediction models are considerably more moderate in scope than the widespread tests and measures upon which previous classification decisions were based. As outlined in Figure 9.1, criteria are limited to relatively few clearly defined and legally based variables that are designed to predict one's institutional adjustment and future behavior. Notable by their absence are indicators related to clinical assessments of offender needs. Objective prediction models are directed more toward

| Factors Used in Classification | Federal | California | NIC |
|---|---|---|---|
| *Current offense* | | | |
| Length of sentence | | X | |
| Expected time served | X | | |
| Seriousness of offense | X | | X |
| *Detainers and warrants* | X | X | X |
| *Criminal record* | | | |
| Prior escapes | | X | X |
| Prior juvenile incarcerations | | X | |
| Prior adult incarcerations | X | X | |
| Prior felony convictions | | | X |
| Prior assaultive offenses | X | | X |
| *Previous institutional behavior* | | | |
| Prior negative behavior | | X | X |
| Prior positive behavior | | X | |
| *Social factors* | | | |
| Age | | X | X |
| Education | | X | X |
| Employment | | X | X |
| Marital status | | X | |
| Military record | | X | |
| Alcohol/drug abuse | | | X |
| *Administrative override factors* | X | X | X |
| *Total number of criterion variables used in model* | 6 | 24 | 8 |

**Figure 9.1** Criteria used in inmate classification systems. *Source:* James Austin, "Assessing the New Generation of Prison Classification Models," *Crime and Delinquency,* Vol. 29, No. 4 (October 1983), p. 566. Reprinted by permission of Sage Publications, Inc.

determining the necessary level of institutional security than individual treatment prescriptions. As a result, their acceptance in the field represents another reflection of the movement from the rehabilitative focus of the medical model to the custodial orientation of the justice model.

Because of the lack of rigorous evaluations, the effectiveness of objective prediction techniques in the inmate classification process has yet to be fully determined.[31] One preliminary study did show that objective classification systems appear to reduce needless overclassification, finding that "the proportion of inmates housed in lower security levels has increased without adversely affecting rates of prison misconduct, escapes, and fatalities."[32]

But there is also some resistance to these techniques, because they change the role of classification personnel from diagnosticians and therapists to something closer to a bookkeeper.[33] Concern has been expressed that such an impersonal approach dehumanizes classification, encouraging an overly bureaucratic process in which staff never have to "exercise any judgment" or "take any risks."[34] A related question raised by prediction models is whether removing the human element from classification decision making is truly more *equitable* or whether *efficiency* is merely disguised as equity. In other words, do the rigors of scientific analysis produce more equitable results than the richness of subjective assessments?

Regardless of the answer, once classified, the inmate is faced with adjusting to the decisions made during the intake process. Offenders may find themselves assigned to a minimum-, maximum-, or medium-security institution; to a facility with a wide range of programs and services or to a place where an hour a day of solitary recreation is the single diversion; to a prison with a variety of employment opportunities or a location where work is confined to routine maintenance duties. Recognizing these variations, in the remainder of this chapter we focus on the types of activities, services, and programs that traditionally have been available in correctional institutions.

---

*LEARNING GOALS*

*Do you know:*

- *What role religion plays in a correctional facility?*
- *To what extent correctional chaplains are accepted by inmates and staff?*
- *How religion is related to correctional treatment?*

---

### ❖ RELIGIOUS SERVICES

Ever since the strong religious emphasis of the Quakers in the first penitentiary at the Walnut Street Jail, religion has played a significant role in prison life.

---

[31]Buchanan et al., p. 289.
[32]Buchanan, et al., p. 286.
[33]Forcier, p. 3.
[34]Gettinger, p. 37, citing John Conrad, former head of classification in California.

To those incarcerated in prison or jail, the availability of chaplains, church services, and religious studies can help to cope with confinement. Courtesy of the Iowa Department of Social Services.

Historically, the chaplain represents the first example of what could be considered treatment staff in correctional institutions. In fact, during the early days of the prison system, the entire administrative staff often "consisted of the chaplain and the warden."[35] Even in facilities with few or nonexistent educational programs, classification procedures, or other rehabilitative services, inmates virtually always have access to a chaplain. Thus, the chaplain is frequently the informal ombudsman in a system where no official inmate representative or grievance procedure exists.[36]

It is the chaplain who is there to share the few joys, soothe the many sorrows, and make life somewhat more tolerable for those incarcerated—who holds out the promise of a future better than the past. It is the chaplain who is among the first to greet the newly arriving inmate. And usually, it is the chaplain who is last to say a final word to the shaven, strapped, and wired person quietly awaiting imminent death in the electric chair.

### Inmate Acceptance

Unquestionably, chaplains play an indispensable role in correctional institutions. But while chaplains have always been involved in prisons, their acceptance has never been complete or unreserved. Many inmates do not attend wor-

[35]Herbert I. Bloom, "Religion as a Form of Institutional Treatment," in Hippchen, p. 209.
[36]*Final Report: Task Force on the Role of the Chaplain in New York City Correctional Institutions* (New York: New York City Corrections Board, 1972).

ship services, and church is considered by some as representing the authority of an "establishment" of which they are not a part. It is therefore not unusual for inmates to take the attitude—well expressed by one prisoner—that "if there's a God, he sure wasn't on my side!" The chaplain is viewed by such inmates as a person who is selling intangibles without much practical usefulness.

On the other hand, inmates who are experiencing guilt and remorse can make use of religious programs for support and forgiveness. With little but time on their hands, even some of the most seemingly hard-core inmates do—in the original Quaker tradition—indulge themselves in reading the Bible and attending religious studies. There are those who undoubtedly find a measure of personal solace in religion. Others find it a useful aid to help them adjust to their situation, or simply a "crutch" to lean on in hard times. Still others may actually use religious conversion as a manipulative tool to convince correctional administrators of their reform and eligibilty for release. But regardless of their motives, it is not uncommon for prisoners to "find God" during their incarceration.

## Staff Acceptance

By the same token, chaplains have not been universally well accepted by either prison staff or administrators. The custodial personnel may look upon the chaplain as a threat to security, since the job calls for being on somewhat "friendly" terms with the inmates. The mere fact that one has elected the clergy as a vocation implies to some that the chaplain is a "do-gooder" or an "easy touch." A chaplain who is naive with regard to the manipulative capabilities of inmates can easily reinforce such perceptions. For example, in one small rural prison, the chaplain was told by the inmates that they did not have pens to write to their loved ones. The prisoner communicating this sad news indicated that his wife would gladly donate pens if the chaplain would pick them up. Inside each of the pens was a small quantity of marijuana. As illustrated by this "con game," chaplains must become skillful at separating legitimate from illegitimate inmate anxieties. They must administer to the religious needs of the population while being alert to the security concerns of the agency by whom they are appointed. Doing so requires maintaining a delicate balance between being useful and being used.

Personal style and professional capabilities will also have much to do with both inmate and staff acceptance. Chaplains who hold a narrowly dogmatic viewpoint or encourage church attendance simply for the sake of "conformity" will be less effective in the correctional setting than those who respect all religious views and recognize the value of treating the deeper causes of maladjustment rather than simply focusing on its symptoms.

## Personnel Recruitment

Most religious personnel serving in corrections are highly committed to their mission, very effective at working with the inmate population, and involved for the spiritual rather than career rewards. But it is often difficult to attract properly trained chaplains to a position that is likely to be underpaid, unappreciated, and overworked. In one study, for instance, a "troubling percentage" of chaplains reported feeling that their work is not valued by others, requires long hours, and isolates them from the mainstream of their faiths.[37] The rural location of many prisons and the unattractiveness of the work environment in comparison to serving a congregation in free society are also not favorable to recruitment.

In addition, as prison populations reflect greater cultural and ethnic diversity, chaplains representing the traditional Catholic/Jewish/Protestant denominations are not as relevant to all religious orientations of the inmates. Although it is no longer assumed that a chaplain's training must reflect the specific religious denomination of the inmate being counseled, it is equally inappropriate to overlook the need for broader diversity among the religious staff. In that regard, some correctional institutions have found it helpful to create a religious advisory board, composed of representatives of the clergy throughout the community. This not only better assures protection of all inmates' constitutional right to exercise religious preferences freely, but also serves as a link between the correctional facility and the community, as well as a potential source of volunteers.[38]

The work of full-time chaplains is frequently supplemented by volunteers from religious organizations. Although they have certainly helped to ease the burden on full-time chaplains, even the best intentioned and most highly qualified part-time volunteers cannot effectively substitute for full-time personnel.

In the absence of adequate staffing and facilities, some institutions have implemented uniquely creative approaches to meeting religious needs. One jail, for example, faced the dilemma of complying with a state mandate to provide inmates with access to religious services. The question was how to do so for 2000 inmates in 15 decentralized housing units, with no chapel and only a handful of volunteer chaplains. The answer—"the same way that religions have reached millions of followers for years: television." Now, both prerecorded and live religious programs are broadcast to all inmates through the jail's 114 television sets.[39]

## Treatment Impact

The chaplain's contribution to treatment can be substantial. As noted in Chapter 8, just having someone to talk to, share grief with, or listen to problems can exert a powerful influence. As one chaplain has observed:

> A chaplain must not only be a preacher but also a listener . . . a listener who really hears and a teacher who is ready to be challenged. . . . This concern and openness hopefully produces a similar openness of the spirit in the inmate. If religion has validity in life outside the "walls," it has more validity and reality within the prison . . . despite the difficulties of resistance and resentment of the inmate. It can and does heal. True love and concern, true honesty, and true confrontation create rehabilitation.[40]

[37]Bruce D. Stout and Todd R. Clear, "Federal Prison Chaplains: Satisfied in Ministry but Often Undervalued," *Federal Prisons Journal,* Vol. 2, No. 4 (Winter 1992), p. 10.

[38]Daniel Burgoyne, "Pima County Adult Detention Center: The Religious Program," *American Jails,* Vol. 6, No. 1 (March/April 1992), p. 93.

[39]Phil Danna, "Lights, Camera, Religion," *American Jails,* Vol. 6, No. 3 (July/August 1992), pp. 60–62.

[40]Bloom, p. 213.

Imprisonment can be a lonely, soul-searching experience. It is often the chaplain who makes existence there more bearable, who offers hope for a more promising future—if not in this world, in the next. Moreover, finding security in religion provides many offenders with the internal stability that permits them to make a successful adjustment to society.

In prisons of the past, the chaplain's function was primarily to convince the inmates of the justness of their sentences. Although some of that role may be retained today, the chaplain's duties have expanded considerably. This is particularly true in institutions that do not have designated counseling and treatment personnel, or where such staff members are not readily available. As the oldest and most consistent representative of treatment in correctional institutions, the chaplain has probably contributed more than any other position to the correctional process.

---

*LEARNING GOALS*  ▨▨▨▨▨▨▨▨▨▨▨▨▨▨▨▨▨▨▨▨▨▨▨▨▨▨▨▨▨▨▨▨

*Do you know:*

- *The extent of functional illiteracy among those incarcerated?*
- *The direct and indirect benefits of providing academic education and vocational training in correctional institutions?*
- *Why computer-assisted instruction is particularly well suited to teaching inmates?*
- *Why availability of a library is important in correctional institutions?*
- *The major deficiency of vocational training programs in corrections today?*
- *How the private sector has become involved in prison industries and what issues this raises?*

---

## ❖ EDUCATION, TRAINING, AND OTHER SERVICES

Following religion and moral teaching, the introduction of education was the second major change in the history of correctional institutions. Based on academic and vocational education, the reformatory movement began in Elmira (NY) in 1876. Nor has the need for inmate education diminished over the years since these early beginnings. As we saw in Chapter 7, over half of the inmates in state prisons throughout the country have not completed high school.[41] Even more alarming, the Correctional Education Association estimates that up to 75% of all inmates may be functionally illiterate.[42]

Many of them have been "nonlearners" in the public schools and uninterested in education, eventually dropping out or being expelled. Lack of education

---

[41]*Sourcebook of Criminal Justice Statistics—1991* (Washington, DC: U.S. Department of Justice, 1992), p. 648.

[42]James E. Duffy, "Illiteracy: A National Crisis," *Corrections Today,* Vol. 50, No. 6 (October 1988), p. 44.

may or may not have been among their motivations for becoming involved in crime. It is nevertheless clear that their postrelease employment opportunities will be severely limited in a culture where a high school educational credential is a minimum requirement for most jobs. In today's society, functional literacy is essential for basic survival—including everything from simply reading a newspaper to filling out a job application.

## Institutional Programs

Although they may well have the same intellectual potential as the general population, many inmates come to prison from a personal background that was economically deprived, culturally disadvantaged, and/or educationally deficient. In fact, even among those in free society, it has been noted that "relatively few students fail for reasons of intellectual disability—the more likely reasons are such factors as self-defeating attitudes of indifference, negativism, and fear."[43] By promoting literacy and marketable skills, society saves "time, money, and lives later, when—like it or not—an inmate will be back on the street."[44] It has even been proposed that convicted offenders be tested before sentencing, with successful completion of institutional literacy programs tied to sentence reductions.[45] As a former governor of Wisconsin has noted, "making inmates productive is the first step to keeping them out of prison. Making them literate is one of the first steps in making them productive."[46]

Many programs in correctional institutions have therefore emphasized *academic education* and *vocational training*. The primary purpose of such programs is to provide offenders with the tools of literacy, a trade, or specific job skills. But important secondary advantages include enhancing the inmate's work habits, pride, dignity, self-esteem, sense of accomplishment, and feelings of self-worth. Merely being able to read a story to a child during visiting can be an uplifting experience for a formerly illiterate inmate. For those who have experienced a lifetime of being "losers" or "misfits"—rejected by schools, employers, and even family—these indirect benefits often prove to be even more significant than the immediate objectives. In fact, it has been found that educational services contribute substantially to the rehabilitative process.[47] For a personal account of just how this happened in one case, see the inmate's story in the next "Close-up on Corrections."

## Basic Education

There is little doubt that *literacy*—simply being able to read and write—is one of the most critical skills needed to function in our current society. On a

---

[43]Stanford C. Ericksen, *Motivation for Learning* (Ann Arbor, MI: University of Michigan Press, 1974), p. 120.

[44]Duffy, p. 45.

[45]"Professor's Proposal Draws Wide Exposure," *Corrections Today*, Vol. 54, No. 5 (July 1992), p. 18, citing an article by Richard Wade in *The New York Times* (May 29, 1992).

[46]"High-Tech Tutors: Wisconsin Uses Literacy Program Statewide," *Corrections Today*, Vol. 52, No. 7 (December 1990), p. 142.

[47]Rick Linden and Linda Perry, "The Effectiveness of Prison Education Programs," *Journal of Offender Counseling, Services and Rehabilitation*, Vol. 6 (1982), pp. 43–57.

Plea from a Prisoner

The youngster appeared in front of my tiny "house" on an afternoon when I was short on patience and long on aggravation. All of his possessions were inside a pillowcase slung over his shoulder.

"I'm your new cellie," he informed me. "Jackson's my name and crack's my game."

"Perfect . . . " I mumbled to myself, looking at a kid half my age. . . . Just what I needed, a 20-year-old street punk sharing my 5′ x 9′ cubicle. . . .

Fortunately, we worked different jobs, and different shifts, allowing occasional cell privacy. . . . Jackson stayed on his bunk, pacified by television. There was no anomosity on my part, just no interest in lame conversation.

One thing I did notice. He would perk up when the guard came around our cell at mail call. But there was never anything for Jackson. A couple of times he had commented sarcastically about all the letters I wrote, and the stack of magazines and books cluttering my shelf space.

A day came when Jackson did get a letter. Lying on my lower bunk, I could hear him above, rattling the pages while I flipped through a new magazine. He swung his bare feet off the upper bunk and hopped to the floor. . . .

With unusual meekness he asked, "Say man, you got a minute?"

"What for?"

"Would you read my momma's letter to me?"

I was just able to hold back the question—*You can't read?* But surprise surely registered on my face. It always comes as an astonishing revelation to encounter an adult American who is functionally illiterate.

"Sure," I told him. The letter was two simple pages from a mother worried about her boy confined in a harsh world of bricks and bars. He was silent after I read the final few words: "We love you son. Be careful and come home soon, Momma."

"Would you help me write back to her?" he asked. Gone was the cocky criminal, replaced by a sad, vulnerable youngster barely out of his teens. I hesitated, then made a decision.

"Yeah, I'll write the letter, but it's going to cost you."

"How much?" he asked suspiciously. Everything costs something in the penitentiary.

"An hour of your time, *every* night at lock up. You're gonna learn to read and write."

He looked hard at me. "What's the catch?"

"You've got nothing but time," I reminded him. "Might as well get something out of being here."

"You won't tell nobody?" he asked sheepishly.

"Isn't anybody's business."

"Deal!" he said, sticking out his hand to seal the bargain. . . .

Jackson obviously hadn't absorbed much in the six years he attended school. The basic alphabet was a cloudy concept. His written vocabulary was barely double digit.

But within a few weeks, two things were readily apparent: I had a lot to learn about patience, and Jackson was a *very* bright young man.

He attacked our project with determination. Instead of watching "Gilligan's Island" reruns, he practiced the alphabet, printing out page after page of characters, then progressing to short words. He copied countless sentences from magazines and tried to decipher the words syllable by syllable. I watched with amusement and a little pride, as he discovered the magic of language....

That was several years ago. Jackson has long since gone back to "the world" on parole. During two years "inside," he became an insatiable reader who kept a tattered paperback dictionary always within reach. Unlike most men who come to prison, he left a little better for the experience....

*Source:* Guy Marble, "Plea from a Prisoner," *Educational Leadership,* Vol. 50, No. 4 (December 1992/January 1993), pp. 61–62.

---

national level, a number of organizations have been active in promoting and improving the quality of basic education programs for inmates throughout the country.[48] In addition to regular classroom instruction, inmates today often have access to correspondence courses, in-cell study, and more recently, computer-assisted instruction which enables students to learn at their own pace. Some minimum-security facilities have even permitted selected inmates to attend regular classes offered in the community. In Canada, peer tutors are used to recruit and work with inmates in an effort to expand their involvement in literacy programs.[49] But however it occurs, the educational environment must be physically and emotionally safe in order to promote learning.

When the educational program is conducted within prison walls, it presents unique challenges in contrast to traditional education on the outside. For one thing, maintaining order in the classroom is essential (as discussed in Chapter 8). It will not be conducive to learning if inmates view classes as a break from normal discipline, where everyone is free to act without regard for the rules and regulations governing the rest of the institution.

Another issue relates to the quality and appropriateness of learning materials. As concerns over the alarming lack of literacy among the adult population in the United States have surfaced, improvements have been made in the textbooks associated with basic education. However, in light of limited correctional budgets, prisons are not always able to take advantage of the latest advances in reading materials. Using outdated books discarded by the public schools can present

---

[48]See Linda R. Acorn, "National Symposium on Partnerships Features Offender Literacy and Training Programs," *Corrections Today,* Vol. 53, No. 1 (February 1991), pp. 72–75.
[49]Karen Dvorak, "Literacy Program Report," *American Jails,* Vol. 6, No. 5 (November/December 1992), pp. 68–69.

Basic education classes are conducted to assist inmates with obtaining a GED and improving their employment opportunities. Courtesy of the Dade County Department of Corrections and Rehabilitation, Miami, Florida.

a considerable problem, since a grown man returning to his cell with a *Run, Jane, Run* textbook under his arm is certain to be ridiculed by other inmates.[50]

It is for such reasons that some institutions reserve separate cellblocks for those involved in various educational activities. Housing all inmates participating in a particular program together enables them to study together and mutually reinforce learning. In addition, it promotes security by minimizing the need for movement to and from classes. But wherever they are housed, it is essential to avoid labeling students in such classes as "stupid" or "illiterate." As was clearly demonstrated in the last close-up, illiteracy is a personal embarrassment that many inmates will attempt to conceal. For such reasons it has been found that those most in need of basic education are "in many cases, the least likely to apply for regular classroom placement."[51]

### Computer-Assisted Instruction

Schools in correctional institutions are also unlike those in free society in another respect—they do not have the capability of running on a regular, September-to-June calendar. Inmates arrive continuously throughout the year. Moreover, unlike the public schools, smaller facilities in particular do not have

---

[50]E. Eugene Miller, "Education at Bucks County Prison," *American Journal of Corrections*, Vol. 29, No. 2 (March/April 1967), pp. 22–25.
[51]Dvorak, p. 68.

the luxury of dividing classes by grade levels. But placing those at the ninth-grade level in classes with others functioning as low as third or fourth grade is hardly motivational.

Addressing the educational needs of inmates who function at varying grade levels was especially difficult prior to the introduction of *computer-assisted instruction* (CAI). With the programmed instruction available through CAI, however, many of the deficiencies in the academic offerings of correctional institutions can be eliminated.[52] CAI has been found to be successful "even for inmates who have failed in traditional attempts to learn to read and write."[53]

As a self-paced instructional tool, CAI enables each student to progress at his or her own rate. It also enables the institution to address widely varying educational levels without the need for separate classrooms for each grade. CAI presents material in short and easy steps, keeps the learner active by calling for responses based on previous steps, and provides immediate feedback of results. Moreover, it is considerably more prestigious to work on a computer than to be in a regular classroom setting. Another major benefit is reduced staffing, which is a significant factor, given the acute shortage of prison teachers everywhere. With CAI, fewer instructors can serve more students.

## College Education

Beyond basic remedial education, a number of correctional institutions have also introduced college coursework through cooperative arrangements with institutions of higher education. Emphasis on college education for inmates began with the federal funding of Project NewGate during the late 1960s, which, as the name implies, was designed to provide new avenues of opportunity for the disadvantaged.

Today, college education for inmates is offered primarily through *correspondence courses* or contracts with community colleges or universities to provide classes within the prison compound. Much less frequently, *study release* might be employed to enable a few selected inmates to attend classes on the campus of a local college or university. Some institutions have used a combination of approaches—for example, offering the first year or two of college coursework at the correctional facility and then busing upper division students to a local campus.[54] In this way, inmates can demonstrate that they have the academic ability, motivation, and discipline to pursue higher education before being entrusted to study release. But on-campus study is rarely provided for a number of reasons, ranging from the increasing costs of tuition to the difficulty of placing short-term offenders in a regularly scheduled semester, along with the security risks of allowing such freedom. Where advanced coursework is available, it is therefore more likely to be conducted within institutional walls.

[52]Frank P. Belcastro, "The Use of Programmed Instruction in Canadian Correctional Institutions," *The Canadian Journal of Corrections*, Vol. 11, No. 4 (October 1969), pp. 233–39.
[53]"High-Tech Tutors," p. 140.
[54]Kenneth L. Hardy and Harland Randolph, *Guidelines for the Administration and Implementation of the Federal City College Lorton Extension College* (Washington, DC: District of Columbia Department of Corrections and Federal City College, 1972).

Aside from the need to maintain order in the classroom and the disadvantage of a somewhat "unnatural" learning environment, there is one additional drawback to offering college classes inside the correctional facility itself. Making courses available to inmates can create resentment on the part of correctional officers or other staff who have a desire to pursue college education but are unable to do so because of shiftwork, insufficient funds, or whatever. An obvious solution is to provide equivalent educational opportunities at the institution for personnel as well as prisoners. That will not, however, overcome similar protests among taxpayers who resent providing inmates with the advantage of college study while they have to pay the costs of educating their children. This argument overlooks the costs of continuing to support recidivating offenders who might be prompted by a college education to make a change in their lifestyle. Nevertheless, it can be a strong deterrent to offering educational programs that go beyond what is available in public secondary schools.

### Library Services

Inmates pursuing advanced academic studies will obviously find it difficult to complete college coursework successfully without access to a library. Even those simply working on basic literacy or GED classes need materials to

The law library is an important component of any correctional institution in light of court rulings that inmates be provided with access to legal materials. Courtesy of the Michigan Department of Corrections.

encourage the development of reading habits. Library services are therefore closely related to and supportive of educational programs. Yet the importance of a library in correctional institutions has long been underestimated.

In the past, most prisons had a small library, stored in a vault to which inmates were not permitted access. Books could be ordered and delivered in two or three days. In contrast to these early beginnings, most modern correctional institutions now have services similar to a public library, where inmates can come, browse through the collections, and check out books.

But that does not mean that prison libraries are equivalent to those on the outside. As one correctional librarian has noted, "A traditional librarian would find the average correctional library very frustrating—an inadequate or non-existent card catalog, limited budget, mechanical breakdowns, high loss rate, high staff turnover, aging physical plants, and few creature comforts."[55] Just as in free society, there are those who fail to return books to prison libraries. However, some institutions have taken book theft off the list of offenses for disciplinary action in order to discourage destruction of the "evidence." Furthermore, regardless of how they have obtained the books, the primary objective is to encourage these nonreaders to begin reading.

Since correctional facilities have been required by the courts to provide inmates with access to legal materials, the law collection is an important part of the library. Not only does a law library comply with mandates that inmates not be restricted from access to the courts, it also may reduce the number of suits claiming denial of access to counsel. Some institutions even provide paralegal assistance with legal research and the typing of legal forms for writs.

While the long-term benefit of a correctional library may be "to rehabilitate or uplift," its more immediate purpose involves providing both a recreational and an educational outlet, along with legal support.[56] As such, the staff members of the library also occasionally assume informal counseling or social work roles. In a prison population "starved for diversion," even the smallest library program can become a "major event" in the lives of inmates.[57]

## Vocational Training

Work has been a central feature of prisons throughout the history of corrections—from the handicrafts assembled in the Walnut Street Jail, to the large prison industries of the nineteenth century, to the contract labor systems used throughout the South. While such employment may have instilled discipline, the demeaning work and dehumanizing manner in which inmates were often supervised on the job did more to degrade self-esteem than to develop skills. Moreover, the primary purpose was not to promote an inmate's potential, but rather, to produce an institutional profit. As a result, "during the first half of the twentieth century, the unregulated use of prison labor led to exploitation of pris-

[55]Barbara Gordon, "Correctional Librarians: Providing Services by the Book," *Corrections Today*, Vol. 51, No. 7 (December 1989), p. 64.
[56]Ibid., p. 62.
[57]Ibid., p. 64.

oners and unfair competition with free-world labor."[58] Although the modern goals of correctional institutions do not involve becoming self-sufficient, there is a useful place for employment in "any well-rounded program directed toward the needs of those confined."[59]

But correctional administrators, work supervisors, and inmates often have conflicting views of what *vocational training programs* are designed to accomplish.[60] Depending upon one's perspective, such activities can be seen as a method of providing meaningful work, teaching skills and work habits, preparing for a trade on the outside, earning wages, overcoming idleness, or simply generating revenue. (See Figure 9.2 for a look at the differences between the perspectives of inmates, the correctional institution, and society in this regard.) Despite these differences, virtually everyone agrees that vocational training is a necessary and beneficial component of correctional institutions.

Today, most prisons and many jails have some type of industrial program. Along with academic education, it was the Elmira Reformatory which also first introduced the concept of developing job skills through vocational training. Since that origin in 1876, vocational training has expanded to include everything from auto mechanics to welding, printing, construction trades, woodworking, agriculture, data processing, key punching, bookkeeping, and cosmetology. The next "Close-up on Corrections" takes a look inside a vocational training classroom, and provides a view of one inmate's enthusiasm for the program.

Some institutions, however, simply define any type of work as "vocational training" or provide a very limited range of opportunities that generally reflect the types of training most convenient or economical to offer. But facilities which take this mission seriously do not disguise routine maintenance work as preparation for a trade. To the contrary, they offer a wide variety of skills-based pro-

| Offender-based | Institution-oriented | Societal |
|---|---|---|
| Good work habits | Reducing idleness | Repayment to society |
| Real work experience | Structuring daily activities | Dependent support |
| Vocational training | Reducing the net cost of corrections | Victim restitution |
| Life management experience | | |
| Gate money | | |

**Figure 9.2**  Goals of prison labor. *Source:* Randall Guynes and Robert C. Greiser, "Contemporary Prison Industry Goals," in *A Study of Prison Industry: History, Components, Goals* (College Park, MD: American Correctional Association, 1986), p. 21.

[58]Barbara J. Auerback, George E. Sexton, Franklin C. Farrow, and Robert H. Lawson, *Work in American Prisons: The Private Sector Gets Involved* (Washington, DC: U.S. Department of Justice, 1988), p. 9.

[59]Timothy J. Flanagan, "Prison Labor and Industry," in Goodstein and MacKenzie, p. 135, quoting F. Flynn.

[60]See *Public Policy for Corrections: A Handbook for Decision-Makers* (College Park, MD: American Correctional Association, 1986), pp. 74 and 78, where it is noted that "a major issue facing prison industry is a determination of its mission."

### The ABC's of Second Chances

Inside [the] cosmetology classroom, women . . . straighten hair, pluck eyebrows, and apply perm solution. And for a few hours, they can almost forget they are inmates. . . .

"I'm glad this facility is here—and this school," said inmate Dawn G. . . . while plucking a fellow inmate's eyebrows. "If ever I'm going to learn something, it will be in here, because it was certainly not out there on the streets." . . .

[Inmates are offered] the opportunity to learn a trade, brush up on basic skills, and earn the equivalent of a high school diploma. . . .

"I always tell them, `Every jail has a silver lining,'" said Brenda Mason, who teaches typing, computer skills and word processing to female inmates. . . . [O]n the walls of Mason's classroom are the words: "Type your way out." . . .

At the Training and Treatment Center . . . [t]here's a waiting list for all the classes—auto paint and body shop, auto repair, welding, air conditioning and refrigeration, cabinet-making and adult education. . . .

In the 14 years Sam Avick has been teaching cabinet-making . . . he has only seen four or five of his students return to the jail. . . . "We save the county a lot of money. And we supply the outside world with qualified people." . . .

After seven months of serving time . . . and four months of cosmetology training, Dawn G. is determined to enroll in a beauty academy when she gets out. . . . And she plans to enroll in a drug support group. . . . "I'm glad I came here," [she] said. "If I had stayed on the street, I would have ended up dead."

*Source:* Luchina Fisher, "The ABCs of Second Chances," *The Miami Herald* (September 14, 1989), pp. 14–16.

grams and make an effort to match training with trades that are marketable in the state or local area. As one manager in the private sector observed: "Let's face it: We can get robots to press license plates. Let's give prisoners meaningful, progressive jobs—jobs with a future."[61]

Obviously, it is of limited benefit for an inmate to become proficient in a job for which there is minimal demand on the outside, or one that involves occupational licensing based on good moral character which essentially restricts ex-offenders (discussed further in Chapter 11). When properly implemented, research indicates that job training and work experience can reduce prison misconduct, increase post-release employment, and lower recidivism.[62]

[61]Duffy, p. 45. See also Howard L. Skolnik and John Slansky, "Prison Industries: A First Step in Helping Inmates Get Good Jobs after Release," *Corrections Today*, Vol. 53, No. 5 (August 1991), pp. 92–94.

[62]William G. Saylor and Gerald G. Gaes, "The Post-release Employment Project," *Federal Prisons Journal*, Vol. 2, No. 4 (Winter 1992), p. 33.

Even where there is considerable program variety, a major deficiency of vocational training today is the inability to accommodate everyone desiring to participate. In most institutions, there are not enough teaching personnel or productive work of any kind to occupy the population to its fullest extent. This dilemma can result in placing more inmates on a work site than are necessary to do the job, thereby not only detracting from the quality of training but also creating conditions that are unrealistic in the environment of the "real" work world.

## Private-Sector Involvement

A promising response to the lack of readily available vocational training is the expanding private-sector involvement in prison industries. Initiated in the early 1970s with the Free Venture project developed by the Law Enforcement Assistance Administration, the trend began toward developing prison industries that are managed by the private sector and closely reflect the conditions of work in outside employment. In addition to removing certain restrictions on the sale of prison-made products, federal legislation in 1979 authorized the establishment of Prison Industry Enhancement pilot projects, which provided the seeds for *private involvement* in prison industries. As is evident in Figure 9.3, by 1988, private-sector prison industries had expanded widely throughout the country, and even more states are participating today.

Such partnerships between public prisons and private enterprises are not, however, problem-free. The challenges of recruiting private industries into prisons and determining salaries and benefits for inmate employees remain major issues. "Most private business people think of prisons, when they think of them at all, as extremely violent and unpleasant places in which an inflexible bureaucracy prevents any kind of normal activity."[63] Thus, it is necessary for administrators to convince the private sector of the merits of correctional industries and perhaps even provide incentives to attract their business into the facility.

Among the "incentives" that generate considerable controversy are inmate wages. Attracting industries into prisons would undoubtedly be facilitated by the payment of lower salaries, and "given the additional costs of doing business in prison . . . some private-sector firms are eager to pare wages as much as possible."[64] But others argue that only union or prevailing wages will protect the free market from the unfair competition of prison-made products.

Furthermore, not all correctional administrators are equally convinced of the merits of prison industries. For example, such accepted practices of the private sector as collective bargaining can conflict with "deeply-rooted correctional management traditions." In other words, "the goals of private enterprise and of running an efficient and safe prison are by no means complementary."[65] These are among the issues that remain to be resolved. But in the

[63]Auerback et al., pp. 15–16.
[64]Ibid., p. 14.
[65]Flanagan, p. 153.

| Active venture | Authority but no plans | Silent or unclear |
| Advanced plans | Statutory prohibition | |

**Figure 9.3** States with private-sector prison industries. *Source:* Barbara Auerback, George E. Sexton, Franklin C. Farrow, and Robert H. Lawson, *Work in American Prisons: The Private Sector Gets Involved* (Washington, DC: U.S. Department of Justice, 1988), p. 12.

meantime, private-sector involvement offers significant potential for expanding the limited opportunities that have characterized vocational training in corrections to date.

## Recreation

Everyone cannot participate in vocational training. Virtually all inmates, however, are entitled to some form of recreation. Even in maximum-security institutions, inmates are afforded recreational privileges, although they may be restricted to an hour of solitary workout under the close supervision of correctional staff.

In lower-security facilities, recreational pursuits generally involve either individual or programmed group athletics. Many correctional institutions have athletic teams in football, basketball, and baseball that play outside teams. But there has been some concern expressed that correctional recreation should not be limited to "high pressure competitive sports . . . designed for the few participants who were fortunate enough to have been gifted with the skills to make the

Football is a popular recreational sport in many correctional institutions. Courtesy of Anthony W. Zumpetta.

teams."[66] A broader view of recreational programming includes everything from arts and crafts to music, drama, table games, hobbies, television, and movies.[67]

The individual sport that has been the most popular in prison is boxing. In fact, some of the leading contenders in this sport have learned their skills in prison or juvenile training school. One of the reasons for inmates' enthusiasm for boxing is that it is an individual activity rather than a team sport, which appeals to those who do not relate well to others.

Regardless of the specific type of activity employed, meaningful recreation may well be one of the most rewarding programs in correctional facilities. In addition to providing worthwhile use of leisure time, recreation can help to alleviate the stress and anxiety of incarceration. Fitness programs in particular can enhance the inmate's self-image and provide a means of coping with confinement.[68] Moreover, people do not get into trouble while busily occupied and working off excess energy. Trouble almost always starts during the boredom caused by too much leisure time.

[66]Darwin E. Clay, "Physical Education and Recreation in Correctional Treatment," in Hippchen, p. 214.
[67]See *Correctional Officer Resource Guide* (Laurel, MD: American Correctional Association, 1989), pp. 112–14.
[68]Michael Jones, "Health and Fitness: Exercise Programs for Inmates Promote Positive Change," *Corrections Today*, Vol. 51, No. 7 (December 1989), p. 96.

LEARNING GOALS

*Do you know:*

- *To what extent correctional treatment was available under the medical model?*
- *Whether inmates have a constitutional right to treatment?*
- *The most commonly available form of treatment in correctional facilities?*
- *The advantages of family therapy and self-help groups?*
- *What sensitivity training, psychodrama, contingency contracting, and therapeutic communities are?*
- *How behavior modification has been misused?*
- *How reality therapy differs from traditional therapeutic techniques?*
- *Why social casework is more frequently used in community-based corrections than institutional settings?*

## ❖ COUNSELING, CASEWORK, AND CLINICAL SERVICES

Everyone would not necessarily agree that religious services, educational programs, libraries, vocational training, or recreation meet a strict definition of "treatment."[69] But there is little doubt that counseling, casework, and clinical services represent traditional long-term approaches to offender rehabilitation. Some 25 years ago, during the height of the medical model, the American Correctional Association acknowledged the prominence of such approaches in the treatment process: "[T]here has been increasing recognition that a major function of a correctional agency is to influence change in the attitude and behavior of the offender. The disciplines of psychiatry, psychology, and social casework have provided corrections with tools which are useful in stimulating [that] change."[70]

Although the mission of corrections has undergone substantial redefinition since then, one might assume that treatment services were generally available in prisons under the medical model. That, however, has not been the case.

### Treatment Availability

Psychological counseling, social casework, and psychiatric therapy have never existed in the bulk of correctional institutions. A survey of state and federal

---

[69]For example, Stan Stojkovic and Rick Lovell, *Corrections: An Introduction* (Cincinnati, OH: Anderson Publishing Company, 1992), pp. 216–24, note that "treatment for correctional clients is not a clear or concise concept," and divide programs into two major categories: "inmate activities" (e.g., recreation, religion, self-help) and "rehabilitation programs," (the primary objective of which is to "alter the post-release behavior of the offender . . . ").

[70]*Manual of Correctional Standards,* Third Edition (Washington, DC: American Correctional Association, 1969), p. 17.

prisons conducted in the mid-1950s,[71] for example, found that the vast majority of staff held jobs related to the security needed to keep prisoners *in*, with less than 8% classified as people who were "there to get them ready to go out and stay out," (and even many of these were clerical positions). At that time, there were only 23 full-time psychiatrists in U.S. correctional institutions—a number that would provide an average of 82 seconds of psychiatric help each month per inmate (assuming equal distribution throughout the country). The psychological staff numbered 67—able to provide about 4 minutes monthly for individual attention. The 257 caseworkers averaged less than 16 minutes per inmate each month.

By the mid-1960s, the percentage of treatment personnel had increased. But it was still estimated that more than 20,000 additional specialists were needed to address the "drastic scarcity" of treatment staff.[72] During a time that represented the peak years of the medical model, these figures do not say much for practical as opposed to ideological commitment to rehabilitation. In fact, most correctional administrators responding to a national survey in 1975 maintained that treatment programs had never really been tried, because they had not been adequately funded.[73] Others have observed that "it is not uncommon for an institution that houses a thousand or more inmates to define itself as being committed to rehabilitation when there is no full-time staff member who holds an advanced degree in any of the helping professions, or, when there are full-time and more or less adequately qualified staff members, to find that the ratio of inmates to qualified treatment staff is a hundred or more to one."[74]

Additionally, it is pertinent to note that during this period of time, treatment represented an "invasion" of what had previously been a custody-dominated system. Those in the custodial ranks tended to view treatment personnel with varying degrees of skepticism, mistrust, or at best, grudging tolerance. Mere acceptance was still a long way off, let alone the establishment of a mutual custody–treatment partnership. For all of these and many other reasons, it would appear that the medical model focused more on rhetoric than rehabilitation.

Undoubtedly, staffing over recent years has increased well beyond 23 psychiatrists, 67 psychologists, and 257 caseworkers—but then so has the inmate population. It is a far cry from the mere 17,280 inmates counted in the mid-1950s to the record high of 823,414[75] confined in 1990. Moreover, as Figure 9.4 illustrates, custodial/security employees still far outnumber educational or professional/technical personnel.

Perhaps even more revealing are the data reporting that in the area of drug treatment alone, some 15,000 inmates were on waiting lists during 1990 in state prisons throughout the country.[76] Yet drug rehabilitation is presumably a high

[71]Alfred C. Schnur, "The New Penology: Fact or Fiction?" *Journal of Criminal Law, Criminology and Police Science*, Vol. 49 (November/December 1958), pp. 331–34.

[72]President's Commission on Law Enforcement and Administration of Justice, p. 97.

[73]Michael S. Serrill, "Is Rehabilitation Dead?" *Corrections Magazine*, Vol. 1, No. 5 (May/June 1975), pp. 3–7, 10–12, 21–32.

[74]Charles W. Thomas and David M. Petersen, *Prison Organization and Inmate Subcultures* (Indianapolis, IN: Bobbs-Merrill, 1977), p. 36.

[75]Tracy L. Snell, "Prisoners in 1991," *Bureau of Justice Statistics: Bulletin* (Washington, DC: U.S. Department of Justice, 1992), p. l.

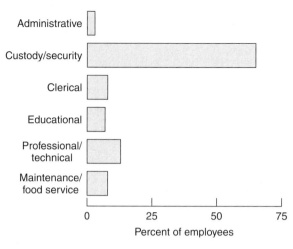

**Figure 9.4** Employees in state and federal correctional facilities. *Source:* James Stephan, *Census of State and Federal Correctional Facilities, 1990* (Washington, DC: U.S. Department of Justice, 1992), cover page.

Administrative

Custody/security

Clerical

Educational

Professional/ technical

Maintenance/ food service

0    25    50    75

Percent of employees

public priority. These data suggest that in terms of "treatment" within correctional institutions, there may actually be very little to discuss. Overall, there has not been enough treatment to counter the negative effects of institutional living or the stigma of being labeled an "offender," much less to go forward with constructive change.

Even where treatment services are provided, patterns vary widely in terms of the number of personnel available and the manner in which their expertise is used. As mentioned earlier, many of these professionals work in the classification unit, where they are *processing* prisoners rather than *counseling* them. Once routine procedures are completed—such as social histories, admission summaries, chronological files, preparole progress reports, and the like—very little time remains for individual attention.

Nor have the courts recognized a universal right to treatment among all correctional clients. As we will see in Chapter 15, constitutional issues have been raised concerning due process, equal protection, and cruel and unusual punishment. Although some initial recognition was given to the right to treatment on statutory grounds,[77] thus far, the absence of universal treatment has not been regarded as cruel and unusual punishment in violation of the Eighth Amendment. The Supreme Court has held that correctional administrators cannot maintain an attitude of "deliberate indifference" to the serious mental, physical, or emotional illness of offenders. But treatment may be limited to those with an identified medical necessity, as well as to procedures that can be provided within reasonable time and costs.[78] In a more recent case, the courts rejected a sex offender's argument that the failure of prison officials to provide a therapeutic

[76]Compiled from *Sourcebook—1991* (Washington, DC: U.S. Department of Justice, 1992), pp. 662–65.
[77]*Rouse v. Cameron,* 373 F.23 451 (1966).
[78]*Estelle v. Gamble,* 97 S. Ct. 285 (1976). In this case, an inmate sued on the grounds that he was denied parole because of a psychological evaluation indicating that he would not complete the parole period successfully, yet the institution had not offered psychiatric services to deal with his problems.

program tailored to his needs constituted cruel and unusual punishment.[79] In short, legal opinion to date has not supported an inherent Constitutional right of inmates to treatment.

On the other hand, it must also be acknowledged that many inmates do not actively seek treatment with any great deal of enthusiasm. They may well procrastinate even in the face of very clear expectations about the types of programs they must participate in to earn various privileges (such as parole, work release opportunities, a lower security classification, etc.). Then, when it becomes apparent that entering a specified program is the only avenue to achieve these objectives, it may be difficult to be accommodated. Under such circumstances, packed "therapy sessions" are more likely to provide attendance certification than an avenue for meaningful change. In essence, treatment means change, and change is contrary to a criminal's established way of life. To abandon one's psychological and economic investment in crime requires a commitment that few may be willing to make.

### Counseling

Counseling represents the one type of treatment that has most commonly been available in correctional facilities. In fact, generally speaking, counseling could be considered an approach used by almost everyone in the correctional setting. As a result, the word *counseling* can be a very misleading term when used within institutions. In the outside world, counselors are considered to be those with appropriate academic credentials and a license to practice, who address a client's problems through such professionally recognized practices as individual or group therapy. In corrections, however, the term can take on a much broader meaning: "[T]he term `counselor' in corrections may or may not refer to a person with formal educational preparation in counseling. The term has been used to refer to nonprofessional staff and to untrained volunteers. . . . "[80]

The title "correctional counselor" within a facility might be attributed to anyone from professionally licensed clinical practitioners to unlicensed civilian personnel who handle inmate requests for commissary items, passes, medical attention, and so on. This does not mean that there are not uncertified personnel who can and do perform generic counseling functions. Correctional officers, for example, probably conduct more "cellblock counseling" than any other staff members, since they are readily accessible to the inmates and are with them for more extended periods of time than the official treatment personnel. Moreover, the greater the compatibility between officers and inmates in terms of such factors as ethnicity, race, or social class, the more likely they are to establish the rapport essential to the counseling function.

In that respect, it is noteworthy that counseling is the establishment of a relationship between the counselor and client in an effort to understand and

---

[79]Daniel Pollak, "Legal Briefs: *Bailey v. Gardebring*, U.S. Court of Appeals, 8th Circuit, 1991," *Corrections Today*, Vol. 54, No. 2 (April 1991), pp. 26–28.

[80]*The National Manpower Survey of the Criminal Justice System, Vol. 3, Corrections* (Washington, DC: U.S. Department of Justice, 1978), p. 77.

help solve the client's problems through mutual consent, rather than by giving advice or admonition. Mutual understanding is therefore a basic ingredient in any counseling session. Because middle-class counselors with middle-class values may find it difficult to relate to the values of those from more diverse backgrounds, matching cases with appropriate therapists makes better use of professional personnel.

Problem solving through counseling in the correctional setting, however, is often confined to "facilitating inmates' adjustment to the institution, rather than to their more long-term adjustment to a normal . . . life on the outside."[81] This does not necessarily mean that counselors take an overly narrow view of their role. But the limited availabilty of trained counselors in correctional institutions can impose a system of prioritizing. And obviously, the difficulties associated with incarceration are the immediate concerns of the inmates.

Besides large caseloads, counselors face a number of additional challenges unique to the institutional setting. Correctional counselors must be able to cope with everything from lack of administrative support and a heavy volume of paperwork to the difficulty of maintaining confidentiality, the potential for being "conned" by manipulative clients, and the necessity to work with those who have been "coerced" into treatment—who "do not see anything wrong with themselves, have no desire to change, and seriously question whether the counselor really wants to help them."[82] Given these considerations, the effective correctional counselor is one who is both patient and persistent; skilled and streetwise; optimistic and realistic.

In addition to the personal talents of the individual counselor, the intervention method used to address client problems will have a substantial impact on the outcome. There are probably as many psychological approaches as there are psychologists. The key, of course, is identifying the appropriate one for the client's needs. If counseling methods could be generalized, they would probably fall into the four broad steps outlined in the next "Close-up on Corrections."

Of course, few people respond to only one specific treatment approach. The counselor must be sensitive enough to the person's problems and sufficiently flexible to shift from one approach to another as the client's needs demand. Changing behavior is less dependent on the system employed than the mutual awareness and responsiveness of those involved. There is, in fact, some opinion among professionals that the ability of the therapist to empathize is much more important than the specific method used. In essence, the function of the counselor comes down to providing the client with strength, understanding, and help in an effort to both recognize and resolve behavioral problems.

## Group Methods

Because individual counseling is conducted in one-on-one sessions between the client and therapist, it does not enable as many inmates to receive services as

[81]Michael Braswell, "The Purpose of Correctional Counseling" in David Lester, Michael Braswell, and Patricia Van Voorhis, *Correctional Counseling,* Second Edition (Cincinnati, OH: Anderson Publishing Company, 1992), p. 25.

[82]Jeffrey Schrink, "Understanding the Correctional Counselor," in Lester et al., pp. 48–53.

Steps in Psychological Counseling

1. The psychologist and the client explore the problem and the total social and psychological situation together, developing a common understanding.
2. A relationship is established, based on acceptance of the client that is neither judgmental nor condoning of criminal behavior.
3. The psychologist confronts the client with the reality of the person's situation to generate awareness and insights necessary for working through the problem—restructuring defenses or eliminating conflicts with social authority. Ideally, this leads the client to both self-acceptance and acceptance of society's expectations.
4. The most important step is successful termination of the relationship, through which the client is no longer dependent on the psychologist and can function effectively alone, without help.

It takes a long time to acccomplish these steps, which are considerably more complex than this abbreviated description may indicate. But successful termination is the most important aspect of the counseling relationship. With appropriate interpersonal relations skills and concerted effort, almost anyone can establish rapport. However, successful termination—bringing the client to the point of being able to function independently—requires exceptional skills.

group methods, where a number of clients can be handled simultaneously. The key difference between group and individual counseling is the presence of other clients during the intervention process.[83] In addition to being more economical and meeting the needs of a greater number of inmates, group techniques provide an opportunity for obtaining feedback and reinforcement from one's peers.

In its pure sense, *group therapy* is a treatment process in which a trained therapist (often a psychiatrist or clinical psychologist) works with small groups, guiding interaction, exploration of problems, and development of social skills through the establishment of supportive relationships within the group. While the "textbook" approach would limit group size to between 8 and 12 members, the number is about twice that in prisons. This is not only a result of resource limitations, but also involves pragmatic reasons. Some will inevitably miss group meetings either voluntarily or involuntarily (e.g., work conflicts, transfers, lock-downs, etc.), and larger numbers generate greater interaction.

[83]David Lester and Patricia Van Voorhis, "Group and Milieu Therapy," in Lester et al., p. 175.

Group techniques are more economical, enable a greater number of inmates to participate, and provide the opportunity to obtain feedback and reinforcement from peers. Courtesy of Daytop Village, Inc., New York City.

Group therapy, group counseling, guided group interaction, sensitivity training, and psychodrama are among the group-oriented techniques that were introduced into correctional institutions in the decades between the late 1940s and the mid-1960s. Group methods have become a widely used alternative in correctional settings, within both institutions and community-based services such as probation, parole, and halfway houses. By the early 1950s, California developed a unique approach to group counseling which involved the training of volunteer personnel to lead groups. Correctional officers, records clerks, and any other prison staff who were interested could participate. Following a four- to six-week training program, each employee became a group leader of inmates in counseling sessions, under the supervision of a professional psychiatrist, psychologist, or social worker. Aside from making group sessions more readily available throughout the institution, an unanticipated benefit of this approach was improved understanding of inmate behavior throughout the correctional system as well as within the personal lives of group leaders. In fact, the wives of participating male correctional officers indicated that their husbands were better fathers and more understanding of human behavior as a result of their experience with the group counseling sessions.

In more recent years, *guided group interaction* has been used, particularly in juvenile facilities, as a therapeutic technique. Guided by an official leader, groups undergo intensive interaction in an environment that is designed to enhance personal decision-making skills through group participation. Groups, for example, may be given the responsibility for deciding whether a group member will be granted a home furlough, how a group member who violates a rule will be punished, and the like.[84] The next "Close-up on Corrections" describes the developmental stages involved in guided group interaction.

There has also been a movement toward making the inmates themselves part of the group leadership process. The idea of using peer pressure to promote self-improvement was an outgrowth of guided group interaction programs during the 1960s as inmates began to provide the leadership to help individual members of the group explore avenues for change. Beyond the economy of this approach, a major benefit of group techniques is that they dilute the threat of authority which can hamper a one-to-one relationship—a threat that can be further diminished by the appropriate use of inmate group leaders.

On the other hand, inmates do not always accept their peers as authorities. It may also be dangerous to one's status among cellmates to be viewed as the leader of an institutionally sponsored program, which (as we will see in Chapter 10) represents a cardinal violation of the inmate code. As described in the "Close-up on Corrections" on page 361, facilities with a therapeutic community approach are likely to be more receptive environments for peer counseling.

### Self-Help Groups

Beyond merely leading groups initiated by the correctional administration, inmates have for many years been involved in *self-help groups* of their own cre-

---

❖ *CLOSE-UP ON CORRECTIONS*

Stages in Guided Group Interaction

- *STAGE 1.* New members gradually relax their defenses as they are encouraged by group members and the leader.
- *STAGE 2.* Residents share their life stories and problems, as they begin to trust the group.
- *STAGE 3.* Offenders frequently examine how they got in trouble and begin to discuss the problems of institutional and street living.
- *STAGE 4.* By the fourth stage, they may feel sufficiently secure to accept reeducation.
- *STAGE 5.* Participants set up their own plans for change. Guided by both their own and the group's evaluations, participants reach a conscious decision about their futures.

*Source:* Clemens Bartollas, *Correctional Treatment: Theory and Practice* (Englewood Cliffs, NJ: Prentice Hall, 1985), pp. 133–34.

---

[84]Clemens Bartollas, *Correctional Treatment: Theory and Practice* (Englewood Cliffs, NJ: Prentice Hall, 1985), p. 133.

Inmate and Ex-offender Involvement in Peer Counseling

For more than 10 years, the Arizona Department of Corrections has . . . provide[d] a counseling program . . . [which] isolates 86 inmates in a therapeutic community, where they work with staff and each other to improve their behavior, attitudes, and self-images. . . .

To be a peer counselor, an inmate must be in the program for a minimum of three months and be doing well in understanding his past criminal behavior and negative behavior patterns. He must also be free of disciplinary write-ups, must pass an exam on transactional analysis philosophy, scoring 90% or better, must be participating in a school or work program, and must have completed or be actively attending education skills group classes, substance abuse counseling or other recommended sessions.

Inmate peer counselors' duties include maintaining client information sheets . . . ; participating in the program rules committee, on treatment teams and group sessions; making recommendations to the unit coordinator concerning inmate behavior contracts; providing one-on-one counseling to other inmates . . . ; writing biweekly progress notes; attending a minimum of nine hours of group sessions; and meeting biweekly with the unit coordinator for supervision purposes.

The goals of the program are to provide inmates with social control, so they can adjust to confinement; to provide an environment in which neither staff nor inmates perceive one another as enemies; to teach inmates to change their negative lifestyles; to develop a community geared for learning; to train inmates to become teachers and counselors; and to help inmates become socially productive. . . .

There have been no independent studies that prove the program . . . guarantees a successful adjustment to society. It does, however, appear that inmates in the program are calmer, less angry, relate better to staff, receive fewer disciplinary reports, file fewer grievances, and are more involved in work and school programs than other inmates in the same institution.

*Source:* Roger W. Crish, "Therapeutic Community Helps Change Inmates for the Better at Rincon," *Corrections Today,* Vol. 53, No. 5 (August 1991), pp. 96–100.

ation. Both within and outside correctional institutions, prisoners and ex-offenders have become involved in such groups as Alcoholics Anonymous, Narcotics Anonymous, and Gamblers Anonymous. In addition to treatment-oriented groups, they have also participated in such social organizations as the Jaycees and various religious groups.

There are a number of advantages to self-help groups. For one thing, although an offender might be assigned to attend self-help sessions, many of those involved have recognized that they have a problem with which they need help. Whether the motivation to change is the result of external intervention or internal self-awareness, these groups involve positive peer pressure through association with other people undergoing similar problems. The person comes to realize that he or she is not alone in experiencing such difficulties, and that others can help in developing the inner strength necessary to overcome the problem. Moreover, they provide a vehicle through which the offender can learn responsibility, decision making, problem solving, and other life skills.

An additional major benefit of these groups is the fact that they operate both in prisons and within the outside community, and can therefore serve as a "bridge" back into the mainstream of life for newly released ex-offenders. For an inside account of how one inmate found help through an AA program at a maximum-security prison (as well as what happened when he relapsed), see the next "Close-up on Corrections."

### Sensitivity Training

Another group method that has periodically been used within correctional facilities is *sensitivity training*, also known as "T-groups" or "basic encounter groups."[85] This approach was originally designed to help people "learn how others perceive their behavior."[86] Sessions are unstructured, based on the assumption that meeting in an open climate—uninhibited by traditional roles and relationships— enables participants to learn a great deal about themselves in terms of how they are perceived by others. Participants discuss their views toward issues and problems as people, rather than from the perspective of any particular ascribed social role. In recent years, the term *sensitivity training* has become more loosely used to include a wide range of experiences in human relations that increase awareness— group dynamics, organizational development, and verbal/nonverbal experiences.

The T-group (training group) generally consists of from 10 to 16 people who meet in a residential setting away from their normal environment for approximately two weeks. The objective is to help people become aware of why both they and others behave as they do. Because such groups can create significant emotional experiences, the sessions verge on therapy, although T-groups can emphasize organizational as well as individual change. Participants have reported improvements in self-understanding, listening skills, and consideration of others.[87] Sensitivity groups involving staff and inmates have also been found to be a valuable resource, especially during times of stress.[88]

---

[85]Carl Rogers, "Client-Centered Therapy," in Silvano Arietti, ed., *American Handbook of Psychiatry*, Vol. 3 (New York: Basic Books, 1966), pp. 183–200.

[86]Paul Hersey and Ken Blanchard, *Management of Organizational Behavior: Utilizing Human Resources*, Fourth Edition (Englewood Cliffs, NJ: Prentice Hall, 1982), p. 129.

[87]John E. Wilkinson, Donald P. Mullen, and Robert B. Morton, "Sensitivity Training for Individual Growth—Team Training for Organizational Development?" *Training and Development Journal*, Vol. 22, No. 1 (1968), pp. 47–53.

[88]Jerrold Lee Shapiro and Robert R. Ross, "Sensitivity Training for Staff in an Institution for Adolescent Offenders: A Preliminary Evaluation," *American Journal of Correction*, Vol. 32, No. 4 (July/August 1970), pp. 14–19.

### Michael's Story

Trouble for me started early. At 12, I started using drugs. At 13, I was put into a county home. At 16, it was a DUI (Driving Under the Influence) and selling drugs. At 19, right up to today, I am in a maximum security prison for committing a violent crime. Alcohol and other drugs played a major part in all of this.

My first year in prison was spent waiting for drugs so I could stay high. Drugs were my security blanket. They were the only thing I could trust. No way did I want to feel guilty for the crimes I committed, or feel anything at all. I was just too damned afraid.

Pressure from others, fear, running away from what I was feeling—these things made me want to stay high. The drugs were the only friend I had. I was lost without them. I couldn't see what I was doing to myself—the hole I had dug. I needed help and I had to find it. . . .

When I finally decided to quit, it was tough. It was hard to part with the only thing that helped me exist inside these walls. . . . How or when it happened, I'm not sure, but I began to understand the AA program. It was a new thing for me to be accepted by others. And a new thing for me to be open and honest with others.

This program was the first thing in my life I ever started and finished. I was so proud of myself. I was on that "treatment cloud." But I soon found out that others were not on that same cloud. Feeling very alone, I began hiding in my cell. I sank deeper into thinking that no one cared, that I was better off high. So that's what I did. . . . I got high.

That was the last time I used drugs. An AA friend helped me back to an AA meeting. After using again, I thought I couldn't go back. I was wrong. The guys at the meeting greeted me with open arms. I had found a home! In the AA program, I didn't need to supply people with drugs to buy friendship. I could be me and be accepted. This was the real awakening for me. It helped me *want* to stay straight.

The Twelve Steps of AA . . . aren't easy, but I need them to stay straight. It was hard at first to believe they work. But then I started seeing the changes in my life.

I began to get in touch with a Higher Power, and I don't mean toting a Bible around. I began to have faith in something other than drugs. I was being "restored to sanity." In the past, it was easier for me to act crazy and make others responsible for my actions. But that old attitude only made *me* suffer.

It's been over two years inside these walls that I've stayed clean. I won't tell you that it's been easy. I will tell you that the single most important thing I can do to stay straight is go to my AA and NA meetings. . . . In this way, I help my recovery and others' at the same time. I carry the message of AA and have a life that I can be proud of.

*Source:* Marie Ragghianti and Toni Glenn, *Breaking Down the Walls: Steps to Freedom for Addicted Inmates* (Center City, MN: Hazelden, 1991), pp. 9–12.

Similar techniques are used in encounter groups, confrontation sessions, and marathon labs. These are generally shorter than sensitivity training but likewise involve direct exposure of beliefs and feelings that are not usually on public display. Within corrections, they can offer potential in terms of providing the basis for follow-up therapy, as well as developing an improved understanding of the correctional process among all participants. But at the same time, they require considerable expense and risk. For example, there are certain issues that may come out in the process of such groups that are better left unsaid within the prison environment. Sensitivity groups have a tendency to strip personal defenses from the participants, leaving them little on which to rely for psychological survival.

### Psychodrama Role-Playing

To a certain extent, *role-playing* is just the opposite of sensitivity training. Whereas sensitivity training requires that group members divest themselves of normal social roles, psychodrama uses role-playing to "act out feelings or behaviors."[89] Through the drama of participating in scenarios, specific roles can be enacted—that of parent, police officer, victim, inmate, warden, or the like. Within the safety of the group, participants can "try on" varying roles to determine how viewpoints differ when seen from these differing perspectives.

The basic idea underlying psychodrama is that behavior reflects one's reaction to other people as determined by the structure of their role. For example, some may view a police officer as a source of help, whereas others see the officer as a symbol of harassment. Thus, feelings of support or suspicion arise on the basis of how one views the role as opposed to the person. Such feelings can be modified as one becomes personally acquainted with the role, thereby producing new insights.

In the correctional setting, there are all sorts of possibilities for role-playing through psychodrama to help the client understand and better appreciate the role of correctional officers, parole agents, counselors, administrators, or even other inmates. Role-playing, for instance, has been used to prepare prisoners for parole by enacting roles that involve coming home to a stressful family situation, a difficult employer, or an unknown parole officer. The possibilities are limited only by the situations that can be replicated.

### Family Therapy

Effective techniques treat the "whole person"—not just emotional or behavioral problems, but also educational, vocational, and other needs as well. It therefore stands to reason that the inmate's family is also an integral part of the total treatment process. Moreover, as we will see in Chapter 12, incarceration places a tremendous strain on the offender's family relationships, which individual therapy may be insufficient to address.

*Family therapy* can include anything from marriage counseling to efforts directed toward improving parent–child relationships. In corrections, it generally refers to working with the family in an attempt to promote social adjustment and acceptance of a member who has been in trouble with the law. This type of thera-

[89]Bartollas, p. 127.

py is complex, and is often far from universally accepted by all participants. But it has greater potential than dealing with the client as an individual outside the family context. Particularly with juveniles, it is obvious that more can be done through such therapy than by working with the offender in isolation. With the counselor's guidance, understanding, and direction, the family can strengthen ties with the offender, and their constructive concern can be an effective therapeutic tool.

## Behavior Modification

Because prisons are closely controlled environments, they represent a setting that is adaptable to the use of *behavior modification*. This treatment technique is based on the assumptions that criminal behavior is learned, that it can be altered through a system of rewards and punishments, and that desirable change can occur within an institutional setting.[90]

As with family therapy, behavior modification has more often been used in juvenile facilities, through the implementation of a "token economy." In this system, tokens that can be used to purchase institutional privileges are awarded for good behavior and taken away for misconduct (as described in Chapter 3). One of the difficulties, of course, has been identifying effective reinforcers of approved behavior, since what may be motivating to one person may have little relevance to another. The process is also vulnerable to manipulation by inmates who quickly "learn the system" and superficially comply without altering deep-seated behavior. As one inmate put it, "you play the game and make them think you are programmed and get out."[91] Moreover, there is concern that even valid changes which do occur may be temporary features of the rigidly controlled environment of prisons rather than long-term behavioral improvements which carry over to the freedom of life on the outside.

In practice, some of the correctional procedures referred to as behavior modification have gone well beyond what was originally meant by the term. Examples of how techniques intended to modify behavior "turned into fiendish forms of punishment"[92] include the use of electroshock, aversive therapy, mind-altering drugs, and psychosurgery. In response to abuse of these techniques, litigation was generated by inmates as well as the Prison Project of the American Civil Liberties Union (ACLU). Such efforts have helped to eliminate many of these forms of "behavior modification" from prison systems.[93]

[90]Steven J. Zimberoff, "Behavior Modification with Delinquents," *Correctional Psychologist,* Vol. 3, No. 6 (September/October 1968), pp. 11–25.

[91]Peter Scharf, "Justice in the Prison: A Developmental Analysis," in Nicholas N. Kittrie and Jackwell Susman, eds., *Legality, Morality, and Ethics in Criminal Justice* (New York: Praeger Publishers, 1979), p. 252.

[92]Wayne Sage, "Crime and Clockwork Lemon," *Human Behavior,* Vol. 3, No. 9 (September 1974), pp. 16–25. See also "Behavior Modification Program Report Released by GAO," *Corrections Digest,* Vol. 6, No. 17 (August 30, 1975), pp. 1–2.

[93]By 1975, sufficient national attention was brought to behavior modification to promote a symposium on the topic. See "Symposium—The Control of Behavior: Legal, Scientific, and Moral Dilemmas, Part I," *Criminal Law Bulletin,* Vol. 2, No. 5 (September/October 1975), pp. 598–636. In addition, court cases have supported the right of an individual to freedom or privacy of the mind [*Stanley v. Georgia,* 394 U.S. 559 (1968)] and raised serious questions regarding "tinkering" with mental processes through the use of drugs [*Mackey v. Procunier,* 477 F. 2d 877 1973)].

Tranquillizing drugs, however, have continued to be used because of their sedative effect in controlling violent, angry, or unruly offenders—despite criticisms that they represent "an inconspicuous form of repression" that "disguises control as therapy."[94] It was only in 1990 that the Supreme Court determined in the *Washington v. Harper* case (110 S. Ct. 1028) that "a prison could not forcibly medicate a mentally ill person as punishment nor . . . forcibly medicate a mentally healthy inmate to achieve security objectives."[95]

The administration of drugs as a substitute for treatment has been one of the unfortunate by-products of an inadequate number of treatment personnel. But even when used more for the control of personality disorders than for managerial convenience, such medications do not specifically attempt to change criminal behavior.

### Cosmetic Surgery

While drug therapy, psychosurgery, and electroshock have been employed in the past without patient consent, *cosmetic surgery* is a more personally acceptable form of treatment which can produce modifying effects on behavior. When a child is born with a physical abnormality that goes uncorrected, it can be influ-

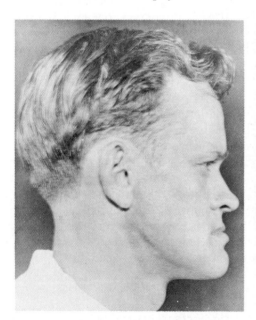 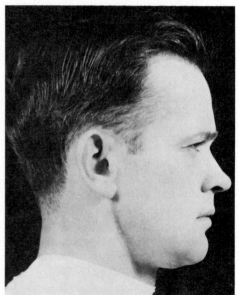

A simple operation setting back the jaw can dramatically change facial features, as seen in these pictures taken before and after the operation. Courtesy of the Michigan Department of Corrections.

[94]Richard Speiglman, "Prison Drugs, Psychiatry, and the State," in Greenberg, pp. 155, 163.
[95]Fred Cohen, "A Closer Look at Mentally Disordered Inmates and Forcible Medication," *Correctional Law Reporter*, Vol. 2, No. 2 (May 1990), p. 20. More recently, the Louisiana Supreme Court held in 1992 that "an incompetent inmate cannot be forced to take drugs that might make him sane enough to be executed." See "National News Briefs," *Corrections Today*, Vol. 54, No. 8 (December 1992), p. 16.

ential in creating a negative self-concept. Someone who has been ridiculed throughout life for being "different" can mature into an adult who has developed a pattern of acting-out against real and imaginary tormentors.

In such cases, behavioral controls can sometimes be promoted by correcting physical abnormalities—from straightening a nose, teeth, or crossed eyes to removing facial scars or body tattoos. Not everyone would agree that cosmetic surgery is an appropriate role for corrections. But to the extent that physical disfigurements contribute to antisocial behavior and lack of self-esteem, plastic surgery can be a productive addition to correctional treatment if supplemented by other social and rehabilitative services.

Given the escalating costs of such medical procedures today, however, their use is generally confined to physical conditions that are actually a threat to the inmate's health. In fact, some correctional systems have policies which prohibit treating any non-life-threatening condition experienced by the inmate prior to incarceration.

## Contingency Contracts

One type of behavior modification that is used less today for entirely different reasons than electroshock or psychosurgery is *contingency contracting* (also referred to as prescriptive treatment programs or MAPS—"mutual agreement programming"). In this approach, both the administration and the inmate sign a contract that calls for the administration to do certain things (such as provide work release or a parole recommendation) when the inmate completes his or her end of the bargain (such as abiding by rules and regulations, attending educational or training programs, etc.). Thus, a mutual agreement is reached concerning expectations on the part of the inmate and what, in turn, the administration agrees to do if these pre-established expectations are met.

Massachusetts, for example, uses a contracting system known as CAPA—Classification and Program Agreements. Through this agreement, the corrections department and the inmate agree to a gradual, prescheduled reduction of the inmate's custodial security level that is contingent on "positive adjustment," as well as participation in programs designated as needed by the inmate.[96] For a sample of the Massachusetts "Classification and Program Agreement," see Figure 9.5.

From an administrative perspective, contingency contracts promote positive behavior. To the inmate's advantage, they also clearly articulate expectations and release criteria. The danger, of course, is that performance may not meet requirements, which reduces effectiveness and increases resentment. Although early assessments were generally positive,[97] and some states still use various forms of contracting, the move away from discretionary parole under the justice model has reduced the usefulness of contracts in recent years.

---

[96]Michael W. Forcier, "The Massachusetts Department of Corrections Classification and Program Agreements System," in Wolford and Lawrenz, p. 39.

[97]Anne H. Rosenfeld, *An Evaluative Summary of Research: MAP Program Outcome in the Initial Demonstration States* (College Park, MD: American Correctional Association, 1975), p. 57.

FORM B

## CLASSIFICATION AND PROGRAM AGREEMENT

Placement _____  Security Level _____  Approximate Arrival Date _____

| Assessment Area | Program |
|---|---|
| Education | Adult Basic Education |
| Substance Abuse | Narcotics Anonymous |
| Financial | Print Shop |

Placement _____  Security Level _____  Approximate Arrival Date _____

| Assessment Area | Program |
|---|---|
| Education | Adult Basic Education (Pre-GED) |
| Substance Abuse | Psych. Services Substance Abuse Program |
| Vocational | Drafting Program |

Placement _____  Security Level _____  Approximate Arrival Date _____

All agreements will be automatically renegotiated upon placement in minimum custody for community programs.

I agree to participate in the programs as stipulated in the agreement. I understand that I will be transferred in accordance with the above schedule contingent upon positive agreement status. I have discussed all classification recommendations with staff.

_____  _____
Inmate Signature                                                                    Date

I have discussed the provisions of this agreement with _____

and believe they are mutual and understood _____

Board Chairperson

I am aware and agree to the above modifications of the agreement.

_____  _____
Inmate Signature                                                                    Date

**Figure 9.5** Classification and program agreement. *Source:* Michael W. Forcier, "The Massachusetts Department of Corrections Classification and Program Agreements System," in Bruce I. Wolford and Pam Lawrenz, eds., *Classification: Innovative Corrections Programs* (Richmond, KY: Department of Correctional Services, 1988), p. 50.

## Reality Therapy

If there is one area of correctional treatment that has been almost as controversial as behavior modification, it is *reality therapy.* Originally, reality therapy was developed by a psychiatrist who became disenchanted with traditional therapeutic techniques and created a system diametrically opposed to orthodox psychiatric approaches.[98] It takes the position that psychodiagnostic procedures and psychotherapy are used as excuses for deviant behavior. An example of this position is illustrated in the following statement: "Plausible as it may seem, we must never delude ourselves into wrongly concluding that unhappiness led to the patient's behavior, [in other words], the delinquent child broke the law because he was miserable, and that therefore our job is to make him happy."[99]

Reality therapy is based on getting involved with the client and encouraging the person to accept responsibility for his or her own actions. Some of the key words in reality therapy are therefore "responsibility," "involvement," "here and now," and "facing the consequences." Focus is on discussing the client's current situation as one of his or her "own choosing," while still making the person feel loved and worthwhile. The idea is that aggressively dealing with reality in a therapeutic frame of reference can communicate love (sometimes called "tough love") and generate self-respect through firm but caring steps.

One strength of reality therapy is that it can be understood by correctional officers, staff, and inmates not trained in therapeutic techniques. Particularly in juvenile institutions, it has also demonstrated success with helping young offenders "take a responsible attitude" toward handling their problems and getting back in control of their lives.[100] On the other hand, its weakness may lie in oversimplification of human behavior and failure to recognize that some types of mental illness may be worsened by expectations that are too demanding. Although reality therapy is successful for a fairly large group of correctional clients who can take such confrontation, it may well be too simplistic for more complex mental problems.

## Psychiatric and Psychoanalytic Treatment

Psychiatric involvement in corrections is generally limited to initial diagnosis, treatment prediction, and subsequent consultation with the psychologists, social workers, and other counselers who make up the bulk of institutional treatment staff. The relatively small number of psychiatrists working in the correctional field suggests that long-term *psychoanalytic techniques* designed to uncover deep-rooted causes of behavior have not frequently been employed in correctional settings. Within the criminal justice system, most psychiatrists function outside corrections in the pretrial and courtroom phases of the process—to

[98]See William Glasser, *Reality Therapy* (New York: Harper & Row, 1965).
[99]Ibid., p. 30.
[100]Alexander B. Smith and Louis Berlin, *Treating the Criminal Offender,* Second Edition (Englewood Cliffs, NJ: Prentice Hall, 1981), p. 69, citing studies conducted by Glasser.

determine whether defendants are of sufficient mental competence to be held legally responsible for their actions.

When an extremely disturbed inmate is in need of mental health services, referral is usually made to a psychiatric hospital for treatment. In fact, some correctional departments, in conjunction with the state mental health agency, maintain a separate forensic facility exclusively for the criminally insane. (For more details on how the mentally ill are handled, see Chapter 12.)

## Social Casework

Historically, the partnership between *social work* and corrections began early in the twentieth century, when private charities and reform groups were becoming increasingly involved in corrections. With the development of the concept of self-determination, social work became the art of "helping people help themselves."

Because of this emphasis on empowerment of the individual client, however, social workers have traditionally experienced difficulties with regard to working in the authoritarian setting of corrections. As a result, social casework is used more frequently in community-based corrections (particularly probation and parole), minimum security institutions, juvenile facilities, and diagnostic processing, as opposed to the direct delivery of services in high-security prisons.

Techniques used in social work include casework, group work, and community organization. The field is largely divided into two schools of thought concerning casework practice—one based on achieving effective client functioning and one based on Freudian diagnostic and therapeutic approaches. But generally, the emphasis is more on adjustment within one's environment than in-depth psychotherapy. As one social worker in juvenile corrections has observed, "My job is to zero in on what adolescence is all about, and to be a mediator with the adult world."[101]

Social work concepts include the idea that constructive use of authority is to withdraw services if the client does not remain eligible by circumstances or motivation. For example, a probationer who does not respond properly to supervision may be discharged as unamenable and subjected to incarceration if law violations continue. But while this approach may be compatible with community-based corrections, the lack of formal and informal authority of social workers in custodial institutions represents a significant limitation.[102]

## Nontraditional and Multiple Techniques

The psychoanalysis practiced by psychiatrists, the casework methods used by social workers, the group and individual therapy performed by psychologists, and the informal counseling conducted by many others all represent traditional approaches to working with people. Those who have become disenchant-

[101]Pete Hansen, "What Is a Social Worker?" *Perspective*, State of Washington Department of Institutions, Olympia, Vol. 13, No. 1 (Summer 1969), p. 12.
[102]See Bartollas, p. 218.

ed with these orthodox procedures have advocated such nontraditional concepts as reality therapy, transactional analysis, primal therapy, systematic desensitization, nondirective therapy—and more recently—even acupuncture, pet therapy, and transcendental meditation,[103] along with many others too numerous to mention. Generally, these new techniques have been directed toward a certain group representing a proportionally small segment of the total correctional caseload.

None of the traditional or nontraditional approaches works with everyone, but each seems to work with someone. Some offenders are reformed through psychiatric help; others because they learned a job skill, others because they found religion; and still others simply because someone took an interest in them. It is apparent that no single type of treatment is demonstrably superior to any other one. No single program or process represents the ideal solution for every client. Each has its unique strengths and weaknesses. Each works better with some offenders or at some point in their lives than others.

Although treatment personnel might like to draw from a broad array of techniques, the extensive training needed to become a professional in any one area creates a narrowly focused perspective. As a result, most identify with one or two approaches, neglecting the larger body of knowledge outside their professional discipline. Similarly, correctional institutions have historically adopted a narrowly limited range of techniques to offer everyone within their custody.[104] It should therefore be of little surprise that researchers have reported disappointing results in correctional treatment.

Some institutional settings have come to use a much wider variety of treatment alternatives that are not based on a single method.[105] An example of such a multifaceted approach is the prison that functions as an overall *therapeutic community*. As the next "Close-up on Corrections" describes, these "communities" are based on the concept that multiple treatment techniques, combined with a treatment-oriented custodial staff, can produce an institutional environment totally directed toward behavioral change.[106]

When correctional officers participate in and support a comprehensive treatment program, the entire team is going in the same direction—with the objectives known and accepted by all. An even more sophisticated therapeutic community is one in which groups of inmates meet daily in peer sessions to work through problems. In this manner, everyone works together toward providing a cohesive, supportive network.

---

[103]See, for example, Marcia Haynes, "Pet Therapy: Program Lifts Spirits, Reduces Violence in Institution's Mental Health Unit," *Corrections Today*, Vol. 53, No. 5 (August 1991), pp. 120–22, and Dana M. Murray, "Transcendental Meditation Can Offer Peaceful Road to Rehabilitation," *Corrections Today*, Vol. 53, No. 7 (December 1991), pp. 112–17.

[104]See Daniel Glaser, "Achieving Better Questions: A Half-Century Progress in Correctional Research," *Federal Probation*, Vol. 39 (1975), pp. 3–9.

[105]Bartollas, p. 281.

[106]The Atlantis Chemical Dependency Program located at the maximum-security prison in Stillwater, Minnesota, for example, is a 24-hour closed unit that stresses "therapeutic living with peer group confrontation and reinforcement," using "a multidisciplinary approach employing techniques from reality therapy, rational-emotive therapy, transactional analysis, behavior modification, Twelve Step concepts, and meditation." Ragghianti and Glenn, pp. 13–14.

### The Therapeutic Community

Therapeutic communities are predicated upon the . . . [basis] that the most effective therapy for the offender is one in which the institutional setting is an experiment in social living, so that by learning to adjust to life within the institution, the offender at the same time learns the necessary values, attitudes, and skills to lead a law-abiding life in free society. Within a therapeutic community, all aspects of the institution are coordinated to the single goal of rehabilitation.

Like prisons, therapeutic communities differ greatly in physical arrangements. Some are small units within larger custodial structures. Others are small, single units, often former residences. However, the full implementation of the concept, of which there are a few examples, involves the establishment of an actual community composed of perhaps 200 residents and a sizable complement of staff. In keeping with the concept of community, the physical arrangement deemphasizes custody. There are no walls or bars, although a fence may surround the facility. . . . The community center is likely to be modeled after a town square—with administrative offices, a school, a vocational training facility, a chapel, a recreation building, and perhaps quarters for visitors. Arranged around the square in a manner to simulate neighborhoods are the cottages for residents. Each cottage is likely to house some 15 to 20 residents in private rooms and to contain a kitchen and dining area.

In comparison to prisons, therapeutic communities are non-bureaucratic. There is a minimum of clearly defined rules, and decision-making is decentralized to facilitate the goal of individualized treatment. The staff are either trained professionals or lay personnel who receive extensive and continuous training in treatment skills, and both groups are expected to be guided by standards of professional expertise in the performance of their functions. . . . In their relations with clients, the staff is expected to minimize status distinctions, to encourage open and spontaneous communication, and to develop close, personal relations in an effort to gain client cooperation and identification with the staff and the goals of the institution. . . . Misconduct by clients is interpreted as symptomatic of an underlying problem, and any punishment is consistent with therapeutic recommendations. Punishment is thus minimized and highly individualized.

The client is expected to develop a life as similar as possible to life in the free community through involvement in the work, educational, religious, and recreational programs provided. Consistent with this orientation to life after release, clients are encouraged to maintain contact with the external world through the mass media and through extensive visits and mail from family and friends. . . . Relations within residential units are expected to resemble family relations. Group therapy sessions are conducted within the residential unit, perhaps on a daily basis. Further, each cottage is largely a self-governing unit, and administrative and maintenance problems are resolved by means of group decisions.

*Source:* Leo Carroll, *Hacks, Blacks, and Cons: Race Relations in a Maximum Security Prison* (Lexington, MA: D.C. Heath, 1974), pp. 217–18.

But with the change from the treatment orientation of the medical model to the incapacitation focus of the justice model, the enthusiasm for prison-based therapeutic communities has diminished. Rehabilitation overall has been deemphasized. Additionally, the movement toward purely voluntary treatment is somewhat inconsistent with the intent of an environment in which the total commitment is toward behavioral change. What the future holds for such rehabilitative efforts remains to be seen. But it is clear that if insufficient resources were available to implement the mandates of the medical model, it is not very realistic to expect more during times of greater fiscal restraint and political conservatism.

Even in terms of a less comprehensive approach to treatment, limited resources and lessened enthusiasm are not the only drawbacks. Prison-based rehabilitative programs are inherently difficult to manage and administer, regardless of the specific modality, qualifications of staff, or sincerity of participants. Moreover, transferring treatment progress to the real world from the artificial environment of a correctional institution represents a significant challenge. In that respect, perhaps "society has asked too much of the handful of idealists working in prison under the general job classification of `treatment.'"[107]

## ❖ SUMMARY

Some would maintain that correctional treatment is limited to therapeutic intervention by licensed professionals following a detailed clinical diagnosis. In contrast, this chapter has reflected a broader perspective encompassing many of the programs and services provided within correctional facilities that promote socializing influences among the inmate population.

Whatever one's perspective of treatment, within corrections, the process begins with initial classification. Through proper classification, the institution is better able to manage large groups of offenders, meet individual requirements, prioritize needs, and distribute scarce resources. We have seen how the emphasis of classification has changed over time from segregation to diagnosis/planning, treatment, and security/custody.

In a number of states, classification is the function of a central reception and diagnostic center—where inmates are interviewed, tested, examined, and evaluated. However, decisions made by classification committees have been criticized as subjective and overly routinized. Prison crowding also can prohibit placing inmates in those facilities and programs best suited to their needs. Nevertheless, classification outcomes have a long-term impact on the offender.

Classification was originally handled by large groups of staff members (preprofessional stage). Later, professional staff were added to prepare a social history report upon which to make more informed decisions (traditional stage). With the greater integration of classification decisions into the total prison program, the process was reduced to a three-person professional classification committee. Team treatment and functional unit management followed, to further integrate

[107]Personal correspondence from Dr. Anthony Zumpetta, West Chester (Pennsylvania) University, October 20, 1992.

classification as well as subsequent service delivery into the institutional environment. Most recently, objective prediction models have been employed which streamline classification by standardized decision making. But concerns have been expressed that such a highly structured process dehumanizes classification, substituting administrative efficiency for an in-depth assessment of needs.

However the inmate is classified, religious services represent one form of treatment to which everyone is entitled. Beginning with the Quakers, religion has always played a key role in corrections. Although chaplains are not always fully accepted by either inmates or staff, they can be very influential. Beyond providing worship services and religious studies, one of the most significant roles of the chaplain is simply being a willing listener.

Following religion, education and vocational training were the next major rehabilitative programs to be introduced into correctional institutions. Because so many inmates have not completed high school or are functionally illiterate, correctional clients are especially in need of remedial education. In recent years, computer-assisted instruction has been helpful in this respect, since it enables classes to be provided on an ongoing basis, tailors learning to the person's capability, and progresses at the student's own pace. Some institutions even offer the opportunity to attend college classes, either within the prison or through correspondence courses or study release. Library services are essential to support such educational programs, as well as to provide a recreational outlet and meet requirements for access to legal materials.

Work has been a central feature of prisons throughout the history of corrections. But it has only been in relatively modern times that employment and vocational training have been directed toward developing marketable job skills rather than making financial profits. Although wide varieties of vocational programs are available throughout corrections today, they are still insufficient to meet the demand. Efforts have been under way to encourage the private sector to become involved in establishing prison and jail industries.

While such vocational opportunities are limited, virtually all inmates have access to recreation—which encompasses everything from team sports to boxing, arts and crafts, music, drama, table games, hobbies, television, and movies. An organized recreation program not only relieves boredom and idleness, but can also help to reduce the stress and anxiety of incarceration.

The more traditional forms of treatment provided in corrections include counseling, casework, and clinical services. Even during the height of the medical model, such programs have not been readily available, and many treatment personnel find themselves more immersed in routine processing than direct service delivery. Of all forms of treatment, counseling represents that which is most commonly available (although the term *counseling* has sometimes been interpreted very broadly in the correctional setting). In contrast to one-on-one counseling sessions, group therapy can serve more clients in a less threatening atmosphere. Guided group interaction, sensitivity training, psychodrama, and family therapy are among the group-oriented techniques that have been employed in corrections. Inmates themselves have been utilized effectively as group leaders, and have also formed self-help groups such as Alcoholics Anonymous and Narcotics Anonymous.

Another form of treatment, behavior modification, was originally designed to change behavior through the conditioning power of rewards and punishments. However, efforts to modify behavior have at times extended to such techniques as psychosurgery, electroshock, aversive therapy, and mind-altering drugs. Although many of these practices have been terminated as a result of legal intervention, tranquilizing drugs are still used in some settings to control violent, angry, or disruptive inmates.

Numerous additional techniques have been attempted at one time or another—ranging from cosmetic surgery, to contingency contracting, to reality therapy. However, long-term psychoanalysis has not been frequently employed in corrections, although institutions can make referrals to psychiatric hospitals for severely disturbed inmates. Similarly, social work has not been a part of the treatment program of many correctional institutions, in part because its focus on self-determination and individual empowerment can conflict with an authoritarian setting. Social casework has, however, been used much more extensively in juvenile facilites and community-based corrections.

Historically, correctional institutions have offered a very limited range of treatment techniques, despite the fact that no one alternative will work equally well with all inmates. In an effort to provide a multifaceted approach that incorporates programs representing a number of disciplines, therapeutic communities direct the total institutional environment toward behavioral change. A broader array of treatment alternatives certainly presents greater potential for meeting the needs of any particular person. But with society's move from the medical model to the more punitive justice model, issues surrounding how best to diagnose, treat, and change behavior are no longer prominent concerns.

# chapter 10

# The Effects
# of Institutional Life

*Day to day, life for any man locked up can be overwhelming. It is generally boring, lonely, and keenly frustrating, as he is deprived of most of his social identity and personal worth. . . . Days seem to devour each other, or run by as if under water. The inmate, segregated from a society that he is simultaneously a part of, exists in a kind of regimented tribal commune with its own rules, hierarchies, and inbred morality. To survive both mentally and emotionally in a prison, one must learn to fear the past more than the future.[1]*

*Anonymous Inmate (confined in a maximum security prison)*

## ❖ CHAPTER OVERVIEW

The effects of being incarcerated are difficult for those in free society to fully appreciate. They range from the simple irritation of being required to eat the same monotonous food at precisely the same time day after day to the serious impact of being restricted from normal social relationships. They include the dehumanizing influence of everything from being subjected to strip searches to losing material possessions, personal privacy, and individual autonomy. They are the product of an environment in which inmates are secluded from the outside, subservient to the staff, subdued by the rules, subjected to the control of other inmates, socialized into the prison subculture, and silenced by the lack of public concern.

Under such conditions, hopelessness, frustration, and alienation find fertile breeding grounds. A few accept their plight as a consequence of their actions. Many either rationalize the situation as a product of circumstances over which they had no control or project blame on their family, friends, lawyers, or the system in general. Some express their feelings in passive resignation; others in physical rebellion. Assaults, homicides, and suicides occur in virtually every correctional institution. Although considerably less frequent, riots represent the ultimate expression of built-up hostilities. The public is inevitably shocked when

---

[1]Cited in Michael Braswell, Tyler Fletcher, and Larry Miller, *Human Relations and Corrections,* Third Edition (Prospect Heights, IL: Waveland Press, 1990), pp. 63–64.

violence flares into a widespread riot. But it is perhaps more surprising that such major disturbances are relatively unusual events.

Just as all inmates do not participate in institutional riots, everyone is not equally affected by the negative impact of incarceration. Those who are older, serving shorter sentences, and more emotionally secure will be more insulated. But relatively few are successfully able to avoid the long-term effects of imprisonment. Some would argue that achieving a long-term impact is exactly what corrections is supposed to accomplish—so that the offender might think twice before reengaging in criminal activities. However, their images of a newfound respect for authority, greater self-control, and resolve to remain law-abiding often conflict with reality. More likely, the result of lengthy confinement is a deep sense of frustration, isolation, and embitterment—hardly feelings that are conducive to effective reintegration into society. "An incarcerated offender is, at best, a financial drain on society, and at worst, a time bomb ready to explode upon release."[2] Although we may wish to separate ourselves physically from criminal offenders, we should not "forget altogether, permanently exclude, or completely dehumanize these people."[3] Unfortunately, that is often precisely what has been done, whether intentionally or not.

Again, those in free society might argue that by stripping the offender of human dignity, imprisonment will make the type of lasting, negative impression that will serve as a strong deterrent to recidivism. Quite the contrary, instead of making them determined to avoid another prison term, incarceration leaves many inmates accustomed to prison life and resigned to the inevitability of returning to it. As we will see in Chapter 11, some become so inured to the prison routine and so apprehensive of their ability to "make it" on the outside, that, ironically, they are reluctant to leave.

Given the fact that even the best of the treatment techniques described in Chapter 9 take place within such a dehumanizing environment, it is little wonder that they have been less than totally successful. Perhaps the most that treatment can be expected to accomplish in such a setting is to counteract the negative effects of incarceration—to release inmates who, if not better, are at least no worse than they were upon entering the institution.

Undoubtedly, there are those who have overcome the effects of prison to become law-abiding citizens. But they may well have done so despite—rather than because of—their experiences in confinement. In many respects, imprisonment represents more an obstacle to overcome than an opportunity to reform. It may simply be illogical to expect corrections to change behavior, given the incongruity of trying to teach offenders to adjust to society by removing them from it.

[2]Rhonda Reeves, "Redefining Punishment: Corrections in the Community," *Corrections Today*, Vol. 54, No. 8 (December 1992), p. 76.
[3]Keith Farrington, "The Modern Prison as Total Institution? Public Perception vs. Objective Reality," *Crime and Delinquency*, Vol. 38, No. 1 (January 1992), p. 15.

## ❖ THE PROCESS OF PRISONIZATION

Through the process of *prisonization*, inmates become socialized into prison life. It involves adapting to the culture, values, norms, and behavioral expectations of the prison environment[4] and begins virtually immediately upon incarceration. The entering inmate is stripped, showered, deloused, given a uniform, assigned a number, and issued the rulebook. Personal property is searched, inspected,

The process of prisonization begins almost immediately upon admission to the facility. It involves adapting to the unique values, norms, and expectations of the prison environment. Courtesy of the Kentucky Department of Corrections.

[4]See Donald Clemmer, *The Prison Community* (New York: Holt, Rinehart and Winston, 1958).

and inventoried. Items that are not allowable are stored or shipped elsewhere. Hair is cut to standardized regulations. Beards may be shaven. Stripped of these sources of individual identity, the depersonalization of imprisonment begins.

Reactions to entering prison range from physical or mental rebellion to abnormal hunger and capacity to sleep. Attitudes toward the prisonization process range from never fully accepting it to an immediate and complete acceptance. But free will and self-direction can be repressed only so far, even in the most regimented institution. In opposition to the authoritative controls of the administration, inmates create their own status hierarchy, code of conduct, and subcultural value system—governing everything from verbal communications to sexual activities. It is not long before new inmates learn how personal autonomy finds expression within confinement. They quickly determine who wields power, controls privileges, and imposes punishments. Nor is it long before those imprisoned realize that they are subject not only to the formal rules and regulations established by the official administration, but also to the informal code imposed by their fellow prisoners. And among the inmate population, violation of the *in*formal code is a far more serious infraction than violation of the official regulations.

## Importation or Deprivation?

Before exploring the intricate process and consequences of prison socialization, a question arises as to how it occurs in the first place. In other words, is it simply a result of confining together large groups of offenders who share similar values, attitudes, and behaviors? If so, the attributes of prisonization are *imported* (i.e., brought into the institution) by the particular types of people who commit crime. Thus, we would not expect to find the same behaviors if prisons confined those of a different socioeconomic class or value background.

> Consider, for example, the case of an inmate who was raised in a lower class family which resided in a large urban area and who had moved from involvement in a delinquent gang into a group of adults [engaged in criminal activity]. One need not be a criminologist to hypothesize that the attitudes, values, motivations, and behavioral patterns that such an individual might well subscribe to would be very similar to those reinforced within the inmate society. Indeed, it would seem most likely that such individuals provided the basis for the content of the inmate subculture when it initially emerged and that . . . [it continues because of] the substantial numbers of these types of persons who are so selectively processed by other elements of the criminal justice system. . . . In many ways, such new arrivals are prisonized before they ever enter the institution![5]

Certainly, one's moral values are bound to be affected by close, continuous association with others who do not reinforce socially acceptable norms. But is there also something about the nature of correctional institutions that creates an

[5]Charles W. Thomas and David M. Petersen, *Prison Organization and Inmate Subcultures* (Indianapolis, IN: Bobbs-Merrill, 1977), p. 53.

unnatural response among those who would otherwise not react the same way in a different environment? If so, the behavior of those confined may reflect a normal response to being abnormally *deprived* of everything from physical amenities to social status and personal self-esteem.[6] Figure 10.1 illustrates the differences between the importation and deprivation models of prisonization; that is, whether inmates become hardened and prone toward deviant behavior:

- Because such characteristics reflect the lifestyle they experienced on the street?
- Or as a result of the frustrations they experience in prison?

Regardless of which theory is ascribed to, it is apparent that prisons produce a unique culture that reflects either "response to the deprivations of prison existence or . . . re-creation of [one's] external environment within the walls."[7] Actually, it may be a little of each, with the two models complementing rather than contradicting each other.[8]

An experiment conducted in the early 1970s with two dozen male college students acting out roles as inmates and officers may shed some light on this

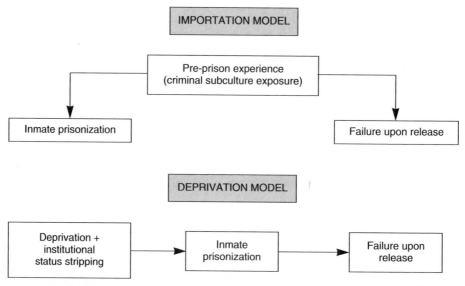

**Figure 10.1**  Models of prisonization. *Source:* Adapted from Richard Hawkins and Geoffrey P. Alpert, *American Prison Systems: Punishment and Justice* (Englewood Cliffs, NJ: Prentice Hall, 1989), p. 238.

[6]See Nicolett Parisi, "The Prisoner's Pressures and Responses," in Nicolett Parisi, ed., *Coping with Imprisonment* (Beverly Hills, CA: Sage Publications, 1982), pp. 9–11, who maintains that both *internal* and *external* stimuli contribute to pressures and strategies of coping in prison.

[7]Jim Thomas, Harry Mike, Jerome Blakemore, and Anmarie Alyward, "Exacting Control through Disciplinary Hearings: 'Making Do' with Prison Rules," *Justice Quarterly*, Vol. 8, No. 1 (March, 1991), p. 41.

[8]Thomas and Petersen, p. 55.

issue.[9] Those selected were mature, emotionally stable, intelligent students from middle-class backgrounds throughout the U.S. and Canada. None had any criminal record. In fact, they appeared to represent the "cream of the crop" of their generation. By the flip of a coin, half were assigned to play the role of "prisoners." The other half were designated as "guards"—instructed to make up their own rules for maintaining law, order, and respect in the mock prison setting established by the researchers. How do you think *you* would react if put into the role of an inmate or correctional officer? According to this experiment, your response might be quite different from what you would expect! See the next "Close-up on Corrections" for the chilling story of what actually happened.

The outcome of that experiment tends to support the deprivation model in a number of respects. The student inmates displayed many of the same prisonization characteristics as their real-life counterparts, despite the fact that their backgrounds were not at all representative of the typical prisoner. Additionally, the officers quickly assumed roles that reflected the organizational environment. As a result, the researchers concluded that we underestimate the power and pervasiveness of situational controls over behavior.[10]

At the same time, it should be kept in mind that this brief experiment involved not "hardened criminals" but defenseless students, who were placed in an environment that was very different from that to which they were accustomed. In contrast, inmates entering correctional institutions today are more likely to have progressed through a number of intermediate sanctions or shorter terms in jail prior to experiencing prison. It would therefore be expected that their "criminal identity" would be better developed. As one therapist has noted, an incarcerated offender "hears new ideas for crime in prison, but *he* is the one who accepts or rejects those ideas. No one forces him to continue a life of crime. . . . He is not a hapless victim who is corrupted by fellow inmates. . . . Criminals exhibit the same behavior patterns inside prison as on the streets."[11]

Nor did those playing the role of "guards" have the benefit of the academy training and more rigorous selection that would be characteristic of a real setting. In that respect, the experiment's most significant message may actually be the danger inherent when unskilled, untrained, and unsupervised personnel control the destiny of the powerless. As a result of such factors, the effects on the students were rather drastic and spontaneous, whereas becoming "prisonized" in reality is a more long-term, gradual process.

Nevertheless, the fact that those incarcerated tend to develop an institutionalized personality and a unique subcultural system appears to be more a function of the abnormal environment to which they are exposed (deprivation) than an outgrowth of personality traits or individual characteristics that they share in common (importation). In other words, "[a]lthough some persons arrive

[9]Philip G. Zimbardo, "Pathology of Imprisonment," in Lawrence F. Travis, Martin D. Schwartz, and Todd R. Clear, eds., *Corrections: An Issues Approach*, Second Edition (Cincinnati, OH: Anderson Publishing Company, 1983), pp. 99–104. (The remainder of the discussion of what has become known as the "Zimbardo experiment" is summarized from this source.)

[10]Ibid., p. 101.

[11]Stanton E. Samenow, "The Criminal Personality Exists before Prison," in Bonnie Szumski, ed., *America's Prisons: Opposing Viewpoints*, Fourth Edition (St. Paul, MN: Greenhaven Press, 1985), p. 62.

The Pathology of Imprisonment

The "prisoners" were unexpectedly picked up at their homes by a city policeman in a squad car, searched, handcuffed, fingerprinted, booked . . . and taken blind-folded to our "jail." There they were stripped, deloused, put into a uniform, given a number, and put into a cell with two other prisoners, where they expect-ed to live for the next two weeks. The pay was $15 a day, and their motivation was to make money. . . .

At the end of only six days, we had to close down our mock prison because what we saw was frightening. It was no longer apparent to most of the subjects (or to us) where reality ended and their roles began. The majority had indeed become prisoners or guards, no longer able to clearly differentiate between role-playing and self. There were dramatic changes in virtually every aspect of their behavior, thinking, and feeling. In less than a week, the experience of imprisonment undid (temporarily) a lifetime of learning; human values were suspended, self-concepts were challenged, and the ugliest, most base, pathological side of human nature surfaced. We were horrified because we saw some boys (guards) treat others as if they were despicable animals, taking pleasure in cruelty, while other boys (prison-ers) became servile, dehumanized robots who thought only of escape, of their own individual survival, and of their mounting hatred for the guards.

We had to release three prisoners in the first four days because they had such acute situational traumatic reactions as hysterical crying, confusion in think-ing, and severe depression. Others begged to be "paroled," and all but three were willing to forfeit all the money they had earned if they could be paroled. By then (the fifth day), they had been so programmed to think of themselves as prisoners that when their request for parole was denied, they returned docilely to their cells. . . . By the last days, the earlier solidarity among the prisoners (systematical-ly broken by the guards) dissolved into "each man for himself." Finally, when one of their fellows was put in solitary confinement (a small closet) for refusing to eat, the prisoners were given a choice . . . : give up their blankets and the incorri-gible prisoner would be let out, or keep their blankets and he would be kept in all night. They voted to keep their blankets and to abandon their brother.

About a third of the "guards" became tyrannical in their arbitrary use of power, in enjoying their control over other people. They were corrupted by the power of their roles and became quite inventive in their techniques of breaking the spirit of the prisoners and making them feel they were worthless. Some of the guards merely did their jobs as tough but fair correctional officers, and sever-al were good guards from the prisoners' point of view, since they did them small favors and were friendly. However, no good guard ever interfered with a com-mand by any of the bad guards; they never intervened on the side of the prison-ers, they never told the others to ease off because it was only an experiment, and they never even came to me as prison superintendent or experimenter in charge to complain. . . .

The consultant for our prison . . . [was] an ex-convict with 16 years of imprisonment. . . . [He] would get so depressed and furious each time he visited our prison, because of its psychological similarities to his experiences, that he would have to leave. A Catholic priest who was a former prison chaplain . . . talked to our prisoners after four days and said they were just like the other first-timers he had seen.

*Source:* Phillip G. Zimbardo, "Pathology of Imprisonment," in Lawrence F. Travis, Martin D. Schwartz, and Todd R. Clear, eds., *Corrections: An Issues Approach,* Second Edition (Cincinnati, OH: Anderson Publishing Company, 1983), pp. 100–101.

---

in prison with prior histories of violent behavior, the prison environment and inmate subculture tend to reinforce such behavior and foster environmental dynamics conducive to violence by those with little prior history of it."[12] While one's prior lifestyle may well have an impact on how quickly and thoroughly prisonization occurs, the concept itself requires exposure to an assimilation process that takes place in prison.

### The Institutionalized Personality

As the mock prison experiment illustrated, the pervasive effects of incarceration can be experienced in even a very brief period of time. Consider, then, how detrimental the effects of long-term imprisonment can be, especially for those in maximum custody: where everyone is subjected to strict regulation for the safety and security of the institution; where inmates are taught to line up and move in unison; where aggression is met with aggression; where orders dictate every movement; where lights never go out; where life is highly structured around a well-regulated routine; where there are few individual decisions to be made—other than whether to go along or resist. In such a setting, close emotional relationships are nonexistent. "Little" things—from the day's menu to an extra candy bar—take on an exaggerated importance. The minimal standard of living drains the very meaning from life. Goals and aspirations become readjusted downward or given up completely. Long-timers learn to live from day to day.

The result is a dehumanizing environment that forms an *institutionalized personality.* Such a personality is characterized by moving like a robot according to a routinized pattern: losing all initiative; living on a day-to-day basis; blocking off the past; avoiding the future. To the extent that the institutionalized inmate looks forward to anything, it is only to such simple diversions from the dullness of routine as the weekly movie.

It may be difficult for those on the outside to appreciate how issues as seemingly minor as getting a smaller portion of food or disagreeing over what TV program to watch can explode into violent attacks. But such apparent over-

[12]"What Prisons Do to People," unpublished monograph (Albany, NY: New York State Defenders Association, 1985), p. 5.

reactions to trivial details are not nearly as irrational when viewed from within a totally controlled environment. For an inmate's account of how swiftly and efficiently disputes can be resolved, as well as the pervasive fear that such a setting creates, see the next "Close-up on Corrections."

This transformation to an institutionalized personality represents the inmate's accommodation to long-term control through processes that have been variously described as "desocialization,"[13] "prisonization,"[14] "imposed socialization,"[15] "total institutionalization"[16] or adapting to the "pains of imprisonment."[17] It is generated by the abnormal features of the prison environment, particularly those tangible as well as intangible things that the prisoner is deprived of, including everything from personal and private property to goods and services, civil rights, heterosexual relationships, personal status, autonomy, and security. Contrary to what those in free society may believe, it is not the extent to which imates are deprived of material possessions that imposes the greatest punishment: "Being locked away from one's family and friends, being totally out of control of one's life, is a deprivation that dwarfs the significance of television, stereos, and designer jeans."[18]

## ❖ CLOSE-UP ON CORRECTIONS

### Settling Disputes

If the issue is worth beefing about, it is done silently and quickly with a knife or a length of pipe. There is a small scuffle, a man lies bleeding; there is the clatter of a shiv or pipe being kicked away. If the weapon is ever found, it is not "on" anyone. There are no fingerprints. That is all.

Everywhere, every minute—like the air you breathe—there is the threat of violence lurking beneath the surface. Unlike the air, it is heavy, massive, as oppressive as molasses. It permeates every second of everyone's existence—the potential threat of sudden, ferocious annihilation. It is as grey and swift and unpredictable as a shark and just as unvocal. There is no letup from it—ever.

*Source:* Bill Sands, *My Shadow Ran Fast* (Englewood Cliffs, NJ: Prentice Hall, 1964), pp. 53–54.

---

[13]Peter O. Peretti, "Desocialization–Resocialization: Process within the Prison Walls," *Canadian Journal of Corrections,* Vol. 12, No. 1 (January 1970), pp. 59–66.

[14]Clemmer.

[15]John J. Vollmann, "Imposed Socialization: A Functional Control in a Total Institution," *Sociological Research Symposium VIII* (Richmond, VA: Virginia Commonwealth University, 1978).

[16]Erving Goffman, *Asylums: Essays on the Social Situation of Mental Patients and Other Inmates* (Garden City, NY: Anchor Books, 1961), who describes a "total institution" as a "place of residence and work where large numbers of like-situated individuals, cut off from the wider society for an appreciable period of time, together lead an enclosed, formally-administered round of life," p. xiii.

[17]Gresham M. Sykes, *The Society of Captives: A Study of a Maximum Security Prison* (Princeton, NJ: Princeton University Press, 1958).

[18]John Irwin and Rick Mockler, "Prison Comforts Make Little Difference," in Szumski, p. 86.

As described in the next "Close-up on Corrections," it is not just the basic deprivation of freedom, but rather, the forfeiture of society's trust that is perhaps the most significant loss. In fact, as we will see in Chapter 12, this social rejection may be felt even more intensely among the small proportion of offenders who are female. In a society unaccustomed to female criminality, women's involvement in crime is not only as socially unacceptable as it is for men, but may additionally be viewed as a "morally distasteful" display of characteristics that do not conform to traditional views of "femininity."

As a result of such rejection, inmates begin to redefine their self-concept and experience a state of helplessness, frustration, and loss of hope—provoked by the necessity to submit to the power of both official staff and other inmates. In fact, it has been noted that this state of submissiveness involves "a profound threat to the prisoner's self-image" because it reduces one to "the weak, helpless, dependent status of childhood."[19] Adapting to "the system" is necessary to meet the requirements of a new social role that demands subservience, awe for authority, and severe self-limitation. It calls for serving time on a day-to-day basis and not bothering anybody else, unless one is powerful enough to do so.

Institutionalized offenders simply attempt to "get along" in a regimented society by "playing the nods" with supervisors and "doing their own time" with peers. They conform to the norms and values considered socially acceptable by other inmates—for example, disdain for the penal system and those in authority,

---

### ❖ CLOSE-UP ON CORRECTIONS

#### The Deprivation of Liberty

The prisoner is never allowed to forget that, by committing a crime, he has foregone his claim to the status of a full-fledged, *trusted* member of society. . . . [T]he inmate is . . . stripped of many of his civil rights, such as the right to vote, to hold office . . . and so on. But as important as the loss of these civil rights may be, the loss of that more diffuse status which defines the individual as someone to be trusted or as morally acceptable is the loss which hurts most. . . .

[T]he wall which seals off the criminal, the contaminated man, is a constant threat to the prisoner's self-concept . . . and the threat is continually repeated in the many daily reminders that he must be kept apart from "decent" men. Somehow this rejection or degradation by the free community must be warded off, turned aside, rendered harmless. Somehow the imprisoned criminal must find a device for rejecting his rejectors, if he is to endure psychologically.

*Source:* Gresham M. Sykes, *The Society of Captives: A Study of a Maximum Security Prison* (Princeton, NJ: Princeton University Press, 1958), pp. 65–67.

---

[19]Karl Menninger, *The Crime of Punishment* (New York: The Viking Press, 1968), p. 75, citing Sykes.

Isolated from free society, many inmates are aware of their social rejection, experiencing feelings of helplessness, frustration, and loss of hope. Courtesy of the Iowa Department of Social Services.

use of vulgar language, name-calling, distrust of fellow prisoners as well as staff, and acceptance of the status quo.

The resulting stereotypical pattern of behavior allows inmates to "get into the routine" with a minimum of irritation and anxiety. In some respects it is similar to breaking the spirit of a wild horse in order to shape its response to the commands of the rider. Like horse and rider—who develop a working accommodation with each other—the subsequent relationship is characterized by routines of dominance, surrender, and behavior on cue. Among inmates, this conformity reinforces the futility of relating to others in a meaningful way. It induces a facade of courtesy to authority figures and promotes flat, noncommital responses to others which are devoid of any emotional investment. In essence, "the most common effect of the prison experience is a slow, water-drip disfigurement of the human spirit. The greatest tragedy is that those who adjust to it best are damaged most."[20]

---

*LEARNING GOALS*

*Do you know:*

- *What types of inmates are most susceptible to the debilitating effects of prisonization?*
- *How long it takes for the average prisoner to become institutionalized?*
- *What factors contribute to an inmate's adjustment to confinement?*
- *What terms inmates use to describe various adaptations to incarceration?*
- *How attitudes and values influence one's behavior in prison?*

---

[20]Charles Campbell, *Serving Time Together: Men and Women in Prison* (Fort Worth, TX: Texas Christian University Press, 1980), p. 229.

To some extent, everyone is affected by this "wearing-down" process of imprisonment. Those who are younger, more emotionally vulnerable, and confined for longer periods of time will be particularly susceptible. But even among the physically strong and emotionally healthy, few escape the long-lasting influence of incarceration. The damage done by institutionalization is generally in direct relation to the length of incarceration. However, some stable personalities can endure confinement for a long time, while others "cave in."[21] It has been estimated that it takes about five years for the average prisoner to become institutionalized to the ultimate point of docile, subservient adaptation.[22]

Of course, not everyone reacts exactly the same way to the dehumanizing effects of imprisonment. Nor do all correctional institutions exert the same impact. Local jails, for example, may have their own forms of inmate socialization. But the shorter terms of confinement in jails—combined with the high turnover of their population—do not provide the intense, long-term interactions that promote prisonization. The treatment or custodial orientation of a facility also can have a positive or negative impact on this process: "Generally, research has suggested that the counterproductive influences of the inmate subculture are greatly diminished in settings . . . [where] less emphasis is placed on maintaining custodial control and relatively greater attention is devoted to the pursuit of change-oriented goals."[23]

As illustrated in Figure 10.2, three factors contribute to one's prison adjustment: *individual characteristics* of the offender, *environmental conditions* of the institution, and the *interaction* between person and environment.[24] Thus, it may be neither the environment itself nor the offender's individual characteristics, but rather, the interactive effects of both which shape how one will adjust to the prison experience.

To some extent, the features of the environment in particular can create a *self-fulfilling prophecy*. When people are mistrusted, they will tend to act in ways that betray our confidence. When violence is met with violence, it has a self-reinforcing effect. When people are locked into cages and treated like animals, it should not be surprising that their behavior is less than civilized. In other words, behavior often conforms to expectations. For a look at how the self-fulfilling prophecy influenced the adjustment of a lifer after 17 years in prison, see the next "Close-up on Corrections."

### Individual Adjustments

Because of the unique nature of this interaction, it is not surprising to find a wide range of *adaptive behaviors*. Some simply try to maximize their personal

---

[21]For a discussion of how prisoners break down under institutional stress, see Hans Toch, *Men in Crisis: Human Breakdowns in Prison* (Chicago: Aldine, 1975).

[22]Tom Runyon, *In for Life* (New York: Norton Press, 1953).

[23]Thomas and Petersen, p. 17.

[24]Kevin N. Wright, "A Study of Individual, Environmental, and Interactive Effects in Explaining Adjustment to Prison," *Justice Quarterly*, Vol. 8, No. 2 (June 1991), p. 219.

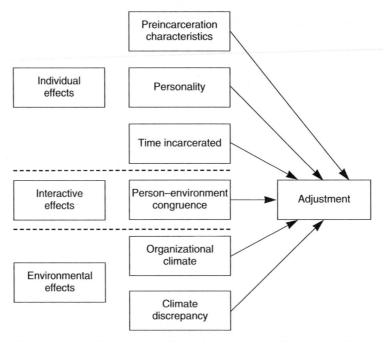

**Figure 10.2** Factors contributing to prison adjustment. *Source:* Kevin N. Wright, "A Study of Individual, Environmental, and Interactive Effects in Explaining Adjustment to Prison," *Justice Quarterly,* Vol. 8, No. 2 (June 1991), p. 223.

benefits and minimize discomforts. Some try to remain aloof, not risking involvement with others and attempting to keep a social distance from the rest of the population. Those exhibiting authoritarian personality traits are likely to rebel, become aggressive, or exploit others—exercising whatever control they can exert over those who are even more powerless.[25] Others rebel passively, sullenly biding their time until release.

First-timers may be particularly vulnerable to intimidation by other inmates, as well as more cautious and apprehensive in their dealings with staff and other inmates. Youthful offenders react to institutional conditioning even more intensely than their older counterparts—often developing antisocial grudges, feelings of inequality, and a diminished self-concept that can shape their outlook for years to come. Among adults, some portray a "tough guy" image. Others attempt to enhance self-esteem by boasting about their criminal past. Still others become crafty, deviant, or secretive. For a look at the terms used by the inmates to describe various adaptive roles, see the "Close-up on Corrections" on page 390.

[25]For more information on this topic, see the classic work of T.W. Adorno, Else Frenkel-Brunswick, Daniel J. Levinson, and R. Nevitt Sanford, *The Authoritarian Personality* (New York: Harper & Row, 1950).

The Self-Fulfilling Prophecy

"I was hurt—frustrated, deprived of hope, regimented, humiliated, punished—I became worse, either deliberately or unconsciously. Each time I was helped—given some small hope or purpose, treated as an individual, given even a small reason to be grateful to authorities—I became, and behaved, better. Each time needless discipline has been relaxed, each time they have been allowed to . . . respect themselves, I've seen men in this prison become better prisoners and better risks as ex-convicts. Each time I've seen men really trusted—not partly trusted, as on the prison farms or other places with guards near—I've seen them try to deserve that trust.

Today I am trusted . . . to a large extent, despite the fact that for over ten years, I was the only man to escape from inside the walls. . . . [The warden] simply accepted my voluntary promise not to escape, and that fact made it impossible for me to let him down. . . .

I believe my experiences and reactions to them have in many ways been the same as those of other convicts—that I have reacted much as any citizen thrown into an utterly unnatural environment might have. Today, treated like a man, I feel compelled to act like a man."

*Source:* Tom Runyon, "Prison Shocks," in Robert G. Caldwell, ed., *Criminology* (New York: Ronald Press, 1956), p. 636.

## Inmate Attitudes and Values

There is little doubt that the coercive nature of imprisonment does much to shape inmate responses to it. Nevertheless, there are also certain attitudes and values prevalent among the population that influence behavior. To some degree, these represent traits that may have brought offenders into contact with the law on the outside, although they can also be further nurtured by the institutional environment.

For example, many inmates have experienced a lifetime of difficulty with appropriately *responding to authority*—particularly if they were products of dysfunctional families or abusive homes, where punishment bore no relationship to behavior, and violence was an acceptable means of exerting power over others. To such offenders, authority has always been something to avoid or be resented because of its association with hostility and aggressiveness.

The constant supervision, adherence to the demands of those in power, and subservient role of inmates in prison further reinforce their distrust and disrespect for authority. Very seldom do inmates view authority in the treatment sense as supportive or protective. Rather, their reference to correctional officers as "screws" is indicative of what the inmates perceive the staff as doing to them. Officers are authority figures who are out to "get" them.

❖ *CLOSE-UP ON CORRECTIONS*

### Inmate Roles

| TERM | CHARACTERISTICS | REACTION BY OTHER IN389MATES |
|---|---|---|
| "Right guys" | Obey the inmate code; oppose staff and institutional rules | Accepted |
| "Square johns" (or) "Straights" | The opposite—"conventional" inmates who obey the rules and regulations; do not adhere to the inmate code | Disliked; not trusted |
| "Con politicians" (or) "Merchants" | Play "both sides"—manipulate staff into trusting them with choice assignments, while professing allegiance to the inmate code; wield power by selling scarce goods and services | Not fully trusted, but respected for their shrewdness |
| "Outlaws" (or) "Toughs" | Overly aggressive; rely on force or physical violence in dealings with others | Isolated; avoided |
| "Squealers" (or) "Rats" | Informants; provide information on illicit inmate activities to authorities; betray fellow inmates; threaten cohesiveness of the inmate code | Rejected; retaliated against |
| "Wolves" (or) "Fangs" | Homosexuals; prone to preying aggressively on inmates (wolves), or submitting passively to advances (fangs) | Feared; rejected; avoided |

*Sources:* Adapted from Clarence Schrag, "Some Foundations for a Theory of Corrections," in Donald R. Cressey, ed., *The Prison: Studies in Institutional Organization* (New York: Holt, Rinehart and Winston, 1961), pp. 345–46; and Gresham M. Sykes, *The Society of Captives: A Study of a Maximum Security Prison* (Princeton, NJ: Princeton University Press, 1958), pp. 87–105.

Nor is it only the correctional staff who "have it in" for them. The very fact that they are in prison is often blamed on someone else—or simply "the system" or society in general. In a social structure where one sees oneself as "born to lose," it is easy to assume the self-concept of a scapegoat. Unwilling or unable to accept personal accountability for their actions, it is convenient for offenders to neutralize blame by *rationalizing* their actions (e.g., "I needed the money." "Politicians steal more than I did."). Through various forms of rationalizing their own guilt and/or projecting the blame on others, they can psychologically:

- *Avoid responsibility* (e.g., "It wasn't my fault." "I just went along with the gang.")
- *Deny injury* (e.g., "They can afford it." "Nobody got hurt.")
- *Blame the victims* (e.g., "They had it coming." "They should have done what I said.")

In part, such attitudes are further reinforced by the inmate's concept of the social system as composed of the *caught* and the *uncaught*. They know and hear of persons who have committed offenses for which they were not convicted or sentenced. Even more tangibly, if inmates see personnel at the institution stealing prison products or "clipping" the system of goods and services, it frustrates them. In their opinion, there is little that distinguishes them from the rest of society. They were just unfortunate enough to get caught (as we saw expressed in the inmate's poem featured in Chapter 3). In a world filled with aggression, exploitation, and perceived injustice, those society has labeled as "offenders" may well come to view themselves as "victims."

An inmate's *tolerance for anxiety* is another factor that must be taken into consideration in predicting behavior. Many are worried about their spouse, family, or loved ones. A disturbing letter from home, (or lack of correspondence) can create a state of severe anxiety. Yet those incarcerated can do nothing about anything on the outside—they are utterly powerless. Anxiety reactions often fall into three phases: initial protest, followed by feelings of despair, and ultimately, resignation to one's situation through emotional detachment.

High levels of anxiety are routinely experienced during the first few months of incarceration. They tend to level off as the offender adjusts to the institution and then rise again nearing release, as the inmate confronts the uncertainties of what will be faced in free society.[26] This helps to explain why some inmates escape or run away only a week or so before they are scheduled for parole. There is little opportunity in prison to reduce one's anxiety. Those who are able to do so generally accommodate by serving their sentence "one day at a time," trying to avoid becoming overwhelmed by either mistakes of the past or uncertainties of the future.

---

*LEARNING GOALS*

*Do you know:*

- *How the inmate subculture functions within prisons?*
- *What purposes are served by the inmate code?*
- *How new inmates are initiated into the informal code of conduct?*
- *Why inmates join prison gangs?*
- *What activities are engaged in by inmate gangs?*

---

## ❖ THE INMATE SUBCULTURE

Those on the outside who share certain values, attitudes, beliefs, ethnicity, or other similar traits often group together into subcultures within free society. The

---

[26]Similarly, a U-shaped pattern of compliance has been observed—with those closest to either the beginning or the end of their sentence more likely to support staff and reject the inmate code. See Stanton Wheeler, "Socialization in Correctional Communities," *American Sociological Review*, Vol. 26 (1961), pp. 697–712.

same occurs within prison walls. And just as different patterns of behavior, standards of conduct, and even language characterize subcultures on the outside, they do likewise within the prison.

While inmates bring a number of common traits into the institution, their organization into a separate *subculture* is largely a response to the conditions they find there. It emerges in reaction to the deprivations and isolation of institutional living, as well as the process by which inmates interact with institutional authority. It serves as an expression of autonomy in a setting that attempts to supress individuality. It provides a self-defensive solidarity in an environment where a "we versus they" social boundary prevails. It is an expected and natural phenomenon in response to unnatural organizational conditions. In other words: "prolonged confinement fosters high levels of integration into an inmate society, within which . . . antisocial attitudes and behavior are systematically reinforced."[27]

## Prison Language (Argot)

This society is manifested in a unique language, as reflected in the previously mentioned terms used to identify various inmate roles (e.g., "straight," "tough," "wolf") and further illustrated in the next "Close-up on Corrections." It should, however, be noted that inmate slang is neither universal nor static, but rather, is continually evolving at each institution. These examples therefore represent prison *argot* in that area of the country at that particular point in time. Like the secret codes of childhood games, learning the inmate argot not only enables prisoners to communicate with each other in a language unfamiliar to outsiders, but also establishes an identity which only they can share. Moreover, within the terms used in the language of the inmate subculture are found elements of:

- *Mockery of the system* (e.g., "the man"; "goon squad")
- *Superficial resignation to authority* (e.g., "play for the gate"; "play the nods")
- *The inmate social hierarchy* (e.g., "right guys" versus "straights")
- *Adherence to the inmate code* ("don't snitch"; "get backs")

But to the extent that language is simply a means of communicating and reinforcing values, it is the inmate *code of conduct* that most significantly identifies the prison subculture. In opposition to the institutional rules and regulations, it sets informal standards for controlling behavior in a manner designed to counteract official authority.

## The Inmate Code

The informal social control held by inmates through adherence to the *inmate code* serves the vested interests of powerful and long-term prisoners. Those who have been around the institution long enough to know the routines

---

[27]Charles W. Thomas and David M. Petersen, "The Inmate Subculture" in David M. Petersen and Charles W. Thomas, eds., *Corrections: Problems and Prospects,* Second Edition (Englewood Cliffs, NJ: Prentice Hall, 1980), p. 85.

## Inmate Slang and Argot Terms

| TERM | MEANING |
|---|---|
| Fish | New inmates. |
| Get-backs | Revenge in prison. "Those guys got some get-backs coming for what they done to Johnny last week." |
| Hard time | A prisoner unable or unwilling to adjust to the normal prison routine will do *hard time*. . . . "I sure hope Bill gets his visit soon, he is really doing hard time this week." |
| The man | Any person in authority. "If the man comes up on the tier, you yell out." |
| Play for the gate | To adjust your conduct so that you can compile a record as a model prisoner and be paroled sooner. |
| Pull your own time | To mind your own business. "You're gonna have to learn to start pulling your own time for a change." |
| Script | Prison "money." |
| Shank | A knife or other sharp-edged weapon. |
| Snitch | A prison informer. |
| Waste | To kill someone. "They're going to get themselves wasted by being caught up in a beef in here." |
| Watch your back | To protect oneself from attack in the prison. "I'm watching my back out in the visiting room . . . " |
| What goes 'round comes 'round | A commonly used expression meaning: "You eventually have to pay for what you do to others in here." |

*Source:* Inez Cardozo-Freeman, *The Joint: Language and Culture in a Maximum Security Prison* (Springfield, IL: Charles C. Thomas, 1984), pp. 480–541.

| TERM | MEANING |
|---|---|
| Bug out | To act crazy. |
| Boss | When spelled backwards, the letters stand for "sorry S-O-B." Used by inmates to address staff and to call them an "SOB" without actually doing so. |
| Cheek it | When inmates do not want to swallow medication, they will "cheek it," spitting it out once they are away from the sight of staff. Occurs when an inmate wants to store psychotropic drugs and take them in mass quantity. |
| Chill out | To take on a low profile for a period of time, stay out of sight, or calm down. |
| Dr. Feelgood | The institution's psychologist. |
| Hack | A correctional officer. |

| TERM | MEANING |
|---|---|
| Hole | The administrative detention unit or the disciplinary segregation unit. |
| Phone is off the hook | Used by inmates to notify each other that a staff member is close enough to overhear their conversation. |
| To roll over | To become an informant. |

*Source:* Eugene Ray, *Dictionary of Prison Slang,* Federal Bureau of Prisons, Computer Printout (November 30, 1986).

and the authority structure can achieve power by gaining the trust of administrative officials and the acquiesence of other inmates. It is through the inmate code that such compliance is maintained.

The code defines what actions are proper or improper, good or bad, right or wrong from the inmate's perspective. By establishing these prescriptions for "do's" and "don'ts," it clearly distinguishes between the values of the official administration and those of the unofficial social system: "The code represents an organization of criminal values in clearcut opposition to the values of conventional society, and to prison officials as representatives of that society. The main tenent of this code forbids any type of supportive or nonexploitative liaison with prison officials. It seeks to confer status and prestige on those inmates who stand most clearly in opposition to the administration. . . ."[28]

In free society, breaking the laws of the community results in punishment, as well as an inferior social status for the offender. In much the same manner, violation of the inmate code produces alienation from fellow prisoners, reduced status on the social hierarchy of the institution, and punitive sanctions. In fact, it can result in severe physical retaliation, as we will see later in the vicious treatment of "snitches" when inmates broke into the protective custody unit during the Santa Fe, New Mexico, riot.

Thus, the inmate code "places a strong emphasis on in-group loyalty and solidarity," as well as "aggressive and exploitative relations" with anyone who does not adhere to it.[29] Although some of its provisions are vaguely supportive of institutional order, most simply serve the self-interests of the inmate population, as illustrated in the next "Close-up on Corrections."

Newly arriving inmates (referred to in a predatory manner as "fish") are rapidly initiated into the code of conduct through exaggerated accounts of what lies ahead, threats and intimidation by other inmates, situations where they are required to "prove themselves," and both real and fabricated stories of what happens to those who are noncompliant. Moreover, visual observations quickly reinforce the power of inmate control, the forced obedience to it, and the inability to rely on official or unofficial intervention:

[28]Lloyd Ohlin, *Sociology and the Field of Corrections* (New York: Social Science Research Council, 1956), p. 28.
[29]Ibid., p. 29.

The Inmate Code

1. DON'T INTERFERE WITH THE INTERESTS OF OTHER INMATES:

   Never rat on a con. Don't be nosey. Don't have a loose lip. Don't put a guy on the spot.

2. DON'T QUARREL WITH FELLOW INMATES:

   Play it cool. Don't lose your head. Do your own time.

3. DON'T EXPLOIT OTHER INMATES:

   Don't break your word. Don't steal from cons. Don't sell favors. Don't welsh on bets.

4. MAINTAIN YOURSELF:

   Don't weaken. Don't whine. Don't cop out. Be tough. Be a man.

5. DON'T TRUST THE GUARDS OR THE THINGS THEY STAND FOR:

   Don't be a sucker. Guards are hacks or screws. The officials are wrong and the prisoners are right.

*Source:* Adapted from Gresham M. Sykes and Sheldon I. Messinger, "The Inmate Social System" in Richard A. Cloward, Donald R. Cressey, George H. Grosser, Richard McCleery, Lloyd E. Ohlin, Gresham M. Sykes, and Sheldon I. Messinger, eds., *Theoretical Studies in the Social Organization of the Prison* (New York: Social Science Research Council, 1960), pp. 6–8.

The first day I got to Soledad, I was walking from the fish tank to the mess hall and this guy comes running down the hall past me, yelling, with a knife sticking out of his back. Man, I was petrified. I thought, what the f--- kind of place is this?[30]

Several times I saw things going on that I didn't like. One time, a couple of guys were working over another guy and I wanted to step in, but I couldn't. Had to just keep moving as if I didn't see it.[31]

Along with being oriented to the inmate code, the new offender is "sized-up." He is evaluated by others according to such features as age, race, offense, fighting ability, and social connections. The prisoner who does not establish his "turf," demonstrate his masculinity, or prove able to defend himself during this initial assessment process is likely to be relegated to a low position on the inmate hierarchy—subject to manipulation, intimidation, and domination throughout his prison term.[32] (See the next "Close-up on Corrections" for a brutal account of

[30]John Irwin, "The Prison Experience: The Convict World" in George G. Killinger and Paul F. Cromwell, Jr., eds. *Penology: The Evolution of Corrections in America* (St. Paul, MN: West Publishing Company, 1973), p. 202, quoting an interview with a Soledad inmate.

[31]Ibid., p. 207.

[32]Because they represent the vast majority of prisoners, as well as the subject of much of the prison related research, this discussion focuses on male inmates. For more information on the unique aspects of socialization in female prisons, see Chapter 12.

this process.) Nor does it take a great deal of insight to realize that those subjected to such brutality in prison "are likely to pass on their trauma once released."[33]

### Inmate Gangs

In such a hostile setting, it is not surprising to find a prevalence of gang-related violence within prison walls. In fact, the "sizing-up" of new "fish" is in some respects similar to the initiation rights performed before accepting new members into a gang—where torturous rituals seek to determine the proposed member's loyalty and manhood.

---

### ❖ CLOSE-UP ON CORRECTIONS

Prison Initiation

Alan entered [the prison] in April, 1970 to serve an 18-month sentence for breaking and entering. He is 5'6" tall and weighs about 135 lbs. At the time he entered . . . he was twenty years old, had graduated from high school, and had never been confined previously. By his own admission, he was "scared to death" at the prospect of sexual assault.

Soon after he arrived, black inmates began to harass him, calling him "white trash," a "white whore," and threatening "to make a little girl out of [him]." When two black inmates cornered him in his cell one evening before lockup and threatened to throw acid over him—it turned out to be orange juice—he submitted to them. . . . Terrified, he requested protective custody.

After one month of protective custody, however, the strain of being locked in a cell for 23 hours a day and never being allowed out of the wing proved to be too much and he requested return to the population. Soon after his return to the population, he was approached by Willie, a large and powerful black inmate. Willie told him that he didn't approve of what the others had done, felt sorry for Alan, and would take care of him. He gave Alan a carton of cigarettes and signed over a five dollar store order to him. Over the next several weeks, the relationship developed into what Alan considered a real friendship. He was no longer harassed and his fears abated. One evening Willie told Alan to "get off" with him. Alan accepted, but when he arrived . . . he found himself confronted with five or six other blacks. Willie demanded that he "take care of us." "I been taking care of you, now you gotta take care of me and my friends." Alan refused and tried to struggle free, but was overpowered. Willie held him down by the head and shoulders while the others took turns. . . .

*Source:* Leo Carroll, *Hacks, Blacks and Cons: Race Relations in a Maximum Security Prison* (Lexington, MA: D.C. Heath, 1974), pp. 182–183.

---

[33]Steve Lerner, "Prisons Are Violent and Dehumanizing," in Szumski, p. 70.

With the emergence of gangs, the prison subculture is no longer as simple as "us" (inmates) against "them" (staff). Inmate solidarity has not disappeared. But beyond overall resistance to institutional authority, specific allegiance to inmate associations has developed, largely along racial, ethnic, or religious lines—as evidenced by such gangs as the White Mafia, Aryan Brotherhood, Afro-American Society, Black Guerrilla Family, Black Muslims, Mexican Mafia, La Nuestra Familia, and Latin Kings. Just as with gangs in free society, such divisiveness further intensifies power struggles within correctional institutions, generating "an almost relentless cycle of violence and vengeance."[34]

The organization of inmates within power-wielding subgroups has long been a feature of prison life. Over 40 years ago, the Washington State Penitentiary at Walla Walla became infamous for being the birthplace of the first documented prison gang, the Gypsy Jokers Motorcycle Club, which banded together in 1950.[35] But it was not until the 1970s that correctional administrators recognized the widespread development of gangs in American prisons.[36] In more recent years, these factions became particularly powerful, with a "new breed" of radical and violent prisoners acting as catalysts in an atmosphere of hopelessness.[37] As one who was unable to deal with this changing social world of the prison expressed it, "[t]he new kinds in prison are wild. They have no respect for rules or other persons. I just want to get out of here and give it all up. I can't take coming back to prison again, not with the kind of convicts they are getting now."[38]

Like their counterparts on the outside, *prison gangs* are often united by a common language and shared values. Moreover, to the extent that gangs in free society tend to attract those seeking acceptance, recognition, or a sense of belonging,[39] it is apparent that fertile recruiting grounds exist among those in confinement. The racial or ethnic pride promoted by a gang can serve as a substitute for lack of personal identity. Status in a gang can upgrade low self-esteem. Viewing those in power as "oppressors" can provide a cause for uniting militant inmates. The protection and excitement offered by a gang can fill voids in an unsafe and boring existence. In essence, gangs meet unfulfilled needs. Whatever the reasons for their existence, they also seriously jeopardize the order and safety of correctional institutions.

Inmate subgroups can, of course, develop around any number of common similarities. Such factions always present the potential for institutional disrup-

[34]Peter Scharf, "Empty Bars: Violence and the Crisis of Meaning in the Prison," in Michael Braswell, Steven Dillingham, and Reid Montgomery, Jr., eds., *Prison Violence in America* (Cincinnati, OH: Anderson Publishing Company, 1985), p. 139.

[35]William Riley, "Taking a Two-Pronged Approach to Managing Washington's Gangs," *Corrections Today*, Vol. 54, No. 5 (July 1992), p. 68.

[36]Harold W. Clarke, "Gang Problems: From the Streets to Our Prisons," *Corrections Today*, Vol. 54, No. 5 (July 1992), p. 8.

[37]See Burton M. Atkins and Henry R. Glick, eds., *Prisons, Protest, and Politics* (Englewood Cliffs, NJ: Prentice Hall, 1972).

[38]Irwin, p. 206.

[39]Suzanne Harper, "LA's Gang Busters—Lessons Learned," *School Safety* (Fall 1989), p. 13. It has also been noted that youths at risk of gang involvement in the community have had little or no positive development experiences—"constructive activities that [would] enhance their feelings of esteem, self-worth and confidence." See Barry Glick, "Governor's Task Force Tackles Growing Juvenile Gang Problem," *Corrections Today*, Vol. 54, No. 5 (July 1992), p. 94.

tion. But gangs differ from other informal inmate groups in several respects. For example, gangs are more likely to:

- Have an organized leadership with a clear chain of command.
- Remain unified during institutional conflict.
- Engage in activities that are criminal or otherwise threatening to institutional operations.[40]

In other words, gangs tend to share such traits as loyalty, unity, and identity. But unlike nonviolent groups that may do likewise, gangs engage in *criminal behavior*. In fact, they reward the antisocial activities of their members.[41] It is for this reason that they are more recently becoming known by the term "disruptive groups" or "security threat groups." For a look at the activities of some of the gangs operating inside a major prison system, see the next "Close-up on Corrections."

Gangs are becoming an increasing problem in all prisons and jails, although there is still considerable denial in some parts of the country that this problem exists.[42] Preliminary results of a national survey conducted in 1992 indicate that 47,445 inmates throughout the country are members of some 755 security threat groups operating within prisons throughout the United States.[43] Large states such as California, Illinois, New York, and Texas are especially susceptible because of the size of their prison populations and the influence of gangs in these highly populated states. For example, it has been estimated that in 1989, between 80 and 90% of the inmates in the Illinois correctional system had some affiliation with street gangs.[44] Among the street gangs that are infiltrating correctional institutions today are the Bloods, Crips, Vice Lords, Hells Angels, Skinheads, and Latin Kings.[45] In fact,there is more and more overlap between groups defined as "prison gangs" and those identified as "street gangs."[46]

While many gangs may originally have been formed for self-protection, finding strength in unity has bolstered their power, and "if allowed, they influence every conceivable aspect of prison life."[47] In Texas alone, the two most violent years in the history of the correctional department resulted in 52 inmate homicides and over 7000 inmate and staff assaults—with 92% of the homicides and 80% of the assaults attributed to gang-related activities.[48] In response, Texas

---

[40]*Management Strategies in Disturbances and with Gangs/Disruptive Groups* (Washington, DC: U.S. Government Printing Office, 1992), pp. 1–2.

[41]Ibid., p. 2.

[42]Dennis G. Baugh, "ACA Gang Survey Examines National Control Strategies," *Corrections Today*, Vol. 54, No. 5 (July 1992), p. 82.

[43]"Gangs in Correctional Facilities: A National Assessment (Preliminary Results)," unpublished handout (Laurel, MD: American Correctional Association, 1993), p. 4.

[44]Michael P. Lane, "Inmate Gangs," *Corrections Today*, Vol. 51, No. 4 (July 1989), p. 99.

[45]Clarke, p. 8.

[46]Craig H. Trout, "Taking a New Look at an Old Problem," *Corrections Today*, Vol. 54, No. 5 (July 1992), p. 64.

[47]Lane, p. 99.

[48]Salvador Buentello, "Combatting Gangs in Texas," *Corrections Today*, Vol. 54, No. 5 (July 1992), p. 58. Data refer to the years 1984 and 1985.

Prison Gangs

## MEXICAN MAFIA

The Mexican Mafia is considered the most powerful gang in the California correctional system. It . . . is totally crime-oriented. As its name suggests, the gang is very homogeneous, with membership composed almost entirely of first or second generation Mexican-Americans. . . . Membership is for life. Voluntary dropouts are prohibited.

Formed in 1958 . . . in a relatively short time, the gang was in control of most illicit activities valued by other inmates, including gambling, narcotics, homosexual relations, and debt collection. Attempts . . . to weaken the gang through transfer resulted in the spreading of membership throughout the correctional system. By the mid-1960's, the gang regulated heroin traffic and controlled much of the inmates' activites. . . .

Beginning in the late 1960's, the Mexican Mafia began to move its operations into the community. Members have ordered "hits" on the street. Gang members have also been involved in numerous bank robberies. In addition, they attempted to take over federally-funded drug abuse programs by getting gang members seated on the boards of directors. . . . Although these efforts were uncovered, gang activity in the community continues.

## BLACK GUERRILLA FAMILY

The Black Guerrilla Family is a black terrorist gang that follows a Marxist-Maoist-Leninist revolutionary philosophy. Its primary goal is to control the destiny of black inmates, particularly through educating them about racism and helping them maintain pride and dignity while incarcerated. The gang also advocates forceful overthrow of the U.S. government. They accept any black inmates, except homosexuals, who are willing to meet their standards.

The Black Guerrilla Family is highly organized. It has a formalized rank structure consisting of a central executive committee, field generals, captains of arms, captains of squads, lieutenants, and soldiers. . . . [It] follows a precise code of ethics, with punishments for violations. . . . Once accepted, a member must take a death oath affirming a lifelong commitment to the gang. . . .

The gang considers law enforcement and correctional authorities to be its number one enemy . . . [and] is responsible for the most serious assaults on and murders of California correctional staff. . . .

Source: *Management Strategies in Disturbances and with Gangs/Disruptive Groups* (Washington, DC: U.S. Government Printing Office, 1992), pp. 3–4.

has implemented strategies ranging from hiring more staff to providing additional training, aggressively prosecuting in-house violence, and placing confirmed prison gang members in administrative segregation. Although these tactics have undoubtedly helped to ease the problem, they have not eliminated it, and Texas officials still continue to view gangs as a "serious and continuous threat."[49]

Active, well-organized gangs can exert considerable control over such illicit prison enterprises as gambling, sex, and drug transactions. They can intimidate other inmates through coercion, threats, and physical violence. In such a setting, even minor interactions can have ominous consequences. As we saw in the last close-up, some of these groups are even directing criminal activities in the outside community as well. But aside from their strong-arm tactics and corrupt activities, one of the greatest threats of gangs to institutional security is their ability to unite the inmate population into *polarized groups* prepared for *collective violence*.

---

*LEARNING GOALS* ▬▬▬▬▬▬▬▬▬▬▬▬▬▬▬▬▬▬

*Do you know:*

- *When and where the first prison riot occurred?*
- *What predisposing conditions can make an institution vulnerable to a riot?*
- *What predisposing conditions and precipitating events were involved in the Attica riot?*
- *What the five stages of a riot are?*
- *How most riots are terminated?*
- *What techniques were used in the negotiated settlement of the Oakdale riot?*
- *What proactive steps can be taken to prevent riots?*

---

## ❖ PRISON VIOLENCE

Correctional institutions may be physically isolated from the outside world. However, they are not immune to the influences of social, political, racial, and ethnic tensions in society—tensions that "have established conditions for revolt and unrest in our prisons at an unprecedented scale."[50]

If nothing else, the 1992 riots in the streets of Los Angeles following the acquittal of police officers involved in the beating of Rodney King provided clear evidence that mounting hostility has been lurking beneath a surface of superficial tranquility. If frustrations can explode into such outrage in free society, the "chemistry for violence" is that much greater in prison—where society temporarily confines those it has chosen to reject.[51] The words of a former director of corrections some 20 years ago echo a warning no less relevant today:

---

[49]Ibid., p. 60. For a further discussion of various gang control strategies, see *Management Strategies in Disturbances*, pp. 9–12; and Robert S. Fong and Salvador Buentello, "The Detection of Prison Gang Development: An Empirical Assessment," *Federal Probation* (March 1991), pp. 66–69.

[50]Israel L. Barak-Glantz, "The Anatomy of Another Prison Riot," in Braswell et al., *Prison Violence in America*, p. 139.

[51]Paraphrased from Lane, p. 128.

All around us, the ghetto streets have periodically burst with violent indignation at the demeaning inequities suffered by the have-nots. If we listen closely to what the ghetto rioters are saying, we find that they are not just angered by their lack of jobs and income, but angered more by those societal conditions and attitudes which frustrate their efforts to improve their lot and enhance their dignity. When such people come into our prisons, they find there a microcosm of the ghetto's frustrations, denied opportunities, and purposeless living. To bring this explosive potential to a critical point needs only the right leadership and the right incident for a spark. The leadership has been lacking or effectively suppressed in the past, but it is increasingly emerging among today's more politically sophisticated prisoners.[52]

Expressions of personal frustration can take many forms. Some seethe inwardly—resisting authority in subtle ways and mouthing "silent words" of defiance that are restrained from verbal expression only to avoid the consequences. Others are much less constrained—belligerently challenging "direct orders" and asserting their individuality at all costs. Still others act-out aggressively by physical attack—destroying property; assaulting staff or other inmates. Between 1984 and 1989, for example, at least 411 people were killed in federal and state prisons.[53] That does not include either jail homicides or the many rapes, aggravated assaults, suicides, and less serious forms of violence committed by those incarcerated. In fact, violence within medium- and maximum-security correctional institutions has to some degree come to be viewed as almost a routine expectation. As one inmate described the situation to a U.S. district judge, "No big deal. With a population of 1,600, we get about 25 murders a year. With the going price for murder at two cartons of cigarettes, I guess that isn't bad."[54]

But these forms of violence are largely *individual*, self-defeating expressions of frustration or discontent. Individual behavior can be—if not subdued—at least punished. As long as inmates are predominantly loners who usually cooperate with institutional procedures, controls can be concentrated on the relatively few mavericks. It is when prisoners unite into close-knit *groups* under leaders promoting intentional, collective violence that the stability of the "fragile truce" between the keepers and the kept is clearly endangered.[55]

## Riots and Disturbances

Among the public, corrections is narrowly judged by its ability to maintain custody and control. Losing either is therefore a correctional administrator's worst nightmare. Unless the prisoner is particularly infamous, there is generally little public attention paid to an individual escapee, and quickly regaining custody of the absconder can restore public confidence. *Riots*, however, are a far

---

[52]Paul Keve, *Prison Life and Human Worth* (Minneapolis, MN: University of Minnesota Press, 1974), p. 6.

[53]"Inmates Who Kill in Prison," *Corrections Compendium*, Vol. XV, No. 9 (November 1990), p. 1.

[54]"Lewisburg Inmate Testifies on Widespread Prison Violence," *Corrections Digest*, Vol. 7, No. 12 (June 16, 1976), p. 7.

[55]Keve, p. 67.

Officers practice techniques for regaining control of the facility in the event of a riot or major disturbance. Courtesy of Capitol Communication Systems, Inc.

more notable threat. Unlike the solitary escapee, riots represent the correctional authority's loss of control over "a significant number of prisoners, in a significant area of the prison, for a significant amount of time."[56]

The intensive media scrutiny occurring when such a widespread disturbance breaks out can devastate the image of corrections. That would be a relatively minor price to pay, however, if instantaneous notoriety generated long-lasting public support for change. If so, it would be possible that productive by-products could result from destructive events. But the impact is more likely to be a fleeting concern expressed by demands for tighter security rather than a fundamental commitment directed toward substantial improvements.

Perhaps because of this inability to learn from the past—and thus being "condemned to repeat it"[57]—riots and disturbances are as old as prisons themselves. In fact, the first recorded U.S. prison riot predates the American Revolution. It occurred in 1774 at the Newgate Prison built over an abandoned mine shaft at Simsbury, Connecticut.[58] Since then, correctional institutions throughout the country have been plagued by hundreds of riots[59] and countless less serious disturbances.

[56]Bert Useem and Peter Kimball, *States of Siege: U.S. Prison Riots, 1971–1986* (New York: Oxford University Press, 1989), p. 4.

[57]Paraphrased from George Santayana. See David Fogel, *We Are the Living Proof . . . The Justice Model for Corrections* (Cincinnati, OH: Anderson Publishing Company, 1979), p. 1.

[58]Steven D. Dillingham and Reid H. Montgomery, Jr. "Prison Riots: A Corrections' Nightmare since 1774," in Braswell et al., *Prison Violence in America*, p. 19.

[59]For example, defining a riot as an incident "involving 15 or more inmates and resulting in property damage or personal injury," one study uncovered 260 riots throughout the country between 1971 and 1983 alone. See Ellis MacDougall and Reid H. Montgomery, Jr. "American Prison Riots, 1971–1983," unpublished paper (Columbia, SC: College of Criminal Justice, University of South Carolina, n.d.), pp. 2, 11.

Inmates have never won a prison riot, either in the short-term sense of maintaining their freedom or in the long-term sense of drawing lasting attention to their plight. Knowing the ultimate outcome, why do they engage in such futile actions? There is no single answer or simple explanation. Although some riots may be well-planned protests, most appear to be more spontaneous events. One study found that riots are more likely in older, larger, and maximum-security institutions, as well as those where there is less recreation, fewer meaningful work opportunities, and less contact between the warden and inmates.[60] But it has also been noted that

> [i]t isn't necessary to have a callous or inept warden to have a riot. It isn't necessary to have sadistic guards, bad food, or any of the other classic grievances that supposedly provoke a riot. Those will be only surface complaints. The real problem is that even in a prison with good food and humane custodians, life is still a put-down, day after day. Boredom, pettiness, and repetitive meaningless activities are inherent in prison existence, and it should be no surprise that at some point the inmate population has had all it can stand.[61]

In other words, prison riots are to a considerable extent natural consequences of unnatural circumstances. Just as an active volcano is bound to erupt, prisons are virtually destined to burst into violence periodically. At the same time, just as geological factors alert us to the potential for volcanic erruption, there are signals that can warn perceptive staff of an impending disturbance. See the next "Close-up on Corrections" for some of the changes in institutional atmosphere that can serve as early warning indicators of inmate unrest.

### Predisposing Conditions

Although there is no single overall explanation that accounts for all prison riots, various features of prisons can either *reduce* or *reinforce* the potential for violent explosion. In other words, there are certain *predisposing conditions* that can serve to make an institution vulnerable to organized violence. For example, the American Correctional Association has identified the following as underlying contributors to institutional disturbances:[62]

- *Environmental stressors:* regimentation, personal deprivations, freedom limitations, boredom, idleness, brutality, racial conflicts, and gangs.
- *Substandard facilities:* overcrowded living quarters, depersonalized surroundings, poor or monotonous food, and inadequate plumbing, heating, lighting, or ventilation.

[60]Dillingham and Montgomery, pp. 23–24, citing the South Carolina Department of Corrections' study of collective violence between 1900 and 1970.
[61]Keve, p. 15.
[62]Summarized from *Causes, Preventive Measures, and Methods of Controlling Riots and Disturbances in Correctional Institutions* (Laurel, MD: American Correctional Association, 1990), pp. 8–13.

Early Warning Signals: Conditions Conducive to Unrest

- Dining hall indicators
  —Alteration of noise levels
  —Removal of food staples
  —Refusals/requests not to attend meals
- Housing unit indicators
  —Increase in contraband
  —Alteration of noise levels
  —Increase in misbehavior reports/incidents
  —Increase in cell change requests
  —Increase in assaults on staff
- Recreation yard indicators
  —Large gatherings of ethnic, racial, or other groups
  —Polarization of known inmate rivals
  —Increase in verbal defiance of staff members
  —Decrease in yard attendance
- Other indicators
  —Increase in buying of staples from commissary
  —Alteration of visiting activity
  —Increase in smuggling of contraband by visitors
  —Increase in manufacture/possession of weapons
  —Increase in sick call attendance
  —Increase in protective custody admissions

*Source:* Condensed from *Early Warning System: Introduction and Implementation Manual for Employees* (Albany, NY: Department of Correctional Services, n.d.), pp. 5–9.

- *Inappropriate staffing:* insufficient numbers of staff to provide basic services, as well as inadequate management, security, and supervision.
- *Public apathy:* indifference, punitive attitudes, singular focus on incapacitation, and lack of concern for treatment—prompting feelings of alienation as inmates see themselves increasingly ostracized from society.
- *Criminal justice and social inadequacies:* perceptions of sentencing disparities, subjective parole decisions, inequitable treatment by the criminal justice system, and discriminatory public policies.

While all of these and many other conditions serve to predispose correctional institutions to riots, perhaps the most pervasive underlying factor is the simple *lack of personal dignity.* As was expressed in the riots at both Attica and Santa Fe, "prisoners came to believe the only way to prove their humanity was by dying; . . . [t]hey saw nothing short of death that would regain their individuality and give them an identity."[63] Stated in their own words, "If we cannot live like people, we will at least try to die like men" (Attica); "If I'm going to die, I'm going to die like a man" (Santa Fe).

Undoubtedly, such alienation exists in many prisons along with the additional institutional conditions and social forces described above. The question thus may be not why there are so many prison riots, but rather, why there are so few.

## Precipitating Event

Inmates may well endure any number of predisposing conditions for quite extensive periods of time without disrupting into organized violence. At some point, however, a completely unanticipated event may *precipitate* mass action in violent response. Creating a strong perimeter with extreme pressure inside is the basic technique for building a bomb. Use the same principles, put society's outcasts inside, and you have a high-security prison.[64] Then, all that is needed is to ignite the fuse.

Any number of *precipitating events* can serve as the spark that ignites a riot. An altercation between an inmate and an officer, a momentary breech of security, a fight between two inmates, or any variety of other random incidents can trigger a riot. Even publicized accounts of events outside the prison can serve as precipitating events, as in the case of immigration actions that set off the Atlanta and Oakdale riots of 1987. In fact, it is probably due to the alert attention of correctional officials that widespread violence throughout the country did not spread into correctional institutions following the verdict in the 1992 trial related to the Rodney King case.

Particularly when a significant number of predisposing conditions come into contact with both a precipitating event and a breakdown in security, the stage is set for a riot. Such was the case in Attica—where in 1971, the most lethal riot in correctional history resulted in the deaths of 32 inmates and 10 staff members.[65] See the next "Close-up on Corrections" for an account of the conditions, events, and bloodshed surrounding a disturbance which over 20 years later remains a vivid reminder that society will not permit reforms to be forced by riots.

## Stages of a Riot

Although riot activities are not easily categorized into uniform patterns, as illustrated in the Attica scenario, they generally tend to proceed in five stages:[66]

1. *Initial explosion:* the spontaneous (or in some cases, planned) uprising during which inmates gain control of part of the institution.

---

[63]Sue Mahan, "An 'Orgy of Brutality' at Attica and the 'Killing Ground' at Santa Fe: A Comparison of Prison Riots," in Parisi, p. 76.

[64]Paraphrased from Vernon Fox, *Correctional Institutions* (Englewood Cliffs, NJ: Prentice Hall, 1983), p. 115.

[65]James A. Hudson, *Attica* (New York: Kimtex Corporation, 1971), p. 3.

[66]Summarized from Fox, p. 120.

### Attica

#### THE SETTING

Serenely located among the orchards and dairylands of upstate New York, the maximum-security Attica Correctional Facility was not a traditional trouble spot among the state's institutions. Yet, the critical events that transpired there between September 9 and 13, 1971, thrust Attica into the national spotlight—symbolizing it as representative of correctional problems everywhere.

Surrounded by a gray concrete wall, with gun towers spaced along the top, this concrete fortress housed some of New York state's most notorious inmates. Many of Attica's 2243 inmates were repeat offenders convicted of violent crimes, and by 1971, the population was increasingly composed of young, black, or Puerto Rican offenders from urban areas.

#### ADMINISTRATIVE SHORTCOMINGS

In contrast to the inmates, Attica's 380 correctional officers were predominately white, recruited from the rural countryside surrounding the facility. With little or no training (three weeks at most, depending on when the person was hired), the officers considered their function to be primarily custodial. In light of the shortage of psychological staff, however, counseling was often their responsibility by default.

Not only were they largely untrained, but by virtue of a 1970 union contract, it was the youngest and most inexperienced officers who were in most frequent direct interaction with the inmates. The contract enabled staff to bid for their assignments, and the older, more senior officers were quick to opt for the choice posts—those which involved the least contact with inmates. Administrative policies enabled the day-to-day changing of duty posts, thereby further deterring any development of inmate/officer rapport. Because of shift schedules, no more than one-third of the officers were on duty at any one time, resulting in considerable apprehensiveness about being understaffed.

Caught in a statewide budget squeeze, employees' salaries were low, and little was spent on inmate programs or rehabilitative efforts. As state corrections commissioner Russell G. Oswald expressed it: "On the one hand, the state budget for . . . government had never been more stringent, and the taxpayers had never been so tax-conscious. On the other hand, the inmates in the maximum security institutions had rarely seemed more dangerous."[a]

[a]Russell G. Oswald, *Attica—My Story* (New York: Doubleday, 1972), pp. 7–11.

Overall, Attica was no better or worse than other maximum-security facilities that were operating with meager numbers of inadequately prepared staff, receiving increasingly militant inmates, and forced by all of these constraints to place greater emphasis on security. The fact that these unfortunate circumstances culminated in the most lethal prison uprising in American penal history may indeed be the only thing that set Attica apart. History made Attica, justifiably or not, symbolic of the plight of corrections nationwide.

## PRECIPITATING EVENTS

To this day, there are conflicting versions of whether the Attica riot was a well-planned attack by an organized group of militants or a spontaneous burst of violence resulting more from angry frustrations than revolutionary plans. The truth may never be known. But regardless of its confusing origins, the outcome was undeniably tragic.

The initial explosion on September 9 occurred in response to an event the previous day from which angry feelings lingered. In that incident, a misunderstanding resulted in an inmate striking a correctional lieutenant—an unheard-of violation of regulations. Two offenders involved were assigned to special disciplinary housing quarters. Rumors that officers retaliated with physical abuse against the disciplined inmates kept the situation tense. Then, as one of the officers involved in the incident attempted to return a group of inmates to their cells after breakfast, he was attacked. The uprising was under way.

At this point, the physical design of the building should have enabled the cellblock where the disturbance originated to be sealed off. But several conditions permitted the violence to spread, including a defective gate, an outdated communications system, insufficient staff, and extensive confusion in the absence of a riot control plan. With these advantages, homemade weapons emerged, and the initial violence spread. Inmates from other areas joined in, got swept along, or fled in search of security. In less than two hours, extensive property had been destroyed, several officers had been critically injured, and over 1200 inmates were in command of four cellblocks and over 40 hostages.

## THE ORGANIZATION PHASE

Now a crucial decision was necessary—whether or not to send state police troopers in to face the rioters directly. Recognizing their limited strength and lacking a feasible supply of the type of tear gas most effective under riot conditions, it was obvious that weapons would have to be fired in a direct attack. Since there would be no way to protect the hostages, offensive moves were postponed.

Intent upon avoiding unnecessary bloodshed, the director of corrections agreed to negotiate with the inmates himself. This violated long-standing policy against negotiations when hostages are being held. It was perceived by many as "giving in," bolstering the inmates' confidence, and possibly encouraging the taking of hostages in future insurrections. When an immediate decision to retake the institution was not made, tensions among both the state police and the correctional employees heightened further, creating an atmosphere of edgy anticipation and nervous strain.

## NEGOTIATIONS

The state police were not yet fully mobilized for an attack. Still hoping that a nonviolent settlement could be reached, the corrections director agreed to additional unprecedented steps—personally meeting with the rioters on territory held by them and conceding to admit the news media. In retrospect, many criticized the decision to open the riot up to the glare of publicity. The media offered inmates a new source of power and reinforced their sense of importance, making it "almost impossible to persuade them to give up the limelight and return to anonymity."[b] But time was needed to assemble a sufficient supply of tear gas, and concern for the safety of the hostages if an attack was launched kept hope alive.

[b]New York State Special Commission on Attica, *Attica* (New York: Bantam Books, 1972), p. 212.

By this time, the list of inmate demands was growing. Added to it were a court injunction protecting them from subsequent administrative reprisals and the names of outside observers with whom they wanted to meet. Still anxious to negotiate a settlement, the state concurred. By the end of the day, there was optimism that a peaceful resolution could be reached.

But the next morning, in a gesture symbolic of their increasing defiance, a rebel leader tore the court injunction in half, accompanied by hearty cheers. As frustrations were vented before the cameras, a shouting, name-calling melee resulted during the next meeting with the corrections director. A move was made to take him hostage, but leaders kept their earlier guarantee of safe passage.

With this ominous change of atmosphere, any remaining confidence in the ability to obtain voluntary release of the hostages shifted to the efforts of the observers' committee. The observers were well-known liberal and radical leaders who had been chosen by the inmates themselves. But the committee's effectiveness was severely limited by its unmanageable size and confusion over its role. Eventually, the committee negotiated a compromise consisting of 28 points regarding physical facility improvements, staff upgrading, and greater freedom from administrative controls. But the committee's tireless efforts ended in the early hours of September 12 with the inmates' refusal to accept any plan that did not include unconditional amnesty, transportation to a "nonimperialist" country for those desiring it, and removal of the existing Attica superintendent.

By this point, tremendous pressure was building to retake the facility. State police, correctional officers, and the national guard had been assembled for two days and were becoming seriously demoralized, impatient, and anxious to get a direct offensive under way. So, following the inmates' rejection of one final message asking for release of the hostages in exchange for the 28 points, preparations were reluctantly initiated for the retaking of Attica.

## TERMINATION

At almost precisely the hour that the rebellion had begun four days previously, the state launched its counterattack. Less than 10 minutes later, 39 people were dead, 80 others wounded—with all deaths the result of firepower, not at the hands of inmates as initially reported.[c] While 28 of the remaining 38 hostages were saved, a variety of flaws contributed to the carnage:

[c]Attica Commission, p. 332.

• Although a general order was issued to use the minimum amount of force necessary, another order to avoid hand-to-hand combat (to prevent the loss of weapons) forced reliance on firepower.

• Final decision making relative to the firing of weapons was left to the discretion of individual troopers, using New York state police firearms policy as their guide. However, the long wait experienced by the officers resulted in considerable stress and tension, potentially intensifying their perception of a dangerous or threatening situation.

- Inadequate advance planning, lack of proper controls, and uncoordinated leadership contributed to confusion and misinterpretation. For example, the wide variety of weapons and ammunition used did not always enable precise firing (e.g., shotguns loaded with "00" buckshot). Moreover, inappropriate plans for evacuation and treatment of the wounded resulted in the availability of only two doctors and eight other medical personnel to provide assistance until the national guard's mobile unit could reach the scene.

- Confusion over who was actually in charge and lack of communication further contributed to the uncoordinated nature of the attack. Even when precise orders were issued, gas masks, (not equipped with communication devices) restricted ability to hear verbal orders. Since no plan was developed for visual commands, it was impossible to transmit orders to begin or halt firing.

## INVESTIGATION

In the days following the complete return of Attica to state control, several investigative missions were launched. Highly critical of the official handling of the incident, the Attica Commission made the following recommendations:

> If the prison can be retaken immediately without lethal force, the authorities should do so . . . the possibility of a negotiated settlement must be fully explored before using lethal force . . . negotiations conducted before hundreds of inmates are not likely to be productive . . . all negotiations [should] take place on neutral ground . . . negotiations must be conducted privately without the presence of the press . . . direct negotiations between inmates and the state are preferable to the use of outsiders [but] if outsiders are required in the negotiations, their function and authority must be clearly defined and agreed upon by them, the state, and the inmates."[d]

[d]Attica Commission, pp. 213–14.

## POSTSCRIPT

If nothing else, Attica thrust corrections into the national spotlight for nearly five days. Americans were forced to become aware of things about its correctional system which had, until Attica, remained secluded from public scrutiny.

In terms of the specific institutional grievances of Attica's rebelling inmates, conditions undoubtedly improved over what existed in 1971. But officials were careful to associate any changes with an existing commitment to prison reform rather than a response to pressures generated by the uprising. In Attica, as elsewhere throughout the country, officers are better trained; administrative controls are generally less stringent; physical facilities have been upgraded; and more inmate programs are available. But progress is relative to previous conditions. As one Attica commentator noted, "no matter how badly we fare, the legacy we pass on cannot be worse than the one we inherited."[e]

[e]D. M. Rothman, "Attica System: You Can't Reform the Bastille," *Nation* (March 19, 1973), p. 366.

2. *Organization:* the emergence of inmate leadership, as staff mobilize to pre-pare to respond.

3. *Confrontation:* the stage when inmates are confronted, either through nego-tiation or by force. This phase can range from long, drawn-out discussions to quickly issuing a warning, followed by an ultimatum and a show of force. Tactics employed may depend on whether hostages have been taken.

4. *Termination:* the point at which custodial control is regained, either through firepower, nonlethal force, or negotiated agreement.

5. *Explanation:* the subsequent investigation, designed to identify the cause of the disturbance and assure the public that necessary remedies are undertaken.

## Riot Control: Planning and Negotiating

To prevent widespread property damage, injuries, and loss of life, the best point at which to intervene in a riot is before the inmates can become organized under strong leadership. Unfortunately, that is also the time at which correction-al staff may be equally disorganized. As a result, institutions have devoted more attention in recent years to developing riot control plans designed to locate and isolate the disturbance, evacuate unsafe areas, and quickly resolve the situation.

The value of riot control planning was perhaps best demonstrated at the Federal Correctional Institution in Talladega, Alabama. On August 21, 1991, 118 Cuban detainees who were about to be deported seized control of a unit and took 11 hostages. After nine tense days of agonizingly slow negotiations, it became apparent that a core of violent, desperate detainees were increasingly likely to harm the hostages. Moreover, their demand for release was "simply not negotiable."[67] The decision was made to use tactical intervention:

> On the morning of day ten, at 3:40 A.M. . . . the FBI Hostage Rescue Team, supported by FBI SWAT (Special Weapons and Tactics) and Bureau of Prisons SORT (Special Operations Response Team) personnel, assaulted the unit. . . . Most of the detainees were surprised by the pre-dawn assault; many were literally caught sleeping. . . . No firearms were discharged and no gas was used as the unit was retaken. . . . No hostages were injured. . . . No detainees [were] killed or seriously injured. . . . The following day, 31 of the detainees were flown to Havana; a second flight of 32 was completed several days later."[68]

Rioting inmates know who has the advantage of weapons and firepower. In such a situation, "negotiation" takes on a different connotation from labor mediation, where the power of both sides is more equally balanced. In prison disturbances, negotiation is more a form of "keeping them talking" until group cohesion begins to break down, then offering an honorable and face-saving way out for the inmate leadership.

[67]Richard Phillips, "Crisis in Talladega," *Corrections Today,* Vol. 53, No. 7 (December 1991), p. 131.
[68]Ibid., pp. 132–33.

Lengthy negotiations with rioters have always been politically unpopular, particularly in light of the disastrous results at Attica following four days of extended discussions. In addition, if disorders are not dealt with instantly and decisively, the initiative is lost. It is for such reasons that, as shown in Figure 10.3, most riots have been resolved in the past by either use of force, show of force, or force combined with other factors.

In a notable exception, hostages were held for nine days during the 1987 riot at the Federal Detention Center in Oakdale, Louisiana. Nevertheless, negotiators employed by the Federal Bureau of Investigation and the U.S. Bureau of Prisons ultimately proved successful in obtaining a peaceful outcome. In fact, on the day of their surrender, the inmates cleaned up the yard, planted flowers, displayed handpainted religious pictures, and formed a gauntlet through which the hostages were released—receiving flowers and open signs of affection as they passed through.[69] The next "Close-up on Corrections" describes the process that resulted in such a tranquil ending to a potentially tragic event.

## Riot Prevention

Once a major disturbance has occurred, there is generally considerable reluctance to "give in" to any demands that were not part of an official negotiation agreement. Nor are any unofficial concessions made by individual hostages considered valid. Anyone held hostage is considered to have "no authority, regardless of rank, while under duress."[70] Especially if lives were lost, the public is not likely to support responses which appear to send a message that endorses violence as a means of achieving change. In fact, during the explanation phase, a "scapegoat" is often identified (such as the warden or director of corrections) whose physical dismissal may also serve as a symbolic dismissal of the entire incident.

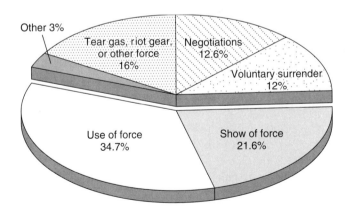

**Figure 10.3** How riots were ended. *Note:* Data reflect reports of 260 prison riots between 1971 and 1983 (for which 93 did not indicate how the riot was ended). *Source:* Ellis MacDougall and Reid H. Montgomery, Jr., "American Prison Riots, 1971–1983," unpublished paper (Columbia, SC: College of Criminal Justice, University of South Carolina), p. 26.

[69]Clinton Van Zandt and G. Dwayne Fuselier, "Nine Days of Crisis Negotiations: The Oakdale Siege," *Corrections Today*, Vol. 51, No. 4 (July 1989), p. 24.
[70]*Causes, Preventive Measures* p. 80.

Nine Days of Successful Crisis Negotiation Techniques

*November 20, 1987:* The U.S. Department of Justice announces the United States has reached an agreement with Cuba to return approximately 2,500 who arrived in the U.S. during the 1980 Mariel boatlift. Many potential deportees are incarcerated in the Federal Detention Center, Oakdale, Louisiana, and the U.S. Penitentiary, Atlanta, Georgia.

*November 21:* 200 inmates at Oakdale riot, resulting in 26 hostages being held for the next nine days.

*November 23:* 1,370 Cuban detainees at Atlanta riot, taking 100 penitentiary employees hostage. . . .

### ALLOWING EMOTIONS TO VENTILATE

Soon after the Oakdale incident began, the U.S. Attorney General declared a moratorium on the deportations. This was immediately conveyed to the inmates, but they were not swayed by this announcement.

It was apparent to negotiators that the inmates had been offered "too much, too soon." The inmates' high frustration level, coupled with mistrust of authorities and fear of deportation, caused them to reject this early resolution. Many of the inmates had been incarcerated since their arrival in the country, and this incident provided them an opportunity to vent their anger and frustration. . . .

### AVOIDING TRICKS AND DISHONESTY

Negotiators continually reassured the inmates that no assault would take place as long as the hostages were not harmed. At the same time, the inmate representatives were told that should tactical entry become necessary to rescue the hostages, tactical teams would enter with automatic weapons. Any attempt to resist or assult members of the tactical team would be met with deadly force—a more serious threat than the riot batons the inmates associated with correctional officers. . . . In this situation, the inmates had to assess their willingness to die for this specific cause. Negotiators were able to maintain a tactical credibility and at the same time negotiate in earnest for a nonviolent solution. . . .

Although initial negotiation sessions were conducted in Spanish, negotiation team leaders decided to conduct all subsequent sessions in English. This denied the inmate representatives emotional spontaneity . . . and forced them to translate their thoughts into English. . . .

### MENTAL HEALTH PROFESSIONALS

One [U.S. Bureau of Prisons] psychologist prepared a psychological profile of the inmate population, which gave FBI negotiators, tactical teams, and the on-scene commanders a unique look at the Oakdale population as a whole. This insight enabled negotiators to develop and recommend appropriate techniques to on-scene commanders that could be used to bring the inmates to the negotiations table.

## MANIPULATION

Manipulative measures included denying the inmates outside sources of food, water, and electricity; allowing them to see an occasional show of force by the authorities; and using cherry picker telephone line trucks to give snipers a view of the compound. . . .

At Oakdale, one FBI negotiator would occasionally act as though he were losing his temper. . . . On one occasion, this negotiator was dressed in camouflage trousers, military-type sweater, and boots. The inmate negotiators feared that he represented the military present at Oakdale and that the military was losing patience with the inmates and might take some precipitous action.

## NON-POLICE NEGOTIATORS

A key issue . . . was the presence at Oakdale of Cuban-born Catholic Bishop Agustin Roman of Miami. . . . On November 28, a videotape was made of the Bishop asking for the release of the hostages and for a peaceful surrender. On November 29, the video was shown at four locations around the perimeter. . . . To obtain the maximum psychological impact, inmate representatives were not forewarned that the tape would be played. The inmates were initially positive about the Bishop's recorded message, but continued to demand his presence as a term of their surrender.

A decision was made to resolve the issue of the Bishop's presence and to provide a final emotional rush for the inmates. Without notifying [them], the Bishop was flown to the detention center . . . and driven around the perimeter of the compound in an open truck in plain view of all the inmates.

By prearrangement, he addressed the inmates . . . [telling] them the agreement to be signed was good and that he wanted them to lay down their weapons and release the hostages. . . . The inmates began to throw down their weapons. . . . The formal agreement, witnessed by the Bishop, was signed shortly thereafter.

## THE SURRENDER RITUAL

The importance of the surrender ritual was clearly evident in this incident. The inmates used handwritten signs and banners to convey their impression that they had been wronged by the U.S. Government and sought only fair treatment for themselves and attention to their common cause.

On the day the incident was successfully concluded, one such banner said, "Dear Citizens of the United States, thank you for your hopes and prayers, we do not want to blow it." This paraphrased an FBI negotiator who constantly warned the inmate representatives "they were too close to blow it now." . . . Negotiators noted the need for . . . an orchestrated, formal "surrender" agreement . . . including a signed document with witnesses and access to the media. . . .

The tactical assets were available and were fully capable of carrying out a hostage rescue mission. But in the Oakdale and Atlanta sieges, the situations were resolved without further violence. Hostage negotiations again proved to be . . . [the] most effective nonlethal weapon.

*Source:* Clinton Van Zandt and G. Dwayne Fuselier, "Nine Days of Crisis Negotiations: The Oakdale Siege," *Corrections Today,* Vol. 51, No. 4 (July, 1989), pp. 16–24.

Obviously, the days following a riot are not the ideal time to address conditions underlying the disturbance. What is needed are not *reactive responses* after the damage has been done, but rather, *proactive procedures* designed to prevent riots from occurring in the first place.

There may admittedly be little that correctional administrators can do to alleviate public apathy, social inadequacies, and stressors inherent in the environment of prisons. Moreover, there is not much at all that can be done without public willingness to support substantial additional funding to improve everything from physical facilities to staff training. But there are some less costly steps that can be taken to reduce the tension, anxiety, and frustration which make an institution particularly vulnerable to rioting. One of the primary examples is simply having in place a *formal grievance procedure* to respond to inmate complaints before minor irritations become major issues. Of course, if inmates do not have confidence that the grievance procedure will result in action, it may only serve as a further source of frustration. Although there will undoubtedly be complaints which are not within the authority or fiscal ability of the administration to resolve, efforts can be made to at least explain the reasons for inaction.

In this regard, *effective communication* with the inmate population represents another area which can be addressed without additional resources that also can reduce the potential for uprisings. In fact, from one perspective, a riot can be viewed as a method of communicating—"a dramatic one that is seldom used unless other forms of communications have been tried and failed."[71] In an atmosphere of open, two-way interaction that is reinforced by staff training, inmates do not have the need to resort to violence to get administrative attention. While even the best communication process is not likely to create an atmosphere of true mutual trust within a prison, listening and responding to inmate problems demonstrates administrative concern, allows for the airing of legitimate complaints, and enables staff to detect signs of impending unrest. In other words, "the most effective approaches to prevention are founded on good management, visibility and accessibility of top administrative staff, and constant alertness to symptoms of possible problems."[72]

This does *not*, however, mean that communication should focus on nurturing sources of intelligence information through informants (or "snitches," as they are disreputably referred to by prisoners). The use of inmate "tipsters" has its proponents among those who argue that (1) better custodial control is possible when prisoners do not trust each other and the inmate code is broken, (2) fewer officers are needed to maintain discipline, and (3) a group of inmates sympathetic to the administration can be developed for informal self-government of the institution. But abdicating responsibility to inmates in this manner can have disastrous effects when those involved abuse their trust and take power into their own hands, as occurred with the "building tenders" system in Texas.[73] Even in systems where inmates are allowed no custodial control functions, rewarding

[71]Ibid., p. 23.

[72]*Management Strategies in Disturbances*, p. 47.

[73]John J. DiIulio, Jr., *Governing Prisons: A Comparative Study of Correctional Management* (New York: Free Press, 1987), pp. 206–12, where the inmate "building tenders" were cited as the "seeds of destruction" of the Texas control model of prison management.

cooperation or information with special privileges enables them to exert their additional authority and "wheel and deal" with both staff and other inmates.

There are considerably more valid arguments opposing rather than supporting the official use of tipsters or informal inmate leaders, including the fact that: (1) the staff become dependent on inmates in matters that should be reserved for administrative authority; (2) an artificial hierarchy of prestige or status is established, with some inmates viewed more favorably and awarded special privileges; and (3) an institution where no one feels that anyone else can be trusted creates a paranoid atmosphere, encourages corruption, and is demeaning to employees and inmates alike.[74]

Better all-round custodial control can be maintained by attending to matters that require official attention than by running down leads given by inmates with dubious motivations. Moreover, the "snitch system" can put the lives of informants in grave danger. The worst example of the sadistic cruelty with which inmates have reacted to informants was demonstrated in the 1980 Santa Fe, New Mexico, disturbance—when rioters broke into the section of the institution holding those in protective custody. (The viciously brutal treatment of informants by the rioters is described in the next "Close-up on Corrections".)

Beyond accounting for 33 inmate deaths, rioters in Santa Fe violently expressed their vengeance through widespread property damage, creating the most costly disturbance in U.S. prison history. Totalling some $36 million, the "cost of the event reached almost exactly one million dollars an hour; the riot lasted thirty-six hours."[75] Undoubtedly, $36 million could have been used much more effectively for remedies directed toward preventing the disturbance than repairs to the resulting damages. Unfortunately, however, it is inevitably easier to generate public concern and fiscal support *after* an institution explodes into all-out violence—when the ambiguity of unheeded warnings is replaced by the clarity of undeniable consequences. As one prison manager has noted: "Every time there's a riot, half of us cries and half is happy because we know it means more attention and probably more money for everything—salaries, programs, you name it"[76]—a benefit of which the inmates may well be equally well aware.

In the face of the immediate fiscal cost of institutional disruptions, it is easy to become distracted from the greater long-term social costs incurred by the more subtle day-to-day threat of brutality and degregation. Some would contend that exposure to such conditions is "just deserts"—that it is fitting for those who were victimizers in the free community to become victims themselves in the prison community. Aside from basic human dignity, what that argument conveniently overlooks is the fact that their membership in the prison community is temporary. Thus, "[p]ermitting them to serve their punishment in an atmosphere at least as free from terror and violence as the outside world is a test of our collective self-respect, and ultimately, a matter of our collective self-interest."[77]

[74]See Perry Johnson, "The Snitch System: How Informants Affect Prison Security," *Corrections Today*, Vol. 51, No. 4 (July 1989), pp. 26–28, and Van Vandivier, "Do You Want to Know a Secret? Guidelines for Using Confidential Information," *Corrections Today*, Vol. 51, No. 4 (July 1989), pp. 30–32.
[75]Mahan, p. 68.
[76]DiIulio, p. 33, quoting an anonymous prison manager.
[77]Lerner, p. 72.

"Get Backs" for "Snitches" in Santa Fe

The first killings took place in Cell Block 3, soon after the block was under inmate control. In one case, inmates armed with steel pipes gathered in front of the victim's cell. One of the assailants said, "We've got to kill this son-of-a-bitch, man. . . . We've got to kill him. . . . He snitched on [inmate's name]." They beat and then knifed him to death. . . .

Another unpopular resident of Cell Block 3, seeing what was coming, jammed the door of his cell so successfully that it couldn't be opened for two days after the prison was recaptured. But it did him no good. He was shot in the face through the window of his cell with one of the grenade launchers taken from the control center.

These murders created a model for retribution against "snitches" and enemies. Thereafter, it was as if inmates vied with each other to produce imaginative modes of murder and mutilation. . . . Begging for his life, [one] victim was kicked and then bludgeoned to death with a pipe. . . . Another victim had his eyes gouged out, a screwdriver driven through his head. . . .

Inmates killed no hostages. . . . [T]he guards may actually have been less hated by the inmates than the "snitches" were. . . . The demonstrative means used to kill "snitches" suggest a virtually ritualistic "purging" of traitorous elements. . . . Guards, on the other hand, however disliked, do what they are expected to do in imprisoning inmates, and do not bear the stigma of treason.

*Source:* Bert Useem and Peter Kimball, *States of Siege: U.S. Prison Riots, 1971–1986* (New York: Oxford University Press, 1989), pp. 105–7.

*Postscript:* Although no correctional officers were killed, it should be noted that they did suffer "stabbings, beatings, and brutal degradation during their captivity."[a]

[a]Adolph B. Saenz and T. Zane Reeves, "Riot Aftermath: New Mexico's Experience Teaches Valuable

## ❖ SUMMARY

Inmates are socialized into the institutional setting through the process of prisonization, by which they adapt to the culture, values, norms, and behavioral expectations of the environment. Some maintain that this process is a feature of similar values, attitudes, and behaviors that offenders bring into the prison setting (importation), while others attribute it to natural adjustments made to an unnatural environment (deprivation). Each explanation holds some validity, and it may be that the prison environment further reinforces preexisting personal traits.

Whatever the cause, the result is often adaptation through development of an "institutionalized personality"—characterized by such noncommital features as routinized behavior, automatic responses, loss of initiative, submission to power, and avoiding any emotional investment. To those exhibiting such a personality pattern, seemingly minor diversions or incidents can take on exaggerated importance. In many respects, those who adjust best to the degrading rituals of imprisonment are psychologically damaged the most. Inmates who are younger, more emotionally vulnerable, and confined for longer periods of time are particularly susceptible.

But everyone does not accommodate to imprisonment in exactly the same manner. Individual characteristics, environmental conditions, and interaction between the two all shape one's adjustment. Defense mechanisms ranging from outright rebellion to rejection of authority, projecting blame on others, and rationalizing behavior also assist the inmate in psychologically coping with confinement.

In response to the dehumanizing nature of institutional conditions, the inmate subculture serves to protect personal identity and autonomy. Through this subculture, inmates reinforce values, attitudes, and standards of conduct that are in direct contrast to those of the administration. The subculture is distinguished by a unique language (argot), as well as an inmate code of conduct that establishes informal regulations in opposition to the formal rules of the institution. Newly arriving prisoners are quickly initiated into the inmate code and sized-up according to how well they fit into the inmate subculture.

Beyond their overall organization into a separate subculture, inmates also unite through gangs. Prison gangs polarize the population along racial, ethnic, and religious lines. In addition to their involvement in corrupt activities both within and outside the institution, gangs present a serious concern for order and safety as a result of their willingness to engage in collective violence. Intentional violence by well-organized, close-knit groups is considerably more difficult to control than individual expressions of frustration.

When correctional officials lose control of a considerable number of prisoners in a sizable area of the compound for a significant amount of time, an institutional riot has occurred. Many underlying conditions can promote the potential for a riot—from the regimentation, deprivations, and lack of personal dignity of the environment itself to crowding, substandard physical facilities, inadequate staffing, public apathy, and perceptions of inequities within the criminal justice system. Such predisposing conditions may be tolerated for long periods of time. Then, a completely unanticipated event can suddenly provide the "spark" that precipitates a riot. This can be anything from an altercation between an officer and an inmate to a momentary breech of security or a fight between two inmates. Once the institution explodes into a violent uprising, riots generally progress in stages—moving from organization under strong inmate leaders, to confrontation with authorities, to termination (through firepower, nonlethal force, or negotiated agreement), and subsequent explanation.

Riots have plagued correctional institutions since as early as 1774, and some have resulted in widespread death, injury, and property damage. The deadliest riot occurred in 1971 at Attica (New York), where 10 staff members and 32 inmates lost their lives. The costliest riot took place in Santa Fe (New Mexico), where—in addition to 33 deaths—damage estimates reached $36 million. In the more recent Oakdale (Louisana) riot, well-trained negotiators were able to reach a peaceful settlement, indicating that traditional reluctance to negotiate with those holding hostages may not always be a wise course of action.

In addition to improved riot control planning, correctional officials can take proactive steps to address predisposing conditions in an effort to reduce the potential for violent explosion of the institution. Examples include implementing formal grievance procedures and providing open, two-way communications between inmates and staff. Care should be exercised, however, to prevent the communication process from deteriorating into a reliance on informants. While some prison officials have used tipsters or informal inmate leaders working on behalf of the administration, these practices entail far more disadvantages than advantages.

Beyond the loss of life and injuries resulting from riots, extensive property damage can require massive fiscal investments to restore the institution to a fully operating condition. Undoubtedly, money could have been spent much more productively to remedy conditions provoking the disturbance, rather than repairing the subsequent damage.

# chapter 11

# Transition from Confinement to Community

*People cannot make it coming out of prison unless two things happen—a change in their heart and somebody on the outside who will help them.*[1]

*Charles W. Colson*

## ❖ CHAPTER OVERVIEW

Given the effects of prison life described in Chapter 10, it is apparent that incarceration is far from the optimal means of preparing offenders for a law-abiding lifestyle in the community. No matter how punitive the public may be in demanding imprisonment, the fact cannot be overlooked that at some point, virtually all inmates are eventually eligible for release. The inevitable may be temporarily postponed. But in most cases, it cannot be totally prevented.

As we saw in previous chapters, those in confinement are isolated from the rest of society, both physically and psychologically. They are constrained by strict rules. They are constantly supervised. Their movements are closely regulated. They "survive" the experience by adaptation. Some become subservient automotons. Others become rebellious activists. Most subscribe to an inmate behavioral code that is counter to the norms and values of official authority.

At the other extreme, those of us in free society are physically integrated with that society. Our actions are unhampered by direct scrutiny. We are free to come and go as we wish. We are able to live our lives much as we please, guided only by self-discipline and the implicit deterrence of social controls. In exchange for these freedoms, however, society requires certain social expectations and respect for legitimate authority. Thus, former inmates rejoining society must be

---

[1]Duncan Clark, "Chuck Colson: Born Again Prison Reformer," *Corrections Today*, Vol. 51, No. 4 (July 1989), p. 81. Mr. Colson, formerly special counsel to President Richard Nixon, served seven months in a federal prison and subsequently became chairman of the board of Prison Fellowship Ministries.

able to replace external with internal constraints. They must substitute compliance with social laws for adherence to inmate codes. In other words, they have to adapt to community integration from controlled isolation.

Needless to say, an inmate cannot be subjected to the rigidities of a tightly controlled institutional environment one day and walk confidently into the freedom of society the next without mishap. Making the transition between these two extremes is obviously not an overnight process that can effectively occur without assistance. In essence, parole represents an effort to provide such help while maintaining some behavioral restrictions. Much like the deep-sea diver who cannot rise too quickly to the surface without proper decompression, the parole process is designed to deescalate external controls gradually in order to ease reintegration into the community.

Parole therefore involves both regulatory and rehabilitative functions. Much like the dual responsibilities of probation discussed in Chapter 5, parole officers face the need to balance their supportive and surveillance duties. But beyond the dual nature of its mission, parole has also encountered vocal opposition, especially as public sentiments have shifted.

Under the medical model, it was assumed that there was an optimum time for releasing an offender from incarceration. To do so too early could present obvious public safety risks. To wait too late could present serious adjustment problems among those confined longer than necessary for their "rehabilitation." With the indeterminate sentences of the medical model, establishing when an inmate should be released was largely the subjective decision of the paroling authority, taking into consideration such factors as the offender's background, prison record, and participation in institutional programs.

In the absence of clear, objective guidelines, eligibility for parole became the source of complaints about apparent inequities. In some cases, parole policies have even been cited as causing prison riots. Attica was a prime example—where the official investigation concluded that "the operation of the parole system was a primary souce of tension and bitterness within the walls."[2] In Attica and elswhere, those who were satisfied with decisions of the parole board were out in the community, while those turned down for parole remained in prison venting their frustrations. Nor was the credibility of the decision-making process enhanced by high rates of recidivism or the public outrage that followed when a parolee engaged in a particularly notorious crime.

Movement to the justice model's determinate sentencing was designed to eliminate the uncertainty of prison terms based on the release-through-parole feature of indeterminate sentencing. As a result, some states have abolished parole, and mandatory release upon expiration of one's sentence is now increasing, while discretionary parole releases are decreasing.

This does not mean that parole no longer exists. However, paroling authorities are now more likely to be responsible for *supervising offenders* in the community following mandated release rather than for *making decisions* about when to release. Despite more restrictive functions and a less supportive public, few

[2]"Prison without Walls: Summary Report on New York Parole Citizens' Inquiry on Parole and Criminal Justice, Inc." in Calvert R. Dodge, ed., *A Nation without Prisons* (Lexington, MA: D.C. Heath, 1975), p. 83, quoting the New York State Special Commission on Attica.

would argue that parole is a needless component of the correctional system. As long as the environment of correctional institutions differs so extremely from that of free society, assistance will be needed in making the transition from confinement to community. Parole certainly cannot guarantee the prevention of recidivism. But without it, released offenders may well be even more destined to become repeat offenders.

---

*LEARNING GOALS*

*Do you know:*

- *The origin and definition of "parole"?*
- *Why legislative authorization of indeterminate sentencing is necessary to implement parole?*
- *Why some states have returned to determinate sentencing?*

---

## ❖ HISTORICAL BACKGROUND

Parole has always been one of the most controversial features of the correctional system. As noted in Chapter 4, Captain Alexander Maconochie experimented with the *mark system*, which enabled inmates to earn freedom through "marks" awarded for hard work and proper behavior. For this and similar progressive but provocative efforts, Maconochie was removed as superintendent of the Norfolk Island (Australia) penal colony. Returned to England, he was subsequently dismissed from prison service "on the grounds that his methods were too lenient."[3] Maconochie's visions lived on, however, in the Irish *ticket-of-leave* pioneered in 1854 by Sir Walter Crofton. Under this system, inmates earned release by gradually progressing through a series of stages involving reduced discipline, which could eventually earn them a ticket of leave—what we now know as parole.

Nor did Zebulon Brockway find America much more receptive to his ideas when he introduced parole at the Elmira Reformatory in 1876. While Brockway did not lose his position for his reform-minded actions, many of the decisions he made regarding persons selected for parole were widely challenged. Deciding who should receive parole was then, and remains, a controversial issue. Nevertheless, by the early twentieth century, a number of events had occurred which gained support for the practice of early conditional release.

### Parole Developments

It was not long after establishment of the first penitentiaries that the idea of parole began emerging. Mirabeau, a French statesman, suggested the function of parole in one of his last reports to the court just before his death in 1791. Having been imprisoned for promoting tax reform and other governmental changes, his

---

[3]Todd R. Clear and George F. Cole, *American Corrections* (Monterey, CA: Brooks/Cole Publishing Company, 1986), p. 372.

suggestions were based on firsthand observations of penal practices while he was confined. In fact, the word *parole* has French origins in the term *parole d'honneur*, which means "word of honor."[4]

In the United States, the term *parole* was first used to refer to a type of conditional release in an 1846 letter written to the Prison Association of New York by Dr. Samuel G. Howe of Boston (husband of Julia Ward Howe, social reformer and composer of *The Battle Hymn of the Republic*). In that same year, Massachusetts was the first state to officially establish parole service when an agent was appointed to assist released prisoners. By legislative action in 1867, Michigan became the first state to introduce the *indeterminate sentencing*. This was necessary in order to enable correctional officials to provide early release on parole, under the philosophy that "the prisoner's destiny should be placed . . . in his own hands; he must be put into circumstances where he will be able, through his own exertions, to better his own condition continually. . . ."[5]

Combined with use of the indeterminate sentence, the possibilities of parole were discussed on a national basis in 1870 during the initial meeting of the National Prison Association. At that meeting, Zebulon Brockway told the assembly that preemptory (fixed) sentences should be replaced with indeterminate sentences. With such a change, prisoners could be released early after exhibiting some evidence that they had been reformed rather than being released on mere lapse of time.[6] He further suggested providing some type of supervision for three years after release from prison. At the time, Brockway was superintendent of the Detroit House of Correction and had been responsible for the passing of Michigan's first indeterminate sentencing law. Later, he was selected to become superintendent of the Elmira Reformatory, where parole was an integral feature from its opening in 1876.

By 1910, thirty-two states and the federal government had established parole systems.[7] By the 1950s, all states had implemented indeterminate sentencing, and all jurisdictions throughout the country had adopted some form of parole. But a quarter-century later, the tide began to turn. Public disillusionment with the medical model's indeterminate sentencing was fueled by reports citing the futility of rehabilitative efforts, along with alarming recidivism rates. As a result, in 1976 Maine became the first state to fully embrace determinate sentencing and abolish parole. Since then, several additional states and the federal government have adopted such sentencing practices and substantially limited the functions of parole.[8]

[4]Belinda Rodgers McCarthy and Bernard J. McCarthy, Jr., *Community-Based Corrections*, Second Edition (Pacific Grove, CA: Brooks/Cole Publishing Company, 1991), p. 244.
[5]Edward Lindsey, "Historical Sketch of the Indeterminate Sentence and Parole System," *Journal of the American Institute of Criminal Law and Criminology*, Vol. 16 (1925), p. 9.
[6]John Lewis Gillin, *Criminology and Penology* (New York: Appleton-Century Company, 1915), p. 510.
[7]George G. Killinger, "Parole and Other Release Procedures," in Paul W. Tappan, ed., *Contemporary Corrections* (New York: McGraw-Hill, 1951), pp. 361–62.
[8]The states with determinate sentencing as of 1988 were California, Connecticut, Florida, Illinois, Indiana, Maine, Minnesota, New Mexico, North Carolina, and Washington, along with the federal government. (Although the U.S. Congress initially abolished the U.S. Parole Commission in 1989, with phase-out planned for 1992, that date has since been extended to 1997). One additional state—Colorado—changed to determinate sentencing in 1979 but returned to indeterminate sentencing in 1985. See *Report to the Nation on Crime and Justice*, Second Edition (Washington, DC: U.S. Department of Justice, 1988), p. 91.

## Parole Defined

While some form of parole remains the primary method through which inmates are released from prison, the nature of parole has changed considerably from its early origins. Generally, parole is considered to be *supervised release* from a correctional institution prior to sentence expiration, under *conditions* that permit reincarceration if violated. In other words, parole is simply a continuation of one's sentence in the community. The inmate is released under supervision and expected to abide by certain provisions, violation of which could result in the revocation of parole. The conditions imposed are quite similar to those required of probationers—such as remaining drug/alcohol-free, reporting periodically to a parole officer, avoiding criminal associations, obeying the law, and the like.

It is the *supervised, conditional release* prior to sentence expiration that distinguishes parole from other forms of custodial release. Unconditional releases obtained by court order, executive pardon, or expiration/commutation of one's sentence do not involve parole. In theory, release on parole could occur from any type of correctional facililty. But in practice, parole is not usually available for those serving time in jail because of the shorter-term nature of jail sentences. Thus, parole is usually an option only for those more serious offenders serving longer sentences in state or federal prisons. Just as convalescence is considered essential after being in a hospital, parole is equally necessary after being in prison. Ideally, both should also include certain prescribed treatments.

---

*LEARNING GOALS*

*Do you know:*

- *In contrast to probation, which branch of government has authority over parole?*
- *How the functions of parole have changed in recent years?*
- *What conflicting objectives are expected of parole?*
- *Who is eligible for parole?*
- *Why parole is preferable to unsupervised release?*
- *On what basis appointments to parole boards have been subject to criticism?*
- *How parole's administrative organization can affect release decisions?*

---

## ❖ PAROLE AUTHORITY

Unlike probation, which is primarily a judicial function of the courts, parole is an *executive function* of correctional authorities. In fact, under previous indeterminate sentencing practices—when parole boards had virtually unlimited discretion to determine release dates—correctional officials in many respects had a greater impact than judges in terms of establishing the length of sentences.

Historically, the functions of parole have involved four phases:

1. *Selection for parole:* reviewing cases to identify which inmates should be released from prison before the expiration of their sentence.
2. *Preparole preparation:* classroom sessions, films, counseling, and other assistance designed to prepare new parolees for the decisions and self-discipline needed to resume life in free society.
3. *Parole supervision:* assistance, treatment, and oversight provided in the ex-offender's home environment to ease transition from the institution, as well as control behavior in the community.
4. *Parole termination:* either through routine dismissal of the case upon successful completion of parole or revocation for violation of parole conditions.

Note, however, that the previous definition of parole refers only to the conditions and supervision accompanying early release from incarceration. It does not address how or by whom the release decision is made. That is because today, correctional authority is more limited to parole preparation, supervision, and termination, with selection now often a function of the judicial or legislative branches of government. Throughout the remainder of this chapter, we explore how and why this change has occurred and whether it actually represents a fundamental departure from past practices, or simply new terms for a similar process.

## Objectives of Parole

Much of the changing nature of parole relates to differing perspectives of just what parole is supposed to accomplish. Traditionally, parole was designed to achieve objectives that were sometimes contradictory. For example, parole has been charged with:

- *Providing the inmate with an incentive* for learning new skills, seeking treatment, and behaving properly in prison, while at the same time . . .
- *Protecting the public* by keeping offenders incarcerated until they are no longer perceived as a danger to society.

As we have seen in Chapter 10, inmates who adapt well to the regimented routines of institutional life may not adapt equally well to the drastically reduced restrictions of free society. Nor does participation in work or treatment programs necessarily guarantee long-term behavioral change. Moreover, placing a priority on protecting public safety demands a conservative approach to making release decisions, whereas serving the best interests of those incarcerated may call for a greater willingness to take risks with borderline cases.

Beyond these conflicting objectives, parole has included the need to:

- Assure *fairness and equity overall,* but also . . .
- Address the *merits of each case individually.*

Despite more determinate sentencing today, parole agents still maintain authority for providing clients with support as well as supervision upon conditional release from confinement. Courtesy of Tom Hudson. Used with permission of the American Correctional Association.

Among its many functions, parole has served as a vehicle for adjusting sentencing disparities. For example, when two offenders convicted of similar crimes receive dramatically different sentences, parole can be used to reduce the discrepancy. On the other hand, no two offenders are exactly alike. When parole decision making takes personal variations into account (such as individual adjustment, behavioral problems, and the like), the result for some can be sentence lengths that differ even more than those originally imposed on others with similar offenses. In addition, with widespread concerns over prison crowding, the integrity of parole is increasingly vulnerable as pressures mount to release offenders prematurely so that space can be provided for new admissions.[9]

[9]In fact, it has been noted that "this pressure may assume the form of a quota system, wherein the number of releases must equal the number of admissions . . . [in which case] the concept of 'earned' parole release is lost." Lloyd G. Rupp, Edward E. Rhine, William R. Smith, and Ronald W. Jackson, "Parole: Issues and Prospects for the 1990s," in *Correctional Issues: Probation and Parole* (Laurel, MD: American Correctional Association, 1990), p. 23.

Parole has been relieved of many of these dilemmas in states where release decisions are now more a result of judicial or legislative decree than parole board discretion. (It should, however, be noted that in most jurisdictions, parole boards retain discretionary authority over release dates.) But ultimately, the major objective of parole has been and continues to be *reducing recidivism.*

In the past, parole attempted to achieve this objective by a combination of selecting the most appropriate candidates for release and providing them with support and supervision as they made the transition into the community. With responsibility for selection diminishing, the focus of parole today is directed more toward postrelease procedures. But that does not mean that its contradictory features have been eliminated, since parole is still expected to:

- *Help the offender* successfully reintegrate into the community, but at the same time . . .
- *Safeguard the public* by continuing to control the parolee under community supervision.

As with probation, parole officers struggle to find a balance between providing supportive assistance and supervising activities so that public safety is not compromised. In fact, it is ironic that the effectiveness of parole is largely judged on the basis of whether its clients return to prison. Yet it is incumbent upon parole authorities to do exactly that when a client is not functioning effectively in society. Moreover, as we will see later, evaluating parole according to recidivism is not only subject to what measures are used, but may be misleading as well, since parole cannot be fully credited with or blamed for its successes and failures.

## Eligibility for Parole

Once an inmate has served whatever minimum sentence was established by state statute or the sentencing court, he or she is generally eligible to be considered for release. Unless the sentence specifically includes a stipulation that it is issued with no possibility of parole, even those with "life" sentences are eligible for parole in a number of states. (In fact, only about 1.3% of the 771,243 inmates in state and federal prisons during 1990 were sentenced to life without parole.[10]) That does not, however, mean that inmates can initiate an application for parole. While they may voluntarily turn down an opportunity to be paroled, they have no direct control over when parole will be offered.

Nor does eligibility mean that parole will be granted automatically. Discretionary parole is legally considered a *privilege* rather than a *right.* Of course, that is not always how it is viewed in practice. This differing perception dates back to the historical development of parole, during which time "both prison administrators and inmates soon accepted the idea that reformed or unreformed, allowance of time for good behavior was automatic and release at the

---

[10]Compiled from figures presented in *Sourcebook of Criminal Justice Statistics—1990* (Washington, DC: U.S. Government Printing Office, 1991), p. 625, and Robyn L. Cohen, "Prisoners in 1990," *Bureau of Justice Statistics: Bulletin* (Washington, DC: U.S. Department of Justice, 1991), p. 1.

earliest possible date was a right rather than a privilege."[11] Nevertheless, the courts have not established any constitutional right to be released on parole before the legal expiration of one's sentence.

Those turned down at their first opportunity for consideration are often routinely scheduled for a rehearing after a designated period of time. Many offenders are paroled at the first opportunity, while particularly notorious criminals may well proceed through numerous rehearings unsuccessfully. For example, the eighth parole hearing was conducted for Charles Manson in 1992, under California's provision for rehearing the cases of those serving life terms every three years. While many doubt the likelihood that someone of his notoriety will ever be paroled, the Los Angeles prosecutor requested an extension to five years between hearings to reduce the chances of his release.[12]

Obviously, inmates repeatedly denied parole are likely to be the most serious, potentially dangerous offenders. But in states that do not provide for life without parole, only death in prison can completely assure the prevention of one's eventual release. In that respect, it is an unfortunate irony that long-termers who ultimately exit prison upon the expiration of their sentence—without community supervision—are often the offenders who need the scrutiny of parole the most.

See the next "Close-up on Corrections" for the tragic account of one such case. As that scenario illustrates, parole represents the most logical and sensible type of release. Although those with a strong custodial orientation may denounce the availability of parole as "too lenient," it is the desire to prevent such unfortunate events that motivates many in corrections to support post-release parole supervision.

## Parole Boards

Parole selections in most states have been administered by a commission or board appointed by the governor (which may be subject to confirmation by the legislature). In the majority of states, serving on the *parole board* is a full-time job. But other jurisdictions have only part-time membership, and still others maintain a combination of some full-time and some part-time members. Most frequently, five people sit on the board, although size varies from two in Minnesota to 19 in New York.[13] Given the relatively small size of most parole boards, it has been noted that "[in] no other part of the system is so much power concentrated in so few hands."[14]

Much of the concern surrounding parole has centered on how that power has been used. Appointments have often been a reward for political service to the successful gubernatorial candidate. It is therefore not surprising that parole

[11]Howard Abadinsky, *Probation and Parole: Theory and Practice,* Second Edition (Englewood Cliffs, NJ: Prentice Hall, 1982), p. 136.

[12]Sally Ann Stewart, "Parole Hearing No. 8 for Manson," *USA Today* (April 20, 1992), p. 3A.

[13]Edward E. Rhine, William R. Smith, and Ronald W. Jackson, *Paroling Authorities: Recent History and Current Practice* (Laurel, MD: American Correctional Association, 1991), p. 54.

[14]Peggy McGarry, *Handbook for New Parole Board Members,* Second Edition (Washington, DC: National Institute of Corrections, 1988), p. 18.

Release without Parole

Every treatment person in the prison, as well as others, predicted that inmate X would kill somebody. He was eligible for parole in 18 months but was kept in prison for the maximum five years remaining on his sentence. As his sentence expired, frantic calls were made to other state officials in a desperate attempt to find a solution. He was not legally insane, so could not be committed to the state hospital. The attorney general ruled that the state could not follow him and keep him under surveillance "on suspicion," since this would violate the Fourth Amendment right to privacy.

After his release, inmate X killed three people who served on the jury that had convicted him and was caught at the farmhouse of his intended fourth victim. Had he been paroled at any time before his release, there would undoubtedly have been a public outcry. The parole board would likely have been severely criticized. But the parolee could also have been under legitimate surveillance, and three lives might have been saved.

---

commissioners in the past have been suspected or accused of corruption—awarding parole on the basis of political and/or financial motivations. In the early part of the twentieth century, such abuses had become flagrant. But few correctional workers were willing to testify about them for fear of retaliation. Where corruption existed, a worker either had to go along with the system or suffer career stagnation at best, dismissal at worst. One of the few people who was willing to document some of these practices wrote:

> In the great Commonwealth of Massachusetts, the sale of paroles during the 1930's was a matter of public documentation. In 1934, I stated at a public meeting . . . that the sale of paroles reached right into the State House, and I was prepared to back up the statement with facts. The Governor, Joseph B. Ely, said [the] next morning, "Fire that man." . . . In 1939, . . . a legislative committee stated in a report to the legislature, "Never in the history of the Commonwealth of Massachusetts has there been so flagrant a sale of pardons and paroles as under the administration of Governor Joseph B. Ely" (Roland D. Sawyer, Secretary of the Pardon and Parole Commission, *Report to the Massachusetts State Legislature*, Boston, 1940). The report listed numerous cases involving such activities and quoted the price paid for them. At least one member of the parole board was forced to resign and left the state.[15]

With more investigative news reporting, greater court interest in the correctional process, more internal controls, and sensitivity to public scandals, these

---

[15]Howard B. Gill, "Community-Based Corrections," *Proceedings of the One Hundredth Annual Congress of Corrections* (Laurel, MD: American Correctional Association, 1971), p. 109.

situations have been either eliminated or drastically reduced since the 1950s. In the intervening years, the vast majority of jurisdictions have substantially improved their methods of selecting persons to be released on parole. But the qualifications of parole board members have remained a source of criticism.

Recommendations of the President's Crime Commission in 1967 called for appointments solely on the basis of merit, with qualifications including "broad academic backgrounds, especially in the behavioral sciences."[16] Yet some 15 years later, parole boards in most states were still being cited for making appointments according to political patronage, without any relevant background or educational requirements.[17] More recently, a 1988 survey found that in 29 states, "there were no professional qualifications, defined by statute, for parole board membership."[18] Even among the remaining 21 jurisdictions, statutes establishing qualifications may be written in "very general terms," thus giving the governor rather "wide latitude" and "generous discretion."[19] As of 1988, only six states required a bachelor's degree for parole board membership; only one required a master's degree.[20]

While being subject to political appointment and legislative confirmation "serves to increase the accountability of the parole board," such practices also "render its decision-making vulnerable to political pressure."[21] The necessity for parole board members to be free of political control or outside interference is therefore still a concern, although it is perhaps a less critical issue in states where their discretionary decision-making power has diminished.

## Administrative Models

In addition to the personal qualifications of the parole board, how parole is administratively organized can have a significant impact on its operations. Two dominant patterns of parole administration have emerged over the years:

1. *Autonomous model.* The parole board is independent of the prison system.
2. *Integrated (or institutional) model.* The institutional staff are significantly involved (i.e., integrated), in making release decisions.

Each of these approaches represents differing points of view about parole decision making. Advocates of the integrated model maintain that it is professional staff within the institution who are most intimately familiar with the inmate and therefore most sensitive to the "right time" for release. But supporters of the autonomous model fear that those who interact with inmates on a daily basis can become *too* personally involved to be objective. In addition, there is concern that they might be tempted to support release to reduce crowding or rid the facility of

[16]President's Commission on Law Enforcement and Administration of Justice, *Task Force Report: Corrections* (Washington, DC: U.S. Government Printing Office, 1967), p. 67.
[17]Abadinsky, p. 146.
[18]Rhine et al., p. 37.
[19]Ibid.
[20]Ibid.
[21]Ibid., p. 35.

problem cases. Most states have therefore embraced the autonomous model. However, it raises apprehension that an independent process may result in decisions that are inconsistent with treatment goals of the institution. As a compromise between these two extremes, some states have moved to a third approach:

3. *Consolidated model.* All correctional services operate under a central department of corrections that includes both the prison system and the paroling authority. Parole decisions are made independently, although staff do provide input. Both custodial and field services operate within the same overall organizational structure.[22]

---

*LEARNING GOALS*

*Do you know:*

- *How the procedures used to grant parole have changed over time?*
- *What (if any) due process protections are involved in parole decision making?*
- *On what basis parole boards make selection decisions?*
- *On what grounds parole decisions have been criticized?*
- *The differences between conditional/unconditional release, commutations/pardons, gain/good time, and mandatory/discretionary release?*
- *How objective prediction instruments have changed parole decision making?*

---

## ❖ SELECTION PROCEDURES

Like their administrative organization, the procedures used by parole boards have also varied over time. In the past, cases were divided among the members. Individual members examined the institutional records, interviewed the inmate(s) being considered, and recommended for or against parole. Each recommendation was then ratified or modified by the full board in executive session. Generally, the board tended to approve the recommendation of its separate members, but sometimes other information would arise to alter it.

Since the mid-1970s, the increasing volume of cases has significantly expanded the workload of parole boards. In response, the U.S. Parole Commission and many of the larger states adopted the use of *hearing examiners,* who are not members of the parole board. Under this system, the board acts in executive session on the recommendations of the hearing examiner.

In almost all cases, the prison or institutional treatment staff prepare a preparole progress report for the board's review. This report generally includes such information as:

---

[22]Summarized from Paul F. Cromwell, Jr., George G. Killinger, Hazel B. Kerper, and Charls Walker, *Probation and Parole in the Criminal Justice System,* Second Edition (St. Paul, MN: West Publishing Company, 1985), pp. 169–70; and McCarthy and McCarthy, p. 249.

- A summary of the inmate's *case history* (including prior record, presentence investigation report, classification results, and the like).
- The *institutional programs* in which the offender has participated.
- Evidence of *adjustment* during confinement (particularly any disciplinary actions taken).
- A *proposed plan* for parole (such as employment and residence).
- Other documents relevant to *behavioral predictions* (such as a psychological profile).
- A *recommendation* by the institutional staff for or against parole, along with supporting reasons.

In some systems, parolees are selected on the basis of written documents alone—the inmate is not interviewed and may not even know that parole is being considered. In other states, parole boards sit as a group while interviewing the inmate. In this case, a majority of the parole board visits each institution at scheduled times. Institutional records, together with preparole progress reports, are reviewed, with each candidate interviewed individually. An institutional representative may also sit in to answer questions for the board as they arise during the hearing. Under both systems, when the final decision is made in executive session, the inmate is officially notified in writing.

## Due Process Considerations

Due process procedures surrounding parole hearings have also undergone changes over the years. Surprisingly, however, these modifications have not been a result of court intervention. Quite the contrary, courts have been reluctant to interfere in what they have traditionally viewed as the administrative decision-making function of parole boards.

Since the courts have not recognized that inmates have a constitutional right to parole, they have not established due process requirements in the parole selection process. For example, in one particular case (*Menechino v. Oswald*),[23] an inmate challenged his parole denial on the basis that he should have been entitled to counsel, the right to cross-examine and to produce witnesses, notice concerning the information being reviewed, and specific grounds for the denial. The court ruled that these due process rights did not apply to parole hearings, under the rationale that (1) denying parole did not alter the status of the inmate (in other words, the inmate did not possess something that was being lost), and (2) the parole board's interests in rehabilitation and readjustment were not contrary to those of the inmate (i.e., the board was not in an adversarial position with regard to the inmate).

Nevertheless, although not legally required, most parole hearings today do allow the inmate to be represented by an attorney and to introduce witnesses. The proceedings are generally recorded in written transcripts, with the inmate advised in writing of the final decision. Recommendations of the American

[23]*Menechino v. Oswald*, 430 F.2d 402, 407 (2d Cir. 1970).

Correctional Association further call for consistently applied written criteria on which to base decisions, along with informing those denied of both their future hearing date and recommendations for improving their prospects at that time.[24]

### Selection Criteria

The popular perception of parole boards may be that they make every effort to select inmates who have good potential for early release. But that is not exactly how the system operates. This does not mean that parole boards do not take their mission seriously or that they are overly lenient. But given the candidates they are faced with assessing, their function is often limited to screening out the *worst*, rather than selecting the *best*. As one parole board member expressed this dilemma, "Given the nature of imprisonment today, there are no good risk prisoners. A parole board must decide *when* to release *bad* risk inmates."[25] Although that statement was made some 20 years ago, it is no less true now in those jurisdictions where paroling authorities still have discretionary power to grant early release.

Despite having access to literally volumes of records, reports, data, interview transcripts, and other information concerning the offender, determining parole eligibility has ultimately been a product of the individual judgments of parole board members. With a few notable exceptions, parole boards have generally not been composed of those with extensive backgrounds or academic preparation in the behavioral sciences. Their decisions have therefore more often been based on personal intuition than professional training. Consequently, factors deemed important by individual members can include anything from cleanliness to church attendance.

Some members refuse to parole anyone who steadfastly maintains innocence despite having been convicted. Others base decisions on rehabilitative factors—reviewing the inmate's outlook, self-improvement, change in work habits, and similar indicators of capacity to adapt to society. Some place heavy emphasis on victim impact statements and anticipated public reaction if the offender is paroled. Still others will reluctantly support releasing a high-risk offender nearing sentence expiration, using the rationale that it is preferable to be released under supervision than unconditionally. In the absence of solid, tangible evidence, parole boards have acted largely on faith in the inmate's intentions and capacity to "make good." While some of those not paroled may also have intended to make good, in the judgment of the board, their capabilities of doing so were in doubt.

In short, all of these varied decision-making criteria reflect the individual preferences, values, beliefs, and biases of parole board members. For an illustration of just how subjective the parole selection process has been, see Figure 11.1, which lists the considerations that have most significantly influenced parole

[24]See *Standards for Adult Parole Authorities* (Laurel, MD: American Correctional Association, 1982).

[25]Donald J. Newman, *Introduction to Criminal Justice,* Second Edition (Philadelphia: J.B. Lippincott, 1975), p. 363, quoting an unnamed parole board member.

| | Percent of board members including this as one of the five most important considerations |
|---|---|
| 1. My estimate of the chances that the prisoner would or would not commit a serious crime if paroled. | 92.8% |
| 2. My judgment that the prisoner would benefit from further experience in the institution program, or at any rate, would become a better risk if confined longer. | 87.1% |
| 3. My judgment that the prisoner would become a worse risk if confined longer. | 71.9% |
| 4. My judgment that the prisoner had already been punished enough to "pay" for his crime. | 43.2% |
| 5. The probability that the prisoner would be a misdemeanant and a burden to his parole supervisors, even if he did not commit any serious offenses on parole. | 35.3% |
| 6. My feelings about how my decision in this case would affect the feelings or welfare of the prisoner's relatives or dependents. | 33.8% |
| 7. What I thought the reaction of the judge might be if the prisoner were granted parole. | 20.9% |
| 8. What I thought the reaction of the local police might be if the prisoner were granted parole. | 12.2% |
| 9. What I thought the reaction of other prisoners might be to the policy which they might ascribe to me from my decision in a particular case. | 12.2% |
| 10. What I thought would be the reactions of my colleagues on the parole board. | 9.4% |
| 11. What I thought the reaction of the press, radio, and TV might be if the prisoner were granted parole. | 8.6% |
| 12. What I thought the consequences of my decision policy might be for the governor or for other officials in the executive branch of government. . . . | 8.6% |

**Figure 11.1** Parole decision-making considerations. *Source:* Joseph J. Senna and Larry J. Siegel, *Introduction to Criminal Justice* (St. Paul, MN: West Publishing Company, 1978), pp. 419–20, citing the 1965 study of the National Parole Institute.

board members. Note the very personal dimensions of decision-making that it reflects (e.g., *"my* estimate of . . . "; *"my* judgment that . . . "; "what *I* thought . . . "; *"my* feelings about . . . "). Given this extensive discretion, combined with concerns about the political independence and professional qualifications of those entrusted with it, it is not surprising that the parole selection process has been subject to complaints and controversy.

### Decision-making Criticisms

The decision-making element of parole has come under fire since the first inmates were paroled from Elmira under Zebulon Brockway. One need go no further than the prison from which parole candidates are drawn to find widespread discontent with the process, among both inmates and staff.

Needless to say, inmates denied parole have often been dissatisfied with what they consider arbitrary and inequitable features of the process. While those denied parole are naturally unlikely to agree with that decision, much of the lack of acceptance for parole decisions may well relate to lack of understanding. As a result, many erroneously believe that selection is based on mere chance—that some are simply "lucky" and others are "unlucky."

Particularly when inmates are not personally involved in parole decision making, it is difficult to appreciate how an anonymous group of people can fairly determine an unknown inmate's destiny. Even those who have an opportunity to present their case through a personal interview are sent out of the room while discussions of the case take place (being recalled only to hear the ultimate decision and a summary of the reasons for it). This common practice protects the confidentiality of individual member's actions. But it does not enable the candidate to hear objective discussions of the case, evaluations of strengths and weaknesses, or prognosis for success or failure. Nor does it provide guidance in terms of how to modify behavior in order to improve subsequent chances for successful parole consideration. Without such insights, it is unlikely that those denied parole understand the basis for the decision or attach any sense of justice to it.

Inmates denied parole are entitled to a subsequent hearing after a certain period of time. But the uncertainty of never knowing precisely when one will be released can create considerable tension and frustration within correctional institutions. When such frustrations result in expressions of violence, the chances for future parole consideration diminish even further.

On the other hand, clever inmates have been known to manipulate the process by superficially "going along with the system," enrolling in institutional programs only to mount an impressive file for parole board review. Such statements as "get [into] a program and you'll get parole"[26] reflect their cynical view of treatment as a ticket to freedom. At least one study has found no support for the theory that inmates can "play games" with parole boards which affect their release dates.[27] Nevertheless, there is evidence that they make the attempt:

> Inmates soon discover what parole board members want. If there is an overly religious board member, the inmate will start going to church to impress him. If group counseling is the "in thing," and if the board is going to repeatedly ask inmates if they have attended "group," the chances are that the inmate will enroll. In fact, California prisoners created a "get-out group," as they themselves termed it. This is a practice group in which the inmates rehearse the "stories" they are going to "lay on" naive board members.[28]

[26]John Kaplan, *Criminal Justice: Introductory Cases and Materials* (Mineola, NY: Foundation Press, 1973), p. 567.
[27]John H. Lombardi, "The Impact of Correctional Education on Length of Incarceration: Nonsupport for New Paroling Policy Motivation," *Journal of Correctional Education*, Vol. 35, No. 2 (June 1984), p. 55.
[28]Lewis P. Carney, *Probation and Parole: Legal and Social Dimensions* (New York: McGraw-Hill, 1977), p. 192. One study in California found 70% of the inmates polled answering "yes" to the question, "Do you believe that therapy and treatment are games?" Jessica Mitford, "Kind and Usual Punishment in California," in Jerome H. Skolnick and Elliott Currie, eds., *Crisis in American Institutions,* Second Edition (Boston: Little, Brown, 1973), p. 513.

Nor are criticisms of parole limited to the inmate population. Parole boards place considerable weight on the inmate's prison record (particularly the presence or absence of misconduct reports). But in one study, the *least* likely factor that parole board members reported considering important was what the reaction of prison officials might be to their decision in a particular case.[29]

Thus, it is not surprising to find that there has been friction between prison wardens and parole boards because of differences in viewpoints. Like the candidates themselves, many prison officials wonder why some were paroled whereas others were not. On the other hand, many parole boards view some of the recommendations of institutional staff as favoring the "warden's pet" or advocating the release of certain inmate leaders in order to manage the facility better. In essence, no matter what the board's decision, it is unsatisfactory to *someone*.

## Impact of the Justice Model

Beyond inmate discontent and staff disagreement, however, it has been ordinary citizens who often express the most vocal dissatisfaction with parole:

> No matter how you look at it, the bottom line is that parole boards let convicted criminals out . . . earlier than their full terms. That kind of undertaking will never get rave reviews. Police are in the business of catching criminals. Prosecutors can boast of being tough crime fighters, and judges have the lofty role of punishing the guilty and letting the innocent go free. But parole boards let admittedly guilty felons out from behind bars every day. . . . [30]

Moreover, it is not the long-term successes but the legendary failures that capture public attention. "The newsworthiness of any parole story is when there has been a serious failure in the system, such as a recently released inmate committing a heinous new crime."[31] As a result of such notoriety, opinions regarding sentencing practices and the related function of parole have had a substantial impact on stimulating change.

Criticisims of parole selection gained little national attention or public interest throughout the time when the medical model dominated criminal justice decision making. In fact, parole was an integral feature of the model. The intent was not to focus on the nature of the *offense*, but rather, on the needs of the *offender*. Yet the courts could not be expected to anticipate how long it would take to diagnose, treat, rehabilitate, and reintegrate an individual offender. It was therefore essential to have the flexibility and discretion of indeterminate sentences, with the judge establishing a minimum and maximum term to be served and the parole board determining exactly when release was most appropriate.

In retrospect, it is perhaps surprising, yet logical, to find indications that it was actually inmates who originally advocated determinate sentences—to avoid

---

[29]Joseph J. Senna and Larry J. Siegel, *Introduction to Criminal Justice* (St. Paul, MN: West Publishing Company, 1978), p. 419, citing the 1965 study of the National Parole Institute.

[30]John J. Curran, Jr., "A Priority for Parole: Agencies Must Reach Out," in *Correctional Issues: Probation and Parole*, p. 31.

[31]Ibid.

being coerced into rehabilitation and to better assure that those convicted of similar offenses received similar prison terms. As one inmate phrased the frustration of his fellow prisoners, "Don't give us steak and eggs; . . . free us from the tyranny of the indeterminate sentence!"[32] But the complaints of inmates about involuntary treatment or sentencing inequities might well have fallen on deaf ears had the public been satisfied with the existing system.

To many observers, however, by the late 1970s and early 1980s, the system simply did not appear to be working:

- The unspecified length of indeterminate sentences created strong suspicion that potential law violators were not being *deterred* by the certainty of punishment.
- High rates of recidivism provided evidence that criminals were apparently not being *rehabilitated.*
- The likelihood of early release on parole generated concern that offenders were not paying their *"just deserts"* to society.

(See the next "Close-up on Corrections" for an amusing commentary on the rueful realities of indeterminate sentencing.)

Parole itself was termed a tragic failure and a cruel hypocrisy. It was viewed as deceiving both the inmate looking for help and the public looking for protection;[33] providing neither security to the law-abiding nor fair treatment to law violators.[34] The premise that parole safeguards society by keeping criminals in prison until they are ready for release was dismissed as nonsense.[35] Although the criminal justice system can never be free of failures, parole was charged with providing more than its share of them. As a result, an increasingly conservative society—lacking trust in rehabilitation and fearful of rising crime rates—called for *fixed, determinate sentences* with a more *objective method* of establishing release dates (preferably upon completion of full sentences).

**Conditional versus Unconditional Release.**   With the transition from the medical model to the justice model, the method by which inmates are released from confinement has changed, although not necessarily in the manner anticipated. Ever since the first indeterminate sentencing legislation was enacted over 125 years ago, inmates have been released from correctional institutions either:

- *Conditionally:* with continued freedom dependent upon adhering to the conditions established by the paroling authority; or
- *Unconditionally:* with no conditions attached, because the offender had served the full sentence, been pardoned, had the sentence commuted, or received some other form of legal modification.

[32]Mitford, p. 512.
[33]"Citizens' Study Calls for End to Parole," *LEAA Newsletter,* Vol. 4, No. 2 (July 1974), p. 23.
[34]Herman Schwartz, "Let's Abolish Parole," *Reader's Digest* (August 1973), pp. 185–90.
[35]Ibid.

Just How Indeterminate *Is* the Indeterminate Sentence?

There are signs posted on the counters of branches of [a] bank in New York which read, in large capital letters, "BANK ROBBERY IS PUNISHABLE BY 20 YEARS IN FEDERAL PRISON."

The signs are a deception. But their impact would be more than a little diminished if they were more accurate, and read: "The symbolic penalty for bank robbery is 20 years in prison. The actual penalty for bank robbery is amorphous, in that it can be anything from probation up to 20 years, depending on the nature of the plea bargain worked out between the offender and the prosecutor, the personal policy of the judge toward bank robbery, the severity of overcrowding in the federal prisons, and the opinion of parole hearing officers on the extent of the rehabilitation and/or dangerousness of the criminal."

This is the American criminal justice system. It is a system in which nothing is certain, in which nothing is clear. It is a system that operates with few hard and fast rules, with only the most vague and undefined standards of conduct, either for the people who administer it or for the people who are subject to it. The amorphousness of the criminal justice system is often the object of public outrage. Many members of the public want the bank robber, and other violent criminals, to go to prison; some even want him to go for 20 years. But no matter how much pressure is applied to make the system more certain and predictable, the effort seems to have no effect. . . .

*Source:* Michael Serrill, "Determinate Sentencing: History, Theory, Debate," *Corrections Magazine*, Vol. 3, No. 3 (September 1977), p. 3.

Beyond the simple expiration of one's sentence, unconditional release can occur as a result of clemency extended by the executive branch of government (i.e., the governor of a state or the president of the United States, although parole boards in some states have this power as well). *Executive clemency* ordinarily takes the form of a:

- *Commutation.* One's sentence is reduced, such as when "time served" is substituted for a longer original sentence. However, a commutation does not necessarily lead to release—as, for example, when life imprisonment is substituted for a death sentence.
- *Pardon.* The offender's conviction is forgiven. Originally designed to undo miscarriages of justice (e.g., when a person was wrongfully convicted), pardons are often unconditional. But conditional pardons can be issued which are dependent upon subsequent performance of the person being pardoned. As illustrated in the next "Close-up on Corrections," pardons may also be requested long after release to restore the offender's civil rights.

Corrections can maintain supervisory authority only over those offenders who are *conditionally released*. In other words, conditional release is similar to the situation of probationers who face the imposition of a suspended sentence for failure to abide by the conditions of probation. Similarly, parolees face the possibility of returning to prison to complete their original term if parole is revoked for failure to comply with the conditions attached. Those receiving unconditional release, however, are no longer under any legal authority of the correctional system.

**Parole Trends Today.** The movement toward determinate sentencing was presumably designed to achieve certainty in punishment—with *fixed, flat terms* replacing *flexible ranges*. One might therefore assume that more full sentences would be served, more unconditional releases would occur, and parole populations would decline. Nothing could be further from reality!

Despite the intent of the justice model, inmates continue to get out of prison before serving their full potential terms. The average time served by those released from state prisons is only one-third of the maximum amount of time imposed by their sentence.[36] Nor are unconditional releases replacing conditional supervision. More than 85% of those coming out of prison are still being released under some form of conditional supervision in the community[37] (see Figure 11.2). Nor is the number of people on parole diminishing. Quite the contrary, the parole population actually grew to over half a million (531,407) by 1990, a 77% increase since 1985.[38] What can account for these apparent discrepancies?

As was described as early as Chapter 1, the major element that public policy changes failed to take into account in moving to determinate sentencing was prison space. Under the justice model, more offenders have been more likely to be sentenced to at least some time in a correctional institution. Yet sufficient funding has not been available to accommodate them through new construction

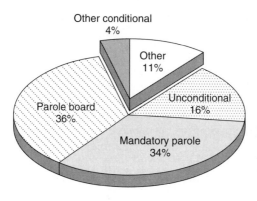

**Figure 11.2** First releases from state prison, 1989. *Source:* Craig Perkins, *National Corrections Reporting Program, 1989* (Washington, DC: U.S. Department of Justice, 1992), p. 31.

Other conditional 4%
Other 11%
Parole board 36%
Unconditional 16%
Mandatory parole 34%

[36]Craig Perkins, *National Corrections Reporting Program, 1989* (Washington, DC: U.S. Department of Justice, 1992), p. 29.

[37]Louis Jankowski, "Probation and Parole 1990," *Bureau of Justice Statistics Bulletin* (Washington, DC: U.S. Department of Justice, 1991), p. 5.

[38]Ibid., p. 5.

or expansion of facilities. It therefore rapidly became apparent that no more prisoners could be admitted until some were released.[39]

As we have seen previously, the primary method for dealing with this escalating inmate population has become the awarding of "gain time" or "good time." These terms are widely used interchangeably. But technically, *gain time* refers to time that is *automatically* deducted by law, based on the length of the sentence, the length of time served, and/or the seriousness of the offense. For example, some states credit an increasing number of days per month the longer a person remains incarcerated. Under such a system, an inmate could earn five days each month during the first year of imprisonment, six days per month during the next year, and so on. On the other hand, *good time* (or what is also called "incentive" or "meritorious" time) is *earned* for proper institutional conduct. In some jurisdictions, it can also be awarded for participation in certain treatment, training, educational, or work programs. The "Close-up on Corrections" on page 441 shows how these various time credits work toward reducing the length of a prison sentence.

**Mandatory versus Discretionary Release.**  If the intent of the justice model was to increase the severity of sentencing, its goal will not be realized until institutional crowding is eliminated. If, however, the intent was to achieve certainty in sentencing, its mission is closer to accomplishment. That does not by any means imply that the full sentence imposed by the court is the one that will be served. But after crediting inmates with time deductions, it is a straightforward mathematical calculation to determine one's earliest possible release date. Assuming that the prisoner does nothing while confined to jeopardize time credits, release is virtually required at that point.

Thus, in states with determinate sentencing, inmates now become eligible for what is known as *supervised mandatory release* when they have served their original sentence minus gain/good time accrued. In that respect, there is more than some truth to the observation that new language has simply been introduced for continuing practices—with "supervised release" replacing "parole," but very little actually changing with regard to the parole officer's supervisory role.[40] Moreover, given the justice model's emphasis on removing coercion from the treatment process, another indicator that meaningful change may not have actually occurred is the earning of good time for program participation—a practice that bears close resemblance to basing parole decisions on treatment progress.

Supervised mandatory release is essentially a form of what has been described earlier in this chapter as conditional release. The ex-offender is subject to conditions which, if violated, could result in reincarceration to serve out the remainder of the sentence (i.e., that portion which was relieved by time credits). It is therefore not the postrelease supervisory function of parole that has changed with the justice model. Nor is that unfortunate, since replac-

---

[39]In fact, the situation has become so desperate that "a number of states are considering changes in their sentencing policies that would link . . . offender sentencing to correctional bedspace." Rupp et al., p. 25.

[40]Orville B. Pung, "Introduction," *Correctional Issues: Probation and Parole*, p. vi.

### Presidential Pardons

One man was jailed for stealing three cases of beer. Another did time for smuggling heroin. A third got in trouble for trying to sneak his Mexican wife into the United States in the trunk of a car.

Now, thanks to Christmas Eve pardons from [former] President Bush—similar to the one granted former Defense Secretary Caspar Weinberger—these three convicted felons and 15 others . . . have had their records wiped clean of criminal wrongdoings. . . .

The continuing price for an old felony conviction was what led Joseph Bear, Jr. . . . a Blackfoot Indian . . . to apply for his pardon. In 1960, he said, "I was 17, and me and my friends were being crazy, and daring each other to do things. We broke into a store and got three cases of beer." Before he got a single sip, he was arrested and sentenced to three weeks in jail and two years' probation. . . . Later he was barred from enlisting in the military. "I felt like I had no country," he said.

He filed for the pardon in 1986, after an opponent publicized the conviction in a successful effort to force Bear from the ballot in an election for the Tribal Council. It bars felons from serving. "The president has given me a new lease on life," Bear said. . . .

Bush granted about 5% of the 1,200 pardon requests received during his administration. While some believe politics dictated the pardon of Weinberger, Bush certainly owed nothing to . . . the others.

*Source:* Mark Thompson, "President Pardons Ordinary People, Too," *The Miami Herald* (January 10, 1993), p. 8A.

---

ing conditional with unconditional releases could create far greater public safety hazards.

What has been fundamentally altered is *how* release decisions are made. As the term "supervised *mandatory* release" implies, more inmates are now coming out of prison because the statutory authority to confine them has expired. In other words, they have served at least their minimum sentence, minus time credits. It is this "mandatory" component of supervised release that distinguishes it from "traditional" parole. Once gain/good time has been deducted from the original sentence, release becomes *mandatory*, as opposed to the *discretionary* decision of a parole board.

In 1977, the majority of those discharged from prison (about 72%) were released as a result of a parole board's discretion. But by 1990, parole boards accounted for less than half (41%) of state prison releases. As illustrated in Figure 11.3, at the same time that discretionary releases have been *decreasing*, mandatory releases have been *increasing*.

### Computing Parole Eligibility

Richard Scott was given a sentence of a minimum of five years and a maximum of ten years for the crime of robbery with violence. At the time of sentencing, he had been held in jail for six months awaiting trial and disposition of his case. Scott did well in the maximum security prison to which he was sent. He did not get into trouble and was thus able to amass good time credit at the rate of one day for every four that he spent on good behavior. In addition, he was given thirty days' meritorious credit when he completed his high school equivalency test after attending the prison school for two years. After serving three years and four months of his sentence, he appeared before the Board of Parole and was granted release into the community.

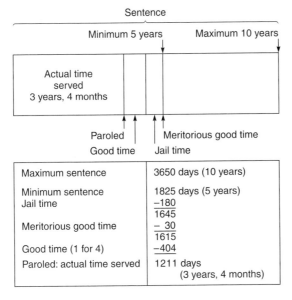

| Maximum sentence | 3650 days (10 years) |
| Minimum sentence<br>Jail time | 1825 days (5 years)<br>−180<br>1645 |
| Meritorious good time | − 30<br>1615 |
| Good time (1 for 4) | −404 |
| Paroled: actual time served | 1211 days<br>(3 years, 4 months) |

*Source:* Todd R. Clear and George F. Cole, *American Corrections* (Monterey, CA: Brooks/Cole Publishing Company, ©1986), p. 376.

**Public and Parole Implications.** Despite the significance of this change, few of those in free society fully understand it. The scenario in the next "Close-up on Corrections" provides a vivid example of how such misperceptions can fuel public anger.

It is easy to see how the public has become confused. Obviously, the trend over recent years has been toward less discretionary and more mandatory supervised releases. But that does not mean that parole board decision making has

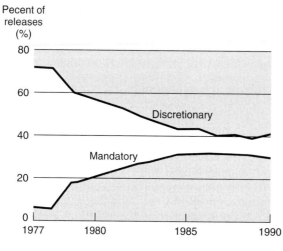

**Figure 11.3** Methods of state prison release, 1977–1990. *Source: Lawrence A. Greenfield, Prisons and Prisoners in the United States* (Washington, DC: U.S. Department of Justice, 1992), p. 18.

been completely abolished. Recall that the vast majority of states still have various forms of indeterminate sentencing. And even in states with determinate sentencing, parole boards must continue to address those inmates sentenced earlier under indeterminate statutes. As recently as 1988, one survey found that paroling authorities in all states except Minnesota retain some statutory responsibility for release.[41]

---

❖ *CLOSE-UP ON CORRECTIONS*

### Let's Get It Straight—Who's Doing the Releasing?

All too frequently, the media fail to understand and clearly distinguish between basic concepts. . . . As a result, the public does not get an accurate story. Few reporters understand the difference between . . . discretionary release and mandatory release, or the function of earned time or gained time and its effect in radically altering a sentence structure.

A recent example provides a valid illustration. A California man who had raped and severed the arms of his victim was widely reported to have been on parole release after serving only a portion of his sentence. The public voiced understandable outrage at the thought that parole board members would consider early release for such an individual. In fact, the inmate was not released as a matter of discretion, but because the law mandated it. Virtually no media reports pointed out that important aspect of the story.

*Source:* John J. Curran, Jr., "A Priority for Parole: Agencies Must Reach Out," *Correctional Issues: Probation and Parole* (Laurel, MD: American Correctional Association, 1990), pp. 34–35.

---

[41]Rhine, et al., p. 33.

While the releasing authority of parole boards has been declining steadily, it has not been completely destroyed. It has, however, been subject to much greater *accountability*—"parole has been called on to be more responsive to the competing concerns of offenders, victims, and the public."[42] Consequently, parole discretion has also been subject to much greater control: "Not only have parole authorities been restricted in choosing whom they may release, but guidelines have been developed to structure release decision-making for offenders eligible for parole."[43]

**Structured Decision Making.** The trend toward structuring the discretion of parole boards reflects much of the same reasoning as the sentencing guidelines and objective classification procedures discussed previously. In other words, it is designed to replace the *subjectivity* of personal decisions with the *objectivity* of formulas that predict risk on the basis of empirical research.

The search for valid instruments to identify what types of offenders represent the best risks for parole began well before current infatuations with the capabilities of computers. As early as the 1920s, rudimentary forms of *parole prediction tables* began to appear. Some of these first studies were based on such dubious sources of information as analyzing the hunches of fellow inmates.[44] Others (like the Burgess scale)[45] endured the test of time to become the foundation for modern risk assessment instruments.

As corrections assumed a more legalistic direction guided by constitutional and civil rights issues during the 1960s and 1970s, increasing emphasis was placed on due process considerations, definable standards, and defensible procedures. Parole was no exception. By the late 1970s, for example, a number of states moved to *parole contracting*, whereby a target date is determined which becomes the parole release date if all provisions are met by the inmate. Described as "contingency contracting" and "mutual agreement programming" in Chapter 9, these contracts set specific goals in such areas as education, training, counseling, and institutional behavior.[46] As the next "Close-up on Corrections" vividly describes, contracts also stipulate that the institution will make available the programs and services needed to fulfill the established goals.

By the 1980s, most states had adopted various other forms of written guidelines governing the granting of parole.[47] Some of these documents are essentially lists of criteria that parole board members are implicitly supposed to take into account in making release decisions. Others are much more explicit statistical tables that assign specific weights to various factors, with one's total score

---

[42]William K. Smith, Edward E. Rhine, and Ronald W. Jackson, "Parole Practices: Survey Finds U.S. Agencies Undergoing Changes," in *Correctional Issues: Probation and Parole*, p. 37.

[43]Ibid., p. 38.

[44]Ferris Laune, *Predicting Criminality* (Evanston, IL: Northwestern University Press, 1937).

[45]A. A. Bruce, E. W. Burgess, and A. J. Harno, *The Working of the Indeterminate Sentence Law and the Parole System in Illinois* (Springfield, IL: Illinois Parole Board, 1928).

[46]Steve Gettinger, "Parole Contracts: A New Way Out," in David M. Petersen and Charles W. Thomas, eds., *Corrections: Problems and Prospects*, Second Edition (Englewood Cliffs, NJ: Prentice Hall, 1980), p. 240.

[47]"Hitting the Boards," *Corrections Compendium*, Vol. V, No. 5 (November 1980), p. 1. (However, using a more rigorous definition, it has recently been found that only 23 states report using "formal, structured guidelines" in making parole release decisions.) See Rhine et al., p. 67.

## Parole Contracting

Harold W. waits in a conference room at a Baltimore community correctional facility. He had been transferred there from the state prison by correctional officials, but somehow the community center had not been warned of his arrival. The center is full. Members of the center's classification committee enter the room. They discuss the case, and tell Harold that he'll have to be transferred to another facility some distance from Baltimore, which is his hometown.

"Wait a minute," Harold declares. "You can't do that. See, here's my contract!"

The committee members look at each other, then get on the phone. . . . It is true. Harold has a legally enforceable contract, signed by the Division of Correction and the Board of Parole, that guarantees him a place at the community facility. . . . He cannot be transferred. He stays at the center.

A Maryland corrections official, in recalling this story, also notes that in several months, under Harold's contract, he will be able to make an even more unusual announcement for an inmate. He will be able to say to the parole board something like this: "Don't forget—I get out tomorrow." And if Harold has done what he promised to do in his contract—like completing his studies, acquiring a job skill, and avoiding disciplinary problems—the board must grant him parole.

*Source:* Steve Gettinger, "Parole Contracts: A New Way Out," in David M. Petersen and Charles W. Thomas, eds., *Corrections: Problems and Prospects,* Second Edition (Engelwood Cliffs, NJ: Prentice Hall, 1980), pp. 238–39.

determining the candidate's prognosis for success or failure on parole. All are designed to make the granting of parole more *objective*.

One of the best known and most widely used of the statistical risk prediction tables is the *Salient Factor Score,* originally pioneered by the U.S. Parole Commission in the 1970s. Under this system, scores of varying weights are assigned to six factors pertaining to the offender's background (shown in Figure 11.4). As that chart indicates, better risks are reflected by high scores (e.g., those who are older, have no prior convictions, etc.). Low scores, on the other hand, reflect greater risk of subsequent violations.

Essentially, such instruments represent another form of parole contracting, since a "presumptive" release date is determined on the basis of one's score and provided to the inmate within several months of being admitted. Although the date may be modified if institutional behavior is unacceptable, basically, these *objective parole criteria* "contractually bind the paroling authority [to a] presumptive release date."[48]

[48]Lombardi, p. 54.

| | | |
|---|---|---|
| **Item A:** | *Prior convictions/adjudications (adult or juvenile)* | _____ |
| | None | = 3 |
| | One | = 2 |
| | Two or three | = 1 |
| | Four or more | = 0 |
| **Item B:** | *Prior commitment(s) of more than thirty days (adult or juvenile)* | _____ |
| | None | = 2 |
| | One or two | = 1 |
| | Three or more | = 0 |

**Item C:** *Age at current offense/prior commitments* _____

Age at commencement of the current offense:
- 26 years of age or more = 2*
- 20–25 years of age = 1*
- 19 years of age or less = 0

*Exception:* If five or more prior commitments of more than thirty days (adult or juvenile), place an "x" _____
here _____ and score this item = 0

**Item D:** *Recent commitment-free period (three years)* _____

No prior commitment of more than thirty days (adult or juvenile) or released to the community from last such commitment at least three years prior to the commencement of the current offense = 1

Otherwise = 0

**Item E:** *Probation/parole/confinement/escape/status violator this time* _____

Neither on probation, parole, confinement, or escape status at the time of the current offense; nor committed as a probation, parole, confinement, or escape status violator this time = 1

Otherwise = 0

**Item F:** *Heroin/opiate dependence* _____

No history of heroin/opiate dependence = 1
Otherwise = 0

**Total Score** _____

NOTE: For purposes of the Salient Factor Score, an instance of criminal behavior resulting in a judicial determination of guilt or an admission of guilt before a judicial body shall be treated as a conviction, even if a conviction is not formally entered.

**Figure 11.4** Salient Factor Score.

While a number of states use the Salient Factor Score in parole decision making, other forms of objective risk assessment are employed as well. Among the most common items that they include are:

- Number of parole revocations
- Number of adult or juvenile convictions
- Number of prison terms served
- Number of incarcerations served

- Whether the current crime involves violence.[49]

Mitigating or aggravating factors that have a bearing on the case are not reflected in the mechanical calculations of statistical scores. As with sentencing guidelines, structured parole guidelines provide the option of overriding the results. Discretion has therefore not been totally eliminated. But deviations from the guidelines are generally restricted to specific reasons that are documented in writing. The result is—like sentencing guidelines—designed to enable some flexibility within a standardized framework.

This does not mean that even the most sophisticated tables, charts, or numbers can fully replace human judgments. Consequently, "it is important that paroling authorities realize that for all the promise of research and statistics, risk assessment tools are only tools. They must be technically sound, and they must be shaped by policymakers in light of policy goals. . . . "[50] While objective instruments can provide valuable tools for human decision making, they cannot replace the human decision maker.[51]

---

*LEARNING GOALS* ▬▬▬▬▬▬▬▬▬▬▬▬▬▬▬▬▬▬▬▬▬▬▬▬▬▬▬

*Do you know:*

- *How the supervisory functions of parole and probation officers differ?*
- *How prerelease centers, work release, and prerelease counseling assist offenders preparing to return to society?*
- *What general conditions are usually established for parolees?*
- *What factors must be taken into consideration in locating housing and employment for the parolee?*
- *How occupational licensing restrictions limit employment for ex-offenders?*
- *What due process protections are required for parole revocation?*
- *Why measures of recidivism are not always valid indicators of parole's success or failure?*

---

## ❖ PAROLE SUPERVISION

In addition to more closely structuring decision making, objective parole guidelines have also been used to determine the level of supervision needed by those released. Again, this is not unlike another practice discussed earlier—the classification of probation caseloads. In Chapter 5 we saw how classifying probationers

---

[49]Joan Petersilia and Susan Turner, "Guideline-Based Justice: Prediction and Racial Minorities," in Don Gottfredson and Michael Tonry, eds., *Prediction and Classification: Criminal Justice Decision Making* (Chicago: University of Chicago Press, 1987), p. 158. (Items listed were found in over 75% of instruments identified.)

[50]Peggy B. Burke, *Current Issues in Parole Decisionmaking: Understanding the Past; Shaping the Future* (Washington, DC: COSMOS Corporation, 1988), p. xii.

[51]Ibid., p. xiv.

according to the level of risk they pose enables staff to more appropriately allocate scarce resources and manage heavy workloads. In much the same manner, objective prediction instruments can serve similar functions for parole officers.

In fact, the supervisory responsibilities of parole staff are in many respects quite similar to those of probation officers. Their clients, however, are not necessarily similar. Parolees are generally more difficult to supervise than are probationers. Whereas probationers have been considered sufficiently hopeful to avoid being sent to prison, parolees have been incarcerated as poor risks for probation. In addition, they have adapted to institutional life. Many have learned to acquiesce to authority on a superficial basis while maintaining a behavior pattern that is basically unchanged. Others have learned to manipulate their way through official contacts with correctional authorities—from prison staff to parole boards. All have been screened out as too difficult for probation and conditioned by their prison experience, where the poker-faced veneer is acquired that makes diagnosis and evaluation difficult.

That does not mean that they are unsalvageable. But the fact that parolees have been removed for some period of time from the community not only increases the difficulty of their supervision but also subjects them to additional personal stresses not encountered by probationers. Despite their indifferent external demeanor, freedom can have an overwhelmingly emotional impact on those institutionalized. Planning for parole should therefore begin well before an inmate exits the prison gate—ideally, "the day the offender enters the institution," although in reality, that is rarely the case.[52]

## Prerelease Planning

From their perspective, ex-offenders have already been rejected for years by the mainstream of society. When they encounter continued rejection upon reentering a hostile environment, feelings of inadequacy and failure are reinforced. It may not take long for even the most hopeful parolee to find the optimism of "starting over" overcome by the realism of being stigmatized. The ultimate effect is often a self-fulfilling prophecy, as those society expects to fail do exactly that.

At the same time, just as the community must be prepared to accept ex-offenders, they, in turn, must be prepared to be realistic about what they will confront and what adjustments they must make upon release. Those who have adapted well to years of institutional life face the formidable challenge of reorienting to an entirely different lifestyle in free society. Few can successfully make that adjustment alone.

For an inside view of the fear and apprehensions of someone being released, read the next "Close-up on Corrections," which puts *you* in the place of a long-term inmate leaving prison (and also illustrates the unrevealing "social veneer" described above). As that scenario points out, in the final analysis, it is in everyone's best interests to extend the help needed to prevent releasees from becoming readmissions.

[52]McCarthy and McCarthy, p. 254.

Hesitant to Go Home

Next Wednesday you will be walking out those front gates as a free man. This last time around cost you ten years. It was your third hitch. You have spent thirty of the last forty years of your life behind bars. Sixty-two years of life's ups and downs have softened your disposition. You have no excuses left; you feel that the time you got was coming to you. In fact, the last hitch was one you purposely set up.

You had been released on a cold gray morning in February. There was no one on the outside waiting for you; your friends were all in prison. You had been divorced for over fifteen years and your former wife had remarried. Your parents were dead, and your two sisters had given up on you long ago. Besides, there were too many decisions to make in the free world. You were not used to all of that freedom; it was frightening. No one cared about you like they did inside the joint.

You got a job as a busboy in a restaurant, but the hustle and bustle was too much, and besides, no one wanted to make friends with an old ex-con. Finally you had all you could take, so you stole all the money from the cash register one night during a lull in the business. You did not spend any of it, but instead went home, had a beer, and waited. In less than two hours, the police arrived at your apartment. Once the restaurant manager realized you and the money were missing, it was not long before you were arrested. You refused an attorney and told the judge that you would keep committing crimes until he sent you back. He reluctantly sentenced you to ten years. You passed up parole each time it came around.

So here you are again. You have been measured for your new suit of street clothes and your one hundred fifty dollar check for transitional expenses has been processed. The labor department representative has arranged for you to have a stock-clerk job in a small grocery store in a nearby town. Your social worker has also arranged for you to stay in a small apartment near where you will work. You remember your last prerelease counseling session with her and how she offered all the words of encouragement a young, energetic, and well-meaning counselor could muster. You just smiled and nodded your approval. What good would it have done to burst her idealistic bubble? She could never understand how frightening the outside world had come to be for you. All of her friends lived in the free world; none of yours did.

You would like to make it on the outside if you could, but the odds are against you. And besides, it's just too lonely out there. You know you ought to feel happy about leaving prison, but the truth is, you are miserable about it. You would like to be able to make it on the outside, but deep down inside, you feel you are doomed before you start.

*Source:* Michael Braswell, Tyler Fletcher, and Larry Miller, *Human Relations and Corrections*, Third Edition (Prospect Heights, IL: ©1990, 1985 by Waveland Press), pp. 83–84. Reprinted with permission from the publisher.

**Preparing the Community.**   Parole is a dual responsibility—to be successful, it requires both serious *commitment* on the part of the *inmate* and sufficient *concern* on the part of *society*. Ideally, release preparations therefore include not only the person about to be paroled, but others in the community as well. For example, continuity should be established between institutional programs and educational or vocational training offerings in the surrounding area. In this way, ex-offenders can continue to attend classes or programs they began while incarcerated. Getting community leaders, influential employers, service agencies, and school officials involved can also assist with obtaining needed resources.

The more those in the community are integrated into prerelease planning, the more likely it is that misconceptions about parole will be reduced. It is only natural to fear and mistrust the unknown. "Public ignorance of a social problem leads to public rejection of the people who personify that problem."[53] The more citizens learn about the parole process and its objectives, the greater likelihood there is for replacing traditionally negative expectations with more cooperative efforts.

But because the reception extended to ex-offenders is often more antagonistic than accepting, it is important for the parolee to locate *supportive peer associations*. Relying on such groups can do much to make the transition from con-

To the extent that inmates can develop a marketable skill, they will be better prepared for parole. Courtesy of Anthony W. Zumpetta.

[53]Paul W. Keve, *Imaginative Programming in Probation and Parole* (Minneapolis, MN: University of Minnesota Press, 1967), p. 255.

finement less frightening. It may be difficult to imagine a "hardened ex-con" fearing anything—much less the expectation of imminent freedom. As we saw in the last scenario, however, even with official assistance from the system, parole can be a very lonely, soul-searching experience. In the next "Close-up on Corrections," an inmate's plea to Ann Landers is further evidence that the prospect of getting out can create more panic than the possibility of staying in. Particularly in terms of the critical role of self-help groups, note her response.

**Preparing the Offender.**   As that inmate's letter indicates, not all institutions offer prerelease guidance before discharge. But some correctional facilities do make an effort to prepare offenders for what to expect and how to cope upon

❖ *CLOSE-UP ON CORRECTIONS*

Prerelease Panic

Dear Ann:

I am coming to the end of a five-year prison sentence in a state correctional facility. I need to know how to deal with society after my release. I'm not sure about how I should conduct myself around people I haven't seen in five years. What will be expected of me? What should I say to women I take out for the first or second time? Should I tell them I've been in prison?

When I apply for a job and am asked if I have a criminal record, what should I say? I'm afraid if I mention this I won't be hired. On the other hand, if I lie and they find out the truth, I will probably be fired.

It seems that there should be some kind of counseling in prison to prepare people like me for the outside. Some inmates I know who have been in prison for a long time are actually afraid to leave because they don't think they'll fit in out there. Almost 90 percent of these prisoners end up coming back, mainly because they were not prepared to face the outside world.

If you can be of any help to people like me, it will be greatly appreciated by the thousands of inmates who are struggling with the same problem.

F.C., Cranston, R.I.

You are not alone. I've dealt with this problem in my column before. There is a self-help group for ex-offenders that can answer your questions and give you more guidance on living on the outside. It can also refer you to local groups around the country that offer job training and placement, as well as counseling. For more information, send a self-addressed, stamped envelope to The Fortune Society, 39 W. 19th St., New York, N.Y. 10011. Its members do an excellent job.

*Source:* Ann Landers, "Support Group Can Help Ex-prisoners," published in newspapers throughout the country on February 7, 1992. Permission granted by Ann Landers and Creators Syndicate.

release. In fact, the success of reintegration "depends on how well the inmate is prepared prior to release."[54] This can be accomplished through a variety of programs offered within the resident institution (e.g., *prerelease counseling*), the outside community (e.g., *work release*), or other correctional facilities (e.g., *prerelease centers*).

• *Prerelease centers.* In some cases, prisoners are phased into release through gradual reduction of their security classification. In this manner, the last months of one's sentence are served in a minimum-security facility or *prerelease center*—where there are fewer rules governing behavior, less staff monitoring, and greater trust placed in the inmate. The goal is to enable those about to be released to take more personal responsibility for decision making, as well as encourage them to replace external staff control with internal self-control.

Inmates being phased out through minimum security may spend daytime hours at work assignments or educational programs in the community. Thus, they are able to become better accustomed to the freedoms of outside life. They can "practice" living in society while remaining under supervision during their unoccupied time. Beyond these general functions of minimum security facilities, prerelease centers provide additional assistance with helping the inmate make plans to obtain housing, employment, transportation, and other essentials for surviving on the outside.

• *Work release.* Not all correctional agencies have a prerelease center or sufficient bedspace in it to meet demands. But arrangements can be made for *work release* without transferring inmates from their assigned institution.[55] Particularly where preparation for parole is viewed as a long-term process, opportunities for work release may be provided well in advance of one's anticipated departure. Work release enables the inmate to be employed on salary in the community during the day, while returning to the facility at night. Generally, transportation is provided by the institution (although a fee may be charged for this service, along with additional fees for room and board).

Work release is an alternative to total confinement that has a number of advantages—among them, enabling offenders to help support their families and reducing the financial burden on taxpayers. Perhaps most important, it enhances the inmate's job skills, confidence, sense of responsibility, and ties with the community. Politically, it has been popular since passage of the first legislation in 1913 authorizing work release in Wisconsin. Conservatives like the economic savings; liberals like the rehabilitative aspects.

Not everyone, however, is equally enthusiastic;[56] nor is work release without risks. Despite its advantages, not all correctional systems have adopted work

[54]Samuel F. Saxton, "Reintegration: Corrections' Hope for the Future," *American Jails,* Vol. 5, No. 3 (July/August 1991), p. 45. Although Chapter 11 focuses on parole from prison, this article addresses the unique aftercare program provided at the Prince George's County (Maryland) Jail, where mentoring, life planning, and inmate support groups are integral features of prerelease planning.

[55]It is, however, preferable to house work release inmates together in a community-based facility in order to avoid both pressures to bring in contraband and the perception among other inmates that some are being "singled-out" for preferential treatment. See Vernon B. Fox, *Correctional Institutions* (Englewood Cliffs, NJ: Prentice Hall, 1983), p. 148.

[56]Elmer H. Johnson, "Work Release: Conflicting Goals within a Promising Innovation," *Canadian Journal of Corrections,* Vol. 12, No. 1 (January 1970), pp. 67–77.

release programs. Even where it is available, the percentage of the total population participating is extremely small (ranging from less than 1% to 14%).[57] Undoubtedly, there have been isolated problems with inmates absconding or returning under the influence of alcohol or drugs. But for the most part, it would appear that the benefits of reintegrating the offender into society through work release outweigh the drawbacks. Except for the extremely few prisoners sentenced to death or confined to life without parole, virtually everyone is subject to potential release at some time. With those who are eligible, it would seem logical that the time to take the risks associated with work release is while they are still subject to continued custody.

• *Prerelease Counseling.* Those successfully participating in work release may be able to continue their same job upon discharge from the institution. If not, or if work release was not available, one of the ex-offender's most immediate concerns will obviously be getting a full-time job. A number of correctional departments therefore provide *prerelease employment counseling,* combined with efforts to locate a position prior to leaving the institution. (In fact, before so many offenders qualified for mandatory supervised release, it was common to withhold parole until employment was verified.) As we will see later, however, locating employment for ex-offenders is more easily said than done.

Beyond the immediate survival needs of finding employment and housing, inmates will have many other personal concerns—from how to establish social relationships to how to buy a used car. As much as possible, issues related to their reintegration should be addressed before leaving the institution through *parole preparation sessions.* During these classes, inmates are advised of the regulations that will govern their behavior while on parole, as well as warned about potential pitfalls—such as resuming the use of alcohol or drugs, taking on debts, getting involved with the wrong types of people, or moving too quickly into a deep relationship. It is, of course, important to make sure that the format is not one of "lecturing," but rather, an open dialogue with opportunities to ask questions and engage in discussions about personal anxieties. As the next "Close-up on Corrections" shows, the topics of interest to inmates in parole preparation sessions are quite diverse—ranging from police harassment to prison jargon.

## Conditions of Parole

For the most part, the conditions of parole require behavior that is normally exhibited by law-abiding people in ordinary living. They are quite similar to the probation stipulations described in Chapter 5. As with probation, *general conditions* refer to the standard requirements governing behavior that are imposed uniformly. Designed to reduce the chances of renewed involvement in crime, they may require steady work, restrict travel, limit personal associations, prohibit the use of alcohol, and the like. Within a particular jurisdiction, these general

---

[57]Bernard J. McCarthy, "Community Residential Centers: An Intermediate Sanction for the 1990s," in Peter J. Benekos and Alida V. Merlo, eds., *Corrections: Dilemmas and Directions* (Cincinnati, OH: Anderson Publishing Company, 1992), p. 182, citing the percentage of each state's prison population on work release in 1989.

Prerelease Preparation: What Every Inmate Should Know

### POLICE HARASSMENT

A common question asked by inmates is to what extent they will be subject to "harassment" by the police, and what they can do to avoid it. Will they be suspect every time a candy bar is stolen from the station where they pump gas? There is, of course, no one uncomplicated answer. But those who understand the role of police in society and how a pattern of offenses already on record can create heightened suspicions are better equipped to resist overreacting when it occurs. If a burglary is committed at two o'clock in the morning and a parolee with a history of burglary is found in the area—several miles from home—it would be reasonable for the police to ask questions. In other words, what may appear to the parolee as random harassment is to the police officer, routine assessment of the situation. To reduce the likelihood of being subjected to law enforcement attention, the parolee must not only *be* law-abiding but must *look* law-abiding as well.

### PAROLE OFFICER RELATIONSHIPS

How well local law enforcement and parole officers work together can also influence how intensively the police will focus on ex-offenders in their investigations. Moreover, to some extent, the parole officer is the client's advocate. It is therefore essential that they get to know and trust each other. If a client makes sure that the parole officer knows him or her, confidence can be built through that knowledge. Then it is possible that the officer can vouch for the parolee when the police initiate contact. On the other hand, if the parole supervisor does not have a well-informed relationship with the parolee, there is nothing on which to base such protective assurance.

The emphasis here is on a practical relationship, unaffected by individual personalities. Parolees do not want to go back to prison—they do not want to lose their freedom. Nor do parole officers want their clients to return—they do not like to have a high proportion of failures on their caseload. Consequently, regardless of how the officer and parolee might view each other personally, their common objective is to enable the ex-offender to remain out of prison and be discharged successfully from parole supervision.

### SOCIAL RELATIONSHIPS

Coming out of prison, it is often hard simply to start a conversation with neighbors, co-workers, or even family members. Part of the problem in communicating results from the fact that inmates unknowingly acquire unique mannerisms, expressions, and vocabulary that are peculiar to the prison setting. Unless ex-offenders "unlearn" prison jargon and customs, they are likely to be quickly identified as "ex-cons" (particularly among others who have served time). But even without displaying prison traits, getting acquainted with the "right" kind of people may well be difficult. Bars and poolhalls are obviously not the best places to meet such people. Although these are legitimate business enterprises patronized by many customers who are fully law-abiding, it is necessary for parolees to avoid areas and situations where they may be vulnerable to liquor, fights, or criminal suggestions.

## ALCOHOL

Among the reasons for refraining from bars is that one of the main trouble areas during the first few weeks on parole involves alcohol. After years of being deprived of it, alcohol often presents an immediate temptation. It is glamorized in advertisements, associated with old memories, or merely a legalized means of temporarily escaping one's troubles. While in prison, those who drank in the past have "dried out," losing some of their former tolerance for alcohol but still recalling its taste. That is why those who leave prison without family contacts or officer supervision have often been picked up shortly thereafter. While doing something as innocent as waiting for a bus, they may walk into a bar for "just one drink" and soon become arrested for public drunkenness. New releasees who intend to drink are therefore well advised to do so at home, testing their tolerance in private for at least a month before drinking in public.

conditions will be imposed on all parolees (as well as supervised mandatory releasees). Although they are not identical throughout the country, some are commonly imposed in the majority of states, as shown in Figure 11.5.

| Condition | Percentage of Jurisdictions |
|---|---|
| Obey all federal, state, and local laws | 98.0% |
| Report to the parole officer as directed and answer all reasonable inquiries by the officer | 96.1% |
| Refrain from possessing a firearm or other dangerous weapon unless granted written permission | 92.2% |
| Remain within the jurisdiction of the court and notify the parole officer of any change in residence | 90.2% |
| Permit the parole officer to visit the parolee at home or elsewhere | 82.4% |
| Obey all rules and regulations of the parole supervision agency | 78.4% |
| Maintain gainful employment | 78.4% |
| Abstain from association with persons with criminal records | 60.8% |
| Pay all court-ordered fines, restitution, or other financial penalties | 52.9% |

**Figure 11.5** General Conditions of parole found in most jurisdictions. *Source:* Edward E. Rhine, William R. Smith, and Ronald W. Jackson, *Paroling Authorities: Recent History and Current Practice* (Laurel, MD: American Correctional Association, 1991, p. 106.

In addition to the general requirements of everyone, *specific conditions* can be added for a particular client to address any unique treatment needs or behavioral restrictions. For example, a habitual DUI (driving under the influence) offender may also be required to attend Alcoholics Anonymous sessions regularly, to abstain completely from the use of alcohol, to refrain from driving a car, and even to submit to random breath, blood, or urinalysis testing.

In the past, parole conditions were often quite lengthy and included restrictions of questionable applicability (such as not getting married or becoming pregnant). More recently, the relevance as well as ambiguity of conditions attached to community supervision have been challenged in court (see Chapter 5). General trends in the overall parole process have also been moving toward greater *objectivity*. As a result, parole authorities have begun to reduce the number of conditions, focusing more on those related to crime control than on those related to social activities.[58] Regardless of what the requirements are, the client must agree in writing to abide by them.

## Functions of Parole Officers

It is the parole board in the state's central office that authorizes both general and specific conditions by which clients must abide. But it is the parole officer in the field who is responsible for assuring that they are upheld. Previously, field services were an administrative unit of the parole board. But since the 1970s, community supervision has become increasingly independent and is now usually housed separately (primarily within the state department of corrections).[59]

On the part of the officer, field services call for—among many other attributes—skills in working with the client and his or her family, developing relationships with law enforcement agencies, and becoming thoroughly knowledgeable of available resources in the area. In fact, the duties of officers involved in community supervision are so varied and their workloads so demanding that guidelines have been developed to assist them with establishing their priorities and managing their time.[60]

Like probation supervision, the parole officer's role involves similar conflicts between providing support and imposing sanctions. But encouraging *change* is actually what both are designed to accomplish.[61] To achieve change, parole officers are simultaneously expected to (1) furnish assistance to help the ex-offender readjust; (2) monitor signs which indicate how well or poorly that adjustment is occurring; and (3) take appropriate action to control behavior when necessary.

---

[58]See Lawrence F. Travis III and Edward J. Latessa, "'A Summary of Parole Rules—Thirteen Years Later': Revisited Thirteen Years Later," *Journal of Criminal Justice*, Vol. 12, No. 6 (1984), p. 598.

[59]Rhine et al., pp. 102–103. See also Eric Carlson, *Contemporary United States Parole Board Practices* (San Jose, CA: San Jose State University Foundation, 1979).

[60]Albert G. Smith, "Organizational Skills for Managing Your Probation and Parole Workload," *Corrections Today*, Vol. 54, No. 5 (July 1992), pp. 136–42.

[61]Barry J. Nidorf, "Probation and Parole Officers: Police Officers or Social Workers?" in *Correctional Issues: Probation and Parole*, p. 73.

**Locating Housing.** While the supportive functions of parole extend throughout the time that the client is on the officer's caseload, more intensive assistance is especially needed during the initial phases. If institutional staff have not already done so, the parole officer must arrange for an approved residence and job. Preference is usually given to locating clients in their own home (with either their marital family or their parents). The reason for this is that parents, spouse, and children are generally more interested in the parolee's success than anyone else. They are therefore more likely to help keep track of the client and make efforts to prevent him or her from getting into circumstances that might lead to trouble. In addition to the greater stability of the environment, living at home is also a more economical alternative.

In the absence of family ties (or in the case of an undesirable home situation) the parole officer will need to make other residential arrangements. A second choice would be the home of close relatives. For the most part, the homes of friends are not approved, since the parolee may not have displayed wise judgment in selecting friends before imprisonment. Although parolees can rent their own apartment, living alone is less preferable than living with family members, since there is less control over what occurs in an apartment.

**Locating Employment.** Along with residence, the client's employment must also be approved. Most parole officers look for a job that places the employee in the mainstream of living—preferably one that includes only day-shift work so there is less social isolation. Because of irregular hours and some of the people with whom employees come into contact, officers would be quite hesitant to approve work in such establishments as bars or discos.

While some jobs are off-limits because of the position's lack of suitability, many others are restricted because of the parolee's ineligibility. Those who have not participated in institutional education programs will especially find many doors closed to them, since even entry-level jobs today tend to require at least a high school diploma.

Moreover, even those with the required educational credentials will find that *occupational licensing* provisions are often based on "good moral character," which effectively excludes ex-offenders. Positions requiring licenses in some states that are difficult to obtain by those with a criminal record include a long list of occupations—ranging from dental hygienists and florists to photographers, manicurists, coal mine inspectors, car dealers, yacht salesmen, tree surgeons, pest controllers, and even sewage work operators![62] Efforts have been made to remove arbitrary statutory restrictions on job opportunities for ex-offenders.[63] The U.S. Labor Department has also compiled a guide for making occupational plans during confinement and identifying employment resources upon release.[64] But the

---

[62]Cromwell et al., p. 286, citing H. Miller, *The Closed Door: The Effect of a Criminal Record on Employment with State and Local Public Agencies,* distributed by the National Technical Information Service (1972).

[63]"Removing Offender Employment Restrictions: A Report on Legislative Developments," *Offender Employment Review* (Washington, DC: American Bar Association, 1973).

[64]*Getting a Job—Another Chance to Make It* (Washington, DC: U.S. Department of Labor, 1993).

fact remains that while individual states vary, many positions still require licensing that would disqualify parolees.

Combined with such state-imposed restrictions is the basic hesitancy of many employers to "take a chance" with ex-offenders. Finding jobs for parolees is also especially difficult in times of high unemployment, when even those without the stigma of being "ex-cons" have a hard time finding meaningful work. Thus, it is readily apparent why it sometimes appears almost impossible to place parolees in jobs with a livable salary, much less career mobility.

When an appropriate job is finally located, there is also the possibility that an employer will take advantage of the powerless status of a parolee (e.g., by requiring more overtime hours or paying lower wages than other workers in the same job with similar experience are making). Knowing that complaints from the parolee would be highly unlikely, officers are expected to keep a careful watch for potential exploitation.

**Field Supervision.**　Once a parolee has settled into a stable residence and a steady job, there is less immediate need for assistance. That does not mean that the officer's helping role has terminated. In addition to any ongoing counseling or therapy being provided, additional problems may well arise with anything from a serious illness to the inability to balance a checkbook. Parole officers' job descriptions may call for planning, assessing needs, establishing goals, and the like. However, the many minor and major emergencies to which they must respond can rarely be planned for or predicted.

Especially during the early months of parole or supervised release, it is important to provide close supervision and support, which will include home visits. Photo by Richard Morrison. Used with persmission of the American Correctional Association.

Consequently, crisis intervention and parole work may often seem to be "synonymous."[65]

But for the most part, once survival needs have been addressed, the officer's attention can turn more toward monitoring the parolee's *reintegration progress*. Much of this component of the job relates to enforcing the conditions established for the client. Particularly during the first months on parole, it is important to provide careful supervision, since that initial period after release is when violations are most likely to occur. (Statistics indicate that "[a]fter the first year, the greater the amount of time a releasee remains in the community without reincarceration, the less are his or her chances of returning to prison."[66]) See the next "Close-up on Corrections" for a humorous but insightful story about what can happen when a parole officer does not closely monitor a client.

It is helpful if both the officer and the client can view parole conditions as *tools* to shape behavior rather than as *limits* being imposed. Of course, that is not often the case. When it is obvious that the parolee is becoming unresponsive and in danger of getting into further trouble, the officer may well recommend revocation. If a new offense is committed, such action will be virtually certain.

As with probation, parole officers might be reluctant to take formal action upon a first violation, especially when it involves a technical or minor matter. But unlike probation, parole officers are dealing with more serious and/or repeat offenders and therefore do not tend to exercise as much discretion. Moreover, officers and their supervisors have become increasingly responsive to the need to protect community safety. Public criticism has not gone unnoticed when a client's criminal actions capture media headlines. Unfortunately, that is when parole is most likely to make the news, since parole "will always be most visible when [it is] most vulnerable."[67]

As a result of such factors, field supervision in recent years has been characterized as having adopted a *sanction orientation* that stresses "swift and uncompromising response to noncompliance."[68] Similar in some respects to the concept of "tough love," the sanction emphasis rests on the belief that "the [re]incarceration of one criminal can be just as much a success as the rehabilitation of another."[69] That does not mean that parole officers have now become police officers, or that they take pleasure in recommending revocation, or that they have abandoned rehabilitative goals. But "[i]f a criminal cannot or will not change within the environment of the community, then the sanction orientation requires that community corrections must, for the sake of community protection, immediately . . . act to change the environment in which the criminal functions."[70]

---

[65]Steven D. Dillingham, Reid H. Montgomery, and Richard W. Tabor, *Probation and Parole in Practice,* Second Edition (Cincinnati, OH: Anderson Publishing Company, 1990), p. 95.

[66]John F. Wallerstedt, "Returning to Prison," *Bureau of Justice Statistics: Special Report* (Washington, DC: U.S. Department of Justice, 1984), p. 2.

[67]Curran, p. 31.

[68]Nidorf, p. 70.

[69]Ibid.

[70]Ibid., p. 74.

### Case Supervision

The parolee had an excellent job, was happily married, was progressing well in all areas, and was within six months of being discharged from parole. As far as the parole officer could determine, there was no prospect that [he] would become involved again in criminal activity.

Nevertheless, after making home calls for a four-month period during which the parolee had been absent, the parole officer's concern could no longer be contained. . . . He asked the wife for an explanation of her husband's long absence. She replied, "I thought you knew. Milton passed away about three-and-a-half months ago." The startled parole officer weakly inquired as to why she had not said anything to him during the intervening four months. She responded that she thought [he] . . . had continued to visit out of kindly concern for *her* well-being.

This true story contains a number of object lessons. [It illustrates that] the professional service of the probation or parole officer is not restricted to the client. . . . But a more important [lesson] is that case supervision is an artistic blend of treatment *and surveillance*. A perceptive officer would not have waited four months before accounting for the wherabouts of his parolee. One can imagine the embarrassment of . . . trying to explain to his supervisor why he had supervised a dead man on his active caseload for almost four months.

*Source:* Louis P. Carney, *Probation and Parole: Legal and Social Dimensions* (New York: McGraw-Hill, 1977), pp. 221–22.

## Parole Revocation

Since parole is a form of conditional release, it can be *revoked* for failure to maintain the conditions upon which it was awarded. Although the supervising field officer can recommend revocation, only the parole board is authorized to revoke one's parole. In other words, those with the authority to grant parole are also those who can repeal it.

In contrast to parole selection, however, inmates *are* entitled to certain *due process protections* in parole revocation proceedings. The rationale for this distinction is, as the Supreme Court has phrased it, that there is a "difference between losing what one has and not getting what one wants."[71] That is, those denied the opportunity to be *released* on parole are not subject to a change in status. They remain in the institution to which they are already confined. On the other hand, those denied the opportunity to *remain* on parole are likely to suffer a substantial change in status.

---

[71]*Greenholtz v. Inmates of the Nebraska Penal and Correctional Complex*, 442 U.S. 1 (1979).

**Due Process Protections.** For many years, parolees had no legal means of challenging the discretion of parole board revocation actions. The concept then was that parole was extended by the "grace" of the executive branch of government and that it could be withdrawn at any time. The granting of parole is still legally considered a privilege. Nevertheless, the Supreme Court determined in the 1972 *Morrisey v. Brewer* case[72] that revocation of parole represents a "grievous loss" which falls within the due process provisions of the Fourteenth Amendment. This does not extend to parolees the full due process protections of defendants facing adjudication in a criminal court. Parole revocation is *not* considered either a stage of criminal prosecution or an adversarial proceeding. But the Supreme Court's ruling did establish that parole revocation must include two stages:

1. A *preliminary hearing*, at which point it is determined if there is *probable cause* to believe that a violation of parole conditions was committed, and if so,
2. A full *revocation hearing*, at which the parolee must be afforded:
   - Written notice of the alleged violation
   - Disclosure of the evidence related to the violation
   - An opportunity to be heard in person and to present witnesses and documentary evidence
   - An opportunity to confront and cross-examine adverse witnesses (unless good cause can be demonstrated for not allowing confrontation)
   - Judgment before a neutral and detached hearing body (such as a parole board)
   - A written statement regarding the evidence relied upon and the reasons for revoking parole.

Note that one of the traditionally fundamental due process protections—the right to counsel—is *not* included among these requirements. This issue was addressed the very next year (1973) in the *Gagnon v. Scarpelli* case.[73] But that ruling did *not* extend due process protections to the provision of counsel for indigent clients facing possible probation or parole revocation. Rather, it was held that the decision to appoint counsel could be made by the state on a case-by-case basis, using its discretion as to whether the parolee's version of an issue being disputed can only be fairly presented by an attorney. Nor have any court decisions thus far mandated the provision of a revocation appeal process. It may therefore be surprising to find that, although not constitutionally required, about half of the states (48%) do offer an opportunity to appeal.[74] Overall, both legally and administratively, trends point toward affording greater due process rights when one's liberty will be restricted.

**Revocation Results.** Once the parolee has been afforded the hearings as described above (along with an appeal in some states), the question becomes

---

[72]*Morrissey v. Brewer*, 408 U.S. 471 (1972).
[73]*Gagnon v. Scarpelli*, 411 U.S. 778 (1973). As was discussed in Chapter 5, in this case, the Supreme Court extended many of the same due process procedures to probationers.
[74]Smith et al., "Parole Practices Survey," p. 42.

what *consequences* occur if parole is revoked. Many would immediately answer that the offender is *returned to prison* to complete the remainder of the original sentence. That is certainly a common outcome, particularly if another crime has been committed. In fact, former parolees are accounting for more than their share of the prison crowding problem—28% of new admissions to federal and state prisons in 1990 were those returning for parole or other conditional release violations.[75] But reincarceration is not the only possibility. To the contrary, in most states (74.5%) the parole board may also elect to *restore parole status*—either with no change or a modification of conditions.[76]

## Recidivism

It is, of course, on the basis of *recidivism rates* that parole—and for that matter, much of the entire correctional system—is judged. As was described beginning in Chapter 1, to recidivate means to "revert" or "repeat." The question is, what is being reverted to or repeated? One of the major difficulties in determining recidivism rates is that different people use differing definitions of it, such as:

- *Rearrest*. Are criminals considered "recidivists" when they are *rearrested*? If so, does the *type of crime* make any difference? Would a juvenile car thief be considered a recidivist if rearrested for running away from home?

- *Reconviction*. What about those rearrested who are not *reconvicted*? Can they be classified as recidivists if they are innocent in the eyes of the court?

- *Reincarceration*. Even if reconvicted, does it matter whether or not they are *reincarcerated*? What if their only punishment is a fine?

- *Parole violation*. Are *parole violators* recidivists? What if they only committed a minor technical violation?

- *Parole revocation*. Are those whose parole is *revoked* recidivists? What if they are not reincarcerated?[77]

In addition to these questions concerning what type of conduct is considered recidivism, there is the further issue of how long a period of time should be taken into consideration after one's prior offense. In other words, how long should offenders be monitored to establish accurate recidivisim rates—one year? two years? ten years? for the rest of their lives?

Using different *failure measures* and *follow-up periods* will obviously produce different outcomes. For instance, one study found that when "arrest within one year" is used as the failure criterion, almost 15% "recidivated." But of those who were still on parole at the end of six years, only 3% failed. Similarly, when more stringent criteria than arrest data are used, results appear to be more encouraging. For example, if "commitment to a correctional institution for 60 days or

---

[75]Louis W. Jankowski, *Correctional Populations in the United States, 1990* (Washington, DC: U.S. Department of Justice, 1992), p. 871.

[76]Rhine et al., pp. 130–31.

[77]For a discussion of such widely varying definitions of recidivism, see Michael D. Maltz, *Recidivism* (Orlando, FL: Academic Press, 1984).

more" is used to measure failure, only about 5% "recidivated" within the first or second year (dropping to 1.1% by the sixth year).[78] By the end of six years, a total of 42% failed if arrest is the criterion, whereas only 19% were unsuccessful if the measure is reincarceration for 60 days or more (see Figure 11.6). These are among the complications that make it not only difficult to measure recidivism, but also virtually impossible to compare studies which use varying definitions of it.

If successful discharge is any indicator, parole may not be as ineffective as sensationalized media accounts might lead us to believe. The majority of first-time parolees in 1989 (over 57%) completed their parole successfully.[79] Yet here again we have a measurement issue, since those reincarcerated after a parole violation are usually eligible to be conditionally released again. When *all* discharges from state parole are taken into account (rather than just first-timers), the figures are not so favorable—only 36% successfully completed their term, with almost 61% returned to prison.[80] Commenting on such less-than-impressive statistics, it has been noted that: "[i]f over 50% of the planes sold by aircraft factory X were to crash within two years of delivery, factory X would have to change the model drastically or else go out of business. Planes falling from the sky are both unpopular and frightening. So are people who commit criminal acts."[81]

Perhaps the most significant (although not unexpected) finding is that those with no prior prison commitments are less likely to recidivate within three years (24.8%) than are those who previously served three or more prison terms (42.5%).[82] Figure 11.7 shows data for those released from prison in 11 states which clearly indicate that offenders with more prior arrests are more likely to be rearrested within three years.

In summary, the effectiveness of parole depends on many factors—from what variables are being measured to what types of offenders are being

| | Follow-up Period | | | | | | |
| Criteria | 1 Year | 2 Years | 3 Years | 4 Years | 5 Years | 6 Years | Total |
| --- | --- | --- | --- | --- | --- | --- | --- |
| Arrest | 14.8% | 9.4% | 7.7% | 3.6% | 3.5% | 3.0% | 42.0% |
| Commitment of 60 days or more | 4.8% | 4.8% | 3.6% | 2.1% | 2.6% | 1.1% | 19.0% |

**Figure 11.6** Measuring recidivism. *Note:* Recidivism rate is given as the percentage with unfavorable outcome each year by differing criteria and follow-up periods for 521 adult parolees. *Source:* Reprinted from *Journal of Criminal Justice*, Vol. 8, No. 1, Peter Hoffman and Barbara Stone-Meierhoefer, "Reporting Recidivism Rates: The Criterion and Follow-up Issues," p. 60, ©1980, with permission from Pergamon Press Ltd., Headington Hill Hall, Oxford OX3 0BW, UK.

[78]Compiled from Peter Hoffman and Barbara Stone-Meierhoefer, "Reporting Recidivism Rates: The Criterion and Follow-up Issues," *Journal of Criminal Justice,* Vol. 8, No. 1 (1980), p. 60.
[79]Perkins, p. 42.
[80]Ibid., p. 41.
[81]Dennie Briggs, *In Place of Prison* (London: Temple Smith, 1975), p. 9.
[82]Wallerstedt, p. 3.

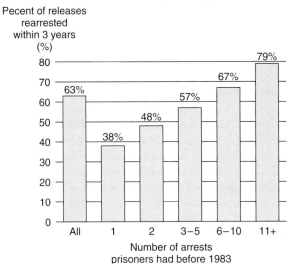

State offenders released from prison in 1983

Pecent of releases rearrested within 3 years (%)

**Figure 11.7** Likelihood of rearrest following release from prison. *Note:* Data reflect inmates released from prison in 11 states in 1983. Among those arrested once before entering, 38% were rearrested within three years of release; among those arrested eleven or more times, 79% were rearrested. *Source: Prisons and Prisoners in the United States* (Washington, DC: U.S. Department of Justice, 1992), p.21.

assessed. It is for such reasons that *standardization* of recidivism criteria is necessary if accurate evaluations of parole are to be obtained.[83] But even with nationally standardized guidelines for determining recidivism, parole cannot be held completely accountable for either its successes or failures.

The willingness or unwillingness of correctional institutions to provide inmates with meaningful programs during confinement will have an impact upon parole's effectiveness. Perhaps most influential, however, is the acceptance or rejection of the client by the community. In that regard, "there is always an instinct to shun the disgraced, expecially when they appear to be blameworthy. . . . But we must help them all, for their sake and our own."[84] Just as the offender cannot make the transition from confinement to community alone, neither can parole be expected to achieve successful outcomes in isolation.

## ❖ SUMMARY

Originating with Maconochie's "mark system" and Crofton's "ticket of leave," parole was initiated in this country by Zebulon Brockway at the Elmira Reformatory in 1876. By the 1950s, every state had implemented the indeterminate sentencing necessary to enable offenders to be released on parole. But some 25 years later, trends began to change. Several states (along with the federal government) moved back to determinate sentencing, abolishing or limiting the functions of parole. Nevertheless, throughout much of the country, parole retains its role of supervising those released from a correctional institution prior to sentence expiration, under conditions that permit reincarceration if violated. In that respect, parole is still grappling with contradictory expectations—e.g., safe-

[83]See Hoffman and Stone-Meierhoefer.
[84]George Ives, *A History of Penal Methods* (Montclair, NJ: Patterson Smith, 1970), pp. 382–83.

guarding the community while servicing the client; extending support without overlooking surveillance.

In states where it has not been abolished, anyone who is not sentenced to death or life without parole is technically eligible for parole. Legally, however, it is considered a privilege rather than a right. Unlike probation, parole is the responsibility of the executive branch of government. In most states it is administered by a board or commission appointed by the governor. Given their extensive power, recommendations have been made to upgrade the educational qualifications of board members, with appointments made solely on the basis of merit, to avoid political interference. Parole has been organized within three distinct administrative models (autonomous, integrated, and consolidated), each of which has implications for how decisions are made.

It has been the decision-making component of parole that has experienced both the greatest criticism and the greatest change over recent years. Extensive information is taken into account in deciding whether or not to grant parole. But personal preferences, values, and backgrounds of individual board members can influence the process. The final selection decision may come down to a basic trust or mistrust with regard to both the inmate's intention and capacity to change. As a result, parole decisions have been vulnerable to criticism by inmates, correctional staff, and the general public. Particularly when a parolee is involved in a serious incident capturing media headlines, the public has questioned its effectiveness. In addition, there has been concern that release on parole from an indeterminate sentence does not provide sufficient deterrence or punishment, has been used to coerce inmates into treatment, and creates disparities in the sentences of offenders convicted of similar crimes.

All of these reservations have generated pressure to return to determinate sentencing, with release specified by sentence length rather than subject to parole board discretion. But in light of the severe prison crowding that followed changes in sentencing practices, good/gain time provisions have been established. Once these time credits are deducted from one's sentence, release is essentially mandatory. But because the full original sentence was not served, release is still conditional on the offender's good behavior under community supervision. Since 1977, trends clearly point toward a significant increase in such mandatory supervised releases. At the same time, discretionary releases are decreasing. Even where parole boards still have discretion over release decisions, objective parole prediction devices (e.g., the Salient Factor Score) are often used to reduce the subjectivity of decision making.

Despite these changes in the selection process, parole retains its postrelease supervisory functions. These include preparing both the community and the offender for release. Much of the parole officer's initial work with a client involves arranging to meet basic survival needs, such as locating housing and employment. The hesitancy of employers to hire ex-offenders, combined with occupational licensing restrictions and educational/experience limitations, often make it difficult to obtain suitable employment for parolees. Once these needs have been addressed, the officer's role shifts toward monitoring the reintegration process.

When the parolee is not adjusting successfully to the freedom of the community, it is also the officer's duty to recommend revocation if warranted by evidence that conditions are being violated. The sanction orientation that such actions reflect maintains that the welfare of all involved requires swift and sure enforcement of parole rules. In contrast to the parole selection process, those facing possible revocation are entitled to certain due process rights. As a result of the *Morrisey v. Brewer* case, it was established that the parole revocation process must occur in two stages. The first phase is a preliminary hearing, and if probable cause is established at that point, a second (full) hearing is conducted. At this revocation hearing, the parolee is afforded a number of due process protections. However, the right to counsel for those who are indigent is considered only on a case-by-case basis, depending on the complexity of the issues being disputed.

Although parole, along with much of the entire correctional system, is judged largely on the basis of recidivism rates, such figures can be misleading. Differing failure measures over differing follow-up periods have produced vastly differing results. The effectiveness of parole is not only difficult to quantify but is subject to variations in terms of programs offered during confinement and community attitudes toward ex-offenders. Beyond the inmate's desire and capacity to change, the success of parole is therefore dependent on everything from correctional practices to community responsiveness.

# Special Topics, Current Issues, and the Future

*[There is a] nagging voice in all of us that says we should be doing more to effect change. Not necessarily change for every inmate. Not necessarily change that attempts to completely reverse damage done by lifelong neglect. But small change. Incremental change. Change that can be built upon—for this generation and for generations to come.[1]*

Margaret C. Hambrick

Courtesy of the Dade County Department of Corrections and Rehabilitation, Miami, Florida.

[1]Margaret C. Hambrick, "Intervention Programs: Setting Change in Motion," *Corrections Today*, Vol. 53, No. 5 (August 1991), p. 6.

Thus far the discussions of correctional services, facilities, and programs herein have primarily described current practices and procedures for dealing with conventional adult offenders. However, this does not provide the entire picture of either where corrections is today or where it should be heading in the future.

Among the major correctional populations that have not yet been addressed are groups which present special problems or unique challenges—from female offenders to those who are aging, AIDS-afflicted, alcoholic, drug-addicted, physically impaired, or mentally disordered. Some of these groups (such as women) have traditionally been in the minority within correctional caseloads and facilities. Others (such as the addicted or mentally ill) represent sizable proportions of correctional clientele. But regardless of their numbers, it is the special difficulties they face within corrections that becomes the focus of Chapter 12. Actually, we encompass only a portion of a much longer list of offenders who could potentially be classified as reflecting special requirements. What those addressed in Chapter 12 have in common is a growing recognition that they present distinct needs which have not always been recognized fully or addressed properly in the past.

Among those who clearly fit that category and whose involvement in the justice system persists at alarming rates are juvenile offenders. Many of the hundreds of thousands of prisoners in correctional institutions or clients on the caseloads of probation and parole officers had their first contact with the law as juveniles. It therefore stands to reason that much of the hope for reducing adult correctional populations rests with the juvenile justice system. In fact, as described in Chapter 13, it was belief in the capacity of young people to change that stimulated the very establishment of a separate process for dealing with juveniles.

As with adults, we will see that even the best intentions are not as readily fulfilled in reality. Nor will we find that youthful offenders have escaped the impact of the justice model. Not only are more juveniles being transferred into the adult criminal justice system, but the juvenile system itself is beginning to look more like its adult counterpart. To some, such changes indicate a failure of the juvenile justice system to live up to its promises. To others, it is the young offenders themselves who are seen as having failed to take advantage of the opportunities offered to them. Whatever one's perspective, the substantial impact of juveniles on the future justifies their significance as a topic of special consideration.

Whether adult or juvenile, special or typical, institutional or community-based, convicted offenders ultimately come under the supervision of correctional staff. We have reviewed everything from the physical plants to the treatment efforts that have been developed to confine and/or change offenders. What we have saved for Chapter 14 is, as the title implies, the key ingredient—staff. Even the most elaborate security systems or sophisticated rehabilitative approaches cannot be implemented effectively without qualified, motivated personnel.

From the director of the department to the entry-level officer in the cell-block or the probation/parole officer in the community, it is the dedication of its employees that enables corrections to function. It is these faceless names on organizational charts who actually operate the system 24 hours a day, seven days a week, often with little compensation and even less recognition. It is they who can make either the most antiquated facility tolerable or the most modern institution unbearable; who can turn probation and parole reporting into either an uplifting encounter or a dull routine. It is therefore fitting that attention turns in Chapter 14 to those who hold the jobs that many others would not want. In addition to finding out who they are and what pressures they face, we look at how they are recruited, selected, trained, compensated, and supervised. Moreover, we determine what changes in personnel procedures can be made to further enhance their capabilities. For it is these thousands of men and women who are the vital factor—not just in terms of how corrections performs today, but more important, what potential it has for tomorrow.

Finally, it is that "tomorrow" which becomes the subject of Chapter 15. To the extent that the past is prologue to the future, a logical starting point for this discussion is legal issues, since past and present correctional practices have often been substantially altered by judicial intervention. Although the courts have been somewhat more restrained in recent years, it is reasonable to assume that the future will continue to be affected by legal actions as well as social change. A prime example is the continuing social debate and legal challenges surrounding the death penalty. Chapter 15 therefore begins with an overview of major legal issues that have influenced the correctional system, along with an agenda of legal controversies that await resolution.

Certainly, no consideration of the future would be complete without devoting attention to the fundamental mission of corrections and how it has changed over time. Again, by looking at past trends, public opinions, and legislative actions, we can begin to glimpse what tomorrow may hold. Will more proactive crime prevention reduce the system's reliance on reactive responses? If not, will we continue to struggle with the dilemma of finding the right balance between punishment and treatment? Will corrections forever be plagued with excessive caseloads and crowded facilities? Will it remain a government function or increasingly become a component of the private sector? And most critically of all, will corrections be able to attract and retain the quality of personnel necessary to meet the challenges of change? If so, there is hope for a future that is brighter than the past. But whatever the outcome, there is no one with a greater stake in assuring its success than each and every one of us.

# chapter 12

# Special Populations
# in Corrections

*Because of the nature of the business, we are responsible for people who are not at liberty to make choices and have fewer options than the larger society, and therefore we should be held to a higher standard. . . .* [1]

*Janie L. Jeffers*

❖ CHAPTER OVERVIEW

Accommodating to society can be especially challenging for those who are distinct in some respect from the majority. In social situations where most people are of a similar race or ethnicity, and generally enjoy good mental as well as physical health, those who do not share such characteristics may encounter difficulties as a result of their minority status. In society overall, the majority is often not overly sympathetic to those who have not had the benefits of their good fortune. Nor is the experience of those under correctional supervision any exception. In Chapters 10 and 11, we saw the ordeals of adjusting to imprisonment and the obstacles to readjusting upon release. Undergoing these processes can be particularly difficult for inmates with special needs—from childbearing females to those who are elderly, physically or mentally disabled, alcoholic, drug-addicted, or AIDS-infected.

If the negative effects of incarceration described previously can be so profound for healthy males—who, within correctional institutions, represent the majority of inmates—the impact can be even more significant for those who differ in some respect from the rest of the inmate population. Women, for example, do not react to the conditions of confinement in the same manner as men. Although the long-term results may be no less devastating, their concerns, social relationships, and adaptation to imprisonment are somewhat different. As has been reflected in the male-dominated discussions of prisonization addressed thus far, females

[1] Janie L. Jeffers, "AIDS at Our Door: Preparing for an Unwanted Guest," *Corrections Today,* Vol. 52, No. 1 (February 1990), p. 36.

have represented an extremely small segment of the prison population. Although still in the vast minority, their numbers are increasing today. Consequently, there is a need for both greater consideration of their unique requirements and greater parity of services in comparison to those extended to men.

Other groups that were also incarcerated in vastly smaller numbers in the past include AIDS-infected and elderly inmates. But with the aging of the U.S. population in general, as well as the spread of AIDS in society at large, more and more of these offenders are appearing in correctional facilities, and administrators are increasingly recognizing their obligation to direct attention toward meeting their special needs.

Still others, such as alcoholics and the mentally ill, have always been represented in sizable numbers among those under correctional supervision. The necessity to provide better care and treatment for them is no less acute today. Now, however, they are joined by growing numbers of drug-addicted offenders. Although corrections has made strides in providing treatment for its clients who are mentally ill, alcoholic, or drug-addicted, demand still exceeds capacity in many such programs.

In fact, regardless of the nature of their needs, those with special requirements have not traditionally received high priority from government in general. Thus, to some extent, the lack of correctional services for such inmates reflects similar shortcomings in the community at large. Once removed from the mass of society through incarceration, they become an even lower public priority—essentially, a minority within a minority.

Some are subject to victimization by other inmates in a subculture where the weak are quickly overcome by the strong. Some simply languish in a system hard-pressed to meet basic necessities of conventional inmates, much less divert scarce resources to special needs. It is an unfortunate irony that in many cases, attention is largely directed toward them reactively in proportion to the growth of their numbers, rather than proactively in an effort to prevent their numbers from growing.

---

*LEARNING GOALS*

*Do you know:*

- *For what types of crimes women are more likely to be arrested?*
- *How the female arrest rate compares to that of men?*
- *What proportion of inmates in prison and jail are female?*
- *What crime is largely accounting for increases in female arrest and incarceration rates?*
- *How women differ from men in terms of their involvement in victim-precipitated crime?*
- *How concerns about their children affect female inmates?*
- *In contrast to men, how women adapt to the conditions of confinement?*
- *What factors distinguish female from male correctional facilities?*
- *The advantages and disadvantages of coed prisons?*

In comparison to males, females have always been (and continue to be) less frequently convicted of crimes and incarcerated in correctional facilities. Some maintain that this reflects a tendency to treat women differently in the criminal justice system, with judges and prosecutors more likely to be lenient with women. For example, when a woman is the sole support for her children, the decisions of criminal justice officials may be influenced by realizing the hardship that imprisonment would create for the family. On the other hand, some believe that females—especially those engaged in the types of violent crimes usually committed by men—are dealt with more severely by a system that views such acts as particularly unacceptable for women: "[W]omen defendants pay for the judges' belief that it is more in man's nature to commit crimes than it is in woman's. Thus when a judge is convinced that the woman before him has committed a crime, he is more likely to overact and punish her, not only for the specific offense, but also for transgressing against his expectations of womanly behavior."[2]

Beyond potentially chauvinistic attitudes, the fact remains that women do not generally pose as clear a danger to society. In comparison to men, they are far more likely to be arrested for property offenses than for violent crimes.[3] Nor are women as likely to be arrested in the first place. Of all police apprehensions in 1990, the vast majority (82%) were male offenders.[4] To some extent, discretionary practices on the part of the arresting officer may account for a portion of this discrepancy. Moreover, society's traditional disdain for aggressiveness on the part of females, as well as dependent, sexually stereotyped social roles, may provide them with fewer criminal opportunities. Much of this, of course, is changing as women are becoming more uniformly accepted in broader roles throughout society.

Whether or not there is any causal connection between social trends and criminal tendencies, females are beginning to appear more often in police reports. While arrests for *violent index crimes* increased 43.3% for men between 1981 and 1990, the same time period witnessed a 61.8% upsurge among women. The differences were even greater in terms of *property index crimes*—with an 8.3% growth in male arrests compared to 31.6% for women[5] (see Figure 12.1). Regardless of the reasons, the female arrest *rate* is increasing at a faster pace than that of their male counterparts. But in comparison to the 7,290,217 males apprehended in 1990 for criminal acts (violent, property, and nonindex offenses), the 1,674,882 females apprehended (18.7%) are still a distinct minority.[6]

---

[2]Rita Simon, *The Contemporary Woman and Crime* (Washington, DC: U.S. Department of Health, Education, and Welfare, 1976), p. 50. (*Note:* HEW is now known as the U.S. Department of Health and Human Services.)

[3]Of all arrests for violent crimes in 1990, only 11.3% were females; of property-related index crime arrests, 25.6% were females. Compiled from figures presented in *Uniform Crime Reports for the United States* (Washington, DC: U.S. Government Printing Office, 1991), p. 179.

[4]Ibid., p. 174.

[5]Ibid.

[6]Ibid.

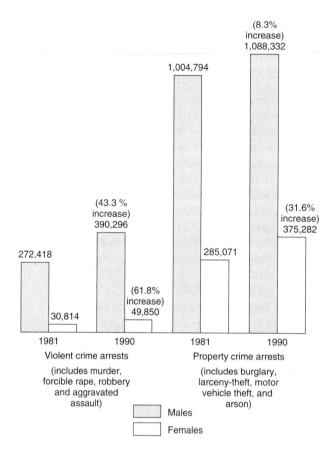

(8.3%
increase)
1,088,332

1,004,794

(43.3 %
increase)
390,296

(31.6%
increase)
375,282

272,418

285,071

(61.8%
increase)
49,850

30,814

| 1981 | 1990 | 1981 | 1990 |

Violent crime arrests
(includes murder,
forcible rape, robbery
and aggravated
assault)

Property crime arrests
(includes burglary,
larceny-theft, motor
vehicle theft, and
arson)

Males
Females

**Figure 12.1** Arrest trends for index crimes by sex. *Source:* Compiled from Federal Bureau of Investigation, *Crime in the United States: Uniform Crime Reports* (Washington, DC: U.S. Government Printing Office, 1991), p. 179.

## Female Inmates

Given their more limited involvement in crime, it is not surprising to find that women comprised less than 6% (43,845) of the 771,243 inmates under the jurisdiction of state and federal correctional authorities in 1990.[7] Looking at the data indicating that about 18% of offenders apprehended were women, it may initially appear that the criminal justice system is, indeed, going easier on females. But beyond those under state and federal jurisdiction, local jails confine another 37,253 females, representing over 9% of the jail population.[8]

In addition, the nonviolent property crimes which female offenders primarily engage in are more likely to make them candidates for probation, community service, restitution, or other nonincarceration alternatives. That does not mean that the system is necessarily more sympathetic to women. Although the

[7]Robyn L. Cohen, "Prisoners in 1990," *Bureau of Justice Statistics Bulletin* (Washington, DC: U.S. Department of Justice, 1991), p. 4.

[8]Tracy L. Snell, "Women in Jail 1989," *Bureau of Justice Statistics Special Report* (Washington, DC: U.S. Department of Justice, 1992), p. 2.

rate of imprisonment for males is about 18 times higher than that of females,[9] the number of women serving time has increased considerably in recent years (see Figure 12.2). Moreover, in the decade between 1980 and 1990, the number of women housed in our nation's prisons increased by 256%; in contrast, their total arrest rate increased by only 60% during that time.[10] To get a better idea of what may be accounting for this discrepancy, we need to take a closer look at what types of female offenders are being incarcerated.

In many respects, the characteristics of female inmates resemble those of their male counterparts. Like male prisoners, females tend to be relatively young and unmarried (either single, separated, divorced, or widowed). As Figure 12.3 reflects, they are only slightly less likely to have graduated from high school, but substantially less likely to have been employed prior to their arrest. As also indicated in that chart, women did not report as much involvement with drug use prior to their arrest. Nor did as many report being under the influence of any drug at the time of their offense.[11] However, it is interesting that they are *more* likely than men to be in prison for drug-related offenses. Assuming that their drug-use reports are as accurate as those of men, this could mean that they are either apprehended more often in proportion to men, or that drug offenses are dealt with more seriously for women—or perhaps both.

In terms of apprehensions, data indicate that during the 1980s, the number of women arrested for drug violations increased at about twice the rate of men.[12]

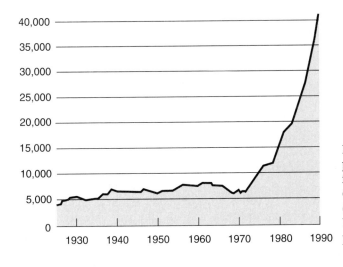

**Figure 12.2** Sentenced female prisoners in state and federal institutions. *Source: Sourcebook of Criminal Justice Statistics—1991* (Washington, DC: U.S. Department of Justice, 1992), p. 634.

[9]Cohen, pp. 4–5. The rate of incarceration for males is 566 per 100,000 males in the resident population, in contrast to 31 per 100,000 females in the resident population.

[10]Meda Chesney-Lind, "Putting the Brakes on the Building Binge," *Corrections Today*, Vol. 54, No. 6 (August 1992), p. 30.

[11]Lawrence A. Greenfeld and Stephanie Minor-Harper, "Women in Prison," *Bureau of Justice Statistics Special Report* (Washington, DC: U.S. Department of Justice, 1991), p. 5. But it should be noted that this report also points out that women were *more* likely than men to report prior use of a *major* drug, as well as to be under the influence of a major drug at the time of their offense.

[12]Ibid., p. 4, where it is noted that between 1980 and 1989, adult arrests for drug violations increased 307% for females in comparison to 147% for males.

|                    |                                        | Females | Males |
|--------------------|----------------------------------------|---------|-------|
| Race/Ethnicity     | White                                  | 39.6%   | 39.5% |
|                    | Black                                  | 46.1    | 45.3  |
|                    | Hispanic                               | 11.7    | 12.6  |
| Age                | Under 25                               | 22.5    | 27.4  |
|                    | Under 35                               | 73.0    | 72.9  |
| Marital status     | Unmarried (or separated)               | 79.9    | 79.6  |
| Education          | Less than high school                  | 56.9    | 61.8  |
| Employment         | Employed full-time                     | 37.1    | 58.4  |
| Drug use           | Ever used any drug                     | 71.8    | 79.9  |
|                    | Used any drug on a regular basis       | 56.5    | 62.6  |
|                    | Under drug influence at time of offense| 33.7    | 35.4  |
| Current offense    | Violent offenses                       | 40.7    | 55.2  |
|                    | Property offenses                      | 41.2    | 30.5  |
|                    | Drug offenses                          | 12.0    | 8.4   |
|                    | Public order offenses                  | 5.1     | 5.2   |
|                    | Other offenses                         | .9      | .7    |

**Figure 12.3** Comparison of male and female state prison inmates in 1986. *Source:* Compiled from Lawrence A. Greenfeld and Stephanie Minor-Harper, "Women in Prison," *Bureau of Justice Statistics Special Report* (Washington, DC: U.S. Department of Justice, 1991), pp. 2, 5.

With regard to how the system treats female drug offenders, the 1980s witnessed a 138% increase of women in local jails (which is also double the increase of men)—with almost half of this growth resulting from more women being held for drug violations.[13] Nor is the problem confined to jails. A prison administrator voices the frustration of many by remarking that it seems every woman inmate in her prison is "under the influence of something."[14] Some have concluded that incarceration figures "suggest that the war on drugs has translated into a war on women."[15]

As with drug offenses, differences are also seen in Figure 12.3 for property and violent crimes. Prison statistics reflect women's greater likelihood of being arrested for property offenses, with a substantially smaller percentage of females incarcerated for violent crimes. It is for such reasons that at least one national study has called for halting the construction of women's prisons in favor of expanding commmunity-based alternatives.[16]

Women also differ from men in terms of their involvement in *victim-precipitated* crime—that is, offenses where the victim played a role in triggering the

[13]Snell, pp. 1–2. (Data reflect the period between 1983 and 1989).
[14]Elaine DeCostanzo and Helen Scholes, "Women behind Bars: Their Numbers Increase," *Corrections Today,* Vol. 50, No. 3 (June 1988), p. 106.
[15]Chesney-Lind, p. 30.
[16]"Study Seeks Alternatives to Incarceration of Women," *CJ: The Americas,* Vol. 5, No. 5 (October/November 1992), p. 14, citing a study conducted by the National Council on Crime and Delinquency.

criminal act. For example, almost half of females serving time in state prison for violent offenses (49.3%) report that they had been physically or sexually abused by their victims.[17] Moreover, violent male inmates are considerably more likely to have victimized strangers, whereas the victims of violent female offenders are more often close relatives or intimate companions.[18]

## Concerns for Children

If there is one major factor that separates female from male inmates, it is worrying about their children. That is not to imply that men are unconcerned, but despite social progress toward achieving sexual equality, childrearing largely remains a female responsibility. The vast majority of women in correctional facilities (76%) are mothers (compared to less than 60% of male inmates who are fathers).[19] Since we have already seen that almost 80% of female prison inmates are unmarried or separated, it is apparent that many of these mothers are single parents.

While male inmates have traditionally counted on the mother of their children to look after them, women cannot necessarily depend on the father to do so. For example, among a national sample of those in state correctional facilities, only 22% of inmate mothers said that their children are living with the father, in contrast to the almost 90% of inmate fathers who reported that their children are living with the mother.[20] Whereas the male offender's family may remain relatively intact, it appears that the woman's family can be seriously disrupted when she is removed from the home. Added to the "pains of imprisonment" for females, therefore, is the further frustration, conflict, and guilt of being both separated from and unable to care for their children. For a sense of this added deprivation, imagine yourself in the place of the inmate who received the letters from her children in the next "Close-up on Corrections."

To nurture the mother–child relationship during visiting, some facilities allow inmates and their children to cook meals in the kitchen, take naps together, and enjoy outside playgrounds or picnic areas.[21] A number of institutions also have more liberal visiting policies for children than adults (even including overnight visits in a few cases). Many allow women to keep their newborn babies in prison for the first few weeks after birth. Despite these brief reprieves, women often find the loneliness of prison filled with anxious thoughts about:

- Where will my kids live?
- Are they getting proper care?
- Will someone bring them in for visits? Or should I not let them see me here?

[17]Greenfeld and Minor-Harper, p. 6.
[18]See *Sourcebook of Criminal Justice Statistics—1990* (Washington, DC: U.S. Department of Justice, 1991), p. 621.
[19]Greenfeld and Minor-Harper, p. 6.
[20]Ibid., pp. 6–7.
[21]See, for example, Gloria Logan, "Family Ties Take Top Priority in Women's Visiting Program," *Corrections Today*, Vol. 54, No. 6 (August 1992), pp. 160–61.

Letters from Children

To Mom,

I Love you. I'm doing good in school. I don't have my school pictures yet. I miss you too also. I got my haircut 1/2 month ago. I hope you can get out for my birthday. Those people must be mean to keep you in there. Well time to go.

(Written by a 6-year-old to a mother serving 5 to 20 years in state prison)

Dear Mom,

I got some money for my birthday. We had cupcakes an brownies. I am 7 years old. I got a hat from Dorthy. I got a silly straw from Linda. I miss you. Will you be out for Christmas?

(Written by the same child after his seventh birthday)

*Source:* Kathryn Watterson Burkhart, *Women in Prison* (New York: Doubleday, 1973), pp. 225, 228.

- Can we keep up a relationship through phone calls and letters?
- Will they remember who their mother is when I get out?
- Will I lose permanent custody?
- What type of relationship will we have when I am released?[22]

This separation and resulting anxiety over how their children are getting along without them can provoke considerable stress, along with threats to the inmate's self-esteem.[23] In a society where women who violate the law are not only social outcasts but almost automatically assumed to be improper parents as well, the inmate mother's self-respect is inevitably bound to suffer. As a result, it has been suggested that counseling and treatment programs for women should address the problems associated with "emotional disturbances, self-confidence, and self-esteem."[24] It is not the burden of children alone, however, that distinguishes male from female inmates.

[22]Summarized and paraphrased from Christine E. Rasche, *Special Needs of the Female Offender: Curriculum Guide for Correctional Officers* (Tallahassee, FL: Florida Department of Education, n.d.), pp. 60–61. See also Phyllis J. Baunach, *Mothers in Prison* (New Brunswick, NJ: Transaction, 1985); Ellen Barry, "Imprisoned Mothers Face Extra Hardships," *The National Prison Journal*, Vol. 14 (Winter 1987), pp. 1–4; and Belinda Rodgers McCarthy, "Inmate Mothers: The Problems of Separation and Reintegration," *Journal of Counseling, Services and Rehabilitation*, Vol. 4, No. 3 (Spring, 1980), pp. 199–212.
[23]J. G. Fox, "Women in Prison—A Case Study in the Reality of Stress," in Robert Johnson and Hans Toch, eds., *Pains of Imprisonment* (Beverly Hills, CA: Sage Publications, 1982), pp. 205–20.
[24]Scarlett V. Carp and Linda S. Schade, "Tailoring Facility Programming to Suit Female Offenders' Needs," *Corrections Today*, Vol. 54, No. 6 (August 1992), p. 154.

## Adaptation to Confinement

Women face many of the same debilitating effects of imprisonment as do men. But there are some differences in the manner in which they adapt to the prison environment. These distinctions result from both dissimilarities between male and female correctional institutions (as we will see shortly) and inherent differences between the sexes.

Women find adjustment more difficult than men do, for a number of reasons. For example, they tend to value privacy more,[25] and consequently, experience greater difficulties adjusting to communal living, the intrusion of rules, and the degrading nature of body searches.[26] At the same time, they do not have as much support from spouses and significant others on the outside. They may fear being abandoned and worry about the inability to cope with the loneliness they might experience upon release. Female inmates are more likely to substitute *emotional intimacy* with other inmates for the loss of family and social ties. These bonds are often expressed in *"quasi-family" patterns*, with certain inmates taking on the roles of mother, father, and children within the institution.

**Inmate Relationships.** The value of family life—and the woman's role within it—are so firmly established in American culture that female inmates try to avoid the alienating and dispiriting effects of imprisonment by creating family structures. Unlike men, who tend to form gangs, women establish power and authority relationships through the model that they were familiar with on the outside—the family.[27] In other words, they imitate the "real world" that they came from:

> This is an affectionate world of families . . . [where] some women play the parts of men . . . cutting their hair short, wearing slacks, walking and talking in a masculine way. . . . Other women play the traditional role of mother or wife. . . . [T]hey wander into relationships . . . much like friendships we have on the outside—where, for instance, you guide and counsel a friend as though he or she were your own child. The difference in prison is that you most often call that friend your "child" or your "mother" openly. It is a family that allows a sense of belonging—and eases the loneliness of feeling isolated. . . . It creates a common bond that eases the pressures of doing "hard time."[28]

Thus, homosexuality in female institutions is characterized more by *mutual affection* and *caring relationships* than the violent submission to force of homo-

---

[25]For example, it has been noted that because of the belief that women need more privacy, they "often have separate rooms rather than cells and dormitories." Joycelyn M. Pollock-Byrne, "Women in Prison: Why Are Their Numbers Increasing?" in Peter J. Benekos and Alida V. Merlo, *Corrections: Dilemmas and Directions* (Cincinnati, OH: Anderson Publishing Company, 1992), p. 91.

[26]See David A. Ward and Gene G. Kassebaum, *Women's Prisons* (Chicago: Aldine, 1965).

[27]John Gagon and William Simon, "The Social Meaning of Prison Homosexuality," in David M. Petersen and Charles W. Thomas, eds., *Corrections: Problems and Prospects* (Englewood Cliffs, NJ: Prentice Hall, 1980), p. 123.

[28]Kathryn Watterson Burkhart, *Women in Prison* (New York: Doubleday, 1973), pp. 365–66.

sexual behavior in male prisons. In contrast to male prison subcultures, the resulting subculture among female inmates is more an attempt to establish a "substitute social world" in which they can play roles related to their lives on the outside.[29]

**Prison Conduct.**　Women are therefore less likely than men to experience sexual attacks during incarceration, and also appear to be less victimized in general by other inmates.[30] That does not mean that women's institutions are peaceful, tranquil environments that are managed with ease. Quite the contrary, correctional staff tend to prefer working in male institutions—despite the fact that they may fear for their safety more when working among male inmates. "The reasons usually given for this preference are that male inmates are perceived as more cooperative and respectful than female inmates, who are usually seen as more manipulating and emotional."[31]

Nor does their conduct appear to result in as many disciplinary infractions. During 1986, for example, almost 53% of male inmates were charged with violating prison rules, in comparison to 47% of females.[32] But the more pertinent question may concern the nature rather than the number of their violations.

In contrast to males, female inmates tend to be cited more often for offenses such as disobedience, disrespect, vulgar language, and the like.[33] To some extent, this might be explained by a greater tendency on the part of women to verbalize their feelings rather than act-out physically. However, the attitudes of officers can play a role as well—particularly if custodial personnel assume a paternal role, expecting female inmates to respond as docile children and writing them up when they do not.

At least one analysis of this possibility suggests that disciplinary differences between male and female inmates can largely be attributed to greater readiness to take official action against women for behavior that would be tolerated in a men's prison.[34] In other words, *petty misbehavior* can take on more significance in female

---

[29]See Rose Giallambardo, *Society of Women: A Study of a Women's Prison* (New York: Wiley, 1966).

[30]See, for example, Candace Kruttschnitt and Sharon Krmpotich, "Aggressive Behavior among Female Inmates: An Exploratory Study," *Justice Quarterly*, Vol. 7, No. 2 (June 1990), p. 384, who found that "fewer than one-quarter of the incarcerated females engaged in acts of aggression toward their fellow inmates."

[31]Rasche, p. 68.

[32]*Sourcebook*, p. 623.

[33]For example, one study found that the infractions committed by male offenders were significantly more serious than those of females. See C. A. Lindquist, "Prison Discipline and the Female Offender," *Journal of Offender Counseling Services and Rehabilitation*, Vol. 4, No. 4 (Summer, 1980), pp. 305–18. Other research notes that in female institutions, disruptive infractions were the most frequently cited, followed by property violations (e.g., possession of contraband) and assaultive infractions. See Joan Petersilia and Paul Honig, *The Prison Experience of Career Criminals* (Santa Monica, CA: Rand Corporation, 1980). However, a study matching male and female prisons on the basis of size and security classification found that, on the whole, females and males did not differ in terms of total number of serious disciplinary offenses. See Chloe A. Tischler and James W. Marquart, "Analysis of Disciplinary Infraction Rates among Male and Female Inmates," *Journal of Criminal Justice*, Vol. 17, No. 6 (1989), pp. 507–13.

[34]Russell P. Dobash, R. Emerson Dobash, and Sue Gutteridge, *The Imprisonment of Women* (Totowa, NJ: Basil Blackwell, 1986), pp. 146–47.

institutions. Minor violations might not generate as much concern in a male institution, where more serious infractions (such as physically assaulting staff members) demand more frequent attention.

## Comparisons to Past Practices

Female inmates today may still be encountering sexism in terms of how they are expected to behave and how they are treated by staff. Yet, any twentieth-century inequities pale in comparison to the sufferings of their ancestors. As was discussed in Chapter 4, early prisons and jails confined men, women, and children together in wretched conditions: "Lashing and other brutal punishments were common, and many people (including children born in prison) died there. Even when women and children were provided areas separate from male inmates, they had no. . . protection from sexual and other abuse. They uniformly received inequitable, inadequate care."[35]

Following efforts pioneered by Elizabeth Fry of England, women in the United States began campaigning for the separation of male and female offenders. As we know, their struggle was eventually successful (although the first separate prison—the Indiana State Reformatory for Women—was not constructed until 1873). But in the long term, the results were not exactly the types of remedies that reformers may have envisioned. Certainly, the conditions of communal confinement could hardly have been worse, and the removal of women was a considerable improvement of their situation. As progressive changes occurred thoughout the years, however, the segregation of women often prevented them from sharing in subsequent correctional advancements.

In the early origins of corrections, female offenders were characterized as everything from witches to morally depraved, unredeemable, or misguided creatures who had "fallen from the pedestal of virtue."[36] By the turn of the century, working-class women—guilty mainly of such outrageous offenses as "promiscuity, vagrancy, and saloon-visiting"—were incarcerated in reformatories designed to "retrain them to become chaste, proper, and domestic."[37] For those who were hopelessly beyond redemption in this regard, there was always the option of being held indefinitely in a custodial asylum for "feebleminded" women. But even these approaches represented considerable progress from the days when women were confined to the large attics of male facilities for 24 hours a day, not only without benefit of recreation or work diversions, but also at the mercy of sexual advances by male personnel.

[35]Joann B. Morton, "Looking Back on 200 Years of Valuable Contributions," *Corrections Today*, Vol. 54, No. 6 (August 1992), p. 76, citing Nicole Hahn Rafter, *Partial Justice: Women in State Prisons, 1800–1935*, Second Edition (New Brunswick, NJ: Transaction Publishers, 1990).

[36]T. A. Ryan, *Adult Female Offenders: A State of the Art Analysis* (Washington, DC: National Institute of Corrections, 1984), p. 3.

[37]Nichole Hahn Rafter, "Chastizing the Unchaste: Social Control Functions of a Women's Reformatory, 1894–1931," in Stanley Cohen and Andrew Scull, eds., *Social Control and the State* (New York: St. Martin's Press, 1983), pp. 288–89. In one such institution, vocational programming consisted of "training charges in home-making, a competency they were to utilize either as dutiful daughters or wives within their own families or as servants in the homes of others" (p. 291).

## Current Conditions of Confinement

Although conditions of imprisonment for women have come a long way from the mistreatment and abuses of these historical origins, they still have a long way to go in many respects. In terms of the facilities in which they are confined, there are both advantages and disadvantages of being a female inmate.

Because they serve a more limited population, female institutions are substantially *smaller* in size. (The average daily population of male prisons in 1990 was 700, in comparison to 390 for female institutions.[38]) With the increasing numbers of females being incarcerated, that does not necessarily mean that they are less crowded. But they are generally less likely to suffer from the impersonal conditions of male facilities. The physical environment in women's prisons is less oppressive, and there is more emphasis on rehabilitation. At the same time, however, female institutions are less likely to be able to economically justify a wide variety of treatment, training, recreational, vocational, and educational programs.[39]

As a result, rehabilitative efforts in women's prisons may be limited to such stereotypical activities as sewing, typing, and the like—or at best, other nontraditional programs that do not need sizable enrollments to be cost-effective. In contrast, the more diverse, large-scale industrial and vocational training offered in male facilities provides better preparation for obtaining jobs and achieving upward mobility upon release. For example, statistics reveal that:

- The average number of educational and vocational programs in correctional institutions for men is 10; for women, it is three.
- Office occupations, food service, and cosmetology are the most common program offerings for female offenders.
- Only 10% of female offenders are enrolled in prison industry programs—the most common is sewing.[40]

Naturally, there are also *fewer female institutions* overall. A total of only some 71 federal and state prisons exclusively house women, which represents just 7% of all prisons.[41] Virtually every state has maximum, medium, and minimum-security institutions for males. But because of their fewer numbers, there is *less custodial classification* among women's prisons.

Those convicted of a wide variety of offenses representing a considerable range of seriousness are therefore often confined together. In fact, many states

[38]Lawrence A. Greenfeld, *Prisons and Prisoners in the United States* (Washington, DC: U.S. Department of Justice, 1992), p. 2.

[39]Lee H. Bowker, *Women, Crime, and the Criminal Justice System* (Lexington, MA: D.C. Heath, 1978), p. 229.

[40]Margaret O'Leary and Don Weinhouse, "Colorado Facility Helps Women Overcome Barriers to Education," *Corrections Today*, Vol. 54, No. 6 (August 1992), citing T. A. Ryan, "A Transitional Education Program for Adult Female Offenders," in the *1989 Yearbook of Correctional Education*, a publication of the Correctional Education Association.

[41]Greenfeld, p. 2, where it is also noted that an additional 77 prisons (7%) contain housing for both sexes.

Facilities for female offenders are generally less likely to suffer from the impersonal conditions of male prisons, but they are also less likely to offer a wide variety of institutional programs. Courtesy of the South Carolina Department of Corrections.

do not have enough female offenders to justify more than one women's prison. This means that they are likely to be *more geographically remote* than male facilities, requiring families to travel considerable distances for visiting.[42] Both physically and psychologically, society appears to be keeping its distance from the female offender. If male prisoners are often forgotten, females may be all but completely abandoned.

In recent years, some improvements have undoubtedly been made to upgrade services provided in female prisons, particularly in such areas of special need as health care and drug treatment. Moreover, the American Correctional Association has developed policy guidelines calling for equity in terms of correctional services for male and female offenders. Women may no longer be incarcerated for visiting saloons. But they still appear to be more likely than men to be serving time for drug violations and property offenses. Socially offensive females may no longer be sent to mental asylums for their failure to become domesticated. But neither are they being provided with the job skills that will enable them to become self-sufficient in free society. Women may no longer be the victims of rigidly enforced conformity. But neither are they the beneficiaries of rational, enlightened change.

---

[42]One national survey found that not only did long-term state facilities for women tend to be in rural areas, but only 24% use specific classification systems for women. See *ACA Task Force on the Female Offender: What Does the Future Hold?* (Laurel, MD: American Correctional Association, 1988), pp. 6, 8.

## Co-correctional (Coed) Prisons

Although it could prove extremely costly to establish services in women's prisons that are equivalent to those received by men, one way to better assure parity between male and female offenders is to incarcerate them together. Thus, there is hope on the horizon for improving the conditions of confinement for women—and, in many respects, men as well—in the form of *co-correctional (coed) prisons*. The first experiments with coed prisons for adults date back only about two decades ago to the Massachusetts Correctional Institution at Framingham (which became coeducational in 1973) and the Federal Correctional Institution at Fort Worth, Texas, (1974), which is operated by the U.S. Bureau of Prisons.

In an effort to provide a more natural environment for both male and female inmates (as well as to attain greater cost-effectiveness), some 77 state and federal prisons now operate on a coed basis, housing some 48,343 inmates of both sexes.[43] Obviously, these facilities do not remotely resemble the communal quarters in which women were housed during the early history of corrections. Yet it is somewhat ironic that after successfully achieving separate institutions, in many respects it has become more desirable today to assign women to facilities that also house men. While such changes undoubtedly reflect shifting social attitudes, they are also to some extent an indicator of the limited potential for achieving full parity between male and female institutions.

In addition to more closely replicating the realities of outside society, coed facilities enable women to take advantage of a greater variety of treatment and job training opportunities. For an inside account of the surprised reaction and civilizing influences experienced by a newly arriving male inmate in one of the first coed prisons, see the next "Close-up on Corrections."

Unlike such correctional facilities in Denmark and Sweden, males and females in U.S. coed prisons are prohibited from sharing living quarters or engaging in sexual contact. They do interact socially during meals, recreational periods, or in the course of various institutional programs. However, as described in the close-up, the rules governing unacceptable conduct are quite specific and closely supervised. Although the public may have visions of these facilities as havens of sexual freedom where rampant promiscuity results in many illegitimate births, nothing could be further from the truth. Naturally, with "normal" conditions, normal consequences can be expected. But, for example, in nearly three years of one coed facility's operation, only four pregnancies occurred—far fewer than most high schools experienced in the same period of time![44] Moreover, the general consensus among correctional personnel is that it is preferable to deal with the few instances of improper heterosexual contact in coed institutions than the widespread homosexuality characteristic of single-sex prisons.

Beyond the potential for sexual misbehavior, there are some further disadvantages of co-corrections. Particularly if one sex outnumbers the other in the

---

[43]James Stephan, *Census of State and Federal Correctional Facilities, 1990* (Washington, DC: U.S. Department of Justice, 1992), p. 8.

[44]Sally Chandler Halford, "Kansas Co-correctional Concept," *Corrections Today*, Vol. 46, No. 3 (June 1984), p. 54.

Co-Corrections

The Federal Correctional Institution [F.C.I.] at Fort Worth had been functioning for a year and a half when Juan Segovia arrived. . . .

The bed to which Juan was assigned was in a big open room. . . . Sprawled out on the bunk to his left . . . was a thin, youthful Chicano. He looked at Juan with tentative friendliness but said nothing. Juan [asked] . . . "What kind of place is this?"

"It's o.k. Best thing about it, you be here long enough, you might make a furlough."

"What about these women?"

The youth smiled before he replied, "They're o.k.; they're just women." He smiled again. . . .

Juan reached for the booklet . . . F.C.I. RESIDENT HANDBOOK. . . . [It] listed in Spanish "Prohibited Acts" and "Rights and Responsibilities." . . . The booklet answered some questions for Juan and raised others that would not have occured to him otherwise. The Warden's greetings on the first page said: "At F.C.I Forth Worth you are part of an important experiment and we need your help. People serving time in prisons all over the country, now and in the future, have a stake in the success or failure of this venture."

Juan was not sure what to make of this. The judge had not said anything to him about his having a responsibility to people in prisons all over the country now and in the future. In another place he read:

> Men and women need each other. There is an important need that men and women have for each other that has no physical aspect. Enjoy the presence of one another but remember that physical contact is prohibited, except for discreet and momentary hand-holding or arm-in-arm contact while walking, standing, or seated on benches. No other type of physical contact between men and women residents is permitted and none whatsoever is permitted while seated or lying on the lawn. . . .

Juan and Tapioca were on the yard together one pretty day just after supper. . . . Tapioca sat on a bench with two of her friends from the Women's Unit. Juan sat near her on the grass. He had been complaining about how stiff and sore he was [from work in the plumbing shop], especially through his neck and shoulders.

"You're a big baby, little brother, you must never have done any hard work before. Move over here; I'll give you a rub."

Juan shifted his back to Tapioca and gratefully moved closer to her. With both hands, she began to knead his shoulders and back. It was a delicious feeling.

[An] . . . officer had been standing under a live-oak tree nearby. He strolled over and made an arc around the group on the bench. Without looking, he said,

"Cool it, Taffy," and kept on walking. Tapioca yelled after him, "Hey, Mr. Murphy, this man has a very sore back!"

Mr. Murphy called back over his shoulder, "Send him to the clinic."

Juan snarled under his breath, but Tapioca said, "Take it easy, little brother, he's a cop; he's got to do his job."

"He's a son-of-a-bitch," Juan insisted.

"Now wait a minute, dear friend, I'm going to tell you something." She was speaking now in intimate Spanish. "Look over there, see those windows?"

"Sure, the Warden's office. No doubt he's in there spying on us too."

Tapioca shook her head despairingly, "Would you want the cop's job? He's got to keep things straight out here. He can't come on too strong. It's a tough job. Would you want such a job, little brother?"

"They got it soft and make a lot of money, but I would never want to be a cop."

"Well, neither would I, little brother." An edge of anger had come into Tapioca's voice. "But something tells me you've decided to be some kind of smartass. Are you tough—now that you're in this real tough prison? Don't you know we're all little children together in here; the hacks, the warden, the convicts? Everybody needs to do the best they can. . . . I'm sick of everybody being angry. God loves us all. What's the matter with you?"

Juan gazed out over the yard. He said nothing.

Long moments passed. Then Tapioca got up from the bench and said, "Let's go, we'll be late to the meeting."

"What meeting?"

"The meeting of the committee for the Cinco de Mayo celebration, man. I'm the chairman and I just appointed you to the committee. I hope you'll do me the honor to accept. Let's go."

Juan grinned hesitantly, then got to his feet. How about this? He had never been on a committee before.

*Source:* Charles Campbell, *Serving Time Together: Men and Women in Prison* (Fort Worth, TX: Texas Christian University Press, 1980), pp. 1–13.

---

institution, jealousies, competition, and rivalries for attention may develop. Of course, since there are more males than females incarcerated nationwide, it is more likely to be women who will be outnumbered. When the difference is greater than a 60–40 ratio, "real integration is difficult, and women can expect to feel conspicuous . . . and to be treated as a minority group."[45] To the extent that female inmates are viewed as sexual objects by their male counterparts, there may also be an element of sexual exploitation in such a setting. In addition, the "look but don't touch" nature of the environment can provoke tension and frustration. Those who are married to someone on the outside may likewise

[45]Sue Mahan, "Co-corrections: Doing Time Together," *Corrections Today,* Vol. 48, No. 6 (August 1986), p. 134.

encounter resentment on the part of their spouse, and a relationship developed within the prison could break up an existing marriage.

But the benefits for both women and men would appear to far outweigh the drawbacks. For women, such facilities provide a greater range of recreational, educational, training, and work programs than would traditionally be available in female prisons. Men, on the other hand, are not pressured to portray the hardened, macho image required to avoid appearing weak in a male institution. They tend to behave better in the presence of women and engage in fewer fights, since proving one's toughness does not become the "badge of honor" that physical prowess demonstrates in male institutions. Both sexes also seem to take more pride in their appearance, and simply having someone of the opposite sex to talk to and share troubles with can itself have a positive effect. But perhaps it is correctional administrators who obtain the greatest benefits, since coed facilities appear to generate both fewer grievances and fewer serious disciplinary infractions.[46] As one male inmate summed it up, "The primitive law of prison isn't in operation here."[47]

---

*LEARNING GOALS*

*Do you know:*

- *What groups are at greatest risk of HIV infection and among whom infection is spreading the fastest?*
- *Why the rate of AIDS is higher within correctional institutions than among the public at large?*
- *What responses correctional administrators have implemented to reduce the spread of HIV/AIDS?*
- *What the arguments are for and against the distribution of condoms in correctional facilities?*
- *What position the courts have taken with regard to the mandatory testing of inmates for HIV/AIDS and the separate housing of those who test positive?*

---

## ❖ AIDS (ACQUIRED IMMUNE DEFICIENCY SYNDROME)

In recent years, a disease that knows no gender, racial, or class boundaries has created a devastating impact on society. Prior to the 1980s, AIDS was virtually unknown, but in the less than two decades since then, the disease has afflicted society in virtually epidemic proportions. There are few people who do not know someone who has died of AIDS, and it is estimated that between 1 and 1.5

---

[46]Halford, p. 54, citing comparisons between the year prior to introducing co-corrections and the year after, when there was a 73% reduction in the number of disciplinary charges overall, a 40% reduction in violent discipline charges, and a 42% reduction in the number of grievances filed.

[47]Mahan, p. 138.

million people are infected with HIV (i.e., carrying the human immunodeficiency virus, which leads to AIDS).[48]

Nor are any social or demographic groups immune. Intravenous (IV) drug users and homosexual or bisexual men remain the largest groups at risk for HIV infection. But the fastest-growing populations being affected by HIV disease are children[49] and women.[50] It should, however, be noted that it is not any particular *groups* that are inherently at risk, but rather, the high-risk *behaviors* in which they engage that place them at risk.[51] Many of those being infected today, such as women and children, are the inadvertent victims of those who have been involved in such high-risk behaviors as sharing drug needles or engaging in unsafe sexual practices, (since AIDS can be transmitted through blood and semen).

## AIDS in Corrections

Like the general population, corrections has experienced a substantial increase of inmates who are either HIV-positive or have active cases of AIDS. Also like the general population, without mandatory testing, it is impossible to know exactly how many inmates are infected with HIV, since the virus can linger undetected for years before developing into AIDS. But it does appear that *AIDS incidence rates* are *higher among prisoners* than in society at large, where the rate of 14.65 cases per 100,000 people is significantly less than the 202 cases per 100,000 inmates in state and federal correctional systems.[52] Moreover, the pace at which AIDS in corrections is growing (up 72%) now exceeds the percentage increase of AIDS cases in the overall population (50%).[53]

Some of this difference may be a result of either reduced rates of increase among the population at large and/or improved reporting and record keeping among correctional systems. Nevertheless, prisons and jails do confine a population with a *higher concentration* of individuals who have histories of high-risk behavior, particularly IV drug use.[54] In fact, the National Commission on AIDS points out that "By choosing mass imprisonment as the federal and state governments' response to the use of drugs, we have created a de facto policy of incarcerating more and more individuals with HIV infection. . . . Clearly, we are thus concentrating the HIV disease problem in our prisons and must take immediate action to deal with it more effectively."[55]

---

[48]Anna T. Laszlo and Marilyn B. Ayres, *AIDS: Improving the Response of the Correctional System,* Second Edition (Washington, DC: National Sheriffs' Association, 1990), p. 5.

[49]Ibid., p. 7, citing W. L. Heyward and J. W. Curran, "The Epidemiology of AIDS in the U.S.," *Scientific American* (October 1988). However, it should be noted that "[m]ost of these children were born to mothers who use IV drugs or are the sexual partners of male IV drug users. . . . "

[50]*National Commission on AIDS Report: HIV Disease in Correctional Facilities* (Washington, DC: National Commission on Acquired Immune Deficiency Syndrome, 1991), p. 5. Although "women comprise only 9% of AIDS cases, they are the fastest growing population to be affected by HIV disease."

[51]Laszlo and Ayres, p. 5.

[52]Theodore M. Hammett and Saira Moini, "Update on AIDS in Prisons and Jails," *AIDS Bulletin* (Washington, DC: National Institute of Justice, 1990), p. 4.

[53]Ibid., p. 2.

[54]Ibid., p. 4.

[55]*National Commission on AIDS Report*, p. 5.

The commission urges the implementation of more educational and drug treatment programs to prevent the spread of HIV infection. In the meantime, data indicate that correctional facilities must accommodate growing numbers of inmates with AIDS. Administrators therefore have an imminent responsibility to meet the needs of active HIV/AIDS cases. But from a broader, longer-range point of view, corrections also has a *proactive duty* to educate all of those under its supervision to the dangers of high-risk behavior. As long as corrections remains the one government agency that intercepts the lives of so many who are at risk, it is essential to seize this opportunity to change their behavior. Given the alarming spread of AIDS, the actions or inactions of corrections in this respect will have a profound impact on health and well-being throughout society.

## Correctional Responses

Since there is not yet a known cure for AIDS, the vital concern of correctional administrators is to reduce expansion of the disease, particularly within institutional populations. A number of approaches have been implemented in response to this concern, primarily:

- *Educating* both inmates and staff with regard to how the disease is spread.
- *Issuing condoms* to protect inmates engaged in homosexual activities from contracting the disease.
- *Testing* (either voluntary or mandatory) to identify those who are infected
- *Separately housing* those in various stages of the disease.

**Education and Training.** Practically everyone agrees that educational efforts are needed. As one national study found, "[m]ost correctional administrators feel strongly that AIDS education and training are not options but absolute requirements," and virtually all prisons and jails reported offering or developing AIDS training or educational materials.[56] Such programs are essential to provide facts concerning how the disease is transmitted—thereby hopefully changing high-risk behaviors. In addition, they can help to eliminate the myths surrounding casual transmission that can lead to overreaction and unwarranted discrimination.

Ideally, programs should be offered for both inmates and staff in a *proactive* manner—well before widespread concern promotes panic. Among inmates, for example, at least one study has found that not only is there considerable confusion about the manner in which AIDS can be transmitted, but lower levels of knowledge were also associated with higher perceptions of the risk of contracting AIDS while incarcerated.[57] In other words, the *less inmates knew* about objective facts concerning AIDS transmission, the *more fearful* they were of acquiring the virus in prison. Nor is there any reason to believe that similar lack of knowl-

[56]Hammett and Moini, p. 4.
[57]Sherwood E. Zimmerman, Randy Martin, and David Vlahov, "AIDS Knowledge and Risk Perceptions among Pennsylvania Prisoners," *Journal of Criminal Justice,* Vol. 19, No. 3 (1991), pp. 239–56.

edge on the part of institutional personnel is any less influential. AIDS training for staff can diminish such unfounded fears while encouraging basic precautionary measures.[58]

**Condom Distribution.**   While support for AIDS education is widespread, there is one particular policy of some facilities that is another matter entirely—the distribution of condoms. On the one hand, this practice has been widely criticized as giving official sanction to unauthorized sexual activities. But on the other hand, there are advocates who maintain that since it is virtually impossible to prevent inmates from engaging in homosexual behavior, it is better to provide them with protection than to risk spreading the disease throughout the institution. As one doctor practicing in corrections has argued: "Facilities that have decided to issue condoms to inmates have not decided to permit sex. Instead, the programs are established as an acknowledgement that sex occurs. In the absence of such programs, I challenge prison administrators to stop sex altogether. Failing that, prison administrators are not meeting their obligation to do everything possible to maintain the health of their wards."[59] For a controversial debate of both viewpoints, see the next "Close-up on Corrections."

**HIV Testing.**   Like the condom issue, testing inmates for HIV has both supporters and critics. Recent advances in HIV treatment that delay the onset of AIDS underscore the need for early detection and intervention. In light of this medical incentive, more people in the general population are undergoing diagnostic tests. But, of course, they are doing so of their own free will. Within corrections, few would argue against providing tests and follow-up medical services on a *voluntary* basis for those requesting such help—as evidenced by data showing that 75% of prisons and 90% of jails make testing available upon request.[60] But it is the *mandatory* testing of everyone that is in dispute.[61]

This involuntary means of identifying HIV-positive inmates has increasingly come under fire from both sides of the issue. On the one hand, some inmates have demanded mandatory mass testing for everyone's protection. In opposition, others have challenged such practices as an invasion of their right to privacy. Thus far, the courts have neither uniformly upheld nor denied either side.

In one case, for example, an appellate court refused to order correctional officials to administer AIDS tests to all inmates and staff on the basis that "the risk alleged by the inmates was based on unsubstantiated fears and ignorance."[62]

---

[58]For information on AIDS-related guidelines see Laszlo and Ayres, pp. 37–75, along with Theodore Hammett, Dana Hunt, Michael Gross, William Rhodes, and Saira Moini, "Stemming the Spread of HIV among IV Drug Users, Their Sexual Partners and Children: Issues and Opportunities for Criminal Justice Agencies," *Crime and Delinquency,* Vol. 37, No. 1 (January 1991), pp. 101–24.

[59]Kim Marie Thorburn, "Health Programs Do Work to Fight AIDS," *Corrections Today,* Vol. 54, No. 8 (December 1992), p. 127.

[60]Hammett and Moini, p. 6.

[61]Nor is this controversy confined to institutions. See Denny C. Langston, "Issues for Probation and Parole Administrators Considering Testing Offenders for AIDS," *Corrections Today,* Vol. 53, No. 1 (February 1991), pp. 92, 96–98.

[62]Barbara A. Belbot and Rolando V. del Carmen, "AIDS in Prison: Legal Issues," *Crime and Delinquency,* Vol. 37, No. 1 (January, 1991), p. 137.

Condoms in Jails?

YES (Sheriff Michael Hennessey, San Francisco County, California)

As the administrator of a jail, it is my obligation to protect the health and welfare of the inmates. . . . To curb the rampant spread of this deadly disease, it is imperative that comprehensive AIDS prevention and education efforts be permitted in county jails, including carefully controlled distribution of condoms as part of the educational process. . . . Introducing prisoners to condoms and changing their behavior while they are in jail has an important multiplier effect: it not only prevents transmission of the disease between prisoners, it curbs the spread of infection from released prisoners in their relationships in the community.

By advocating the use of condoms in jails, I am *not* condoning sex in jail. According to California state law and our jail policy, sexual activity is prohibited in the jail. Our deputies are instructed to arrest and book any inmates caught having sex. However, we must face reality. As much as we try to prevent it, sex does occur in jail, most of it consensual. . . .

Condoms need not be distributed randomly. As a part of our departmental policy, health educators provide counseling with each condom they distribute. An element of the counseling program is the reminder that sexual relations while incarcerated is a felony and a violation of jail rules and regulations. . . . County jails present a prime opportunity to educate a large population of individuals at risk of HIV infection. It is incumbent upon sheriffs to honor the professional imperative to protect the public—in this case by providing AIDS education to inmates, including the limited distribution of condoms.

NO (Dr. John Clark, Chief Physician, Los Angeles County Sheriffs' Department)

The arguments against distribution of condoms have generally been based on the fact that in most jurisdictions, sexual activity in the correctional environment is a felony; and the issuance of condoms delivers a mixed message to inmates. Also, much concern has been expressed over the fact that a condom makes an excellent receptacle for contraband, especially illegal drugs. Such contraband can easily be ingested or inserted internally. . . .

Few individuals are incarcerated [in jail] long enough that meeting sexual needs is a high priority. Obviously, sexual activity does occur in jails. However, with overcrowding, there are fewer opportunities for intimate activity; and much of the activity in jails is gang rape, where condoms are not likely to be used. . . .

In the few jurisdictions that are distributing condoms, the controls are either too strict to accomplish the desired effect of reduced HIV transmission or so lax that the potential for misuse as contraband receptacles is exacerbated. . . .

The majority of the instances of viral transmission behind bars are related to intravenous drug use. . . . Are we obliged to protect the IV-drug users by giving out bleach and needles, lest we be guilty of "deliberate indifference" to the highest risk group behind bars?

In summary, the epidemiological data, the unique operational characteristics of the jails and the laws that govern our jurisdictions do not provide a rational basis for distribution of condoms in jails. . . .

Source: "Condoms in Jail," *The National Sheriff,* Vol. 41, No. 6 (December 1989/January 1990), pp. 9–10.

From the opposite perspective, a prisoner in another jurisdiction challenged the constitutionality of the state's policy of testing all inmates for the AIDS virus. In this case, the court ruled that the inmate's invasion of privacy was "far outweighed" by the prison's interest in treating those infected and taking steps to prevent further transmission of the disease.[63] In yet another case, the outcome was more ambiguous, with the court finding that the prison administrators had no evidence on which to base an AIDS testing procedure.[64]

Overall, however, the courts have been relatively consistent in upholding the constitutionality of state laws permitting mandatory testing. But at the same time, they have supported the right of correctional administrators to refuse to implement mandatory testing. Thus, current judicial reasoning appears to be that testing is not constitutionally *required* under the Eighth Amendment (which prohibits cruel and unusual punishment); but neither is it *prohibited* under the Fourth Amendment (which protects privacy).[65]

As a compromise between the extremes of mandatory and voluntary screening, some states target AIDS testing toward *high-risk* groups (such as IV drug users, homosexual men, and prostitutes). In fact, mandatory mass screening has been conducted primarily in small states with few inmate AIDS cases, making it a costly practice in comparison to the benefits derived. Some jurisdictions have discontinued the practice for reasons ranging from funding shortages to the realization that it was "creating more problems than it was intended to solve."[66] It is notable that as of 1991, none of the five states with the highest cumulative incidence of AIDS—New York, New Jersey, Florida, California, and Texas—were screening new inmates for HIV on a mandatory basis.[67] Similarly, the Federal Bureau of Prisons abandoned its mandatory screening "when results of 16,372 tests showed that only 3% of the prisoners tested positive."[68] The American Correctional Health Services Association has also gone on record as opposing mandatory testing, based on the concern that it is "costly and serves no useful public health function."[69]

With less mass testing, there are undoubtedly inmates in prison who have

[63]"Court of Appeals 10th, Rejects Fourth Amendment Challenge to Blood Testing of Prison Inmates for AIDS," *Criminal Law Reporter,* Vol. 45, No. 20 (August 23, 1989), p. 2360.
[64]"Prisons and Jails—Mandatory AIDS Testing," *Criminal Law Reporter,* Vol. 48, No. 7 (November 14, 1990), pp. 1150–51.
[65]Belbot and del Carmen, p. 138.
[66]Hammett and Moini, p. 6.
[67]National Commission on AIDS, p. 22.
[68]Belbot and del Carmen, p. 136, citing Martin Gunderson, David J. Mayo, and Frank S. Rham, *AIDS: Testing and Privacy* (Salt Lake City, UT: University of Utah Press, 1989).
[69]"Inmate HIV Testing," *American Jails,* Vol. 6, No. 5 (November/December 1992), p. 87.

undetected AIDS. But that does not mean that they necessarily *contracted* the disease in prison. Quite the contrary—although correctional facilities may be perceived as "fertile breeding grounds" for the spread of HIV, a number of studies suggest that this is not the case. In reality, research to date indicates that actually, *very few* inmates have become HIV-positive as a result of activities that took place within a correctional facility.[70]

**Separate Housing.** Regardless of whether inmates are screened upon arrival or submit to testing voluntarily, once AIDS is detected, the issue becomes what actions are appropriate to take. As the National Commission on AIDS has observed, "[t]here is certainly no point in screening without a clear notion of what is to be done with information uncovered in the screening process."[71] From a humanitarian point of view, it is obviously essential to provide appropriate *medical care* (although meeting this obligation can create serious financial difficulties, particularly as the number of cases escalates). Moreover, because of the overwhelming emotional impact of AIDS, most would agree that *counseling* and other *supportive services* are equally critical.[72] But it is the question of *where to locate* inmates who have tested positive that has become most controversial.

As with mandatory/voluntary testing, correctional administrators are again caught between two contradictory arguments in this regard. On the one hand, inmates free of AIDS have raised Eighth Amendment challenges, maintaining that it is "cruel and unusual punishment" to be unprotected from others with this communicable disease. But at least one court has held that prisoners must specifically show how the conditions of confinement they are challenging put them at risk of contracting AIDS.[73] In a similar case, inmates demanded mandatory screening and housing segregation of those who test positive. The judge rejected their arguments, ruling that the state had taken reasonable precautions to minimize the risk that inmates would contract the virus.[74]

At the same time, HIV-positive inmates have questioned whether it is a violation of *their* rights to be housed separately from the general population. In this respect, one court has declared that inmates shall not be segregated solely because they are HIV-positive, although they may be isolated on a case-by-case basis according to security or medical needs.[75] But in another case, the court supported the argument of correctional administrators that "the segregation of infected prisoners was mandated to protect both the AIDS victims and other prisoners from tensions and harm that could result from fears of other

[70]Mark Blumberg and Denny Langston, "Mandatory HIV Testing in Criminal Justice Settings," *Crime and Delinquency*, Vol. 37, No. 1 (January 1991), pp. 12–13. Also see Zimmerman et al., who indicate that "intraprison transmission rates are less than 1%" (p. 249).

[71]National Commission on AIDS, p. 22.

[72]See, for example, Mary Winifred, "Program Helps Inmates with AIDS Battle Illness Together," *Corrections Today*, Vol. 53, No. 5 (August 1991), p. 182.

[73]A. F. Anderson, "Aids and Prisoners' Rights Law: Deciphering the Administrative Guideposts," *Prison Journal*, Vol. 69, No. 1 (Spring/Summer 1989), p. 21.

[74]The state's practice is to offer voluntary AIDS tests to all inmates upon entry into the system, along with later testing "if a doctor has reason to think an inmate is infected." See "Inmates' Request for Mandatory Testing Denied," *On the Line*, Vol. 15, No. 2 (March 1992), p. 2.

[75]National Commission on AIDS, p. 22, citing *Smith v. Meachum* (1989).

inmates."[76] While most judicial rulings have upheld the constitutionality of separate housing, as with testing, "the courts have concluded that the Constitution neither requires nor prohibits segregation."[77]

**Legal Implications.**   As these cases reflect, such disputes have raised a number of legal issues.[78] In fact, along with *mandatory screening*, measures aimed at the *segregated housing* of those with HIV represent the major types of AIDS-related cases filed by inmates.

An immediate legal implication of a separate housing assignment policy is that it readily identifies those with HIV, thereby compromising the confidentiality of AIDS testing. State laws and court rulings vary in terms of how strictly they protect the confidentiality and anonymity of those tested for HIV.[79] States with such protections generally limit notification to the inmate and attending physician. Only a few jurisdictions have official policies of notifying correctional officers. Staff, however, are not always satisfied with these confidentiality provisions. As one officer has argued, "[t]he nation now has right-to-know laws dealing with dangerous and toxic substances in the workplace; . . . an inmate with AIDS is a dangerous person, and his or her blood is definitely a toxic substance."[80] In response, it has been pointed out that educational programs can reduce concerns about the transmission of AIDS (which is often what prompts demands for disclosure). Moreover, "disclosures may, in fact, lull correctional officers into a false sense of security, leading them to believe that all infected prisoners have been identified."[81]

In addition to revealing the confidentiality of their health status, separately housing those who are HIV-positive can have further repercussions. The National Commission on AIDS notes that not only is there "no legitimate public health basis for segregating prisoners with HIV disease," but also, those who are so isolated:

- Often lose access to religious services, work programs, visitation rights, libraries, educational and recreational programs, and drug/alcohol treatment.

[76]M. J. Olivero, "The Treatment of AIDS behind the Walls of Correctional Facilities," *Social Justice*, Vol. 17, No. 1 (Spring 1990), p. 114.

[77]Belbot and del Carmen, p. 147.

[78]For a brief but comprehensive summary of the major due process, equal protection, privacy, and Eighth Amendment cases concerning AIDS/HIV, see Belbot and del Carmen, pp. 135–55; and Gina Caruso and Howard Messing, "AIDS Caselaw Slowly Developing in Favor of Institution, but Cases Still Surprisingly Few," *Correctional Law Reporter*, Vol. 2, No. 2 (May 1990), pp. 1, 22–24.

[79]For instance, state statute in Iowa provides that "correctional personnel are to be notified if a prisoner is found to have a contagious infectious disease. . . . The Michigan statute allows for test results to be disclosed to only those persons who demonstrate to the department of corrections a need to know the results. In Florida, a prisoner's test results are confidential except that they may be shared with [correctional] employees . . . [who] need to know such information." However, in a significant exception, an Alabama judge "concluded that prisoners have no right to privacy in [terms of] their medical conditions because they have made themselves public by virtue of having committed crimes." But most cases addressing confidentiality suggest that although disclosure "may be appropriate and even necessary in certain circumstances, the disclosure must be limited in scope." Belbot and del Carmen, pp. 139–43.

[80]Curtis R. Davis, "AIDS and an Officer's Right to Know," *Corrections Today*, Vol. 53, No. 7 (December 1991), p. 28.

[81]Hammett and Moini, p. 7.

- Serve in virtually solitary confinement within small prisons, and in larger institutions, are often grouped together indiscriminately, regardless of their security classification.[82]

It is therefore not surprising that such practices have represented a sizable proportion of the lawsuits related to AIDS. Undoubtedly, these cases have generated some of the impetus toward the current trend away from segregation—toward the "mainstreaming" of HIV-positive inmates with the rest of the general population. But beyond the threat of legal action, this change in housing policy has resulted from a combination of additional factors, including increased costs, less fear, more compassionate attitudes, and the rising numbers of inmates with HIV infection or AIDS—which is making segregation both impractical and unfeasible.[83]

A realistic compromise between the extremes of complete integration and total segregation has been recommended that would take into account both high-risk behavior and HIV/AIDS infection. As shown in Figure 12.4, this approach would classify the person according to a continuum reflecting institutional behavior as well as the health status of those who are HIV-positive. Housing and supervision would then be designed to both *reduce opportunities* for high-risk activities and provide for the *medical needs* of those who are becoming progressively ill.[84]

In summary, there are no clearcut guidelines on how corrections should respond to the threat of AIDS. As a result, some administrators have experimented with preventive measures, ranging from providing condoms to promoting education. Identification approaches likewise have varied from requiring mandatory mass testing, to selectively screening high-risk groups, to simply making tests available on a voluntary basis. In reaction to the results, some systems have implemented housing segregation policies. Others have explored compromises, such as increasing segregation on the basis of how far the disease has progressed. Many have either continued or returned to mainstreaming those who are HIV-positive with the rest of the population. The only thing that is sure

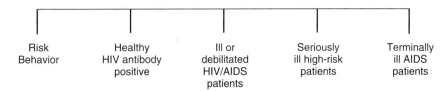

| Risk Behavior | Healthy HIV antibody positive | Ill or debilitated HIV/AIDS patients | Seriously ill high-risk patients | Terminally ill AIDS patients |

**Figure 12.4** HIV disease continuum. *Source:* James E. Lawrence and Van Zwisohn, "AIDS in Jail," in Joel A. Thompson and G. Larry Mays, eds., *American Jails: Public Policy Issues* (Chicago: Nelson-Hall, 1991), p. 123.

[82]*National Commission on AIDS Report,* p. 3.
[83]Hammett and Moini, p. 8.
[84]James E. Lawrence and Van Zwisohn, "AIDS in Jail," in Joel A. Thompson and G. Larry Mays, eds., *American Jails: Public Policy Issues* (Chicago: Nelson-Hall, 1991), pp. 122–24.

about AIDS is that until there is a cure, the issues surrounding this disease will undoubtedly continue to create further conflict, confusion, and court cases. As one inmate has so well expressed the dilemma, "I am not as afraid of death as I am of what you will allow to happen to me in the process of dying."[85]

---

*LEARNING GOALS* ▒▒▒▒▒▒▒▒▒▒▒▒▒▒▒▒▒▒▒▒▒▒▒▒▒▒▒▒▒▒▒▒▒▒▒▒▒▒▒▒▒▒

*Do you know:*

- *What age groups are most at risk of drug addiction?*
- *Through what stages drug use progresses?*
- *For those convicted of drug offenses, what sanction is most often imposed by the justice system?*
- *To what extent those in prison or jail are participating in drug treatment programs?*

---

### ❖ OTHER SPECIAL OFFENDER POPULATIONS

Beyond females and those who are afflicted with HIV/AIDS, there are any number of inmates with special needs in the correctional setting. It is apparent that discussion of the extensive treatment requirements of many such offenders is well beyond the introductory scope of this book. There are, however, several special groups that are addressed throughout the remainder of this chapter: alcoholic, drug-addicted, mentally disordered, physically impaired, elderly, and sex offenders.

Some (such as those who are alcohol/drug-addicted or mentally disordered), have been included because of the sizable proportion of the correctional population which they represent. Others merit attention either because they have often been overlooked as a result of their limited numbers (e.g., the physically impaired), or their growing numbers are causing increasing concern (e.g., the elderly). While the groups focused on herein certainly do not exhaust all categories of special offenders, they do illustrate the scope of unique problems with which correctional administrators must cope.

Particularly in times of fiscal shortages, it is difficult for the average correctional agency to offer specialized services or treatment programs without compromising basic operations for the bulk of the population. Nevertheless, it is essential from a humanitarian, practical, and in some cases, even legal perspective to make every effort to accommodate the requirements of those with special needs.

### Drug Abusers

We have already seen that IV drug use with unsanitary needles is a major transmitter of AIDS, and that drug involvement is an increasing problem among female offenders. It goes without saying that drug abuse is hardly limited to these

---

[85]Anonymous inmate, cited in Madeleine LaMarre, "AIDS Inmates: A Management Dilemma," *Corrections Today*, Vol. 50, No. 3 (June 1988), p. 100.

two groups. Not only have arrests for drug violations increased 70% between 1981 and 1990,[86] but there is little doubt that any number of additional property crimes are linked to the need for ready cash to support drug habits.[87] In addition, as Figure 12.3 reflected, about one-third of both female and male prison inmates reported being under the influence of drugs at the time of their offense.

Those most at risk of narcotic addition are *adolescents and young adults*. Although many young people do not see any dangers in "casual experimentation" with drugs, they fail to realize that "drug use frequently progresses in stages—from occasional use, to regular use, to multiple drug use, and ultimately to total dependency. With each successive stage, drug use intensifies, becomes more varied, and results in increasingly debilitating effects."[88]

Perhaps because poverty and discrimination can be so degrading to self-esteem, drug abuse has traditionally been associated with low-income and minority groups. The use of drugs knows no social or racial boundaries today, but minorities are still disproportionately affected. Increases in the minority population of juvenile detention facilities, for example, have been linked to the "extremely large increase in the number of these youth referred to juvenile court for drug offenses," along with "a substantial change in how juvenile courts respond to [such] cases."[89] As with adults, the juvenile justice system is becoming more inclined to incarcerate those involved in drug offenses. And if they do not find effective treatment for their problem in juvenile facilities, it can be anticipated that they will later appear in the adult correctional system.

**Institutional Profiles.** In fact, there is already evidence that such trends are occurring among the nation's jails. Because they are more likely than state prisons to house young, first-time, or minor drug offenders, it is not surprising to find significant percentages of drug users among the jail population. About three-fourths (78%) of jail inmates report having used illegal drugs, with 58% indicating that they are regular users.[90]

Between 1983 and 1989, the percentage of inmates in jail charged with drug offenses more than doubled—to approximately one-fourth of the total jail population. As in the case of juveniles, minorities were overrepresented, with black inmates accounting for 48% of those in jail for drugs.[91] Also like its juvenile counterpart, the adult criminal justice system is becoming tougher on drug crimes. The majority of adults convicted of drug offenses are being *sentenced to confinement* (80%)—either in jail (57%) or prison (23%).[92]

[86]*Uniform Crime Reports*, p. 173.

[87]One national survey, for example, found that almost one-third of jail inmates convicted of robbery and burglary admitted having committed their crime to obtain money for drugs, as had about one-fourth of those in jail for larceny and fraud. See Caroline Wolf Harlow, "Drugs and Jail Inmates, 1989," *Bureau of Justice Statistics: Special Report* (Washington, DC: U.S. Department of Justice, 1991), p. 9.

[88]*What Works: Schools without Drugs* (Washington, DC: U.S. Department of Education, 1987), p. 7.

[89]Howard N. Snyder, "Growth in Minority Detentions Attributed to Drug Law Violators," *Office of Juvenile Justice and Delinquency Prevention: Update on Statistics* (Washington, DC: U.S. Department of Justice, 1990), pp. 1–2, 5.

[90]Harlow, p. 4.

[91]Ibid.

[92]*Sourcebook*, p. 521.

**Treatment Programs.**   The next logical question naturally is: What help do inmates obtain for combatting drug habits once they are incarcerated? If 1989 is any indicator, the answer may well be "not enough." In that year, only about 5% of inmates in a national survey were receiving drug treatment in jail.[93] Nor were 1990 data substantially better within prisons. Estimates indicate that approximately 13% of state and federal prison inmates were in drug treatment programs during that year, with many more on waiting lists.[94]

Although they may not be widely available, there are a number of innovative drug rehabilitation efforts being provided within correctional institutions. In terms of focus, they range widely—from group counseling, intensive therapy, and self-help groups to the use of acupuncture.[95] One of the most prominent comprehensive programs is the therapeutic community technique. Typically, this treatment model is based on the concepts of Synanon (a program developed by a recovering alcoholic). The next "Close-up on Corrections" features some insights into what recovering addicts experience through such a therapeutic community approach.

**Treatment Results.**   While such efforts to treat drug abuse are undoubtedly commendable, their long-term effectiveness is another matter entirely. In this respect, programs offered in correctional institutions are probably not much different from those provided in the community. For example, one 20-year follow-up of an in-patient hospital treatment program found only 10% of those released abstaining from drugs for five or more consecutive years.[96] Within correctional institutions, the numbers of those incarcerated who have already undergone treatment is indicative of unimpressive results. Among jail inmates who admit regular use of a major drug, for instance, almost half (45.7%) had participated previously in drug treatment—some as often as six or more times.[97] Within prisons, almost one-third (30%) of all inmates reported that they had participated in a drug treatment program at some point—12% more than once.[98]

The fact that drug-related behavior was not changed in prison is further demonstrated by figures indicating that two-thirds of drug offenders fail to com-

[93]Harlow, p. 11. See also Robert L. May, Roger H. Peters, and William D. Kearns, "The Extent of Drug Treatment Programs in Jails: A Summary Report," *American Jails*, Vol. 4, No. 3 (September/October, 1990), pp. 32–34.

[94]Compiled from *Sourcebook*, pp. 626–29. There are, however, some conflicting data in this regard. For example, one study citing self-reports of over 1000 state and federal correctional facilities found that enrollment in various drug treatment/intervention programs was substantially less than reported capacity. See Caroline Wolf Harlow, "Drug Enforcement and Treatment in Prisons, 1990," *Bureau of Justice Statistics Special Report* (Washington, DC: U.S. Department of Justice, 1992), p. 11.

[95]For guidelines on designing relevant drug/alcohol treatment programs in prison, see George Pratsinak and Robert Alexander, eds., *Understanding Substance Abuse and Treatment* (Laurel, MD: American Correctional Association, 1992); and *Intervening with Substance-Abusing Offenders: A Framework for Action* (Washington, DC: National Institute of Corrections, 1991).

[96]George E. Valliant, "A Twenty-Year Follow-up of New York Narcotic Addicts," *Archives of General Psychiatry*, Vol. 29 (August 1973), pp. 237–41.

[97]Harlow, "Drugs and Jail Inmates," p. 11.

[98]Steven D. Dillingham, *Bureau of Justice Statistics Data Report, 1989* (Washington, DC: U.S. Department of Justice, 1990), p. 33.

Drug Treatment through the Therapeutic Community Approach

[T]he therapeutic community model . . . generally require[s] clients to remain in treatment for periods ranging from several months to a few years. Recovery, in fact, is viewed as a lifelong process.

The treatment provided in these settings involves drug abstinence, work, and . . . adoption of the 12 steps (of Alcoholics Anonymous). It also focuses on rebuilding the personality of the addict. Drug abuse is viewed as a symptom of a larger problem within the individual that must be treated. . . . The treatment regimen is intense and all-encompassing. Encounter groups are used extensively: they focus on breaking down the client's resistances so that a rebuilding process may begin. The rebuilding phase involves a self-help process assisted by the efforts of the group, which has experienced similar problems. . . .

In the final stages of treatment, the client is gradually released to community life through daily passes that enable him/her to obtain employment and housing, and to reunite with supportive friends and family. The last step is . . . return to the community and independent living outside the program.

*Source:* Bernard J. McCarthy, "Community Residential Centers: An Intermediate Sanction for the 1990's," in Peter J. Benekos and Alida V. Merlo, eds., *Corrections: Dilemmas and Directions* (Cincinnati, OH: Anderson Publishing Company, 1992), p. 184.

plete their parole successfully.[99] This does not necessarily mean they have returned to drug use. But to the extent that drugs were the source of their involvement with the criminal justice system, it is reasonable to conclude that they have probably resumed former habits. On the other hand, corrections often tends to focus exclusively on its failures (perhaps because there seem to be so many of them), while overlooking the admittedly fewer but nevertheless significant successes.

Nevertheless, the fact remains that although some are undoubtedly helped back into a productive lifestyle, many are not. In part, these mixed results and limited availability of drug treatment reflect changing ideologies from the medical model to the justice model: "Current correctional strategies do not reward rehabilitation. Rather, they reward quiet control and trouble-free days. In order to realign the system, then, correction[s] . . . must be rewarded for creating credible opportunities for inmates to improve their lives, for sustaining that opportunity in the community after release, and for achieving significant reductions in recidivism."[100]

[99]Complied from Craig Perkins, *National Corrections Reporting Program, 1989* (Washington, DC: U.S. Department of Justice, 1992), p. 41. Data reflect all 1989 state parole discharges for those convicted of drug offenses.
[100]Douglas S. Lipton and Harry K. Wexler, "Breaking the Drug–Crime Connection: Rehabilitation Projects Show Promise," *Corrections Today*, Vol. 50, No. 5 (August 1988), p. 146.

In other words, reducing drug use among criminal offenders cannot be accomplished in the absence of a rehabilitative orientation. That does not, however, mean that treatment is the only component of drug rehabilitation. As shown in Figure 12.5, careful *screening* and appropriate *intervention* must be followed by close *supervision,* including both continued support and surveillance upon release.[101] In fact, it has been noted that a major weakness of many drug rehabilitation efforts in corrections is that they operate without the benefit of follow-up treatment and continuing care.[102]

Moreover, support must be practical as well as emotional. It will do little good to send an abuser home drug-free and presumably "cured" without any prospect of employment. Incarceration can compel abstinence from drugs and address withdrawal symptoms. But it is unlikely that long-term effectiveness will be achieved if the underlying social and psychological causes of physically addictive behavior are not confronted—or if interventions end with one's institutional sentence.

Today, it cannot even be automatically assumed that confinement will insulate offenders from drug use, as reflected by the fact that inmates are now being tested for drugs in almost all state and federal prisons.[103] Illegal substances are popular contraband items within correctional facilities, and they are not all brought in from the outside. To the contrary, drug abuse within institutional

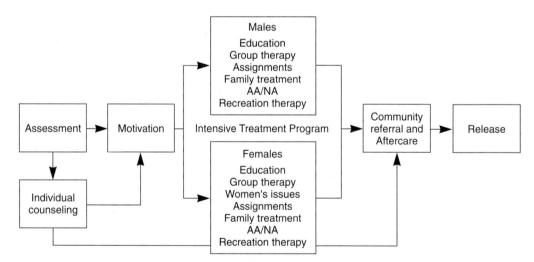

**Figure 12.5** Addiction treatment model. *Source:* Tom Sherron, "Minimum Security and Chemical Dependency Treatment: A Functional Model for Corrections," *American Jails,* Vol. 5, No. 5 (November/December 1991), p. 76.

[101]See also Charles R. Messmer and Henry A. Brown, "Beyond the '80's: The Emergence of a Model Substance Abuse Treatment Program within the Correctional Setting," *American Jails,* Vol. 4, No. 5 (January/February 1991), pp. 114–20.

[102]*Intervening with Substance-Abusing Offenders,* p. 35.

[103]"Inmates Tested for Drugs in about 90% of State, U.S. Prisons," *Narcotics Control Digest* (July 29, 1992), p. 7.

walls has extended to the misuse and abuse of prescription medications dispensed by prison infirmaries. Many of the inmates who had been drug abusers on the street find themselves undergoing the pains of withdrawal in prison, during which "they will attempt to obtain anything and everything possible from the hospital in the hopes of relieving the tension, anxiety, and other unwanted symptoms they're experiencing."[104]

Regardless of the source, addicted inmates can be expected to make concerted efforts to continue their drug use while incarcerated, just as would be expected if they were forced to undergo involuntary abstinence in the community. In that regard, correctional facilities are plagued by the same difficulties as drug control agencies on the outside, and "[u]ntil there is a greater effort to remove drugs from the free society, there is little hope of removing the problem from within the walls of America's prisons."[105]

---

*LEARNING GOALS*

*Do you know:*

- *Why alcohol is in many ways a greater threat than the use of illegal drugs?*
- *How extensively alcohol is involved in status offenses?*
- *How the use of alcohol compares to the use of illegal drugs among inmates?*
- *What role psychological, sociological, and physiological factors play in terms of promoting vulnerability to alcoholism?*

---

## Alcohol Abusers

Among the many unfortunate by-products resulting from the nation's epidemic of drug abuse is that it has diverted attention away from a number of other significant social issues, such as the poverty and neglect that can create inducements for drug experimentation. But even more directly related is a long-standing problem which has plagued society well before the current "war" on *illegal* drugs was waged. We are, of course, referring to the abuse of and/or addiction to a *legal* drug—alcohol. Because it is so widely, inexpensively, and legally available (at least for adults), alcohol in some ways may actually be a greater threat. This does not mean that many people do not consume alcohol in a socially responsible manner. It is when the overuse of this drug begins to damage health, deteriorate family relationships, affect employment, and generate crime that it becomes a problem.

Like illicit drugs, the use of beer, wine, or hard liquor often begins at young ages, even though alcoholic beverages are legally restricted for those under 21 in all states.[106] But illegality does *not* prevent consumption. Of all noncriminal (sta-

---

[104]Leo Pierini, "Biting the Hand That Feeds Them: The `Other' Prison Drug Problem," *Police* (November 1991), p. 35.

[105]Harry E. Allen and Clifford E. Simonsen, *Corrections in America: An Introduction,* Sixth Edition (New York: Macmillan, 1992), p. 644.

[106]*Sourcebook,* p. 134.

tus) offenses, liquor violations represent the greatest number of cases processed by juvenile courts.[107] Alcohol, in fact, is the "drug of choice" among young people. While less than 5% of those between 12 and 17 report using hard drugs within the past year, almost half (45%) admit to the use of alcohol.[108] By the time they are in the 18- to 25-year-old age category, less than 10% say that they never used alcohol.[109] For many, that does not mean an occasional drink—to the contrary, over one-third of young adults report consuming "five or more drinks in a row" within the previous two weeks.[110] Again, as with illegal drugs, all use of alcohol does not necessarily lead to addiction. But among those who are particularly susceptible as a result of *personality* maladjustments or even inherited *physical* tendencies, abuse can lead to addiction.

**Institutional Profile.**   In comparison to those who use illegal drugs, it appears that alcohol abusers may even be more heavily concentrated in some correctional institutions. For example, a higher percentage of convicted inmates in jail reported being under the influence of alcohol (41%) than drugs (28%) when they committed their crime.[111] Approximately equal proportions of prison inmates reported that they were under the influence of alcohol (37%) or drugs (35%) at the time of their offense.[112] The combination of alcohol with other drugs (polydrug use) is also appearing more frequently among correctional populations, as well as the public at large.

Of course, being "under the influence" during the commission of a crime does not inherently mean that the person is an alcoholic. It may only indicate that the offender becomes more susceptible to criminal suggestions or cannot control behavior when drinking. On the other hand, there are alcoholics who are completely convinced of their ability to "handle" increasingly large amounts of liquor, managing to function without detection in society and not seeking help until alcoholism has begun to destroy their life. As a result, alcoholism is to a great extent a *hidden disease,* with no accurate measures of its prevalence within either corrections or the outside community.

**Treatment Programs.**   As with drug addiction or any other social problem, prevention is a far better remedy than intervention after the fact. Also like these other maladies, behavior is often symptomatic of deeper underlying problems. Treatment of alcoholism must therefore be based on the realization that drinking may be a *manifestation of other difficulties* (although recently, there is additional evidence emerging that there may actually be a *genetic link* through which alcoholism is inherited).

In any event, conventional therapy emphasizes strengthening the patient psychologically so that alcohol is no longer a convenient "crutch" for solving problems or relieving emotional tensions. As with drug intervention, treatment

---

[107]Ibid., p. 548.
[108]Ibid., p. 335.
[109]Ibid., p. 337.
[110]Ibid., p. 333.
[111]Harlow, "Drugs and Jail Inmates," p. 10. (Data reflect 1989 statistics.)
[112]Christopher A. Innes, "Profile of State Prison Inmates, 1986," *Bureau of Justice Statistics: Special Report* (Washington, DC: U.S. Department of Justice, 1988), p. 6. (Data reflect 1986 statistics.)

approaches range from psychotherapy to special diets designed to counteract vitamin deficiencies, along with self-help groups. In both cases, treatment is more likely to be effective if it is not conducted in isolation, but rather, includes a family-focused approach that involves relatives and significant others.

---

*LEARNING GOALS*

*Do you know:*

- *How society has responded over the years to those with mental disorders?*
- *How the developmentally disabled differ from the mentally ill?*
- *Why staff need special training for dealing with the developmentally disabled?*
- *Where those declared criminally insane are confined?*
- *Why it is difficult to transfer mentally ill inmates to state mental health facilities?*

---

## Mentally Disordered Offenders

Throughout history, society has reacted to those who have mental disorders with a mixture of fear, mistrust, and repulsion. In the Middle Ages, it was thought that they were possessed by evil spirits, and if fortunate enough to escape burning at the stake, they faced banishment from society. In later years, ashamed families would secrete mentally disordered relatives in basements or attics. When society began to assume more public responsibility for their care, they were again secluded—in large remote institutions closed off from public scrutiny. Eventually, concerns were voiced about both the conditions in which they were being confined and the types of disorders for which they were being held. Mental institutions were criticized as dumping grounds where the elderly, handicapped, and undesirable were virtually imprisoned.[113] Even among those with legitimate mental problems, it was determined that many suffered from conditions that could be treated as effectively on an outpatient basis.

Much of this criticism came to a climax during the civil rights movement of the 1960s—when widespread support was generated for protecting the interests of the disenfranchised, including the mentally ill. As a result, the *deinstitutionalization* of large mental hospitals began with various forms of community mental health legislation in the 1970s. However, somewhere along the way to replacing *institutional confinement* with *community-based treatment*, society ran out of money or interest or both. In Chapter 6, we already saw the impact of this transition in terms of how jails in particular have become something of a "second-rate mental institution": Wandering aimlessly in the community, psychotic much of the time, and unable to manage their internal control systems [these chronically homeless, previously

---

[113]Barbara Gordon, *I'm Dancing As Fast As I Can* (New York: Bantam Books, 1979), p. 98.

institutionalized mentally ill people] found the criminal justice system was an asylum of the last resort."[114]

As with alcoholics and drug addicts, those whom society cannot or will not care for effectively often become correctional clients. In that respect, public attitudes toward the mentally ill have not changed dramatically over the years—still reflecting a combination of suspicion and aversion. But despite fears of being victimized by a violent criminal psychopath, "generally, persons identified as mentally ill represent no greater risk of committing violent crimes than the population as a whole."[115]

Admittedly, to speak of "mentally disordered" offenders encompasses a wide range of behaviors, from the mildly disoriented or neurotic to those who are severely psychotic and completely out of touch with reality. This umbrella term is used broadly to relate to mental conditions that differ from what is considered "normal." It is important to make clear distinction between the developmentally disabled and the mentally ill.

**Developmental Disability (Mental Retardation).** Previously known by such terms as "mentally defective" or "feebleminded," and more recently, as *developmentally disabled,* mental retardation is a clinical classification resulting from an *abnormally low IQ,* (usually in the area of 70 or below). There is not necessarily any relationship between retardation and criminal behavior. However, the limited intelligence of the developmentally disabled severely restricts their employment opportunities, which can lead to stealing for survival. It also tends to make them susceptible to being led into crime by others. And when they do break the law, they often do not have the mental capacity to do so without being detected. Thus, it is not surprising that they are quickly apprehended—as we see in the next "Close-up on Corrections."

Because of their nominal intelligence, when such persons do engage in crime, they may be found incompetent to stand trial. Or they may not be held accountable for their actions in a court of law, just as a small child would not be held criminally responsible due to lack of ability to distinguish right from wrong. As a result, it is not surprising to find that their proportion of the institutional population in corrections is quite small.[116] Moreover, because of their limited numbers, programs for them are very scarce. Although there is no "cure" for mental retardation, with special assistance, some can be helped to improve the level of their development toward achieving greater social independence.

But a far greater danger for them than lack of treatment is their potential for being victimized in prison. Not only are they subject to verbal ridicule and

[114]J. R. Belcher, "Are Jails Replacing the Mental Health System for Homeless Mentally Ill?" *Community Mental Health Journal,* Vol. 24, No. 3 (1988), p. 193.

[115]National Commission on the Causes and Prevention of Violence, *Crimes of Violence* (Washington, DC: U.S. Government Printing Office, 1969), p. 444.

[116]One report found that only about 10% of all incarcerated inmates are mentally retarded. Bertram S. Brown and Thomas F. Courtless, *The Mentally Retarded Offender and Corrections* (Washington, DC: U.S. Government Printing Office, 1971). Others have put the estimate as low as 5%, although noting that the figure could be far higher. Bruce DeSilva, "The Retarded Offender: A Problem without a Program," *Corrections Magazine* Vol. 6, No. 4 (August 1980), p. 25.

Developmentally Disabled Offenders

Eddie, a fat 43-year-old Providence, RI, man with an IQ of 61, holds up Dunkin' Donuts shops. He walks up to the counter, pretends he has a gun inside the pocket of his tattered green coat, and demands "all your money and a dozen donuts." He has done it at least a half-dozen times. The police catch Eddie every time walking down the sidewalk eating the donuts. Eddie has served at least two prison sentences for such offenses. . . .

Everyone has read about them. They are the hapless, inept criminals who do things like rob a bank and sign the note they give to the teller; who run out of the liquor store they just robbed, jump in their getaway car and discover they have lost the keys; who burglarize the same store or home at the same time every week until the police catch them.

Such incidents make humorous fillers for newspaper columns. But if one looks into them more deeply, the facts are not always so funny. Some of these offenders are merely clumsy; many, however, are mentally retarded. They commit their crimes ineptly because they don't have the mental capacity to plan them. They are easily caught and a disproportionate number of them end up in jails and prisons.

*Source:* Bruce DeSilva, "The Retarded Offender: A Problem Without a Program," *Corrections Magazine*, Vol. 6, No. 4 (August 1980), pp. 24–25.

physical abuse by other inmates, but to conceal their deficiencies, they rarely participate in rehabilitation programs.[117] In addition, they are "slower to adjust to routine" and have "more difficulty in learning regulations."[118] Often, they simply do not understand what is expected of them. Staff who are not sensitive to the developmentally disabled can therefore mistakenly assume that an inmate is being defiant when actually, the person could not mentally comprehend the officer's instructions. (See the next "Close-up on Corrections.")

As illustrated in that story, officers who are not trained to recognize the behavioral characteristics of the developmentally disabled will assume that the inmate has normal ability to grasp instructions. This is a particular problem for these offenders, since many of them are skillful at hiding their disability in an effort to appear "normal."[119] As a result, they tend to accumulate more disciplinary infractions and are more likely to be denied parole (serving on average two or three years longer than others with the same offense).[120]

[117]Miles Santamour and Bernadette West, *Sourcebook on the Mentally Disordered Prisoner* (Washington, DC: U.S. Department of Justice, 1985), p. 70.
[118]Ibid.
[119]Thomas Tiberia, "Helping Correction Officers Recognize and Interact with Handicapped Offenders," *American Jails,* Vol. 6, No. 2 (May/June, 1992), p. 32.
[120]Santamour and West, p. 70

### Dealing with the Developmentally Disabled

On one particular hot summer weekend, fifteen minutes before he was to be relieved, Officer Terry . . . asked inmate Ness to assist him [in cleaning up the mess hall]. . . . About twenty minutes later, C.O. Terry returned to the mess hall to check on the work. When he saw what inmate Ness was doing, he first couldn't believe it and then he got angry. Inmate Ness had continued to sweep the garbage back and forth all over the floor, but was not putting it in a pile. In fact, the area that needed cleaning was now larger. Barely able to control his anger, C.O. Terry yelled, "NESS, WHAT THE HELL IS WRONG WITH YOU? WHAT ARE YOU—STUPID? WHAT DO YOU THINK YOU'RE DOING?" Inmate Ness became visibly nervous and stammered, "I, I, I ain't stupid." C.O. Terry disregarded the inmate's remark and stated, "YOU'RE TRYING TO BUST MY CHOPS BECAUSE YOU KNOW I WANT TO GET OUT OF THIS PLACE. LISTEN, NESS, I'M NOT GONNA TELL YA AGAIN, GET THIS MESS PICKED UP NOW!" C.O. Terry then walked out. . . .

Inmate Ness then grabbed a garbage can and began walking around the mess hall picking up a handful here and there, never really making any progress on the scattered mess. After five minutes, Officer Terry returned and once again. . . screams, "O.K., YOU MORON, THAT'S IT, GET OVER HERE." Before the inmate moves, he yells back, "I, I AIN'T NO MORON." C.O. Terry yells, "YOU ARE TOO, NOW GET OVER HERE." Inmate responds, "I AIN'T NO MORON." C.O. Terry yells, "I'M GIVING YOU A DIRECT ORDER TO GET YOUR BUTT OVER HERE RIGHT NOW." Inmate Ness shakes his head violently side to side, indicating that he's not moving. C.O. Terry then calls for officer assistance. . . .

*Source:* Thomas Tiberia, "Helping Correction Officers Recognize and Interact with Handicapped Offenders," *American Jails,* Vol. 6, No. 2 (May/June, 1992), pp. 31–32.

To prevent such difficulties, some departments have established procedures for identifying developmentally disabled offenders and placing them in special units where they can receive appropriate care, equitable discipline, and life skills training that will help them become more independent upon release.[121] But unfortunately, they are more likely to be either unrecognized or mainstreamed with the general population and supervised by personnel who are not aware of their special condition.

[121]See, for example, descriptions of two such programs in South Carolina and Texas: William J. Deemer and Adrienne D. Conine, "An Institutional Programming Model for the Adult Developmentally Disabled Offender," *Corrections Today,* Vol. 46, No. 3 (June 1984), pp. 30–31; and Miles B. Santamour, "Mentally Retarded Offenders: Texas Program Targets Basic Needs," *Corrections Today,* Vol. 52, No. 1 (February 1990), pp. 52, 92, 106.

**Mental Illness.** Unlike the simplicity of identifying mental retardation by one's score on an IQ test, the complexities of mental illnesses defy easy classification. In terms of seriousness, mental illness can range from harmless senility to violent-prone psychosis. The term "criminally insane" was used at one time to classify severely mentally ill offenders, but they are now more often included within broader categories such as mentally ill or mentally disordered. In fact, legal and medical definitions of various mental conditions can still differ significantly. At least in part because of such confusions in terms of definitions, an accurate number of the mentally ill who are incarcerated is virtually impossible to obtain. For purposes of this discussion, we will use the term *insanity* to differentiate such offenders from those with varieties of less severe conditions that could also be encompassed under "mental illness."

It has become common to hear of defendants entering pleas of "not guilty by reason of insanity" at the trial stage, particularly when well-publicized cases employ this defense successfully (e.g., John Hinkley, who attempted to assassinate former president Ronald Reagan). Indeed, "madness" has been a criminal defense since the thirteenth century. Although it obviously has a medical interpretation, in the criminal justice system, insanity is a *legal* term—a status that is decided by the court, taking into consideration the opinions of medical experts. The criminally insane, then, are those who have been so declared by the court.

In the past, defendants ruled incompetent to stand trial or declared legally insane during trial could be confined in a *mental health institution* for an indeterminate period of time. But a 1977 Supreme Court ruling (*Jackson v. Indiana*) held that those found incompetent for trial cannot be held indefinitely and established that any such commitment must be justified by treatment progress. However, even if released under criminal law, the patient may be recommitted under civil law. But if at some point the mentally insane are determined by medical staff to be "cured," there may well be nothing to prevent their release, since technically, they were not "convicted" in a court of law. In an effort to prevent untimely releases from mental health institutions of those who could otherwise be held in a correctional institution, Michigan passed the first Guilty but Mentally Ill legislation in 1972. Several other states have followed suit. Although these statutes vary, the basic intent is to establish factual guilt or innocence in a court of law (regardless of the insanity outcome), which would therefore enable a correctional sentence to be imposed, thus preventing the offender who is declared mentally insane from escaping criminal responsibility.

In addition to mental health institutions, the criminally insane may be confined in a special *forensic hospital* (i.e., a psychiatric hospital that is also a secure correctional institution). In smaller states and localities, a separate *psychiatric ward* may be set up within an existing prison to accommodate them. Contrary to past practices, the legally insane are no longer confined indiscriminately with the general population.

But that certainly does not mean that there are no mentally ill inmates among the general population. An inmate may suffer from any number of mental disturbances without being declared legally insane. Aside from the relatively few who are so designated, many others with varying forms of mental disorders are confined within correctional facilities. There are no valid statistics documenting exactly how many mentally ill offenders are behind bars. According to the National Commission on the Causes and Prevention of Violence, "the popular idea that the mentally ill are overrepresented in the population of violent criminals is not suggested by research evidence."[122] On the other hand, a summary of the psychiatric evaluations of prison inmates over an almost 50-year period found that nearly half (49%) needed psychiatric attention.[123] Regardless of the numbers, whether or not they get such help is another matter.

Treatment is both essential from a compassionate point of view and a practical management necessity—given the fact that "certain types of psychiatric impairment increase the likelihood of . . . violent behavior within the general prison population."[124] But as was discussed in earlier chapters, sophisticated psychiatric and psychological treatment is costly. When available, it may be limited to the most severe cases, with participation "contingent upon the inmate being found psychotic, acutely disturbed, in need of immediate psychiatric care, or a sex offender."[125] Even at the height of the medical model, treatment was not as prevalent as the supposedly rehabilitative emphasis of that era would suggest. Response to mental illness in financially pressed agencies may therefore be limited to efforts directed toward simply *containing* their behavior.[126] But as one doctor in charge of mental health services in a correctional system has noted, "[t]reatment programs must include more than separation, close supervision, and administration of medication."[127]

It might seem that an obvious solution would be to transfer such cases to a state mental health hospital which is better equipped for their care. But since the deinstitutionalization movement, that is far more easily said than done. Before accepting an inmate, state mental health laws now often require that in addition to being legitimately mentally ill, "clear objective evidence must also exist that the inmate is a real and immediate danger to himself or herself or to others; or that the inmate is unable to attend to his or her basic needs. . . . This standard, when rigidly applied . . . effectively precludes the transfer of many inmates . . . to mental institutions."[128]

[122]National Commission on the Causes and Prevention of Violence, p. 444.

[123]Lawrence A. Bennett, Thomas S. Rosenbaum, and Wayne R. McCullough, *Counseling in Correctional Environments* (New York: Human Sciences Press, 1978), p. 76.

[124]Deborah R. Baskin, Ira Sommers, and Henry J. Steadman, "Assessing the Impact of Psychiatric Impairment on Prison Violence," *Journal of Criminal Justice*, Vol. 19, No. 3 (1991), p. 278.

[125]Stephen L. Hardy, "Dealing with the Mentally and Emotionally Disturbed," *Corrections Today*, Vol. 46, No. 3 (June 1984), p. 17.

[126]For an overview of the challenges facing corrections with regard to the staffing, monitoring, and documenting of services to the mentally ill, see Richard M. Austin and Albert S. Duncan, "Handle with Care: Special Inmates, Special Needs," *Corrections Today*, Vol. 50, No. 3 (June 1988), pp. 116–20.

[127]Max J. Mobley, "Mental Health Services: Inmates in Need," *Corrections Today*, Vol. 48, No. 3 (May 1986), p. 13.

[128]David Kalinich, Paul Embert, and Jeffrey Senese, "Mental Health Services for Jail Inmates: Imprecise Standards, Traditional Philosophies, and the Need for Change," in Joel A. Thompson and G. Larry Mays, eds., *American Jails: Public Policy Issues* (Chicago: Nelson-Hall, 1991), p. 81. There are, however, some communities that are making concerted efforts to coordinate their mental health and correctional services. See, for example, Gary Long, "A Multidisciplinary Mental Health Services Delivery Team," *American Jails*, Vol. 5, No. 4 (September/October 1991), p. 107.

Moreover, without a sizable complement of psychiatric staff, it may be difficult to determine just who is mentally ill—since manipulative inmates may feign symptoms in order to get attention or a different housing assignment. For a perceptive illustration of how one mental health worker distinguishes between the truly mentally disturbed and the traditional malingerer, see the next "Close-up on Corrections."

---

**LEARNING GOALS**

*Do you know:*

- *How prostitution differs from other "sex" crimes?*
- *How the criminal justice system generally responds to prostitution?*
- *What the relationship is between the victims of child molestation and subsequent perpetrators of this crime?*
- *What behavioral patterns are involved in child molestation?*
- *Why rape is considered to be more closely related to assault than other forms of sexual misconduct?*
- *What approaches characterize the development and treatment of sexual offense patterns?*

---

## Sex Offenders

Like the confusion surrounding classification of various forms of mental illness, states have differing definitions of sexual crimes (e.g., "lewd and lascivious behavior," "carnal knowledge," "unnatural acts," etc.). As with special offender populations in general, this discussion could include an extremely wide variety of behaviors, but will be limited to the most common sexually oriented offenders in the correctional system— prostitutes, rapists, and child molesters.

**Prostitutes.** A major difference between prostitution and other sex crimes is that it is an offense which is committed for *financial gain*. Particularly among young juvenile runaways, drug addicts, alcoholics, and others who have minimal legitimate employment opportunities, selling one's body offers a desperate means of survival.[129] Social attitudes vary toward prostitution throughout the world, and even within different states in the U.S. Some areas legalize and regulate the trade, while others strictly prohibit it. Most jurisidictions vacillate between these two extremes—officially outlawing prostitution, but not vigorously enforcing it.

In part, these differences reflect the fact that prostitution is considered a *"victimless"* crime—that is, a crime committed by two consenting parties. But that does not mean that prostitution does not generate victims. Customers can become robbery victims. Prostitutes themselves can be abused by either customers or their "pimps." And with the spread of AIDS, both are subject to an

---

[129]See, for example, the compelling stories of children on the streets of New York in Bruce Ritter, *Sometimes God Has a Kid's Face: The Story of America's Exploited Street Kids* (New York: Covenant House, 1988).

Managing Malingerers

By simply making a vague threat such as "I don't know what I'll do," an inmate will be brought to the institutional psychologist. If the inmate sticks to that line, there is a very good chance he will be sent to the mental health unit. If he continues to threaten suicide when he gets to the unit, we put him on restrictive suicide precautions—we take all his clothing and possessions, give him a paper gown, and place him in a bare cell with nothing to lie on but a paper sheet. We then observe him at 15-minute intervals.

While this may sound cruel, it is actually quite useful. If a person is truly depressed and suicidal, he may use any available means to kill himself. I know of inmates who have cut open the bottoms of their mattresses, crawled inside and suffocated. Others have hung themselves with braided toilet paper.

However, the greatest use of these strict precautions may be their diagnostic potential—they separate the truly suicidal from the malingerer. Suicidal inmates barely notice the conditions of their confinement; they are withdrawn and continue to brood about whatever it is that is bothering them.

But not so the malingerers. Usually within an hour of being placed in the cell they begin to complain. Many an inmate who absolutely convinced me of his depression and hopelessness will, a day later, let on that he didn't want to do his segregation time or that he was having trouble with another inmate. And since he really isn't suicidal, can't he have a mattress and just stay here for a while? . . . [But] [i]f they're not suicidal, they don't belong in the mental health unit. We encourage them to return to the general population and deal with their problems. . . .

*Source:* Roy Clymer, "Managing Malingerers: Power Stems from Active Involvement, Not Control," *Corrections Today,* Vol. 54, No. 6 (August 1992), pp. 22–24.

even greater threat today. However, because prostitution is not a high priority within the criminal justice system, offenders are rarely sentenced to more than short terms in jail. As a result, prostitution generally receives negligible attention throughout the crimnal justice system.

**Child Molesters.**   In contrast to its ambivalence toward prostitution, society holds clearly despicable attitudes toward the molesters of innocent children. Even among jail and prison inmates, these offenders are at the bottom of the social hierarchy—rejected, scorned, and threatened by other inmates. As the public has become increasingly concerned with taking action against such violators, more vigorous efforts have been made to report, prosecute, and punish their actions. Despite these efforts, however, many cases remain hidden by fear and shame.[130]

[130]See Debra Whitcomb, Elizabeth R. Shapiro, and Lindsey D. Stellwagen, eds., *When the Victim Is a Child: Issues for Judges and Prosecutors* (Washington, DC: U.S. Department of Justice, 1985).

But perhaps the most tragic element of the sexual abuse of children is that many of its victims grow up to perpetuate the crime, becoming abusers themselves. This, of course, does not mean that all of those who are abused will become molesters, but it has been estimated that the vast majority of such offenders were former victims.[131] Many of these offenders victimize children in an attempt to resolve their own abusive experiences.[132] In terms of their *behavioral patterns*, it has been found that these offenders are:

- "Often a member of the family, rarely a stranger.
- Almost always male, rarely female.
- Sometimes extremely domineering and authoritative in their homes, but mostly passive and ineffectual individuals outside the family.
- From all socioeconomic classes . . . not only very poor families as is commonly believed.[133]

Some correctional facilities may separate child molesters from the general population for their own protection. But unless they are identified as having some other problem that would give them a higher priority for treatment (such as drug addiction or mental illness), there is often little offered to them in terms of therapy. In fact, even when programs are available, it has been found that to be effective, they must be accompanied by a change in prison norms among both staff and inmates. "The present correctional approach . . . forces them to hide in prison, say they are incarcerated for other charges, and not take part in sex offender programs. [But] when sex offenders do not participate in sex offender specific treatment, they are at risk of reoffending."[134]

**Rapists.**   For many years, rape was considered a sexually oriented offense, which (like the myths about child molestation) was associated with excessive sexual drives. Similar to the prison homosexual rapes discussed in Chapter 10, however, there is now increasing recognition that heterosexual rape is also committed more for the desire to *control* and *dominate the victim* than for sexual gratification. As one former prosecutor has phrased it, "People who think rape is about sex confuse the weapon with the motivation."[135]

Forcible rape is classified as a *crime of violence* involving aggressive, hostile behavior that is directed toward degrading and dominating another person. It is a crime more closely related to assault than to other forms of sexual miscon-

[131]Albert Ellis and Ralph Brancale, *The Psychology of Sex Offenders* (Springfield, IL: Charles C Thomas, 1956). See also Robert L. Gerser, *Hidden Victims: The Sexual Abuse of Children* (Boston: Beacon Press, 1979).

[132]Paraphrased from Eve Krupinski and Dana Weikel, *Death from Child Abuse and No One Heard* (Winter Park, FL: Currier-Davis, n.d.), p. 104.

[133]Ibid., pp. 104–107.

[134]Garry P. Perry, Bob Wilson, and Steve Boechler, "Development of Sexual Abuse Programming within a Correctional Centre," *American Jails,* Vol. 6, No. 2 (May/June, 1992), p. 82.

[135]Alice Vachss, "Rapists are single-minded sociopathic beasts . . . that cannot be tamed with understanding," *Parade Magazine* (June 27, 1993), p. 5.

duct.[136] Not only are the majority of rape victims injured, but more than almost any other violent offenders, rapists are likely to have had prior criminal charges against them.[137]

During the 1930s, most states adopted *criminal sexual psychopath* laws to identify chronic rape offenders and commit them to state hospitals for treatment. However, since these laws generally defined sexual psychopaths as those who have a "mental derangement," coupled with a propensity toward committing "sex offenses," the most serious and dangerous rapists were sometimes not covered by the law. Rather, minor sex offenders (such as voyeurs or "peeping Toms," exhibitionists, etc.) were more likely to be targeted in many cases. Moreover, because of medical and legal variations, accurately determining sexual psychopathy is quite difficult.[138] In recent years, a number of states have replaced the sexual psychopath term with "mentally disordered sex offender" or "dangerous sex offenders." Whatever they are designated, *chronic rapists* by their very definition can be expected to continue criminal behavior if appropriate treatment is not provided. For an overview of the psychological problems experienced by sex offenders and an account of one program designed to deal with them, see the next "Close-up on Corrections."

While all sex offenders need some form of treatment, "not all sex offenders need the same type, intensity, or duration of treatment." For example, among 73 sex offender programs, it was found that "785 different therapies were employed."[139] Matching the needs of the offender with the capabilities available can be very challenging, although overall results reveal significantly lower recidivism rates for treated versus untreated offenders.[140] Like mental health services, the intensive therapy that may be required is costly, especially in financially pressed times. As with many other areas of corrections, needs far outdistance resources.

---

### LEARNING GOALS

*Do you know:*

- *What is meant by the term "physical impairment"?*
- *How those with physical impairments have traditionally been accommodated within correctional facilities?*
- *What impact the Americans with Disabilities Act is expected to have?*

---

[136]See Susan Brownmiller, *Against Our Will: Men, Women, and Rape* (New York: Simon and Schuster, 1975), pp. 367–77.

[137]Fifty-six percent of the female victims of rape reported sustaining injuries. *Sourcebook*, p. 271. Of all violent felony defendants with one or more prior charges, only those currently charged with robbery represented a higher percentage (55%) than rapists (53%), although this does not necessarily mean that their prior crime(s) also involved rape. *Sourcebook*, p. 440.

[138]See Thomas J. Meyers, "Psychiatric Examination of the Sexual Psychopath," *Journal of Criminal Law, Criminology, and Police Science*, Vol. 56, No. 1 (March 1965), pp. 27–31.

[139]Arthur Gordon and Frank J. Porporino, "Canada Targets Sex Offenders According to Treatment Needs," *Corrections Today*, Vol. 53, No. 5 (August 1991), p. 162. See also William E. Prendergast, *Treating Sex Offenders in Correctional Institutions and Outpatient Clinics: A Guide to Clinical Practice* (Binghamton, NY: Haworth Press, 1991).

[140]Christopher S. Norris, "Sex Offender Treatment," *Federal Prisons Journal*, Vol. 2, No. 4 (Winter 1992), p. 30.

### Missouri's Sexual Offender Program

Experts in the field are the first to acknowledge that treatment of sexual offenders is no simple task. . . . Very often, sexual offenders have had some unusual and disturbed conditioning experiences that make it difficult for them to learn acceptable and effective living skills. . . . [W]hile the offender has been practicing these destructive patterns for coping with life, he/she has been . . . neglecting to practice or learn alternative, more constructive strategies. . . .

Sexual offense patterns can be modified if two issues are addressed adequately:

- The offender must be taught to become aware of the active role he/she takes in the sexual offense behavior and to accept responsibility for his/her actions and for changing them.
- The offender must be taught alternative skills for coping with life to use as substitutes for offense patterns, which he/she begins to learn to control through awareness and reinforcement for practicing other behaviors. . . .

*Source:* Marie Clark, "Missouri's Sexual Offender Program," *Corrections Today*, Vol. 48, No. 3 (May 1986), pp. 85, 89.

## Physically Impaired Offenders

The needs of *physically impaired offenders* obviously differ substantially from the requirements of those who are psychologically damaged, but in both cases, correctional systems are likely to be ill-equipped to meet them. The physically impaired (or disabled) include those who do not enjoy the benefits of being able to see, hear, speak, walk, or who in some other way face a major restriction as a result of a physical condition (which can include mental retardation). In the past, such persons were referred to as "physically handicapped," terminology that has changed with greater realization that there is often nothing "handicapping" them more than social attitudes toward their condition.

There is not anything about those with disabilities that inherently makes them any more or less likely to become involved in crime.[141] But when they are, correctional services and facilities that were designed with only the physically unimpaired in mind experience severe difficulties in meeting the needs of those who do not share similar good fortune. In the past, disabled

---

[141]However, there is some evidence that for a variety of reasons, handicapped juveniles are overrepresented in correctional institutions, serve longer sentences, and are more likely to be placed in segregation units. See Carolyn A. Buser, Peter E. Leone, and Mary E. Bannon, "Prison Segregation Units and the Educational Rights of Handicapped Inmates: Problems and Some Potential Solutions," *Issues in Correctional Training and Casework*, Vol. 3 (October 1987), pp. 1–3.

offenders had to adjust as best they could. Now, as a result of the *Americans with Disabilities Act*, it is correctional agencies that have to adjust (along with any other public or private establishments in free society that have more than 25 employees).

Signed into law in 1990, the act took effect in 1992. It defines the disabled as "anyone with a physical or mental impairment substantially limiting one or more major life activities, [who] has a record of such impairment, or is regarded as having such an impairment."[142] The law prohibits denying an otherwise qualified person a job or promotion, as well any other type of discrimination with respect to salary, benefits, and so on.

In terms of institutional populations, its most far-reaching provisions may be those related to the requirement that *reasonable accommodations* must be made for the disabled unless it would pose an "undue hardship" on the organization. The law specifically refers to making such accommodations for workers who request them, so it is not entirely certain at this point to what extent inmates in correctional facilities will be affected. But it does clearly require that new buildings be constructed in a manner that is accessible to those with disabilities and that existing buildings be made accessible.

An additional feature of the law prohibits a public entity from denying program benefits because facilities are inaccessible. It has been pointed out that this provision focuses on "making *programs*, not *buildings*, accessible,"[143] which is obviously a more comprehensive challenge. If nothing else, the publicity surrounding enactment of this legilsation has generated greater awareness of the special needs of the disabled: "[T]he very presence of the ADA [Americans with Disabilities Act] ensures that handicapped inmates will become more aware of their rights to equal opportunities for participation in prison life."[144] As is vividly illustrated in the next "Close-up on Corrections," accommodating the needs of the disabled and providing them with equal opportunities can have far-reaching implications within a correctional facility.

---

*LEARNING GOALS*

*Do you know:*

- *To what extent the elderly are increasing among correctional populations?*
- *Why there are increasing proportions of older inmates in prison?*
- *What special needs are required by elderly prisoners?*
- *What alternatives to incarceration have been proposed for geriatric prisoners?*

---

[142]"Agencies and Facilities Must Comply with New Federal Law on Disabled," *Corrections Today*, Vol. 54, No. 6 (August 1992), p. 143.

[143]Randall Atlas, "Is Accessibility a Disability? The Impact of ADA on Jails," *American Jails*, Vol. 6, No. 5 (November/December 1992), p. 55.

[144]Herbert A. Rosefield, "Enabling the Disabled: Issues to Consider in Meeting Handicapped Offenders' Needs," *Corrections Today*, Vol. 54, No. 7 (October 1992), p. 110.

Meeting the Needs of Disabled Offenders

### CUSTODY AND SECURITY

Training must be provided to increase sensitivity to disabled inmates' special needs and overcome any aversion to viewing stumps, colostomy bags or other manifestations of a handicap. Officers should be taught how to properly strip search a wheelchair-bound paraplegic, disassemble wheelchairs and prostheses, and otherwise conduct a proper shakedown. . . .

Questions will arise concerning requirements for leg cuffs on paraplegics, waist chains across colostomy bags and even handcuffs for those on crutches. Custody should consult medical personnel when making these decisions. . . .

### PERSONAL SAFETY

The need to protect handicapped inmates from exploitation leads directly to safety issues. First, disabled inmates need to be protected from other inmates. . . . Second, handicapped inmates need to be protected in case of fire or natural disaster. Building evacuation planning and emergency response must include special consideration for the disabled. Wheelchairs and crutches can block exits, leading to panic and injury. Plans must include the steps to be taken to safely evacuate this population without slowing the evacuation of the other inmates. . . .

### PROGRAMS

A major challenge . . . is providing the disabled with meaningful work, study and recreational opportunities. It is difficult to find prison jobs for handicapped inmates that provide an opportunity to earn sentence reduction credits. . . .

While finding appropriate jobs may be difficult, handicapped inmates frequently prove to be excellent workers. All too often, no attempt has been made to put these inmates to work, and they have been forced to sit back and watch other inmates earn incentive wages and days off their sentences without an opportunity to do likewise.

### MEDICAL SERVICE

A major issue is helping with activities of daily living. These include dressing, bathing, feeding, and transporting. . . . Ideally, medical staff such as nurses' aides provide all such required assistance. However, in the real world of limited budgets and insufficient staff, inmates frequently are used for these activites. . . . Any inmate involvement in daily living assistance must be closely monitored by professional staff to ensure inmates are properly trained and that they do not exploit those they are assigned to assist.

### HOUSING

[H]ousing requires many special accommodations for the disabled. Obviously, it must be handicapped-accessible, but today, that means a great deal more than it used to. Simply putting up handrails in the showers is no longer adequate. . . . The square footage requirement for handicapped inmates is greater. Lockers must be low enough to be reached from a wheelchair, and writing tables must be high enough for a wheelchair to pull under. . . .

ONGOING CHALLENGE

Like all special populations in our correctional systems, managing disabled inmates presents an ongoing challenge. While their numbers are few and their needs are great, the system must be prepared to accommodate them. If we do not, we will be forced to do so through civil lawsuits.

*Source:* Herbert A. Rosefield, "Enabling the Disabled: Issues to Consider in Meeting Handicapped Offenders' Needs," *Corrections Today*, Vol. 54, No. 7 (October 1992), pp. 111–14.

---

## The Elderly in Prison

Just as the population in general is aging, so is that of our correctional institutions. As a result of medical advances and healthier lifestyles, the average life expectancy continues to climb. Moreover, senior citizens are already a rapidly growing segment of the population, and as those in the post–World War II "baby boom" approach retirement, the percentage of the elderly in the population will expand even further. At one time, an inmate in South Carolina—at 103 years of age—was the oldest prisoner in the United States.[145] But in just another decade or two, he will probably not be so unique.

Young people still are far more disproportionately likely to be criminal offenders, although crime among the elderly is no longer as totally unheard of as it was in the past. This does not mean that a crime wave is occurring among older Americans. Quite the contrary, less that 3% of those arrested in 1990 were over the age of 55.[146] But in light of trends toward *longer sentences*, prison populations are getting older, and "some see in the longer mandatory sentences handed out these days a need for special accommodations in prison for the elderly and sick, who require therapy, medication, wider cell doors for wheelchairs, even Braille signs on doors."[147]

Between 1979 and 1986, the percentage of state prison inmates over the age of 25 increased from 64% to 73%. Such collective statistics do not appear to be very startling. However, figures for individual states more clearly reflect aging trends, particularly in areas of the country with large percentages of the elderly in their population. For example, since the early 1980s, the growth rate of inmates over the age of 50 in Florida has been double (51%) that of the prison population overall (25%).[148] In Florida, "data clearly show that the number of older inmates . . . [in prison] is increasing at a much faster rate than the number of younger inmates."[149]

---

[145]"Growing Old in Prison," *Corrections Magazine*, Vol. 5, No. 1 (March 1979), p. 32.
[146]*Uniform Crime Reports*, p. 185.
[147]Mary Cronin, "Gilded Cages," *Time* (May 25, 1992), p. 54.
[148]Richard L. Dugger, "The Graying of America's Prisons: Special Care Considerations," *Corrections Today*, Vol. 50, No. 3 (June 1988), p. 28. (Data reflect fiscal years 1981–1982 to 1986–1987).
[149]Ibid.

As the elderly become a larger percentage of prison inmates, correctional administrators will be faced with unique challenges to address their needs. If aging inmates are simply mainstreamed with the overall population, they will be vulnerable to being preyed upon by younger, healthier inmates—as is seen in the plight of one geriatric inmate in the next "Close-up on Corrections." They are also less likely to be able to participate physically in the recreational and vocational programs that are traditionally offered in correctional facilities. Nor can they in many cases eat the same foods as other inmates, since aging is often accompanied by more restrictive diets. Meeting the housing, recreational, rehabilitative, and even dietary needs of geriatric inmates presents issues that corrections will be confronting in the years ahead.

But perhaps most significantly in terms of costs, as more and more older offenders are confined behind bars, *long-term health care* will become an increasingly greater concern—just as it is already within the general population in free society. "Nearly every geriatric inmate has some long-term chronic debilitation that requires frequent medical attention,"[150] and meeting such needs is costly. In 1989 it was estimated that the average expense of medical care and maintenance for inmates over 55 was $69,000 a year—about three times the norm.[151]

## ❖ CLOSE-UP ON CORRECTIONS

### Growing Old behind Bars

On a steamy June day in 1973, a 50-year-old drifter named Quenton Brown robbed a bread store in Morgan City, La., of $117 and a 15-cent cherry pie. He walked across a dusty street, crawled under a house and ate the pie. When the police showed up a few minutes later, he surrendered his .38 pistol and the handful of money without resistance. Brown, whose IQ is 51, told the cops he had bummed his way to the Cajun outback to find work on an oil rig. Unable to find a job, he robbed. The jury gave short shrift to his claim of insanity. The judge gave him 30 years without parole.

Brown has pulled 17 years in the Louisiana State Prison at Angola, one of the nation's toughest. At 67, he is feeble, suffering from emphysema, a crushed esophagus and bleeding ulcers. His prison record is free of all but minor infractions, none involving drugs, sex or violence. . . . Over the years, he has watched former death-row murderers walk to freedom while his bids for release have been repulsed. As he grows older, the worst part of doing time is the younger, bolder prisoners: "They call you names. You go to the prison store, they snatch the bags from your hands as you leave. You're living in a jungle among savages."

*Source:* Ginny Carroll, "Growing Old behind Bars," *Newsweek* (November 20, 1989), p. 70.

[150]O. W. Kelsey, "Elderly Inmates: Providing Safe and Humane Care," *Corrections Today,* Vol. 48, No. 3 (May 1986), p. 56.
[151]Ginny Carroll, "Growing Old behind Bars," *Newsweek* (November 20, 1989), p. 70.

Some might advocate that *early release* should be extended to the elderly, for financial if not humanitarian reasons. In that regard, at least one agency has implemented a "compassionate release program" for terminally ill inmates who are no longer a risk to society, thereby "giving them an opportunity to live out their remaining days in relative dignity."[152] But many older prisoners have outlived their relatives and used up their savings. With no prospect of employment, where are they to go? For these types of cases, others have proposed that *secure nursing homes* and *electronic monitoring* would be more suitable alternatives. Such options would obviously be agreeable to the many offenders reflected in the dejection of one aging inmate: "I know I don't have many more years. I'd like to spend a few of them outside prison."[153]

## ❖ SUMMARY

Because of their "minority" status among institutional populations, the needs of special offenders have not often been a high priority. Females in particular have historically been arrested, convicted, and incarcerated less frequently. In comparison to men, they are more likely to be involved in property offenses and victim-precipitated crimes. However, the rate at which females are arrested and imprisoned is escalating considerably faster than that of their male counterparts. Much of the increase is attributable to drug-related offenses. Some maintain that such changes reflect greater involvement of women in crime. Others believe that the criminal justice system is becoming more punitive in its response to female criminality. But regardless of the reasons, women are becoming a larger proportion of correctional clientele, although they are still in the distinct minority.

In contrast to male inmates, females are more likely to suffer from the frustration of being both separated from and unable to care for their children. Separation anxiety can create considerable tension, stress, and reduced self-esteem. Also unlike males, female inmates tend to adapt to the deprivations of confinement by developing quasi-families, through which emotional intimacy with other inmates is substituted for the loss of family and social ties. In comparison to men, females tend to commit fewer serious disciplinary infractions. But there is some concern that women may be more frequently cited for misconduct that would be tolerated in a male institution.

Female institutions are smaller and more remote than male facilities. They are therefore not generally able to offer the diversity of programs provided within men's prisons. In an effort to address this problem economically—as well as create a more normal institutional environment—some facilities are now coed, with male and female inmates confined within the same compound. They do not share living quarters but are allowed to interact socially and share in the same programs. While there are both advantages and disadvantages of such arrange-

---

[152]Jeffers, p. 38, citing a program initiated in New York City directed toward selectively releasing terminal or end-stage AIDS patients from custody.
[153]Carroll, p. 70.

ments, overall, they have been found to generate fewer grievances and serious disciplinary citations.

Like women, those with HIV infection are appearing more frequently within institutional populations. With the spread of AIDS throughout society, it is not suprising to find that this disease is on the increase among inmates, particularly since those convicted of drug offenses are likely to be sentenced to prison or jail terms. Although IV drug users and homosexual/bisexual men are the largest groups at risk of HIV infection, it is spreading rapidly among women and children as a result of secondary infection.

Correctional responses to reducing the transmission of HIV have included educational programs, issuing condoms, HIV testing, and separate housing. Legal challenges have focused primarily on mandatory testing and the segregation of HIV-positive inmates. Thus far, the courts have ruled that mandatory testing is neither required under the Eighth Amendment nor prohibited under the Fourth Amendment. Similar judicial findings have resulted from cases challenging the segregation of HIV-positive inmates. Again, the courts have held that it is neither required nor prohibited.

Along with women and AIDS victims, drug abusers represent another component of correctional clientele that is growing at alarming rates, particularly among minority groups. Drug treatment programs are available in most correctional facilities, but they are reaching relatively small percentages of inmates, and the punitive emphasis of the justice model does not encourage participation. While the long-term success of such programs is not always impressive, it is important to note that treatment is not the only component of drug rehabilitation. Careful screening and appropriate intervention must be followed by close supervision—including both supportive assistance and continued monitoring.

Despite current concerns with the abuse of illicit drugs, alcohol has historically been the most abused substance and remains the "drug of choice" among young people. Although many are able to use alcohol in a socially responsible manner, others become addicted to it. Treatment programs for this disease generally emphasize strengthening the patient psychologically so that alcohol is no longer a convenient "crutch" for solving problems or relieving tensions.

Along with those experiencing problems with alcohol, mentally disordered offenders represent a sizable component of correctional populations—especially since the deinstitutionalization of mental health services. The developmentally disabled differ from the mentally ill in that their mental capacity has been retarded at an early stage of development. They are usually identified by an IQ of less than 70, which renders them easily susceptible to apprehension when they engage in crime. Within correctional institutions, the developmentally disabled represent special problems, since they are slower in adjusting and learning what is expected of them. Their behavior can also be misinterpreted as defiance.

In contrast, the criminally insane are those so designated by the courts, using legal criteria related to one's capacity to distinguish right from wrong. Those determined to be criminally insane may be confined in mental health facilities, forensic hospitals, or the separate psychiatric ward of a prison. But there are also many others incarcerated who are not legally designated "insane" but suffer from various forms of mental illnesses. In recent years, it has become more difficult to transfer such inmates to a mental health hospital, but correctional facilities are generally ill-equipped to meet their needs.

Like the mentally ill, sex offenders defy simple classification. They encompass conduct ranging from prostitution to rape or child molestation. Prostitution differs from other sexually oriented crimes in that it is committed for financial gain. Because both parties engage in this offense voluntarily, it often receives a low priority within all components of the criminal justice system. On the other hand, child molesters have become an increasing public concern. Many cases nevertheless remain hidden by fear and shame. Effective correctional treatment programs for molesters must be accompanied by a change in prison norms which traditionally force them to conceal their offense out of fear of victimization. Like myths about child molestation, rape was considered a sexually oriented crime in the past. Now there is greater realization that rape is a violent offense, committed more from a desire to control and dominate the victim than for sexual gratification. Without treatment, chronic rapists can be expected to continue their behavior. But identifying the proper intervention is difficult, since all sex offenders do not necessarily need the same type, intensity, or duration of treatment.

In the past, corrections as well as the general public has been slow to respond to the needs of the physically impaired. Following implementation of the Americans with Disabilities Act in 1992, both public agencies and private employers are now legally prohibited from discriminating against the disabled. It is still uncertain what direct impact this legislation will have on the inmate population, but it has generated widespread publicity calling attention to the special needs of the disabled throughout society.

While the physically impaired are still a small proportion of the correctional population, the elderly represent a rapidly expanding group. Along with the overall aging of the population in general, longer prison sentences are resulting in greater numbers of older inmates. As this trend continues, corrections will be faced with meeting their unique requirements in terms of everything from housing assignments to dietary restrictions, recreational provisions, and rehabilitative programs. Moreover, the long-term health care of geriatric inmates will become increasingly costly. In fact, meeting the special needs of all groups of offenders discussed in this chapter presents a significant challenge for correctional programs and facilities that are already hard-pressed to meet even the basic needs of more "traditional" offenders.

# chapter 13

# Juvenile Corrections

*To say that juvenile courts have failed to achieve their goals is to say no more than what is true of criminal courts in the United States. But failure is most striking when hopes are highest.*[1]

President's Commission on Law Enforcement and Administration of Justice

## ❖ CHAPTER OVERVIEW

The future ambitions and far-reaching aspirations of any society depend on its children. The children of today will become tomorrow's leaders, workers, and parents. Unfortunately, some will become its criminals as well.

In addressing any social problem, prevention holds far greater promise than intervention after the fact, and crime is certainly no exception. When prevention fails and young offenders confront social authority, they are sending a signal that something has gone wrong. Many will overcome their difficulties simply by maturing and growing up. Others will not. For them, encounters with authority will escalate if that "something" is not corrected. For a certain number of them, confrontations will become increasingly serious and frequent, until any hope for change is all but abandoned.

Before that point of no return is reached, children who come into contact with the justice system present more promise than their adult counterparts. By their very definition, "juveniles" are considered different from adult "criminals." If nothing else, they are younger—and therefore presumably less responsible for their actions, as well as more amenable to change. Involvement in the juvenile justice system can therefore offer the potential for addressing their problems and redirecting their behavior at an early stage. On the other hand, it can further

---

[1]President's Commission on Law Enforcement and Administration of Justice, *Task Force Report: Juvenile Delinquency and Youth Crime* (Washington, DC: U.S. Government Printing Office, 1967), p. 7.

**519**

alienate and embitter them, fostering the resentment and frustration that propel juvenile offenders toward adult criminality.

In fact, it was in recognition of the unique needs and potential for change among young people that the juvenile court was originally established. In an effort to create an environment wherein the "best interests" of the child were of greater significance than the interests of serving justice, the juvenile court was meant to be an advocate rather than an adversary of the offender. In such a system, there would be no need for lawyers or constitutional rights or the procedural formalities of the adult court. The intent was to promote the welfare of the child rather than to punish the offender for wrongdoing. But somewhere along the path toward serving their best interests, it became apparent that children were receiving neither the benevolent protection promised by the juvenile court nor the due process protections afforded in adult courts.

At the same time, juveniles were engaging in far more serious offenses than the original founders of the juvenile court had ever envisoned. To their victims, it makes little difference whether it was a juvenile or an adult who had raped, assaulted, or robbed them. Thus, demands for greater procedural protections in juvenile court, combined with increasing fear of juvenile crime, have resulted in a juvenile justice system today which more closely resembles its adult counterpart.

Although the most serious, chronic violators are now more likely to be transferred into adult court, the juvenile justice system still maintains many distinctions in terms of how it deals with less violent or habitual offenders. Society has not completely abandoned hope for turning young offenders away from a life of crime. But neither is it willing to tolerate the continued criminality of those whom the juvenile court has proven unsuccessful in rehabilitating. As a result, the question of whether juveniles should be punished or protected remains a continuing source of debate. Although it is unlikely that this basic issue will be resolved, the manner in which it is addressed will have long-term implications—not only for young offenders themselves, but more important, for the collective future of our entire society.

---

*LEARNING GOALS*

*Do you know:*

- *How children were treated historically in comparison to adults?*
- *Why houses of refuge and reform schools were established?*
- *How industrialization, immigration, and urbanization influenced the child-saving movement?*
- *When and where the first juvenile court was created?*
- *The definition of* parens patriae *and how it relates to the original intention of the juvenile court?*
- *Why procedures are more informal in juvenile than adult court?*

While we are now accustomed to thinking of children as different from adults, that was not always how young people were treated. Throughout medieval society, the idea of childhood simply did not exist.[2] In fact, it has only been within relatively recent history that children have clearly been distinguished from grown-ups. Previously, young people were considered virtually "miniature adults"—they were dressed like adults, employed in the same backbreaking work, and subject to similar (or in some cases, even more severe) punishments for misbehavior. For example, in colonial New England, children could receive the death penalty for cursing (or "smiting") their natural father or mother.[3]

In English common law, a child became an adult at the *age of 7*, when he could supposedly make his own living in the economy of England at the time. Before the advent of child labor laws, however, making a living often exposed children to long hours of heavy manual labor and monotonous routine for meager wages. During the Industrial Revolution, sweatshops, mines, and factories were notorious for their exploitation of youngsters. Not only were children exposed to dangers at work, but they were also expected to be subservient to anyone in authority, with severe consequences for the unruly. As early as 1660, colonial law gave magistrates the power to punish disobedient or disorderly children through "corporal punishment, by whipping or otherwise, . . . not exceeding ten stripes for one offense."[4]

One 12-year-old apprentice in 1665 "was so mistreated by his master that he died of the beatings he received."[5] Schoolteachers were likewise authorized to administer corporal punishment indiscriminately. In a school with 250 pupils, an observer as late as 1837 witnessed "an average of over 65 floggings a day."[6] And since children were considered the property of their parents, there was virtually no concept of child abuse. Clearly, the legal system favored *adults*, and the courts generally upheld the reasonableness of parental action in almost all cases.[7] As we saw in earlier chapters, violators who were not physically punished were jailed side by side with adult criminals. In fact, it is a sad commentary on the plight of children to note that the Society for the Prevention of Cruelty to Animals was established in 1824—exactly 50 years *before* creation of the Society for the Prevention of Cruelty to Children in 1874.[8]

---

[2]Philippe Aires, *Centuries of Childhood: A Social History of Family Life* (New York: Alfred A. Knopf, 1962), p. 128.

[3]Wiley B. Sanders, ed., *Juvenile Offenders for a Thousand Years* (Chapel Hill, NC: University of North Carolina Press, 1970), p. 46.

[4]Joseph M. Hawes, *Children in Urban Society: Juvenile Delinquency in Nineteenth Century America* (New York: Oxford University Press, 1971), p. 41.

[5]Paul H. Hahn, *The Juvenile Offender and the Law*, Third Edition (Cincinnati, OH: Anderson Publishing Company, 1984), p. 3.

[6]Joan Newman and Graeme Newman, "Crime and Punishment in the Schooling Process: A Historical Analysis," in Keith Baker and Robert J. Rubel, eds., *Violence and Crime in the Schools* (Lexington, MA: D.C. Heath, 1980), p. 11, citing observations of Horace Mann.

[7]See Francis Barry McCarthy and James G. Carr, *Juvenile Law and Its Processes* (Indianapolis, IN: Bobbs-Merrill, 1980), pp. 18–20.

[8]Vernon Fox, *Correctional Institutions* (Englewood Cliffs, NJ: Prentice Hall, 1983), p. 200.

## Houses of Refuge and Reform Schools

By the nineteenth century, society began to intervene in the lives of errant children whose families either could not or would not adequately care for them. Early institutions for children were voluntary and privately operated, often run by religious or charitable organizations. In these settings, little distinction was made between children who presented behavioral problems and those who were confined for nothing over which they had any control, such as being orphaned or abandoned. The term "juvenile delinquent" was virtually unknown, since families were still primarily responsible for disciplining misconduct.[9]

Beginning with the New York City *House of Refuge* established in 1825, similar public institutions began to spread throughout the country. As the name implies, houses of refuge were developed for the protection of children who were destitute, abandoned, neglected, or orphaned. Conditions were not, however, as benevolent as the term "refuge" might indicate. In exchange for food, clothing, and shelter, residents were expected to work hard, and strict compliance with institutional regulations was physically enforced: "For example, there is ample evidence of the use of solitary confinement, whipping and other forms of corporal punishment. The labor system within the houses of refuge was managed by outside contractors who sometimes abused the children. . . . [Work] . . . was mostly menial in nature. Violence was commonplace . . ."[10]

Not long thereafter, Massachusetts opened the first public *reform school* for delinquent boys in the mid-1840s. But at this time, there were no juvenile courts, so youthful offenders were sent to such reformatories to avoid a convic-

In an effort to build self-confidence and discipline, military drill teams were an important part of early juvenile reformatories. Courtesy of Anthony W. Zumpetta.

[9]Robert M. Mennell, "Attitudes and Policies toward Juvenile Delinquency in the United States: A Historiographical Review," in Michael Tonry and Norval Morris, eds., *Crime and Justice: An Annual Review of Research* (Chicago: University of Chicago Press, 1983), p. 198.

[10]Barry Krisberg, "The Evolution of the Juvenile Justice System," in John J. Sullivan and Joseph L. Victor, *Criminal Justice 92/93* (Guilford, CT: Dushkin Publishing Group, 1992), p. 152.

tion that would otherwise result in a sentence to be served in an adult prison. This procedure led to litigation on the part of aggrieved parents when children were informally sent to a juvenile institution without having been officially convicted. Although houses of refuge and reform schools provided alternatives to incarceration with adults, the treatment of boys and girls confined there remained harsh. Children were subjected to strict discipline, long hours of work, and severe punishments.

Many of these institutions were actually designed more for industrial production than for nurturing or rehabilitation, and their exploitation of child labor was shameful.[11] At one point, disenchantment with existing institutions was so great that it stimulated the practice of *placing-out* children—arranging for their transportation to rural farming communities or western ranches: "Child-saving societies employed agents to take groups of delinquent or vagrant children west by train. The children were then parceled out in towns along the way."[12] In this way, the brutalities of reform school life could be avoided by sending youngsters to the countryside for service in agriculture.

## The Child-Saving Movement

Toward the end of the nineteenth century, there was little doubt that conditions cried desperately for improvement. By this time, *industrialization* was taking hold. Factories were rapidly beginning to replace agriculture as the country's economic base. Combined with virtually unrestricted *immigration*, cities were attracting vast numbers of foreigners as well as farmers to the promise of a better life in urban factories. But the life they found waiting for them was hardly an improvement.

As cities expanded, *urbanization* required accommodating a continuous influx of people, many of whom did not share the same customs or even speak the same language. Thus, it is not surprising that urban areas encountered problems of a variety and magnitude unknown in the past. Crime, poverty, overcrowding, and unemployment escalated dramatically. But perhaps more important, these trends toward industrialization, immigration, and urbanization threatened what had become well-entrenched standards of the "American way of life," firmly rooted in middle-class, rural values.[13]

No longer were many of America's youth able to enjoy the advantages of the "wholesome atmosphere" of rural tranquility—where hard work, fresh air, and an uncomplicated lifestyle could shape personal development in a positive manner. Rather, they were exposed to the "contaminants" of urban living, under the guidance of parents faced with cultural barriers that made mere survival difficult, much less ability to provide proper direction and middle-class socialization for their children.

[11]See, for example, Steven L. Schlossman, *Love and the American Delinquent* (Chicago: University of Chicago Press, 1977), pp. 113–23.

[12]Clifford E. Simonsen, *Juvenile Justice in America,* Third Edition (New York: Macmillan, 1991), p. 22.

[13]Anthony M. Platt, *The Child Savers: The Invention of Delinquency* (Chicago: University of Chicago Press, 1969), pp. 36–43.

Under such conditions, it became increasingly apparent that the economic, social, and physical impact of life in crowded ghettos of urban immigrants was creating a negative influence on childhood development. Intervention into the lives of such economically and culturally deprived children was therefore justified as essential to "rescue" them from a destiny of doom, which became known as *child-saving:* "Child-saving . . . was . . . an affirmation of faith in traditional institutions. Parental authority, home education, rural life, and the independence of the family . . . were emphasized because they seemed threatened at this time by urbanism and industrialism."[14]

In retrospect, some have criticized the motives of the child-saving social reformers as a hostile reaction against urban development that was largely based on self-serving rather than child-saving interests. But at the time, child-savers were cast as righteous campaigners responding to the immorality that was viewed as the cause of delinquency among immigrant children. Nor could their timing have been better.

Beyond the social disruptions occurring in urban America, child-saving emerged at a time when the role of women was expanding and long-held beliefs about the nature of criminality were changing. As women began to demand rights and seek careers outside the home, intervention into the welfare of children became an acceptable employment or public service option for them. Moreover, new theories of criminology provided fresh optimism for changing behavior. In contrast to the *classical* emphasis on free will and determinism, the newly emerging *positive* school of thought provided hope that behavior is amenable to change. And who better to begin with than the youngest?

## Origin of the Juvenile Court

As a consequence of these widespread social influences supporting a different approach to wayward children, the state of Illinois passed legislation in 1895 and 1897 establishing a separate juvenile court. Although these initial efforts were declared unconstitutional, the rising political influence of women resurrected the effort. The Cook County (Chicago) Women's Clubs mobilized to provide the driving force that motivated the Chicago Bar Association to draft a law that finally passed constitutional scrutiny—establishing the first *juvenile court* in Chicago in 1899. Entitled "An Act to Regulate the Treatment and Control of Dependent, Neglected, and Delinquent Children," it was enthusiastically endorsed.[15]

The title of the legislation reveals the spirit behind it. Focusing on *dependency* and *neglect* as well as *delinquency*, reformers envisioned truly "rescuing" the child from a host of undesirable conditions. To accomplish this, the law provided:

"(1) for the separate hearing of children's cases in a court having chancery rather than criminal jurisdiction;

(2) for the detention of children apart from adult offenders; and

[14]Ibid., p. 98.
[15]Helen Rankin Jeter, *The Chicago Juvenile Court* (Washington, DC: U.S. Government Printing Office, 1922), p. 5.

(3)  for a [juvenile] probation system."[16]

Separate detention and probation had already existed in some locations, and the concept of chancery (i.e., civil) jurisdiction had also been established previously.[17] But whereas the individual elements of the Illinois legislation may not have been so revolutionary, the impact of their combined effect has been felt throughout the country—resulting in the development of a distinct *juvenile justice system* in virtually every state in the United States.

**The Power of *Parens Patriae*.**   To achieve its wide-ranging mission, the new juvenile courts emphasized an *individualized approach* to justice. A prominent objective of the court was to develop a diagnosis and personalized treatment plan designed to meet each child's specific needs. The priority was therefore to determine the needs of the child rather than to decide "guilt" or "innocence."

In its efforts to protect rather than prosecute, the court relies on the authority of *parens patriae*—a Latin term that refers to the king as the ultimate parent (*parens*) over all subjects in the country (*patriae*).[18] In this country the concept of *parens patriae* derived from the state's power to sever children from their pauper parents under the Poor Laws. With no welfare support available in the nineteenth century, the only alternative for indigents was refuge in the poor houses. Since that was obviously not a healthy atmosphere in which to raise children, the state could remove children from indigent families and place them out as apprentices.

With the power of *parens patriae,* the state could assume parental authority over a juvenile (similar to the concept of *in loco parentis,* which enables teachers to act temporarily "in the place of parents" while a child is in school). Under *parens patriae,* the juvenile court is invested with responsibility for and authority over the welfare of its clients. In fact, the notion that parental perrogatives can be superseded by the state in the interest of the child's welfare was well entrenched by the time the juvenile court was created. As the Pennsylvania Supreme Court noted in an 1838 case challenging that power: "The right of parental control is a natural, but not an unalienable one. . . . [M]ay not the natural parents, when unequal to the task of education, or unworthy of it, be superseded by the *parens patriae,* or common guardian of the community?"[19]

The burden of this premise clearly fell heavily on the lower classes, whose poverty illustrated an incapacity to provide proper direction for their offspring. Moreover, the jurisdiction of the juvenile court extended well beyond offenses that would be considered criminal if committed by an adult—into such nebulous

[16]Ibid., p. 5.

[17]In fact, it has been argued that the act itself represented no significant innovations. See Sanford J. Fox, "Juvenile Justice Reform: An Historical Perspective," *Stanford Law Review,* Vol. 22 (June 1970), p. 1187.

[18]Precedent for the doctrine of *parens patriae* was set in the Napoleonic Decree of 1811, indicating that the state was responsible for the welfare of its children. In the United States it can be traced back to our English heritage through the crown's power to maintain the feudal structure by intervening in guardianship problems to maintain the existing social structure. See Douglas R. Rendlemen, "Parens Patriae: From Chancery to the Juvenile Court," in Frederic L. Faust and Paul J. Brantingham, eds., *Juvenile Justice Philosophy* (St. Paul, MN: West Publishing Company, 1974), pp. 74–75.

[19]*Ex parte Crouse,* 4 Whart. 9 (Pa, 1838).

areas as truancy, begging, and incorrigibility. In many cases, the behaviors targeted were "most directly relevant to the children of lower class migrant and immigrant families."[20] As a result, the conduct of youth need not be considered particularly serious to justify juvenile court processing. In the name of *parens patriae*, the power of the state assumed priority over the rights of the parents, and the broad but vague authority of the juvenile court far exceeded its adult counterpart.

**Procedural Informality.** According to this philosophy, the juvenile court did not require an adversarial model of justice, wherein the defendant competes against the prosecution. To the contrary, juvenile court was designed to be the defendant's *advocate* rather than *adversary*. Like a reasonable and knowledgeable parent, the court's intent was to serve the "best interests" of the child.

Underlying this concept is the assumption of youthful dependency and vulnerability, which entitles children to certain privileges and protections not afforded to adults. But at the same time, it restricts the child from legal safeguards provided in the adult criminal justice system. According to this view, the state—serving in the parental role—is in the best position to determine what treatment is needed to guide the child back on a proper path. The basic philosophy is that "erring children should be protected and rehabilitated rather than subjected to the harshness of the criminal system."[21]

Much of the justification for this diversion from the adversarial model of justice is based on the desire to *prevent stigmatizing* the child and to *provide flexibility* in prescribing treatment. Removed from a punishment orientation, the court was committed to avoiding the labeling of children as "criminal." In exchange, less formal procedures would be employed to determine the facts of the case. Since the ultimate outcome was to benefit the child, there would be no need for the traditional conflict between prosecutor and defense. It was the well-being of the child that was to be served, uninhibited by procedural formalities.

In this frame of reference, rigid due process considerations would be both cumbersome and unnecessary. The court would serve as "friend and moral guardian," personalizing the dispensation of justice according to individual needs.[22] Distinctions between the adult and juvenile justice systems were reflected not only in procedure, but in terminologies as well:

- There would be no criminal complaint, but merely a "petition."
- "Summons" would replace warrants.
- "Hearings" would occur instead of trials.
- No one would be convicted of a crime, but rather, found to be "involved" in a delinquent act.
- "Disposition" would replace sentencing.
- "Aftercare" would serve the function of adult parole.

---

[20]Anthony M. Platt, "The Rise of the Child-Saving Movement," in Paul Lerman, ed., *Delinquency and Social Policy* (New York: Praeger, 1970), p. 18.

[21]Julian Mack, "The Juvenile Court," *Harvard Law Review*, Vol. 23 (1909), p. 104.

[22]Schlossman, p. 126.

(See Figure 13.1 for a summary of the terminology differences between the adult and juvenile systems.)

## Prevention and Treatment

Under this unique approach, it was not the specific offense bringing the child to the attention of juvenile court that was of primary concern, but rather, the underlying circumstances. Since the individual's behavior was seen as the product of preexisting causes, the court's mission was directed toward discovering and altering what was actually causing misconduct. But its potential to do so was limited unless intervention occurred early in the young person's development.

Thus, an important component of the juvenile court related to the ability to identify "predelinquent" children and impose upon them treatment designed to "correct their wayward tendencies."[23] It was for this reason that the court's mandate included a wide variety of deviant behaviors directed toward "children who occupy the debatable ground between criminality and innocence."[24] The rationale for such intervention was largely based on the desire to prevent more serious infractions in the future.

The court's preventive function fit well with the medical model—both emphasize "early identification, diagnosis, prescription of treatment, implementation of therapy, and cure or rehabilitation under 'aftercare' supervision."[25] Based on circumstances surrounding the child's behavior, the court would determine the source of the problem and develop an individualized treatment plan.

| Criminal Justice System | Juvenile Justice System |
| --- | --- |
| Crime | Delinquent act |
| Arrest | Take into custody |
| Warrant | Summons |
| Criminal complaint/indictment | Petition |
| Plea bargain | Adjustment |
| Trial | Hearing (or adjudication) |
| Guilty verdict | Adjudicated delinquent |
| Convicted | Found involved |
| Sentencing | Disposition |
| Incarceration | Commitment |
| Jail | Detention center |
| Prison | Training school |
| Inmate | Resident |
| Parole | Aftercare |

**Figure 13.1**  Contrasting terminologies.

[23]J. Lawrence Schultz, "The Cycle of Juvenile Court History," *Crime and Delinquency*, Vol. 19, No. 4 (October 1973), p. 460.
[24]Platt, p. 107, quoting from the Illinois Board of Public Charities, *Sixth Biennial Reports* (Springfield, IL: H.W. Rokker, 1880), p. 104.
[25]Faust and Brantingham, p. 147.

Treatment could be carried out either in the community (through probation or referral to community services), or within a juvenile correctional institution. Once a juvenile is confined to an institution, it makes little difference that the intent was for treatment. Nevertheless, the court's objective was "not so much to punish as to reform, not to degrade but to uplift, not to crush but to develop. . . ."[26] Equally glowing pictures were painted of the juvenile court's advantages over its adult counterpart: "The old courts relied upon the learning of lawyers; the new courts depend more upon psychiatrists and social workers. . . . Justice in the old courts was based on legal science; in the new courts it is based on social engineering."[27]

With its innovative emphasis on prevention and diagnosis, its noncriminal basis in the doctrine of *parens patriae,* and its ability to deviate from procedural formality, the juvenile court held out promising hope—for personalizing the justice process and making a substantial impact on the delinquency problem. Unfortunately, its promise did not measure up in practice.

## ❖ JUVENILE JUSTICE TRANSFORMATION

As the National Commission on Criminal Justice Standards and Goals observed by the early 1970s, "today's juvenile court personnel have shed the naive expectations of early reformers."[28] After more than half a century of experimentation, the juvenile court had neither curtailed the growth of juvenile crime nor fulfilled its commitment to protect rather than punish its clients. In fact, it was becoming all too apparent that in juvenile court, the child actually receives "the worst of both worlds," getting "neither the protections accorded to adults nor the solicitous care and regenerative treatment postulated for children."[29]

As described in earlier chapters, the 1960s represented an era of increasing litigation, and the juvenile justice system was not overlooked. The "first revolution" in juvenile justice which occurred at the turn of the century resulted in a new children's court with expansive powers. In contrast, the "second revolution" some 60 years later was directed toward exactly the opposite—reducing the intrusion of the court into children's lives.[30] Spearheaded by the *due process movement,* the power and intervention of the court were restricted, based on the notion that rights should not be sacrificed in the name of "rehabilitation."

---

[26]Mack, "The Juvenile Court," p. 104.
[27]Bernard Flexner, Reuben Oppenheimer, and Katharine F. Lenroot, *The Child, the Family, and the Court: A Study of the Administration of Justice in the Field of Domestic Relations* (Washington, DC: U.S. Government Printing Office, 1939), p. 66, citing the Children's Bureau of the U.S. Department of Labor.
[28]National Commission on Criminal Justice Standards and Goals, *Courts* (Washington, DC: U.S. Government Printing Office, 1973), p. 289.
[29]*Kent v. United States,* 383 U.S. 541, 86 S. Ct. 1045, 16 L.Ed.2d 84 (1966).
[30]Krisberg, p. 154.

## Due Process Considerations

As a result of growing concerns over the arbitrary manner in which cases were being handled, a number of significant decisions regulating juvenile court practices have been handed down by the Supreme Court. These changes have generally brought juvenile courts more in line with procedures used in the adult system. But as we will see in the landmark cases highlighted below, they have not fully transformed the juvenile court into a miniature version of adult criminal courts. However, like the sentencing guidelines, objective classification procedures, and parole-decision making models addressed earlier, they have introduced greater *structure* into what was previously a highly discretionary process.

Among the first of the juvenile court practices to be challenged before the Supreme Court was the transfer of juvenile cases to criminal court. Prior to the *Kent v. U.S.* decision, juvenile court judges had virtually unlimited discretion in determining whether or not to *waive jurisdiction*. From the juvenile's point of view, it would be advantageous to be transferred to adult court if the offense were significant enough to justify some type of confinement but not so serious that a lengthy prison term could be expected. In other words, both the *least* and the *most* serious offenders were better off under the jurisdiction of the juvenile court, but not those in-between the two extremes:

- For very minor violations (particularly on the part of first-time offenders), the delinquent could expect to be dealt with relatively leniently in juvenile court.
- For somewhat more serious offenses, adult court would probably be preferable, since confinement under the juvenile justice system could last for several years—until the age of majority—for a crime that might well receive a much shorter sentence in adult court.
- For extremely serious crimes (such as murder, rape, or robbery), the offender would probably be better advised to remain under the jurisdiction of the juvenile court rather than face the lengthy prison terms that could be imposed in adult court for such offenses.

***Kent v. U.S.*** Clearly, Morris Kent's case fit into the last category—as a 16-year-old charged with housebreaking, robbery, and rape, under the juvenile court, he faced a maximum incarceration of five years (until reaching the age of 21). In contrast, the maximum that could be levied for his crimes in adult court at that time was the death penalty. The juvenile court waived jurisdiction and he was tried in the criminal justice system. Found guilty on six counts of housebreaking and robbery,[31] he was sentenced to a total of 30 to 90 years in prison.

While the discrepancy in possible sentences no doubt motivated his appeal, it was not this issue that was raised, but rather, the constitutionality of his transfer from juvenile to adult court. Although his attorney had petitioned the court to obtain access to the social history file that was used in considering the waiver, the judge transferred the case without making reference to the motion, without indicating any reasons, and without conferring with the defendant, his parents, or his counsel.

On appeal, however, the Supreme Court in 1966 held that the juvenile court's duty "to function in a 'parental' relationship is not an invitation to procedural arbitrariness," noting that the waiver decision was "as important . . . as the difference between five years' confinement and a death sentence."[32] As a result of this ruling, juveniles being considered for transfer to criminal court are now *entitled to a hearing* (including access by counsel to social records and probation reports) and to a *statement of reasons* for the juvenile court's decision.

***In Re Gault.*** A number of questions regarding juvenile court procedures that still remained unanswered following the Kent decision were to be addressed one year later in the case of *In Re Gault*.[33] Gerald Gault was not in the same category as Morris Kent. In fact, he was among those juveniles for whom it would have been more advantageous to be processed as an adult in terms of the severity of the sentence that could be imposed. At the age of 15, Gault was charged with making lewd phone calls to a neighbor and committed as a delinquent to the state industrial school "for the period of his minority [which at the time was 21] unless sooner discharged by due process of law." Thus, he was facing *up to six years* of confinement. But if he were an adult, the penalty in criminal code for his offense was a $5 to $50 fine or incarceration for *no more than two months*.

Moreover, when Gault was first taken into custody, his parents were not advised of his arrest and did not receive a copy of the petition. At the juvenile court hearing, no sworn testimony was taken and the complainant did not appear in person to testify. Nor was Gault advised of the right to counsel or the right to remain silent. On appeal to the Supreme Court, a momentous decision regarding the constitutional rights of juveniles was handed down. Specifically, the court ruled that:

- Juveniles are entitled to a *notice of the charges* against them.
- In proceedings that may result in "commitment to an institution," notification must be provided of the *right to counsel,* with counsel appointed if the child or parents are unable to afford such services.

[31]Interestingly, Kent was found "not guilty by reason of insanity" on the rape charge.
[32]*Kent v. United States.*
[33]A number of juvenile appellate cases differ in format from adult appeals, being cited as "*In Re*" rather than the traditional *Name v. Name* (or jurisdiction). This is a result of the fact that a number of states have not provided an appellate process for juvenile court cases. An appeal in such states therefore must be filed as a writ of *habeas corpus* rather than through the traditional appellate route.

- Juveniles have the *right to remain silent.*
- In the absence of a valid confession, a determination of delinquency and commitment to a state institution cannot be made without *sworn testimony,* subject to the opportunity for *cross examination.*[34]

***In Re Winship.*** As far-reaching as it was, though, the Gault decision did not address the issue of differing standards of proof prevailing between juvenile and adult courts. But in the 1970 *In Re Winship* case, this became the focus of Supreme Court review. Samuel Winship was a 12-year-old who had been charged with entering a locker and stealing $112 from a woman's purse. Upon a finding of delinquency, he had been placed in a training school for an initial period of 18 months, subject to annual extensions until his eighteenth birthday.

Like other delinquents adjudicated in juvenile court, the judge's decision in the Winship case was based on a lower standard of proof—*preponderance of evidence*—than that used in the adult system—*beyond a reasonable doubt.* But the Supreme Court held that "the same considerations which demand extreme caution in factfinding to protect the innocent adult apply as well to the innocent child." In upholding Winship's appeal, the court ruled that when a 12-year-old child is rendered "liable to confinement for as long a six years, as a matter of due process . . . the case against him must be proved beyond a reasonable doubt."[35]

***Due Process Impact.*** The Supreme Court has not, however, given notice that it intends to make blanket application of constitutional safeguards to delinquency cases. For example, in the case of *McKeiver v. Pennsylvania,* the right of juveniles to a jury trial was rejected. In that ruling, the court declared that its desire was *not* to remake juvenile proceedings into a full adversary process,[36] thereby indicating that it hopes to preserve at least some of the unique features of the juvenile court. Although this case made it clear that juries are *not required* in the juvenile justice system, some states do permit their use.

Juvenile courts still retain considerable discretion in comparison to the adult system. But it is clear that the rationale of individuality, informality, and interests of the child will no longer protect them from the scrutiny of appellate review. Some still hold out hope that, ideally, the court could "guarantee the child's legal rights through procedural safeguards" without losing "the individualized treatment approach."[37] But over the years, it has become increasingly clear that balancing constitutional rights with individual needs is at best a difficult endeavor; at worst, a hopeless dream.

[34]*In Re Gault,* 387 U.S. 1, 87 S. Ct. 1428, 18 L.Ed.2d 527 (1967).
[35]*In Re Winship,* 397 U.S. 358, 90 S. Ct. 1068, 25 L.Ed.2d 368 (1970).
[36]*McKeiver v. Pennsylvania,* 403 U.S. 528, 91 S. Ct. 1976, 29 L. Ed. 2d 647 (1971).
[37]Robert C. Trojanowicz, *Juvenile Delinquency: Concepts and Control* (Englewood Cliffs, NJ: Prentice-Hall, 1973), p. 168. For a description of how the juvenile court has been altered in the wake of Supreme Court decisions of the 1960s, see William E. MacFaden, "Changing Concepts of Juvenile Justice," *Crime and Delinquency,* Vol. 17, No. 2 (April 1971), pp. 131–41.

LEARNING GOALS

*Do you know:*

- *How delinquents differ from status offenders?*
- *What the relationship is between age and the commission of violent crimes?*

## Status Offenders and Delinquents

Much of the difficulty experienced by juvenile courts relates to the widespread array of behaviors that can bring a child into the justice system. Unlike adult criminality, which involves violation of criminal codes, the nature of juvenile delinquency is not prescribed as clearly. Delinquency in the 1899 Illinois legislation was narrowly defined to encompass only those acts that would be considered "criminal" if committed by an adult—what we would officially term *delinquency* today.

But just two years later, the law was amended to include what we now know as *status offenses*—behavior that is illegal only for those under the age of majority. At that time, these offenses ranged from incorrigibility to frequenting a house of ill fame or patronizing gambling establishments. Six years afterward, the definition was broadened again to include such ambiguous behavior as associating with thieves, vicious, or immoral persons; growing up in idleness or crime; patronizing a public poolroom; wandering the streets at night; using vile, obscene, vulgar, profane, or indecent language in public; or displaying indecent or lascivious conduct.[38]

Clearly, concern was not only about violations endangering public safety, but also about far less serious activities. Some 50 years following these amendments, an analysis revealed that truancy, incorrigibility, being beyond parental control, and growing up in idleness or crime continued to be frequently cited status offenses.[39] As recently as 1990, more than 127,000 people under the age of 18 were arrested for running away from home, and almost 60,000 for curfew and loitering law violations.[40]

That does not, however, mean that juvenile offenders are not frequently engaged in serious criminal activities. Quite the contrary, teenagers and young adults are responsible for a disproportionate share of such offenses. Those under 18 years of age represented over 16% of the arrests in 1990 for violent personal crimes. If the age limit is expanded to those under 21, the figure doubles to almost 31%. By 25, it expands to over 47%.[41] In other words, young people under the age of twenty-five account for almost half of the arrests for violent crimes. When arrests for *all* crime index offenses are taken into account, the picture becomes even worse: 28% are under 18; 43% are under 21, and almost 57% are under 25 years of age (see Figure 13.2).

[38]Vaughan Stapleton and Lee E. Teitelbaum, *In Defense of Youth* (New York: Russell Sage Foundation, 1972), p. 22.
[39]Frederick Sussman, *Law of Juvenile Delinquency* (New York: Oceana, 1959), p. 21.
[40]Federal Bureau of Investigation, *Uniform Crime Reports for the United States* (Washington, DC: U.S. Government Printing Office, 1991), p. 182.
[41]Ibid., p. 190.

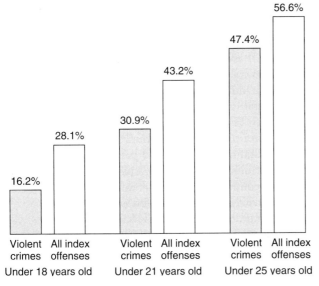

**Figure 13.2** 1990 arrests for violent crimes and crime index offenses by age. *Note:* "Violent crimes" include murder, forcible rape, robbery, and aggravated assault. "All index offenses" include violent crimes, as well as burglary, larceny-theft, motor vehicle theft, and arson. *Source:* Federal Bureau of Investigation, *Crime in the United States: Uniform Crime Reports* (Washington, DC: U.S. Government Printing Office, 1991), p. 190.

Worse yet, in almost all categories of serious crime, arrests of those *under* 18 years of age are increasing at a faster pace than for the over-18 group.[42] There may be some argument that young people's lack of criminal sophistication may make them more susceptible to apprehension. In addition, the fact that juveniles are more likely than adults to commit crime in groups also makes them more vulnerable to arrest. Nevertheless, it appears that the involvement of juveniles in relatively serious offenses has certainly not declined since implementation of the "preventive" approach associated with the creation of a separate juvenile justice system.

---

*LEARNING GOALS*

*Do you know:*

• *What factors are taken into account in deciding whether to transfer a juvenile to adult court?*
• *How juveniles are dealt with in adult court?*
• *What categories of cases fall within the juvenile court's jurisdiction?*

---

## Juveniles in Adult Court

Needless to say, it was not these types of extremely serious offenses that reformers had in mind when the first juvenile court was created in 1899. As one frustrated police officer has observed, "The law says a kid should be treated differently because he can be rehabilitated, but they weren't robbing, killing, and

---

[42]Among those under 18, there were higher percentage increases in arrests between 1989 and 1990 for every category of index offenses except burglary, which decreased. But even here, the decrease was less than that for those over 18. *Uniform Crime Reports,* p. 182.

raping when kiddie court was established."[43] In most states, the juvenile court's jurisdiction extends only until the age of 18.[44] But as we have seen from the data above, that does not by any means exclude the possibility that youngsters with very serious charges can come before the court.

Obviously, the public has become increasingly concerned about the growing involvement of teenagers in violent crime. Although relatively few in number, these hardcore offenders make up a disproportionate share of juvenile crime. Many of them have already been processed through juvenile court for earlier offenses, often at quite young ages, and continue their criminal patterns as adults: "Not only do we know that a small group of young males is responsible for most violent crime by juveniles; we also know that these offenders start early and finish late. Studies have demonstrated that a substantial proportion of the violent few continued to commit crimes as adults and, of those who did, most had been arrested for the first time at the age of twelve or even younger."[45]

More punitive social attitudes are creating demands that experienced juvenile offenders, like adult criminals, be held responsible for their actions and pay their "just deserts." While the juvenile justice system has not dismantled the medical model to the same extent as in the adult system, there is little doubt that the justice model has had an impact here as well.

For example, there has been a growing trend in recent years toward transferring juveniles accused of serious offenses to adult court. In some cases, this is accomplished by discretionary *waiver*, through which the juvenile court relinquishes its jurisdiction. But a number of states now automatically exclude certain violent offenses from being heard in juvenile court. In others, transfer to adult court is mandated when a young offender has already been adjudicated a specified number of times in juvenile court or has had a prior conviction in adult court. In cases where waiver is a discretionary decision, the factors generally taken into account include the juvenile's *age*, nature of the *offense*, and considerations related to both *rehabilitative prospects* and *public protection*.[46]

Because of variations in practices, it is difficult to determine exactly how many cases are actually being transferred to criminal courts, although it is estimated to be a very small proportion of the total juvenile court workload. One study, for instance, found that even among those charged with violent crimes, only 5% of the cases where formal action was taken involved transfer to adult court.[47] Surprisingly, it appears that most of the juveniles referred to criminal court are charged with property offenses. However, those who are charged with violent crimes or who have serious prior offense histories are more likely to be transferred.[48]

---

[43]Cited in Charles E. Silberman, *Criminal Violence, Criminal Justice* (New York: Vintage Books, 1978), p. 421.

[44]*Report to the Nation on Crime and Justice,* Second Edition (Washington, DC: U.S. Department of Justice, 1988), p. 79. In 10 states, it is lower (16 or 17) and in Wyoming, it is higher (19).

[45]Rita Kramer, *At A Tender Age: Violent Youth and Juvenile Justice* (New York: Henry Holt and Company, 1988), p. 18.

[46]See Hahn, pp. 179–80.

[47]Verne L. Speirs, "The Juvenile Court's Response to Violent Crime," *Office of Juvenile Justice and Delinquency Prevention Update on Statistics* (Washington, DC: U.S. Department of Justice, 1989), p. 4.

[48]*Report to the Nation,* p. 79.

What may be of even greater surprise to those advocating transfers in an effort to "toughen up" on young offenders is that juveniles tried as adults do *not* tend to get lengthy sentences. Although more than 90% are convicted, the majority are not sentenced to confinement at all, but rather, receive probation or fines.[49] This is usually because juveniles are viewed in criminal court as "first offenders," regardless of their prior juvenile court history, and the sentencing judge may also take age into consideration as a mitigating factor.

But just as they are more likely to be transferred into the adult system, juveniles convicted of *serious violent crimes* in adult court also appear to be more likely to be institutionalized. In one study, 63% of such offenders were sentenced to prison, for an average of 6.8 years.[50] In most states, those sentenced to confinement in adult court serve their time in adult correctional institutions. A few states restrict their confinement to juvenile facilities until the age of majority is reached, at which time they are transferred to an adult institution for the remainder of their sentence.

## Juvenile Court Jurisdiction

Undoubtedly, it is the criminal involvement of hard-core, chronic delinquents that captures media headlines and thereby creates a distorted perception of the "typical" juvenile lawbreaker. But although they are responsible for a disproportionate share of violations (particularly the more serious offenses), habitual violent juveniles do not by any means represent the bulk of clients coming to the attention of juvenile courts.

Until one reaches the age of majority, juvenile courts generally have jurisdiction over three basic types of cases:

1. *Delinquency:* offense committed by someone under the age of majority that would otherwise be classified as a crime if committed by an adult.
2. *Status Offense:* offense that is illegal only for those under the age of majority (e.g., underage drinking, truancy, running away from home, etc.). Those exhibiting "ungovernable," "incorrigible," or "uncontrollable" behavior can also be included. A number of states have adopted a separate classification for status offenders to more clearly distinguish them from delinquents—for example, CHINS (children in need of supervison), PINS (persons in need of supervision), or MINS (minors in need of supervision).
3. *Dependency, Neglect or Abuse:* situations in which the child is either without means of support (i.e., dependency) or is being neglected or abused. In some jurisdictions, these matters are handled by agencies outside the juvenile court, until such point that a change in legal guardianship is necessary.

As Figure 13.3 indicates, most referrals to juvenile court are for *property crimes* (46%, primarily larceny or burglary), followed by *public order offenses*

[49]Ibid. See also David Reed, *Needed: Serious Solutions for Serious Juvenile Crime* (Chicago: Chicago Law Enforcement Study Group, 1983), and Elizabeth T. Schack and Hermine Nessen, *The Experiment That Failed: The New York Juvenile Offender Law—A Study Report* (New York: Citizen's Committee for Children of New York, 1984).

[50]*Report to the Nation*, p. 79.

| | | |
|---|---|---|
| 11% | *Crimes against persons* | |
| | Criminal homicide | 1% |
| | Forcible rape | 2 |
| | Robbery | 17 |
| | Aggravated assault | 20 |
| | Simple assault | 59 |
| | | 100% |
| 46% | *Crimes against property* | |
| | Burglary | 25% |
| | Larceny | 47% |
| | Motor vehicle theft | 5 |
| | Arson | 1 |
| | Vandalism and trespassing | 19 |
| | Stolen property offenses | 3 |
| | | 100% |
| 5% | *Drug offenses* | 100% |
| 21% | *Offenses against public order* | |
| | Weapons offenses | 6% |
| | Sex offenses | 6 |
| | Drunkeness and disorderly conduct | 23 |
| | Contempt, probation, and parole violations | 21 |
| | Other | 44 |
| | | 100% |
| 17% | *Status offenses* | |
| | Running away | 28% |
| | Truancy and curfew violations | 21 |
| | Ungovernability | 28 |
| | Liquor violations | 23 |
| | | 100% |
| 100% | *Total all offenses* | |

**Figure 13.3** Reasons for referrals to juvenile courts. *Note:* Percents may not add to 100 because of rounding. *Source: Report to the Nation on Crime and Justice,* Second Edition (Washington, DC: U.S. Department of Justice, 1988), p. 78.

(21%) and *status offenses* (17%, primarily running away or ungovernability). Only 11% of juvenile court referrals concerned *violent crimes,* and simple assault was by far the most frequent offense in this category. Although violent juvenile crime remains a concern, these figures indicate that the bulk of cases appearing in juvenile courts are considerably less serious. But public expectations of the juvenile court far exceed its capacity to respond, as reflected in the wide array of responsibilities that many of these judicial agencies must undertake: "The juvenile court operates foster homes, detention facilities, aftercare programs and welfare services for children; handles traffic offenses involving juveniles; administers child welfare funds; and serves as a disciplinary officer for the schools and those parents who cannot cope with the behavioral problems of their children."[51]

Despite the introduction of greater due process procedures resulting from the court cases discussed previously, the juvenile court still places considerably more emphasis on a rehabilitative philosophy than criminal courts. Thus, for many years there was debate over whether juvenile court judges should be *social*

[51]Richard W. Kobetz and Betty B. Bosarge, *Juvenile Justice Administration* (Gaithersburg, MD: International Association of Chiefs of Police, 1973), p. 246.

workers or *psychologists* who learn the law, or whether they should be *lawyers* who learn treatment techniques. In most many cases, this issue has been resolved by having a judge who is trained in law, with treatment recommendations handled by the probation and casework staff.

## ❖ THE JUVENILE JUSTICE PROCESS

Regardless of how it is organized and staffed, the juvenile court does not operate in isolation. As part of a larger justice system and society in general, it is affected by law enforcement, correctional agencies, and private organizations, as well as resources available in the community. To determine how all of these elements influence the juvenile offender, it is essential to examine how juveniles are processed through "the system"—from initial contact to final disposition.

---

*LEARNING GOALS*

*Do you know:*

- *Who can refer children to juvenile court?*
- *What discretionary options are available to the police in the handling of young offenders?*

---

### Initial Contact and Referral

Like adults, the justice process for juveniles begins with a *complaint* against the child. But unlike adults, the police are not the only authorities who can refer a child to juvenile court. Schools, parents, and other social agencies can also file juvenile complaints. For example, schools might refer a chronic truant or a student involved in vandalism; parents might refer a child they cannot control; and social welfare agencies might refer an abandoned or neglected youngster. Most complaints (or *referrals*) for delinquency cases (84%) come from law enforcement agencies. In contrast, however, the police are responsible for less than half (45%) of referrals for status offenses.[52]

We saw in Chapter 1 that police discretion plays a significant role in the processing of adult offenders, and the same is true to an even greater extent for juveniles.[53] The police have a variety of options available in the handling of young offenders, which range considerably in terms of their impact:

- *Outright release:* giving a verbal warning or reprimand, without officially recording the incident.

---

[52]*Juvenile Court Statistics: 1987* (Pittsburgh, PA: National Center for Juvenile Justice, 1990), pp. 12, and 35. Among status offenses, those most likely to be referred by non-law-enforcement agencies are truancy and ungovernability.

[53]John P. Kenney and Dan G. Pursuit, *Police Work with Juveniles and the Administration of Justice,* Fourth Edition (Springfield, IL: Charles C Thomas, 1970), p. 80.

- *Release to parents:* releasing the child to the custody of parents, which may be accompanied by a conference with the family in an effort to assure that the behavior is not repeated.
- *Informal referral:* diverting the case to a social service agency in the community without further official processing.
- *Conditional release:* releasing the child to the custody of parents on the condition that the offender meet certain requirements, such as participating in a particular community program.
- *Take into custody:* what would be considered an arrest in the criminal justice system, which is followed by referral to the intake unit of juvenile court.[54]

As with adults, the action taken by the police is based largely on the offender's attitude and the seriousness of the violation. In addition, the person's age, prior contact with enforcement officials, and family situation are taken into account. Whether or not one even enters the juvenile justice system therefore depends on a variety of factors and circumstances, although the seriousness of the offense is most likely to assume primary importance.

---

*LEARNING GOALS*

*Do you know:*

- *What alternatives are available at the intake stage?*
- *On what basis intake decisions are made?*
- *Why so many cases are disposed of at intake?*

---

## Intake Procedures

As illustrated in Figure 13.4, the juvenile court's intake officer also has considerable discretion with regard to what happens next. Even after initial screening by the police, the majority of cases referred to the court are dismissed nonjudicially through informal arrangements and community referrals at the *intake stage*. Thus, intake represents another screening device. At this point, the court determines whether it should take further action, and if so, whether official or unofficial action is needed. As such, intake reflects the original intent to individualize each case and provides treatment alternatives.

Upon receiving a complaint or referral, a juvenile court *probation officer* or *intake counselor* investigates the case. The circumstances of the complaint are recorded. If it is not an extremely trivial matter, the facts are investigated by contacting the child, the parents, the victim if one was involved, school personnel, and others who might be able to contribute information. A brief social history

---

[54]See Simonson, p. 195; and Richard W. Kobetz, *The Police Role and Juvenile Delinquency* (Gaithersburg, MD: International Association of Chiefs of Police, 1971), p. 104.

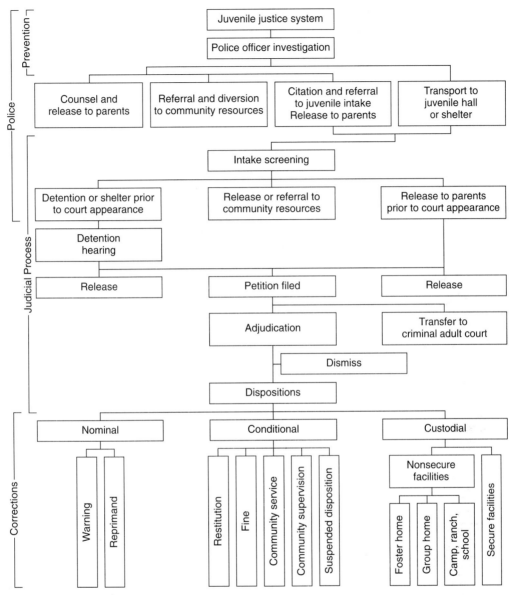

**Figure 13.4** Juvenile justice process. *Source:* National Advisory Committee on Criminal Justice Standards and Goals, *Juvenile Justice and Delinquency Prevention: Report of the Task Force on Juvenile Justice and Delinquency Prevention* (Washington, DC: U.S. Government Printing Office, 1976), p. 9.

report is prepared for use by the court. Like the police officer in the field, the intake unit has a number of discretionary options at this point:

- *Dismissal* of the case (which may be accompanied by a warning).

- *Informal adjustment* through such alternatives as diversion to another agency or informal probation without official processing.
- *Filing a petition* to initiate formal processing.

Given the range of these options, it is apparent that intake has a significant impact on the ultimate fate of the juvenile before the court. Because of the greater informality of the juvenile justice system, however, intake decisions are not generally structured by written guidelines. The intent is to maintain the flexibility needed to make decisions on a case-by-case basis. But some criticisms have been raised that, without written guidelines, intake decisions "may be based upon the 'personal whim' of overworked intake officers [or] may be socially and racially biased. . . ."[55] Since the basic notion of individualized treatment for the child largely revolves around the casework function of intake, the issue is to what extent the process can be *routinized* and *regulated* while preserving the *flexibility* necessary to maintain a personalized approach.

As with discretionary decisions made by the police, intake decisions are made on the basis of such informal criteria as the nature of the offense, prior involvement with the juvenile justice system, attitudes of the child and his or her parents, age of the child, and desire of the complainant to press charges.[56] Obviously, in cases where a violent felony crime is involved, a petition is filed and the case progresses through the formal system. But we have already seen that these represent relatively few of the cases referred to juvenile court.

With well over a million total cases presented annually (1,226,000), it is not surprising to find that *over half* (54%) of delinquency matters are handled *informally* at the intake stage[57] (see Figure 13.5). In fact, it has been charged that such nonjudicial processing operates more as an expedient means of preventing the court from bogging down under the burden of its caseload than as a benevolent method to personalize justice and offer the juvenile a "second chance."[58]

---

*LEARNING GOALS*

*Do you know:*

- *On what basis a juvenile might be detained prior to court appearance?*
- *What the difference is between protective custody and secure detention?*
- *The impact of the Schall v. Martin case?*
- *Why the Juvenile Justice and Delinquency Prevention Act has not been fully successful in removing juveniles from adult jails?*
- *What percentage of those in short-term detention are being held in predisposition status?*

---

[55]Kobetz and Bosarge, p. 246.
[56]Ibid., p. 249.
[57]*Juvenile Court Statistics*, pp. 5 , 31.
[58]Robert D. Vinter, "The Juvenile Court as an Institution," in President's Commission,  pp. 87–88.

## Juvenile Detention

Assuming that intake elects to file a petition and continue with formal processing, another decision must be made at this point. Prior to court appearance, the child can either be *released* to the custody of parents or *detained*. Detention can be either in *protective custody* (such as a foster home or runaway shelter) or in a *secure custodial facility* (what would be termed "pretrial detention" for adults). Again, this is a discretionary matter that is usually not bound by written guidelines. The National Advisory Committee for Juvenile Justice and Delinquency Prevention has recommended that detention be reserved for those who:

- Are *fugitives* from another jurisdiction.
- Voluntarily *request protection* from circumstances that present an immediate threat of serious physical injury.
- Are charged with *murder*.

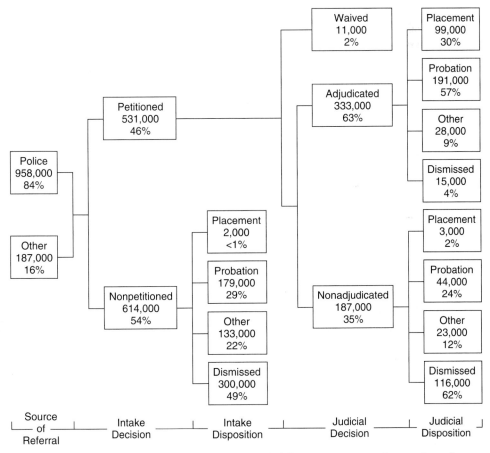

**Figure 13.5** *Juvenile court processing of delinquency cases. Source: Juvenile Court Statistics: 1987* (Pittsburgh, PA: National Center for Juvenile Justice, 1990), p. 14.

- Are charged with a *crime of violence* or *serious property crime* and are already on conditional release for another offense, have demonstrated failure to appear in court, or have a record of recent serious property crimes or violent conduct resulting in injury.

- Present a *risk of flight or serious harm* to either property or the physical safety of others (assuming there is no less restrictive alternative that will reduce the risk they pose).[59]

Detaining juveniles prior to their court disposition has been legally challenged. But in the 1984 *Schall v. Martin* case, the Supreme Court upheld the preventive detention of juveniles for their own or society's protection.[60] Juveniles charged with *delinquent acts* are much more likely to be restrictively detained (24%) than are *status offenders* (8%).[61] Among status offenders, runaways are more apt to be securely detained than are those in any other offense category.[62]

This does not mean that juveniles can be held indefinitely merely on the discretionary decision of intake personnel. When intake recommends preadjudication custody, the child is entitled to a subsequent *detention hearing*, as shown in Figure 13.4. At this hearing, the judge determines whether to release the juvenile or whether sufficient reasons exist to continue with confinement.

### Juveniles in Adult Jails

A major issue facing the juvenile justice system in recent years has become *where* those held prior to disposition of their case are being confined. Because of the small numbers of offenders requiring custody, many jurisdictions in the past did not provide for separate juvenile detention facilities. Rather, they housed juveniles in adult jails—where they could face deplorable conditions and even death, as described in the next "Close-up on Corrections." Given the impact of such an environment, it is not surprising to find that the rate of suicide among juveniles in adult jails has been found to be almost eight times higher than that of young offenders held in juvenile detention centers.[63]

While conditions have improved over the past two decades, jails are still not an appropriate environment for housing impressionable youngsters. Yet, as recently as 1990, there were over 2000 juveniles confined in adult jails.[64] Among those included in this number are violent offenders being transferred to adult court. There is a valid argument that extremely serious, chronic delinquents can

[59]National Advisory Committee for Juvenile Justice and Delinquency Prevention, *Standards for the Administration of Juvenile Justice* (Washington, DC: U.S. Government Printing Office, 1980), p. 297 (emphasis added).

[60]*Schall v. Martin*, 104 S. Ct. 2403 (1984).

[61]*Sourcebook of Criminal Justice Statistics—1990* (Washington, DC: U.S. Department of Justice, 1991), pp. 546, 549.

[62]Melissa Sickmund, "Runaways in Juvenile Courts," in *Office of Juvenile Justice and Delinquency Prevention Update on Statistics* (Washington, DC: U.S. Department of Justice, 1990), p. 5.

[63]Michael G. Flaherty, "An Assessment of the National Incidence of Juvenile Suicide in Adult Jails, Lockups, and Juvenile Detention Centers," in Ralph A. Weisheit and Robert G. Culbertson, eds., *Juvenile Delinquency: A Justice Perspective* (Prospect Heights, IL: Waveland Press, 1985), p. 131.

[64]*Sourcebook*, p. 578.

Juveniles in Adult Jails

It was a typical, quiet Friday night when the phone rang. On the other end of the line was a seventeen-year-old boy calling from the county jail. It seems that the $73.00 in traffic fines that he owed were more serious than he thought. He tells his dad that if he does not pay his fine, he will have to stay in jail overnight. His dad decides that a night in jail might do him some good. Consequently, his son is put in a cell with five other youths. Sometime during that night, his son's cellmates gang up on him, and he is beaten and tortured. In the morning the phone rings again. This time it is the hospital. The boy is dead. . . .

*Source:* Thomas A. Nazario, *In Defense of Children* (New York: Charles Scribner's Sons, 1988), pp. 328–29.

be an intimidating threat to others if they are confined in juvenile facilities. But jails are certainly unsuited for those charged with status offenses or minor delinquencies: "Jails lack adequate physical plant facilities, adequate numbers of appropriately trained staff members, as well as adequate health, recreational, and other programs to meet the minimum standards of juvenile confinement. . . ."[65]

Recognizing the negative influence which jail confinement can have on juveniles, the federal *Juvenile Justice and Delinquency Prevention Act of 1974* restricted the confinement of juveniles in adult facilities to limited situations. When the Act was amended in 1980, its provisions went even further—requiring the removal of all juveniles from adult jails and lockups by the end of 1985. But because so many states were not in compliance by the deadline, it was extended three years until 1988, and several exceptions were added—primarily allowing for short-term detention in certain serious juvenile cases, provided that they are separated from adult inmates by "sight and sound." In other words, juveniles and adults must be kept completely separate in terms of all institutional activities (e.g., sleeping, eating, recreation, education, health care, etc.), and direct-contact staff must be separate from those who service the adult population.[66]

However, there are no federal juvenile courts or detention facilities. Responsibility for the juvenile justice system is a state or local function. Although this federal legislation therefore does not carry the weight of law, it does provide funding in exchange for an agreement to comply with its provisions. Compliance is monitored by the U.S. Department of Justice, Office of Juvenile Justice and Delinquency Prevention (OJJDP). States in violation face the possibility of having their federal juvenile justice funds terminated. In addition, lawsuits have also been filed challenging state violation of the federal requirements. In one such case

[65]Ira M. Schwartz, *Justice for Juveniles* (Lexington, MA: Lexington Books, 1989), p. 82.

[66]For a description of how one state has implemented "sight and sound" restrictions, see Brad Black, "Juvenile Confinement in Kentucky—A Step in the Right Direction," *American Jails*, Vol. 4, No. 5 (January/February, 1991), pp. 32-36.

(*Hendrickson v. Griggs*), the judge issued an injunction to stop the state from detaining any more delinquent children until a plan was submitted to remove them from adult jails, noting that "[i]t makes little difference . . . that these values were embodied in a funding program rather than a nationwide prohibition. If the state did not share Congress' priorities or did not wish to implement them, it could merely have refused to seek the OJJDP funding."[67]

Nevertheless, reaction has been "slow and incomplete," and by 1987, "at least 40 states had failed to achieve full compliance."[68] Among the reasons cited are factors ranging from deliberate defiance to lack of commitment, ignorance of the law, insufficient resources, processing errors, and conflict between state and federal regulations.[69] There are also some who contend that the sluggish pace of compliance can be attributed to the failure of federal officials to push hard enough for it.[70] But regardless of the reasons, some 20 years after the initial legislation, state and local realities have yet to fully reflect the ambitions of federal reform.

**Short-term Detention Facilities.** Short-term *detention facilities* are the juvenile equivalent of adult jails. Currently, there are fewer than 500 state and locally administered detention centers throughout the United States, which house just under 20,000 children.[71] Like adult jails, some of those in detention are awaiting disposition of their case, while others have already been adjudicated. In Chapter 6 we found that pretrial and postconviction offenders in adult jails are approximately equal in number. That is not the case in juvenile detention centers. Some of those being held in detention have been committed following adjudication in juvenile court. But the vast majority (85%) are confined in predisposition status (in adult terms, "pretrial").[72] It is for this reason that they are called "short term," since most residents are awaiting either adjudication, disposition, placement, or transfer. As might be expected, the bulk of those being temporarily detained are charged with *delinquencies*, (offenses that would be considered crimes if committed by an adult). However, 6% are being held as a result of abuse, neglect, status offenses, or unknown offenses.

Regardless of what brought them there, short-term detention is the first institution to which the child is often exposed. Because this exposure can be a traumatic experience, it is important that the facility be staffed by personnel who are properly trained and suited for working with children. *Diagnosis, education, and treatment* must be maintained if the juvenile justice system is to take full advantage of this opportunity to intervene in a preventive or corrective manner. Moreover, because most of the residents fall under compulsory school attendance

[67]Michael J. Dale, "Children in Adult Jails: A Look at Liability Issues," *American Jails*, Vol. 4, No. 5 (January/February 1991), p. 31, citing *Hendrickson v. Griggs*, 672 F. Supp. 1126 (N.D. Iowa 1987).

[68]Charles E. Frazier and Donna M. Bishop, "Jailing Juveniles in Florida: The Dynamics of Compliance with a Sluggish Federal Reform Initiative," *Crime and Delinquency*, Vol. 36, No. 4 (October 1990), pp. 427–28.

[69]Ibid., pp. 427\208>41. For an account of the specific difficulties encountered by one state in achieving compliance, see Ruth B. O'Donnell, "Getting Juveniles Out of Kansas Jails," *American Jails*, Vol. 4, No. 5 (January/February 1991), pp. 16–22.

[70]Frazier and Bishop, p. 429.

[71]*Sourcebook*, p. 574.

[72]Compiled from *Sourcebook*, p. 574.

laws, provision of education is mandatory. However, some maintain that it is wasteful to offer much treatment in detention facilities, since clients are not there long enough to take advantage of extensive programs. In fact, at least one study has found that superintendents of juvenile detention considered custody to be their primary orientation.[73]

But while children are in detention, there is an opportunity to learn as much as possible about them. For this reason, progressive facilities employ intelligence, aptitude, and personality testing, along with other diagnostic procedures. It is also at this point that information from the immediate family and relatives, schools, and other social service agencies can be integrated into a social history that will subsequently be useful in the treatment process.

Recreation and religious programs are also very important. Many detention clients are isolated children, handicapped by feelings of inferiority, who have never competed successfully anywhere. Thus, recreation programs should focus on building self-esteem creatively rather than only through competitive athletics. Arts and crafts, films, music lessons, board games, and other alternatives should be provided in addition to athletic sports and play. In fact, one juvenile detention center has found that exposure to the creative arts has promoted both treatment and socially acceptable behavior:

> Often from socially and economically impoverished homes . . . this population [in juvenile detention has] never seen a play, . . . played an instrument, . . . been to an art show, . . . learned to draw, . . . written a story. . . . [T]hey have never had the opportunity to put their hands into clay, paint their feelings, draw a portrait, or dance for an audience. By engaging in the communicative, cooperative and playful dimension of the arts, [they] . . . can learn new ways to express themselves. . . . [W]e have seen the fruits of our labors in [their] pride, self-confidence and creativity. . . . [74]

Although religion may not play as great a role as in adult facilities, it is another essential ingredient. With young people, such programs must be realistic, since adolescents experiencing difficulty with the law cannot be expected to readily accept religion. Religious programs must be selected and supervised carefully to offer the greatest potential for reaching out to communicate with these troubled youths.

Because separation from society can create even more anxieties for youngsters than for adults, it is especially critical that those in detention be kept in contact with supportive relationships. This can be particularly difficult if the source of the child's problem was an uncaring, neglectful, or abusive home environment. Regardless of any hostility expressed by the children or their parents, the detention staff must maintain assurance of society's constructive interest in the child.

[73]Nicholas Reuterman, *A National Study of Juvenile Detention Facilities* (Edwardsville, IL: Southern Illinois University, 1970), p. 35.

[74]Robert E. King and Brenda Voshell, "Imagery for Adolescence," *Journal of Correctional Training* (Fall, 1992), pp. 8-9.

Needless to say, many of these considerations can be addressed more effectively in an *open setting* than in a *closed institution*. Moreover, secure detention has long been plagued by problems ranging from substandard care to insufficient resources. In terms of their ability to satisfy the physical and emotional needs of adolescents, it has been observed that "the conditions in many places are not much better than those in adult jails."[75] For these reasons, public or private *shelter care* is often a preferable option to secure confinement for short-term detention. Shelters are a type of residential home environment for dependent children, those who are neglected, or status offenders. In addition, several states are also using shelter care successfully for cases of minor delinquency pending court disposition. For those with special needs, such options as group homes, mental health facilities, or other programs for juveniles with emotional disturbances often can provide more effective help than can detention.

---

*LEARNING GOALS*

*Do you know:*

- *What the difference is between fact-finding and dispositional hearings?*
- *What is meant by the "balanced approach" to juvenile justice?*

---

## Adjudication

Thus far, we have addressed intake procedures and short-term detention, but have yet to focus on the judicial functions of the court itself. Once a petition has been filed, a *hearing* before a juvenile court judge is scheduled. Juvenile court hearings are divided into two types: *fact-finding* (adjudication) and *disposition* (sentencing). These may be conducted in two separate proceedings or as two parts of a consecutive hearing.

Under the original philosophy of the juvenile court, the intent was to give personalized attention to determining the facts involved and the needs of each offender. That, however, was long before the juvenile justice system was handling well over a million cases each year. Although there has been a movement to establish independent family courts, many juvenile matters are still handled within a circuit, district, county, or municipal court. Under such arrangements, the demands of other cases restrict the amount of time available to deal with delinquency cases. Even where juvenile cases are heard in a separate court, the workload volume can severely limit the attention devoted to each case. One study, for example, revealed that most juvenile court cases are heard in approximately 15 minutes.[76] Obviously, such assembly-line "justice" inhibits the ability to provide the kindly, parental guidance envisioned by early reformers, as we

[75]Hahn, p. 194.
[76]James D. Walter and Susan A. Ostrander, "An Observational Study of a Juvenile Court," in Weisheit and Culbertson, p. 113.

see from the inside account of the manner in which justice is dispensed in the next "Close-up on Corrections."

But no matter how well organized the court or how competent its personnel, the juvenile justice system cannot fulfill its mission in isolation from the community. Local agencies control many of the services needed by its clients: employment opportunities, vocational training, special education, rehabilitative therapy, and so on. That such resources are in short supply even for the general public, much less the delinquent population, further constrains the court's effectiveness. Given these external and operational limitations, it would appear that the juvenile court never had a fair chance to implement the mandates of its founders.

As we have seen, *procedural informality* was the basis of the original juvenile court, so that the interests of the child could be served without becoming encumbered by the technicalities and uniformity of the adult criminal justice system. From this point of view, the court has been relatively successful. Despite the introduction of greater due process protections, most cases are still heard by a judge rather than a jury. Strict rules of evidence are not imposed. The general atmosphere is one of noncombativeness. At issue, then, is not whether the original intent of procedural informality has been met, but whether the concept underlying that intent—serving the best interests of the child—has been compromised in the process.

One point of view holds that it is juveniles who have been victimized by state-imposed treatment. Others maintain that it is the public that has been vic-

---

## ❖ CLOSE-UP ON CORRECTIONS

### The Tragedy of Juvenile Court

It is overcrowded and understaffed, a jerry-built justice system where social workers with no training in law are required to write legal petitions; where lawyers with no training in social work are supposed to know what treatment is best for a 9-year-old mugger.

Parents and children . . . sit silently while lawyers talk about them in jargon. . . . Much of the time, neither parents nor children know when their case is over. They must be told by the bailiff to leave the courtroom. . . . A case may last 20 minutes or 20 seconds. . . .

Defense lawyers and some prosecutors say they see far too many cases that have no business being in a court. They say neighborhood disputes, school problems, small-time marijuana cases and minor misdemeanors could be better handled by principals, mediators, or social workers, rather than lawyers and judges. "The statistics show the kids grow out of it," says [one public defender]. "In fact, I'm not sure we can show that we're achieving anything."

*Source:* Marc Fisher, "Shame on Us All: The Tragedy of Juvenile Court," *Tropic Magazine* (*The Miami Herald*, November 17, 1985), pp. 10–27.

timized by the "child-saving" focus of the juvenile justice system.[77] Society is concerned that juvenile justice not only serve the needs of the child, but also be in keeping with the public good. As one advocate of the recent trend toward a more *balanced approach* has observed, "[w]e didn't want to assume that 'in the best interest of the child' always meant an adversarial relationship with the best interest of the community. When a crime occurs involving a juvenile, we should try to come up with a penalty that is best for the kid and best for the community."[78]

For a look at how some communities are accomplishing this, see the next "Close-up on Corrections." As that account demonstrates, the balanced

---

### ❖ CLOSE-UP ON CORRECTIONS

#### A "Balanced Approach" to Juvenile Justice

Known as "The Balanced Approach," [this effort] . . . is a significant departure from traditional programs that emphasize counseling over restitution to victims or community protection. It challenges the notion that counseling alone can reform juvenile offenders. . . .

The law [on which it is based] requires juvenile justice programs to be "in the best interest of the child," but also requires that programs be "consistent with the public good." . . . Under The Balanced Approach, every program for a juvenile offender has three elements: community protection, restitution to the victim and the community, and skills development. The three are aimed at holding youths accountable while providing them with help to change their behavior.

Community protection involves an effort to prevent future offenses, whether that is [through] counseling, house arrest or detention. And because crime affects the community and the victim, both are entitled to restitution.

Offenders, however, need help, too. They receive counseling and training to make better choices and learn skills such as how to apply for a job, open a checking account, or find an apartment.

The program uses a scale of increasingly restrictive measures . . . to change behavior. If juveniles continue to offend, the consequences become increasingly harsh. Juvenile offenders with little or no past records can be referred to diversion programs. . . . If offenses continue, or if early offenses are serious, the youth faces curfew, house arrest, probation, court appearances, mandatory counseling, behavior contracts, court wardship, and eventually detention, either short- or long-term. . . .

*Source:* Greg Bolt, "Other States Mimicking Juvenile System," *Oregon Corrections Association Reports* (Fall 1991), p. 17.

---

[77]Francis T. Cullen, Kathryn M. Golden, and John B. Cullen, "Is Child Saving Dead? Attitudes toward Juvenile Rehabilitation in Illinois," *Journal of Criminal Justice,* Vol. 11, No. 1 (1983), p. 1.

[78]Greg Bolt, "Other States Mimicking Juvenile System," *Oregon Corrections Association Reports* (Fall 1991), p. 17, quoting Dennis Maloney, director of the Deschutes County (Oregon) Community Corrections Department.

approach maintains a heavy emphasis on establishing accountability and responsibility. But there are some who argue that it also is open to misinterpretation in the absence of guidelines for judicial decision making, and that: "[w]ithout such guidelines, judges and correctional officials are likely to rely on their own values, and the 'balance' may become skewed by personal bias or community pressures."[79]

It should also be noted that achieving a balanced perspective does not necessarily mean uniformly employing middle ground between leniency and repression. Rather, it implies providing a more diverse range of options for responding to a similarly wide-ranging array of problems and behaviors. As we saw in Chapter 9, no single approach works equally effectively with all adult offenders. Given the greater variety of law-violating offenses for which young people can come to the attention of authorities, the same could be stated with even more certainty in juvenile corrections. In the absence of a wider assortment of meaningful treatment and programming alternatives, it has been observed that "[a]gencies are caught between naive reformers who believe all juveniles should be handled in the community and reactionary citizens and officials who demand an increase in confinement measures."[80]

---

*LEARNING GOALS*

*Do you know:*

- *What three general categories of disposition alternatives are available to juvenile courts?*
- *The difference between secure and open custodial facilities?*
- *What impact the justice model has had on the custodial confinement of juveniles?*

---

## Disposition

What type of approach is used in the disposition of juvenile cases is largely a function of judicial discretion. The judge has a number of options at the *disposition hearing* (or what would be called sentencing in adult court). Dispositional alternatives range in severity from nominal to conditional or custodial (as shown in Figure 13.4):

- *Nominal.* Particularly for first-time delinquents or those involved in less serious offenses, the judge may simply elect to issue a warning or reprimand, with no further repercussions if the child avoids future contact with the law.
- *Conditional.* As the term implies, these sanctions require that the child comply with some type of requirement (e.g., paying a fine, providing community

[79]Martin L. Forst and Martha-Elin Blomquist, "Punishment, Accountability, and the New Juvenile Justice," *Juvenile and Family Court Journal,* Vol. 43, No. 1 (1992), p. 8.

[80]Lloyd W. Mixdorf, "Juvenile Justice: We Need a Variety of Treatment, Programming Options," *Corrections Today,* Vol. 51, No. 4 (July 1989), p. 120.

service, making restitution to the victim, or completing a training, educational, or treatment program). Among the most frequently used conditional dispositions is *official probation.* Almost one-third of all delinquency cases and 20% of all status offenders receive probation.[81] Like its adult counterpart, juvenile probation sets conditions that the child must abide by—such as attending school, maintaining a curfew, avoiding associations with known criminals or delinquents, and reporting to a probation officer. Also like the criminal justice system, the judge can suspend formal disposition, dropping the charges if the juvenile complies with the conditions established. Designed to incorporate counseling and casework with a certain amount of surveillance, probation represents the court's initial intent of individual treatment within the community. But the use of probation is limited by excessively high caseloads, forcing greater reliance on the practical requirements of efficiency than the treatment needs of the child. In this respect it has been observed that probation often becomes "a token effort," which, in terms of its potential has been underused, but in terms of its funded strength has been badly overused.[82]

- *Custodial.* If custodial commitment is warranted, the court has two choices: *secure* or *nonsecure* facilities. Nonsecure or "open" facilities include such residential services as foster homes, group homes, camps, ranches, and marine institutes. These are options for those who need some guidance, structure, and supervision, but not as much restraint and limitation as are found in juvenile correctional institutions or training schools. See the next "Close-up on Corrections" for some of the creative dispositions that are being used as alternatives to secure confinement in one state.

Although the juvenile justice system has become more adversarial, there is still a presumption that to preserve its rehabilitative mission, it need not comply with all due process protections of the criminal justice system. According to this fundamental premise, the major guideline for determining disposition focuses more on the needs of the offender than on the nature of the offense. In that respect, the punishment orientation of adult courts under the justice model can be viewed as imposing unpleasant consequences as a result of one's *past offense(s).* On the other hand, the treatment emphasis of juvenile courts under the medical model seeks to improve the offender's *future welfare.* One would therefore assume that adult courts would impose determinate sentences proportional to the offense, whereas juvenile courts would tend to employ open-ended, indeterminate dispositions focusing on the needs of the offender. That may well have been the case in the past. But research is beginning to reveal that "juvenile court dispositional practices increasingly resemble those of punitive criminal courts."[83] The question then becomes whether such an approach serves the best interests of the child, the community, or neither.

[81]*Sourcebook,* pp. 546, 550.
[82]Paul W. Keve, "*Some Random Reflections on the Occasion of a Barely Noticed Anniversary,*" Crime and Delinquency, Vol. 24, No. 4 (October 1978), p. 456.
[83]Barry C. Feld, "The Punitive Juvenile Court and the Quality of Procedural Justice: Disjunctions between Rhetoric and Reality," *Crime and Delinquency,* Vol. 36, No. 4 (October 1990), pp. 446–47.

Alternatives That Work

In Marion County, Indiana, alternative dispositions for troubled youths include a wide variety of unique programs:

- *Project Challenge:* six-week program aimed at breaking the behavior cycles that lead youths to trouble, including a three-week wilderness camp that encourages youths to trust themselves and their peers, and provides vocational, family, and individual counseling.

- *Ivy Tech:* offers vocational education for youths who are functionally illiterate or in need of remedial education or extra attention in the classroom.

- *Electronic Surveillance:* enables the county to make sure students are home when they are supposed to be. The electronic device allows them to assume responsibility while ensuring community safety.

- *Run, Don't Run:* aimed at youths who have literally run from encounters with law enforcement officers, the program is intended to establish respect between young offenders and law enforcement officials. Participants learn how fleeing, resisting, or striking a police officer influences the officers' actions.

- *Visions:* designed for serious first referrals or repeat offenders, youths are admitted to the juvenile detention center for one night, followed by a morning lesson about the juvenile justice system. That afternoon, they tour the Indiana Boys/Girls School and the Marion County Jail.

- *Operation Kids Can (Care About Neighborhoods):* youths spend mornings learning about the juvenile justice system. Then, they work in structured community service projects such as cleaning vacant lots and picking up garbage. (In 1989, this program received a United Way award for outstanding community service.)

- *Paint It Clean:* requires youths associated with destructive gang activities to paint over gang graffiti in local neighborhoods, parks, and buildings, thereby helping to eliminate gang claims to territory and allowing communities to reclaim their neighborhoods.

- *Summer Youth Program:* gives children the chance to go canoeing, horseback riding, camping, hiking, and caving. Monthly field trips are also conducted throughout the year.

- *Near Peer Tutoring:* targets junior high school probationers having trouble in at least one class. High school honor students and adult volunteers tutor youths weekly at neighborhood probation offices.

*Source:* Adapted from James W. Payne and Joe E. Lee, "In Indiana: A System Designed to Accommodate Juveniles' Needs," *Corrections Today,* Vol. 52, No. 6 (October 1990), pp. 103–4.

*Do you know:*

- *How many children are being held in custodial confinement?*
- *What percentage of confinements are for nondelinquent reasons?*
- *How juvenile custody rates are changing and what demographic groups are most affected?*

## Children in Custody

As in criminal court, the severity of the offense and the juvenile's past record are taken into account in determining the appropriate disposition. However, one major seven-year study of judicial decision making in a metropolitan area discovered that even when controlling for the seriousness of the offense, males, blacks, dropouts, and those from broken homes were treated more punitively.[84] Some of these groups (such as school dropouts) may admittedly represent greater risk to the community, and overall, dispositions may be no more inequitable in juvenile than adult courts. Nevertheless, the impact is likely to be more severe, given the vulnerability of youth and the lifelong stigma attached to incarceration as a juvenile. Moreover, institutionalization of juveniles could potentially extend to a time period in excess of what adults would receive for a similar offense, since a juvenile in most jurisdictions can be detained indeterminately until the age of majority, as opposed to the more determinate, fixed sentences usually imposed by criminal courts.

The juvenile justice system may still in some respects adhere more to the philosophy of the medical model than that of the justice model. But like their adult counterparts, greater numbers of juveniles are being confined in correctional institutions. At the same time that the proportion of young people in the general population has been declining in recent years, the population of children being held in juvenile facilities has been increasing.[85]

By 1989, over 56,000 children were being held in 1100 public juvenile facilities alone.[86] Additionally, over 38,000 were held in some 2195 private facilities.[87] These figures represent a substantial *growth in custody rates* in recent years, with

[84]Charles W. Thomas and Anthony W. Fitch, *An Inquiry into the Association between Respondents' Personal Characteristics and Juvenile Court Dispositions* (Williamsburg, VA: Metropolitan Criminal Justice Center, College of William and Mary, 1975), p. 17.

[85]Even while the number of juvenile arrests was dropping, police were referring a higher proportion of those arrested to juvenile court, which in turn was imposing stiffer sentences. See Barry Krisberg, Ira M. Schwartz, Paul Litsky, and James Austin, "The Watershed of Juvenile Justice Reform," *Crime and Delinquency*, Vol. 32, No. 1 (January 1986), pp. 5-38.

[86]Barbara Allen-Hagen, "Public Juvenile Facilities: Children in Custody, 1989," *Office of Juvenile Justice and Delinquency Prevention Update on Statistics* (Washington, DC: U.S. Department of Justice, 1991), pp. 2–3.

[87]Terence P. Thornberry, Steward E. Tolnay, Timothy J. Flanagan, and Patty Glynn, *Children in Custody, 1987: A Comparison of Public and Private Juvenile Custody Facilities* (Washington, DC: U.S. Department of Justice, 1991), p. 1.

most of the increase occurring among blacks (up 14%) and Hispanics (up 10%).[88] Today, it would be relatively accurate to estimate that over 100,000 juveniles are in some type of correctional confinement.

As shown in Figure 13.6, most of those confined are males (79%), and minorities are also overrepresented (48%).[89] Although the majority are being held for delinquent offenses (69%), the remainder are detained for *nondelinquent* reasons—the most common of which are status offenses (11%) and abuse, neglect, or dependency (9%). These small percentages, however, obscure the fact that over 28,000 children are in confinement for reasons *unrelated* to behaviors that would be considered criminal if committed by an adult. Those being held for delinquent offenses are predominately male (88%). In contrast, females represent a sizable proportion (41%) of those in custody for nondelinquent reasons.

|  | Total | Male | Female |
|---|---|---|---|
| *Total* | 91,646 | 72,611 (79%) | 19,035 (21%) |
| Public facilities | 53,503 (58%) | 46,272 (86%) | 7,231 (14%) |
| Private facilities | 38,143 (42%) | 26,339 (69%) | 11,804 (31%) |
| *Delinquent offenses* | 63,261 (69%) | 55,955 (88%) | 7,306 (12%) |
| Public facilities | 50,269 (79%) | 44,757 (89%) | 5,512 (11%) |
| Private facilities | 12,992 (21%) | 11,198 (86%) | 1,794 (14%) |
| *Nondelinquent reasons* | 28,385 (31%) | 16,656 (59%) | 11,729 (41%) |
| Public facilities | 3,234 (11%) | 1,515 (47%) | 1,719 (53%) |
| Private facilities | 25,151 (89%) | 15,141 (60%) | 10,010 (40%) |

**Figure 13.6** Children held in public and private facilities. *Note:* "Delinquent offenses" include crimes against persons, along with property, alcohol, drug-related and public order offenses, probation/parole violations, and unknown offenses. "Nondelinquent reasons" include status offenses, dependency, neglect and abuse cases, emotional disturbances, retardation, other nondelinquent acts, and voluntary admissions. *Source:* Compiled from Terrence P. Thornberry, Steward E. Tolnay, Timothy J. Flanagan, and Patty Glynn, *Office of Juvenile Justice and Delinquency Prevention Report on Children in Custody, 1987: A Comparison of Public and Private Juvenile Custody Facilities* (Washington, DC: U.S. Department of Justice, 1991), pp. 40–41.

[88]Allen-Hagen, p. 3.
[89]Thornberry et al., p. 6.

What all of this adds up to are *increasingly crowded* juvenile correctional facilities—where residents are disproportionately minority youths, where status offenders are comingled with delinquents, and where underpaid staff are expected to meet the needs of those ranging from drug abusers to depressed runaways. Worst of all, because they are overshadowed by a crowding crisis in adult prisons that has dominated the public agenda, it is next to impossible to get society to care about the plight of children.[90] Yet in terms of the conditions in which they are confined, it is essential to be especially vigilant with juveniles, "because we are dealing with a population that is politically powerless, socially rejected, and easily exploited."[91]

---

*LEARNING GOALS*

*Do you know:*

- *How public and private training schools differ?*
- *What types of programs and services are provided in juvenile facilities?*
- *To what extent juveniles have a right to treatment in correctional institutions?*

---

### Juvenile Institutions

During the early origins of juvenile corrections at the beginning of the nineteenth century, private and public training schools developed side by side. As a result, juveniles today are held in both private and publicly operated state training schools, as well as locally operated city training schools, detention centers, and various types of camps, ranches, and shelters. A recent national survey assessed the *conditions of confinement* in 984 of these diverse facilities.[92] Results were somewhat mixed. Apparently, juvenile institutions on average may be neither as bad as we might fear nor as good as we might hope. For example, facilities were assessed as "generally adequate" in several important areas:

- Food, clothing, and hygiene.
- Recreation.
- Living accommodations.

However, "substantial and widespread deficiencies" were found in terms of:

- Crowding.
- Security.

---

[90]Allen F. Breed and Barry Krisberg, "Juvenile Corrections: Is There a Future?" *Corrections Today*, Vol. 48, No. 8 (December 1986), p. 16.

[91]David Shichor and Clemens Bartollas, "Private and Public Juvenile Placements: Is There a Difference?" *Crime and Delinquency*, Vol. 36, No. 2 (April 1990), p. 297.

[92]Dale G. Parent, "Conditions of Confinement," *Juvenile Justice*, Vol. 1, No. 1 (Spring/Summer 1993), pp. 2–7.

- Suicide prevention.
- Health screenings and appraisals.

Just as in the adult system, crowding has become a pervasive problem in juvenile confinement. By 1991, almost half (47%) of the juvenile population was living in overtaxed facilities—where rates of injuries were higher, making them more dangerous for both clients and staff.[93] In that regard, crowding may also be related to security deficiencies, to the extent that it diminishes the ability to "adequately separate predators from victims."[94] Suicidal behavior likewise remains a serious problem. Juveniles in confinement are taking their own lives at roughly double the rate of young people in the general population, (and that does not include additional thousands of attempted suicides or self-mutilations).[95] Although the majority of clients are held in facilities that screen for indicators of suicide risk at the time of admission, health screenings and appraisals frequently are "not completed in a timely manner."[96]

Perhaps reflecting their reform school heritage, a combination of education, work, and discipline has characterized many juvenile training schools. Courtesy of the California Youth Authority.

[93]Ibid., p. 4.
[94]Ibid., p. 5.
[95]Ibid., p. 6.
[96]Ibid., p. 6.

As a result of these findings, it was concluded that "improving conditions significantly will require broad-scale reforms affecting routine practices in most facilities."[97] That will be a considerable challenge, especially given the varieties of clientele, funding arrangements, and administrative structures that characterize juvenile corrections. For example, as mentioned above, juveniles are confined in both public and privately-operated facilities.

While *private training schools* are supported by contributions, donations, and charitable foundations, they function under state license to assure compliance with minimum standards regarding health, sanitation, residential care, and institutional programming. But because they are private, these schools generally have greater latitude than state schools. They can therefore be somewhat selective in terms of the children admitted so that their resources can be concentrated on specific types of problems. Although Supreme Court decisions prohibit racial discrimination in the selection process, private institutions do have the flexibility of setting minimum intelligence or educational requirements, prohibiting the admission of serious offenders, or restricting admission to only certain types of cases. As a result of such practices, the majority of juveniles in private facilities are white, whereas most in public facilities are black or Hispanic.[98] Private facilities also hold proportionately more females and status offenders, as shown in Figure 13.5. *Public facilities*, of course, do not have these options. State training schools must accept everyone committed to them.

Judges send children to private institutions when, for any of a variety of reasons, the service they provide is deemed to be more desirable for the child than what can be offered in the state's training school. But the number of applications to private institutions often exceeds the number that can be admitted. Consequently, the courts and these institutions have developed procedures to identify special types of cases for admission. Private schools are thus better able to gear their programs to the particular category of boy or girl whom they can best serve. On the other hand, state institutions have no selective admission process. Public facilities must therefore be equipped to handle a much *wider range of behavioral problems.*

Whether public or private, the superintendent or director of a juvenile institution is responsible for its operation. Like the wardens in charge of adult prisons, superintendents supervise a staff of specialists in such areas as security, social services, education, recreation, treatment, food services, maintenance, and administration. Some facilities are organized around a series of "cottages" housing 20 to 50 residents, with cottage parents supervising individual living quarters. Others, such as Boys Town in Nebraska, are mini-communities, where residents elect their own mayor and other governmental representatives, have their own monetary system, and in essence, replicate the community in miniature.

In addition to state-mandated education for those of compulsory school attendance age, the counseling, group therapy, and other treatment programs

[97]Ibid., p. 3.
[98]Thornberry et al., p. 8. For a further discussion of differences between public and private juvenile placements, see Shichor and Bartollas, pp. 286–99.

discussed in Chapter 9 are even more important for juveniles.[99] A number of public juvenile institutions also operate vocational training programs. This is particularly beneficial for those who are already high school dropouts and need marketable employment skills.

In contrast to short-term detention, *long-term institutions* for youthful offenders have a "general mandate" to control the residents, protect the community, provide treatment, and rehabilitate.[100] In practice, a combination of education, work, and discipline represents the typical approach of many state training schools, perhaps reflecting their reform school heritage. Unlike adults, however, the courts have recognized that juveniles committed involuntarily for rehabilitative purposes have a statutory and constitutional *right to treatment*.[101]

> In various jurisdictions, the courts have found that if a juvenile is confined for the purpose of care and rehabilitation, that juvenile must receive the needed psychiatric or other care, and cannot simply be confined with no adequate services provided. These cases have concentrated primarily on status offenders and neglected children, and the courts have required the states to provide the treatment or move the child to a less confining setting. This trend toward the protection of youths who are incarcerated rests on the belief that juvenile correctional programs are primarily rehabilitative and not punitive.[102]

Precisely what is meant by "treatment" is, of course, another issue entirely. We have already seen in Chapter 9 that a wide variety of programs and activities have been loosely defined as treatment in adult prisons and jails. Moreover, despite the fact that rehabilitation is supposedly the major emphasis of the juvenile justice system, "[j]uvenile corrections professionals speak sparingly these days about correcting the behavior of young offenders and much more about education, skill training, social survival skills, community service and self-discipline. The word 'rehabilitation' is used less and less, and the word 'treatment' is almost extinct. . . . "[103]

Some might characterize such trends as reflecting a new approach that is more functional—equipping residents with the social accountability and personal skills that they lack. But to others, they imply an enduring custodial orientation—emphasizing punishment, discipline, and control. Support for the latter view is

[99]Virtually all facilities (97%) offer educational programs, and most (90%) also provide counseling. The most common types of treatment programs are family counseling, employment counseling, peer-group meetings, and behavior modification through contingency contracts. Thornberry et al., p. 31.

[100]Peter C. Kratcoski and Lucille Dunn Kratcoski, *Juvenile Delinquency*, Third Edition (Englewood Cliffs, NJ: Prentice Hall, 1990), p. 303.

[101]See *Nelson v. Heyne*, 491 F.2d 352 (7th Cir. 1974) and *Morales v. Turman*, 383 F. Supp. 53 (Ed. Texas 1974).

[102]Robert C. Trojanowicz and Merry Morash, *Juvenile Delinquency: Concepts and Control*, Third Edition (Englewood Cliffs, NJ: Prentice Hall, 1983), p. 391.

[103]Hunter Hurst, "Turn of the Century: Rediscovering the Value of Juvenile Treatment," *Corrections Today*, Vol. 52, No. 1 (February 1990), p. 49.

found in evaluations of juvenile correctional facilities, which reveal "a continuing gap between the rhetoric of rehabilitation and its punitive reality."[104]

Yet for children who have been denied the security and stability of a nurturing home environment, there remains a desperate need for the kind of positive interaction which they have been denied. As one correctional youth counselor has somberly observed, "these kids don't have dreams. They don't even understand the concept."[105] Without dreams, ambition dies. And in the absence of ambition, there is no motivation to comply with society's rules: "The cruel irony of this is that America is the 'land of opportunity,' the place immigrants came to make their dreams come true. And we are raising millions of children *who don't even know how to dream.*"[106]

---

*LEARNING GOALS*

*Do you know:*

- *What impact juvenile institutions have on their residents?*
- *Why stealing is so prevalent in juvenile facilities?*
- *Why the negative effects of institutionalization are even greater for children than for adults?*

---

### Effects of Confinement

Regardless of what types of treatment programs are available or how nonpunitive the facility's orientation is, there is little doubt that juvenile institutions generate significant negative effects. Despite efforts to deemphasize the institutional atmosphere, training schools are, in fact, *custodial environments*: "[T]he inescapable fact is that a cottage that houses twenty, forty, or more inmates can never be homelike, no matter how many 'homelike touches' are added. No home that a youngster came from [is] so lacking in privacy. . . . The sense of constraint, inherent in mass living under regulated authority, permeates the institutions.[107]

In addition to the negative influence of custodial constraints, training schools have been cited as breeding grounds for abnormal behavior patterns of all sorts—from homosexuality to theft. In this environment are concentrated varieties of delinquents who see life as socially unjust in the first place. Then these negative values are reinforced by their peers in a setting that too often lacks adequate responses to their problems. Association with other delinquents can intensify hostility as well as raise one's status among delinquent peers. Separation from familiar environments promotes feelings of abandonment. Many have been rejected by their home, their school, and now, by their commu-

---

[104]Feld, p. 453.

[105]Jeanne Edna Thelwell, "Teach Someone to Dream," *Corrections Today*, Vol. 50, No. 6 (October 1988), p. 48, quoting Sandy Polacow.

[106]Ibid.

[107]Rose Giallombardo, *The Social World of Imprisoned Girls* (New York: Wiley, 1974), p. 240.

nity as well. Such feelings of rejection can lower self-esteem, further underscoring failure.[108] In that regard, it has been noted that: "[i]nstead of being a constructive and maturing experience, incarceration in a juvenile institution is often harmful. . . . Nonconstructive time spent away from family and community leads to a lessening of the sense of belonging and responsibility."[109]

Especially for first-time or status offenders, interaction with the institutional population itself *reinforces negative values*. And just as in adult prisons, the weak are preyed upon by the strong. In one juvenile facility, 72% of the residents were found to have been victimized in some way—from sexual assault to exploitation for material items.[110] In fact, even those serving brief stays in short-term detention are vulnerable to abuse: "The weaker juvenile who is sentenced to detention may be subject to violent acts, victimized by extortion, and emotionally scarred. These youths need treatment and services, not a vindictive punishment."[111]

Stealing is a common problem in juvenile facilities. Many who are insecure want to stockpile things, whether or not what they are accumulating has any useful value or not. Acquiring property provides them with some of the security they are not getting any other way. Others react to their problems by repeated attempts at running away or by engaging in aggressive fights. Still others develop a close relationship with another resident, which can create emotional strain when one of them is released.

Virtually everyone is subjected to the negative impact of institutional confinement discussed in Chapter 10 with regard to adult prisoners—from lack of privacy to resentment of authority. In contrast to adults, however, the intensity of that impact can be considerably greater for children, who are confined in the midst of their emotional and physical development. Even if the programs offered in such settings were implemented as originally intended, they would be hard-pressed to overcome the combined detrimental effects of the repressive institutional atmosphere and the preexisting problems of the clients themselves. Suffice it to say that reports summarizing numerous individual studies "generally come to negative conclusions about the effectiveness of institutional interventions."[112]

---

*LEARNING GOALS*

*Do you know:*

- *What correctional boot camps are designed to achieve?*
- *Some of the advantages as well as the drawbacks of correctional boot camps?*

---

[108]Kenney and Pursuit, p. 258. See also Dennis C. Bliss, *The Effects of the Juvenile Justice System on Self-Concept* (San Francisco: R&E Research Associates, 1977), pp. 54–60.

[109]Harry E. Allen and Clifford E. Simonsen, *Corrections in America*, Sixth Edition (New York: Macmillan, 1992), p. 417.

[110]Clemens Bartollas, Stuart J. Miller, and Simon Dinitz, "The Exploitation Matrix in a Juvenile Institution," in Weisheit and Culbertson, p. 164.

[111]J. Steven Smith, "Detention Is an Invaluable Part of the System, But It's Not the Solution to All Youths' Problems," *Corrections Today*, Vol. 53, No. 1 (February 1991), p. 59.

[112]John T. Whitehead and Steven P. Lab, *Juvenile Justice: An Introduction* (Cincinnati, OH: Anderson Publishing Company, 1990), p. 346.

## Shock Incarceration Programs

Because lack of self-discipline and disrespect for authority are common among youthful offenders, a number of states have recently begun to experiment with an entirely different type of environment structured around a military-style *boot camp*. Also known as "special alternatives to incarceration" or "shock incarceration," such programs are generally reserved for older adolescents and young adults, some of whom would otherwise be facing their first term in prison or jail. (In fact, they generally operate through the adult corrections department rather than the juvenile justice system.) Like their military counterparts, correctional boot camps emphasize strenuous physical training and strict discipline, with an underlying theme of individual/group survival.

Compared to inmates serving time in traditional institutions, offenders successfully completing a boot camp experience appear to have lower recidivism rates.[113] Those released to community supervision after graduation are also reported to make better probationers, being "more likely to obey instructions, to keep appointments, and to seek, obtain and maintain employment."[114] The graduates themselves generally have positive feelings about their experiences, particularly in terms of achieving better self-control.[115] Despite the promise of these early results, however, there are potential negative side effects.

A survey of boot camp administrators found that "rehabilitation" and "recidivism reduction" were cited most often as very important goals.[116] Although "punishment" was generally ranked lower (or not at all), concerns have been expressed that boot camps are vulnerable to creating increased aggression, abuse of power, and other adverse by-products of a we-versus-they authoritarian atmosphere.[117] Moreover, as we see in the next "Close-up on Corrections," the discipline instilled in boot camps is only one component of what such offenders need to make long-term changes in their behavioral patterns upon return to the community. As one boot camp director has accurately noted:

[113]"Boot Camps Seen Lowering Recidivism," *Law Enforcement News* (May 31, 1991), p. 3. However, preliminary results of some program data raise questions about shock incarceration's capacity to reduce recidivism. See Dale G. Parent, *Shock Incarceration: An Overview of Existing Programs* (Washington, DC: U.S. Department of Justice, 1989), p. 4.

[114]Parent, p. 33.

[115]Ibid.

[116]Doris Layton MacKenzie and Claire C. Souryal, "Boot Camp Survey: Rehabilitation, Recidivism Reduction Outrank Punishment as Main Goals," *Corrections Today,* Vol. 53, No. 6 (October 1991), pp. 90–91.

[117]Merry Morash and Lila Rucker, "A Critical Look at the Idea of Boot Camp as a Correctional Reform," *Crime and Delinquency,* Vol. 36, No. 2 (April 1990), pp. 204–22. However, others have found "no evidence that those who complete boot camp programs are angrier or negatively affected by the program." Doris Layton MacKenzie, "'Boot Camp' Programs Grow in Number and Scope," *National Institute of Justice Reports,* (November/December, 1990), p. 7. See also Peter J. Benekos, "Shock Incarceration: The Military Model in Corrections," in Peter J. Benekos and Alida V. Merlo, eds., *Corrections: Dilemmas and Directions* (Cincinnati, OH: Anderson Publishing Company, 1992), p. 132.

Experiments in Boot Camp

Plagued by overcrowded penitentiaries, the high cost of new prison construction and a rising tide of drug-related crime, some states are packing young offenders off to the correctional equivalent of boot camp . . . a chance to swap their sentences for several months of 4 A.M. reveilles, double-time marches through chow lines, push-ups on command and hours of backbreaking labor. The camps vary in format, but recruit from essentially the same group: young felons, many with long juvenile rap sheets, who are facing their first state prison terms, usually for nonviolent crimes. Officials hope the regimen will shock them out of criminal careers, leaving penitentiaries for only the most hardened. . . .

[But] correctional experts are concerned that they are long on physical punishment and short on offering the skills inmates will need on the outside. "The fear is they could return to the streets in very good shape, strong, hostile, unemployed and with no prospects," said Dale Parent, a correctional analyst. . . .

Critics suggest that legislators nostalgic for their own [military] service experience "forget boot camp was followed by two years in the military and training in skills," says Mark Mauer, assistant director of the Sentencing Project, which promotes alternative jail sentences. "And when they were released, they returned to a community which supported them and welcomed them." For kids . . . making it out of boot camp only means beginning another battle for survival.

*Source:* Eloise Salholz and Frank Washington, "Experiments in Boot Camp," *Newsweek* (May 22, 1989), pp. 42–44.

Within 90 to 120 days, the length of most boot camp programs, we cannot correct all of these young offenders' problems. Nor can we provide them with all the educational and vocational skills they have missed. . . . Boot camps were never intended to do all that. Consider military boot camps. The are not intended to make a young person into a fully functional soldier. Rather, they provide a foundation of discipline, responsibility and self-esteem [which] the military can build on during the advanced training that follows. Correctional boot camps are designed to do much the same thing. They provide a strong foundation [that] parole and probation officers can build on in guiding young offenders into the necessary community-based programs that will help them. . . . Boot camps are a viable alternative . . . if they are accompanied by appropriate aftercare."[118]

[118]Donald J. Hengesh, "Think of Boot Camps as a Foundation for Change, Not an Instant Cure," *Corrections Today,* Vol. 53, No. 6 (October 1991), pp. 106–8.

At boot camps, drill instructors bark out rapid-fire commands with a no-nonsense demeanor. Courtesy of the New York City Department of Correction.

---

*LEARNING GOALS*

*Do you know:*

- *What is meant by "aftercare" in the juvenile justice system?*
- *Why aftercare is often a low priority?*
- *Why follow-up continuity is necessary when a youngster leaves a juvenile facility?*

---

## Aftercare Programs

As the critics of boot camps note, it is not just what occurs within confinement that shapes behavior, but equally important, what follow-up services are available upon release. In adult terms this is what is referred to as "parole" or "supervised mandatory release." In the juvenile justice system it is called *aftercare*. As the name implies, it is intended to provide continuing care for the child after release from a juvenile correctional facility.

Unfortunately, aftercare has historically been the function of an already overburdened juvenile justice system. With resources focused on the immediate needs of new cases and younger clients coming before the court, it is a luxury to divert attention to existing cases lingering in the system. Moreover, by the time they are released, some are close to or have already exceeded the age of majority. Thus, any further offenses they commit will be under the jurisdiction of the criminal justice system.

In recognition of these shortcomings, some states now administer aftercare through a youth commission, youth services bureau, rehabilitative services agency, or the department that administers the state's juvenile training schools. Under this arrangement, the same caseworker can maintain offices in the institution as well as in the community, thereby developing a greater familiarity with the children by working with them both during confinement and during their transition to the outside: "While the teenagers are in residence, an aftercare counselor develops a relationship with them and their families. The counselor works intensively with youths during the two months before they leave . . . through a series of transitional activities. Once they return to their families, the counselor helps secure them education, training or jobs, and gets them counseling if necessary."[119]

The caseworker can thus maintain continuity in terms of nurturing an ongoing relationship with the client and his or her family. This offers greater security for the child and eases the transitional process. But it is not always administratively feasible, particularly in large state programs where training schools may be hundreds of miles away from the urban centers to which children are returning.

Aftercare is not provided in all jurisdictions, and as the discussion above illustrates, when available, it is often plagued with administrative and operational difficulties. But even the most progressive, sensitive, and well-endowed aftercare program cannot erase the effects of confinement. Nor is the "rehabilitative ideal" of the juvenile justice system an excuse for "deluding ourselves into the belief that imprisonment is therapy or . . . treatment."[120] In the end, the negative impact of incarceration is no less severe merely because the institution is called a "training school" or "detention center" rather than a prison or jail.

---

> *LEARNING GOALS*
>
> *Do you know:*
>
> - *Why the labeling effects of the juvenile justice system are not limited to those who are incarcerated?*
> - *What a noninterventionist strategy is?*

---

[119]Ron Stepanik, "The Eckerd Youth Program: Challenging Juveniles to Change," *Corrections Today*, Vol. 53, No. 1 (February 1991), p. 50.
[120]James C. Hackler, "The Need to Do Something," in Weisheit and Culbertson, p. 195.

## Alternative Approaches

The detrimental effects of contact with the juvenile justice system are not limited to those who are institutionalized. Simply being officially processed through the system labels the child as a "juvenile delinquent"—a stigma that will be confronted well into adulthood. Under the original philosophy of the juvenile court, of course, this was not supposed to happen. One of the fundamental reasons for establishing a separate juvenile justice system was precisely to *avoid the labeling* that inevitably accompanies involvement in the criminal justice system.

Many states do have provisions for sealing one's record as a juvenile and/or expunging it after a certain time period. In fact, offenders processed in juvenile court are not actually supposed to have a criminal record at all, since they have not technically been "convicted" of anything. But in reality, even sealed records are open to scrutiny by those with a "legitimate interest." In addition, the FBI has recently been authorized to begin collecting and distributing the arrest and conviction records of juveniles charged with serious or significant offenses.[121]

As we saw earlier, the due process movement called attention to the fact that young offenders were not receiving the solicitous care that had been the original philosophy of the court. To the contrary, it was becoming apparent that for many, formal processing often produces more harm than good. Willingness to make referrals to this benevolent protector of the child's welfare might be greater if, indeed, such action would truly be nonstigmatizing, rehabilitative, and as paternalistic as originally envisioned. That not being the case, there are many who advocate *noninterventionist* strategies—keeping the child out of the system whenever possible, or at least minimizing the extent of penetration into the system. Reducing the court's intrusion into the lives of children has been promoted by efforts directed toward *diversion, decriminalization,* and *deinstitutionalization.*

---

*LEARNING GOALS*

*Do you know:*

- *What functions youth services bureaus perform and why they do not necessarily eliminate labeling?*
- *What is meant by the "least restrictive means" of dealing with juvenile offenders?*
- *What legal issues are raised by diversion?*

---

## Diversion

One of the obvious ways to avoid the negative impact of being processed in the juvenile justice system is to divert troubled children out of it through referral

---

[121]"Barr Widens Access to Juvenile Records," *Crime Control Digest,* Vol. 26, No. 29 (July 20, 1992), p. 1.

to a nonjudicial agency better equipped to handle their problems. This is what is known as *diversion*—the disposition of a case without formal adjudication, on condition that the child fulfill some type of obligation, such as obtaining counseling.

Of course, diversion requires that the court have access to other options. Yet one national poll of juvenile court judges revealed that few had psychological or psychiatric services accessible to them on a regular basis "over half a century after the juvenile court movement set out to achieve the coordinated application of the behavioral and social sciences to the misbehaving child."[122] As early as 1967, the President's Crime Commission called attention to the court's very limited choices: "The dispositional alternatives available even to the better endowed juvenile courts fall far short of the richness and the relevance to individual needs envisioned by the court's founders. In most places, indeed, the only alternatives are release outright, probation, and institutionalization."[123]

As illustrated in Figure 13.7, it was a recommendation of the President's Commmission that a separate community-based *Youth Services Bureau* be established for dealing with the difficulties experienced by less serious offenders. Under this proposed alternative, only serious or repeat offenders referred by the police are brought directly into juvenile court. All others proceed through a Youth Services Bureau, which serves as both a *screening mechanism* to divert status offenders out of the system, and a *referral option* from juvenile court for delinquency cases that are better handled in the community.

The potential of this approach, however, has never been fully realized. Although federal funding helped to launch Youth Services Bureaus throughout the country, one study found that over a half-dozen years later, the majority of states were still not even differentiating between status offenders and delinquents, and were subjecting both to the same dispositions.[124] Moreover, there has been evidence that diversion programs often "widen the net" of social control— "drawing clients from youth who previously would have had their cases dismissed or would not even have been referred."[125]

Research also indicates that Youth Services Bureaus have primarily been *supplements to* the juvenile justice system rather than *substitutes for* it.[126] In this respect, it has been noted that the word "diversion" itself has two meanings: diversion *from* something or diversion *to* something. Simply diverting children from court to some other juvenile justice-affiliated program or service does not remove them from the system. It only directs them into another part of it, and "there is no reason to believe that the labels imposed by Youth Services Bureaus and other instruments of diversion will be nonstigmatizing."[127]

[122]President's Commission, p. 7.

[123]Ibid., p. 8.

[124]Mark M. Levin and Rosemary C. Sarri, *Juvenile Delinquency: A Comparative Analysis of Legal Codes in the U.S.* (Ann Arbor, MI: University of Michigan, 1974), p. 12.

[125]Krisberg, p. 158.

[126]Harjit S. Sandhu and C. Wayne Heasley, *Improving Juvenile Justice: Power Advocacy, Diversion, Decriminalization, Deinstitutionalization, and Due Process* (New York: Human Sciences Press, 1981), p. 158.

[127]Bruce Bullington, James Sprowls, Daniel Katkin, and Mark Phillips, "A Critique of Diversionary Juvenile Justice," *Crime and Delinquency,* Vol. 24, No. 1 (January 1978), pp. 63-64.

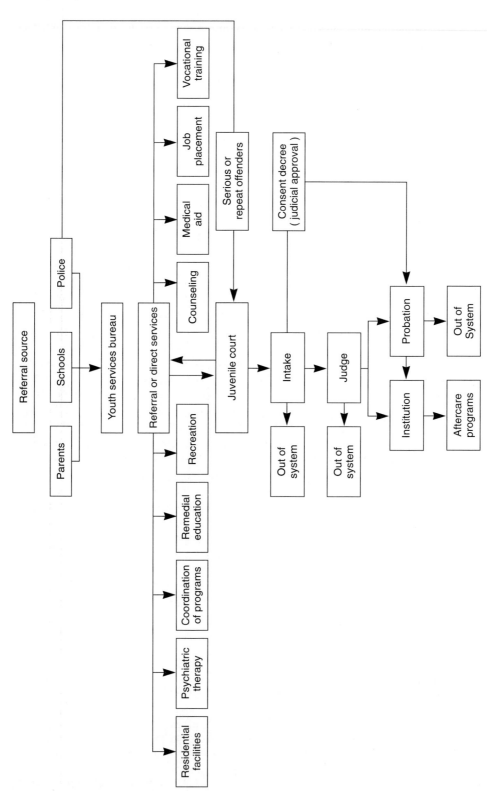

**Figure 13.7** Juvenile court diversion: the Youth Services Bureau. *Source:* President's Commission on Law Enforcement and Administration of Justice, *The Challenge of Crime in a Free Society* (Washington, DC: U.S. Government Printing Office, 1967), p. 89.

Nor does diversion mean the wholesale removal of cases from juvenile court jurisdiction. Rather, it represents only one component of a *continuum of services* that range from the least restrictive to the most restrictive options, in an effort to properly match available resources with the requirements of each situation.[128] The concept underlying diversion is to employ the *least restrictive means* of dealing with the case that is in keeping with the welfare of the child and the protection of the community. But in many communities, the range of services available is unfortunately still quite limited—and weighted heavier on the side of "most" rather than "least" restrictive alternatives.

Even where energetic attempts have been made to expand community treatment opportunities, invoking diversion raises the question of what legal rights the juvenile is entitled to when informal options are used. Informal adjustment of cases removes the stigma of court adjudication and the long-lasting negative impact that it can produce. At the same time, it subjects the child to certain restrictions (e.g., informal probation) or treatment requirements in the absence of due process protections that would accompany formal hearings. With more informal processing, "protections against unjustified treatment" can become as important as "protections against unjustified punishment."[129] This dilemma has been addressed in Canada by formalizing the procedures and rights granted to young people who either appear in court or participate in pre-trial diversion.[130]

On the other hand, there are those who maintain that providing alternative opportunities represents the original mission of serving the child's best interests. After all, the basic concept of diversion is not new. Throughout history, every change and innovation made with regard to juveniles has been "diversionary"—from the separation of children and adults in prisons and jails to the formation of a separate court in order to divert juveniles from the criminal justice system.[131] In the viewpoint of some, that basic mission of the juvenile justice system has been replaced by the legalistic aim of securing the child's freedom—which means "sending him back where he came from, to everything that has brought him where he is."[132] Again, as with the juvenile justice system in general, the issue comes down to whether children are gaining more than they are losing.

[128]See Tom English "Improving Juvenile Justice at the Local Level," *Juvenile Justice Bulletin* (March/April 1990), p. 1.

[129]Simonsen, p. 197.

[130]John Wass and Ron Marks, "Young Offenders Act Revamps Juvenile Justice in Canada," *Corrections Today*, Vol. 54, No. 8 (December 1992), p. 88.

[131]Whitehead and Lab, p. 309.

[132]Kramer, p. 94. The story of a young drug dealer who, at the completion of two months of intensive training did not want to go home is illustrative in this regard. Asking for special permission to stay longer, he said that he did not want to go home because "home was part of his problem." The suspicion was that his relatives were involved with drugs and that he would be forced back into the drug trade upon return. See Richard J. Ward, "Military and Civilians Working Together," *American Jails*, Vol. 6, No. 5 (November/December 1992), p. 91.

*Do you know:*

- *What is meant by decriminalization?*
- *What the arguments are for eliminating the court's jurisdiction over status offenders?*

## Decriminalization

From the standpoint of *minimizing intrusion* of the juvenile justice system into children's lives, obviously, the most desirable approach would be to keep kids out of the system entirely—formally as well as informally. Aside from specific programs directed toward delinquency prevention, one way to do so is to restrict the wide range of behaviors over which the juvenile court has jurisdiction.

Earlier, it was mentioned that one of the original justifications for a separate juvenile court was based on identifying "predelinquent" children in order to deal with their difficulties before these preliminary tendencies could escalate into more serious violations. That, however, was when considerable optimism still prevailed that official intervention would be more beneficial than harmful. Quite the contrary, it has been suggested that court intervention may actually increase rather than reduce the future likelihood of engaging in serious criminal activity.[133] As it became increasingly apparent that faith in good intentions was not justified in reality, many began to question whether "borderline" delinquent behavior, such as status offenses, should actually be dealt with in the juvenile justice system at all.

It has already been noted that a number of states have created separate legal categories for status offenders (e.g., CHINS, PINS, etc.), designating that such children are in need of "supervision" rather than "prosecution." But using different terms to classify their behavior does not necessarily translate into substantial differences with regard to how they are treated. Moreover, simply attaching new labels to their behavior may be no less stigmatizing.

To address these problems, the National Council on Crime and Delinquency in 1975 called for complete elimination of court jurisdiction over status offenders, based on the belief that community-based services are more beneficial than court-mandated supervision in addressing their needs.[134] This is what is known as *decriminalization*—removing non-criminal behaviors (i.e., status offenses) from juvenile court jurisdiction. Decriminalization is based on the belief that there is a need to confine the boundaries of official authority more appropriately. Supporters of this approach believe that sanctions currently extend "too far into the regulation of moral conduct and various minor forms of deviance," and that if regulation or treatment is necessary, it should occur outside the official system.[135]

[133]See, for example, Marvin E. Wolfgang, Robert M. Figlio, and Thorsten Sellin, *Delinquency in a Birth Cohort* (Chicago: University of Chicago Press, 1972), p. 252.

[134]National Council on Crime and Delinquency, "Jurisdiction Over Status Offenses Should Be Removed from the Juvenile Court," *Crime and Delinquency*, Vol. 21, No. 2 (April 1975), p. 97.

[135]Raymond T. Nimmer, *Diversion: The Search for Alternative Forms of Prosecution* (Chicago: American Bar Foundation, 1974), p. 46.

Further justification for decriminalization is cited by those who note that eliminating status offenses from juvenile court can reduce racial and economic disparity within the justice system. This is not necessarily meant to imply that the system deliberately discriminates against the poor or minorities. But such groups have fewer options and resources available to them. They are less likely to be able to get decent jobs, afford private treatment, or take advantage of nonjudicial alternatives. As a result, their unaddressed problems are more likely to come to official attention. Some maintain that in the absence of other choices, something is better than nothing. This argument is based on the premise that if no one else is willing or able to fulfill the needs of status offenders, the juvenile court is obliged to do so. But to others, "doing nothing"—at least judicially—may not be such a bad idea, as one appellate court judge states in no uncertain terms:

> The situation is truly ironic. The argument for retaining beyond-control and truancy jurisdiction is that juvenile courts have to act in such cases because "if we don't act, no one else will." I submit that precisely the opposite is the case: *because* you act, no one else does. Schools and public agencies refer their problem cases to you because you have jurisdiction, because you exercise it, and because you hold out promises that you can provide solutions.[136]

Moreover, added to recommendations for the decriminalization of status offenses is the weight of evidence pointing to the ineffectiveness of current practices. In contrast to the belief that court referral will change behavior by directing status offenders to the help they need, research shows that "the juvenile courts possess neither the expertise nor the resources to help youths who commit status offenses; that [those] processed by the court are less likely to benefit from the services of agencies outside the justice system; and [that] youths who participate in programs under court orders, or under threat of incarceration if they fail, become more delinquent."[137]

It has now been some 20 years since the National Council on Crime and Delinquency called for removing status offenders from juvenile courts. But we have seen obvious indications throughout this chapter that most states have yet to do so. Status offenses still outnumber violent crimes in terms of cases referred to juvenile courts (Figure 13.3). Over 28,000 juveniles are still confined for nondelinquent reasons (Figure 13.6). Youth Service Bureaus (Figure 13.7) have been slow both to develop and to fulfill their potential. What all of these and many other indicators point to is the fact that even the most pressing demands for action have often dissolved into apathy. As one observer has ruefully noted, "children don't form much of a constituency in this country, and that isn't likely to change."[138]

---

[136]National Council on Crime and Delinquency, p. 98, quoting Judge David Bazelon, U.S. District Court of Appeals.

[137]Sandhu and Heasley, p. 78.

[138]Hurst, p. 50.

## Deinstitutionalization

Reformers have generally been unsuccessful in diverting status offenders from the system or decriminalizing their behaviors. But perhaps there is greater hope that such offenders can at least be provided with more appropriate forms of treatment than custodial institutions. Just as decriminalization sought to remove less serious cases from the juvenile court, *deinstitutionalization* (or "decarceration") is directed toward removing low-risk, noncriminal offenders from secure confinement. In place of incarceration, the idea is to provide services through community-based resources.

In Chapter 10 we looked in depth at how negatively the institutional environment affects adult prisoners. Earlier in this chapter we saw that these results can be even more devastating for those who are still in their developmental years. In recognition of such disadvantages, the National Advisory Commission on Criminal Justice Standards and Goals recommended that states not only "refrain from building any more state institutions for juveniles" but also "phase-out present institutions over a five-year period."[139] But these were only the well-intentioned recommendations of a national study group. It was not until passage of the Juvenile Justice and Delinquency Prevention Act of 1974 that there was any real motivation for states to deinstitutionalize. Like the removal of juveniles from adult jails, federal juvenile justice funding has been used as an incentive to promote the removal of status offenders from secure detention facilities, as well as longer-term juvenile institutions. In their place, it encourages the establishment of nonsecure, community-based services.

There are naturally disagreements over just what types of community resources are best for status offenders. Traditional alternatives have included foster care, probation, and various forms of community-based residential and nonresidential programs. More recently, a number of nontraditional options have emerged—ranging from wilderness excursions to wagon train expeditions and maritime adventures. Through teamwork under difficult situations, such unique experiences are designed to build trust, confidence, and self-esteem.[140]

[139]National Advisory Commission on Criminal Justice Standards and Goals, *A National Strategy to Reduce Crime* (Washington, DC: U.S. Government Printing Office, 1973), p. 121.
[140]See, for example, "On Board, Not Behind Bars," *Corrections Today*, Vol. 53, No. 1 (February 1991), pp. 32–38.

Beyond debates over what alternatives are most appropriate for what types of individuals, questions have been raised about the federal government's role in promoting deinstitutionalization. Some feel that this is overstepping the bounds of authority. Others steadfastly maintain that status offenders should not be in the juvenile justice system in the first place.

Just as diversion attempts to provide the *least restrictive* means of processing a case, deinstitutionalization attempts to offer the *least restrictive disposition*. The concept recognizes that there is still considerable support for the potential deterrent effect of early intervention, but tries to assure that official intervention is as *nonpunitive* as possible. In fact, it was not actually the detrimental effects of incarceration that prompted Congress to pass the 1974 juvenile justice legislation, but rather "the argument that deprivation of liberty for persons who have not violated the criminal code is unjust and unwarranted."[141]

Considering the fact that the cost of housing *one resident* for a full year in a juvenile facility ranges from $25,300 to $47,300,[142] it is apparent that such sizable expenditures could be directed elsewhere more productively. For that amount of money, a youngster could attend any of the most prestigious private schools in the country. Yet it is difficult for options to incarceration to coexist in a society that continues to place so much emphasis on institutional construction. As long as incarceration is a primary goal, commitment to alternatives will not be a high priority.[143] This dilemma was recognized in Massachusetts when, in the early 1970s, the state closed virtually all of its large secure juvenile correctional institutions. For a look at some of the reasons behind this unprecedented step, see the next "Close-up on Corrections."

Massachusetts did reserve secure placements in small treatment centers for a relatively few chronic, violent offenders. But the vast majority of its juvenile population was deinstitutionalized. By 1975, only 10% of those not in aftercare were in secure settings. The remainder were primarily in nonresidential programs, group care, or foster care.[144] Clearly, this change placed young offenders in closer contact with the community. Perhaps more significantly, doing so *did not appear to create any increased danger to the public.* The state's network of community-based alternatives featured intensive supervision and surveillance, and despite concerns to the contrary, "[t]he Massachusetts youth correction reforms did not unleash a juvenile crime wave. In 1985, Massachusetts ranked 46th among the 50 states with respect to their rate of serious juvenile crime. . . . [F]or those who did commit new offenses, there was a tendency to commit less serious crimes. . . . The overall rates of recidivism . . . were as low or lower than any other state. . . ."[145]

[141]Anne L. Schneider, *Reports of the National Juvenile Justice Assessment Centers: The Impact of Deinstitutionalization on Recidivism and Secure Confinement of Status Offenders* (Washington, DC: U.S. Department of Justice, 1985), p. 1.

[142]Allen-Hagen, p. 7.

[143]See David J. Rothman, *Incarceration and Its Alternatives in 20th Century America* (Washington, DC: U.S. Department of Justice, 1979).

[144]Alden D. Miller, Lloyd E. Ohlin, and Robert B. Coates, "The Aftermath of Extreme Tactics in Juvenile Justice Reform: A Crisis Four Years Later," in David F. Greenberg, ed., *Corrections and Punishment* (Beverly Hills, CA: Sage Publications, 1977), p. 230.

[145]Ira M. Schwartz, "Correcting Juvenile Corrections," *Criminal Justice 92/93* (Guilford, CT: Dushkin Publishing Group, 1992), p. 179, citing Barry Krisberg, James Austin, and P. A. Steele, *Unlocking Juvenile Corrections: Evaluating the Massachusetts Department of Youth Services* (San Francisco: National Council on Crime and Delinquency, 1989).

A Radical Strategy:
The Closing of Training Schools in Massachusetts

Before 1969, the Massachusetts Division of Youth Services [DYS], like correctional agencies in most states, relied on the use of youth training schools to handle a
substantial number of their problem youths. The DYS training schools had the
usual educational and vocational programs; however, these schools were basically custodial and authoritarian in nature, with emphasis on conformity and
obedience to rules. There were some reports of brutal and punitive treatment . . .
which led to a series of investigations, studies, and recommendations. In the
wake of all these inquiries, the director of DYS resigned and the board begain a
national search for a new director. The choice was Dr. Jerome Miller . . . an advocate of therapeutic communities [which are] supposed to [prepare] residents of
an institution for adjustment to social life and work conditions outside. . . .
Participants of this community play an active role in changing themselves and
also in helping their coparticipants. . . . This treatment model requires a democratic atmosphere; . . . staff and youths interact in small units. Youths are allowed
to wear their own street clothes rather than institutional garments. . . .

Miller concluded that therapeutic communities could be run more successfully in small group homes located in the community—not in the institutions. He
also felt that professional services . . . could be provided more effectively in the
community and that community-based group homes would attract more volunteers. . . . Ironically, Massachusetts, which was one of the first states to start a
training school in 1846 [thus] became the first to abolish such institutions.

*Source:* Harjit S. Sandhu and C. Wayne Heasley, *Improving Juvenile Justice: Power Advocacy, Diversion,
Decriminalization, Deinstitutionalization, and Due Process* (New York: Human Sciences Press, 1981), pp.
152–53.

Although deinstitutionalization is also having an impact in other locations,
it has yet to fully achieve its goals. As shown in Figure 13.8, the percentage of
status offenders held in secure (versus open) facilities has declined rather steadily since 1974, dropping to 28% by 1979. But that figure remained unchanged
through 1983, and progress toward decarceration appears to be leveling off. As
recently as 1990, one out of five runaway cases still involved secure detention.[146]
Regardless of federal funding initiatives and success of the Massachusetts experiment, confining status offenders in correctional institutions has by no means
been eliminated.

Nor are all decarceration efforts equally successful. Overall, findings are
mixed. As seen in Figure 13.9, the majority of programs made no difference

---

[146]Sickmund, p. 5. (Data reflect only those jurisdictions reporting detention information and
indicate that runaways "are more apt to be securely detained than other types of status offenders".)

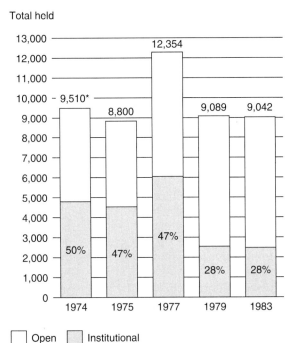

Total held

**Figure 13.8** Total number and proportion of status offenders held in "institutional" (secure) versus "open" (nonsecure) facilities, 1974–1983. *Note:* Facility type for 103 juveniles in private facilities was undisclosed for reasons of confidentiality. *Source:* Anne L. Schneider, *Reports of the National Juvenile Justice Assessment Centers: The Impact of Deinstitutionalization on Recidivism and Secure Confinement of Status Offenders* (Washington, DC: U.S. Department of Justice, 1985), p. 15

in terms of recidivism. The remainder were equally divided between those which achieved a positive impact and those which indicated a negative effect.[147]

However praiseworthy in theory, some are concerned that decarceration has produced unintended side effects. As it has become more difficult to institutionalize status offenders in training schools, there is some evidence that parents have become more likely to coerce children into such alternatives as psychiatric hospitalization—in which case "youngsters are merely being shunted to different forms of institutional placement."[148] Others assert that status offenders are "being cast to the urban streets, where they are exploited and victimized," as reflected in the findings of a task force which concluded that deinstitutionalization policies were directly contributing to the growing numbers of missing children.[149] From the opposite perspective, still others have found evidence of net widening and "relabeling" (which refers to cases that previously might have been treated as status offenders being "relabeled" as minor delinquencies).[150] Again, as with the juvenile justice system in general, it appears that even the best intentions can produce consequences that are contrary to original ambitions: "It

[147]It shoud be noted, however, that a number of these studies experienced serious methodological problems.

[148]Whitehead and Lab, p. 348–49, citing a study conducted by Ira M. Schwartz, J. Jackson-Beeck, and R. Anderson, "The `Hidden' System of Juvenile Control," *Crime and Delinquency*, Vol. 30 (1984), pp. 371-385.

[149]Breed and Krisberg, p. 17.

[150]Schneider, p. vi.

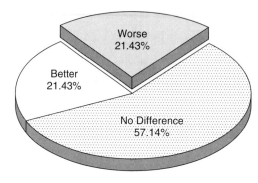

**Figure 13.9** Summary of recidivism findings from 14 deinstitutionalization of status offender programs. *Source:* Anne L. Schneider, *Reports of the National Juvenile Justice Assessment Centers: The Impact of Deinstitutionalization on Recidivism and Secure Confinement of Status Offenders* (Washington, DC: U.S. Department of Justice, 1985), p. 7.

must be said that at best we have been inefficient, and at worst we have been inhumane, and at all times we have been confused."[151]

## ❖ SUMMARY

Social policies related to our treatment of children have emerged from a bleak history marked by harsh conditions. Throughout much of the nineteenth century, children were expected to fulfill many of the same responsibilities as adults without enjoying the freedoms of adulthood. In the absence of social welfare, houses of refuge emerged as shelters for those who were destitute, abandoned, neglected, or orphaned. But even here, children were often exploited through long hours of work and severe punishments.

By the turn of the century, industrialization, immigration, and urbanization had combined to create problems of growing magnitude in American cities. The resulting poverty, overcrowding, unemployment, and crime obviously did not provide the best environment for raising children. Rather than addressing these underlying conditions, social reform was directed toward intervening in the lives of children in an effort to "rescue" them from the contaminating influences of urban life. Thus, the child-saving movement created the impetus for establishing the first separate juvenile court in 1899, based on the concept of *parens patriae*, which enabled the state to intervene in the place of parents to assure the welfare of the child. Serving the "best interests" of the child required that procedures be kept informal and flexible, since the court was designed to be the child's advocate rather than adversary. The court's mission included early identification of predelinquent behavior, personalized diagnosis, and prescription of rehabilitative treatment. To further avoid the stigma of criminal processing, the court relied on civil procedures and created a vocabulary of tranquilizing terms to distinguish the juvenile justice system from its adult counterpart.

But some 60 years later, serious questions were raised about the court's fulfillment of its commitment to protect rather than punish. Given concerns that juveniles were sacrificing their rights in the name of rehabilitation (and that their "rehabilitation" often amounted to little more than incarceration), the

---

[151]Hahn, p. 220, quoting Don M. Gottfredson.

due process movement sought to reduce the court's power and intrusiveness. During this period, a number of landmark Supreme Court decisions considerably extended the rights to which juveniles are entitled. These rulings have not, however, fully transformed proceedings into the adversarial nature of the criminal justice system. There is still hope that ideally, the juvenile court can guarantee legal rights through procedural safeguards without losing its personalized approach.

But that potential is difficult to achieve in a system which is empowered to take action in response to wide-ranging behaviors. In addition to violations that would also be criminal for an adult (delinquencies), the juvenile court has jurisdiction over conduct that is unlawful only as a result of one's status as a minor (status offenses), as well as dependency, neglect, and abuse cases. Juvenile courts have been accused of being too punitive in their handling of minor delinquents and status offenders, while at the same time being too lenient with serious delinquents. With increasing public concern focusing on chronic juvenile offenders engaged in violent crime, many high-risk cases are being transferred to adult court.

For those who are handled within the juvenile justice system, the process begins with the filing of a complaint. Whereas most delinquent referrals are originated by the police, the majority of referrals for status offenses are made by others, such as parents and school officials. During intake screening, it is determined whether a formal petition should be filed or if the case can be adjusted informally through another alternative. Intake personnel also recommend whether or not to hold the child in protective custody or secure detention prior to adjudication. Despite federal funding initiatives, juveniles still have not been removed from all adult jails.

Whether or not the child is detained prior to court appearance, a fact-finding hearing is ultimately scheduled. If the case is not dismissed, a disposition hearing follows. Although children now enjoy greater due process protections, proceedings are still more informal than in adult court. Dispositions can range in severity from nominal warnings to conditional programs or custodial confinement. In contrast to its original emphasis on the medical model's belief in rehabilitation, the juvenile court is now coming closer to resembling the justice model in terms of its dispositional practices. As a result, juvenile correctional facilities are witnessing a substantial growth in custody rates, particularly among minorities.

Juvenile institutions include both public and privately operated training schools. Public facilities must accept anyone committed to them, whereas private schools can be more selective, focusing on specific programs for a particular type of offender. If children are confined for the express purpose of getting treatment, the courts have recognized their legal right to receive it. Unlike adult prisons, the focus of juvenile corrections is still assumed to be primarily rehabilitative rather than punitive. That does not, however, mean that the effects of confinement are not as detrimental for juveniles. Quite the contrary, the negative impact can be even greater for children, who are confined in the midst of their emotional and physical development.

Because official intrusion into the lives of children appears to do more harm than good in many cases, there are those who advocate a noninterventionist strategy. Supporters of this approach would keep children out of the system whenever possible, or at least minimize the extent of their penetration into it. One way to do so is by diverting cases informally into nonjudicial community-based programs and services. Another is to decriminalize status offenses so that juvenile courts do not have jurisdiction over noncriminal conduct. Yet another alternative is to avoid institutionalizing status offenders. All of these proposals involve using the least restrictive means of dealing with minor indiscretions of adolescents. But they depend upon community resources which are not always available and can create unanticipated negative consequences.

We have undoubtedly come a long way since the time when the concept of childhood simply did not exist. Yet in many respects, we still have a long way to go toward treating wayward children with more of the care that should be reserved for sensitive kids than the contempt which should be restricted to sophisticated criminals. First, of course, we must distinguish between the two.

# chapter 14

# Staff: The Key Ingredient

*Never underestimate the expertise of your staff. After all, they do a pretty good job of running our facilities 24 hours a day, seven days a week.*[1]

*Samuel F. Saxton*

## ❖ CHAPTER OVERVIEW

Throughout this book, numerous correctional processes, programs, and procedures have been discussed. They have focused on a wide variety of topics from an equally broad range of perspectives. At this point it may seem that there is nothing whatsoever in common among these distinct and sometimes conflicting facets of the correctional conglomerate. But however diverse, they all have one basic ingredient in common. There is one element that is essential to providing correctional services, regardless of the type of client being processed or the type of approach being provided.

That crucial component is, quite obviously, people. Those who make the decisions, establish the policies, and administer the correctional system are extremely influential. It is their knowledge and expertise that shape the overall goals and direction guiding correctional practices. Those who carry out the policies and deliver the operational services are in the long run even more influential. It is they who have the direct, day-to-day contact with correctional clients. Through them, prevailing theories, public opinions, and political actions are translated into practice. It is their level of professionalism and personal skill that can either help or harden an offender; promote or subvert operational programs; strengthen or weaken correctional effectiveness: "Correctional administrators can (and do!) manage with crowded conditions, insufficient funding, political

---

[1]Samuel F. Saxton, "A Participatory Approach to Management," in *Correctional Issues: Correctional Management* (Laurel, MD: American Correctional Association, 1990), p. 35.

setbacks, and conflicting priorities. They cannot, however, manage without qualified, dedicated personnel."[2]

This does not mean that line-level staff are exclusively responsible for the system's successes or failures. Under the best of circumstances, it is difficult to implement policy intentions. But it can be virtually impossible when line personnel are faced with insufficient resources, uncooperative clients, and unsupportive supervisors. Staff members cannot achieve desired results without the fiscal resources necessary to do so. Being constantly short-handed, overworked, underpaid, and inadequately equipped eventually takes its toll on dedication and commitment. Nor can operational personnel be held accountable for offenders who are unwilling to accept help or unmotivated to change their behavior. Dealing with reluctant clients is an acknowledged fact of life for correctional workers.

Confronting these inherent obstacles would be considerably less frustrating, however, within a supportive administrative environment. It is one thing to persevere in the face of an apathetic public and an unappreciative clientele. But line staff cannot be expected to perform competently in an organizational environment that is plagued with contradictory goals, unclear policies, inequitable rules, inconsistent administrative procedures, or autocratic management techniques.

If lack of endorsement on the part of society and offenders is not counterbalanced by a nurturing organizational climate, it should not be surprising to find correctional employees experiencing anger, resentment, and eventually, alienation. When job stress leads to burnout, it is obvious that work is affected. Some react to such conditions by doing the minimum to get by—resigning themselves to a shoulder-shrugging "who cares?" existence while biding time until retirement. Others overreact—making the smallest issues into major incidents while venting their frustrations on co-workers and clients. Many simply leave—unable or unwilling to cope with the ultimate insult of an organization that appears to be no more supportive than clients or the community.

While operational personnel are charged with direct delivery of services, it is the upper-level administrative and managerial staff who set the tone for how well those services will be delivered. It is they who determine how line staff will be recruited, selected, trained, and supervised. Because tomorrow's supervisors and managers are recruited primarily from within today's rank and file, these personnel practices will have long-term implications. Thus, it is an important role of administrators to protect that investment in the future. It is they who establish an atmosphere that will either encourage or discourage employees throughout the organization. And it is that atmosphere which will have much to do with the long-term results of the entire correctional system.

Again, this does not mean that correctional personnel should be held responsible when society pursues inappropriate policies or provides insufficient funding. Even high-quality, motivated staff members who are fully committed to their mission will not enable deficient programs to succeed. But deficient staff will undoubtedly inhibit the success of even the most promising programs.

[2]Jeanne B. Stinchcomb, "Introduction," *Correctional Issues*, p. vi.

## ❖ CORRECTIONAL PERSONNEL

If there is one thing that is common among the wide variety of correctional programs and facilities operating throughout the United States, it is that in one way or another, they all deal with people. In today's litigation-conscious society, dealing with people also means carefully documenting what is being done. In the midst of the volumes of paperwork that are generated, it is sometimes easy to lose sight of the fact that corrections is not a paper-pushing bureaucracy, but rather, a people-serving business.

Because it is in the "people business," corrections is a very labor-intensive enterprise. But as the numbers of correctional personnel expand to keep pace with growing client populations, it is also sometimes difficult to keep in mind that every number on every agency's table of organization represents an individual employee—a person with strengths and weaknesses; capabilities and limitations; satisfactions and frustrations. The field of corrections spends a tremendous amount of money on hiring and training these people. From half to three-fourths of the operating budget is devoted to personnel.[3] It therefore "does not appear very prudent to throw all of that away with the flippant attitude that people are expendable."[4]

### Numbers and Characteristics

As recently as 1990, there were 555,813 workers staffing the correctional system throughout the United States.[5] Although we saw in earlier chapters that the bulk of correctional *clients* are under some form of community supervision, slightly less than 14% of correctional *employees* work in probation or parole. The overwhelming majority (83%) hold jobs in correctional institutions.[6] It is appar-

---

[3]F. Warren Benton and Charlotte A. Nesbitt, eds., *Prison Personnel Management and Staff Development* (Laurel, MD: American Correctional Association, 1988), p. 1.

[4]Tod Kembel, "Cultivating Our People: The Art of Leadership," *American Jails,* Vol. 5, No. 1 (March/April 1991), p. 90.

[5]Sue A. Lindgren, "Justice Expenditures and Employment, 1990," *Bureau of Justice Statistics Bulletin* (1992), p. 6.

[6]*Sourcebook of Criminal Justice Statistics—1991* (Washington, DC: U.S. Department of Justice, 1992), p. 34. (*Note:* The remaining 3% work in other corrections-related capacities within state government.)

ent that secure facilities are not only costly to construct, but also more expensive to staff.

Some of these institutional employees are supervisors, managers, or administrators. Some are teachers, counselors, or other professional/technical staff. Some are clerical, maintenance, or other supportive employees. But as shown in Figure 14.1, the vast majority are *correctional officers* who hold custodial/security positions in local, state, and federal correctional facilities. Moreover, in recent years, the increase of employment opportunities within institutional corrections (up 70.5%) has far outdistanced staffing increases within community-based corrections (up 39.7%).[7]

With the growth of the correctional workforce in recent years, a number of changes in the characteristics of these employees have occurred. Today, the stereotypical image of a correctional officer as a middle-aged, white male with less than a high school education could hardly be further from reality. That profile was typical of line staff in the past, but since the 1970s, the characteristics of correctional officers have been undergoing a significant transition:

1. Correctional workers are entering all phases of correctional work at *younger ages* . . . especially in adult institutional corrections.

2. Correctional workers are entering all phases of correctional work with *higher levels of education.* Again, this is especially noticeable in adult institutional corrections.

3. *Minorities and women* are entering the correctional work force in increasing numbers . . . [8] [emphasis added].

Although white males still predominate among those on the correctional payroll, female representation has expanded to one-fourth of the total paid staff

| | Custody/Security (CO's) | Administrative | Clerical, Maintenance, Food service | Professional/ Technical | Other | Total |
|---|---|---|---|---|---|---|
| Local jails | 73,280 | 6,727 | 11,711 | 7,393 | 520 | 99,631 |
| State and federal facilities | 169,587 | 7,382 | 41,867 | 45,365 | n/a | 264,201 |
| Total | 242,867 (66.8%) | 14,109 (3.9%) | 53,578 (14.7%) | 52,758 (14.5%) | 520 | 363,832 |

**Figure 14.1** Number of employees in correctional institutions. *Note:* Data include all full-time, part-time, payroll, nonpayroll, and contract staff. *Source:* Adapted from *Census of Local Jails, 1988* (Washington, DC: U.S. Department of Justice, 1991), p. xi; and James Stephan, *Census of State and Federal Correctional Facilities, 1990* (Washington, DC: U.S. Department of Justice, 1992), p. 14.

[7]James Stephan, *Census of State and Federal Correctional Facilities, 1990* (Washington, DC: U.S. Department of Justice, 1992), p. 15. Data reflect comparisons between 1984 and 1990.
[8]William G. Archambeault and Betty J. Archambeault, *Correctional Supervisory Management* (Englewood Cliffs, NJ: Prentice Hall, 1982), p. 19.

working in both jails (27%) and prisons (25%). In terms of race and ethnicity, comparable gains have been made, with minorities composing slightly more than a fourth of those on jail (30%) and prison (26%) payrolls. Similar patterns emerge when looking more specifically at those employed as correctional officers, where minorities represent 32% of line staff within jails and 29% within prisons.[9]

Expanding the employment of females and minorities in corrections is beginning to produce a workforce that is more reflective of the people and communities being served. Beyond the issue of better representing the demographic characteristics of the correctional population, there is also the argument that staff who share the client's cultural background may be better able to relate. Furthermore, with the implementation of equal employment opportunity, agencies are now prohibited from discriminatory hiring practices which had restricted some groups in the past.

## Implications of a Changing Workforce

These changes have not been easy to adjust to within correctional agencies. In addition to having to accommodate to a "new breed" of employee in terms of race, gender, or ethnicity, many of those beginning correctional work today are entering at younger ages and bringing with them higher educational credentials than their predecessors.[10] In fact, amendments to the 1990 Comprehensive Crime Control Act—designed to encourage students into criminal justice careers—may well produce additional future changes in this regard.[11]

This combination of an increasingly younger, better-educated workforce composed of more minorities and women has created challenges for administrators. Previously, correctional employees were considerably more homogeneous, sharing similar job-related values and attitudes. That was obviously disadvantageous in terms of generating change or meeting the needs of diverse clientele. But it was advantageous in terms of managing, supervising, and accommodating to like-minded employees. Along with the benefits of a more varied workforce, corrections is now faced with the challenge of adapting to the differences they represent. Nor are these differences confined to gender or ethnic distinctions. Today's employees appear to be considerably less likely than their predecessors to quietly endure an autocratic management style or to routinely implement unreasonable policies sent down through the chain of command: "Line employees have become much more sensitive to treatment they receive from supervisors. They are less apt to tolerate the old authoritarian style of command.

[9]Data compiled from Stephan, p. 16, and *Census of Local Jails, 1988* (Washington, DC: U.S. Department of Justice, 1991), pp. 22–23.

[10]That does not, however, mean that agencies are necessarily requiring higher education, (although agency directors who themselves possess advanced degrees do tend to rate formal education as important for officers seeking job advancement). See Tod W. Burke, Elaine Rizzo, and Charles E. O'Rear, "National Survey Results: Do Officers Need College Degrees?," *Corrections Today*, Vol. 54, No. 5 (July 1992), p. 174.

[11]"House Passes Corrections, Police Education Bill," *Crime Control Digest* (October 22, 1990), p. 4. (Under the Perkins loan cancellation provisions of this legislation, students and in-service officers who qualify for federal educational loans can have their repayments fully canceled after five years of service in local, state, or federal law enforcement or correctional agencies.)

Instead, union grievances and complaints…are on the increase."[12] No longer are line staff as willing to subserviently accept managerial practices that do not recognize their worth as individuals. "Mechanisms need to be developed to meet rising employee expectations and needs. The term `public servant' is too often taken literally . . . by management. Public employees cannot be treated as some sort of second-class worker."[13]

Today's employees can be expected to be more vocal about expressing job dissatisfaction. In comparison to many of their predecessors, this "new breed" has less to fear in doing so, since they often have greater potential for seeking employment elsewhere. And if correctional administrators do not recognize and respond to their concerns, seeking employment elsewhere is exactly what many of the most qualified will do.

## Staff Turnover and Retention

Although today's correctional employees may more readily leave employment that is not satisfying to them, corrections has long been plagued by high rates of turnover. In fact, one recent national survey of prison wardens, jail directors, and juvenile superintendents found turnover among correctional officers ranked between "continues to be a problem" and "is becoming more of a problem lately."[14] Annual turnover among institutional employees averages around 25%.[15] In comparison, average turnover rates do not generally exceed 9% among police departments and are usually much lower.[16] For a correctional agency to experience a 25% turnover means that in any given year, one-fourth of the entire workforce is being replaced. Moreover, within individual institutions, it is not uncommon to find rates far in excess of the overall average.

Needless to say, no stable business could run efficiently with a continuous transition of employees coming and going. Especially when personnel leave within the first few years of employment, turnover is also very costly, in light of the investment made in recruiting, selecting, and training them for the job. There are some *expected separations* that corrections can do little about—in any agency, people are inevitably going to retire, become seriously ill, die, get fired, move when a spouse relocates, and so on. General *economic conditions* also have an impact on resignations—more people are naturally going to be inclined to leave when employment opportunities are plentiful throughout the economy. Within corrections, there are also inherent *factors in the work environment* that are conducive to turnover—shift work, physical dangers, verbal abuse, low pay, uncooperative clients, and an unsupportive public are part of the nature of the

[12]David E. Kaup, "Attitude Change," *American Jails,* Vol. 6, No. 5 (November/December 1992), p. 36.
[13]William C. Collins, "Labor Relations and Dispute Resolution," in Benton and Nesbitt, p. 162.
[14]Marilyn McShane, Frank P. Williams, David Shichor, and Kathy L. McClain, "Examining Employee Turnover," *Corrections Today,* Vol. 53, No. 5 (August 1991), p. 220.
[15]Ned Benton, "Strategies for Staff Development," in *Correctional Issues,* p. 13.
[16]*Sourcebook of Criminal Justice Statistics—1990* (Washington, DC: U.S. Department of Justice, 1991), p. 39.

job. But there are other reasons that employees voluntarily leave which *are* amenable to change.

The long-term selective retention of good staff is essential for building an effective organization. It is therefore necessary to determine why qualified employees leave. According to one study, managers assessing the reasons for employee turnover tend to assume one of two different perspectives:

> One group believed that there was nothing wrong with the job, but there was something wrong with the employee or the employee's choice of the job. . . . Part of this group blamed the personnel office and selection policy for hiring the "wrong" person. The second group admitted to the problems of the job and the job's potential to discourage employees. This group cited poor working conditions, offenders' aggressiveness, long hours, and the stress of crowding as reasons for employee turnover.[17]

The basic drawbacks of correctional employment are undoubtedly more discouraging to some than others. But it is interesting that neither group of managers responding to this survey appeared to accept any personal responsibility for the dissatisfactions that cause employees to quit. Yet in a study during which resigning correctional officers were given an exit questionnaire that asked their reasons for leaving, 8 of the 11 most frequently cited reasons were related to supervisory or managerial problems, such as:

- No feeling of accomplishment.
- Poor promotional opportunities.
- Few incentives for good work.
- Poor relations with supervisor.
- Lack of support from supervisor.
- Unfair treatment by supervisor.
- Supervisor overly critical.
- Management did not treat employees fairly.[18]

Moreover, when the exiting employees were asked to make specific recommendations concerning changes that could make the agency a better place to work, most categories of responses (20) addressed problems with supervisors or management, rather than problems with inmates (6). While working with certain inmates may simply be troublesome, working under certain management and supervisory practices may simply be intolerable.

---

[17]McShane et al., pp. 224–25.

[18]N. G. Peterson, J. S. Houston, M. J. Bosshardt, and M. D. Dunnette, *A Study of the Correctional Officer Job at Marion Correctional Institution, Ohio: Development of Selection Procedures, Training Recommendations, and Exit Information Program* (Minneapolis, MN: Personnel Decisions Research Institute, 1977), pp. 49–66.

## ❖ ADMINISTRATIVE PRACTICES

With a few exceptions that occasionally occur at the highest ranks, virtually all correctional managers, administrators, and supervisors are selected from within the agency. (In fact, most systems have restrictions against lateral entry into all but the uppermost levels). This pattern has major implications for how entry personnel are recruited, selected, and trained, since it is largely from the ranks of line-level officers that command staff are chosen.

Throughout the remainder of this section we briefly review these administrative practices. Our focus will be not only on how they operate currently, but also on how they can be changed to improve existing procedures, especially in light of their long-term implications for the future of correctional management and leadership.

### Recruitment

Historically, the field of corrections has tended to limit its officer recruitment to establishing minimal requirements and accepting anyone who could meet them. The rationale typically given for such rudimentary practices often relates to the pressures induced by lack of public prestige, high turnover, and traditionally low salaries. But each of these justifications is amenable to change.

**The Image Issue.** In terms of prestige, many agencies are locked into the despair of believing that it would be fruitless to set higher entrance standards. This perspective is based on the reasoning that because the field suffers from an inferior image, it is relegated to taking virtually anyone who is willing to work in it. Restricting standards to the lowest acceptable denominator, however, results in recruiting precisely that. Few of the best suited or most educated will be attracted to a job with requirements that are far below their level of qualification. Thus, a self-fulfilling cycle is created—if only the least qualified are recruited, only the least qualified tend to apply. On the other hand, an agency which expects a high caliber of employee will be considerably more likely to attract better applicants.

Of course, as standards are raised, more candidates will naturally be rejected. That is why the organization must be willing to search aggressively for applicants. Once an agency is recognized as a good place to work where people are proud to be employed and only the best are selected, it will be easier to appeal to suitable candidates. But even under these ideal circumstances, it is essential to put considerable energy into the recruitment process, beyond just distributing posters and brochures.[19] Making personal contacts by attending job fairs, establishing college internships, and the like, are key ingredients of successful recruitment.

Furthermore, recruitment is not just a one-way "public relations" activity, but rather, a two-way communication process in which the potential candidate shares his or her expectations of what the job entails.[20] If recruiting is limited to "selling" the job, it may well generate a lot of applicants, but many will be sadly disillusioned later, when they find that reality does not match their initial perceptions. With high visibility, a respected reputation, and intensive (but realistic) recruitment, agencies will find their pool of prospective employees expanding, therefore enabling them to be more selective.

**Vacancy Pressures.**   With regard to turnover, much of the strategy for keeping entrance standards at minimal levels is designed to enable the organization to fill numerous vacancies promptly. Departments that are not at full capacity will often be required to employ officers on overtime, which quickly becomes very costly. Unfortunately, some agencies have come to accept high turnover as the price of doing business in corrections. In many cases, it is not. Dealing with the turnover problem requires a twofold approach: first, finding out why employees are leaving, and then doing something about it.

As noted previously, some terminations are "expected separations," many of which can be anticipated. With proactive planning, an agency can identify approximately how many people will be retiring within upcoming years and schedule recruitment efforts accordingly. Even among those who leave unexpectedly, much more can be done to determine why and to deal with the findings. As mentioned earlier, this does not necessarily mean trying to pry higher salaries from the taxpayers. Although better pay would undoubtedly help, people who enjoy their jobs will be more reluctant to leave, despite the attraction of more money elsewhere. Throughout much of the remainder of this chapter, we address administrative techniques that could increase satisfaction without spending one additional dime. What is involved in reducing voluntary turnover is not higher

[19]For more information, see Carlos M. Sanchez, "Attracting a Top-Notch Staff," in *Correctional Issues*, pp. 1–6, Dennis J. Molyneaux, "Recruiting the Best," *Corrections Today*, Vol. 48, No. 5 (July 1986), pp. 96, 102–4, and "New Recruitment Strategy Shows Promise in Canada," *CJ: The Americas*, Vol. 5, No. 4 (August/September, 1992), pp. 18–19.
[20]Roy R. Roberg and Jack Kuykendall, *Police Organization and Management: Behavior, Theory, and Processes* (Pacific Grove, CA: Brooks/Cole Publishing Company, 1990), pp. 428–29.

costs but greater commitment. And the more that corrections can decrease voluntary resignations, the more it can increase entrance requirements.

**Compensation Concerns.**  At the same time, it is readily apparent that few enter corrections for the monetary compensation it offers. Many states and localities are making significant strides toward improving entry-level salaries. For example, between 1986 and 1990—a time when the U.S. economy was not especially healthy—starting correctional officer salaries increased an average of about 19%.[21] But overall, given the nature of the job and the qualifications necessary to do it properly, they are not generally paid adequately.

This issue likewise has been used as a justification for reducing entrance standards. Yet there are any number of professions—from teaching to nursing or social work—that have traditionally not been well compensated. Nevertheless, in most states these occupations have established and maintained relatively rigorous educational and training requirements. Even within corrections, the majority of probation, parole, and juvenile caseworker positions require a bachelor's degree, sometimes with additional experience as well.[22] In any event, if the job satisfaction concerns discussed above are addressed, salary may not be as significant a drawback to effective recruitment.

## Selection

Naturally, the purpose of active recruitment is to identify a sufficiently sizable pool of applicants to facilitate choice in the selection process. Without such choices, an agency may be tempted to fill positions with applicants who would not be considered suitable if there were a larger group from which to draw.

Once the applicant pool is assembled, the selection *screening process* begins. Screening encompasses all of the procedures used to determine who meets the established entrance qualifications and possesses the greatest potential. Ultimately, all of the various screening procedures employed should be designed to accurately predict the candidate's ability to succeed on the job. It is therefore essential that the measurements are *related to the job* to be performed.

One of the most prevalent screening instruments is a written civil service exam, which is used by almost 80% of state agencies in the selection of correctional officers.[23] Probably the next most common procedure is an oral interview. Some agencies have also begun to employ various forms of psychological evaluations, to guard against hiring those with personality disorders. Others also conduct background checks, polygraph tests, medical exams, physical agility tests, and the like. But written exams and oral interviews remain the most widely used screening devices. The usefulness of both largely depends upon how carefully they were structured.

---

[21]*Vital Statistics in Corrections* (Laurel, MD:  American Correctional Association, 1991), p. 31.
[22]Ibid., pp. 35, 40.
[23]Ibid., p. 32.

**Written Tests.** Written exams have the advantage of being easy to administer, relatively inexpensive, and simple to score. Like SATs and college entrance tests, they are useful for determining a candidate's general level of knowledge and written communication skills. Good writing capabilities are undoubtedly important in correctional work, where preparing memos, reports, and other forms of written communication are a daily feature of the job. But just because a person is a good "test taker" does not necessarily mean that he or she will work out well on the job. That is especially true if test items are not directly job-related. Moreover, those rejected on the basis of an irrelevant test may well have grounds for legal action.

The question then becomes how to make written tests more reflective of the actual knowledge needed to perform the job. Ideally, this is done through a *job-task analysis*, which:

- Identifies the tasks being conducted by those already holding the job.
- Determines the knowledge, skills, and abilities necessary to effectively perform job tasks (particularly those that occur frequently and/or are significant to successful performance).[24]

The relationship between job-task analysis and selection screening is based on a simple concept—that is, if you do not know what you are looking for, how

Job-related written tests, practical exercises, and training are all necessary ingredients in selecting and grooming professional correctional officers. Courtesy of the Dade County Department of Corrections and Rehabilitation, Miami, Florida.

[24]For further information on analyzing job tasks and developing valid performance-based criteria, see Candice Skrapec, "Assessment and Selection," in Benton and Nesbitt, pp. 54–55.

will you know when you find it? The analysis of job tasks is therefore designed to identify what specific types of knowledge and skills are needed to perform the job properly. Then it is possible to construct written test items that reflect more accurately what a candidate needs to know. But the major disadvantage of even the most carefully constructed, job-related written test is that it is limited to measuring knowledge. Written tests can determine what applicants *know* intellectually, but that may or may not reflect what they are actually able to *do*.

**Oral Interviews.**   Many employing agencies require an oral interview in order to meet prospective employees face to face and get a better feeling for whether or not they will work out on the job. The primary drawback of oral interviews is exactly that—they are based more on personal feelings or subjective judgments than on objective evaluations of one's capabilities. Like the decision making of parole boards, employment interview panels are open to criticism—and in this case, potentially to legal challenge as well.

Even when interviewers use standardized score sheets and numerical scales to record their ratings, the numbers are subject to individual interpretation. For example, a "3" on a 1-to-5 scale measuring "appearance" presumably reflects an average score. But what is "average appearance" to one interviewer may be below or above average to another. Furthermore, these rating criteria also may encounter problems in terms of job relevance (as discussed above with regard to general-knowledge written tests).

Another limitation of the oral interview is the tendency of candidates to respond to questions in a manner that they consider socially or organizationally acceptable. It is only natural to tell the interviewers what the applicant thinks they want to hear, regardless of whether or not such responses are truly accurate reflections of one's personal opinions.

**Innovative Alternatives.**   In an effort to address the shortcomings of traditional selection devices, progressive organizations have implemented more job-related procedures, such as *assessment centers*. Based on a job-task analysis, the assessment center technique is designed to predict more accurately which candidates actually do, in fact, have the ability needed to perform the job properly. Assessment is based on the concept that the best way to find out if someone can do a specific job is to place them in the job and see how well they perform. Obviously, that is impossible in corrections—where legal restrictions, certification standards, and liability concerns prohibit such an option. But assessment does the next best thing, through a series of written exercises, videotaped scenarios, and/or live role-playing interactions with the candidate.[25]

For example, information might be provided about a hypothetical problem in a correctional facility, with the candidate instructed to write a memo describing the situation and making a recommendation to correct it. In this way, a number of dimensions can be assessed, such as judgment, decisiveness, and written communication. A similar process could be used to set up a role-playing situa-

[25]See Jeanne B. Stinchcomb "Why Not the Best? Using Assessment Centers for Officer Selection," *Corrections Today*, Vol. 47, No. 3 (June 1985), pp. 120–124.

tion in which, for instance, two "inmates" (actors) wish to speak to the "officer" (job applicant) about their inability to get along together in the cell they share. Trained assessors would then observe and measure the resulting interactions on such dimensions as leadership, verbal communication, judgment, and so on.

This is a very brief description of a rather complex process. Nevertheless, the advantages of using assessment should be apparent. Unlike written exams, they are not limited to testing knowledge. Unlike oral interviews, they are not the product of a subjective process or unstructured opinions. By placing the applicants in simulated, job-related situations and evaluating their reactions, assessment comes as close as possible to reflecting real life, as well as measuring the "common sense" that is so elusive in paper-and-pencil testing.

However, also unlike traditional approaches, assessment centers can be costly to develop and operate. As a result, some agencies are experimenting with modified variations of assessment, such as video-based situational exams and situational interviews.[26] In fact, assessment is even more appropriate and cost-effective for making promotional decisions, since it can be fine-tuned to the specific requirements of the job while eliminating complaints about favoritism or subjectivity that often surround the promotional process.

Whether agencies use written exams, oral interviews, psychological evaluations, assessment techniques, or a combination, it is becoming increasingly critical that the screening process be able to demonstrate that it is:

- *Valid*: true, accurate measurement of the dimensions of the job.
- *Reliable*: consistent measurement that does not fluctuate arbitrarily (e.g., according to who is doing the rating).
- *Job-related*: relevant to the actual job that the candidate will be performing.
- *Legally-defensible*: able to withstand the test of outside scrutiny by the courts (which will be much more likely if the prior three conditions are met).

Otherwise, the agency is not only vulnerable to needless and costly litigation, but more importantly, is not accurately predicting who will and will not perform effectively on the job. In that case, some good candidates are being overlooked, while some inappropriate candidates are being selected.

## Training

Regardless of how good the selection process is at bringing the most qualified recruits into the agency, they cannot be expected to know what is required of them on the job without proper training. Gone are the days when an officer was given a uniform, a badge, and a set of keys—sent to work with no further instruction than "good luck!" In most jurisdictions, officers are no longer relegated to learning the job through "helpful" inmates. Correctional work is not only more complex today, but is also governed by a multitude of legal restrictions and organizational policies

[26]See, for example, Mary K. Stohr-Gillmore, Michael W. Stohr-Gillmore, and Nicholas P. Lovrich, "Sifting the Gold from the Pebbles: Using Situational Interviews to Select Correctional Officers for Direct Supervision Jails," *American Jails,* Vol. 3, No. 4 (Winter 1990), pp. 29–34.

with which the officer is expected to comply. As we will see later, because of the potential for liability and costly litigation, correctional management "does not have the luxury of treating staff training as a peripheral or nonpriority concern."[27]

Even recruits who enter the agency from previous work as correctional officers elsewhere should not be exempt from the basic training academy. Every correctional organization is somewhat unique, and there is no guarantee that a person who performed acceptably in one place will do so in another. No matter how well experienced, recruits must learn the specific rules, regulations, operational procedures, and behavioral expectations of the department that they are entering. When an untrained officer is involved in a situation that results in liability claims, the courts are increasingly holding the employing agency liable for damages, using a "failure to train" rationale.[28]

**Mandated Training.**   Despite the importance of training to effective job performance, not all states require entry-level correctional officer training. Virtually all states have statutes mandating police training, and most also have standards for state correctional officers. But officers employed in local jails are still not included in the training mandates of many states. Fortunately, in most cases, training is provided on a voluntary basis, even when mandatory state standards are lacking.[29]

The American Correctional Association's correctional officer training standards call for a minimum of 40 hours of orientation prior to job assignment, followed by 120 hours within the first year of employment (along with an additional 40 hours each year thereafter).[30] Given the complex demands and legal liability of correctional work today, these standards are just that—minimal. Moreover, unlike state certification statutes, ACA standards do not carry the weight of law. Although any correctional facility hoping to achieve ACA accreditation must meet these standards, the minimum required often becomes the maximum provided. A 1984 survey by the National Institute of Corrections, for example, found that most states were requiring only the minimum hours required by ACA.[31]

Since then, some states and localities have voluntarily begun to provide more training than is mandated by either ACA or even state law. For example, between 10 and 16 weeks of training are required in Florida, Michigan, and Vermont,[32] and at the local jail level, Dade County (Florida) requires 16 weeks of classroom preparation.

Determining just how much entry-level training is actually mandated can become confusing, since some agencies define training strictly in terms of class-

[27]Jess Maghan and William C. Collins, "What Staff Doesn't Know *Can* Hurt Them: Correctional Law Training," *Corrections Today*, Vol. 50, No. 5 (August 1988), p. 164. See also Randy Borum and Harley Stock, "Excessive Force Prevention Programs: An Essential Tool to Properly Train Staff and Protect against Litigation," *Corrections Today*, Vol. 54, No. 4 (June 1992), pp. 26–30.

[28]See John Sample, "Civil Liability for Failure to Train to Standard," *Educational Technology* (June 1989), pp. 23–26.

[29]Dianne Carter, "The Status of Education and Training in Corrections" (Part II), *Journal of Correctional Training* (Spring 1992), p. 7.

[30]*Standards for Adult Correctional Institutions* (Laurel, MD: American Correctional Association, 1990), pp. 79–81.

[31]Carter, p. 6.

[32]*Vital Statistics*, p. 33.

room hours, while others include various types of "field training" or "on-the-job" training as well. As illustrated in Figure 14.2, expanding the definition brings more agencies into the 5 to 9 week range. Yet even when training is restricted to that which occurs in the classroom, the majority of agencies report mandating between 5 and 9 weeks.

**Training Curriculum.** Distinguishing between classroom and outside activities raises the question of just what *is* considered proper training. Good training—like good screening—focuses on the knowledge, skills, and abilities needed to be successful on the job.[33] It therefore stands to reason that the entry-level training curriculum should be based on the same job-task analysis that is used to develop selection procedures.[34] Today, this generally means that the curriculum will include everything from human behavior and interpersonal skills to constitutional law, legal issues, ethics, operational policies and procedures, and such high-liability areas as CPR/first aid, firefighting, defensive tactics, driving, and firearms.[35] The observations of the director of officer training in England bear no less relevance in this country: "We ask a lot from new officers in training, and precisely because we do, we get it."[36]

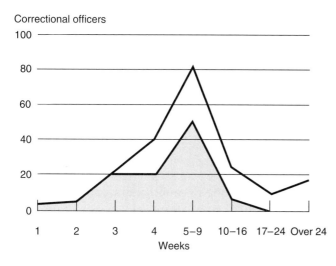

Correctional officers

**Figure 14.2** Mandatory training for correctional officers. *Source: Vital Statistics in Corrections* (Laurel, MD: American Correctional Association, 1991), p. 33.

[33]John E. Southern and Jerry A. Nosin, "Mandatory Pre-Employment and Training Standards for Jail Officers," *American Jails*, Vol. 5, No. 3 (July/August 1991), p. 62.

[34]For more information on using a job-task analysis to develop a training curriculum, see Steven D. Falkenberg and C. Randall Baird, "Developing Job Validated Training Curricula in Corrections: Methods and Procedures," *Issues in Correctional Training and Casework*, Vol. 3 (October 1987), pp. 8–13.

[35]Some of the recently recognized needs in correctional officer training have been identified by Larry S. Fischer, "Correctional Training: Critical Topics for the 1990's," *American Jails*, Vol. 6, No. 2 (May/June 1992), pp. 17–21; and Judith Quinlan and Elaine Motte, "Psychiatric Training for Officers: An Effective Tool for Increased Officer and Inmate Safety," *American Jails*, Vol. 4, No. 2 (July/August 1990), pp. 22–25.

[36]David Waplington, "The Selection and Training of Prison Officers in England and Wales," *American Jails*, Vol. 5, No. 6 (January/February 1992), p. 60.

Once the curriculum is established, the next question is how it will be offered. Undoubtedly, classroom instruction is a central feature of training, but we all know that learning skills occurs through a combination of hearing, seeing, and doing. Participants can benefit tremendously from being provided with opportunities to try out their classroom learning through practical role-playing exercises.[37]

Academy training should also be integrated with field experience, so that what is learned in the classroom can be applied to the realities of the job. Yet it is equally necessary to assure that training which occurs in nontraditional settings is, in fact, a structured learning experience. All too often, what may pass for on-the-job training (OJT) is, in reality, either on-the-job reading of policy manuals or simply doing the job, with no more guidance or instruction than a good supervisor would normally be expected to provide in a regular work setting.

Regardless of where it is offered physically, to qualify as "training," the program must meet three fundamental criteria. That is, valid training is:

1. Properly *developed*: based on actual job tasks, as reflected in a written lesson plan.
2. Properly *delivered*: taught by qualified instructors.[38]
3. Properly *documented*: including both attendance records and measures of satisfactory completion.

Programs that meet these guidelines can legitimately be considered "training." Otherwise, it is somewhat misleading to count on-the-job experiences among training hours.

**Preservice Training.** It is one thing to mandate a certain number of training hours and develop an appropriate curriculum, but quite another to assure that the training is provided in a timely manner. With pressures to fill existing vacancies immediately, the *historical approach* to training has been to place new recruits directly on the job, postponing their enrollment in the academy until they could be spared to attend. Needless to say, once employees become a part of the workforce, they tend to become "indispensable," and sparing them at any time creates a hardship.

Some states now prohibit this approach, requiring all preemployment training to be completed before job assignment. But others allow a designated grace period during which the new recruit can legally work prior to being enrolled in the training academy. The numerous disadvantages of postponing training include increased liability. When training is relegated to on-the-job experience,

---

[37]For a description of how role-playing that involves inmate "actors" can be used, see Jeanne B. Stinchcomb and Sally Gross-Farina, "Command Performance: Inmate Involvement in Training," *American Jails*, Vol. 1, No. 3 (Fall 1987), pp. 6–9. For information on scenarios for in-service training, see George Giurbino, "Are Corrections Officers Becoming Over-Familiar with the Inmates?" *Training Aids Digest* (February 1992), pp. 9–10.

[38]For more information on the development and delivery of valid training, see Michael J. Gilbert, "The Challenge of Professionalism in Correctional Training," *Issues in Correctional Training and Casework* (October 1986), pp. 4–10.

Training programs include drill and ceremony to build teamwork, discipline, and *esprit de corps*, along with classroom work to develop intellectual capabilities and practical exercises to refine skills. Courtesy of the Dade County Department of Corrections and Rehabilitation, Miami, Florida.

"Violation of an inmate's rights becomes almost inevitable, and with the violation comes officer liability. If the officer's actions or inaction can be traced back to a lack of training, higher-ranking officials may also be found liable."[39]

Beyond legal vulnerability, lack of preemployment training puts officers in a very tenuous position. In essence, they are struggling to cope with a job where they are unsure of what rules to enforce, what behaviors are prohibited, what actions to take, and so on. As we saw earlier, this can promote a dangerous reliance on the inmates for guidance. In addition, untrained officers do not tend to make receptive recruits when they finally do get to training, especially if they have already developed inappropriate work habits which must then be "unlearned" at the academy.

For these and many other reasons, correctional organizations today are moving toward what is becoming acknowledged as the *traditional approach* to training. As shown in Figure 14.3, the procedure that is now more traditionally accepted is to send recruits to training immediately upon employment. Thus, they are not put to work until successful completion of the academy curriculum. This is certainly a vast improvement over historical practices.[40] But there are two fundamental drawbacks to the traditional approach: first, what it is costing the

[39]Maghan and Collins.

[40]For more details on the advantages of training before job assignment, see David W. Hayeslip and Derral Cheatwood, "Problems with Correctional Officer Trainees: Designing a Training Program to Best Counter These Problems," *Issues in Correctional Training and Casework*, Vol. 5 (October 1988), pp. 10–13.

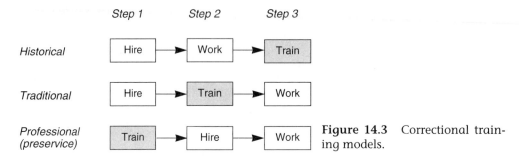

Step 1          Step 2          Step 3

Historical      Hire → Work → Train

Traditional     Hire → Train → Work

Professional    Train → Hire → Work
(preservice)

**Figure 14.3** Correctional training models.

organization fiscally, and second, what it is costing the field in terms of recognition as a profession.

Fiscally, the traditional approach is very costly. Since recruits are hired before training, everyone is on full salary throughout the program. Even for an "average" program of only 6 to 7 weeks, at a relatively low starting salary of $16,000 (plus benefits), training is costing well over $2000 per person. Assuming a class size of 25 to 30 recruits, this one academy class alone will run up a bill of at least $50,000 to $60,000, and that is using rather conservative figures for compensation and training time. Given the fact that corrections has routinely been underfunded, the potential for reducing such expenditures is appealing, especially during tight economic times.

But perhaps even more important is what the traditional approach is costing in terms of corrections becoming recognized as a *profession*. The professionalization of corrections is a commendable goal that has been supported vigorously by virtually every state and national organization representing correctional personnel throughout the country. But realistically, it takes far more than vocal support to make it happen. Among other things, procedures for enacting and enforcing standards, licensing, and certification must be implemented.[41]

One of the consistent hallmarks of any "established" profession is that the education, training, and certification mandated for entrance are required before employment. A person interested in teaching would not apply to the school board and then expect to be sent to college. A person interested in nursing would not apply to a hospital and then expect to be enrolled in nursing school. Occupations with state licensing requirements must meet established provisions before they can obtain their "license to practice."

It is therefore for both fiscal and professional reasons that some agencies are now turning to the *professional (or preservice) approach*. As with the traditional approach, recruits are fully screened to assure that they meet state and agency hiring standards before academy entrance. But that is where the similarity ends. Like existing professions, recruits are not hired under this model until they successfully complete the training necessary to be certified as correctional officers. The major advantage of preservice training is a combination of fiscal savings and the promotion of corrections as an acknowledged profession. As shown in Figure 14.3, the priority of training also increases correspondingly as the field

---

[41]Robert Barrington, "Introduction," in *Report of the Working Group on Professional Standards in Corrections Staffing* (Marquette, MI: International Association of Correctional Officers, 1990), p. 3.

moves from the historical to the traditional, and finally, to the professional/pre-service approach.[42]

**Probation and FTO Programs.**   Whether employees are hired in the traditional manner before attending training or after academy graduation through the professional approach, most agencies establish some period of time for *probation*. During this time (generally, six months to one year), new employees are "on trial," with the agency examining their performance to determine whether their appointment should be continued. But the probationary period does not always achieve its full potential. In some cases, it functions as a "rubber stamp," which results in virtually all new hires becoming permanent members of the workforce. A good selection process will naturally produce fewer probationary terminations. Yet when everyone always completes probation satisfactorily—regardless of their work record—the purpose is defeated.

That does not mean that probation's only function is to weed out unsuitable employees who have inadvertently slipped through the hiring process. To the contrary, the probationary period should be an on-the-job extension of the training academy—where knowledge and skills learned in the classroom are put into practice, with the newcomer exposed to a wide variety of operational positions and assisted with becoming effectively integrated into the organization. Without a structured postacademy program that provides performance feedback, the effect of training "will be short and of little impact on the organization."[43] Probation offers an opportunity to *assist* as well as *assess* the new recruit in the work environment.

Since training needs do not end with graduation from the basic academy, in-service classes are necessary to keep updated, prepare for advancement, and learn new skills. Courtesy of the Dade County Department of Corrections and Rehabilitation, Miami, Florida.

[42]June Damanti and Jeanne B. Stinchcomb, "Moving toward Professionalism: The Preservice Approach to Entry-Level Training," *Journal of Correctional Training* (Summer 1990), pp. 9–10.
[43]Michael J. Gilbert, "Evaluation," in Benton and Nesbitt, p. 135.

This dual mission is precisely what *field (or facility) training officer* (FTO) programs are designed to accomplish. In other words, they enable the agency to evaluate the trainee closely as well as to bridge the gap between formal training and on-the-job application of the skills learned in the academy.[44]

FTO programs are essentially a structured phasing-in of the new employee. The trainee is rotated systematically through various job assignments under the direction of a seasoned employee (FTO). The FTO serves as a mentor and is responsible for training, supervising, and evaluating the recruit. This reduces the trauma and anxiety of the first days on the job and also provides feedback from the FTOs which can be used to identify any weaknesses in the selection process or the training curriculum.[45] Without an FTO to link academy training to operational practices, a recruit's first experience on the job can be confusing and bewildering. As a veteran sergeant tells it, "[y]ou report to your first post, are given a set of keys and your instructions go something like this, 'You'll be working 'C' Wing and I'll be busy pulling people for yard. If you have any questions, ask the Wing trusty, he's been here a while and knows his way around.' Needless to say, this type of on-the-job training is by no means the ideal format for the development of the professional correctional officers that we need. . . . "[46]

As FTO programs demonstrate, training does not end with graduation from the basic academy. It should continue not only through OJT during probation, but also periodically throughout the officer's career in order to keep updated with changing policies and procedures, prepare for advancement, and learn the new skills needed as one progresses in rank.

---

*LEARNING GOALS*

*Do you know:*

- *The difference between line and staff supervisors?*
- *How internal and external motivation differ?*
- *What is meant by a progressive disciplinary continuum?*
- *The difference between a supervisor's task and relationship behavior?*
- *What four supervisory styles are included in situational leadership and when they should be used?*
- *What factors should be taken into account in determining one's leadership style?*

---

[44]Tod B. Rawles, "Field Training Officers—Bridging the Gap," *American Jails,* Vol. 3, No. 2 (Summer 1989), pp. 72–74.

[45]For more details on FTO programs, see Richard J. DeGraff, "Five Ways to Develop a Skilled Staff," *Corrections Today,* Vol. 54, No. 5 (July 1992), pp. 108–9; and Donald W. Moose, "Maricopa County Detention Cadets Participate in 20-Day Field Training Program," *Training Aids Digest,* Vol. 12, No. 12 (December 1987), pp. 1, 3–7.

[46]Jose D. Alejandro, "Training's Missing Link: The Facility Training Officer (FTO) Program," *Connection,* Vol. 2, No. 2 (Summer 1990), p. 4 (Dade County, FL, Department of Corrections and Rehabilitation Newsletter).

In most jobs, a new employee would have to work for some period of time at the operational level of the organization before becoming a supervisor. But unlike entry-level employees in other occupations, beginning correctional, probation, and parole officers are immediately charged with supervisory functions. That is because, technically speaking, "every correctional employee who exercises legal authority over offenders . . . *is a supervisor,* even if the person is the lowest-ranking employee in the agency or institution."[47] In that sense, officers are *line* or *field supervisors*—that is, they supervise offenders at the line level of institutional operations or in the field (as in the case of probation or parole). They, in turn, are supervised by personnel at the next level of the organizational hierarchy, who are considered *staff (or first-level) supervisors,* since they represent the first level in the chain of command which has supervisory responsibility over other staff members. Within institutional corrections, staff supervisors are generally personnel at the rank of corporal or sergeant.

To supervise inmates, an officer must be able to motivate, discipline, direct, train, and evaluate behavior. To do so, the officer must be skilled in oral and written communication, judgment, sensitivity, leadership, and the like. The next logical question, then, is: What is required of the first-level staff supervisor? The answer is essentially the same. Undoubtedly, staff supervisors have certain additional responsibilities, such as communicating with upper-level management, allocating personnel on a shift, and maintaining payroll records. But in terms of their fundamental personnel supervisory functions, there is a great deal of similarity. In essence, both are supervising people—regardless of whether those people are offenders or officers. If a punitive or autocratic approach is learned at the entry level when supervising inmates, it is likely to be passed on to subordinates as one is promoted up the ranks. In that regard, officers are likely to reflect the supervisory style of their own supervisor. Improving the *supervision of offenders* is therefore, in many respects, closely related to improving the *supervision of officers.* Staff members are entitled to be treated with no less equity and respect than would be expected of them in their supervision of offenders. And they are more likely to fulfill those expectations if they, in turn, receive appropriate treatment from their supervisors.

## Motivation

One of the most critical elements of good supervision is stimulating subordinates to carry out their jobs in the manner prescribed. This is what is known as *motivation.* People can be motivated either *externally* or *internally.* In Chapter 8 we found that the primary function of custody is to provide external controls for those who lack sufficient internal controls to function in free society. In Chapter 10 we saw what negative effects that can have on the inmates. Needless to say, staff function in the same debilitating environment ("serving their sentence," as some say, "in eight-hour shifts"). When personnel are treated in a similar man-

[47]Archambeault and Archambeault, p. 5.

ner that relies heavily on external inducements, they can become just as "institutionalized" as the inmates.

On the other hand, when internal motivations are tapped, personnel are considerably more likely to do a good job simply for the intrinsic benefits of doing so—such as feeling good about themselves, taking pride in their accomplishments, and enjoying a sense of personal satisfaction. Of course, not everyone is equally internally motivated. As we will see later, there are also factors in the work environment that can reduce or even destroy the self-satisfaction of doing a good job. In fact, a new approach to management known as *continuous quality improvement* (or "total quality management") is based on the belief that "most employees want to perform well but are hindered by systematic issues that interfere with their ability to get the job done."[48] Rather than address organizational impediments, however, most supervisory motivational efforts rely on various sources of external incentives.

External motivators are rooted in the theory of behavioral conditioning discussed in Chapter 3. That is, they assume that behavior is shaped by how the supervisor responds to it. Supervisory-related responses include either *rewards* or *punishments*. Traditionally, rewards have been rather narrowly interpreted as obtaining a higher salary, job promotion, more benefits, or preferred assignments. What is often overlooked is the simple reward of a "pat on the back" for a job well done—in other words, some indication that the supervisor knows and cares about the quality of work being done.

As illustrated in Maslow's hierarchy, people who are beyond basic physiological and safety levels are not inclined to be motivated by money or similar extrinsic rewards. As the correctional workforce is increasingly composed of those with higher education and greater career options, the strength of these motivators is diminished. If supervisors are not able to create the type of environment where such employees feel needed, appreciated, and recognized, even the most lucrative benefits are unlikely to be powerful enough to motivate them to do their best. Unfortunately, many supervisors dismiss their responsibility in this regard with a self-excusing rationale which maintains "that's what your paycheck is for!" But instilling the pride and sense of fulfillment that characterize motivation is the function of personnel supervisors, not predetermined salaries.

## Discipline

Added to the drawback of external motivators is the fact that from the subordinate's perspective, it appears that punishments are employed more readily than rewards. It may well take years for even the most competent employee to obtain a salary increase, promotion, or added fringe benefits. On the other hand, when something inappropriate is done, the disciplinary system is activated much more rapidly. This is not, of course, meant to imply that some form of discipline is not at times warranted and necessary. Even when that is the case, how-

---

[48]Peggy Ritchie-Matsumoto, "Using CQI Techniques to Benefit Corrections," *Corrections Today*, Vol. 54, No. 8 (December 1992), p. 158.

ever, the employee is considerably more likely to view disciplinary action as equitable when the supervisor's focus is not limited to punishing what was done wrong on a few occasions, but also includes praising what was done right on far more occasions.

Focusing on fear, threat, or intimidation can become counterproductive. Rather than stimulating proper work-related behavior, such negative conditions are more likely to generate low levels of morale, commitment, and effort. Again, that does not mean that the supervisor should avoid criticizing or correcting the employee. But criticism should be constructive rather than destructive, emphasizing growth and development as opposed to suspicion and mistrust.

Typically, punishment falls on a *progressive continuum* from least to most severe, which includes such sanctions as:

- Informal counseling
- Verbal warning or reprimand
- Written warning or reprimand
- Fine
- Suspension
- Demotion
- Dismissal.[49]

In some states there is even an additional penalty beyond termination—that is, *decertification.* Without such a provision, there may be nothing to prevent an employee who is fired for excessive misconduct in one correctional agency from seeking employment in another (especially if a thorough background investigation is not part of the hiring process). The concept behind decertification is that professionalism in corrections is not something that can be issued like a uniform or a badge. Rather, the employee's professional certification must be maintained on a continual basis. Just as lawyers can be disbarred and doctors can have their license revoked, an officer's "license to practice" in the field of corrections can also be removed in states with decertification procedures.

Decertification is, however, on the highest end of the range of disciplinary options. In the majority of routine cases, disciplinary action follows that escalating path—beginning with the least severe response and moving progressively up the continuum if the behavior continues. The obvious exception is when the employee has engaged in a very serious infraction that immediately calls for a corresponding level of punishment.

Overall, the process of disciplining staff is not unlike that advocated in earlier chapters for inmates—that is, it should be carried out in a manner which is:

- *Firm*: unwavering
- *Fair*: proportional to the seriousness and/or frequency of the infraction
- *Consistent*: uniformly administered without personal bias.

---

[49]Archambeault and Archambeault, p. 129.

It is, however, somewhat more difficult to ensure that these criteria are met when disciplining staff. Because supervisors are selected from the officer ranks, a co-worker today can become one's boss tomorrow. Under such a situation, it is not always easy for a newly promoted supervisor to maintain neutrality and objectivity. In other words, "to exercise authority fairly, the new supervisor is forced to alter relationships with former peers,"[50] which is not easy to do.

## Direction

With most employees, the need to invoke the disciplinary process occurs relatively infrequently. In contrast, both line and staff supervisors are required to provide ongoing direction for their subordinates on a continual basis. Because staff supervisors in particular represent the organizational rank through which *managerial policies* are translated into *operational practices,* their ability to provide appropriate direction will have much to do with how effectively policies are implemented.

The next logical question, of course, is just how much direction is enough— and conversely, how much direction is too much? At one extreme is the supervisor who insists on scrutinizing the subordinate's work so closely that the effect is stifling in terms of initiative and motivation. At the other extreme is the *laissez-faire* supervisor, who provides little if any direction at all, which can result in uncertainty, confusion, and anxiety. But the problem is not simply finding the proper balance between too little and too much direction. Searching for the "one best" supervisory style is a fruitless task. Such all-encompassing perfection simply does not exist. With some staff members and in some circumstances, a more directive approach is needed. With other people and different circumstances, considerably less oversight may produce a better response.

The issue is not identifying the one most appropriate supervisory technique. Rather, the challenge is to select properly from a repertoire of approaches after determining which is best suited to the situation, particularly with regard to the needs of the employees. This is what is called *situational leadership.* It is not maintaining one constant, unchanging style. Under situational leadership, the person's supervisory approach varies in order to meet the demands of the situation. As described with regard to the management of inmates, consistency is achieved by responding to a similar circumstance or type of behavior in a similar manner whenever it occurs, as opposed to treating all staff and all situations alike.[51]

Situational leadership styles range according to how much *task behavior* (guidance) or *relationship behavior* (support) the supervisor provides. As shown in Figure 14.4, they range from high to low emphasis on giving task-related guidance *to* subordinates, and also range from high to low emphasis on developing supportive relationships *with* subordinates.

More specifically, the four situational leadership styles encompass the following approaches:

[50]Harry K. Singletary, "The Race for Promotions," in *Correctional Issues,* p. 27.
[51]Paul Hersey and Kenneth H. Blanchard, *Management of Organizational Behavior: Utilizing Human Resources,* Fourth Edition (Englewood Cliffs, NJ: Prentice Hall, 1982), p. 100.

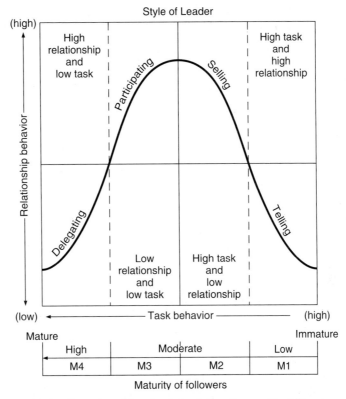

Figure 14.4  Situational leadership styles. *Source:* Paul Hersey and Kenneth H. Blanchard, *Management of Organizational Behavior: Utilizing Human Resources* (Englewood Cliffs, NJ: Prentice Hall, 1982), p. 152.

1. *Telling* (high task; low relationship). The supervisor provides specific instructions with regard to what is to be done and how it is to be accomplished, and maintains close oversight over job performance.

2. *Selling* (high task; high relationship). The supervisor explains decisions and provides opportunity for clarification. Rather than merely giving instructions on *what* to do, the supervisor describes *why* it should be done, enabling the employee to better understand the merits of the task being undertaken.

3. *Participating* (high relationship; low task). The supervisor shares ideas and decision-making responsibility with subordinates. The main role of the supervisor is communicating with subordinates and facilitating the process through which they participate in making job-related decisions.

4. *Delegating* (low relationship; low task). The supervisor turns over authority for making and implementing decisions to subordinates. But delegating does *not mean abdicating*. While the authority to make and carry out decisions may be delegated, the supervisor still maintains ultimate responsibili-

ty for the end results. Because of the personal maturity of subordinates, neither a high level of relationship nor a high emphasis on task is needed.[52]

Needless to say, no single approach is equally suitable for all situations or all employees. During an institutional riot, fire, hostage-taking situation, or other emergency, it is apparent that those with ranking authority must be firmly in command—issuing orders and taking charge in accordance with the "telling" style. In routine, day-to-day circumstances, however, the supervisor may find the need to employ each and every one of these approaches. Selecting the right leadership style for the situation involves determining the employee's level of maturity with regard to the specific task to be done. In other words, the supervisor must assess the employee's:

- *Job-related maturity*: the knowledge and skill necessary to be *able* to do the task.
- *Psychological maturity*: the confidence and commitment necessary to be *willing* to do the task.[53]

Thus, depending on the particular task being undertaken, a given employee may range from very "mature" to very "immature." New recruits and those being transferred to unfamiliar assignments will generally be expected to be relatively low in terms of maturity level, at least initially. This is why a more directive, *telling* approach is likely to be appropriate with such employees. The problem is that some supervisors get "locked into" the telling model (or do not know how to implement any other style), despite changes in the subordinate's level of maturity over time. Seniority on the job does not necessarily equate directly with maturity. But as maturity progresses, the supervisor's style should move from telling to selling, then to participating, and ultimately, to delegating.

---

*LEARNING GOALS*

*Do you know:*

- *The definition of management?*
- *For what reasons planning is needed?*
- *The difference between leaders and managers?*
- *What crisis management is and why it is often characteristic of correctional agencies?*
- *The relationship between proactively planning and reactively responding?*
- *What the organizational budget communicates to employees?*
- *Why written policies and procedures are essential?*

---

[52]Ibid., pp. 152–54.
[53]Ibid., pp. 151, 157.

It is, of course, at the upper managerial ranks where overall direction is provided for the entire correctional system. Some correctional managers are appointed through the internal promotion process. Others are recruited from outside the agency. But regardless of whether they are promoted or imported, correctional administrators are dependent on the fiscal and programmatic support of a public that generally remains unwilling to provide either. When society neither demands nor is willing to pay for the best programs and people to run them, it should be of little surprise that the result is less than ideal. Yet there are those who persevere in the face of these constraints and frustrations, somehow maintaining devotion and commitment. In fact, a former inmate who has worked with correctional administrators throughout the country following his release has high praise for those he has met: "I have found correctional administrators to be among the most dedicated, competent professionals I've run into. I have a great deal of empathy for them, because they take all the political heat, and they don't deserve it. If everything is running well, no one pays any attention, but if there's the slightest problem, the wrath of the whole political structure descends on them."[54]

Just as line officers may tend to emulate the style of their supervisor, upper-level managers set the tone for the entire organization. However, managers also have much more comprehensive responsibilities than supervisors with respect to the administration of the total agency. Management is the process of *organizing, administering, and coordinating a system that is designed to achieve organizational goals and objectives*. As such, managers and administrators serve as facilitators to expedite the action necessary to accomplish the organization's mission. They are responsible for systematically guiding each phase of the administrative process—from planning to budgeting, staffing, and program supervision. But it should also be noted that although certain officials carry the title of "managers," management is not the sole responsibility of any particular office. In essence, everyone throughout the organization contributes to the process of managing it.[55]

### Planning and Decision Making

A considerable part of the manager's job will be devoted to deciding what the organization's goals and objectives should be and planning how to achieve them. "Planning gives us a sense of some control over our own destiny."[56] In fact, it is this planning element of the job that largely sets *leaders* apart from *managers*. The next "Close-up on Corrections" features three basic strategies that distinguish leaders from managers.

[54]Duncan Clark, "Chuck Colson: Born Again Prison Reformer," *Corrections Today*, Vol. 51, No. 4 (July 1989), p. 84.

[55]John Klofas, Stan Stojkovic, and David Kalinich, *Criminal Justice Organizations: Administration and Management* (Pacific Grove, CA: Brooks/Cole Publishing Company, 1990), p. 7.

[56]Saxton, p. 33.

The Art of Leadership

### COMPONENT 1. A LEADER KNOWS WHERE HE [OR SHE] IS GOING

In any organization, people need strong leaders. . . . Often many . . . people feel that they are wandering around in a fog in their organization. They have no sense of vision or direction in their areas of responsibilities. If our top management has no sense of vision or direction, how can we ever expect our people to know where we are going?

### COMPONENT 2. A LEADER KNOWS HOW TO GET THERE

In order for any organization to know where it is going, it is necessary to have a plan. This plan takes the form of goals and objectives. . . . Our people need to know what to strive for. They desire to know what is expected of them in the performance of their duties. Goals and objectives help an organization stay on target to meet the overall mission and purpose. Without them, we have no path or direction. Without any direction, our purpose becomes clouded. . . . [and] motivation is affected. . . .

Many organizations take the necessary time and steps to put together their goals and objectives, but forget to communicate them to the people who actually do the work. The people who perform the functions . . . are the ones who need the information most. . . . A lack of communication begins to breed discontent which leads to downward trends in morale. . . .

### COMPONENT 3. A LEADER KNOWS HOW TO TAKE PEOPLE ALONG

[P]eople want to know and feel that they are needed. . . . An organization that strives to develop that sense of need . . . will see their employee morale grow by leaps and bounds. People will take a stronger interest in their work and a strong bond of unity and cohesiveness will develop between staff members. . . .

*Source:* Tod Kembel, "Cultivating Our People: The Art of Leadership," *American Jails,* Vol. 5, No. 1 (March/April 1991), pp. 87–90.

---

Managers focus on keeping the existing system running smoothly, measuring their success by how well goals and objectives are met. But they may get so inextricably involved in the mundane and immediate matters that their view of the "big picture" is blocked. Leaders, on the other hand, focus more of their efforts on determining where the organization *should be headed* in the future. That is not meant to imply that they do not oversee the process for achieving goals and objectives. But in contrast to the technical emphasis of managers on controlling what is happening "here and now," leaders are creative visionaries who are already contending with the challenges on the distant horizon. In other words, they direct more of their energies toward *leading* the path to the future than *managing* the process of keeping the organization on its present course. Particularly in the private sector, "the dominant principle of organizations has shifted from management in order to control an enterprise, to leadership in order to bring out the best in people and to respond quickly to change."[57]

As in many other public services, however, the field of corrections has traditionally been administered more from a management than a leadership perspective. While the mechanics of long-range planning are undertaken at the upper levels of the organization, daily operations are often governed by the old adage, "if it ain't broke, don't fix it," especially in times of fiscal cutbacks—when managers are forced to do more with less. But aside from fiscal limitations, entrenched veteran managers who find change threatening frequently just want to "keep the lid on." This is understandable in view of external pressures from a turbulent political climate. Political instability contributes to an unwillingness to take risks, and in that type of climate, precedence becomes a good defense. Thus, tradition has a way of becoming ingrained in policy and procedure.

Moreover, in the short run, it takes much less effort to wait until things fall apart before taking action. It may also be more personally stimulating to respond to crisis situations immediately at hand than to plan ahead methodically so that crises can be prevented. For these and many other reasons, concerns have been raised that corrections is predominantly a "reaction-oriented business."[58] *Proactively planning* is not nearly as enjoyable a task as *reactively responding*. But the less we do of the former, the more we will need of the latter.

Management by crisis is not really "managing" anything. It is simply reacting to a situation that is blown out of proportion because of earlier reluctance to be proactive. In other words, the more proactive planning is put off, the more crisis reaction is needed. If nothing was fixed yesterday because it was not yet broken, today and tomorrow will find the manager continually trying to dig out of the resulting "reactive rut."

In addition, the manner in which plans are developed will have much to do with how well they can be implemented. Decisions guided by plans that are made by a select few at the top of the organizational hierarchy are likely to encounter resistance—and possibly even active sabotage—as they move down the chain-of-command toward the point of execution. A paramilitary, "telling" approach may be appropriate for jobs that require few discretionary decisions, but work in corrections certainly does not fit that description. Broader representation of more ranks in the planning and decision-making process can help substantially in gaining the acceptance needed to accomplish the resulting plans.

In this regard, many agencies have adopted *participatory management* techniques. Often, however, these approaches are modified versions of what is actually meant by participation: "For example, managers may solicit input from employees but not really involve them in the decision-making."[59] As noted in

[57]Helen G. Corrothers, "A Guide to Managing Success in Today's Corrections Career," *Corrections Today*, Vol. 54, No. 6 (August 1992), p. 178, citing the authors of *Megatrends 2000*.
[58]Peter Perroncello, "The Role of the Jail Supervisor: Proactive or Reactive?" *American Jails*, Vol. 3, No. 3 (Fall 1989), pp. 74–76.
[59]Frank P. Williams, "An Analysis of Factors Affecting Management Styles in American Prisons and Juvenile Institutions," paper presented at the Academy of Criminal Justice Sciences, Pittsburgh, PA (March 1992), p. 4.

earlier chapters with regard to participatory management, people are more likely to be committed to assuring the successful implementation of decisions they were involved in making. Quite simply, "people tend to support what they help to create."[60]

Nor is the need to expand participation limited to those within the agency itself. Correctional administration differs from other types of public administration in terms of the many external "publics" to which it must respond, which represent varying attitudes, opinions, and beliefs concerning crime and the treatment of criminals. A significant part of the correctional manager's job is interacting with that external environment to obtain public support for correctional policies and practices.

The implementation of any number of noble plans in the field of corrections has also been frustrated by poor organization, insufficient resources, self-interest groups, or inadequate administration. Without proper follow-through, good plans at the top can fail at the point of execution. Delivery systems are the means through which resources and services are channeled to those who need them. Optimum *allocation of resources* is therefore another crucial aspect of the administrative system required for carrying out plans effectively.

## Budgeting and Resource Allocation

Because it is through the budget that resources are allocated, budgeting is integrally related to planning and decision making. If plans have not been properly made to meet upcoming challenges, or if essential resources to implement those plans are not forthcoming, organizational effectiveness will suffer. In essence, the budget sets *priorities* that determine what emphasis will be placed on what part of the correctional process. In this regard, it has been noted that "organizations clearly communicate how they value training and education by the resources directed toward staff preparation."[61] Another example is whether the institutional budget emphasizes custodial or treatment personnel, which will determine the types of programs that will be carried out. Managing the budget is one of the most widely recognized means of controlling an organization's operations.

Obtaining the necessary fiscal resources to manage the organization and fulfill its mission is a primary responsibility of top management. This goes beyond simply establishing what the agency needs to operate and fighting for that level of funding during budget negotiations. To the contrary, the budgetary process is an ongoing procedure that involves a continual effort to familiarize the public with correctional operations, gain support for both routine and innovative programs, and establish a correctional constituency. Administrators must interpret the correctional program to political leaders, the news media, and the general public. Political, economic, and social pressures must be addressed before public policy issues—such as reform and progress—can be considered.

In this respect, the criminal justice process is somewhat like a marriage in terms of visibility. During the courtship and the marriage ceremony, there is

---

[60]Saxton, p. 31.
[61]Dianne Carter, "The Status of Education and Training in Corrections" (Part I), *Journal of Correctional Training* (Winter 1992), p. 6.

considerable social interest, which diminishes during the long-term marital adjustment. In criminal justice, the visibility is in the arrest and trial phases. It ends with the verdict and the sentence, after which there is a tendency to forget the offender. Yet it is "after the ceremony" that the correctional function occurs. The subsequent process that takes place has low visibility and constitutes a public relations challenge for the correctional administrator.

Consequently, corrections is never likely to be as popular an item to fund as, for instance, education, transportation, or law enforcement services. But if corrections resides in the dark, unknown, or mistrusted recesses of public consciousness, it is even less likely to obtain necessary fiscal support. Public policy as expressed through the budget is always a trade-off between social and economic goals. If an agency is to prevail in the budgetary process, it must keep society and its political representatives informed of just what *is* being traded off when corrections is not funded adequately. In that respect, the distinction between fundamental managers and forward-thinking leaders becomes even more apparent.

### Organization and Administration

Once plans are made and a budget is allocated to implement them, the manager's task becomes one of creating an organizational process through which *funds are allocated* and *work is divided* in a manner that enables resources and services to be delivered where they are needed. The use of computers has facilitated efficiency in this respect, since a rapid information retrieval system enhances administrative decision making by providing immediate access to more information on which to base decisions. But although computers can improve the *efficiency* of the correctional system, the issue of how *effectively* resources are distributed and work is divided cannot be divorced from human judgment.

Distributing resources involves both personnel and physical plant facilities. It has been said that a good correctional program can be run in an old red barn, reflecting the emphasis that should be placed on personnel.[62] Administrators have to make basic decisions concerning whether to put their money into the horses or the barn. Although both are necessary, a barn never won a horse race. In other words, even the most elaborate and sophisticated physical facilities cannot operate effectively without an appropriate quantity and quality of staff. While the reverse is not equally true, it is undoubtedly demoralizing to work in a physical environment that is outdated, cramped, lacking proper equipment, or otherwise deficient. Distinctions between operating conditions among various units of the organization essentially reflect budget priorities, and employees are quick to observe where the preferences are being placed.

Merely putting an organizational process into place does not, of course, assure that it will function as intended. Ongoing administration of the process is therefore necessary to *maintain* and *evaluate* the service delivery system. In the field of corrections, these services consist of the treatment and supervision procedures needed to change the behavior of the offender in order to readjust to an

[62]This statement, "I can run a good correctional program in an old red barn," has been attributed to the late Austin MacCormick.

orderly society. Sufficient external controls must be provided to protect society. But at the same time, adequate internalized controls must be developed so that external controls can be safely withdrawn.

Thus, the fundamental issue in correctional administration comes down to whether the organization should direct its efforts toward changing or controlling behavior. The dilemma may be especially evident within prisons and jails, where basic administrative decisions must be made concerning how much of the delivery system will be devoted to incapacitation versus rehabilitation. But even within community corrections such as probation and parole, administrators must determine to what extent and with what clients supervision, surveillance, and control will be emphasized over support, strengthening, and change.

Whatever the specific focus, there are certain essentials that must be incorporated into administrative practices or provided to correctional clients. These are outlined in manuals prepared by the American Correctional Association, which provide *standards and guidelines* governing correctional administration and operations. More details concerning the content and implemention of ACA standards will be forthcoming in Chapter 15. But it is pertinent to note here that most of the items on the ACA standards compliance checklists begin with the statement, "Written policy, procedure, and practice provide that. . . ." The point is that organizational practices must be committed to writing. Regardless of the extent to which an agency is in compliance with ACA standards, *written policies* are essential, along with descriptions of the *procedures* by which they are to be implemented.

Needless to say, it is of no value to create such documents if they are not distributed—and more important, understood—by everyone throughout the organization. All administrative, middle-management, and operational personnel should receive not only copies of written policies and procedures but also training on how they are to be carried out. Simply signing-off on a paper which indicates that the employee received and read the document is not sufficient. Even the best written policies and procedures are not always completely clear and cannot prescribe exactly what should be done in each and every circumstance. They must leave some room for interpretation on a case-by-case basis according to the situation. Training is therefore essential to assure that the intent of policies and procedures is fulfilled when they are operationalized in practice.

Finally, once policies are established, communicated, and implemented, they must be evaluated. This requires both day-to-day feedback and long-term evaluation research. Operating a correctional agency without research is like operating a business without bookkeeping. In neither case do administrators know their profits and losses, where they have been, or where they are going. Rather, they are operating on faith and hope.

## ❖ PERSONNEL ISSUES

Regardless of how many policies are written or how much training and evaluation are conducted, in the daily administration of a correctional organization, issues are bound to arise that generate conflict or confusion. Inadequate managers either make efforts to avoid confronting these challenges or retreat into a rigid "that's the way we've always done it" pattern of response. Good managers turn controversial issues into opportunities to make progressive change. True leaders proactively anticipate and deal with issues on the horizon before they actually surface and require reaction.

The capabilities of managers and leaders notwithstanding, there remain a number of unresolved matters that have created conflict or confusion throughout correctional organizations. Although many more issues than can be presented here could fit that description, the remainder of this chapter explores some of the most visible controversies of recent years. They range from the legal liability of employees to job stress, unionization, and the integration of females into a male-dominated workplace.

---

*LEARNING GOALS*

*Do you know:*

- *The difference between civil and criminal liability?*
- *What types of damages can result from being held civilly liable?*
- *What vicarious liability is and under what conditions it occurs?*

---

## Legal Liability

Lawsuits filed by offenders are a constant source of concern to both administrative and operational staff. In the United States, inmates may petition the courts to seek redress for damages or to challenge practices on the basis that constitutional or civil rights have been violated. Thus, both the employing agency and its individual employees are subject to being named in lawsuits when their actions or inactions caused harm, injury, or death.

Litigation can take the form of civil or criminal liability (or both), depending on whether or not a criminal law was violated. *Criminal liability* applies when in the course of performing one's job, the employee is found to have broken the criminal law and is therefore held accountable in a criminal court. For example, an officer who assaults and severely injures an inmate could be held criminally liable if the officer cannot establish that he or she was acting in *self-defense*. Being prosecuted for a criminal act is not, however, the only form of liability that could result from this situation. Whether or not the officer is charged, convicted, and/or punished by the state, the injured inmate can still file a *civil liability* claim. As illustrated in Figure 14.5, there are several fundamental differences between criminal and civil law.

Criminal law is prosecuted by the state for the purpose of seeking punishment for a violation against the social order. In contrast, civil action is initiated by the individual victim in order to obtain compensation for damages, medical bills, pain, suffering, lost wages, and so on. Whereas a conviction of guilt in a criminal court may assist in establishing a subsequent civil case, acquittal in

| | Criminal | Civil |
|---|---|---|
| Action initiated by | The state | The victim |
| Invoked as a result of harm caused to | Society overall | A particular person |
| For the purpose of | Punishment | Compensation |

**Figure 14.5**  Criminal and civil law comparisons.

criminal court does not automatically absolve the defendant of possible civil liability. If an inmate is successful in pursuing a civil case against a correctional employee or agency, the court can award one of three types of damages:

1. *Nominal*: an insignificant amount of money (such as $1), which may be accompanied by a "cease and desist" injunction order to prohibit similar behavior in the future.
2. *Compensatory*: a monetary award which is generally equated with the expenses incurred by the victim—that is, an award designed to compensate for fiscal losses.
3. *Punitive*: a substantial monetary award which goes beyond mere compensation in an effort to punish the offender or offending agency "through the pocketbook," under the theory that suffering a major economic setback will prevent the behavior from reoccurring.

Since the ability of individual staff members to pay a large monetary award or settlement is limited, civil suits are often directed toward the employing governmental agency, which obviously has far greater capability to make such a payment. Moreover, "most inmates do not file lawsuits directly against line officers; instead, they challenge rules and policies established by administrators or other officials."[63] This raises the question of how an employing agency, a supervisor, or an administrator can be held liable for the actions of a subordinate. The answer involves another form of civil liability, which encompasses wrongdoing beyond one's own direct actions or inactions. It is what is known as indirect or *vicarious* liability.

Vicarious liability is created when:

- Someone else (such as the employee's supervisor) *knew or should have known* what was occurring or about to occur, but
- *Did nothing*, and
- That lack of action was the *proximate cause* (as opposed to the direct cause) of subsequent harm, injury, or death.

Vicarious liability can result from such circumstances as:

- *Failure to train*. If, for example, in the above-mentioned case, the assaulting officer had recently been employed and had not yet been sent to the train-

---

[63]*Correctional Officer Resource Guide,* Second Edition (Laurel, MD: American Correctional Association, 1989), p. 13.

ing academy, the officer could claim that he or she was not properly prepared for what to expect on the job and how to react appropriately. If successful in doing so, liability could transfer to the employing agency.

- *Negligent supervision.* Again using the case above, if the employee's supervisor witnessed the assault and did not intervene, the supervisor could incur liability as well. But a supervisor would not necessarily need to observe the incident visually to be held vicariously liable, if, for instance, the supervisor was well aware that this employee had engaged in assaultive behavior in the past and had taken no corrective action.

- *Negligent employment or retention.* Like the supervisory example, this is a form of the "known or should have known" feature of vicarious liability. Let us say that the employee had a long history of being fired by other correctional institutions for assaulting inmates. The courts could well maintain that the pattern of behavior was apparent had any effort been made to look into previous employment, thus holding the organization liable for negligent employment. If, on the other hand, the employee came into the agency with a clean record, but demonstrated a history of assaultive attacks following employment, the agency could be held liable for negligent retention.

Unfortunately, in the daily press of business, organizations and their employees do not always take these possible sources of liability into consideration. Look at the scenario presented in the next "Close-up on Corrections" and see if you can determine what, if any, consequences in terms of civil or criminal liability could result.

Under vicarious liability, agency administrators are responsible for all activities within their jurisdiction. In response to such vulnerability, some administrators seek to protect themselves with insurance or bonding. Others have even gone so far as to put all of their property in their spouse's name. Still others have filed *counter*suits when the courts have ruled that a claim was wrongful, with the hope that such actions will deter those who might otherwise file unwarranted or frivolous claims.[64]

But the best protection against liability is a proactive rather than a reactive approach. It is being continually aware of what is going on within the organization, making it clear what is and is not acceptable through written policies and procedures, and taking all reasonable measures to assure that everyone fully recognizes the client's constitutional and civil rights. As in sports, the best defense is a good offense. Administrators, supervisors, and operational staff who avoid taking shortcuts, stay abreast of legal issues, and treat inmates with the same respect that they would desire if roles were reversed will achieve far more insulation from liability than any insurance policies could hope to provide.

---

[64]See Charles Friend, "Protection against Civil Liability," *The National Sheriff*, Vol. 41, No. 6 (December 1989/January 1990), pp. 34–35.

Liable or Not?

Officer Johnson arrives on duty for the 11:00 P.M. to 7:00 A.M. shift. Immediately, he realizes that it is not going to be a good night. The sergeant is barking out a constant stream of orders. Phone lines are ringing incessantly. Officers are scurrying off to their posts. Metal is clanging against metal as sallyport gates continually open and close to admit and release coming and going staff. More seem to be going out than coming in, and things look even more chaotic than usual at shift change.

Johnson receives his orders—transporting an inmate from "D" wing to the downtown hospital. The inmate's condition is not exactly an emergency, but has been ranked as a high-priority case. Officer Johnson realizes that to do an outside transportation run, he will be required to carry a weapon, and his annual firearms qualification card expired last month. Momentarily, he debates over whether to just do the run without telling the sergeant, but decides against it.

"Sarge, I hate to say this, but remember last month when they couldn't spare me to go to the range? Well, my firearms qualification is up."

The sergeant is in no mood to hear complaints or excuses:

"Yeah, well, this is sure a fine time to tell me that! You know what I have here tonight? Nowhere near enough to run this shift, that's what—3 out sick, 4 on leave, and 2 more off for some training class."

"But sarge, you know I have to check out a weapon for this run. Can't you give it to someone with a card?"

"Listen, I don't even know where the list is, and does it look like I've got the time to hunt for it? Besides, the problem around here is we have too many stupid rules anyway. If that damn phone would just stop. . . . "

"But sarge. . . . " The sergeant answers the phone, "Control Desk, hold on." Turning to the officer, "Johnson, that's enough! Get going!" The sergeant goes back to the phone; the officer leaves for the transportation detail.

Officer Johnson pulls up to the hospital admission area. It is close to midnight and only a few people are milling around in the vicinity. They appear to be harmlessly going about their business. He breathes a sigh of relief and begins to remove the inmate from the vehicle. Without warning, two armed men emerge out of the shadows. They hit Johnson, force him to the ground, and take off with the inmate. One turns around briefly, pointing his weapon in the officer's direction. Johnson fires his revolver, and an innocent bystander is shot.

In this case, are there grounds for charging:

- The officer with criminal liability?
- The officer with civil liability?
- Anyone else with criminal or civil liability?
- If so, what type of liability would apply? Why?

ANSWERS:

- *Criminal liability.* Since the officer did not intentionally shoot the bystander, it is unlikely that it could be proven that a crime was committed.

- *Direct civil liability.* Since Johnson raised objections to completing the transportation detail and made it very clear that he was not currently firearms-qualified, it is unlikely that he could be held civilly liable. Even if the sergeant later denies remembering Johnson's verbal objection, the courts could maintain that it is the supervisor's duty to make assignments in a manner cognizant of the requisite qualifications (i.e., the supervisor "should have known").

- *Vicarious liability.* Because the sergeant persisted with assigning Johnson inappropriately despite his protests, grounds do exist for holding the sergeant vicariously liable. In other words, the sergeant *knew* what the situation was, *did nothing* about it, and that inaction could potentially be construed as the *proximate cause* of the resulting injury. It is also possible that the agency or other upper-level administrators could be held vicariously liable for "failure to train," since the officer indicated that he had been unable to go to the firearms range when scheduled because the shift was also short-handed at that time. Here, however, it gets somewhat more complicated. If, for instance, the organization had a clearcut written policy requiring annual firearms requalification and strictly prohibiting the issuance of weapons to anyone without it, liability could be limited to those who actually violated the policy.

---

*LEARNING GOALS*

*Do you know:*

- *How Title VII of the Civil Rights Act has affected the correctional workforce?*
- *What is meant by a BFOQ and under what circumstances it may be invoked?*
- *How the courts have decided the issue of women's right to work versus male inmate privacy?*
- *To what extent women are employed as correctional officers today, and what, if any, restrictions are placed on their duty posts?*

## Sexual Integration

Just as correctional agencies are liable for their actions with regard to offenders, organizations that do not adhere to the provisions of equal employment laws are subject to litigation. Thus, women and minorities cannot be denied correctional positions if they meet the qualification requirements. Particularly with respect to female employees, this has created a major issue in which the male inmate's right to privacy has confronted the female applicant's right to employment.

Women were employed in corrections long before this concern surfaced. But during their early entrance into the institutional workforce, they were confined to duties within female facilities. As we saw in Chapter 12, there are far fewer correctional institutions for females. As a result, employment opportunities for women were quite limited. Moreover, because of the lack of job variety and promotional opportunities in these facilities, advancement potential for female employees was further restricted.

All of this changed in 1972 with the passage of amendments to the 1964 Civil Rights Act. Title VII of this act prohibits employment discrimination on the basis of race, religion, sex, or national origin. The amendments added in 1972 "were crucial to women's advancement in corrections work in two separate ways: First by covering public sector employment, and second by increasing the enforcement power of the EEOC [Equal Employment Opportunity Commission]."[65]

The law does, however, provide for one exceptional circumstance under which some discriminatory practices might be allowed. That exception occurs when the employing agency can demonstrate that a particular race, religion, sex, or national origin is a *bona fide occupational qualification* (BFOQ) required to perform the job. This does not mean that employers can discriminate on the basis of general assumptions about women's suitability for correctional work. In fact, the law very narrowly defines BFOQ to apply only to certain unique situations, such as a movie role calling for a male actor.

Nor have discrimination suits been limited to females working in male institutions. Comparable questions have also been raised by male officers employed in female prisons, and the results have been similar. That is, the "courts generally have concluded that employees' equal employment opportunity rights and institutional security take priority over inmates' limited privacy rights."[66] In fact, a recent study reveals that in most women's prisons in the United States, males are both employed as correctional officers and routinely assigned to supervise inmate living units, and that the female inmates respond positively to their presence.[67]

Aside from the legal issues involved, prisons have never been the most adaptable environments for accommodating massive change. The integration of females into traditionally male-dominated institutions and job assignments has been especially controversial. In part, resistance has been based on fears that women would jeopardize safety and security, as expressed in the true story told in the next "Close-up on Corrections." It has also reflected general opposition to management practices within tightly controlled, bureaucratic structures that impose changes without allowing for input or feedback from lower levels in the chain of command. Most fundamentally, however, females represent a threat to the pride, homogeneity, and male ego associated with the close-knit world of correctional officers. To the extent that women can perform the job successfully, a serious challenge is posed to conventional beliefs that masculinity is a necessary

[65]Linda E. Zimmer, *Women Guarding Men* (Chicago: University of Chicago Press, 1986), p. 6.

[66]Barbara W. Jones, "Relevant Rulings: Examining the Case for Women in Corrections," *Corrections Today*, Vol. 54, No. 6 (August 1992), p. 104.

[67]Linda L. Zupan, "Men Guarding Women: An Analysis of the Employment of Male Correction Officers in Prisons for Women," *Journal of Criminal Justice*, Vol. 20, No. 4 (1992), p. 297.

### The Gender Gap

[M]en frequently see corrections as a dangerous profession requiring machismo. They believe it is a place where women are especially unsafe. Because men are conditioned to protect women, they may feel that, in addition to working with the inmates, they have an added responsibility to protect the women officers.

These feelings can make men and women uncomfortable with each other. Women may feel patronized, as if they are merely being tolerated rather than appreciated and affirmed for their work. . . .

A woman corrections officer recently told me she enjoyed counseling inmates who were close to release or community placement. She said that if she made a difference in the lives of even a few inmates, she felt her efforts were worthwhile.

However, some of her male counterparts thought she was getting too personally involved with the inmates. This baffled her, since she considered much of their contact with the inmates—bantering and favoring some inmates over others, for example—less professional than her counseling. To the male officers, her actions seemed too intimate and were thus inviting danger. . . .

The officer was comfortable with her approach. She was encouraging inmates' participation in an integrated community, a new experience for most of them. The inmates responded to her differently than they did to the men. To her, they expressed fears and confessed weaknesses they did not share with male employees.

Was she protecting the public by her actions or placing lives in jeopardy? The men viewed her activities as unnecessary and in a negative light. She saw her actions as positive. The differences here may be a result of differences in how each gender views the world.

*Source:* Adria Libolt, "Bridging the Gender Gap," *Corrections Today,* Vol. 53, No. 7 (December 1991), pp. 136–38.

---

requirement. As one male supervisor noted: "It really hurts these guys to think that a woman can do their job. They've been walking around town like big shots—like they're doing a job only `real men' can do. Well, if the woman next door can do your job, then maybe you're not so tough after all. . . . [T]hese men have been going home to their wives for years saying `you don't know what it's like in there.' Now some of their wives are joining up. The jig is up, so to speak."[68]

Ironically, one of the most unlikely sources of support for greater equality in the assignment of women came from correctional officer labor unions.[69] Union leaders themselves may or may not have been personally in favor of female inte-

---

[68]Zimmer, p. 57.
[69]The following information is summarized from Zimmer, pp. 65–69.

Female correctional officers are now undergoing the same training and being deployed to the same job assignments as men. Courtesy of the Dade County Department of Corrections and Rehabilitation, Miami, Florida.

gration. But in one state at least, their interests in protecting seniority provisions of the union contract overrode any conflicting personal considerations.

During the time that women were fighting for equality, the union contract in the state of New York provided that seniority would be the sole criteria for making job assignments. In other words, officers could bid for their duty posts, and longevity was to be the only factor considered in selecting those to fill the most preferential assignments. However, when women began to join the corrections department, posts were classified as suitable or unsuitable for females in order to limit their direct contact with male inmates. The problem was that the noncontact posts designated as appropriate for women also happened to be among those most sought after by men, who were being denied their seniority rights under the contract as more and more women were joining the workforce. The union therefore demanded an integrated seniority list.

The outcome is typical of the balance being pursued by many other agencies facing similar issues—that is, attempting to minimize intrusion of inmate privacy while balancing the rights of all employees with equal employment opportunities for women. The resulting compromises include such provisions as restricting opposite-sex strip searches and shower duty, teaming female and male officers in housing units, requiring opposite-sex officers to announce their presence, using partial shower and toilet screens, and the like.

Despite widespread initial resistance, female officers today are the beneficiaries of a legacy of over two decades of employment in a variety of correctional positions. The vast majority of correctional agencies (72.6%) now report that women are being assigned to all types and locations of posts.[70] Thus, they now tend to be more readily—although not unconditionally—accepted by their male co-workers. Ambivalence in this regard is reflected in a recent ACA telephone opinion "hotline" which sought reactions to the question, "Should inmates be supervised by correctional officers of the opposite sex, even at the risk of invading their privacy?" Responses to the hotline were almost evenly divided, with 54% in favor and 46% opposed.[71]

Inmate reaction has also been mixed but tends to be somewhat more positive. Some have neutral attitudes about the presence of women, under the theory that the rules are the same no matter who is enforcing them. While in the minority, others remain opposed—degraded by having a female "boss," concerned about lack of privacy, or frustrated by the presence of women in an environment where sex is prohibited. But it appears that the majority favor female officers, feeling that they treat inmates with more respect, professionalism, and compassion.[72]

Regardless of staff or inmate attitudes, the fact remains that more and more women are becoming employed as correctional officers. As of 1991, females composed 22% of the correctional officers in jails and approximately 15% within prisons. This compares to only 8% of all sworn police officers, despite the more pressing legal issues facing female employment in corrections.[73] But women have been relatively recent additions to the workforce, and still represent only small percentages of the upper and midlevel managers.[74]

As they progress in seniority and upward advancement, there is little doubt that the future will see considerably greater involvement of women in management positions. Moreover, such changes may have significant implications for the organization's management style. It has been noted that women tend to "structure organizations as a web or network, rather than a hierarchy." That is, in contrast to men, the female executive places herself "in the center reaching out, rather than at the top reaching down."[75] However, it may still take

[70]Michael J. Gilbert, "Recruiting," in Benton and Nesbitt, p. 38.
[71]"CT's Opinion Hotline," *Corrections Today*, Vol. 53, No. 1 (February 1991), p. 16.
[72]Summarized from Zimmer, pp. 60–65.
[73]Data reflect figures presented by Linda L. Zupan, "The Employment and Deployment of Women Correction Officers in the Nation's Largest Jails," *American Jails*, Vol. 4, No. 5 (January/February 1991), p. 60.
[74]Ibid.
[75]Corrothers, p. 178, quoting Sally Helgesen, *The Female Advantage* (New York: Doubleday, 1990).

decades before women are fully accepted within corrections, much less have such a widespread impact on the organizational environment.

---

### LEARNING GOALS

*Do you know:*

- *The difference between episodic and chronic stress?*
- *How agencies have traditionally responded to officer stress and why such responses have been inadequate?*
- *What can be done proactively to prevent correctional officer stress?*

---

## Officer Stress

If there is one thing that is virtually a universal complaint among both male and female correctional employees, it is the issue of job-related stress. Everyone experiences a certain amount of personal stress in the course of daily living. In fact, some degree of stress may actually be beneficial, since a totally stress-free lifestyle would become a rather boring routine. Everyone also has differing levels of internal strength for coping with stress. But when stressful conditions on the job exceed the person's coping abilities, debilitating effects emerge in terms of health, safety, and job performance.

In determining what creates such debilitating effects for correctional staff, it is important to distinguish between two types of stress:

1. *Episodic stress.* As the name implies, episodic stress is generated by traumatic incidents (or "episodes") that occur on the job. Anything from breaking up a dangerous fight to being involved in a riot, becoming a hostage, or witnessing a death in the line of duty represents a potential source of episodic stress. Because of the extensive publicity and notoriety produced by such events, they are often assumed to be the major source of stress in correctional work. However, there are two considerations that cast doubt on this assumption. First, despite their high profile, stress-inducing episodic incidents occur relatively infrequently. Second, their duration is relatively short-lived—that is, these incidents begin and end quickly. That is not meant to imply that they cannot create long-term effects in the form of *posttraumatic* stress. But on a daily basis, it is not likely that one would encounter many episodic events, and when such incidents do arise, they affect a proportionately small number of staff. In contrast, there is another form of stress that has a longer, more continuous impact on a far greater number of people.

2. *Chronic stress.* Like a chronic cough or illness, "chronic" stress is that which is constantly present in the day-to-day work environment. Unlike its episodic counterpart, chronic stress is not the result of a one-time crisis or emergency situation. Rather, it the product of a slow, continual process of erosion that occurs over a period of years. The differences between these

two sources of stress are apparent in the simple analogy of driving to work, as described in the next "Close-up on Corrections."

That comparison is not meant to imply that commuting is a unique source of stress in corrections any more than it is for any other occupation. It is dealing with inmates that immediately comes to mind as a potential source of chronic stress within correctional institutions. Again, however, it is a mistake to jump to the conclusion that inmates represent the primary source of long-term job-related stress in corrections.

Research reveals that it is actually *other staff* that are more chronically stress provoking: from operational co-workers to supervisors, managers, and administrators. For example, one study reports that officers actually outranked inmates in terms of those creating major, continuing pressures and problems. Furthermore, in terms of how they are treated by supervisors, many indicate that they are either not recognized or are given attention only "when something goes wrong."[76]

---

### ❖ CLOSE-UP ON CORRECTIONS

Episodic versus Chronic Stress

Let us say that you are driving down a crowded interstate highway at 45 mph on your way to work. Suddenly, a car cuts over from the middle lane to get onto the exit ramp and comes within inches of hitting your car. You immediately hit the brakes and swerve the wheel to avoid a crash. What is happening to you physiologically? Most likely, your heartbeat has increased, your adrenalin is pumping, and your palms are sweaty. When you realize the danger is over, it probably feels as if all of the blood is draining from your body. That is an example of episodic stress. Fortunately, it is not something that you encounter every day on the way to work!

Contrast that experience with what *does* occur every day during your drive to work. You get up at 5:30 A.M. Still half-drousy, by 6:10 you are in a long line of traffic. You continually maneuver for a good position, keeping a constant eye on the clock, trying to stay alert, hoping nothing farther down the road will delay traffic even more.

There is no big tie-up today, but everyone slows down to watch a police officer issuing a ticket in the service lane. You mutter something about why people do that, watching the clock even closer. You are due for shift change at 7:00 A.M. It is 6:52 as you slide into the employee parking lot. You made it. Exhausted, but on time—already feeling like you've put in a full day's work. That is the routine you complete twice a day, 5 days a week, 50 weeks a year—over 10,000 times until you retire. The toll it is taking over those years is an example of chronic stress.

---

[76]Julie A. Honnold and Jeanne B. Stinchcomb, "Officer Stress: Costs, Causes, and Cures," *Corrections Today*, Vol. 47, No. 7 (December 1985), pp. 49–50.

Additional research confirms that the difficulty of work in correctional institutions is related more to problems involving staff relationships than to problems in dealing with inmates.[77] It has been found that interactions with fellow officers heighten stress.[78] Moreover, even when officer–inmate interaction has been identified as a major stress inducement, the underlying source of the stress has been attributed to administrative problems such as unclear guidelines, inadequate communication, conflicting orders, lack of opportunity to participate in decision making, and the like.[79] In fact, "lack of support from administration" ranked among the highest sources of stress in all three states included in a national study of correctional officer stress.[80]

There is little doubt that correctional administrators have begun to recognize the debilitating impact of stress among their personnel. But that does not mean that they necessarily accept any personal responsibility for it. To the contrary, the primary organizational responses to employee stress are vivid illustrations of why it is so important to accurately determine the nature of a problem before implementing solutions. Among the two most common organizational efforts that have been established in response to stress are employee assistance programs and stress reduction training, both of which have significant limitations:

- *Employee assistance programs (EAPs)*: Designed to offer counseling, therapy, and various forms of treatment, EAPs assist employees in coping with problems in their lives—whether those problems are related to work, family, substance abuse, or whatever. Undoubtedly, such programs are beneficial in general, and they can be very helpful in dealing with the posttraumatic stress resulting from critical incidents. But we have already seen that episodic stress is not the most frequent stress inducer in corrections. Those suffering from chronic stress might also benefit from EAPs. But counseling is not likely to be helpful in permanently resolving their job-related stress, since it is treating the *symptoms* rather than dealing with the *causes* of stress.

- *Stress reduction training*: Training programs addressing stress traditionally include information on diet, nutrition, exercise, meditation, self-relaxation, and similar techniques for dealing with stress. As with EAPs, however, the emphasis is on improving the employee's ability to cope with stress by reducing its debilitating *effects*.[81] In other words, it is "teaching people how

[77]Barbara A. Owen, *The Reproduction of Social Control: A Study of Prison Workers at San Quentin* (Westport, CT: Praeger, 1988).

[78]Francis T. Cullen, Bruce G. Link, Nancy T. Wolfe, and James Frank, "The Social Dimensions of Correctional Officer Stress," *Justice Quarterly*, Vol. 2, No. 4 (December 1985), pp. 520, 522.

[79]Frances E. Cheek and Marie Di Stefano Miller, "The Experience of Stress for Correction Officers: A Double-Bind Theory of Correctional Stress," *Journal of Criminal Justice*, Vol. 11, No. 2 (1983), pp. 105–120.

[80]Gerald W. McEntee and William Lucy, *Prisoners of Life: A Study of Occupational Stress Among State Corrections Officers* (Washington, DC: American Federation of State, County and Municipal Employees, n.d.), p. 22 and Table 25. (The three states included in this study were Pennsylvania, Illinois, and Washington). For a review of the current status of stress research, see Robert G. Huckabee, "Stress in Corrections: An Overview of the Issues," *Journal of Criminal Justice*, Vol. 20, No. 5 (1992), pp. 479–86.

[81]See Jeanne B. Stinchcomb, "Correctional Officer Stress: Is Training Missing the Target?" *Issues in Correctional Training and Casework* (October 1986), p. 22.

to put up with an intolerable situation rather than taking steps to change it."[82] Again, the underlying *causes* remain unaddressed.

When employees return from EAP counseling or stress training, where do they go? Right back into the same work environment that created their stress in the first place! True, they may be better equipped to cope with it (at least in the short term). But long-term chronic stress will not be resolved without a dedicated commitment to *proactive prevention*—that is, eliminating the work-related stressors, rather than treating the stressed-out workers.

The next "Close-up on Corrections" outlines simple techniques designed to address some of the administrative causes of stress. Notice that the emphasis is on keeping employees informed and *involved*. A proactive organizational approach to stress prevention requires the inclusion of all ranks in the agency's problem-solving and decision-making network.

The ironic thing about focusing on causes as opposed to effects is that it may not be nearly as expensive. EAPs and stress reduction training programs can be quite costly to implement, especially for a large agency. In contrast, it is relatively inexpensive to uncover the supervisory, managerial, and administrative practices that are creating stress and take appropriate action to change

---

### ❖ CLOSE-UP ON CORRECTIONS

Administrative Tactics for Reducing Stress

1. *Provide clear guidelines for job performance.* Make sure that written rules and procedures are clearly stated, developed with those who will use them, and kept up-to-date. . . .
2. *Give support.* Explain why you are backing a decision or clarify why you are not. Praise staff members for jobs done well.
3. *Allow input into decision-making from all staff concerned.* This can be achieved through staff conferences.
4. *Foster good communication, up and down.* Provide clear and up-to-date downward communication . . . and develop informal methods of getting information upward.
5. *Foster interdependence.* Use a team approach, including custodial and ancillary personnel. Reinforce group-centered attitudes and behaviors, as well as individual achievement.
6. *Clarify and stress basic organizational goals.* Clarify the relation of decisions to be made to the facility's basic goals. . . .

*Source:* Francis Cheek and Marie Di Stefano Miller, "Reducing Staff and Inmate Stress," *Corrections Today,* Vol. 44, No. 5 (October 1982), p. 73.

---

[82]Ralph Gardner, Jr., "Guard Stress," *Corrections Magazine,* Vol. 7, No. 5 (October 1981), p. 12.

them.[83] Rather than money, what it really costs to respond effectively to employee stress in a proactive manner is the willingness of managers and administrators to confront their own shortcomings. But in many agencies, that is considered too high a price to pay.

---

*LEARNING GOALS*

*Do you know:*

- *Why correctional officers have begun to join labor unions?*
- *How economic conditions and membership changes may affect the concerns expressed by unions?*
- *What impact unions have had on correctional agencies?*

---

## Labor Unions

When an organization is unwilling or unable to respond to the stress-inducing concerns of its employees, it should not be surprising to find frustrated workers turning to other avenues for the resolution of their complaints. One such alternative has undoubtedly been employee unions. Correctional officer unions have been strong for a number of years in some states. Today, employees in about 86% of the states have the right to organize.[84]

In some areas, unions are quite active and include virtually all employees. In others, they attract much smaller percentages, often reflecting limited union membership among other occupations in the state. Many prisons actually have several unions—such as those that include teachers, nurses, craftsworkers, building trades, social workers, or clerical staff. However, correctional officer unions have traditionally been the strongest. Among the largest unions that include correctional personnel is the American Federation of State, County, and Municipal Employees (AFSCME).

Originally, unions were concerned predominantly with such *extrinsic* matters as salaries and working conditions. These items still remain serious issues on the bargaining table in a number of states. But union interests have also begun to expand well beyond money and fringe benefits. Unions are now becoming more actively involved in a wide range of issues affecting the health, safety, and well-being of their membership—ranging from equipment and training to disciplinary actions, promotional policies, and other administrative practices. Among the officer stress studies cited earlier, for example, was one sponsored by AFSCME, and in some locations, employee assistance programs have been created in response to union pressures.

---

[83]See, for example, the guidelines presented in Richard M. Ayres, *Preventing Law Enforcement Stress: The Organization's Role* (Washington, DC: National Sheriffs' Association, 1990), which presents stress reduction management strategies that can readily be adapted to corrections.

[84]*Vital Statistics,* p. 57.

These more *intrinsic* concerns are likely to become even more significant bargaining issues in the future for two reasons. First, unions are increasingly aware of the fact that in a sluggish economy, demands for higher wages or additional benefits are often simply unrealistic. Second, as union membership becomes increasingly composed of the "new breed" of correctional workers described at the beginning of this chapter, it can be expected that their concerns will begin to shift. In place of the extrinsic matters which had been emphasized by their predecessors, today's employees are more likely to fight for intrinsic issues surrounding work satisfaction, personal autonomy, job enrichment, and self-fulfillment. As with proactively responding to stress, managers could take a preventive position that would decrease the need for union intervention. Again, however, many do not.

From some perspectives, unionization has been viewed as reducing the capacity of administrators to manage the system,[85] although less than half (47.2%) of the prison wardens in one survey reported that unions restrict their management style.[86] Labor unions have won such concessions as higher salaries, overtime pay, compensation for being called back to duty, protection against extra-duty requirements, scheduling restrictions, and many other actions that have been perceived as infringements on management prerogatives. Organizing through collective action has clearly resulted in many benefits for correctional officers. What is often overlooked, however, are the benefits that have accrued to the organization itself. Not everyone would agree that union-generated changes are beneficial. But to the extent that unions have limited traditional autocratic authority in personnel matters, they have helped to promote greater sharing of decision making, decentralized power, negotiation, and review of management decisions.

That is not a comfortable or pleasant transition to make, and unions are open to the allegation that self-centered employees are subverting the reasonable intentions of management. In that regard it has been observed that correctional officers "will get little sympathy from the administrators and the public until they show concern for the overall mission of the institution as well as their personal needs."[87] Unfortunately, what both sides often forget is that the most effective organizations and the most satisfied employees are found in an environment where personal and organizational goals merge. That cannot occur in an atmosphere of labor–management divisiveness, where all power and authority are concentrated in the hands of a few and the legitimate complaints of employees are ignored.

To some degree, it has been management's reluctance to share control and address grievances that has prompted employees to organize collectively. But in the long run, both have mutual concerns at stake—the employee's best interests are served by working in a good organization and management's best interests are served by organizing a good workforce. The more that each can fulfill their complementary roles, the less those roles will conflict.

[85]Hervey A. Juris and Peter Feuille, *The Impact of Police Unions—Summary Report* (Washington, DC: U.S. Department of Justice, 1973), p. 9.

[86]Marilyn D. McShane, Frank P. Williams, and David Shichor, *Correctional Management in the 1990's: A National Survey of Correctional Managers,* Volume II (San Bernardino, CA: California State University, Department of Criminal Justice, 1990), p. 10.

[87]Harry E. Allen and Clifford E. Simonsen, *Corrections in America,* Sixth Edition (New York: Macmillan, 1992), p. 458.

Of the nearly half-million correctional employees throughout the United States, the majority work as correctional officers in prisons and jails. The stereotypical image of correctional officers is changing as younger, better-educated people and more minorities and women are entering the field. Such trends are both a benefit and a challenge to administrators, who must adjust to greater diversity in the workplace as well as meet changing demands.

Although a "new breed" of employees with expanded career options may be more likely to leave unsatisfactory employment, corrections has historically been plagued by high turnover rates. Some separations are to be expected for natural reasons, but there are also factors inherent in the work environment that are conducive to turnover, many of which relate to administrative complaints. When management can identify and rectify such problems, employees experience greater job satisfaction and the organization experiences less attrition.

Because there will always be some turnover, there will always be a need for active recruitment. Correctional recruitment has traditionally been hampered by constraints surrounding image, vacancy pressures, and compensation. Although these issues have often been used to justify reduced entrance standards, they are subject to change.

Once recruitment has assembled a sufficient pool of applicants to facilitate choice, the most qualified must be selected. Typically, screening has included written tests and oral interviews, both of which have serious drawbacks in terms of their ability to predict job performance accurately. Selection can be enhanced by using methods that are valid, reliable, job related, and legally defensible.

Like selection procedures, basic training should be structured around the knowledge, skills, and abilities reflected in a job task analysis. Even where officer training is not mandated, most agencies provide it voluntarily through both classroom sessions and OJT. The point at which entry-level training is offered varies—from the historical approach (following time on the job), to the traditional practice (immediately upon hire), to the emerging professional model (prior to employment). After graduation from the academy, officers undergo a probationary period, which is most effective when accompanied by an FTO program that is designed to both assist and assess the new recruit.

Unlike most entry jobs, officers become line supervisors immediately upon assignment. Like staff supervisors, they must therefore be able to motivate, discipline, and direct subordinates. Externally, both rewards and punishments can be used to shape behavior, although the latter unfortunately tend to be employed more frequently. When such disciplinary action is warranted, it should be implemented progressively in a manner that is firm, fair, and consistent.

It is through supervisors that management policies are translated into operational practices. Ongoing direction is best provided through situational leadership—that is, adjusting one's style according to the demands of the situation, particularly with regard to the follower's level of maturity in terms of the task at hand.

While supervisors implement policy, upper-level managers are responsible for developing it through the process of planning, decision making, budgeting, and allocating resources. Proactive planning is essential to avoid the reactive response pattern that creates management by crisis. In fact, it is largely vision and planning foresight that distinguish leaders from managers. Plans and decisions should be made with the active participation of those who will be affected or charged with implementation.

Plans are achieved through the budget, which determines where emphasis will be placed. Because corrections is not very visible or popular to fund, it is essential for management to develop informative relationships with the public and those responsible for the political process. Once funding is obtained and resources are distributed, operational practices designed to achieve goals and objectives must be outlined in written policies and procedures.

Although proper written standards may help to protect against litigation, correctional agencies and their employees are subject to civil liability when their actions or inactions result in harm, injury, or death. Beyond direct liability, vicarious liability can occur for failure to train, negligent supervision, or negligent employment/retention.

Under Title VII of the Civil Rights Act, employers are prohibited from discriminating against anyone on the basis of race, religion, sex, or national origin, unless they can document that a BFOQ exists. As a result, women have been employed increasingly in correctional agencies, creating conflict between equal employment rights and inmate privacy. Initially, this was resolved by restricting female job assignments to noncontact posts. But that practice has been opposed by males who were denied such preferential positions. The outcome has been a compromise involving broader integration of women throughout the workforce while minimizing intrusion on inmate privacy.

Another personnel-related issue that is causing increasing concern is officer stress. Although officers are occasionally exposed to episodic stress, it is the chronic stress induced by day-to-day conditions in the work environment that is taking a greater long-range toll. Organizational responses to stress have focused on providing EAPs and stress reduction training—both of which are limited to coping with the effects of stress rather than eliminating its causes.

Many of the frustrating work conditions that provoke stress also promote collective organization through labor unions. While managers often view unions as infringing on their authority, collective action has also achieved organizational benefits. Ultimately, both management and labor have mutual concerns at stake—concerns that relate not only to the demands of unions but also to the desires of organizations to reduce personnel turnover, improve supervisory styles, enhance motivation, and alleviate stress. In the long run, what benefits one, benefits both.

# chapter 15

# Current Trends
# and Future Issues

*There is a Latin proverb that says: "If there is no wind, row." And row we will, and we will make it upstream, because we have . . . vision, vigor and values.*[1]

*Helen G. Corrothers*

## ❖ CHAPTER OVERVIEW

With the rapid pace of change in terms of everything from technology to social policy, there has never in the history of corrections been such a need for the type of farsighted, creative, and proactive leadership discussed in Chapter 14. The challenges that will accompany the beginning of the twenty-first century demand visionary leaders. New approaches, alternatives, and innovations will be needed as traditional practices come under closer examination. That is not meant to imply that administrators should arbitrarily succumb to pressure groups, popular fads, or impractical expectations. But while corrections will probably never be highly visible, neither is it any longer isolated from scrutiny. When legitimate questions are raised, they will require legitimate responses. Otherwise, frustrated clients, correctional workers, and constituents will be persuaded to turn to those who *will* respond—such as the courts, unions, and legislators.

Perhaps nowhere is this more evident than in the area of inmate litigation. Throughout this chapter, numerous examples are cited of how vigorously the courts have emerged from a long period of reluctance to address correctional operations. In fact, the years of most active intervention generated concern that the judiciary may have been overextending its interference. In more recent years, the general trend in correctional law has been directed toward achieving an equitable balance between inmate rights and institutional security. Nevertheless,

[1]Helen G. Corrothers, "Facing Future Challenges," *Corrections Today*, Vol. 54, No. 7 (October 1992), p. 62.

the courts have made it clear that they will respond to valid inmate complaints when administrators are unable or unwilling to do so.

By no means are all of the controversies that result in litigation a reflection of inadequate or uncaring management, however. There are fundamental differences concerning issues ranging from the morality of the death penalty to methods of inmate discipline that will ultimately be settled in the courts. Additionally, as overcrowding and underfunding continue to plague the system, conflict will continue to surround such issues as community-based programs versus new prison construction, front- versus back-door alternatives, and treatment versus punishment. But it is also important to note that remedies do not need to be strictly dichotomous, "either-or" choices. For example, intensive supervision probation has developed as a compromise between the limited supervision of traditional probation and the rigid controls of incarceration. Similarly, an emphasis on offender accountability through victim restitution is a middle-range option between the perceived "liberalism" of treatment and "conservativism" of punishment.

In an effort to address current challenges, correctional agencies have employed various strategies. Some have turned to greater involvement of the private sector, on the theory that the competitiveness and cost-efficiency characteristic of private industry can be used productively in corrections. Others have sought to reduce litigation by adhering to the administrative and operational standards required for accreditation. Still others have made efforts to enhance the training, education, and compensation of their personnel; to improve physical facilities, work conditions, and administrative practices; to devote more attention to experimentation, research, and evaluation.

Some are beginning to take proactive measures to address potential problems before they become pressing crises. But many others are still *re*acting. When buffeted and confused by the winds of change, it is often tempting to respond with an overreliance on high-tech equipment, short-term fads, or quick-fix solutions. Yet the fundamental issues facing corrections are not amenable to shortcut resolutions. They have not developed, nor will they be resolved, overnight. To the extent that corrections is reluctant to anticipate the future or unwilling to seriously address what *can* be anticipated, the legacy that is passed on will be of limited improvement over the one that was inherited. Whatever actions are taken or postponed today will shape both the problems and prospects passed on to our successors. How we respond to today's difficulties will shape tomorrow's destinies.

❖ LEGAL ISSUES

As we saw in Chapter 4, the courts were somewhat hesitant to intervene in correctional operations until the 1960s. During this lengthy *hands-off period,*[2] the inmate's

---

[2]Terms used to describe these three phases of correctional law development are from William G. Archambeault and Betty J. Archambeault, *Correctional Supervisory Management: Principles of Organization, Policy, and Law* (Englewood Cliffs, NJ: Prentice Hall, 1982), p. 195.

legal status was virtually a "slave of the state"—who, upon conviction, no longer enjoyed the rights, privileges, and immunities of law-abiding citizens.[3] Beyond a limited view of inmate rights, the hands-off phase reflected judicial concerns about disrupting the balance of power between the executive and judicial branches of government, as well as a general acceptance of the presumed expertise of correctional administrators. In other words, during the hands-off phase, correctional managers functioned relatively independently, because it was assumed that:

1. While criminal suspects were entitled to constitutional rights at the trial phase, they somehow lost any rights upon conviction.
2. Since corrections was designed to benefit the offender, correctional staff would know what was best for the inmate.
3. Whatever was given to an offender was a "privilege"—not a "right"—and as such, could be subject to conditions or taken away for any reason.[4]

During the 1960s, however, widespread challenges to traditional authority emerged. Suddenly, the actions and decisions of those in power became the subject of massive social reactions, from antiwar demonstrations to civil rights protests. Previously disenfranchised groups began to demand equal rights, a voice in government, and protection under the law. It was therefore not surprising to find the courts also directing attention toward those most powerless and unprotected—correctional clients. This expanding recognition of individual rights prompted the *involved-hands phase* of judicial activism, opening corrections to widespread constitutional review. Under such scrutiny, many of the inmate rights discussed throughout the remainder of this section were enacted. Moreover, the emergence of a receptive audience was not overlooked by the inmates. Between 1966 and 1988, the number of suits they filed in federal courts throughout the country skyrocketed—from 218 to 24,421.[5]

As the more conservative social climate of the 1980s replaced the liberalism of the 1960s, judicial intervention has begun to reflect more of a compromise between the extremes of the two earlier phases. That does not mean that flagrant violations which prompted the hands-on stage are being tolerated. But neither does it mean that management is as severely curtailed as was characteristic of the involved-hands phase. Rather, the current *restrained-hands approach* is more likely to attempt to seek a reasonable balance between the rights of clients and the security interests of correctional administrators. Under this "balancing test," the Supreme Court has ruled that certain restrictions on an inmate's constitutional rights are allowable if they are reasonably related to a "legitimate peno-

---

[3]*Ruffin v. Virginia*, 62 Va. 790 (1871). However, it has also been argued that "the *Ruffin* case itself does not particularly support the restrictive view attributed to it," and that other cases decided in the same time period "do not indicate that the judiciary had no interest in the welfare of prisoners. . . ." See Donald H. Wallace, "*Ruffin v. Virginia* and Slaves of the State: A Nonexistent Baseline of Prisoners' Rights Jurisprudence," *Journal of Criminal Justice*, Vol. 20, No. 4 (1992), pp. 334, 340.

[4]Paraphrased from William C. Collins, *Legal Responsibility and Authority of Correctional Officers* (Laurel, MD: American Correctional Association, 1982), p. 5.

[5]William C. Collins, *Correctional Law for the Correctional Officer* (Laurel, MD: American Correctional Association, 1990), p. 23.

logical interest," such as promoting institutional safety and security.[6] Nor are today's courts as quick to impose their own solutions. When a violation occurs now, they are somewhat more likely to give correctional administrators an opportunity to correct the problem.

Nevertheless, whenever the courts redefine inmate rights, the outcome produces an accompanying redefinition of the power, authority, and liability of correctional staff (as illustrated in Figure 15.1). For example, when inmate rights are *expanded*, a substantial impact on personnel results. Their power and authority are subsequently *reduced*, since they no longer have the autonomy to maintain practices that the courts have ruled as unconstitutional. At the same time, employees' liability is *increased*, as those in violation of constitutional provisions find themselves more vulnerable to civil litigation. To determine just how legal rulings have affected both inmates and correctional staff, it is necessary to review the significant areas in which the courts have shaped correctional law.

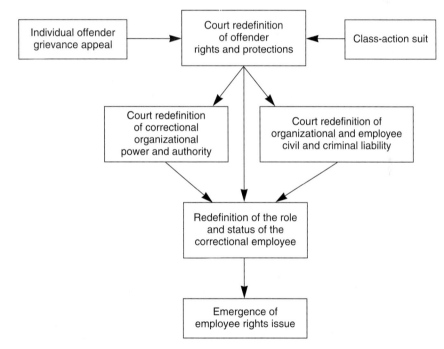

**Figure 15.1** Impact of court decisions. *Source:* William G. Archambeault and Betty J. Archambeault, *Correctional Supervisory Management: Principles of Organization, Policy, and Law* (Englewood Cliffs, NJ: Prentice Hall, 1982), p. 197.

---

[6]Ibid., p. 59, citing *Turner v. Safley*, 107 S. Ct. 2254 (1987), and *O'Lone v. Estate of Shabazz*, 107 S. Ct. 2400 (1987).

## Freedom of Religion

Under the First Amendment of the U.S. Constitution, the right to exercise religious beliefs is protected and government is prohibited from establishing any specific religion. Those in free society are likely to take this freedom for granted. We are readily able to attend whatever religious services we desire, to regulate our diet in accordance with religious practices, to wear or display religious materials, and so on. But enabling inmates to maintain such widespread freedoms would be extremely difficult in a large institution encompassing many different religions, and in some respects, could jeopardize security as well. In keeping with the balancing test, their freedom to fully exercise First Amendment rights may be reasonably restricted. In deciding to what extent such restrictions are constitutional, the courts must address a number of related questions:

1. *To what extent can (or should) government subsidize religious activities*? We have seen in Chapter 9 that both paid and voluntary chaplains have been an integral feature of prison life since the Quakers introduced Bible reading in the Walnut Street Jail. Technically, the First Amendment prohibits state establishment of any religion, which could be interpreted as prohibiting the use of government funds for religious activities. Yet at the same time, government itself deprives some citizens of the full exercise of their religious rights—when, for example, they are stationed in remote areas on a military base or confined in a correctional facility. To compensate for this state-created deprivation, the Supreme Court has held that provision of compensatory services in the form of prison chaplains is justifiable.[7]

Whether inmates must be provided with state-compensated clergy representative of their *specific faith* is, however, another issue. In that respect, it has been ruled that corrections is not expected to maintain a "full complement" of religious personnel on the payroll, but rather, that a "representative selection" would suffice. This decision is based on the premise that chaplains "are hired to serve the spiritual needs of all prisoners and are not intended to be merely the emissaries of their particular churches."[8]

[7]Barbara B. Knight and Stephen T. Early, Jr., *Prisoners' Rights in America* (Chicago: Nelson-Hall, 1986), p. 188.
[8]Ibid., pp. 188–89.

2. *Exactly what qualifies as an actual religion?* To be safeguarded under the First Amendment, it is necessary to establish that the protections being sought do, in fact, represent the practices of a religion. The definition of "religion" is not limited to conventional faiths. For example, the courts have held that witchcraft meets the test of qualifying as a religion. On the other hand, the courts have refused to grant First Amendment protections to an inmate-created group called Church of the New Song (CONS), whose principles require them to be "served steak and wine from time to time."[9]

3. *To what extent is the free exercise of religion protected?* Once it has been established that certain beliefs represent an acknowledged religion, the issue becomes to what degree correctional institutions can interfere with the unrestricted exercise of religious practices. This raises difficult issues, since accommodating religious beliefs essentially means providing special treatment for certain groups.

Some religious principles are relatively uncomplicated and easy to comply with in confinement. When Catholics were prohibited from eating meat on Fridays, for instance, it was not any major imposition to schedule fish to be served. On the other hand, pork has long been inexpensive and therefore frequently used in institutional meals. Both Jewish and Black Muslim religions have challenged this practice, although their claims "have met with mixed success because the dietary requests may pose both logistical and economic problems to prison administrators."[10]

Generally, the courts have favored accommodating pork-free diet restrictions where those holding such religious principles represent a significant portion of the inmate population. However, it has also been held that eliminating pork completely from institutional menus is not required if inmates are provided with a sufficient variety of foods to enable them to "obtain a nutritionally adequate diet without violating their religious beliefs."[11] In deciding these cases, the administrative ease or difficulty of providing special diets will be a significant factor, as vividly portrayed in the next "Close-up on Corrections."

Unique diets have been a major factor in First Amendment litigation, but they are not the only source of controversy in terms of the free exercise of religious beliefs during incarceration. Other challenges have included such issues as:

- *The right to attend religious services.* Given the wide diversity of religions represented within large institutions, it is difficult to provide formal services for every conceivable group. When such services are offered, however, they cannot be confined to traditional faiths. On this issue, the Supreme Court has noted that an inmate is entitled to a "reasonable opportunity of pursuing his faith comparable to the opportunity afforded fellow prisoners who adhere to conventional religious precepts. . . ."[12]

Religions that represent sizable numbers of inmates have traditionally been permitted to gather for services, provided that doing so does not represent a risk

---

[9]Collins, *Correctional Law*, p. 61.
[10]Knight and Early, p. 201.
[11]Collins, *Correctional Law*, p. 63.
[12]Collins, *Legal Responsibility*, p. 19, citing *Cruz v. Beto* 405 U.S. 319 (1972).

Diet Too Complicated

A New York federal court refused to order the New York Department of Correctional Services to meet the dietary demands of Rastafarians (. . . a religion with roots in the culture of Jamaica). The demands were quite complex and included such things as no meat, sometimes (depending on the sect) no canned foods or dairy products, no foods treated with nonorganic pesticides or fertilizers, and food only cooked in natural materials, such as clay pots.

It made no difference to the court that the prison system provided Orthodox Jewish inmates with kosher or neutral diets and some special dietary accommodations for Muslims. The complexity of the Rastafarian's dietary requirements and the financial and administrative burdens that those requirements would create justified the differences [*Benjamin v. Coughlin*, 708 F. Supp. 570 (S.D.N.Y. 1989)].

*Source:* William C. Collins, *Correctional Law for the Correctional Officer* (Laurel, MD: American Correctional Association, 1990), p. 63.

to institutional order and security. In fact, the Calgary Correctional Centre in Alberta, Canada, has extended the practice of religion to enabling native inmates to participate in Sweat Lodge ceremonies.[13] In the United States, courts have upheld the order-and-security constraint, ruling that "freedom to exercise religious beliefs is not absolute, but is subject to restriction for the protection of the [inmate] society as a whole."[14] In other words, while everyone has the right to maintain their own personal religious *beliefs*, inmates do not have an unconditional right to *exercise* those beliefs during confinement. On the other hand, using the same reasoning, it has been held that a prison cannot arbitrarily prohibit the practice of an established religion unless it can prove that such practice creates "a clear and present danger to the orderly functioning of the institution."[15]

• *Exemptions from hair and beard regulations.* Those serving time in correctional institutions are often required to maintain short haircuts and a clean-shaven face. Prison and jail officials have justified prohibitions against long hair and beards on the basis that they inhibit ready identification of inmates, are unsanitary, and provide potential hiding places for contraband. Some groups, such as American Indians, have challenged these regulations as a violation of their religious beliefs. Court decisions have been somewhat diverse on this issue. When it is clearly established that religious beliefs are sincere, it is possible that the inmate's First Amendment argument will prevail. For instance, in one case involving a Cherokee Indian, "[t]he court ruled . . . that even if the justifications themselves were legiti-

[13]Dave McIeod, "The Raising of a Sweat Lodge," *Keepers' Voice*, Vol. 10, No. 1 (March 1989), p. 15.
[14]Palmer, p. 85.
[15]Ibid., citing *Banks v. Havener*, 234 F. Supp. 27 (E.D. Va. 1964).

mate, they were not warranted in this instance because less restrictive alternatives were available. The inmate could be required to pull his hair back from his face in a ponytail, for example, which would prevent his using it as a mask. . . ."[16]

But other rulings have upheld haircut and beard rules. Most recently, for example, a 1992 appellate court decision in the case of a Rastafarian hairstyle illustrates the greater discretion that is currently being delegated to correctional administrators. In that case, the court ruled that "it is not for us to impose our own ideas about prison management upon those who attempt the reasonable regulation of that nearly impossible task. . . . [T]he loss of absolute freedom of religious expression is but one sacrifice required by . . . incarceration."[17]

• *The right to wear or use various types of special attire or articles* (e.g., religious medallions, prayer rugs, shawls, peace pipes, etc.). Concern for safety and security has also been used as a rationale for prohibiting the use or display of certain religious artifacts (especially those which could potentially be used as or shaped into weapons). In these areas, courts have tended to uphold reasonable regulations which are "substantially justified by the needs of prison discipline and order."[18] But again, institutional policies cannot be used to discriminate against a particular religion. When something—such as the wearing of a medal—is permitted for one group, the same consideration must be extended to all denominations under the *equal protection* clause of the Fourteenth Amendment. Nor can the issue be avoided by arbitrarily prohibiting medals for everyone, unless sufficient reason to do so can be demonstrated.

In summary, various restrictions on the exercise of religious freedom within correctional facilities have been upheld when they are justified on the basis of:

• The need to maintain *discipline or security*
• The proper exercise of *authority and official discretion*
• The fact that the regulation is *reasonable*
• The *economic considerations* involved.[19]

The extent to which correctional practices are defensible according to these criteria will, of course, continue to be defined by the courts.

---

*LEARNING GOALS*

*Do you know:*

• *Under what conditions inmate mail can be censored or restricted?*
• *What due process procedures are required when an inmate's mail is rejected?*

---

[16]Knight and Early, p. 207, citing *Gallahan v. Hollyfield*, 670 F.2d 1345 (C.A.8 1982).
[17]Daniel Pollack, "Legal Briefs," *Corrections Today*, Vol. 54, No. 8 (December 1992), p. 156, citing *Scott v. Mississippi Department of Corrections*, U.S. App. (5th Cir. 1992).
[18]Ibid., p. 205.
[19]Palmer, p. 73. For a summary of related court cases, see Michael J. Dale, "Religion in Jails and Prisons: Defining the Inmate's Legal Rights," *American Jails*, Vol. 5, No. 3 (July/August 1991), pp. 30–34.

## Mail Privileges and Freedom from Censorship

Another First Amendment right enjoyed by those in free society that is subject to modification during confinement is freedom of the press. The nature of incoming mail has been subject to regulation in order to detect contraband, uncover escape plans, avoid material that would ignite violence, and the like. Because of the labor-intensive and time-consuming process of implementing these constraints, further restrictions have often been placed on the volume of incoming mail that an inmate can receive. In addition, outgoing mail has been subject to such limitations as an approved correspondence list, under the theory that doing so promotes rehabilitative goals.

Correctional officials are now being required to more clearly justify such procedures as legitimate reactions to a "clear and present danger." When justification can be demonstrated, it appears that restrictions will be upheld, provided that they do not exceed necessary limits. For example, the Supreme Court has held that prison officials "must show that a regulation authorizing mail censorship furthers . . . interests of security, order, and rehabilitation. Second, the limitation . . . must be no greater than is necessary . . . to the protection of the particular government interest involved."[20]

Moreover, when an inmate's mail is rejected, case law has established certain due process procedures that must be followed:

- The inmate must be notified of the rejection.
- The letter's author must be allowed to protest the refusal.
- The complaint must be decided by an official other than the one who made the original decision to refuse delivery.[21]

As noted in Chapter 8, such restrictions do *not* apply to correspondence with the courts, attorneys, or public officials. While these types of "privileged" mail cannot be read or censored, they can be opened and physically inspected for contraband in the presence of the inmate.

What is not so apparent, however, is how to handle sexually explicit publications. The First Amendment does not protect either pornographic material or that which "involves a clear and present danger of inciting . . . imminent lawless action."[22] Clearly, materials offering advice on such illegal acts as smuggling contraband, concocting homemade drugs or liquor, and the like can be prohibited. Sexually explicit publications can also be banned "on the grounds that the material is detrimental to rehabilitation and leads to deviate sexual behavior."[23] But just what is harmful enough to be considered obscene or pornographic has been subject to debate, as illustrated in the next "Close-up on Corrections."

---

[20]Palmer, p. 41, citing *Procunier v. Martinez*, 94 S. Ct. 1800 (1974).
[21]Ibid., p. 41.
[22]Ibid., p. 50, citing *Brandenburg v. Ohio*, 395 U.S. 444, 48 Ohio Op.2d 320 (1969).
[23]Ibid., p. 52, citing *Carpenter v. South Dakota*, 536 F.2d 759 (8th Cir. 1976).

### Sexually Oriented Publications

One publication censorship issue that still remains uncertain is the rejection of sexually oriented materials. Some such materials are easily banned, but for others, the question is a close one. For instance, mail came to an inmate from the North American Man/Boy Love Association (NAMBLA) and was rejected on security grounds. The material espoused consensual sexual relationships between adult and juvenile males. In court, officials pointed out various ways in which the material could promote violence in the institution and in which it could be detrimental to the rehabilitation of the inmate to whom it was sent as well as many other pedophiles in the prison. The court approved the prohibition. *Harper v. Wallingford*, 877 F.2d 728 (9th Cir. 1989).

*Source:* William C. Collins, *Correctional Law for the Correctional Officer* (Laurel, MD: American Correctional Association, 1990), p. 65.

---

> ### LEARNING GOALS
>
> *Do you know:*
>
> - *When frisk, strip, cell, and body-cavity searches may be conducted without violating constitutional protections?*
> - *To what extent visitors can be subjected to searches?*
> - *Under what circumstances employees can be required to undergo drug testing?*

## Freedom from Unreasonable Search and Seizure

The right to be free from "unreasonable" search and seizure is guaranteed by the Fourth Amendment. But as we saw in Chapter 8, the necessity to maintain institutional security through the detection of contraband severely limits this right within correctional facilities. In that earlier discussion, it was noted that frisk and cell searches can be conducted randomly at any time without cause, unless they are being used for an illegitimate purpose such as abuse or harassment. Inmate patdowns and cell searches therefore do not tend to fall within Fourth Amendment protections. In contrast, there is a degree of protection against body-cavity searches. Because of their greater intrusiveness, such searches must be based on reasonable suspicion and performed only by authorized medical personnel.

Strip searches fall in between these two extremes. The Supreme Court has approved strip searches of inmates "following their exposure to the opportunity to obtain contraband" (e.g., after work release or a contact visit).[24] Moreover, at

[24]Collins, *Correctional Law*, p. 73.

least one appellate court has ruled that "the correctional institution's interest in maintaining security and deterring and discovering contraband permitted it to conduct strip searches without reasonable suspicion or probable cause."[25]

**Visitor Searches.**   Although visitors are entitled to greater protections than inmates, the degree of protection will again depend on the intrusiveness of the search. Visitors can be required to walk through a metal detector, to surrender any articles they are carrying to be searched (e.g., briefcases, umbrellas, purses, etc.), and to submit to a frisk search. But a strip search cannot be conducted without reasonable suspicion. Moreover, a visitor can refuse to be strip searched even when reasonable suspicion exists. Although the visitor would then be denied admission to the facility, he or she could simply elect to leave. Nor is it permissible for an institution to require that visitors consent to a strip search as a condition for being admitted:

> A requirement that every visitor "agree" to a strip search as a condition of being allowed to visit jail inmates resulted in an award of $177,000 [in] damages against a Massachusetts sheriff. The court quickly rejected the argument that the visitor "consented" to the searches, saying that . . . the state cannot condition the granting of . . . a privilege (such as visiting) on someone giving up a constitutional right (in this case, the right to be free from unreasonable searches).[26]

**Employee Searches and Drug-Testing.**   Like visitors, the searching of employees is held to a higher standard than that of inmates. As noted in Chapter 8, employees can be frisk-searched for reasonable suspicion. But for a body-cavity search, probable cause is needed, along with a search warrant.

Undoubtedly the most controversial area of employee searches in recent years has been the analysis of body fluids for the purpose of detecting drugs. While drug testing is used less frequently in corrections than in law enforcement,[27] it is becoming a standard phase of selection screening in some states. There are no legal prohibitions against *preemployment* urinalysis for job applicants. Once candidates are hired, however, they enjoy greater due process protections in this regard.[28] Although a few agencies test on a *random* basis, the vast majority restrict testing to those employees who are under *suspicion* of engaging in drug use.[29] But even when drug testing is based on suspicious behavior (such as work performance, physical appearance, absenteeism, etc.), the *reasonableness* of that suspicion under provisions of the Fourth Amendment may be in question.

[25]Daniel Pollack, "Legal Briefs," *Corrections Today*, Vol. 54, No. 2 (April 1992), p. 28.

[26]Ibid., p. 76, citing *Blackburn v. Snow*, 771 F.2d 556 (1st Cir. 1985).

[27]As of 1988, 19 states (38%) and the Federal Bureau of Prisons were conducting drug testing of either correctional staff or applicants. However, this is far less than the 73% reported by police departments. Randall Guynes and Osa Coffey, "Employee Drug-Testing Policies in Prison Systems," *National Institute of Justice: Research in Action* (Washington, DC: U.S. Department of Justice, 1988), p. 1.

[28]Nevertheless, research indicates that the general public is relatively supportive of mandatory substance abuse testing, particularly "for workers whose impairment would jeopardize public safety." Edward J. Latessa, Lawrence F. Travis, and Francis T. Cullen, "Public Support for Mandatory Drug–Alcohol Testing in the Workplace," *Crime and Delinquency*, Vol. 34, No. 4 (1988), p. 379.

[29]Guynes and Coffey, p. 1.

There are some who maintain that there should be no constitutional issue here. According to their argument, employees who have nothing to fear from the results of a urinalysis would have no reason to object to being tested. But applying that line of reasoning to other search and seizure situations reveals the weakness of its logic. For instance, it is doubtful that anyone would want to give the police unrestricted power to search their home at any time on the basis that the search would not yield anything illegal. If the state can indiscriminately require employees to submit to drug tests, the boundary between personal privacy and public intrusion shifts considerably, inviting the potential for increasing government penetration into private domains.

The primary questions raised in Fourth Amendment challenges to employee drug tests are whether they constitute an actual "search," and if so, to what extent they are "reasonable." The first matter has been clearly settled—courts have established that urinalysis falls within the provisions of being a search (of the person) and seizure (of bodily fluids).[30] Legal decisions have not, however, been quite so unambiguous in terms of the reasonableness measure. The New York City Department of Corrections, for example, encountered conflicting decisions about its random testing policy. Initially, the state supreme court found that the program did not adequately protect employee's rights.[31] But later, an appellate court upheld the tests, maintaining that the department's compelling interest in employee drug abuse outweighed privacy expectations.[32]

In that regard, other courts have similarly held that the duties of correctional officers in medium- and maximum-security prisons involve a "diminished expectation of privacy," and therefore that drug testing is a reasonable intrusion, due to the nature of the job.[33] A summary of these and other cases concludes that the courts appear to be permitting random testing of correctional personnel who have:

- Regular contact with inmates
- Opportunities to smuggle drugs into a facility
- Access to firearms
- Responsibilities that frequently involve driving vehicles that transport passengers.[34]

In other words, these job functions are such that the agency's interest in detecting drug use supersedes the employee's right to privacy. But for all other personnel, testing based on reasonable suspicion is the rule, and future litigation will undoubtedly continue to shape the definition of reasonableness.

[30]*Allen v. City of Marietta*, 601 F. Supp. 482 (N.D. Ga. 1985).
[31]"N.Y. Judge Bans Drug Tests for Corrections Officers," *Corrections Digest* (July 13, 1988), p. 2.
[32]"N.Y. Appeals Court Upholds Drug Testing for Jail Officers," *Corrections Digest* (November 15, 1988), p. 9.
[33]Guynes and Coffey, p. 6.
[34]J. Devereux Weeks, "Jail Employee Drug Testing under Fourth Amendment Limitations," *American Jails*, Vol. 4, No. 3 (September/October 1990), p. 30.

## Freedom from Cruel and Unusual Punishment

Under the Eighth Amendment, U.S. citizens are protected against the infliction of cruel and unusual punishment. This provision is designed to assure that government's power to punish is "exercised within the limits of civilized standards."[35] Thus, it has been the basis of inmate challenges to a wide variety of correctional practices, including disciplinary procedures, use of force, and various conditions of confinement ranging from crowding to smoking. Court decisions concerning what does and does not constitute cruel and unusual punishment have also varied over time. During the hands-off period, judicial definition of "cruel and unusual" was limited primarily to situations involving extreme barbarity, torture, or excessive cruelty. In more recent years, however, legal judgments have reflected changing standards of decency in society.[36]

In making decisions about cases raising Eighth Amendment challenges, courts today are applying certain guidelines that focus on whether the matter being contested:

- Shocks the conscience of the court.
- Violates the evolving standards of decency in a civilized society.
- Imposes punishment that is disproportionate to the offense.
- Involves the wanton and unnecessary infliction of pain without penological objective.
- Shows deliberate indifference to the needs of the inmate.[37]

Generally, the use of force has been upheld in situations involving self-defense, defense of other persons, enforcement of institutional regulations, and prevention of escape or a criminal act.[38] This, of course, is assuming that the

---

[35]Alvin J. Bronstein, "Prisoners' Rights: A History," in Geoffrey P. Alpert, ed., *Legal Rights of Prisoners* (Beverly Hills, CA: Sage Publications, 1980), p. 26.
[36]*Correctional Officer Resource Guide*, Second Edition (Laurel, MD: American Correctional Association, 1989), p. 16.
[37]Collins, *Correctional Law*, p. 81.
[38]Palmer, p. 25.

amount of force used was not excessive under the particular circumstances involved. As recently as 1992, the U.S. Supreme Court made it clear that the standard for using force in a prison setting is governed by the Eighth Amendment. In that case (*Hudson v. McMillian*),[39] the court held that force becomes excessive when it is applied "maliciously and sadistically to cause harm," rather than in a "good faith effort to maintain or restore discipline."

In some situations, an individual action or a particular correctional practice has failed to pass the scrutiny of judicial review. But recently in *Wilson v. Seiter* (1991),[40] the U.S. Supreme Court has taken into account the potential for a combination of conditions to produce "the deprivation of a single, identifiable human need such as food, warmth, or exercise; for example, a low cell temperature at night combined with a failure to issue blankets." On the other hand, overall conditions of confinement do not constitute cruel and unusual punishment when no deprivation of a specific human need can be verified.

**Conditions of Confinement.**   Within the limits of their income, those in free society have the liberty to decide such things as what food they will eat, what clothes they will wear, in what type of residence they will live, with whom they will associate, and when they will visit a doctor or dentist. Needless to say, those incarcerated do not have the freedom to make such choices. As the Supreme Court underscored in one ruling: "An incarcerated person loses more than free-

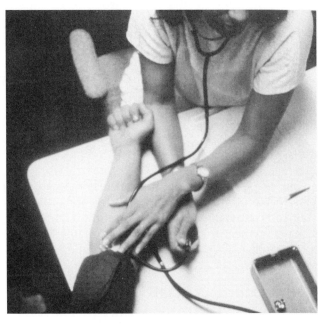

Although inmates have no right to a specified level of care, denial of necessary treatment for serious medical needs is a constitutional violation. Courtesy of the Dade County Department of Corrections and Rehabilitation, Miami, Florida.

[39]*Hudson v. McMillian*, 112 S. Ct. 995 (1992).
[40]*Wilson v. Seiter*, 111 S. Ct. 2321 (1991). For a full interpretation of this case, see Rolando del Carmen, Susan E. Ritter, and Betsy A. Witt, *Briefs of Leading Cases in Corrections* (Cincinnati, OH: Anderson Publishing Company, 1993), pp. 6–8.

dom. The prisoner must depend on the state to make the most basic decisions vital to his or her health and safety."[41]

Everyone, of course, does not agree on how adequately the state makes such decisions. Consequently, inmates have challenged a host of institutional conditions as being in violation of cruel and unusual punishment—particularly when they are confined in an aging, overcrowded facility or subject to inadequate food, clothing, sanitation, or health care. It is obviously beyond the scope of this chapter to consider each of these issues in detail. But when inmates can demonstrate "deliberate indifference or intentional mistreatment," it is likely that the courts will afford them a remedy.[42] The next "Close-up on Corrections" examines how this has been interpreted in the area of medical care.

The inadequacy of specific living conditions is often a result of the overall deterioration of services that accompanies institutional crowding. In and of itself, crowding has not been found to be an Eighth Amendment violation, as was illustrated in two landmark cases on this subject:

- In *Bell v. Wolfish*[43] the court held that there is no constitutional principle requiring "one man, one cell."
- In *Rhodes v. Chapman*[44] no evidence was found that double-celling either "inflicts unnecessary or wanton pain" or is "grossly disproportionate" to the severity of crimes warranting imprisonment.

Double-bunking has not been considered unconstitutional *unless* "in combination with other factors, it yields a situation that may be intolerable."[45] In such cases, the primary question is whether the "totality of conditions" resulting from a crowded institution meets the test of being cruel and unusual; for example:

> Not only can overcrowding have adverse effects upon the psychological and mental health of inmates, but it also often brings to light institutional shortages and defects. . . . Confinement may be rendered unduly hazardous as security systems and personnel, heating, ventilation, sanitation, and fire protection systems become incapable of meeting the expanded demands made upon them.[46]

It is one thing to be confined in tight living quarters. That situation the courts seem relatively willing to accept. It is a completely different matter, however, when accommodating too many inmates also jeopardizes some other aspect of their well-being—such as health, safety, sanitation, or the like. That additional complication the courts have been increasingly reluctant to tolerate.

---

[41]Daniel Pollack, "Legal Briefs," *Corrections Today*, Vol. 53, No. 4 (July 1991), p. 27, citing *Hutto v. Finney* (1978).
[42]Bronstein, p. 37.
[43]*Bell v. Wolfish*, 441 U.S. 520, 542 (1979).
[44]*Rhodes v. Chapman*, 452 U.S. 337, 348 (1981).
[45]Dale K. Sechrest and William C. Collins, *Jail Management and Liability Issues* (Coral Gables, FL: Coral Gables Publishing Company, 1989), p. 109.
[46]Knight and Early, p. 131.

### Medical Care and the Eighth Amendment

It may appear surprising that there is a constitutional right to any level of medical care. But this is a necessary result of the total control [that] the government must exercise over those it imprisons. . . .

The prisoner's ability to obtain medical assistance is at the mercy of his or her keepers; access to medical care is totally within the hands of the officials. Thus, they have the duty to provide sufficient care to meet constitutional standards. . . .

If it can be shown that the prisoner had (1) a known medical ailment or other acute physical problem, (2) which officials deliberately ignored or refused to treat, (3) causing the prisoner pain or injury, then a constitutional violation is established. . . . It is almost impossible for a prisoner to succeed on an Eighth Amendment ground if *some* treatment, no matter how inappropriate or inadequate, was provided. For, to violate the Constitution, the medical care must "shock the conscience," not be "mere negligence." . . .

[T]he Constitution prohibits only the most extreme deprivations; it establishes minimums, a floor. Everything that is wrong is not a constitutional violation. Only inadequate treatment under circumstances that would produce the "unnecessary and wanton infliction of pain" amounts to cruel and unusual punishment. . . .

The finding that inadequate care is not cruel and unusual punishment in no way indicates a stamp of approval. A low level of treatment does not necessarily qualify as a reasonable standard of care; it is simply not so extremely horrendous as to fall below the constitutional floor.

*Source:* Penelope D. Clute, *The Legal Aspects of Prisons and Jails* (Springfield, IL: Charles C Thomas, 1980), pp. 82–85.

**Legal and Administrative Remedies.**   When it appears futile to contest such allegations, correctional officials can enter a *consent decree*, essentially agreeing to take remedial action (as we saw in terms of jail crowding in Chapter 6). If the agency elects to contest the issue and the inmate's claim is ultimately successful, the court can issue an *injunction* requiring that specified deficiencies be corrected within an established timeframe.

Moreover, injunctions can declare a whole facility to be unconstitutional. In fact, they can even extend to include all of the institutions within the state's entire department of corrections (as had occurred in some 11 jurisdictions by mid-1990).[47] Throughout the country, *more than one out of every four* state correc-

---

[47]*Vital Statistics in Corrections* (Laurel, MD: American Correctional Association, 1991), p. 52. As of 1990, the entire adult correctional system was under court order in six states: Kansas, Louisiana, Mississippi, Nevada, South Carolina, and Texas. The juvenile correctional system was under court order in another two states (Alabama and Oklahoma), along with the District of Columbia. Both adult and juvenile systems were under court order in Florida and Rhode Island.

tional facilities were under a court order or consent decree by mid-1990.[48] Nor do those figures include the nearly 400 jails operating under court order.[49]

Federal courts can hold correctional officials in contempt of court for failure to comply with an injunction or consent decree.[50] Moreover, they have "the power to order the release of persons who are being held under conditions which deprive them of rights guaranteed . . . by the Constitution, unless such conditions are corrected within a reasonable time."[51]

Some inmates have not been willing to wait for the courts to act, essentially releasing themselves by absconding. Needless to say, most escapes are not justifiable. But under certain circumstances, the duress of confinement under conditions posing extreme danger to life and personal safety can be used as a defense against punishment for escape. For instance, such a defense may be used when it can be demonstrated that the inmate:

- Was faced with seriously threatening danger of death, sexual attack, or serious bodily injury.
- Attempted and unsuccessfully exhausted appropriate remedies within the institution.
- Lacked any further course of action short of escape.
- Surrendered as soon as the threatening danger had been avoided.[52]

Escape, of course, represents one of the most extreme means of seeking relief from unsafe or inhumane conditions in correctional institutions. Far more common is the filing of lawsuits. It is apparent that legal actions challenging numerous conditions of confinement have achieved a significant influence in terms of making improvements in the standard of living within correctional institutions. Perhaps the most significant contribution of legal action, however, has been the efforts it has generated to avoid lawsuits by more proactively addressing legitimate complaints. Without inmate access to the courts, there might never have been as much incentive to employ *administrative remedies* to reduce litigation, such as formal grievance procedures.

Today, many courts will not elect to hear a case until the complainant has exhausted all such internal administrative remedies. For the inmates, this alternative can produce desired results more quickly, without having to go to court. For correctional officials, it can reduce the costly and time-consuming process of becoming entangled in lengthy litigation. In fact, the Canadian government has taken this concept a step further by establishing an independent office to investigate and report on problems expressed by inmates confined throughout Canada's

[48]James Stephan, *Census of State and Federal Correctional Facilities, 1990* (Washington, DC: U.S. Department of Justice, 1992), p. 7.

[49]*Vital Statistics*, p. 68. As of mid-1988, 387 jails across the country were under court order, primarily for conditions related to crowding.

[50]But a recent Supreme Court ruling has now made it easier for administrators to obtain changes in federal court decrees governing correctional facilities. See "High Court Eases States' Ability to Modify Decrees," *On the Line*, Vol. 15, No. 2 (March 1992), pp. 1–2.

[51]Palmer, p. 242.

[52]Knight and Early, p. 136.

penitentiaries. Insights into the unique duties involved in this ombudsman position of "correctional investigator" are contained in the next "Close-up on Corrections."

Whatever the form of remedy implemented, no longer is there any doubt that corrections cannot overlook the legitimate health and safety needs of those entrusted to its care. While court decisions prompting correctional reforms are often limited to individual facilities or particular circumstances, "in the aggregate, they have created a wave of change that has rippled through other institutions and systems."[53]

But that is not meant to imply that all inmate-initiated litigation has been either fruitful or meaningful. (In fact, the "Close-up on Corrections" on page 644 features some of the frivolous claims that would be humorous were it not for the time and costs which they consumed.) Nor does it mean that lawsuits have been successful in changing the basic nature of the correctional process. It has been noted that society would be making a serious misjudgment to assume that litigation alone "can remedy the many fundamental shortcomings of our correctional systems."[54]

---

### ❖ CLOSE-UP ON CORRECTIONS

Canada's Correctional Investigator

The Correctional Investigator is appointed . . . to conduct investigations . . . concerning problems that relate to confinement in a penitentiary or supervision upon release. . . .

[T]he Correctional Investigator:

- May enter into and remain within any public office or institution, and shall have access to every part thereof;
- May examine all papers, documents, vouchers, records and books of any kind belonging to the public office or institution; and
- May summon before him any person and require that person to give evidence, orally or in writing, including the authority to subpoena evidence and to take evidence under oath.

The Correctional Investigator does not have the authority to order change. The power of the office . . . lies with its ability to investigate complaints independently, to publish its findings and conclusions . . . and to make recommendations to the appropriate government authorities to address the area of complaint. . . .

*Source:* R. L. Stewart, *Annual Report of the Correctional Investigator* (Ottawa, Canada: Minister of Supply and Services, 1992), pp. 1, 17.

---

[53]Jim Thomas, *Prisoner Litigation: The Paradox of the Jailhouse Lawyer* (Totowa, NJ: Rowman & Littlefield, 1988), p. 252.

[54]Charles W. Thomas, "The Impotence of Correctional Law," in Alpert, p. 245.

Frivolous Inmate Lawsuits

The whole thing started in 1989 when Kenneth D. Parker, a convicted armed robber in the Nevada State Prison in Carson City, ordered a jar of chunky peanut butter and other items from the prison store. When the order was delivered, there was no peanut butter, but he claims he was charged for it. The next day, he received a jar of creamy peanut butter, but he rejected it. He wanted crunchy. Then Parker was transferred to the new state prison in Ely. The crunchy peanut butter, apparently, never caught up with him.

Parker sued in U.S. District Court in Reno, claiming his civil rights and rights to property (his $2.50) were violated. U.S. District Judge Edward C. Reed dismissed the case, saying, "Plaintiff is out one jar of crunchy peanut butter worth $2.50 and should seek relief through the prison grievance system of the Nevada small-claims court."

*Source:* "Worst Legal News," *Parade Magazine* (December 29, 1991), p. 18, citing the *Reno Gazette-Journal.*

An inmate appealed the dismissal of his 38th federal civil rights lawsuit against a Texas prison. The appeals court characterized his latest suit as consisting of "vague and largely incomprehensible claims," which included such complaints as:

- The showers are too distant, and he gets cold walking to them;
- He needs a television in his cell because the other inmates talk too loudly;
- He is denied equal protection of the laws because he can only have two boxes of matches a week; and
- The prison needs a chorus of all races to sing together.

The trial court found that most of the claims were frivolous, and that the few which were not had already been dealt with in a class action suit. The appeals court agreed, finding the case to be a "waste of judicial resources" which cannot be tolerated. The appeals court therefore barred the inmate from filing any further lawsuits or appeals unless he first obtained permission from a trial or appellate court judge.

*Source:* Summarized from "Frivolous Suits," *Jail and Prisoner Law Bulletin* (Chicago: Americans for Effective Law Enforcement, n.d.), p. 4, citing *Mayfield v. Collins,* 918 F.2d 560 (5th Cir. 1991).

**Capital Punishment.** Thus far, this discussion of inmate litigation has been limited to challenges directed toward some aspect of the restraints or conditions accompanying incarceration. Obviously, inmates also initiate lawsuits in an attempt to overturn their conviction or alter their sentence. These types of cases do not affect the management or operation of correctional facilities. However, because of its Eighth Amendment implications, as well as the widespread controversy it has generated, one particular focus of such appeals requires further consideration—that is, of course, the death penalty.

Capital punishment has endured since ancient times. Primitive people actually used death sparingly, or at least indirectly. It was seldom that an offender was killed for a crime. More often, a child or a maiden was sacrificed to the gods. The offender was usually banished from the tribe (or exiled), which in the absence of group protection, presumably resulted in death. By the Greek and Roman periods, execution became more commonplace, but not necessarily for the types of offenses to which the death penalty is applied today.

Ancient people used capital punishment less in response to crime than in reaction to political or other deviant ideas that threatened to damage society. This is apparent in two of the most prominent early executions—Socrates and Jesus of Nazareth. Socrates was sentenced by the court to drink poisonous hemlock because the ideas he taught "corrupted the morals of youth" insofar as they varied from local custom and values in Athens. Jesus was sentenced to die by crucifixion (the penalty reserved for blasphemy), because he claimed to be the son of God.

Conventional criminals were also put to death in ancient times. However, the high point of capital punishment occurred in England between 1533 and 1603, when Queen Elizabeth was on the throne. During her reign, about 72,000 people were put to death—for offenses ranging from murder to failing to remove one's cap in church. Nor were children spared. As late as 1801, a 13-year-old child was hanged in England for stealing a spoon.[55]

Today, capital punishment is applied much more discriminately. Nevertheless, there were some 2482 inmates under sentence of death throughout the United States in 1991,[56] and a record number of executions (27) were carried out in 1992.[57] Virtually all prisoners currently under sentence of death have been convicted of murder, and the majority had at least one prior felony conviction.[58] Most are also male (99%) and white (59%).[59] Although blacks (nearly 40%) are disproportionately represented, the Supreme Court has been reluctant to address the potential of racial discrimination in sentencing decisions.[60]

As a result of the lengthy appellate process involved in capital cases, some have been awaiting their fate on death row for a decade or more. (Not only do inmates often file appeals on their own behalf, but a sentence of death is subject to automatic review. On average, those executed in 1991 spent almost 10 years

[55]Arthur Koestler, *Reflections on Hanging* (New York: Macmillan, 1957), p. 15.

[56]Lawrence A. Greenfeld, "Capital Punishment 1991," *Bureau of Justice Statistics Bulletin* (Washington, DC: U.S. Department of Justice, 1992), p. 1.

[57]"1992 Marks Record Number of Executions," *On the Line*, Vol. 16, No. 1 (January 1993), p. 1.

[58]Greenfeld, p. 1.

[59]Ibid.

[60]Michael J. Sniffen, "No Reversal of Fortune for Blacks on Death Row," in John J. Sullivan and Joseph L. Victor, eds. *Criminal Justice 92/93*, Sixteenth Edition (Guilford, CT: Dushkin Publishing Group, 1992), p. 227. See also Paige H. Ralph, Jonathan R. Sorensen, and James W. Marquart, "A Comparison of Death-Sentenced and Incarcerated Murderers in Pre-*Furman* Texas," *Justice Quarterly*, Vol. 9, No. 2 (June 1992), p. 185, whose study concludes that it was not the defendant's race but "the victim's race [that] was the primary extralegal variable affecting sentencing decisions."

on death row.[61] To better appreciate the long-term impact of capital punishment, envision spending a decade under the "living death" isolation that is portrayed in the following "Close-up on Corrections."

All states do not, however, authorize the death penalty. As early as 1847, Michigan became the first state to abolish capital punishment, and by 1990, some 14 states had done likewise. Even in those jurisdictions that have death row

---

## ❖ CLOSE-UP ON CORRECTIONS

### Life on Death Row

The essence of death row confinement was captured by a condemned prisoner who observed, "A maggot eats and defecates. That's all we do: eat and defecate. Nothing else. They don't allow us to do nothing else." Such an existence, he maintained, amounts to a "living death."[a]

Condemned prisoners are permitted to do more than simply eat and defecate in solitary confinement, but the powerful perception persists among the condemned that they cannot do much more than that. The psychological impact of death row confinement is such that most condemned prisoners gradually waste away as human beings. By the time they reach the death-watch, the condemned lead lives not much richer than that of a maggot. In short, though a bit exaggerated, our prisoner's description is basically correct. Death row is indeed a living death, a place where the body is preserved while the person languishes and ultimately dies awaiting execution. . . .

The peculiar silence of death row stems from the empty and ultimately lifeless regimen imposed on the condemned. These offenders, seen as unfit for life in even the prison community, are relegated to this prison within a prison. . . . Typical maximum security prisoners spend about eight to twelve hours a day in their cells; typical death row prisoners spend twenty to twenty-two hours a day alone in theirs . . . Deemed beyond correction, they are denied access to even the meager privileges, amenities, and services available to regular prisoners. . . .

Security is a virtual obsession with the death row commander. Working on death row is, in his words, a "battle of minds," and the lines of conflict . . . are clear: "They want out; we must keep them in." In this continuing battle of wits and wills, no one can afford to be casual or relaxed. Or friendly. . . . There is no such thing as small talk here. . . . [D]eath row . . . is seen by both the keepers and the kept as cold, lonely, and often frightening . . . "a psychological nightmare that very few survive."

*Source:* Robert Johnson, *Death Work: A Study of the Modern Execution Process* (Pacific Grove, CA: Brooks/Cole Publishing Company, 1990), pp. 35, 38, 44–45.

[a]Robert Johnson, *Condemned to Die: Life under Sentence of Death* (Prospect Heights, IL: Waveland Press, 1989), p. 116.

---

[61]Greenfeld, p. 13.

inmates, years can go by without an execution. But when an inmate is put to death, particularly a high-profile offender, the heated debate over this issue is frequently renewed. Capital punishment is an emotional issue that polarizes people into extreme positions. As shown in the next "Close-up on Corrections," there are staunch advocates both for retaining and for abolishing the death penalty.[62]

The death penalty has yet to be argued conclusively on the basis of empirical evidence demonstrating that it is a deterrent to crime.[63] It is apparent that capital punishment—at least in the manner in which it is presently administered—does not appear to accomplish the purpose of protecting society through general deterrence: "When studies have compared the homicide rates for the past 50 years in states that employ the death penalty and in adjoining states that have abolished it, the numbers have in every case been quite similar; the death penalty has had no discernible effect on homicide rates."[64] In that regard, a former correctional administrator who has observed the perpetrators of this act for over half a century has concluded that murderers are "often chronic misfits with years of failure behind them," who are "driven by the towering impulse of the moment and incapable of making any fine distinction between [the] consequences of imprisonment versus death."[65]

Regardless of the public's views supporting or opposing the death penalty, the Supreme Court is ultimately the arbitrator of its constitutionality. Numerous challenges have been filed by death row inmates claiming violation of the cruel and unusual punishment protections of the Eighth Amendment. For many years, these appeals had been largely unsuccessful, until the 1972 *Furman v. Georgia* case.[66] In that ruling, the Supreme Court did not actually hold that capital punishment in and of itself was cruel and unusual, but rather that the arbitrary, capricious, and unfair manner in which it was being applied had become unconstitutional.

As illustrated in Figure 15.2, this decision had a significant impact on the death row population throughout the country as unconstitutionally imposed death sentences were commuted. Since the Court's action did not ban the death penalty outright, however, a number of states made efforts to rewrite their statutes governing capital punishment in a manner that would be constitutionally acceptable. As reflected in Figure 15.2, many of these revised statutes have withstood legal scrutiny, and consequently, the death row population has now climbed to an all-time high.

Throughout this section on legal issues, emphasis has focused on the extensive impact of court decisions on correctional practices and populations. While the implications of such legal actions cannot be denied or diminished, they must also be placed within the context of an even larger picture. From that perspec-

[62]For a more complete discussion of both sides of this issue, see Ernest van der Haag and John P. Conrad, *The Death Penalty: A Debate* (New York: Plenum Press, 1983).

[63]For a more complete discussion of both sides of this issue, see Ernest van der Haag and John P. Conrad, *The Death Penalty: A Debate* (New York: Plenum Press, 1983).

[64]Hugo Adams Bedau, "The Death Penalty as a Deterrent: Argument and Evidence," *Ethics*, Vol. 80, No. 3 (April 1970), pp. 205–17.

[64]Hoekema, p. 317.

[65]Paul W. Keve, "The Costliest Punishment—A Corrections Administrator Contemplates the Death Penalty," *Federal Probation*, Vol. 56, No. 1 (March 1992), p. 13.

[66]*Furman v. Georgia*, 408 U.S. 238 (1972).

## The Death Penalty Debate

| SUPPORTERS ARGUE THAT THE DEATH PENALTY: | OPPONENTS COUNTER THAT: |
| --- | --- |
| | Deterrence |
| Has a deterrent effect (or would be a deterrent, if it were carried out with greater speed and certainty). | Studies tend to indicate there is little significant difference in murder rates between states with and without the death penalty.[a] Moreover, this argument raises the question of whether executions can be justified "by the good which their deaths may do the rest of us."[b] |
| | Protection |
| Is needed to best protect society from the most serious and feared offenders. | The public could be adequately protected by life without parole, and in any event, murder is a crime with relatively low rates of recidivism.[c] |
| | Retribution |
| Is fitting retribution or "just desserts"—that is, the most (perhaps the only) appropriate punishment for murder. | Human life is sacred and society does not have the moral right to take it—especially given the potential that an innocent person could be wrongfully executed, as well as indications that the death penalty may be applied in a discriminatory manner.[d] |
| | Social Utility |
| Is not completely useless—even if it cannot be defended on other grounds, it may be a legitimate expression of vengeance or aggression by collective society. | If so, the issue becomes one concerning how many people are expendable for this purpose, along with the extent to which such a violent response may be reinforcing further violence rather than strengthening respect for life. |

[a]See, for example, William J. Bowers and Glenn Pierce, "Deterrence or Brutalization: What Is the Effect of Executions?" *Crime and Delinquency*, Vol. 26 (1980), pp. 453–84; and Brian Forst, "Capital Punishment and Deterrence: Conflicting Evidence?" *Journal of Criminal Law and Criminology*, Vol. 74 (1983), pp. 927–42.

[b]David Hoekema, "Capital Punishment: The Question of Justification," in John B. Williamson, Linda Evans, and Anne Munley, eds., *Social Problems: The Contemporary Debates*, Third Edition (Boston: Little, Brown, 1981), p. 318.

[c]Gennaro F. Vito and Deborah G. Wilson, "Back from the Dead: Tracking the Progress of Kentucky's Furman-Commuted Death Row Population," *Justice Quarterly*, Vol. 5, No. 1 (1988), pp. 101–11.

[d]Although it is difficult to document the extent of racism in capital punishment, research indicates that those who murder whites are more likely to receive the death penalty than the killers of blacks. Among the many studies in this area, see, for instance, M. Dwayne Smith, "Patterns of Discrimination in Assessments of the Death Penalty: The Case of Louisiana," *Journal of Criminal Justice*, Vol. 15, No. 4 (1987), pp. 279–86.

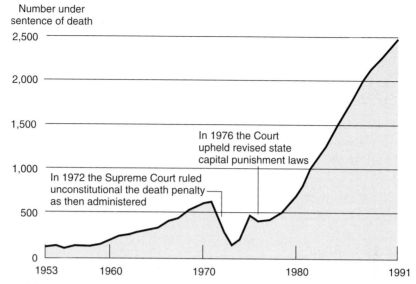

**Figure 15.2** Offenders under sentence of death, 1953–1991. *Source:* Lawrence A. Greenfeld, "Capital Punishment 1991," *Bureau of Justice Statistics Bulletin* (Washington, DC: U.S. Department of Justice, 1992), p. 2.

tive, although much progress has been made in one sense, the overall effect may not be quite as overwhelming as it initially appears:

> While convicted offenders no longer confront a high probability of execution . . . and while the conditions of confinement today are a good deal less harsh than those of even a few short decades ago . . . the likelihood that inmates will leave the prisons of today any more improved than those who left a century ago is too small to calculate. . . .[67]

## ❖ CURRENT TRENDS

Court decisions will continue to shape correctional policies and practices as long as differences remain between the rights of free citizens and convicted offenders. However, there are also a number of trends beyond changes produced by legal procedures that are shaping the nature of corrections. Some of these have been described in previous chapters—to mention just a few, we have already addressed trends involving intermediate sentencing alternatives, new generation jailing, caseload classification, voluntary treatment, reduced parole discretion, and due process rights in the juvenile justice system.

In addition to the changes and emerging issues discussed previously, corrections is heading in new directions as a result of such catalysts as accreditation and privatization. Of course, these are not by any means the only current trends

[67]Thomas, "Impotence of Correctional Law," pp. 248, 253.

that have been unaddressed thus far. But they have been singled out for special attention here as a result of a combination of factors, largely related to either the substantial contribution or significant controversy that they have generated.

---

*LEARNING GOALS*

*Do you know:*

- *What types of standards must be met to achieve correctional accreditation?*
- *Whether accreditation is voluntary or mandatory in corrections?*
- *Why so many agencies have initiated the accreditation process?*
- *To what extent accreditation may be a defense in liability lawsuits?*

---

## Accreditation

Every year, an increasing number of correctional institutions and programs undertake the lengthy process of seeking *accreditation* by the American Correctional Association (ACA) Commission on Accreditation for Corrections. These efforts represent a voluntary desire to upgrade the field of corrections, as well as a proactive means of seeking some protection against litigation. Accreditation is important in correctional services, just as it is in hospitals, universities, and other services interested in maintaining appropriate standards and levels of performance.

ACA has developed over a dozen manuals that provide *standards and guidelines* governing correctional administration and operations—for everything from food services to health care, correctional industries, juvenile facilities, adult institutions, small jails, probation, and parole. These guidelines represent minimum requirements that must be met for a facility or program to become accredited (as described in Chapter 4). Thus, they provide a measurement of the quality of service being provided.

The first correctional standards were published by ACA almost a half century ago, in 1946. They have undergone periodic changes since then and are under continuous revision. Standards regarding correctional administration include such areas as staffing, training, fiscal management, record keeping, legal rights of offenders, and the like. With regard to the direct delivery of services, the guidelines govern basic living conditions, health care, and safety concerns. As such, they cover a wide variety of topics, including:

- The physical plant
- Classification
- Custody and security
- Inmate discipline
- Counseling, education, and recreation
- Health and medical care

- Food services
- Property control
- Library services
- Inmate activities and privileges.

In each of these areas, ACA has established minimum standards with which those pursuing accreditation must be in compliance. However, it is also important to note that the intent is to define fundamental levels of service and operation below which accredited agencies, facilities, or programs must not fall. Because standards are applicable uniformly throughout the country, they are set at a level that is within reason to achieve, rather than a higher level that might ideally be more desirable. There is nothing to prevent organizations from exceeding the standards, but neither is there a great deal of incentive to do so.

Although seeking ACA accreditation is voluntary, over 800 correctional facilities have been involved in the process, and accredited facilities exist in 45 states.[68] Yet there are no legislative or legal mandates requiring accreditation. Nor is any additional funding necessarily forthcoming for accredited agencies. The question then becomes why so many have apparently elected to undertake this rather costly and time-consuming process. There are any number of answers, among them:

- *Self-improvement.* By examining the organization's existing practices against nationally accepted minimum standards, the agency can better determine in what areas it is lacking and take appropriate steps to make improvements. Of those involved in accreditation, the vast majority (93%) report that "the overall quality of their facilities and programs have improved" as a result of this process.[69] As correctional managers themselves have stated: "Accreditation's major benefit to top administration comes from the knowledge that every aspect of operations and administration are now routinely and regularly reviewed. It confirms the organization's strengths, identifies its weaknesses, and enables the organization to develop a systematic resolution to those weaknesses."[70]
- *Pride and morale.* Working toward accreditation is a lengthy process that requires commitment and teamwork on the part of everyone from top management to line staff and even inmates. In an agency that suffers from divisiveness, unclear direction, or simply general lack of cooperation, pulling together toward this common goal can generate a "team spirit" that enhances pride and morale when it is successfully accomplished: "Staff no longer wonder about a direction or philosophical goal. The standards provide goals and directions—goals that require them to stretch to the limits of their professional abilities."[71]
- *Legal defensibility.* By meeting ACA standards, correctional agencies can proactively reduce some of the expensive litigation that could otherwise result

---

[68]*ACA Directory* (Laurel, MD: American Correctional Association, 1990), p. 596.
[69]Ibid.
[70]M. Wayne Huggins and Charles J. Kehoe, "Accreditation Benefits Nation's Jails, Juvenile Detention Centers," *Corrections Today*, Vol. 54, No. 3 (May 1992), p. 42.
[71]Ibid.

from unsafe, unsanitary, or unacceptable conditions. While accreditation will not, of course, fully protect an organization from legal liability, having achieved accredited status can be a strong asset in defending certain types of liability claims. For example, a research project that reviewed thousands of pages of court decisions concluded that

> [c]ourts often consult ACA standards when attempting to determine appropriate expectations in a correctional setting. . . . [However], while there is no doubt ACA standards are a primary reference source for courts, they are not considered the only source, nor are they always adopted as the measure of adequacy. . . . [C]ompliance with ACA standards does not automatically ensure acceptance in court."[72]

In summary, accreditation is pursued for a variety of reasons that relate primarily to the voluntary desire of correctional managers to improve their facilities, services, and administration.[73] In that respect, accreditation demonstrates that the agency "has accepted a basic set of standards that have been worked out by professionals on a nationwide basis," and that it is moving in the direction of developing the types of policies and procedures that are beneficial not only to the inmates, but ultimately, to staff and the public as well.[74]

---

*LEARNING GOALS*

*Do you know:*

- *How the private sector has influenced corrections historically?*
- *What correctional services are provided today by religious groups and private organizations?*
- *What change the concept of privatization has undergone in recent years?*
- *The arguments in support of and opposition to the privatization of corrections?*

---

## Privatization

Not everyone would agree that accreditation is being implemented properly or setting standards high enough. Nevertheless, it is difficult to find fault with the basic concept. The same cannot, however, be said of privatization. Although privatization is emerging as both a trend and a source of controversy today, private individuals and groups have always played a major role in the field of corrections. See the next "Close-up on Corrections" for a few of the many examples of

---

[72]Rod Miller, "Standards and the Courts: An Evolving Relationship," *Corrections Today,* Vol. 54, No. 3 (May 1992), p. 60.
[73]See, for example, Kathy Briscoe and Joyce Kuhrt, "How Accreditation Has Improved Correctional Health Care," *American Jails,* Vol. 6, No. 4 (September/October 1992), pp. 48–52.
[74]*ACA Directory,* p. 596, quoting Samuel Sublet.

influential efforts that the private sector has exerted throughout history in the field of corrections.

As is apparent by these illustrations, the pattern of social action has typically been that private efforts initiate programs which are ultimately taken over by government. When needs arise, it is often the private sector that is the first to respond. Then, as the problem becomes too great to be handled by individuals or philanthropic groups, governmental agencies either subsidize or assume the entire function. At the point that problems become of sufficient magnitude to threaten the general welfare, governmental assistance is traditionally provided. As we have seen in recent years, the process comes full cycle when governmental agencies later request help from private sources in terms of volunteer services, contractual assistance, and so on.

In short, private corrections has always been involved in filling gaps in government services as needs arise. Nonprofit organizations also serve as watchdogs over government functions. In that respect, probably one of the greatest contributions of private organizations is the political influence they can bring to bear in a field generally devoid of political advantage in obtaining appropriations, program improvements, and resources. Voluntary organizations also support and complement services offered by public agencies.

**Religious Groups.** Perhaps because of the relationship between reforming offenders and the humanitarian philosophy of religious organizations, such

---

❖ *CLOSE-UP ON CORRECTIONS*

Influence of the Private Sector in Correctional History

- Victims and their families were the early forerunners of the justice system, seeking personal revenge against offenders.
- In the feudal system, the lord of the manor maintained arbitration courts for the serfs under his control as part of his private enterprise.
- The first permanent home for wandering children was built by the Society of St. Vincent de Paul in 1648.
- John Howard used his own resources to travel throughout Europe examining jail conditions, which resulted in reform of the English penal system.
- The American penitentiary, established in 1790, was based on the philosophy of a private Quaker-affiliated group.
- John Augustus took it upon himself to provide bail, supervise, and redeem petty criminals assigned to him by the courts.
- Houses of refuge for delinquent, dependent, and neglected children were originally operated by charitable or religious organizations.
- The modern juvenile court was initiated as a result of pressures on the part of the Chicago Women's Clubs.

groups have traditionally been active in correctional work. Examples range from the early efforts of the Quakers to the much more recent Jewish Family Services and the sizable correctional component of today's Salvation Army—which provides ex-offenders with material assistance in the form of shelter, food, and clothing, as well as counseling services and job placement. Many of these and other similar groups offer their services in slums and ghettoes, bars and skid rows—wherever the people who need assistance live.

The juvenile field in particular has attracted private-sector involvement, as illustrated by the large number of privately operated juvenile facilities and programs discussed in Chapter 13. Of course, many of these are not affiliated with religious groups, although Father Flanagan's Boys' Home is among the best known, and the Salvation Army maintains juvenile homes and shelters as well. Other religious groups work primarily in the area of delinquency prevention or treatment, such as Youth for Christ and the Juvenile Rehabilitation Ministry of the Southern Baptist Convention. In the adult system, most of the volunteer chaplains in jails and prisons represent private religious organizations.

**Private Organizations.**   The number of private organizations providing correctional services is far too numerous to describe individually. Among the most prominent on the national level are the John Howard Societies, named after the first jail reformer. In Chapter 4 we saw how the improvements advocated by Howard affected correctional reform. His work, along with that of Elizabeth Fry on behalf of female inmates, lives on through the organizations that carry their names.

Through such efforts as its training and accreditation programs, the American Correctional Association has been instrumental in promoting professional advancements. Courtesy of Richard J. DeGraff.

Among the organizations providing legal assistance to offenders are the many legal aid societies. Private legal aid societies practice not only in the courts, but also in correctional institutions. Perhaps best known are the chapters of the American Civil Liberties Union (ACLU), which have been active on behalf of inmates, particularly in capital punishment cases, as well as other challenges to the Eighth Amendment's prohibition against cruel and unusual punishment.

Throughout the United States, a variety of prisoner aid associations has been prominent in assisting discharged inmates with readjustment to society. Primarily, they offer assistance in terms of counseling, financial aid, and obtaining employment. Some also devote attention to working within the political process to encourage correctional improvements. A few have long historical ties, such as the Pennsylvania Prison Society (an offspring of the Philadelphia Society for Alleviating the Miseries of the Public Prisons). Others are of more recent origin, such as Virginia's Offender Aid and Restoration program, which started in 1971 to bring assistance to the local jail and has since expanded statewide to work with jails, prisons, and ex-offenders throughout the state.

At the national level, the American Correctional Association emerged in 1954 from what had formerly been known as the National Prison Association. ACA has been instrumental in promoting correctional advancements, as noted earlier in the discussion of accreditation. Other nationwide membership groups working to stimulate progress include both the American Jail Association and the National Sheriffs' Association. Similarly, the National Council on Crime and Delinquency (formerly the National Probation and Parole Association) is instrumental in disseminating information and conducting research to advance the field of corrections.

**Privatization Today.** In addition to the many religious and secular groups that have traditionally been involved in some aspect of correctional work, the *privatization of corrections* has taken on new meaning today. Publicly funded correctional enterprises are turning with increasing frequency to the private sector in a wide variety of ways.

When government either does not have the specialized expertise necessary to accomplish a particular project, or finds that certain services can be provided at less cost by the private sector, it is not uncommon to *contract* with private industry. In corrections, for example, the preparation of meals and provision of health care are typically contracted out when it is determined that private enterprise is better equipped to offer the service more economically. Particularly for small institutions, it may be cost-prohibitive to hire the personnel and invest in the sophisticated equipment necessary to sustain such services independently.

In addition to ongoing operational contracts, the private sector is often engaged in short-term *technical assistance* when corrections is faced with undertaking something highly technical or beyond its existing capabilities. A typical example is the design, construction, or expansion of a facility. From a cost–benefit point of view, the correctional payroll cannot be expected to maintain a permanent staff of architects, engineers, designers, and other professional personnel needed for these major, one-time projects.

But specific service contracts or short-term consulting assistance represent the privatization of only selected components of the correctional system, which has been commonplace for some time. What has changed in recent years is the movement toward *contracting the full operation* of entire facilities to the private sector.[75] Needless to say, this practice has raised a number of controversial issues, and its advantages as well as disadvantages have been debated extensively. On the one hand, privatization of correctional facilities has been supported on the grounds of efficiency and cost-effectiveness. This rationale maintains that the private sector has a number of advantages over government, including:

- *Reduced costs.* Because of the competitive nature of private industry and its profit motive, there is more incentive to reduce waste, eliminate duplication, and otherwise streamline activities in a more cost-effective manner. "Since private sector companies function in a competitive environment, they must offer high-quality services at minimum cost."[76] Thus, it is maintained that government can obtain more service for less money by opening the management of correctional facilities to a competitive bidding process.

- *Flexibility and creativity.* Bureaucracies are traditionally slow to experiment with new approaches or even respond to immediate needs. In contrast, "[w]hen a need is identified for audiovisual monitors or two-way, portable radios, for example, a corporate decision can be made in minutes and the equipment can be immediately forthcoming."[77] Advocates of privatization therefore cite additional advantages in terms of greater flexibility, creativity, and responsiveness. As one executive has noted, "when you are looking for innovation, you don't look to government, you look to business."[78]

- *Competitive choice.* When there is dissatisfaction with the manner in which corrections is performing, it may not be easy to do anything about it through the existing system. By bringing in a "clean slate" through privatization, corrections is no longer burdened with "positions remaining from old, out-dated programs . . . or particular management preferences from a long-gone administrator."[79] Moreover, if the performance of a private company is unacceptable, government has the choice of resuming operation of the facility itself or contracting with a competitor. Knowing this presumably generates further incentive to provide high-quality service.

In short, proponents of privatization maintain that economy, flexibility, and competition enable private companies to be more innovative and efficient at

---

[75]As of the end of 1992, some 62 private adult correctional facilities were in operation throughout the world, with an additional 7 scheduled to open in 1993–1994. Charles W. Thomas and Suzanna Foard, *Private Adult Correctional Facilities Census* (Gainesville, FL: Center for Studies in Criminology and Law, University of Florida, 1992), p. 2.

[76]T. Don Hutto, "Corrections Partnership: The Public and Private Sectors Work Together," *Corrections Today*, Vol. 50, No. 6 (October 1988), p. 20.

[77]Ibid.

[78]Michael A. Kroll, "Prisons Cannot Rehabilitate," in Bonnie Szumski, ed., *America's Prisons*, Fourth Edition (St. Paul, MN: Greenhaven Press, 1985), p. 26.

[79]James D. Henderson, "Private Sector Management: Promoting Efficiency and Cost-Effectiveness," *Corrections Today*, Vol. 50, No. 6 (October 1988), p. 100.

less cost. Not everyone would agree with that glowing assessment, however. Opponents of the full privatization of correctional facilities cite such concerns as:

- *Quality assurance.* Given the fact that the profit motive is such a strong incentive in the private sector, fear has been expressed that "private operators may be tempted to take shortcuts that could compromise safety" or "reduce the quality and quantity of staff and services."[80] When government contracts with private industry to operate a prison or jail, it is obviously important to specify clearly what minimum standards the contractor must adhere to, as well as to establish procedures for monitoring and enforcing compliance. But even if care is taken in that regard, there is always the danger that the *minimum required* will become the *maximum provided* in an effort to lower costs while raising profits. Advocates of privatization counter that "good services and competitive prices are not mutually exclusive."[81] Opponents warn that "the best policy is, buyer beware!"[82]

- *Selectivity.* A related argument concerns the types of clients and facilities with which the private sector is willing to become involved. To the extent that low-risk populations and minimum-security institutions are more appealing to private companies, government may find itself in a position of being left with the least desirable correctional workload. As the "last resort," public corrections could ultimately be limited to dealing with the most hard-core clients or managing the highest-security institutions. In Chapter 13, trends in this direction have already been noted in the juvenile justice system.[83] Questions have therefore been raised about "whether private facilities actually operate less expensively or whether they have contracted only for services that can be provided easily . . . [leaving] operation of the more expensive programs to the public sector."[84]

- *Liability.* Initially, it might appear that an enticing feature of privatization would be reduced liability for government. However, that attractive potential may only occur to the extent that a privately managed facility is subject to fewer lawsuits than those under public management. In other words, government cannot simply transfer liability to a private corporation through a contractual arrangement. Government is ultimately responsible for its actions, whether they are carried out directly or indirectly through a private company. If an incident occurs in a privately run facility and someone dies or is hurt, "both the private operator and the state can be sued."[85] The bottom line is that

[80]Allen L. Patrick, "Private Sector: Profit Motive vs. Quality," *Corrections Today*, Vol. 48, No. 2 (April 1986), p. 68.

[81]Hutto, p. 22.

[82]Patrick, p. 74.

[83]It has, for instance, been observed that private agencies "typically accept only those clients or cases that are most likely to succeed and, therefore, are unable [or unwilling] to handle the most difficult cases historically handled by public agencies." Verne L. Speirs, *A Private-Sector Corrections Program for Juveniles: Paint Creek Youth Center* (Washington, DC: U.S. Department of Justice, 1988), p. 1.

[84]Byron R. Johnson and Paul P. Ross, "The Privatization of Correctional Management: A Review," *Journal of Criminal Justice*, Vol. 18, No. 4 (1990), p. 356.

[85]Patrick, p. 74. However, it has been noted that government liability "can be reduced by wise contracting, specifying [that] it be indemnified against damage awards and for the cost of litigation." Samuel F. Saxton, "Contracting for Services: Different Facilities, Different Needs," *Corrections Today*, Vol. 50, No. 6 (October 1988), p. 18.

the state is responsible for every institution operated under its authority—whether private or public.[86]

• *Appropriate roles.* Few would question the involvement of private industry in providing selected services or short-term technical assistance. But whether the entire operation of a correctional facility should be turned over to private enterprise is another issue entirely. Some contend that corrections is essentially a government obligation that should not be divorced from the democratic process in which society formulates public policy through elected officials.

Others carry this line of reasoning further to question the appropriateness of private-sector decision making in such sensitive matters as "[inmate] discipline, use of force, good time forfeiture, and parole recommendations."[87] Additionally, the issue of whether privatization will encourage the overuse of institutions has been raised, especially if compensation is based on a per inmate fee. As the John Howard Association has argued, "[s]hort of the death penalty, incarceration is the state's most intrusive control over a citizen's life. It is inappropriate to relinquish this authority to an organization operating with profit as its primary goal."[88]

In response to this concern, privatization contracts have been written in a manner prohibiting the contractor from "making final determinations that could have an adverse effect on the liberty interests of prisoners."[89] Under such contractual provisions, "private firms have no power to determine who will or who will not be committed to their facilities, to shape determinations of when those who are committed to their facilities will be released, or to control disciplinary processes whose outcome could alter significantly the conditions of confinement."[90]

As these wide-ranging positions on both sides demonstrate, privatization is neither good nor bad; right nor wrong.[91] Nor is it even clearcut whether or not privately operated facilities are less expensive. As one correctional administrator has observed: "A well-run correctional facility is a well-run correctional facility—no matter who runs it. A good administrator, whether in the private or public sector, should—and must—be conscious of cost. It is taxpayer money, whether it's being spent by a private contractor or a public sector manager."[92]

Some studies indicate that going private has resulted in "more and better prison services for less money."[93] Similarly, one review of the limited research in

[86]For further information on the legal aspects of privatization, see Sechrest and Collins, pp. 158–62.

[87]Michael J. Mahoney, "Prisons for Profit: Should Corrections Make a Buck?," *Corrections Today*, Vol. 50, No. 6 (October 1988), p. 107.

[88]Ibid.

[89]Charles W. Thomas and Charles H. Logan, "The Development, Present Status, and Future Potential of Correctional Privatization in America," in Gary W. Bowman, Simon Hakim, and Paul Seidenstat, eds., *Privatizing Correctional Institutions* (New Brunswick, NJ: Transaction Publishers, 1993), p. 223.

[90]Ibid.

[91]For a more thorough discussion of this issue, see C. H. Logan, *Private Prisons: Cons and Pros* (New York: Oxford University Press, 1990).

[92]Charles H. Logan and Bill W. McGriff, *Comparing Costs of Public and Private Prisons: A Case Study* (Washington, DC: U.S. Department of Justice, 1989), p. 7. See also Robert W. Poole, Jr., "Privately Operated Prisons Are Economical," in Szumski, pp. 123–26.

[93]Saxton, p. 17.

this area concludes that private management is not only significantly less expensive, but that the cost savings can be achieved without any sacrifice in terms of the quality of correctional services.[94] But other evidence claims that retaining public management has produced cost savings.[95] Still other studies conclude that there is insufficient research "to warrant making the choice of one over the other in every circumstance."[96] In that regard, the American Correctional Association's policy has been to encourage open discussion, research, and evaluation. ACA's position has been criticized on the grounds that since the association has not opposed privatization, ACA must therefore favor it; however,

> [t]his ignores a third possibility. In the Scottish courts, defendants can be found either "guilty" or "not guilty," but the jury can also return a verdict of "not proven." This finding best characterizes ACA's policy on privatization. Not enough objective research has been reported; consequently, any viewpoint either "for" or "against" privatization lacks demonstrable external support. Neither side has proven its case. On privatization, the jury is still out."[97]

---

*LEARNING GOALS* ▓▓▓▓▓▓▓▓▓▓▓▓▓▓▓▓▓▓▓▓▓▓▓▓▓▓▓▓▓▓▓▓▓▓▓▓▓▓▓▓▓

*Do you know:*

- *How urbanization, economics, and drug-related crime can be expected to influence the future of corrections?*
- *What mistakes were made during implementation of the justice model that can be avoided when making future policy changes?*
- *What the concept of restorative justice is?*
- *Why greater efficiency and cost-saving measures will continue to be high correctional priorities?*
- *In what seemingly opposite directions the juvenile justice field is moving and why these changes are not as contradictory as might appear?*

---

## ❖ FUTURE ISSUES

Needless to say, speculating about the future with any degree of accuracy is a rather inexact science. It is difficult enough to predict what the weather will be tomorrow, much less what the horizon holds for a vast and varied enterprise

---

[94]Thomas and Logan, p. 231.
[95]Thomas J. Purvis, "Private versus Public Management of Metro Jail Service," *American Jails*, Vol. 5, No. 5 (November/December 1991), pp. 28–32.
[96]Johnson and Ross, p. 358.
[97]Robert B. Levinson, "Privatization: The Jury Is Still Out," *Corrections Today*, Vol. 50, No. 6 (October 1988), p. 6.

such as corrections. Even today, the multiple goals, diverse practices, and emerging issues in the correctional conglomerate are neither clearly defined nor easily resolved. But simply because the future cannot be anticipated with complete accuracy does not mean that we cannot be alert to the implications of current trends for shaping future issues.

Unfortunately, crisis is frequently the major catalytic agent in stimulating social progress. But changes rarely occur overnight in a revolutionary manner. To the contrary, they tend to come about over time through a slower, evolutionary process. Nor are changes in the field of corrections generally extreme diversions from the present. Rather, they tend to be gradual modifications of what currently exists. To the extent that the past is prologue to the future, there is much that we can anticipate about tomorrow from what is occurring today. It is therefore necessary to take a closer look at some of the general trends being experienced in both society overall and corrections in particular to determine in what directions they may be leading.

## Urbanization, Economics, and the Quality of Life

Everything from the demographic makeup of society to changing population distributions, economic conditions, political affiliations, and social values can ultimately be expected to have an impact on corrections. Because crime is predominantly a feature of younger people, for example, the general aging of the population might be expected to produce lower crime rates, and therefore, fewer correctional clients. But despite the fact that the post–World War II "baby-boomers" have now reached middle-age, crime has not necessarily been declining for a variety of reasons.

As the cities and suburbs of major U.S. metropolitan areas continue to absorb population growth, people are brought closer together physically, generating greater potential for irritation, conflict, and declining public services. The resulting social problems take a toll on everyone—from traffic congestion on saturated roadways to overburdened schools, welfare and unemployment programs, health services, and criminal justice systems. Moreover, these problems have been placing an increasing burden on the taxpayers at a time that economic conditions have created a decreasing ability to pay for the maintenance of existing services, much less new or expanded programs. In short, it is becoming more apparent that the ever-expanding quality of life in the United States may have reached its limit. It is an unfortunate fact that the next generation is unlikely to have as high a standard of living as its predecessors.

At the same time, public perceptions of what represents minimally acceptable levels of government service have also been undergoing a transition. Some of today's concerns were not defined as problems a generation ago. Greater social and political awareness, pressures from activists, and exposure by the mass media have all brought increasing awareness and a new frame of reference to the public's social conscience. What many may see as a deteriorating quality of life today may actually be more a reflection of changing perceptions and escalating expectations that are not in alignment with harsh realities.

## Drugs and Related Crime

One of the harshest realities that Americans have had to face in recent years has obviously been the drug epidemic. The prevalence of drugs throughout all socioeconomic classes is undoubtedly among the major explanations for why high crime rates persist despite demographic changes. As drugs have begun to affect a broader segment of society, attitudes concerning appropriate responses to the problem are beginning to shift. But there remains a heavy emphasis on enforcement, as reflected in a national report which notes that despite measurements showing a downward trend in drug use, drug arrests increased 25% between 1986 and 1991.[98]

Although the "war on drugs" has attempted either to restrict supply or to reduce demand at various points in time, both efforts have largely been unsuccessful. Drug cases have fueled rising probation and parole caseloads and continue to contribute significantly to jail and prison crowding.[99] Moreover, this dilemma has created a vicious cycle. The burden of accommodating ever-increasing numbers of drug-related offenders has forced corrections into a regression back to the basics—often limiting probation and parole services to "monitoring and reporting," and concentrating institutional resources on security and space allocations at the expense of program initiatives.[100]

Until more proactive efforts are targeted toward identifying and responding to the underlying causes of both alcohol and drug abuse, little hope exists for achieving substantial reductions in crime and delinquency rates. In the meantime, what to do with violators of drug laws—or for that matter, whether the laws themselves should be changed—will remain a source of continuing public debate, as both community-based caseloads and institutional populations overflow with drug-related offenders.

## Implications for the Justice Model

As reflected in the drug issue, it is not crime alone that determines the size of correctional caseloads and institutional populations, but rather, the manner in which society responds to criminal behavior. In that regard we have watched social trends shift from the medical model to the justice model.

Yet many of the same conditions that generated movement toward the justice model are equally prevalent today—for example, increasing concern over crime rates and a widespread belief that current practices are not working properly. Moreover, as drug use affects broader socioeconomic groups, opinions concerning appropriate sanctions may be subject to change. It is one thing to advocate "toughening up" through stern punishment for anonymous criminals, but quite another to maintain punitive attitudes when the offender is one's own fami-

---

[98]"ABA Report Finds National Overemphasis on Drug Cases, Less on Violent Crime," *Crime Control Digest*, Vol. 27, No. 8 (February 22, 1993), p. 1, citing the *First Annual Report on the State of Criminal Justice* by the American Bar Association.

[99]Charles B. DeWitt, "Assessing Criminal Justice Needs," *National Institute of Justice: Research in Brief* (Washington, DC: U.S. Department of Justice, 1992), p. 2.

[100]Ibid.

ly member or co-worker. As shown in Figure 15.3, some practitioners in the juvenile justice system have been experimenting with an integrated justice/treatment model for several years, and similar trends are emerging in the adult system.

Whether shifts in political opinions or social values will stimulate corresponding changes in such public policies as sentencing practices remains to be seen. A society content with the status quo is unlikely to support—much less pressure for—change. But in many respects, determinate sentences and sentencing guidelines may not be achieving much better success than their earlier counterparts. It is apparent that the public is becoming both increasingly disenchanted with existing procedures and more amenable to new suggestions.

## Learning from Past Mistakes

If there is one lesson that has hopefully been learned from the self-defeating impact of transition to the justice model, it is the necessity to plan properly in advance of making significant policy changes. In fact, it is actually impossible to determine whether the justice model might have been more effective if it had not been confronted with the massive institutional crowding that resulted in such widespread early release that its original intent was severely compromised. The same argument could be made with respect to the medical model—in which case, the original intent was never fully operationalized in practice with the funding necessary for the treatment programs it envisioned.

As these breakdowns between ambition and actuality illustrate, public policy cannot be fulfilled effectively in the absence of planning and resource allocation. It is insufficient simply to change policy in order to appease political constituencies. Public opinion and political leadership have too often reacted emotionally to crime,

| | Treatment model | Justice model | Justice/treatment model |
|---|---|---|---|
| Philosophy | Parens patriae | Criminal law | Integration |
| Sanctions | Sanctions fit the offender | Sanctions fit the crime | Sanctions must fit both offender and crime |
| Determinateness | Indeterminate consequences | Determinate consequences | Determinate consequences but allowances for treatment flexibility |
| Releases | Released when rehabilitated | Released when specific time is served | Release guidelines; Specific release review date, but may be released earlier if goals are met |

**Figure 15.3** Combining medical (treatment) and justice models. *Source:* Gerald T. O'Rourke, "Minnesota Combines Justice and Treatment for Juveniles to Create Best of Both Worlds," *Corrections Today*, Vol. 51, No. 4 (July 1989), p. 102.

calling for severe and simplistic solutions that have overloaded the corrections component of the system without commensurate funding. Even the best intentions are doomed to failure in the absence of informed decisions based on projections of expected impact, including the resources required for implementation.

Before establishing a new policy, serious consideration of fiscal and operational repercussions is critical to achieving success. But even with careful foresight, plans do not always materialize in practice as they were anticipated in theory. Thus, the need for ongoing study and empirical evaluation cannot be overlooked. In this field, such research has largely been haphazard—conducted on an ad hoc basis, often as an afterthought. Attempts at evaluation have frequently precluded making comparisons, focused on small populations, and provided disconnected bits of information rather than cumulative knowledge.

Before conclusions can be drawn about any program, evaluation must be routinized.[101] Few employers would advocate keeping employees on the payroll without periodic, standardized performance evaluations. Yet major criminal justice policies are implemented routinely without giving thought to how their effectiveness will be measured. Evaluation research should be an essential component included in the planning of policy changes—if for no other reason, because people who are paying the bills have a right to know what is and is not working.

### International Implications

Although the public's "right to know" is an inherent principle of government in the United States, that has not necessarily been the case in other countries with centralized rule by a strong dictatorial leader. But one of the most significant international trends in recent years has been the downfall of many such government structures. As the "iron curtain" has lifted and the "cold war" has thawed, massive changes are also occurring within correctional systems throughout the world. It is well beyond the scope of this book to embark on a review of these emerging adjustments to more democratic forms of government. Additionally, it is too soon to determine exactly what shape they will take or what impact they will have.

One thing, however, is certain. Many countries will be studying how corrections operates in established democracies as they launch the formidable effort of converting from autocratic forms of government to those that give considerably greater weight to the rights and dignity of individual citizens. As long as the United States remains in a vital leadership position within the free world, this country has a tremendous responsibility to fulfill as the acknowledged standard bearer of democracy. Mutual assistance between nations is one way to increase effective and humane treatment for all societies, and correctional systems seeking to revise their practices will undoubtedly be turning with greater frequency to the United States for guidance. As they do, it is our obligation to assure that they have models to review that can be proudly displayed as repre-

---

[101]See Daniel Glaser, *Routinizing Evaluation: Getting Feedback on Effectiveness of Crime and Delinquency Programs* (Rockville, MD: National Institute of Mental Health, Center for Studies of Crime and Delinquency, 1973), p. 182.

sentative of the most advanced correctional practices of a democratic society. The question then becomes to what extent the U.S. correctional enterprise is capable of serving effectively in that critical leadership capacity.

## Projecting Correctional Trends

To answer that question requires further consideration of what present trends portray for the future of corrections. Beyond the legal issues, accreditation, and privatization discussed herein, a number of emerging trends have been addressed throughout the earlier chapters of this book. It is useful at this point to recap briefly some of these transitions and consider what implications they pose for the future direction of corrections.

**Intermediate Sentencing Alternatives.** Initially developed as a "front-door" option for reducing jail and prison crowding, such alternatives as electronic monitoring/home confinement and intensive supervision probation have become recognized as legitimate approaches in their own right. As a compromise between the lesser restrictions of traditional probation and the severity of incarceration, they provide a reasonable middle ground—addressing the concerns of those who advocate more punitive practices, as well as those who object to the futility of imprisonment. On a practical level, both crowded facilities and the exorbitant cost of new construction are inspiring a growing interest in intermediate sanctions.[102] Moreover, intermediate punishments provide an opportunity to fulfill two correctional objectives that have been gaining popularity within in recent years: *restitution and restoration.*

**Restorative Justice Concepts.** In contrast to earlier periods of time, government today has assumed full responsibility for apprehending, prosecuting, and punishing criminal behavior. As a result, crime is viewed by the state in almost an abstract manner—as a violation against the interests of society. Such an approach does little to reinforce any sense of either personal responsibility on the part of the offender or personal involvement in the justice process on the part of the victim. In an effort to address these issues, a new concept of *restorative justice* has been emerging. Using various forms of victim–offender mediation, alternative dispute resolution, or what has been termed the "balanced approach" in our previous discussion of juvenile justice, the restorative focus is twofold:

- Restoring at least some of the tangible losses experienced by the victim through negotiated restitution arrangements.
- Restoring the offender's sense of personal accountability for the harm caused by his or her actions.

For a closer look at how restorative justice differs from the more conventional concept of retributive justice, see the next "Close-up on Corrections."

[102]DeWitt, p. 3.

### Changing Concepts of Justice

| RETRIBUTIVE JUSTICE | RESTORATIVE JUSTICE |
|---|---|
| • Crime defined as violation of the state. | • Crime defined as violation of one person by another. |
| • Focus on establishing blame, on guilt, on past behavior. (Did he/she do it?) | • Focus on problem solving, on liabilities and obligations, on the future. (What should be done?) |
| • Relationships are adversarial. | • Relationships involve dialogue and negotiation. |
| • Imposition of pain to punish and deter/prevent. | • Restitution as a means of restoring both parties; reconciliation/restoration is the goal. |
| • Interpersonal, conflictual nature of crime is obscured; conflict seen as individual versus state. | • Crime is recognized as interpersonal conflict. |
| • Victim is ignored; offender is passive. | • Victim rights/needs recognized; offender encouraged to take responsibility. |
| • Offender accountability defined as taking punishment. | • Offender accountability defined as understanding impact of action and helping decide how to make things right. |
| • Response focused on offender's past behavior. | • Response focused on harmful consequences of offender's behavior. |

*Source:* Adapted from Howard Zehr, "Restorative Justice," *IARCA (International Association of Residential and Community Alternatives) Journal* (March 1991), p. 7.

Programs based on restorative justice principles can be expected to proliferate in the future, especially as victims continue to demand greater representation in the justice process. Moreover, such alternatives will become increasingly attractive to the extent that social attitudes and values continue to move in a more moderate direction, while still expressing discomfort with absolving offenders of individual responsibility for their conduct.

**Changing Nature of Treatment.**   Even with considerably diminished support for the medical model over past decades, belief in the potential benefits of treatment has not been demolished completely. The difference today is that it is more likely to be offered on a *voluntary basis* rather than an inducement for early release. Like restorative justice, this reflects a trend toward placing more individual responsibility on the offender, recognizing that rehabilitation is unlikely to be successful in the absence of personal motivation.

Additionally, the nature of "treatment" is taking on a more *pragmatic orientation*. In contrast to counseling, group therapy, and other forms of psychological treatment, emphasis today is being placed on developing productive employment skills. Evidence of this shift is apparent in the reinstatement of jail and prison industries, as well as the shift from counseling/casework to brokerage/service delivery models in probation and parole. Society's continuing expression of concern over adult illiteracy can only be expected to further strengthen a more pragmatic approach to treatment, with additional emphasis on basic education programs. Beyond expanded vocational training and educational opportunities, more specifically targeted treatment programs can also be anticipated in the future. As opposed to the counseling-for-everyone approach, treatment tailored to the particular needs of such offenders as alcoholics, drug addicts, and sex offenders will be increasingly necessary.

**Changing Features of Institutions.** In addition to the nature of programs offered, indications are already on the horizon that the physical features of correctional institutions are beginning to change as well. These modifications are currently most apparent among local jails—where some of the most antiquated facilities are being abolished or modernized, small jails are being consolidated through *regionalization*, and new architecture and management styles are reflecting the principles of *direct supervision* (new generation) jailing.

Correctional facilities are becoming more electronically sophisticated, and new architcture and management styles are reflecting the principles of direct supervision jailing. Courtesy of the Nassau County Sheriff's Department, East Meadow, New York.

Both jails and prisons are also becoming more electronically sophisticated—as keys, locks, and staff monitors are giving way to computers, video cameras, and other electronic devices. One of the dangers of extensive reliance on high-tech hardware, of course, is that it further promotes the dehumanizing effect of incarceration. Direct-supervision facilities overcome this drawback, since officers are stationed directly inside housing units, interacting with the inmates on a continual basis.

**Efficiency and Cost-Saving Measures.** As in other components of government, corrections is being expected to do more with less, especially during times of economic downturn. It is therefore becoming a necessity to explore means of using both personnel and resources more efficiently. Examples of creative means of doing so exist in both institutional and community-based corrections. Within correctional facilities, for instance, labor-intensive methods of tracking inmate movements and purchases through passes, checklists, and cumbersome paperwork are giving way to the use of *electronic scanning devices*. In community-based corrections, *electronic monitoring* is reducing the need for numerous field visits and home checks, while *caseload classification* is enabling officers to concentrate their efforts on clients most in need of careful supervision.

Electronic equipment and program initiatives that enhance productivity will continue to be attractive as long as fiscal limitations require maximizing available resources. But one of the most promising areas for achieving direct cost savings may well be movement toward the *professional* approach to training entry-level personnel. In addition to several locations within the United States, an entire province in Canada has already made this transition. Since 1992, completion of basic training has been required prior to employment in British Columbia—and the estimated $700,000 in annual savings is earmarked to fund advanced in-service and management training, which would otherwise not have been available as a result of budget cutbacks.[103]

**Objectivity in Decision Making.** The expanded use of computers has made a substantial impact throughout the field, both directly and indirectly. In a wide variety of capacities, computers are now performing what had previously been very time-consuming and labor-intensive efforts. What is somewhat less apparent is how reliance on computers and other technological innovations has shaped decision making in a more quantifiable direction. No longer is the system as willing to accept individual judgments or personal opinions. Rather, we have limited judicial discretion through *sentencing guidelines*, streamlined parole decision making through *prediction tables*, and in some jurisdictions, replaced discretionary parole with *mandatory supervised release*, based on the figures generated by good/gain time schedules.

In fact, "hard numbers" are more and more often replacing human judgments in the decision-making process at various points in the criminal justice system. This transition has reduced the potential for abuse, disparity, and

[103]Murray Finlay, "Corrections Worker Employment Readiness Program," *Journal of Correctional Training* (Fall 1992), pp. 11–12.

favoritism. But it has also contributed to a false sense of security—a belief that data alone can make proper determinations while overlooking the fact that the figures themselves are inherently a product of human values.

**Juvenile Justice Transitions.**   If there is one aspect of the system that still makes an attempt to cling to the more personalized, discretionary decision making of the past, it is juvenile justice. Despite the greater *due process protections* now afforded young offenders, the juvenile field has yet to abandon its inherent emphasis on *parens patriae* and the medical model. That does not, however, mean that serious juvenile offenders are escaping the wrath of public consternation. Indeed, it appears that responses to juvenile law violators are splitting in opposite directions. On the one hand, hard-core, violent juvenile offenders can increasingly expect to be dealt with in a manner commensurate with the seriousness of their offenses—that is, through adult courts and more punitive sentencing.

At the same time, responses to the least serious status offenders include options ranging from *removing* them from secure institutions, to *diverting* them out of the system, to *decriminalizing* their behavior completely. Again, as in the adult system, it is not simply benevolence that is driving such changes, but also the necessity for efficiency and cost-effectiveness in the face of increasing workloads without accompanying resource allocations. While dealing with status offenders outside the official juvenile justice system meets such objectives, it will be essential to assure that appropriate services are provided to them through alternative avenues. Otherwise, they risk becoming the youthful equivalent of the deinstitutionalization of mental health—in which case the egalitarian objectives of reformers were never fulfilled in practice or provided for in terms of funding.

**Changing Correctional Populations and Personnel.**   As society becomes more responsive to the needs of special groups within the larger population, so is the changing nature of correctional populations generating more specific attention. Corrections will especially be challenged to meet the needs of increasing numbers of female offenders, along with those who are AIDS afflicted, physically impaired, or elderly. Nor is there expected to be any decline in the already sizable numbers of correctional clients suffering from alcohol/drug addictions or mental disorders. To what extent such special populations will receive distinct treatment considerations will depend on how willing taxpayers are to support specialized efforts. In that regard, standards that the public sets for acceptable levels of care and service in free society will have much to do with determining how far correctional programs will progress.

It is not, however, only those on the inside of the bars who have been undergoing change. In recent years, the correctional labor force itself has experienced a significant transition. The white-male-dominated tradition of correctional employment is being dismantled by a more diverse workforce that is also more likely to reflect a greater prevalence of higher education. This "new breed" of workers is both introducing new perspectives on the job and creating new challenges for their supervisors. Today's workers are rightfully demanding a voice in making decisions and establishing policies that affect them.

Today's "new breed" of correctional officers reflects more cultural diversity, demands more organizational participation, and represents tomorrow's managers. Courtesy of the Dade County Department of Corrections and Rehabilitation.

Moreover, it is today's operational personnel who represent tomorrow's managers and administrators. Line employees who have never had experience with anything but passively responding to orders do not make very likely candidates for displaying the leadership skills that will be necessary to guide corrections into the twenty-first century.

**Leadership and Professionalism.**   The ability of corrections to recruit and retain the quality of personnel needed in the upcoming century will largely depend on how well it accommodates broader participation, decentralized decision making, and ongoing career development—in other words, how much emphasis and confidence are placed in its most valuable asset. Further stimulus toward professionalism can be expected from state standards agencies, as they increasingly encompass correctional personnel within the categories of employees who must meet minimum employment and training requirements. Additionally, if corrections begins to embrace the preservice approach to entry-level training, a significant step will be taken toward obtaining recognition as a profession. However, the wrong person trained is still the wrong person for the job. Serious attention to valid, reliable, and job-related selection screening will therefore take on greater significance as the field moves toward professionalism.

A recent national survey identified *institutional crowding, staff and funding shortages,* and resulting *workload increases* as the key problems that corrections is anticipated to face in the immediate future.[104] Maximizing the quality of personnel cannot be expected to miraculously resolve these challenges. But it can contribute considerably toward minimizing their negative impact. Notice that each of these issues represents a *quantifiable* aspect of correctional work. As focus shifts more and more in that direction, it is easy to lose sight of the fact that people are changed by other people. They are not changed for the better by a "program" or a "system," although they can be changed for the worse by being regimented and dehumanized. Overall, the system is much less important than the people who breathe life into it.

As the issue of grooming future leadership illustrates, before it is feasible to deal effectively with the future, it is essential to address more effectively the here-and-now. Yet focusing exclusively on the present also perpetuates a continuously reactive cycle. To use an analogy, the first priority for a drowning person is obviously being rescued. Only by learning how to swim, however, will the potential for further near-misses be avoided. The field of corrections may not yet be "drowning." But as noted at the beginning of this chapter, it is rowing upstream amid strong currents. In such a situation, there are three choices: give up; row harder; or reduce the strength of the currents.

Most of today's correctional administrators are undoubtedly rowing harder. They are, for the most part, making vigorous efforts to cope with limited resources and a constantly changing legal, social, and political environment. But as at least one self-critic of correctional leadership has observed, "[w]e still spend too much time . . . complaining about how little control we have over our own destinies and not enough time actively . . . planning regarding the future. . . . It is time for us not merely to respond to issues which others put before us, but rather, to identify those issues and be persuasive as to how they should be addressed and resolved."[105]

Only to the extent that vigorous efforts today are combined with a far-reaching vision of tomorrow can we hope to reduce the strength and impact of changing currents for our successors in the upcoming century. In the long run, future generations will judge us not by what obstacles we have or have not faced today, but rather, by what opportunities we have or have not seized today to shape tomorrow's destiny.

That represents a hefty challenge. It is a lot to expect. It is why corrections is both fascinating and frustrating. Perhaps it is also "why they call it corrections, . . . not perfection."[106]

## ❖ SUMMARY

One of the most prevalent forces shaping correctional policies and procedures in recent years has been the impact of court decisions. As the courts began to inter-

---

[104]DeWitt, p. 8.
[105]Richard G. Kiekbusch, "Leadership Roles: How Are We Doing?" *American Jails*, Vol. 6, No. 5 (November/December 1992), p. 6.
[106]Geno Natalucci-Persichetti, "Maybe That's Why They Call It Corrections," *Corrections Today*, Vol. 53, No. 1 (February 1991), p. 26.

vene more actively after a long "hands off" period, constitutional rights during incarceration were redefined and expanded. Among the First Amendment rights now recognized by the courts are various freedoms related to the practice of religion. However, such protections can be restricted when justified on the basis of institutional order, safety, discipline, or security. Additionally, the freedom to communicate through the mails can be limited. Nor do Fourth Amendment protections against unreasonable search and seizure generally encompass frisk or cell searches. But searches of any kind cannot be employed to abuse or harass inmates. The courts have also recognized personnel drug testing as falling within the definition of "search and seizure." Although job applicants can routinely be tested, employees enjoy greater safeguards.

Numerous legal challenges have been raised under the Eighth Amendment's prohibition against cruel and unusual punishment. Many of these cases involve institutional crowding. The courts have held that crowding in and of itself does not constitute an Eighth Amendment violation, unless it produces a "totality of conditions" that jeopardizes the inmates' health, safety, or well-being. Some such cases have been settled by voluntary consent decrees. In others, the courts have issued injunctions ordering correctional officials to remedy deficiencies within a given period of time. In an effort to reduce inmate litigation, correctional institutions are initiating more proactive administrative remedies.

In addition to challenging the conditions of confinement, inmate litigation has also sought to overturn the death penalty. Although some states have abolished capital punishment, nearly 2500 prisoners remain on death row today. Because of the extreme emotion on both sides of this issue, the death penalty continues to generate considerable controversy. Although the Supreme Court overturned a number of death sentences in 1972 as a result of the manner in which they were implemented, it has yet to specifically find capital punishment itself an Eighth Amendment violation.

Aside from the influence of court-generated legal issues, other forces that have had a substantial impact on corrections in recent years include accreditation and privatization. In an effort to improve services and institutional conditions voluntarily, agencies are increasingly pursuing accreditation. By meeting the level of standards required for accreditation, they are not only seeking self-improvement, but also enhanced pride, morale, and legal defensibility.

Few could argue with the merits of accreditation, but privatization is a much more controversial issue. The nature of private sector involvement has been changing dramatically in recent years. Beyond the voluntary efforts, specific service contracts, or short-term technical assistance that have been common for some time, privatization now refers to contracting the full operation of entire correctional facilities. Again, strong sentiments exist on both sides. There have also been reservations expressed about whether the administration of correctional institutions is an appropriate role for private industry. As the field obtains more experience with privatization in the future, more evidence will be forthcoming.

In the meantime, corrections will also be affected by everything from urbanization, economics, and the quality of life to drug-related crime and the resulting burdens on both correctional facilities and caseloads. In that respect, the justice model does not appear to be functioning much more effectively than its predecessors. However, it must also be acknowledged that like earlier models, its implementation was hampered by lack of proper foresight, planning projections, evaluation research, and resource allocation.

Among the trends that are expected to continue to exert an impact are intermediate sentencing alternatives, the emerging concept of restorative justice, more pragmatic treatment orientations, regionalization of jails, and direct supervision strategies. Increasingly sophisticated electronic devices, workload classification, and objectivity will also characterize the future—particularly as pressures mount for greater efficiency, productivity, and cost-savings. Similarly, the juvenile justice system can be expected to concentrate more of its resources on serious hard-core delinquents while divesting responsibility for less serious status offenses through diversion, deinstitutionalization, and even decriminalization.

The most significant key to the quality of future correctional services, however, will be the quality of future correctional personnel. Much of the capability of tomorrow's leaders will depend on the extent to which today's administrators pursue such avenues toward professionalization as improved selection screening; preservice training; decentralized decision making, and participatory management. By maximizing the quality of personnel, much of the negative impact of upcoming challenges can be minimized. Most important, effectively accommodating the future requires both a current commitment to immediate improvements and the clear vision necessary to proactively intercept forces on the horizon.

# Index

## A

Abrahamsen, David, 84
Accreditation, 650–52
Adjudication:
    criminal justice process, 19–20
    juvenile justice process, 546–49
Administration, 607–8
    jails, 206–26
    prisons, 255–68
Administrative segregation, 284
Aftercare programs, juveniles, 562–63
Aggravating circumstances, and sentencing, 22
AIDS (acquired immune deficiency syndrome), 85–94, 668
    condom distribution, 488, 489–90
    correctional responses, 487–94
    in corrections, 486–87
    education/training, 487–88
    HIV testing, 488–91
    legal issues related to, 492–94
    separate housing, 491–92
Alcohol abusers, 499–501
    institutional profile, 500
    treatment programs, 500–501
Alcoholics Anonymous (AA), 361–62, 363
Alternative dispute resolution, 145
American Bar Association, Criminal Justice Committee, 29
American Civil Liberties Union (ACLU), 365, 655

American Correctional Association (ACA), 262, 278, 327, 590, 655
    standards/guidelines, 590, 608
American Federation of State, County, and Municipal Employees (AFSCME), 622
American Jail Association, 211
Andersonville Prison, 120
Arraignment, 17–19
Arrest, 14–15
Assessment centers, 588
Assize of Clarendon, 103
Attica (N.Y.) Correctional Facility, riot at, 406–9, 420
Auburn Correctional Facility, self-governance at, 264
Auburn system, 116–18, 124
    discipline in, 117, 286

## B

Banishment, 106–7
Beccaria, Cesare, 111
Becker, Howard, 93
Behavioralism, 85–86
Behavior modification, 85, 365–66
*Bell v. Wolfish*, 640
Bentham, Jeremy, 111
Bill of Rights, 112, 114–15
Biochemical theories of criminal behavior, 79–80

Blackstone, William, 111
Blood feuds, 97–98
Body types, and crime, 77–78
Bona fide occupational qualification (BFOQ), 614, 625
Booking process, 15, 193
Boot camp, 560–62
Branding, 107
Bridewell workhouse, 106
Brockway, Zebulon, 123, 135, 421, 422, 463
Budgeting, 606–7

## C

Capital punishment, 21, 56, 107, 644–49
Caseload classification, 667
Cell searches (shakedowns), 291, 293–94
Censorship, freedom from, 634–35
Chain gangs, 124
Children in custody, 552–54
CHINS, 535, 568
Chromosome abnormalities, and crime, 78–79
Chronic stress, 618–19
    episodic stress vs., 619
Church of the New Song (CONS), 631
Civil liability, 609, 613
Classical School of criminology, 74, 111
Classification:
    in jails, 219–20
    of probation cases, 175–76
Clinical psychology, 84–85
Cloward, Richard, 92
Co-correctional (coed) prisons, 482–85
Code of Hammurabi, 41, 54, 98
Collective incapacitation, 60
Community-based alternatives, 140–83
    home confinement/electronic monitoring, 150–55
    pretrial intervention, 142–50
    probation, 156–82
Community residential centers. See Minimum-security facilities
Compensatory damages, 610
Conditional dispositions, 549–50
Conditional release, 538
Conditioning, 85
Condom distribution, and AIDS, 488, 489–90
Confinement:
    adaptations to, 387–91
        individual adjustments, 387–89
        inmate attitudes/values, 389–91
    conditions of, 554, 639–40
    effects on juveniles, 558–60
Conflict model of criminal law, 42, 43–44
Conjugal visits, 203–4
Consensus model of criminal law, 42–43
Consent decree, 222, 641
Contact visits, 302
Containment theory, 92–93
Contingency contracts, 367–68
Continuous quality improvement, 598

Contraband, 291, 292–93, 298
Control procedures, 281–91
    controlled movement, 284–88
        external transportation, 287–88
        system of passes, 285–87
    escapes, 289–91
    headcounts, 288–89
    segregation, 283–84
Co-opted officers, 315
Corporal punishment, 107
Correctional clients, 6–7, 70–95
    behavioralism, 85–86
    early criminological thought, 74–76
        Classical School, 74
        Positive School, 75–76
    identifying, 72–73
    nature of, 71–73
    physiological approaches, 76–81
    psychological approaches, 81–87
    responding to, 73
Correctional management, 603–8
    budgeting/resource allocation, 606–7
Correctional population, changes in, 668
Correctional trends, 664–70
    efficiency/cost–saving measures, 667
    institutions, changing features of, 666–67
    intermediate sentencing alternatives, 664
    justice concepts, restoring, 664–65
    treatment, changing nature of, 665–66
Corrections:
    correctional clients, 6–7
    correctional conglomerate, 5–13
    correctional employees, number of, 6
    cost of, 5–6
    and criminal justice system, 13–23
    custodial institutions, 7–8, 11–12
    defined, 11–13
    development of, 96–139
    hands-off period, 627–28
    impact of the 1960s, 130–34
    involved-hands period, 628
    juvenile programs/facilities, 10–11
    legal issues, 627–49
    noncustodial alternatives, 8–10
    rehabilitative era, 129–30
    restrained–hands approach, 628–29
    special populations in, 469–518
Corrupt alliance, 313–14
Cosmetic surgery, 366–67
Counseling/casework/clinical services, 353–73
    behavior modification, 365–66
    contingency contracts, 367–68
    cosmetic surgery, 366–67
    counseling, 356–57
    family therapy, 364–65
    group methods, 357–60
    nontraditional and multiple techniques, 370–73
    psychiatric/psychoanalytic treatment, 369–70

psychodrama role–playing, 364
reality therapy, 369
self-help groups, 360–62
sensitivity training, 362–64
social casework, 370
treatment availability, 353–56
County sheriff, 208
Crime, 38–69
crime index, 47–48
definition of, 44–46
deterrence, 57–58
extent of, 46–54
incapacitation, 59–61
National Crime Survey (NCS), 51
perspectives on, 40–42
rehabilitation, 61–67
reintegration, 67–68
relativity of, 46
retribution, 54–56
society's response to, 54–68
sociological approaches, 88–95
statistics, implications for corrections, 51–54
Uniform Crime Reports (UCR), 47–49
Crime rate, factors affecting, 49–51
Criminality, determining, 42–44
Criminal justice system:
adjudication phase, 19–20
arraignment, 17–19
arrest, 14–15
correctional goals, conflicts in, 30–36
and corrections, 13–23
functional fragmentation, 25–26
governmental branches, 24–25
impact assessment, 27–29
initial appearance, 17–19
interactions within, 26
jail, 15–17, 23
jurisdictional separation, 25–26
preliminary hearing, 17–19
sentencing, 20–23
trial, 19–20
Criminal liability, 609, 613
Crofton, Sir Walter, 123, 463
Crowding:
jails, 220–26, 664
systemwide strategies to alleviate, 224–25
juvenile correctional facilities, 554
prisons, 242–45
Cruel and unusual punishment, freedom
from, 638–49
Custodial dispositions, 550
Custodial institutions, 7–8, 11–12
Custodial supervision, 298
Custody, 274–322. *See also* Inmate
Management
architectural design, 278–81
external security, 278–80
cell searches (shakedowns), 291, 293–94
contraband, 291, 292–93
control procedures, 281–91
custody/treatment relationships, 276–77

functions of, 275–78
inmate management, 309–20
inmate supervision, 2978
institutional rules/discipline, 305–9
internal security, 280–81
key control, 296–97
outside contacts/visits, 299–305
conjugal visits, 203–4
furloughs, 304–5
mail, 301
telephone, 300
visiting, 301–3
personal (body) searches, 291, 294–96
purposes of, 276
rates, growth in, 552–53
security techniques, 277
tool control, 296–97
Customs, 41

D

Damages, types of, 610
Day fines, 56
Death penalty. *See* Capital punishment
Debtors' prisons, 105–6
Decertification, 599
Decision making, 256, 603–6
objectivity in, 667–68
Decriminalization, and juveniles, 568–70,
Defense mechanisms, 84
Deferred prosecution, 145
Deinstitutionalization, and juveniles, 570–74
Delinquency, 532–33, 535, 544
Detention:
detention centers, 11
hearings, 542
juvenile, 541–42
pretrial, 191–93
short-term detention facilities, 544–46
Determinism, 75
Deterrence, 57–58
types of, 57
Deviance, and the law, 39–44
Differential association, 90
Direct supervision (new-generation) jails,
198–206
architecture and inmate supervision,
199–201
costs/effectiveness of, 203–4
philosophy behind, 198–99
physical features of, 201–2
suicide prevention in, 217
training/management, 205–6
Disciplinary action reports, 307
Disciplinary segregation, 284
Discretion, 14–15
Discretionary waiver, 529, 534
Disposition, and juvenile justice process, 546,
549–52
Diversion, 143–50, 564–67

Diversion (*continued*)
  advantages/disadvantages of, 145–50
    costs, 147–48
    discretion, 148–49
    efficiency/flexibility, 148
    leniency/effectiveness, 146–47
    net widening, 149
    normal environment, 147
    stigma, 146
  formal/informal diversion, 144–45
Double-bunking, 640
Double-door security, 281
Drug abusers, 494–99
  institutional profiles, 495
  treatment programs, 496
  treatment results, 496–99
Drug testing, correctional employees, 636–37
Due process:
  due process movement, 528
  and juvenile justice, 529–32, 668
  and parole, 431–32, 460

### E

Early American corrections, 107–9
  correctional institutions, 108–9
  punishment, 107–8
Early criminological thought, 74–76
  Classical School, 74
  Positive School, 75–76
Economic insecurity, 89
Ectomorph body type, 77
Education/training, 340–53
  basic education, 341–44
  college education, 345–46
  computer-assisted instruction, 344–45
  institutional programs, 341
  library services, 346–47
  private-sector involvement, 350–51
  vocational training, 347–50
Ego, 83
Elderly inmates, 514–16
Electronic monitoring/surveillance. *See* Home
          confinement/electronic monitoring
Electronic scanning devices, 667
Elizabethan Poor Law (1601), 55
Elmira Reformatory, 327, 421
Employee assistance programs (EAPs), 620–21
Employee searches, 636–37
Endomorph body type, 77
Enlightenment ("Age of Reasoning"), 109
Episodic stress, 618–19
Escapes from prison, 276, 289–91, 642
Executive branch of government, 24–25
Exile, 106–7

### F

Family therapy, 364–65
Father Flanagan's Boys' Home, 654

Federal Bureau of Investigation (FBI), 47
  crime clock, 48
Federal Bureau of Prisons, 327
Fee system, jails, 108–9
Female correctional personnel, 613–18
Female offenders, 471–85
  and children, 475–76
  co-correctional (coed) prisons, 482–85
  confinement
    adaptation to, 477–79
    current conditions of, 480–81
  inmate relationships, 477–78
  inmates, 472–75
  prison conduct, 478–79
Field supervision, 457–58
Field training officer (FTO) programs, 596
Fines, 56
Fingerprinting, on intake, 213
Folkways, 41
Formal diversion, 144–45
Fort Jefferson, 120
Free will, 74
Freud, Sigmund, 81
Frisk search, 212, 294–95
Furloughs, 304–5
Future issues, 659–70
  correctional trends, 664–70
  drugs and related crime, 661
  international implications, 663–64
  justice model, implications for, 661–62
  learning from the past, 662–63
  urbanization/economics/quality of life, 660

### G

Gain time, 135
Gamblers Anonymous, 361–62
Gaols, 101, 184, 191
General deterrence, 57
Goring, Charles, 77
Group homes, 12

### H

*Harper v. Wallingford*, 635
Hawes-Cooper Act (1929), 124
Hayes, Rutherford, 121
Headcounts, 288–89
Hearing, 530, 546
Hedonism, 74
Herrnstein, Richard, 81
Hierarchy of needs, 267–68
HIV testing, 488–91
Home confinement/electronic monitoring,
          150–55, 551, 664, 667
  advantages of, 152–54
  disadvantages of, 154–55
  eligibility criteria, 152
Hooten, Ernest, 77
House arrest, 10

Houses of Refuge, 327
Howard, John, 110–11, 113

# I

Id, 83
Imprisonment, and crime rate, 63–64
Incapacitation, 59–61
    types of, 60
Indeterminate sentencing, 122
Indigent transients, 194
Indirect surveillance, 200
Informal diversion, 144–45
Informal referral, 538
Informal social control, 263
Initial appearance, 17–19
Injunctions, 641–42
Inmate classification, 325–36
    classification decisions, 328–29
    functional unit management, 332–33
    historical developments, 326–27
    institutional implications, 330–31
    integrated stage, 331–32
    medical model, relationship to, 329–30
    objective prediction models, 333–36
    preprofessional stage, 331
    professional stage, 332
    purposes of, 326
    reception/diagnosis, 328
    team treatment concept, 332
    traditional stage, 331
Inmate management:
    balanced enforcement, 315–16
    changing supervisory styles, 315
    consistency, 316
    corrupt alliance, 313–14
    informal controls, 317
    interpersonal communications, 318–20
    overenforcement, 311–12
    rules/relationships, 310–11
    social distance, 317–18
    underenforcement, 312
Inmate roles, 390
Inmate self–governance, 264–68
    critique, 265–68
Inmate subculture, 391–400
    inmate code, 392–96
    prison gangs, 396–400
    prison language (argot), 392–93
    prison violence, 400–415
*In Re Gault*, 530–31
*In Re Winship*, 531
Institutional instability, 89
Institutionalized personality, 383–86
Institutional life, 376–418
    confinement, adaptations to, 387–91
    inmate subculture, 391–400
    prisonization process, 378–86
Institutions, changing features of, 666–67
Intake, of juvenile offenders, 538–40

Intensive supervision probation (ISP), 176–79
Intermediate sentencing alternatives, 664
Intermittent surveillance, 199
Internal body–cavity searches, 294–96
Ivy Tech, 551

# J

*Jail Operations/Management Bulletins,* 211
Jails, 11, 15–17, 23, 184–227. *See also* Direct
            supervision (new-generation) jails
    administration, 206–26
        models of, 208–9
    administrator's role, 209–11
    classification, 219–20
    convicted offenders, 191–93
    crowding in, 220–26
    direct supervision (new-generation) jails,
            198–206
    fee system, 108–9
    functions of, 191–98
    inmates, offenses of, 194–97
    intake procedures, 212–13
    jail population, accounting for, 187–89
    length of time served, 197–98
    medical services, 214–15
    mentally ill, 218–19
    number/types of, 186–91
    old jails
        conditions in, 188–89
        eliminating, 186–87
    operations, 206–26
    pretrial detention, 191–93
    small jails, consolidating, 189–90
    staff roles, 211–12, 338
    suicide vulnerability, 215–17
    treatment and industrial programs, 213–14
Job-task analysis, 587
Judicial branch of government, 24
Justice model, 31, 33–34
    compared to medical model, 35
Justinian Code, 41, 98
Juvenile corrections, 519–76
    child-saving movement, 523–24
    historical background, 521–28
    houses of refuge, 522–23
    juvenile court, origin of, 524–27
    *parens patriae*, 525–26
    prevention and treatment, 527–28
    procedural informality, 526–27
    reform schools, 522–23
Juvenile detention, 541–42
Juvenile institutions, 554–58
Juvenile justice, 528–37
    balanced approach to, 548
    due process
        *In Re Gault*, 530–31
        *In Re Winship*, 531
        *Kent v. U.S.,* 529–30
    juvenile court jurisdiction, 535–37

Juvenile justice (*continued*)
    juveniles in adult court, 533–35
    process, 537–74
        adjudications, 546–49
        aftercare programs, 562–63
        alternative approaches, 564
        children in custody, 552–54
        decriminalization, 568–70
        deinstitutionalization, 570–74
        disposition, 549–52
        diversion, 564–67
        effects of confinement, 558–60
        initial contact/referral, 537–38
        intake, 538–40
        juvenile detention, 541–42
        juvenile institutions, 554–58
        juveniles in adult jails, 542–46
        shock incarceration programs, 560–62
    programs/facilities, 10–11
        detention centers, 11
        treatment programs, 12
    status offenders/delinquents, 532–33
    transitions in, 668
Juvenile Justice and Delinquency Prevention
        Act (1974), 543, 570
Juvenile Rehabilitation Ministry (Southern
        Baptist Convention), 654
Juveniles, 194
    in adult jails, 542–46


**K**

*Kent v. U.S.,* 529–30
Key control, 296–97
Kretschmer, Ernest, 77


**L**

Labeling theory, 93–95
Labor unions, 622–23
Laissez-faire supervisors, 600
Law of retaliation. *See* Retribution
Laws, and deviance, 39–44
Leadership, 669–70
Legal issues, 627–49
    freedom from censorship, 634–35
    freedom from cruel and unusual
            punishment, 638–49
    freedom from unreasonable search and
            seizure, 635–38
    freedom of religion, 630–33
    mail privileges, 634–35
Legal liability, 609–13
Legislative branch of government, 24, 28–29
*Lex talionis,* 54, 98–99
Linear remote surveillance, 199
Line and staff supervision, 597–602
    direction, 600–602
    discipline, 598–600

    motivation, 597–98
Lombroso, Cesare, 75, 77, 88
Long-term institutions, for youthful offenders,
        557


**M**

*McKeiver v. Pennsylvania,* 531
Maconochie, Alexander, 121–22, 421, 463
Magna Carta, 102, 103
Mail privileges, 634–35
Management by crisis, 605
Mandated training, 590–91
Mandatory sentencing, 22, 134
Mandatory supervised release, 667
Mark system, 121, 421, 463
Maslow, Abraham H., 267–68
Material witnesses, 194
Maximum-security facilities, 7
Medical model, 31, 32–33, 64, 329–30
    compared to justice model, 35
Medieval law, 100–107
    Anglo-Saxon England, 100–101
    banishment and exile, 106–7
    church influence, 100
    confinement practices, 103
    early English jails, 103–4
    feudal system, breakdown of, 104–6
    punishments, 101–2
Menninger, Karl, 83
Mentally disordered offenders, 501–7
    developmental disability (mental retarda-
            tion), 502–4
    mental illness, 505–7
Mentally ill, and jail, 194, 218–19
Merton, Robert, 92
Mesomorph body type, 77
Metropolitan correctional centers (MCCs), 8,
        206
Minimum-security facilities, 7
MINS, 535
Mitigating circumstances, and sentencing, 22
Mutilation, 107


**N**

Narcotics Anonymous (NA), 361–62, 363
National Crime Survey (NCS), 51
National Manpower Study (1978), 133
Negligent employment/retention, 611
Negligent supervision, 611
Net widening, 149
Newgate prison, 105, 109
*Nolo contendere* (no contest), 18
Nominal damages, 610
Nominal dispositions, 549
Noncustodial alternatives, 8–10
    sentencing, 21

# O

Objective prediction models, 333–36
Officer stress, 618–22
Ohlin, Lloyd, 92
Operation Kids Can (Care About
       Neighborhoods), 551
Organization, 607–8
Outright release, 537

# P

Paint It Clean program, 551
*Parens patriae*, 528, 574, 668
Parole, 12, 123, 416–65
   administrative models of, 429–30
   conditional vs. unconditional release, 436–38
   current trends in, 438–39
   defined, 423
   developments in, 421–22
   eligibility for, 426–27
      computing, 441
   mandatory vs. discretionary release, 439–41
   objectives of, 424–26
   parole authority, 423–30
   parole boards, 427–29, 455
   parole contracting, 444
   parole supervision, 446–62
   presidential pardons, 440
   recidivism, 461–63
   selection procedures, 430–46
      decision-making criticisms, 433–35
      due process, 431–32
      impact on justice model, 435–36
      selection criteria, 432–33
   structured decision making, 443–46
   violators, 194
Parole revocation, 459–61
   due process protections, 460
   revocation results, 460–61
Parole supervision, 446–62
   conditions of parole, 452–55
   employment, locating, 456–57
   field supervision, 457–58
   housing, locating, 456
   parole officers, functions of, 455–59
   prerelease centers, 451
   prerelease counseling, 452
   prerelease planning, 447–54
   work release, 451–52
Participatory management, 263–64, 605
Passes, system of, 285–87
Pat down, 212, 294
Pauling, Linus, 79–80
Pavlov, Ivan, 85
Penitentiaries, 113–18
   Auburn system, 116–18, 124
   Walnut Street Jail, 113–16
Pennsylvania Prison Society, 655
Pennsylvania system, 116

Penn, William, 113, 135
Personal (body) searches, 291, 294–96
Personal violence, 48
Personnel issues, 608–23
"Philadelphia's Society for Alleviating the
      Miseries of the Public Prisons," 113
Photographing, on intake, 213
Physical abnormalities, and crime, 77
Physically impaired offenders, 511–14
Physiological approaches to criminal behavior,
      76–81
   biochemical theories, 79–80
   biology and the environment, 80–81
   body types, 77–78
   chromosome abnormalities, 78–79
   physical abnormalities, 77
Pillories, 108
PINS, 535, 568
Planning, 603–6
Plea bargain, 18
Pleas, 18
Policymaking, public's role in, 31
Population caps, 134
Positive School of criminology, 75–76
Posttraumatic stress, 618
Preliminary hearing, 17–19
Preponderance of evidence, 531
Prerelease centers, 451
Presentence investigations (PSI), 23, 164–67
   defined, 164
   PSI reports
      contents of, 165–67
      preparation/disclosure of, 165
Preservice training, 592–95
Presidential pardons, 440
President's Commission on Law Enforcement
      and Administration of Justice, 131
Pretrial detention, 191–93
Pretrial intervention, 142–50
   defined, 142
   diversion, 143–50
      advantages/disadvantages of, 145–50
      formal/informal diversion, 144–45
Pretrial release programs, 9–10, 12
Primitive law, 97–100
   blood feuds, 97–98
   Code of Hammurabi, 41, 54, 98
   Justinian Code, 41, 98
   *lex talionis*, 54, 98–99
   religions, rise of, 99–100
Prison gangs, 396–400
Prison industries, developments in, 128
Prisonization process, 378–86
   importation vs. deprivation, 379–83
   institutionalized personality, 383–86
Prison reforms, 110–11
Prisons, 11, 228–70
   administration, 255–68
      informal social control, 263
      inmate control, 260–63

Prisons (continued)
   inmate self-governance, 264–68
   operational impact, 257–60
   participatory management, 263–64
   styles of, 256–57
  administrative (support) services, 253–55
  career opportunities, 255
  costs of imprisonment, 230–32
  federal/state/military facilities, 230
  industrial era, 124–27
  number/types of institutions, 229–34
  offender fees, 232–33
  operations, 253
  prison organization, 251–55
   institutional organization, 252–55
   political influence, 251–52
  prison population, 241–48
   crowding, 242–45
   inmate characteristics, 245–46
   inmate offenses, 246–47
   number of inmates, 241–42
  program services, 253
  purpose of, 248–51
   public opinion, 250–51
   social compromise, 248–50
  reform era, 121–23
  regional developments, 119–20
  security classifications, 234–41
   classification procedures, 239–40
   maximum security, 235–36, 237
   medium security, 236
   minimum security, 236–38
   security distribution, 238–39
  time served, 233–34
Prison violence, 400–15
  precipitating event, 405
  predisposing conditions, 403–5
  riots, 401–3
   controlling, 410–11
   preventing, 411–15
   stages of, 405–10
Private training schools, 350–51, 556
Privatization, 652–59
  current trends in, 655–59
  private organizations, 654–55
  religious groups, 653–54
Probation, 156–82
  caseloads, 175–82
  classification of cases, 175–76
  conditions of, 160–61
  costs of, defraying, 179–80
  current status of, 158–60
  defined, 156–57
  discharge/revocation of, 172–74
  eligibility criteria, 161–63
  history of, 157–58
  intensive supervision probation (ISP), 176–79
  presentence investigations (PSI), 164–67
  probation officers, role of, 167–75
  shock probation, 180–82

  violators, 194
Probation officers, 538
  effectiveness, assessment of, 170–72
  role enforcement/investigation, 172
  role of, 167–75
  supervisory role, 168–70
Probation period, new employees, 595–96
Professionalism, 669–70
Project Challenge, 551
Projection, 84–85
Property crimes, 48, 535
Protective custody, 194, 284, 541
Psychodrama role-playing, 364
Psychological approaches to criminal behavior, 81–87
  clinical psychology, 84–85
  intelligence and education, 86–87
  psychoanalytic theory, 81–84
Public order offenses, 535–36
Public policies, changing, 31–34
Punishment, 56, 560
  subordinates, 599
Punitive damages, 610

## Q

Quakers, 113–16, 124, 336, 630, 654
Quinney, Richard, 93

## R

Ragen, Joseph E., 258
RAPS system, 334
Reality therapy, 369
Reasonable doubt, 531
Recidivism, 461–63, 560
Reckless, Walter, 92
Recreation, 351–52
Recruitment, 584–89
  compensation concerns, 586
  image issue, 584–85
  selection, 586–89
   innovative alternatives, 588–89
   oral interviews, 588
   written tests, 587–88
  vacancy pressures, 585–86
Red Eagle Honor Farm, 252
Referrals, delinquency cases, 537–38
Rehabilitation, 61–67, 257, 557, 560, 563
  forms of, 64
Reinforcement theory, 85
Reintegration, 67–68
Relationship behavior, 600
Release:
  conditional, 538
  mandatory supervised, 667
  outright, 537
  parole
   conditional vs. unconditional release, 436–38

mandatory vs. discretionary release, 439–41
pretrial release programs, 9–10, 12
temporary, 304–5
to parents, 538
work, 451–52
Religion:
  freedom of, 630–33
  in juvenile detention facilities, 545
Religious services, 336–40
  inmate acceptance, 337–38
  personnel recruitment, 338–39
  staff acceptance, 338
  treatment impact, 339–40
Remote surveillance, 200
Resource allocation, 606–7
Restitution, 21
Restorative justice, 664–65
Retention, 582–83
  negligent employment/retention, 611
Retribution, 54–56
*Rhodes v. Chapman*, 640
Right to treatment, 557
Roman law, 41
Run, Don't Run (alternative disposition program), 551
Rush, Benjamin, 113

## S

Salient Factor Score, 444–46, 464
Sallyport, 280
*Schall v. Martin*, 542
Secure custodial facility, 541, 550
Segregation, 283–84
Selective incapacitation, 60
Self-defense, 609
Self-fulfilling prophecy, 94, 389
Self-help groups, 360–62
Sensitivity training, 362–64
Sentencing, 20–23
  mandatory sentencing, 22, 134
  sentencing guidelines, 22, 134, 667
  suspension of, 145
Sex offenders, 507–11
  child molesters, 508–9
  prostitutes, 507–8
  rapists, 509–10
Sexual integration, 613–18
Sheldon, William, 77
Shelter care, 546
Shock incarceration programs, 560–62
Shock probation, 180–82
Short-term detention facilities, 544–46
Situational leadership, 600
Skinner, B. F., 85
Social casework, 370
Sociological approaches to criminal behavior, 88–95
  alienation/adaptation/opportunity theory, 90–92

Chicago School's ecological theory, 88–90
  containment theory, 92–93
  differential association, 90
  labeling theory, 93–95
Special inmate populations, 220, 469–518
  alcohol abusers, 499–501
  drug abusers, 494–99
  elderly, 514–16
  female offenders, 471–85
  mentally disordered offenders, 501–7
  physically impaired offenders, 511–14
  sex offenders, 507–11
Specific deterrence, 57
Staff:
  administrative practices, 584–96
    recruitment, 584–89
    training, 589–96
  changes in, 668–69
  changing workforce, implications of, 581–82
  correctional management, 603–8
    budgeting/resource allocation, 606–7
    organization/administration, 607–8
    planning/decision making, 603–6
  correctional personnel, 211–12, 579–84
    numbers/characteristics, 6, 579–81
  line and staff supervision, 597–602
    direction, 600–602
    discipline, 598–600
    motivation, 597–98
  personnel issues, 608–23
    labor unions, 622–23
    legal liability, 609–13
    officer stress, 618–22
    sexual integration, 613–18
  training, 589–96
    curriculum, 591–92
    mandated training, 590–91
    preservice training, 592–95
    probation and FTO programs, 595–96
  training models, 594
  turnover/retention, 582–83, 585
Staff supervisors, 597
Standards of proof, 531
*State of the Prisons in England and Wales, The* (Howard), 110–11
Status offenses, 532–33, 535, 536, 542
Statutes of Westminster, 103
Stocks/pillories, 108
Stress, 618–22
  chronic stress, 618–19
  employee assistance programs (EAPs), 620
  episodic stress, 618–19
  posttraumatic, 618
  stress reduction training, 620–22
Strip search, 294
Suicide:
  and adults in confinement, 215–17
  and juveniles in confinement, 555
Summer Youth Program, 551
Superego, 83
Sutherland, Edwin, 90

# T

Taken into custody, 538
Task behavior, 600
Task Force on Corrections, 131–33
Temporary release, 304–5
Ticket-of-leave system, 123, 421
*Time to Act, A* (report), 132–33
Tool control, 296–97
Training. *See* Education/training; Staff
      training
Training schools, 12, 340–53, 558
    private, 350–51
Treatment, 323–75, 557
    changing nature of, 665–66
    counseling/casework/clinical services,
        353–73
    education/training, 340–53
    inmate classification, 325–36
    religious services, 336–40
    right to, 557
Treatment alternatives to street crimes (TASC),
    145
Treatment availability, 353–56
Trends. *See* Correctional trends
Trial, 19–20
Tuned-out officers, 315
Turnover, staff, 582–83, 585

# U

Uniform Crime Reports (UCR), 47–49
Unions, 622–23
Unreasonable search and seizure, freedom
    from, 635–38

Unsecure custodial facility, 550
U.S. Constitution, 111–12
    Bill of Rights, 112, 114–15

# V

Vicarious liability, 610–11, 613
Victim-offender reconciliation, 145
Violent crimes:
    defined, 533
    and juveniles, 533–36
Visions program, 551
Vocational training, 347–50

# W

Waiver, discretionary, 529, 534
Walnut Street Jail, 113–16, 124, 327, 336, 630
Warehousing, 256
*Washington v. Harper,* 366
Wickersham Commission, 47
Wilson, James Q., 81
Withholding adjudication, 145
Work release, 451–52

# Y

Youth for Christ, 654
Youth Services Bureaus, 565, 569

# Z

Zone of transition, 89